Microeconomics for Manage

This fully updated fourth edition explores microeconomic concepts, with a distinctive emphasis on the "economic way of thinking" and its applicability to sharp managerial thinking, productivity, and good decision-making. It stands apart due to its strong focus on practical and applied knowledge from the business context and its unique structure (Part A of each chapter develops key economic principles; Part B draws on those principles to discuss organizational and incentive issues in management, focusing on solving the "principal–agent" problem to maximize the profitability of the firm). There are plentiful real-life scenarios and provocative examples in each chapter. Accessible to MBA students, other graduate students, and undergraduates, it is ideal as a core text for courses in managerial economics. Requiring an understanding of only basic algebra, this new edition is more concise, with a wealth of online resources, including additional online chapters and an online appendix with more-advanced mathematical applications.

Richard B. McKenzie is the Walter B. Gerken Professor of Enterprise and Society Emeritus in the Paul Merage School of Business at the University of California, Irvine.

D. Eric Schansberg is Professor of Economics at Indiana University Southeast.

Dwight R. Lee is a Professor Emeritus at the University of Georgia.

"This book fills a niche and is written by leaders and experts in the field. It prepares students to become competent, efficient partners in the decision-making of organizations and is rich in public policy and managerial applications. The knowledge it imparts will benefit those who seek greater insight into budgeting, pricing strategies, and the gaining of competitive advantage."

Walter G. Park, *American University*

"*Microeconomics for Managers* remains the best textbook for teaching economics to MBA students. The authors' method of treating economic subjects as people rather than lines on a spreadsheet will inoculate MBA students against economic mistakes. The updates of this 4th edition show how the economic way of thinking remains vital in the post-pandemic business world."

Jonathan Murphy, *Western Carolina University*

Microeconomics for Managers

Principles and Applications

Fourth Edition

Richard B. McKenzie
University of California, Irvine

D. Eric Schansberg
Indiana University Southeast

Dwight R. Lee
University of Georgia

CAMBRIDGE
UNIVERSITY PRESS

Shaftesbury Road, Cambridge CB2 8EA, United Kingdom

One Liberty Plaza, 20th Floor, New York, NY 10006, USA

477 Williamstown Road, Port Melbourne, VIC 3207, Australia

314–321, 3rd Floor, Plot 3, Splendor Forum, Jasola District Centre, New Delhi – 110025, India

103 Penang Road, #05–06/07, Visioncrest Commercial, Singapore 238467

Cambridge University Press is part of Cambridge University Press & Assessment, a department of the University of Cambridge.

We share the University's mission to contribute to society through the pursuit of education, learning and research at the highest international levels of excellence.

www.cambridge.org
Information on this title: www.cambridge.org/highereducation/isbn/9781009354783

DOI: 10.1017/9781009354790

First published 2006
Second edition 2010
Third edition 2017

Printed in the United Kingdom by CPI Group Ltd, Croydon, CR0 4YY

A catalogue record for this publication is available from the British Library

Library of Congress Cataloging-in-Publication Data
Names: McKenzie, Richard B., author. | Schansberg, D. Eric, author. | Lee,
    Dwight R., author.
Title: Microeconomics for managers : principles and applications / Richard
    B. McKenzie, University of California, Irvine, D. Eric Schansberg,
    Indiana University Southeast. Dwight R. Lee, University of Georgia.
Other titles: Microeconomics for MBAs.
Description: Fourth Edition. | New York, NY : Cambridge University Press,
    [2024] | Revised edition of Microeconomics for MBAs, 2017. | Includes
    bibliographical references and index.
Identifiers: LCCN 2023038081 | ISBN 9781009354783 (hardback) | ISBN
    9781009354790 (ebook)
Subjects: LCSH: Microeconomics. | Managerial economics.
Classification: LCC HB172 .M396 2024 | DDC 338.5–dc23/eng/20230814
LC record available at https://lccn.loc.gov/2023038081

ISBN 978-1-009-35478-3 Hardback
ISBN 978-1-009-50719-6 Paperback

Additional resources for this publication at www.cambridge.org/mckenzie4.

Cambridge University Press & Assessment has no responsibility for the persistence or accuracy of URLs for external or third-party internet websites referred to in this publication and does not guarantee that any content on such websites is, or will remain, accurate or appropriate.

Short Contents

Contents

Figures

Tables

Further Reading Online

The Further Readings are all available on the Cambridge online resources website www.cambridge.org/mckenzie4 as files and (in the case of those with an external source marked in brackets) as links.

We are grateful to Getty for the use of their lightbulb/open book icon (© Sobahus Surur/Creative/iStock/Getty Images Plus).

Recommended Videos Online

The videos marked with minutes are lectures by Richard McKenzie; the other videos are supplemental. The lectures and, in the case of the supplementary videos, the links are available on the Cambridge online resources website www.cambridge.org/mckenzie4.

1 Microeconomics: A Way of Thinking about Business
1 Video course introduction (17 minutes)
2 Introduction to the economic way of thinking, 1 (28 minutes)
3 The economic way of thinking, 2 (29 minutes)
4 Property rights, markets, and tragedies of the commons (33 minutes)
5 Prisoner's Dilemma (28 minutes)
6 Comparative advantage (21 minutes)
7 Tragedies of the anticommons (18 minutes)

2 Principles of Rational Behavior in Society and Business
1 Rational behavior and the law of demand (31 minutes)
2 Rational behavior, continued (26 minutes)

3 Competitive Product Markets and Firm Decisions
1 Supply and demand (33 minutes)
2 Market efficiency (26 minutes)
3 Adding features to products (32 minutes)
4 The logic of queues, 1 (24 minutes)
5 The logic of queues, 2 (25 minutes)
6 Executive pay and overpayment (33 minutes)
7 Both Curves; Shifts in Supply and Demand; Supply; Demand; Surplus (Marginal Revolution University @ Practice.MRU.org/)

4 Consumer Choice and Demand in Traditional and Network Markets
1 Elasticity of demand (29 minutes)
2 Rational addiction (21 minutes)
3 Network effects (27 minutes)
4 Trust me (Freakonomics.com #266)
5 How Airbnb designs for trust (Joe Gebbia; TED talks)

We are grateful to Getty for the use of their video play glyphs flat circle icon (© Naveed Anjum/Creative/iStock/Getty Images Plus).

Preface for Teachers

The man who solves complex problems in the space of five minutes on the intuitive basis of "sound" ... judgment [may] sleep easily at night while the analyst who devoted two years to the same topic may sleep badly, but only because he has become acutely aware of all the pitfalls in the problem.

  Malcolm Hoag[1]

Most textbooks used in a microeconomics course for graduate business students – and in a second microeconomics course for undergraduate business students – are designed with undergraduate economics *majors* (or first-year Ph.D. economics students) in mind. Accordingly, business students are often treated to a conventional course in intermediate microeconomic theory, full of arcane mathematical explanations. The applications in such textbooks deal primarily with the impact of government policies on markets. There is little discussion about real-world managers using microeconomics to make better decisions in response to market forces – or how market forces can be expected to affect the structure of firms. These textbooks pay scant attention to the *economic way of thinking* (which differs dramatically from how other professors think about business issues) and what it offers managers – a way to improve their thinking and decision-making on enhancing profits or achieving other organizational goals.

  This is because much microeconomic theory simply assumes firms into existence, with little or nothing about why they are needed in the first place. Moreover, managers and their staff are assumed to do exactly what they are employed to do (e.g., maximize owner profits) with little discussion of how organizational and financial structures affect incentives – and how incentives affect production and profit outcomes. And managers are presumed to think through business problems and make decisions with great (even perfect) care and precision – a premise that leaves less room for teaching students how they can improve their thinking and decision-making.

---

[1] *The Worlds of Herman Kahn: The Intuitive Science of Thermonuclear War* by Sharon Ghamari-Tabrizi, Cambridge, Mass.: Harvard University Press, Copyright © 2005 by the President and Fellows of Harvard College. Used by permission. All rights reserved.

These deficiencies are a problem for serious business students: They typically attend business schools to improve their management skills and learn how to enhance their ability to extract more productivity and profit from the scarce resources available to their firms. They do not want to become economic theorists. As such, *Microeconomics for Managers* breaks from the standard textbook mold. As the title suggests, we have designed this textbook for (future) managers in graduate and undergraduate programs.

The Organization of the Book

In Part A of every chapter, we cover standard microeconomic theory in an accessible way. (We have more technical details in an Online Math Appendix for those who are interested.) Microeconomics adds much to an understanding of firms, consumers, and markets. Such knowledge is valuable – and professors in other business fields will expect their students to have a firm grounding in conventional microeconomic theory. We also provide an array of applications to government policies that business students should understand. After all, managers everywhere face the constraints of government-imposed laws and regulations – and must work to maximize profits within those constraints.

In Part B of every chapter, we go where other microeconomics textbooks seldom, if ever, go with much depth. We drop the usual assumption that firms magically come into existence and automatically maximize profits by simply following maximization rules. Instead, we directly address crucial problems that pervade management decision-making. For example, the "principal–agent problem" is that both owners and workers are more interested in pursuing their own well-being. Owners ("principals") want to maximize their income streams and wealth through the firms they create by getting the most from their employees. Managers and other employees ("agents" of the owner) seek to maximize some combination of income, perks, and job security, which are often in conflict with maximizing profits for the owners. Without effective firm policies that align the incentives of owners and workers for their *mutual benefit*, the work in a firm can be a self-destructive tug of war, with the demise of the firm virtually assured (especially in more-competitive markets).

Getting hourly and monthly pay systems right is obviously an important means of aligning the interests of owners and managers. However, we also explain how the structure of firms, in terms of both people and finances, can affect owner and worker incentives. And make no mistake: both owners and their employees have a stake in finding the right alignment. Jobs can hang in the balance. A firm's ability to thrive and even survive can be greatly impacted by a cost-effective alignment of incentives. As such, we focus student attention on thinking through the complex problems of getting incentives right. *There is as much (maybe more) profit to be made from creatively structuring incentives (and prices) as from developing and marketing products for sale.*

Accordingly, this book places a great deal of emphasis on an increasingly important field within economics, especially as the subject relates to the business world and business programs: *organizational economics* – the study of the design of organizational and financial structures in firms, using the analytical tools of microeconomic analysis. The mode of thinking presented in these pages is crucial for managers who want to ascend their corporate hierarchy or create successful companies of their own. Many of these topics are covered in *organizational behavior* courses which are grounded in psychology. With the economic approach developed here, students will understand how business topics can be approached from different disciplinary perspectives, often with complementary insights.

In between Parts A and B of every chapter, we have inserted a "Perspective" – a short section that provides a novel take on a business or policy issue. For example, everyone *knows* (don't they?) that the "first mover" in any market has a competitive advantage. But in Perspective 9 for Chapter 9, we discuss a startling research finding made by management scholars: there is no "first-mover advantage" (or it appears rarely). First movers can even be at a decided disadvantage, which explains why so many well-known firms that dominate their industries today were "followers."

Many authors and their publishers play textbook development "safe" by taking up only those topics that have become fixtures in the profession's "conventional wisdom." Such an approach sucks the life out of a discipline and its textbook treatments. Topics that have not yet been fully settled by decades of professional debate can give life to a discipline by showing students how disciplines have an organic quality, in that they are constantly evolving through debate. As a consequence, you can expect many topics in this book to spark lively and constructive discussions among students and professors. This is how we want the book to be received.

Toward the end of each chapter, we insert a short series of "Practical Lessons" which are designed to show how the concepts in each chapter can help managers solve workplace problems – all with an eye toward enhancing firm profitability (or the achievement of other firm goals). We believe that theory at its best is a guide to improved thinking, decision-making, and profitability – as well as welfare gains for consumers, workers, owners, and society. Each chapter also has a section titled "The bottom line" – a list of *key takeaways* or succinct statements of the most important points to be drawn from the chapter.

The scholarly and policy literature in economics and management related to most of the topics considered in this volume is massive. We have tried to give credit where credit is due, especially where "classic" or seminal treatments are concerned. However, we have tried to limit references and footnotes so the flow of the argument is not constantly disrupted. Given space constraints, we have a modest select bibliography at the end of the book, but a full bibliography online.

This textbook is well designed to work in undergraduate managerial economics courses, MBA programs, and the growing number of one-year masters programs in management and in accounting – with online, hybrid, or in-person instruction. To help students learn the material, we have provided links to fifty-four video lectures by Richard McKenzie with an average length of 26 minutes (and a range of 8–37 minutes). These are listed at the end of each chapter and are hosted at the Cambridge resources website for the text, www.cambridge.org/mckenzie4. These videos often closely follow the text of the chapter, providing something of a "second reading" of chapter materials. McKenzie also has shorter (3–10 minute) videos that deal with concepts and modes of analysis that are often difficult to comprehend the first time they are presented in a text or lectures. These collectively have had more than two million views and are freely available on YouTube for streaming (not downloading) by searching under his name.

The videos are designed to meet the needs of students in three types of courses:

1 students in online courses organized around this textbook;
2 students in hybrid courses that require watching video lectures to free up in-class time for additional course coverage; and
3 students in conventional face-to-face courses who want additional video resources to learn microeconomics.

Also on the Cambridge website for this book, www.cambridge.org/mckenzie4, we have an array of additional online reading and twenty-two supplemental videos, tied to the various chapters, which can expand the learning experience. Instructors have access to a wealth of (password-protected) materials, including test banks, suggested lines of answers to many of the "Review questions" at the end of each chapter, and several weekly discussion problems that can be assigned to students (with suggested lines of answers to many questions). Thus, a nearly complete course in microeconomics is provided with the textbook, videos, and the online reading suggested for each chapter. (We also encourage you to consider a paper and/or presentation from students on how the course concepts apply to their jobs.)

Embracing Theory and the "Economic Way of Thinking"

You may be interested to know that, between us, we have more than 120 years of university teaching experience, with most of our careers spent in business schools and decades of teaching MBA students. This should tell you that we have a good fix on our readers and their interests, including a course that is intellectually challenging and full of practical applications.

We often start our courses with a question that puzzles our students – many of whom are mid-level and upper-level managers, in firms from a broad range of industries, who remain employed while completing their degrees. The question seems simple on the surface: "Why are you here?" Invariably, student interest is piqued, but they typically require an elaboration: "Why are you in this classroom and enrolled in this program?"

The answers are quick in coming and varied. "I'm here to make more money," one student always confesses with an uneasy laugh. But many other answers share a common theme: "To learn how to *do* business." This is quite understandable. Business students are a focused lot, with their eyes typically fixed on the objective of improving their career paths. Much business education provides instruction in business skills – for example, how to develop business plans and to secure funding for new business ventures.

But invariably the answers leave an important part of our question unanswered because the answer – "to learn how to do business" – does not explain why students are in their seats and we are behind the lectern. We have much to offer here, but the irony is that what *we do* in class is radically different from what *they do* in firms. Indeed, students come to class in a context removed from their work to get away from what they do at work – putting aside the many details of business dealings that are a part of their everyday world. In fact, the class is a world apart from the world of business – and intentionally designed this way for one strategic purpose: to look at how business is done from a broad perspective without the clutter of daily details.

In no small way, the purpose of our class (or any other business course worthy of academic respect) is to explore ways to *think* critically and creatively about how business is done and can be done better – rather than to actually *do* business. In this regard, we take to heart an observation made by Kenneth Boulding (1970, 2):

It is a very fundamental principle indeed that knowledge is always gained by the orderly loss of information; that is, by conducing and abstracting and indexing the great buzzing confusion of information that comes from the world around us into a form we can appreciate and comprehend.

This way of thinking is necessarily *abstract* (to one degree or another) – that is, without the clutter of many business details. We use abstractions principally because no one's brain is sufficiently powerful to handle all the complex details of everyday business life. Productive thought requires that the complexity of business life is reduced enough to allow us to focus on the few things that are most important to the problems at hand by finding meaningful relationships between those things. This is why Professor Boulding insists that knowledge can so often (if not "always") be gained by the "*orderly loss* of information."

We understand that some may worry about our emphasis on theory, because they have read theory-grounded books that seemed sterile or irrelevant – given their heavy reliance on highly technical mathematics or complicated charts. This is not the case in our book. People in business often spurn theory on the grounds that it lacks practical value. We insist, "not so at all." The abstract way of thinking that we develop in this textbook has a *very* practical, overriding goal – to afford students more understanding of the business world than they could if they tried to keep the analysis cluttered up with the "buzzing confusion" of facts from their workplaces.

There is another highly practical goal to be achieved by theory – or, rather, thinking with the use of theory. If people can *think* through business problems in some organized way, albeit abstractly, they might be able to avoid mistakes when they actually *do* business. In economic terms, business mistakes imply a regrettable misuse and loss of firm resources. *Thinking* before doing offers the prospect of reducing waste in doing business.

Our main interest in asking "Why are you here?" is to stress the obvious: If the class is about *thinking* (not doing), then professors have some justification for being in front of the class. And if the class is about the thinking process, there must be some method for thinking through problems – business-related or otherwise. The development of this *method* is the focus of our classes and this textbook. As such, our goal in this volume is to develop the *economic way of thinking* in the context of a host of problems that business students, as (future) managers of real-world firms, will find relevant to their daily work and their career goals.

Sometimes the most productive way to gain insight is to develop models that are "unreal" to one degree or another. For example, we cover "perfect competition," which is an idealized version of competitive markets. We employ this market model not because we think it is "real." It is not, and cannot be, as we stress in Chapter 9. Rather, we use the model as a device to understand *directional forces* in all competitive markets that might otherwise escape revelation – and to offer the prospect of adding predictability in some market environments. If we can see how firms will price their products and seek to maximize their profits (or minimize their losses) under intense competition, we can gain insights into what real firms might do in less competitive environments. We point out how firms under such "perfectly competitive conditions" will inevitably earn only a normal rate of return (when the good and the market for it have already been developed). As such, entrepreneurs would be well advised to avoid markets with more attributes of "perfect competition."

This textbook carries the subtitle, *Principles and Applications*, for good reason. In the following pages, we bring together a host of large and small principles from economists that have transformed the way we think about how the business world works. And we stress how theory can suggest ways in which thinking and decision-making can be improved within firms.

We expect that reactions to these large and small ideas will change significantly by the time students have read the last words of this volume. Three of those large questions are as follows:

- How can microeconomic theory be used to develop rules for improved thinking and decision-making – and, thus, firm profitability?
- How should organizations and incentives be structured to best encourage maximization of firm goals – most notably, profit maximization?
- How does competition – in the markets for products, labor, credit, corporate control, etc. – discipline workers, managers, and executives?

The small questions are no less important and can be just as intriguing. For example:

- Should used cars really be expected to be "better deals" than new ones (as so many people seem to think)?
- If competitive markets are expected to "clear" (with quantity demanded equaling quantity supplied), why do we observe so many queues in grocery stores and at concerts? And if queues are not mutually beneficial to buyers and sellers, then why aren't they eliminated?
- Why are Fruit Loops and popcorn at movies so expensive, relative to their apparent costs?

We expect that readers will finish this book the way our students finish our courses: changed for life in the way they see the (business) world around them. But then, this is what business students typically want – or should want – from every course in their business programs. We often tell our students, "Economics is as much a disease as it is a discipline – and it can be terminal: once you 'catch it,' it's hard to let it go."

Thanks and Updates

When this textbook was first published in 2006, our students made innumerable and invaluable suggestions for improvement. We remain indebted to them – as well as other students and professors who used the first edition and freely advised us about how the book could be improved. (Special thanks are due to Barry Keating at Notre Dame who provided vital editorial guidance.) We have continued to receive counsel from users since then. The most encouraging advice came from one professor who insisted, "Remember, you have a very good book, the best for serious business students on the market. Don't mess with success." Accordingly, we have carefully crafted succeeding editions with the intent of better positioning the textbook for the evolving role of microeconomics in business programs – and by presenting a useful and interesting array of economic events, policies, and problems to consider.

We have made important revisions in this fourth edition. Beyond the additions one would expect with a new edition, we continue to evolve (and hopefully improve) our presentation in the text and through online resources (available at www.cambridge.org/mckenzie4). We have added a new Chapter 6: a discussion of political economy with applications of the theories to the workplace. One cannot discuss economics for long without talking about public policy. And detailing public policy without some understanding of the relevant behavioral models in politics and bureaucracy can be needlessly frustrating. Beyond this, thankfully, there are many applications of political models to the everyday workings of firms.

Perhaps the most important change is that the book has become much more concise. We have eliminated three chapters from the text and reduced the writing within chapters by an average of 15 percent. We have moved the bulk of the previous chapters 5 (international) and 6 (environmental) into Online Chapters 2 and 3. (Both topics get a brief mention in the new Chapter 6 and then supplemental coverage online.) We also have two substantial online chapters that could be used to support an entire class period: we combined chapters 14 and 15 from the previous edition into "behavioral economics" in Online Chapter 1; and we have added a new Online Chapter 4 with an overview of basic macroeconomic concepts. Both topics were candidates for in-text coverage given their importance, but we decided to make them available online to keep the book at a more manageable length.

We have also beefed up our discussion of labor markets in Chapter 12. The material is inherently interesting, relevant to employees, and useful to better understand firms and markets. It also allows us to continue our discussion of market structure throughout the second half of the book – for example, the monopoly power of some firms in labor markets and labor unions as cartels. We have also added a highly applicable discussion of two types of discrimination in Perspective 12 for that chapter.

We love the cover for this edition. It combines references to business, technology, communication, transportation, and the increasingly global competition that managers face. The surrounding buildings and open airspace allude to the prevalence of blinkered thinking and the prospects of something much more expansive through the economic way of thinking. And the arrow is a great metaphor for the progress we hope that students enjoy after a semester of managerial economics with this text and your teaching.

This edition adds the work (and writing) of D. Eric Schansberg – a long-time user of the text in the School of Business at Indiana University Southeast. For better and for worse, most of the edits in this edition are his. We are especially indebted to Valerie Appleby and Emma Collison, our tireless editors at Cambridge University Press, who guided the development of this edition of *Microeconomics for Managers*. We are most grateful to Cambridge for recognizing the critical need for a microeconomics textbook devoted to business students. They know our audience as well as we do.

Preface for Students

If you think education is expensive, try ignorance.

Unknown

Economics is an easy subject and a difficult subject at the same time. It is easy in the sense there are only a few principles that really guide most economic analysis. It is simple and yet it's obviously very difficult. I have dealt a lot with Nobel laureates in physics, chemistry and other fields who have very strong opinions on economic issues and usually they are terrible. These are obviously first-class minds, but they have not given economic issues much attention. They believe that they can casually talk about an economic issue and come up with the right answer, that one just has to be intelligent. This is obviously not the case. There are economic principles. If you do not use these principles, you are likely to come to the wrong answers.

Gary Becker[1]

Students of economics face a difficult task. They must learn many things in a rigorous manner that, on reflection and with experience, amount to common sense. To do this, however, they must set aside – or "unlearn" – some preconceived notions of the economy and the course itself. The problem of "unlearning" can be especially acute for graduate students who are returning to college after years of experience in industry. People in business rightfully focus their attention on the immediate demands of their jobs and evaluate their firms' successes and failures with reference to production schedules and accounting statements – a stark contrast to the perspective developed in an economics class.

As all good economics teachers must do, we intend to challenge you to rethink some of your views on the economy and the way firms operate. We will ask you to develop new methods of analysis, to use abstract and deductive reasoning, and to master a distinctive "economic way of thinking." We will not tell you how or what you must think. However, we will ask you to think differently with the expectation that practicing the economic way of thinking will, to one degree or

---

[1] Clement, Douglas, 2002. Interview with Gary Becker, available in February 2023 at Minneapolis Fed, www.minneapolisfed.org/article/2002/interview-with-gary-becker.

another, become more natural and useful. We understand that you might never be as precisely *rational* as we assume people are in the economic models developed throughout the book. But this way of thinking will help you *consider* how you can improve your thinking and the profitability of your business decisions. A prominent theme of this book is that money (and careers) can be made by developing better "mousetraps," but also through clear and focused thinking about incentives and how businesses function.

In light of this, we will also ask you to reconsider policy issues – both inside and outside the firm – about which you may have relatively fixed views. This will not always be easy, but we are convinced that the rewards from the study ahead are substantial. This text and this course will help you to better understand how the world works and how businesses may be made more efficient and profitable.

The Organization of the Book

Each chapter is divided into three sections. Part A will always develop micro-economic concepts and theories, applying the concepts and theories to social, economic, and business concerns. Here, you will learn conventional microeconomics – from concepts such as property rights and externalities to models such as demand and supply and profit maximization within various market structures. And we will strive to make these relevant by applying them to everyday business problems. For example, in the opening chapter, we will define the basic concept of property rights and then apply it to a range of business contexts.

Part B will always apply the theory developed in Part A to issues that mid-level and executive-level managers confront. For example, in Chapter 11, we explore how monopoly power can be practiced *within* firms – when key departments exercise control over resources and processes as the sole provider of certain services. We also discuss how outsourcing, takeovers, and the threat of such actions can reduce the impact of such monopoly power in practice.

Sandwiched between Parts A and B, we provide a "Perspective" that extends the discussion in the chapter, covers some public policy or management subject, or describes a novel take on a topic that many people have mistakenly accepted as settled. In two cases, we include classic and incisive treatment of key economic arguments. For example, in the opening chapter, we provide a great essay by the late economic journalist Leonard E. Read. In "*I, Pencil,*" Read describes how no one in the world – literally, nobody – knows how to make a pencil totally from scratch. All of the producers use their specialized knowledge and skills, while participating for their own reasons (e.g., to earn money). Yet, pencils by the billions are produced each year, benefiting hordes of people around the world.

We understand that time is a scarce commodity for students, especially those who must balance their studies with a full-time job and a family. Accordingly, we conclude each chapter with a section in which we identify key "Practical Lessons" that emerge from the analysis in each chapter. Here, we show how the economic way of thinking can be used to understand workplace problems and devise profit-enhancing solutions to common managerial problems. Before the review questions, we close with "The bottom line," which summarizes the most important points in the chapter. We also provide videos and other reading online, for those who want more help or are curious about additional applications of the economic principles at hand.

Throughout the volume, we have one goal: *to improve the way you think about the world in large and small ways.* When you complete this book, your view of how markets work (and fail to work) should be greatly clarified, with an improved ability to understand and predict market outcomes. You will see more clearly the manager's role as one of coping with and responding to competitive market forces and internal incentives. These encourage owners, executives, and managers to pay as much attention to the structure of incentives as to how products are created, developed, and marketed. Along the way, we will describe the "competitive market forces" that strongly urge people to find ways to cooperate in mutually beneficial ways.

By thinking through problems with greater clarity, you will be able to avoid the waste of resources that comes from making errors in judgment which are bound to arise when people make decisions from "gut feelings" or wrong-headed presumptions about how the world works. After all, Mark Twain was on target when he mused, "It's not ignorance that does so much damage; it's knowin' so darn much that ain't so."

Some Examples to Whet Your Appetite

We began revising the second edition of this book as the United States slid into the worst economic recession since the early 1980s. The downturn was set off by a housing and financial crisis that left many major banks, investment houses, and insurance companies struggling to stay alive because of the (bursting) "housing bubble" and the subsequent meltdown in the market for mortgage-backed securities. When you complete this book, you will better understand the microeconomic foundations of the chief catalyst for the "Great Recession": the "moral hazard" problem and the ways in which investments based on borrowed money can inspire unfortunate risk-taking.

With this revision of the book, we have recently emerged from the Covid-19 pandemic, with its wide array of policy responses. After reading the text, you will know various principles from economics and political economy that will help you understand what happened and why. Communicable disease, masks, and vaccines can be seen more clearly through the lens of "externalities" (which we will describe in Chapter 6 and detail in Online Chapter 2). Working from home can be modeled as a fringe benefit that workers do not want to give up without other forms of compensation. And we will develop tools to comprehend the cautious responses of government bureaucrats; the often-well-intentioned activism of politicians; and the highly disproportionate impact of special interest groups. From stay-in-place orders and extended school closures to mandates, subsidies, and "stimulus" spending, students will understand more about why policies were chosen and why they had limited effectiveness.

When you complete this book, you will more naturally be able to make observations that might otherwise escape your attention. For example, most people understand that we face an expanding obesity problem – and thus, growth in obesity-related health problems. In turn, this drives up health insurance costs to firms, depriving workers of greater increases in money wages. In part, obesity has been caused by the growing competitiveness of world markets, reducing the price of food, increasing food consumption, and expanding waistlines. Will managers reduce pay offers for prospective workers who are overweight, since the health care costs of such workers can be expected to feed into a company's health insurance costs? Will competitive market forces put upward pressures on the wages of workers who maintain a healthier lifestyle? Excess body weight increases the use of jet fuel. Why do airlines charge thin passengers for their overweight bags, but do not add extra charges for obese passengers?

You might understand how economics (and geopolitics) can drive military conflicts. Conquest results in control over natural resources and the revenue streams they represent, which can make conquest more profitable. How does the growth in retrievable natural gas reserves in the United States impact the financial payoffs from conquests in Ukraine or the Middle East? How did the 9/11 terrorist attack on the World Trade Center towers impact individual decisions, management decisions, and the macroeconomy? The attack increased the perceived risk of flying and lengthened security lines at airports – with both risk and wait times increasing the total cost of plane trips. You will understand why economists have found that the greater cost of flying has led to more people driving – along with more automobile accidents, injuries, and deaths (Blalock, Kadiyali, and Simon 2005a, 2005b). Whether preventing attacks or encouraging people to drive, airport security turns out to be a management problem with life-and-death consequences.

In the realm of personal finances, you may have heard people dogmatically claim that buying a house is better than renting an apartment, because you are buying something rather than giving your money away. But what about "pouring money down a hole" for maintenance, homeowner association fees, mortgage interest (even if subsidized a bit by the government), and the opportunity costs of tying up so many financial resources in a low rate-of-return investment? Or someone might defend leasing to avoid property taxes, not understanding that those taxes are absorbed into the rent. In both cases, a limited understanding of the benefits and costs can lead to poorly-reasoned (if not poor) decisions.

The list goes on and on and on. After the course, you will use the economic way of thinking in much of your daily life. In many cases, thinking like an economist will yield more sophisticated reasoning and better decisions – whether personal choices, public policy preferences, or business decisions. We dedicate this edition to those who have loved economics for a long time and those who will enjoy it greatly for the first time in this course. Thanks for choosing this program, this course – and thus, this book. We hope you enjoy the ride!

Book I
The Market Economy, Overview, and Applications

. . . .

In Chapters 1 and 2 of *Microeconomics for Managers*, we develop the broad outlines of the "economic way of thinking." We explore what economists mean by markets and "rational behavior" and show how "economic thinking" can illuminate many public and management policies. In Chapters 3 and 4, we will develop supply and demand analysis, which will allow us to explore the market consequences of an array of governmental and organizational policies in Chapters 5 and 6. Our goal throughout Book I is to better understand the market economy and consider how market forces can affect management decisions. In Book II (Chapters 7 and 8) and Book III (Chapters 9–12), we will examine many of the theoretical details underpinning supply and market structure. In these later chapters, we will develop concepts about production and costs; explain how firms behave in markets with different levels of competitiveness; and focus on how market structure impacts managerial decisions.

1

Microeconomics: A Way of Thinking about Business

Working hard to think clearly is the beginning of moral conduct.

Attributed to Blaise Pascal

Economics is a way of thinking about problems, not a set of answers to be taken off the shelf.

Unknown

The opening chapters of economics textbooks are notoriously scattered. We'll open with a discussion of how and why markets emerge – out of consumer preferences and the willingness of entrepreneurs to serve those consumers, often for money and profit. Then, we'll move to more-conventional introductory concepts. We'll define the constraint at the crux of all economic behavior: the "scarcity" of money, time, and other resources. We'll describe how scarcity leads to choices that have inherent trade-offs. And we'll discuss how the presence (or absence) of property rights impacts those choices – from the perspective of individuals and society.

We'll also discuss the role of theory – in particular, "the economic way of thinking." The kind of thinking that will be central to this book starts from an innocuous observation: *people have a basic drive to improve their lot in life because they don't have everything they want.* Much of this introductory chapter and the book (and the course), both in theory and in application, is directed at driving home this easily overlooked point. Oddly enough, many lessons in this book are crystallized in a classic story about what happened in a German prisoner-of-war (POW) camp during World War II, as related by a prisoner who happened to be a trained economist.

Part A Theory and Public Policy Applications

The Emergence of a Market

Economic systems spring from people's drive to improve their welfare. R. A. Radford, an American soldier who was captured and imprisoned during World War II, left a vivid account of the primitive **market** for goods and services that grew up in the most unlikely of places, his POW camp in

> A **market** is the process by which buyers and sellers determine what they are willing to buy and sell – and on what terms.

Italy (Radford 1945). Because the inmates had few opportunities to produce the things they wanted, they turned to a system of exchange based on the cigarettes, toiletries, chocolate, and other rations distributed to them periodically by the Red Cross.

The Red Cross distributed the supplies equally among the prisoners, but "very soon after capture ... [the prisoners] realized that it was rather undesirable and unnecessary, in view of the limited size and the quality of supplies, to give away or to accept gifts of cigarettes or food. Goodwill developed into trading as a more equitable means of maximizing individual satisfaction" (Radford 1945, 190). As the weeks went by, trade expanded and the prices of goods stabilized. A soldier who hoped to receive a high price for his soap found he had to compete with others who also wanted to trade soap. Soon, shops emerged and middlemen began to take advantage of discrepancies in the prices offered in different prisoner bungalows.

A priest was one of the few prisoners allowed to move freely among the bungalows. He was able to exchange a pack of cigarettes for a pound of cheese in one bungalow; trade the cheese for a pack-and-a-half of cigarettes in a second bungalow; and return home with more cigarettes than he had started with. Although he was acting in his own self-interest, he had also provided people with something they wanted – more cigarettes or cheese than they would otherwise have had. In fact, prices for cheese and cigarettes differed because prisoners in different bungalows had different desires and they could not all interact freely. To exploit the discrepancy in prices, the priest moved the camp's cheese from the first bungalow (where it was worth less) to the second bungalow (where it was worth more). Everyone involved in the trade benefited from the priest's enterprise.

> An **entrepreneur** is an enterprising person who discovers potentially profitable opportunities and organizes, directs, and manages productive ventures.

A few **entrepreneurs** in the camp hoarded cigarettes and used them to buy up the troops' rations shortly after issue – and then sold the rations just before the next issue, at higher prices. Although these entrepreneurs were pursuing their own private interest, like the priest, they were providing a service to the other prisoners. They bought the rations when people wanted to get rid of them and sold them when people were running short. The difference between the low price at which they bought and the high price at which they sold gave them the incentive to make the trades, hold on to the rations, and assume the risk that the price might not rise.

Soon, the troops began to use cigarettes as money, quoting prices in packs or fractions of packs. (Only the less desirable brands of cigarettes were used this way; the better brands were smoked.) Because cigarettes were generally acceptable, the soldier who wanted soap no longer had to search out those who might want his jam; he could buy the soap with cigarettes. Even nonsmokers began to accept cigarettes in trade.

This makeshift monetary system adjusted itself to allow for changes in the money supply. When the Red Cross distributed new supplies of cigarettes, prices in terms of cigarettes rose, reflecting the influx of new money. After nights spent listening to nearby bombing, when the nervous prisoners had smoked up their holdings of cigarettes, prices fell. Radford saw a form of social order emerging in these spontaneous, voluntary, and completely undirected efforts. Even in this unlikely environment, the human tendency toward mutually advantageous trade had asserted itself.

Today, markets for numerous new and used products spring up spontaneously in much the same way. At the end of each semester, college students can be found trading books among themselves or standing in line at the bookstore to resell their books. Used-book buyers can save students the time in line by roaming dormitory and classroom hallways offering to buy student books (as well as the textbooks collected by professors) – sometimes at better prices than campus bookstores pay. These buyers then become sellers – for example, on Amazon, where they compete with new copies to future students – the result being an increase in the competitiveness and efficiency of textbook markets and fewer new copies of textbooks sold.

Garage sales are common in practically all communities – with eBay and Facebook Marketplace as large-scale internet equivalents. Indeed, like the priest in the POW camp, many people go to garage sales to buy what they believe they can resell – at a higher price, of course. "Dollar stores" have sprung up all over the U.S. for one purpose: to buy surplus merchandise from manufacturers and sell it at greatly reduced prices to willing customers.

There are even firms that make a market in getting refunds for other firms on late overnight deliveries. Many firms don't think it is worth their time to seek refunds for a few tardy packages. (Overnight delivery firms have an economic incentive to keep late deliveries in check.) However, there are obviously economies to be had from other firms collecting the delivery notices from several firms and sorting the late ones out, with the refunds shared by all concerned.

Gift cards have become a big and profitable business for retailers, partially because many of the cards go unused. Recipients lose them or don't care to shop where the card is redeemable. Companies have created exchanges for gift cards – for example, offering recipients $80 for a $100 gift card. It will then put the card up for sale on its website for more than $80. Recipients can also donate their unused balances to charity through DonorsChoose.org.

Today, we stand witness to a "new economy" on the Internet; many students reading this book will, like the priest in the POW camp, help to develop it. This has obviously brought gains to many firms – most notably Microsoft, Apple, Google, and Amazon – and their customers have gained from higher-quality products and lower prices through competition. But the internet economy has wreaked havoc on other firms – most notably, brick-and-mortar stores and newspapers – that have lost market share or have closed. The expansion of some industries – regardless of whether they are seen as a part of the "old" or "new" economy – and the contraction of others are interrelated for a reason that lies at the heart of economics: we simply can't do everything.

The Economic Problem

Our world is not nearly as restrictive as Radford's POW camp, but it still faces limits. Indeed, if we think seriously about the world around us, we can make two general observations.

First, the world is more or less fixed in size and limited in its known and usable **resources** (given available technology). We can plant more trees, find more oil, and increase our stock of human talent. But there are limits on what we can accomplish with the resources at our disposal, at least within some defined time limit.

> **Resources** are things used in the production of goods and services. There are only so many acres of land, gallons of water, trees, rivers, wind currents, oil and mineral deposits, trained workers, and machines that can be used in any one time period to produce the things we want.

Economists have traditionally grouped resources into four broad categories: land (the surface of the world and everything in nature), labor (the human and mental efforts devoted to production), capital (also called investment goods – for example, machines, buildings), and technology (the knowledge of how resources can be productively combined). To this list, some economists would add a fifth category, *entrepreneurial (and intrapreneurial) talent*. The entrepreneur is critical to the success of any economy, especially if that economy relies heavily on markets. Because entrepreneurs discover more effective and profitable ways of organizing resources to produce the goods and services people want, they are often considered a resource in themselves. Entrepreneurs not only create "better mousetraps," they often do nothing more than what the priest did in the POW camp: find novel ways of redistributing available (but scarce) resources to the benefit of everyone.

Second, in contrast to the world's physical limitations, human wants abound. You might want a top-of-the-line tablet, a self-driving car, more clothes, a big-screen television, seats at a big concert or ballgame. And that's on top of what you already have – the "basics" (e.g., three good meals a day) that you normally take for granted. Even if we had all the money we wanted to spend, save, and give away, we're still short on time. Consider the Garden of Eden: Even in the middle of "plenty," Adam and Eve (as limited humans) had to allocate their scarce time. If they were picking apples, then they weren't pruning the orange trees or laying underneath the shade of a tree.

Bottom line: people want far more than they can ever have. One of the unavoidable conditions of life is the fundamental condition of **scarcity**. Put simply, there isn't enough of everything to go around. Consequently, society must face unavoidable questions: (1) What will be produced? (2) How will those things be produced? (3) Who will be paid what – which relates to who will produce the goods? (4) Perhaps most important, who will determine how the above questions shall be answered?

> **Scarcity** is the fact that we all cannot have everything we want all the time; we have unlimited wants and limited resources.

These questions have no easy answers. We spend our lives attempting to manage them on an individual level. In terms of public policy, the question is always whether to let markets and individuals do what they want or to constrain them through government policy (and if so, how so?). In terms of firms and markets, how do individuals and groups allocate their resources? These questions are fundamental to all fields in business and the social sciences, but to economics in particular. Indeed, economists see the fact of scarcity as the foundation of **economics**. More to the point, economics is a way of *thinking* about how people, individually and collectively in various organizations (including firms), cope with scarcity.

> **Economics** is a method of thinking, founded on the study of how people cope with the pressing (individual and social) choice problems associated with scarcity – with their efforts directed (primarily) toward satisfying as many wants as possible.

The problem of allocating resources among competing wants is not as simple as it may first appear. A key problem is that we have information about our wants and the resources at our disposal that may be known to nobody else. This is a point Leonard Read made concerning what it takes to make a product as simple as a pencil (Read 1983) – and that F. A. Hayek stressed in many of his writings that ultimately gained him a Nobel Prize in Economics (Hayek 1945).

In his short article (in Perspective 1 after this Part A), Read makes the startling observation that no one knows how to make a product as seemingly simple as a common pencil (from scratch). But tens of billions of pencils are made each year, all through markets that mysteriously guide the economic decisions of millions of producers and consumers through multiple layers of production. Hayek stressed that the mystery of production (whether pencils or more complicated goods and services) can be understood by viewing the pricing system as a *decentralized information system* that is critical to coordinating many people's decisions to employ and redeploy the world's scarce resources to satisfy people's wants. Since these wants are known in detail only by the people who have them, this means they can't be known by centralized authorities – who might imagine that they can do what markets do, but can't absorb the vast information required to produce efficiently.

Hayek argued that market prices are especially important because they reveal the relative values of resources and goods, directing people's efforts in optimizing the allocation of resources across space and time. You may know you want a calculator because your statistics class requires you to have one, but even your friends (much less the people at Hewlett-Packard or Samsung) do not yet know your purchase plans. You also may be the only person who knows how much time you want to offer in the labor market – which is determined by how long and intensely you want to devote time to school, work, socializing, etc. At the same time, you know little about the wants and resources of other people around the world (or even colleagues in your study groups).

Before resources can be effectively allocated, the information we hold about our individual wants and resources must somehow be communicated to others. This means that economics must be concerned with systems of communications – for example, the priest in the POW camp who used both words and prices to convey information about how the troops in various bungalows assessed the value he had offered. The field is extensively interested in how information about wants and resources is transmitted through prices in the market process and votes in the political process. Indeed, the "information problem" is often acute within firms, given that the chief executive officer (CEO) often knows little about how to do the jobs at the bottom of the corporate "pyramid." The information problem is one important reason that firms must rely extensively on *incentives* to get their workers (and managers) to use their local information in pursuit of the firm's goals.

Markets such as the POW camp and firms operating within markets emerge in direct response to scarcity. Because people want more than is immediately available, they produce goods and services for trade. By exchanging things they like less for things they like more, they reallocate their resources and enhance their welfare as individuals. As we will see, people organize firms, because the firms are more cost-effective than markets. Firms can be expected to expand only as long as things can be done more cost-effectively through firms than through competitive market trades. This means that many firms fail not only because of things they do wrong (e.g., allow costs to get out of control), but also because market trades between firms become less costly (e.g., through improved telecommunications), causing firms to outsource services and shed employees.

It's tempting to assume that *scarcity* is exclusively a construct of the external physical world. The irony is that the scarcest resource in the world is internal to each of us: the human brain. It is not much larger than a softball and weighs, on average, three pounds. It has about a hundred billion neurons (give or take a few billion), most of which are tied up keeping our complex bodily systems functioning. The relatively small portion of the neurons available for thinking about the external world of scarcity must be used with great care – in the most efficient way we know how. This is where microeconomics comes into the picture. It is a subject that seeks to improve our thinking, so that our brains can economize on themselves and then economize on all the scarce resources in the world around us. We offer this book and course as a way to improve your brainpower and thereby improve business decision-making, productivity, and profitability.

We have heard critics – most recently, behavioral economists and behavioral psychologists – lament the various limitations of people's brains, including those of economics professors! We gladly embrace the criticisms (and cover them in Online Chapter 1), because they suggest that people's brainpower and thinking can be improved. In fact, the criticism gives greater purpose to microeconomics: our limitations should cause people to seek simplified and more efficient ways of thinking about the world.

The Scope of Economics

Business students often associate economics with a rather narrow portion of the human experience: the pursuit of wealth; money and taxes; commercial and industrial life. Critics often suggest that economists are oblivious to the aesthetic and ethical dimensions of human experience. Such criticism is partly justified. Increasingly, however, economists are expanding their horizons and applying the laws of economics to the full spectrum of human activities. For example, the appreciation of a poem or play can be the subject of economic inquiry. Poems and plays, and the time in which to appreciate them, are also scarce.

Jacob Viner, a distinguished economist in the first half of the twentieth century, once defined economics as "what economists do." Today, economists study an increasingly diverse array of topics. As always, they are involved in describing market processes, methods of trade, and commercial and industrial patterns. They also pay considerable attention to poverty and wealth; to racial, sexual, and religious discrimination; to politics and bureaucracy; to crime and criminal law; and to revolution and terrorism. There is even an economics of group interaction, in which economic principles are applied to marital and family issues. And there is an economics of firm organization and the structure of incentives inside firms – where we will focus much of our attention throughout the book.

What is the unifying factor in these diverse inquiries? What distinguishes the economist's work from that of other social scientists? Economists take a distinctive approach to the study of human behavior and use a mode of analysis based on certain presuppositions. For example, much economic analysis starts with the general propositions that people prefer more to fewer of the things they value – and they seek to maximize their welfare by making reasonable, consistent choices in the things they buy and sell. These propositions enable economists to derive the "law of demand" (people will buy more of any good at a lower price than at a higher price, and vice versa, all else constant) and many other principles of human behavior.

One purpose of this book is to describe the economic approach in considerable detail – to develop the commonly accepted principles of economic analysis and demonstrate how they can be used to understand a variety of issues (e.g., pollution, ticket scalping), as well as firms' organizational and financial structures. In every case, economic analysis is useful only if it is based on a sound theory that can be evaluated in terms of real-world experience. This mode of analysis – we dub it the "economic way of thinking" – will appear time and again as you move through your business programs, most prominently in your finance, accounting, marketing, and strategy courses. (And it should make economics come to life as you engage with the media. For example, consider Online Reading 1.1 and 1.2: *New York Times* articles on "The economics of suspense" and "The cost of paying attention." See also: the inherent disincentives created by trying to help the poor in Online Reading 1.3.)

Developing and Using Economic Theories

The real world of economics is staggeringly complex. Each day, billions of people engage in innumerable transactions, only some of them involving money (about 30 percent), and many of them undertaken for conflicting reasons (McMillan 2002, 168–169). To make matters more complicated, people are confronted with terabytes of data coming from their five senses – far more than can be absorbed by the brain. To make sense of all this, people must first economize on their scarce mental powers before they seek to economize on resources in the external world, partially by ignoring or filtering out much sensory data before it has a chance to throttle thinking altogether with "sensory overload." Additionally, we all turn to **theory** to further economize on our highly constrained brainpower.

> A **theory** is a model of how the world is put together; it is an attempt to uncover some order in the complex and often seemingly random events of daily life. Theory is how we make sense of the world.

Economic theory is abstract, but not in the sense that its models lack concreteness. On the contrary, good models are laid out with great precision. Theories are simplified models *abstracted from* the complexity of the real world. Economists deliberately simplify their models to best concentrate attention on the problems of greatest interest. As a guiding principle of analysis, economists accept a widely repeated quip from physicist Albert Einstein: "Theories should be as simple as possible, but no simpler."

As explained in Chapter 2, economists assume that people are *rational*, which is to say that they weigh the costs and benefits of options available to them, consistently choosing in such a way as to maximize their well-being. *We even assume that people are more rational than we know them to be*, but only because such an abstraction promotes understanding and offers insights that might not otherwise be achieved.

As a road map is useful because it ignores most of the details between the various points along our route of travel, so models, theories, and statistics are useful because they ignore details that are not (as) relevant to the questions being investigated. A statistic is only a proxy for the world it attempts to measure. Reducing a complex aspect of the world to a series of numbers is ridiculous at some level. But it can be helpful if we understand the statistic's value and its limits. Even powerful models such as "demand and supply" are absurd and wooden if taken too literally or without understanding their limits. But they can still have tremendous explanatory power. Although a theory is not a complete and realistic description of the real world, a good theory will incorporate enough to simulate real life. It should provide some explanation for past experiences and permit reasonably accurate predictions of the future. When you evaluate a new theory, ask yourself:

- Does this theory explain what has been observed?
- Does it provide a better basis for prediction than other theories?

If a theory is "complete," so much the better. But such theories don't come along often – and never in economics (or other social sciences). This would involve explaining amazingly complex interactions among and between many people in their various settings, with much of it driven by subjective evaluations that are largely unknown and unknowable.

Microeconomics and Macroeconomics

The discipline of economics is divided into two main parts that are typically covered in two different business courses: microeconomics and macroeconomics. This book will deal almost exclusively with microeconomic theory, policy implications, and applications inside firms.

Questions of interest to microeconomists include the following:

- Why do individuals choose as they do in "markets"?
- What determines the price and output level of particular goods and services?
- What determines wages, interest rates, and profits?
- How do government policies – such as price controls and excise taxes – affect the price and output levels of individual markets?
- Why and how do incentives matter inside firms?

These questions are relevant to the performance of the entire economy, but they are also questions that concern the managers of individual firms. Decisions on what goods and services to produce, how to produce them, what prices to sell them for, and how much to pay employees are obviously important to the profitability – and, indeed, the viability – of firms. The competitiveness of a firm is determined by the decisions its managers make on:

1 how best to compensate employees (*personnel management*);
2 the best mix of debt versus equity financing (*financial management*);
3 how best to promote a good or service (*marketing management*);
4 how to transport and distribute the product (*supply chain management*); and
5 whether to purchase a productive input from an outside supplier or expand the firm through vertical integration by producing the input in-house (*organizational management*).

In many respects, the firm faces the same problems as the overall economy. In both cases, success depends on somehow motivating a large number of people to take action that promotes the general interest of all, when those people have:

1 widely different abilities and interests;
2 mixed concern for the interests of others; and
3 limited knowledge about how to serve the interests of others.

By keeping this problem in mind when examining the structures, strategies, practices, and procedures of firms – and applying the insights of the economic way of thinking – we can and will advance toward a better understanding of business management.

Economists also study broad macroeconomic sectors of the economy, such as the total output of all firms that produce goods and services. Instead of concentrating on how many bicycles or smartphones are sold, macroeconomists watch overall production level and overall price level. These and similar issues are of much more than academic interest – whether the high inflation of the 1970s and early 2020s; the post-inflation recession of the early 1980s; the "Great Recession"; the impact of 9/11, terrorism, immigration, and Covid; or mounting concerns about government budget deficits and the national debt.

Some MBA programs offer courses in "macroeconomics" given its relevance and importance. But an understanding of macroeconomics is necessarily dependent on an understanding of microeconomics. And many of the microeconomic concepts developed in this book – supply and demand, adverse selection and moral hazard, risk aversion, incentives, etc. – will speak to significant macroeconomic problems. (For interested teachers and students, we have Online Chapter 4.) Likewise, the understanding of "political economy" that we'll develop in Chapter 6 – why and how agents in political markets make choices – is helpful.

Private Property Rights, Game Theory, and the Prisoner's Dilemma

Microeconomics is replete with graphical and mathematical devices for illuminating people's interactions inside firms and markets with various levels of market competition. Supply and demand curves, which we introduce in Chapter 3, are devices for discussing price and output determination under intense *competition*. But as we will see, much microeconomic analysis is about achieving *cooperation* among people to produce and purchase goods and services cost-effectively. Indeed, competition in markets among many buyers and sellers is, at its core, concerned with settling which buyers will cooperate with which producers – both members of groups competing among themselves, to see who will participate with the goal of achieving their mutual ends.

Buyers and sellers must first settle on the terms, including the limits, of their cooperation (Rubin 2014). Cooperation may not always be "natural" in the sense that people may have personal incentives to choose noncooperative strategies. To illustrate the problems of achieving cooperative solutions, we use **game theory**, another tool from microeconomics, which comes from applied mathematics and is often portrayed as a decision matrix (as we'll see in

> **Game theory** is a matrix-based tool used to discuss people's decisions when their most preferred course of action depends on the choices of others.

Table 1.1). Such a matrix permits us to imagine the problems people face in achieving cooperation when their decisions must be made strategically – that is, when their optimal choices depend upon the choices of others. We start with a discussion of the emergence of property rights in a game-theoretic setting, because property rights are necessary for trade to flourish (one of our opening themes) and to ease students into familiarity with game theory (a tool we use throughout the text).

Private Property Rights and the Games Economists Play

In microeconomics, we start with the fact that all actions are constrained by *scarcity*. Private "property rights" are among the institutional mechanisms people have devised to help alleviate the pressing constraints of scarcity, which is why we take them up at this early stage in the course. **Property rights** in economics extend far beyond the control and use of land; they pertain to the permissible use of any resources, goods, and services. Property rights are a social phenomenon; they arise out of the

> **Property rights** in economics extend far beyond the control and use of land; they pertain to the permissible use of any resources, goods, and services; they define the limits of social behavior – what can and cannot be done by individuals in society. They also specify whether resources, goods, and services are to be used privately or collectively by the state or some smaller group.

necessity for individuals to "get along" within a social space in which all wish to move and interact.

The existence (and extent) of property rights has obvious ethical considerations. But an important practical attribute of private property rights is that they make owners into **residual claimants**: they receive whatever "residual" is left over from revenue streams or from property sales after all other "claims" (costs) have been

> A **residual claimant** is one who receives the leftover gains (or losses) after all other claims have been satisfied.

satisfied. For example, if a property owner incurs costs to upgrade a property, the owner can lay claim to any additional revenue stream or to the higher sale price caused by the upgrade. By the same token, the owner will also suffer the loss in revenue or sale price caused by the misuse and abuse of the property. As a residual claimant, the owner therefore has an incentive to improve the private property and to protect it from misuse and abuse (subject to costs and benefits).

Where individuals are isolated from one another by natural barriers or are located where goods and resources are extremely abundant, property rights have no meaning. In the world of Robinson Crusoe, shipwrecked alone on an island, property rights were inconsequential. His behavior was restricted by the resources found on the island, the tools he was able to take from the ship, and his own ingenuity. He still had a problem of efficiently allocating his time within these constraints – procuring food, building shelter, and plotting his escape. However, the notion of "property" did not restrict his behavior; it was not a barrier to what he could do. He was able to take from the shipwreck, with impunity, stores that he thought would be most useful to his purposes.

After the arrival of Friday, the native whom Crusoe saved from cannibals, a problem of restricting and ordering interpersonal behavior immediately emerged. The problem was particularly acute for Crusoe because Friday, prior to coming to Tibago, was himself a cannibal. (Each had to clearly establish property rights to his own body!) The system that they worked out was simple: Crusoe essentially owned everything. Their relationship was master and servant, with Crusoe dictating to Friday how the property was to be used.

In common speech, we frequently speak of someone "owning" this land, that house, or these bonds. This conventional style is undoubtedly economical from the viewpoint of quick communications, but it masks the variety and complexity of the ownership relationship. What are owned are *rights* to *use* resources, including one's body and mind – and these rights are always circumscribed by social or legal restrictions on certain actions. To "own land" usually means to have the right to till (or not to till) the soil, to mine the soil, to *offer* those rights for sale, etc. – but not to have the right to throw soil at a passerby, to use it to change the course of a stream, or to force someone to buy it. What are owned are *socially recognized rights of action* (Alchian and Demsetz 1973).

Property rights are not necessarily distributed equally, meaning that people do not always have the same rights to use the same resources. Students may have the right to use their voices (i.e., a resource) to speak with friends in casual conversation in the hallways of classroom buildings. But they do not, generally speaking, have the right to disrupt class with a harangue on their political views. In other words, property rights can be recast in terms of *behavioral rules*, which effectively limit and restrict our choices. Behavioral rules determine what rights we have with regard to the use of resources, goods, and services. These rights may be the product of the legislative process and may be enforced by a third party, usually agents of government. In this case, property rights emerge from legislation.

Private Property Rights and the Market

In the market economy, people are permitted to initiate trades with one another. Indeed, when people trade, they are actually trading "rights" to goods and services. For example, when a person buys a house in the market, she is actually buying the right to live in the house under certain conditions – as long as she does not disturb others, for example. The market economy is predicated upon establishing patterns of *private* property rights; those patterns have legitimacy because of government enforcement – and, perhaps just as important, because of certain social norms regarding the limits of individual behavior that are commonly accepted, observed, and self-enforced (with locks and alarm systems, for example). Without recognized property rights, there would be nothing to trade – that is, no market.

How dependent are markets on government enforcement for the protection and legitimacy of private property rights? Our answer must be somewhat speculative.

We know that markets existed in the "Wild West" (in the nineteenth-century U.S.) when *formally* instituted governments were nonexistent. Further, it is highly improbable that any government can be so pervasive in the affairs of people that it can be the arbiter of all private rights. For example, cases in which disputes over property rights within a neighborhood are settled by "associations" (or "local councils" in the U.K.) are relatively rare, and disputes that end up at police headquarters are rarer still. Most conflicts over property rights are resolved at a local level between two parties, and many potential disputes do not even arise because of generally accepted behavioral limits.

Finally, the concept of property rights helps clarify the relationship between the public and private sectors of the economy – that is, between the section of the economy organized by collective action through government and the section organized through the actions of independent individuals. When government regulates aspects of the market, it redefines behavioral limits (in the sense that people can no longer do what they once could); this can be seen as realigning the property rights between the private and public spheres. For example, when the government imposes price ceilings on goods and services (as it does with rent controls) – or price floors (as it does with minimum wages and agricultural price supports) – it is redefining the rights that sellers have regarding the property they sell. One purpose of economics is to analyze the effect that such realignment of property rights has on incentives, behavior, and efficiency.

The Emergence of Private Property Rights

In an idealized world where people are fully considerate of each other's feelings – and adjust their behavior to others, without recourse to anything resembling a dividing line between "mine" and "thine" – property rights are likely no more necessary than they were for Crusoe alone on Tibago. But in the world as it now exists, there is great potential for conflict. The development of property rights, held communally by the state or held privately by individuals, can alleviate the potential for conflict. These rights can be established in ways that are similar but which can be conceptually distinguished: (1) *voluntary* acceptance of behavioral norms with no third-party enforcer (e.g., police and courts); and (2) the specification of rights in a legally binding social contract, meaning that a third-party enforcer is established. Most of what we say for the remainder of this chapter applies to both modes of establishing rights. However, for reasons developed later in the book, the establishment of rights through voluntary acceptance of behavioral norms has distinct limitations, especially in relation to the size of the group (growth in group size undermines the norms).

To develop the analysis in the simplest terms possible, consider a model of two people, Fred and Harry, who live alone on an island. They have, at the start, no behavioral rules or anything else that "naturally" divides their spheres of interest – that is, they have nothing that resembles property rights. Further, being rational, they are assumed to want more than they have or can produce by themselves. Their social order is essentially anarchic. Each has two fundamental options for increasing his welfare: He can use his labor and other resources to produce goods and services, or he can steal from his fellow man. With no social or ethical barriers restricting their behavior, Fred and Harry should be expected to seek the allocation of their resources between these options in the most productive way. This may mean that each should steal from the other as long as more is gained that way than through the production of goods and services.

If Fred and Harry find stealing a reasonable course to take, each will have to divert resources into protecting that which he has produced (or stolen). Presumably, their attacks and counterattacks will lead them toward a social equilibrium in which each is applying resources to predation and defense and neither finds any further movement of resources into those lines of activity profitable (Bush 1972, 5–8). This is not an equilibrium in the sense that the state of affairs is a desirable or stable one; in fact, it may be characterized as a "Hobbesian jungle" in which "every man is Enemy to every man" (Hobbes 1968, first published in 1651).

In an economic sense, resources diverted into predatory and defensive behavior are wasted; they are taken away from productive processes. If these resources are applied to production, total production will rise, and both Fred and Harry can be better off; both can have more than if they try to steal from each other. Only through winding up in a state of anarchy, or seeing the potential for ending up there, do they question the rationality of continued plundering and unrestricted behavior. Because of the prospects of individual improvement, there exists potential for a "social contract" that spells out legally defined property rights. Through a social contract, they may agree to restrict their own behavior, allowing them to do away with the relatively more costly restraints that, through predation and the subsequent defense, each imposes on the other. The fear of being attacked on the streets at night can be far more confining than laws that restrict people from attacking one another. This is what John Locke meant when he wrote, "The end of law is not to abolish or restrain but to preserve and enlarge freedom" (Locke 1690, 23).

Once the benefits from the social contract are recognized, there may still be, as in the case of voluntary behavioral norms, an incentive for Fred or Harry to chisel (cheat) on the contract. Fred may find that he is better off materially by agreeing to property rights rather than remaining in a state of anarchy. But he may be *even* better off by agreeing and then violating the agreed-upon rights of the other. Through stealing, or violating Harry's rights in other ways, Fred can redistribute the total wealth of the community toward himself.

Consider Table 1.1, which illustrates the kind of "games" – involving actions and reactions of individual players – that economists use to draw out strategies people will (or should) use to deal with given situations. Table 1.1 contains a matrix of Fred and Harry's hypothetical "utility" (satisfaction) levels if either respects or fails to respect the rights established by the contract. There are four cells in the matrix, representing the four combinations of actions that Fred and Harry can take. They can both respect the agreed-upon rights of the other (cell 1); they can both violate each other's rights (cell 4); Harry can respect Fred's rights while Fred violates Harry's rights (cell 3); or vice versa (cell 2).

Table 1.1 **The games Fred and Harry can play with property rights**

	Harry respects Fred's rights		Harry violates Fred's rights	
Fred respects Harry's rights	Cell 1		Cell 2	
	Fred	Harry	Fred	Harry
	15 utils	10 utils	8 utils	16 utils
Fred violates Harry's rights	Cell 3		Cell 4	
	Fred	Harry	Fred	Harry
	18 utils	5 utils	10 utils	7 utils

Note: The payoffs (measured in "utils" – units of satisfaction) from the choices of Fred and Harry are indicated in the four cells of the matrix. Each has an incentive to violate the other's rights. If they do violate each other's rights, they will end up in cell 4 – the worst of all possible states for both of them. The productivity of the "social contract" can be measured by the increase in Fred's and Harry's utility resulting from their moving from cell 4 (the "state of nature") to cell 1 (a state in which a social contract is effective).

Clearly, by the utility levels indicated in cells 1 and 4, Fred and Harry are both better off by respecting each other's rights than by violating them. However, if Harry respects Fred's rights and Fred fails to reciprocate, Fred has 18 utils, which is greater than he will receive in cell 1. Harry is similarly better off if he violates Fred's rights while Fred respects Harry's rights: Harry has 16 utils instead of the 10 utils he will have if they respect each other's rights. The lesson to be learned: inherent within an agreement over property rights is the possibility for each person to gain by violating the rights of the other. But if both follow this course, they both will end up in cell 4 – that is, back in the state of anarchy.

There are two reasons why this may happen. First, as we stated above, both Fred and Harry may violate each other's rights in order to improve their own positions; the action may be strictly *offensive*. Second, each must consider what the other will do. Neither would want to be caught upholding the agreement while the other one violates it. If Fred thinks that Harry may violate his rights,

Fred may follow suit and violate Harry's rights: he will be better off in cell 4 (i.e., anarchy) than in cell 2. Thus, Fred and Harry can wind up in anarchy for purely *defensive* reasons.

Many wars and battles, at both the street and international levels, have been fought because one party was afraid that the other would attack first in order to get the upper hand. The same problem is basically involved in our analysis of the fragile nature of Fred and Harry's social contract. The problem of contract violation can grow as the community grows in number because violations are more difficult (more costly) to detect.

Game Theory: Prisoner's Dilemmas

Fred and Harry's situation is a classic example of a powerful game-theoretic setting called the *Prisoner's Dilemma*, in which both parties in two-person games have built-in incentives to take noncooperative solutions. This dilemma represents a common problem in achieving cooperation in any number of social settings, not the least of which is business – a topic that will come up repeatedly in this book. The name "Prisoner's Dilemma" comes from a standard technique of interrogation to obtain confessions from two or more suspected partners to a crime. The suspects are taken to different rooms for questioning, and each is offered a lighter sentence if he confesses. But each is also warned that if the other suspect confesses and he does not, his sentence will be more stringent.

Prisoner's Dilemmas are especially problematic when the parties are unable to communicate. Here, each suspect has to guess, without the benefit of communication, how the other suspect will stand up to the pressure. Worried that the other may confess, each may confess because he cannot trust his partner to avoid the temptation. The problem for a suspect becomes more complicated as the number of captured partners increases. He must count on more people – and he must consider whether others may confess because *they* cannot count on all of the partners to hold under the pressure.

Game theory pops up in places where you might least expect its application. In football (the U.S. version, not soccer), consider a coach's decision to punt or fake a punt on fourth down. In politics, a contested primary drains resources from the victorious candidate, weakening her for the general election. In the Cold War, the U.S. and U.S.S.R. had to decide about the accumulation and use of nuclear weapons. And so on. (See Online Reading 1.4 where game theory says Pete Carroll's infamous call at the goal line in Super Bowl XLIX is defensible. See Online Reading 1.5 where game theory came into play in international negotiating strategies when Greece was in search of debt relief from the European Union in 2015. Fortunately for Greece, its chief negotiator was a notable game theorist.)

Prisoner's Dilemma Solutions: Enforcement and Trade

To prevent violations of both an offensive and a defensive nature, a community may agree to the establishment of a police, court, and penal system to protect the rights specified in the social contract. The system may be costly, but the drain on the community's total wealth may be smaller than if it reverts back to anarchy (as resources are diverted into predatory and defensive behavior). The costs associated with making the contract and enforcing it will determine just how extensive the contract will be – a matter considered later in the book.

The social contract, which defines property rights, establishes only the limits of permissible behavior; it does not mean that Fred and Harry will be satisfied with the exact combination of property rights they have been given through the contract. To the degree that some other combination or distribution of the existing property held by Fred and Harry will give them both more satisfaction, trades are not only possible, but likely. Mutually beneficial exchanges can be expected to emerge.

For example, suppose that the only goods on Fred and Harry's island are coconuts and papayas. The social contract specifies the division of the fruits between them. We need not concern ourselves with the total number of the fruit each has; we need only indicate the relative satisfaction that Fred and Harry receive from the marginal units. Suppose the marginal utilities in Table 1.2 represent the satisfaction they received from the last coconut and papaya in their possession. Fred receives more utility from the last papaya (15 utils) than the last coconut (10 utils). He would have a higher level of utility if he could trade a coconut for a papaya. On the other hand, Harry receives more utility from the last coconut than the last papaya; he would gladly give up a papaya for a coconut.

Table 1.2 **Relative satisfaction from marginal units consumed**

	Coconut (utils)	Papaya (utils)
Fred	10	15
Harry	90	30

The two should continue to exchange *rights* to the coconuts and papayas until one or both of them can no longer gain via trade.

The trades are comparable to those that took place in the POW camps described at the start of the chapter. If the social contract also allocates the right to *produce* the fruit, we can demonstrate that both can be even better off through specializing in their production and trading with each other. Consider the

Table 1.3 **Specializing in production and trade**

	Coconut production	Papaya production
Fred	4	8
Harry	6	24

information in Table 1.3, which indicates how much Fred and Harry can produce with one hour of labor.

With one hour of labor, Fred can produce either four coconuts or eight papayas; Harry can produce either six coconuts or twenty-four papayas. Even though Harry is more productive in both lines of work – and thus has an *absolute advantage* in both goods – we can show that they can both gain by specializing and trading with each other. This is because each has a *comparative advantage* in one good: each can produce one good at a *relatively* lower cost than the other person.

If Fred produces four coconuts, he cannot use that hour of time to produce eight papayas. In other words, the "cost" of the four coconuts is eight papayas – or one coconut for every two papayas. Fred would be better off if he could trade one coconut for *more than two* papayas, because this is what he has to give up to produce the coconut. To determine whether there is a basis for trade, we must explore the cost of coconuts and papayas to Harry. The cost of one coconut to Harry is four papayas, because he has to give up twenty-four papayas to produce six coconuts. If Harry could give up fewer than four papayas for a coconut, he would be better off. He could produce the four papayas, and if he has to give up fewer than that for a coconut, he will have papayas left over to eat, which he would not have had without the opportunity to trade.

To summarize: Fred would be better off if he could get more than two papayas for a coconut; Harry would be better off if he could give up fewer than four papayas for a coconut. If, for example, they agree to trade at the exchange rate of one coconut for three papayas, both would be better off. Fred will produce one coconut, giving up two papayas, but he can get three papayas for the coconut. Harry can produce four papayas, giving up one coconut, and trade three of the papayas for a coconut. He has the same number of coconuts, but has an additional papaya.

Although simple, the above example of *exchange* is one of economists' most important contributions to discussions of social interaction. Many people seem to imagine that, when people trade, one person must gain at the expense of another. If people in France trade with people in Japan, someone must be made worse off in the process – or so it's often imagined. We will deal with such arguments (briefly in Chapter 6 and at length in Online Chapter 3) when we take up international trade. For now, we have demonstrated that, through trade, both Harry and Fred can be better off – even though we postulated that Harry was more efficient than Fred in the production of both fruits.

Trades that emerge from exploitation of comparative advantages among traders can have even more profound effects than those already indicated. This is due to efficiency benefits of specialization of labor (or any other resource). By specializing in the production of papayas, Harry can become more skilled in their production and waste less time moving back and forth between the production of coconuts and papayas – thus, producing more papayas in a given time period. The same can be said for Fred because of his specialization in coconuts.

As such, restrictions on market trades (e.g., tariffs and quotas) have two adverse effects. First, they reduce the ability of traders to exploit their comparative advantages in production. Second, they narrow the scope of markets, thereby reducing the potential specialization gains in resource use. (These insights go back to the venerable Adam Smith, author of *The Wealth of Nations* (Smith 1937, originally published 1776), in his opposition to trade restrictions.)

In short, there are potential economies with freer trade in many products through the expansion of markets. Greater production ultimately translates into greater real income, which is divided among those involved in the trades, according to the terms of trade (the prices of goods going both ways). This holds for both the production of final and intermediate goods and services, as well as inputs to production.

While this argument has been couched in terms of two people trading coconuts and papayas, similar gains are fully evident within business firms. CEOs might be more talented and productive in accounting, law, and advertising than the assistants they hire. However, they hire assistants to exploit their comparative advantage in running entire firms. Accountants hire bookkeepers not because their bookkeepers are more talented and productive in recording transactions, but because they have comparative advantages in understanding what summary accounting statistics convey about the overall operation of their firms. Firms are full of people with specialized talents who are exploiting those talents at a higher level than would be possible if all sought to be "jacks of all trades." Indeed, the very survival of firms depends upon their understanding the gains from trades and resource specialization. Most business students who read this book have already recognized the benefits of specialization in their efforts (at least at some level). They are specializing in the study of business topics, rather than physics, dentistry, and horticulture.

Communal Property Rights and the "Tragedy of the Commons"

To many, the ideal state of affairs may appear to be one in which everyone has the right to use all resources, goods, and services and in which no one (not even the state) has the right to exclude anyone else from their use. We may designate such rights as "communal rights." Many rights to scarce property have been and are still allocated in this way. Rights to the use of a university's facilities are held communally by the students; no one admitted to the university has the right to keep you off campus paths or lawns or from using the library according to certain rules and regulations. (Such rules and regulations form the boundaries, much as if they were natural, within which the rights are truly communal.) The rights to city parks, sidewalks, and streets are held communally. Before the United States was settled, many Native American tribes held communal rights to hunting grounds; that is, at least within the tribe's territory, no one had the right to exclude anyone else from hunting on the land. During most of the first half of the nineteenth century, the rights to graze cattle on the prairies of the western United States were held communally; anyone who wanted to let his cattle loose on the plains could do so. Granted, the U.S. Government maintained the right to exclude cattlemen from the plains; but as long as it did not exercise this right, the land rights were communal. Looking into the future, nobody owns the Moon or other natural objects in space. For now, that works well enough; down the road, this will probably not suffice.

Communal property rights can be employed with tolerably efficient results if one of two conditions holds:

1 there is more of the resource than can be effectively used for all intended purposes (in other words, there is no cost to its use); or
2 people within the community fully account for the effects that their own use of the resources has on others (the concept here is "externalities" – a topic we address in Chapter 6 and Online Chapter 2).

Without the presence of one of these conditions, the resources will tend to be "overused." Under communal ownership, if the resource is not presently being used by someone else, no one can be excluded from the use of it. Consequently, once in use, the resource becomes, for that period of time, the private property of the user.

The biologist Garrett Hardin (1968) characterized the problem of overused (and abused) communal resources as "the tragedy of the commons" and considered why a pasture might be overgrazed if cattle rancher access to an immense pasture was unimpeded by property rights. In deciding how many cattle to add, each cattleman will be likely to reason that the addition of his cattle – and his cattle alone – will make no difference to the amount of feed available to the cattle of other herdsmen. But the grass eaten by one rancher's cattle is grass that can't be eaten by the cattle of other ranchers. This means that he can impose a portion of the costs of his cattle grazing on other ranchers. This is justification enough for all ranchers to put more cattle on the pasture than they would if they individually incurred the full grazing costs of their cattle. The result is that the cattlemen can collectively face an outcome – a "tragedy" in the form of overly thin cattle – that none of them would want (Hardin 1968):

Therein is the tragedy. Each man is locked into a system that compels him to increase his herd without limit – in a world that is limited. Ruin is the destination toward which all men rush, each pursuing his own best interest in a society that believes in the freedom of the commons. Freedom of the commons brings ruin to all.

Water is potentially another (worldwide) tragedy of the commons. The world's thirty-seven major aquifers, which support the lives of two billion people, are fully common-access resources, with people in various nations able to tap them for whatever use they want, no matter their relative value. People who tap the aquifers have to pay the drilling cost but do not have to pay for the water they individually pump. Each person who drills a well into the aquifers can individually reason that their *individual* withdrawals are the proverbial "drop" taken from a very large underground "bucket." Each person can also reason that any water not withdrawn will also be trivial. However, with a multitude of drillers thinking this way, their individual "drops" become much more consequential.[1]

California has experienced the same problem: the draining of the State's aquifers to replace the reduction in surface water. A farmer crystallized the nature of the inherent problem of this water commons tragedy in a comment to a *New York Times* reporter: "[M]y livelihood depends on pumping that water – if I stop pumping it, my neighbor keeps pumping it" (Barringer 2015). The problem can only be addressed by multiple parties coordinating their groundwater policies – no mean task, given the difficulty of collective decision-making problems among large groups of people (a topic we cover in Chapter 2). One possible solution is to charge a price for water drained from the aquifers.

Another example is the use of roads. Drivers may consider most of the (personal) costs involved in their use of the road, but will likely overlook (social) costs imposed on others. Their presence increases highway congestion and the discomfort of other drivers. Their driving creates pollution that does not impact them directly. Their use of the roads will increase costs of road maintenance. If they do not bear these costs, they will overextend the use of the resource, driving as long as the additional personal benefits are greater than the additional personal costs, but (mostly) ignoring the social costs they have created.

There are three ways that social costs can be internalized:

- First, people can be considerate of others and account for the social cost in their behavior.
- Second, the government can prompt the driver to consider the social costs of driving in an indirect way by imposing a tax on the driver's use of the road

---

[1] Because of individual thinking, and no price for the water pumped, scientists at the University of California, Irvine, have determined that one-third of the world's aquifers are being depleted faster than they are being replenished, with the result that the underground water levels around the world are falling (Richey 2015).

(through a tax on gasoline or a tax on the miles driven as determined by GPS-based monitoring devices), causing less driving and fewer costs imposed on others. This is called "internalizing the social cost." Once the state does this, the right to the freeway is no longer "communal"; the rights have been effectively attenuated by the state.

- Third, the right to the road can be turned into *private property* – individuals are given the right to exclude others from the use of the road. This may seem undesirable, unless we recognize that private owners can then charge for the use of the road: They can sell "use rights," in which case the marginal cost of driving will rise, resulting in a decrease in another cost that individual drivers incur from traffic congestion (a tragedy of the commons all too familiar to students commuting to work or class in urban areas).

The prime difference between private ownership and government taxation is that the revenues collected go into the coffers of individuals or the government. This is "good" or "bad," depending upon your attitude toward government versus private uses of the funds. Furthermore, under private ownership and without viable competitors (in an example where competition may not be practical), the owners may attempt to charge an amount that is greater than the social costs – in the jargon of economists, to acquire monopoly profits, and, in so doing, cause an *underuse* of the road. (We'll discuss this in Chapter 10.)

For that matter, the state-imposed taxes may be greater than the social costs. But the state may also act like a monopolist. State agencies may not be permitted to make a "profit" as it is normally conceived, but this does not exclude the use of their revenues for improving the salaries and the working conditions of state employees. Monopoly profits may be easy to see on the accounting statements of a firm, but may be lost in bureaucratic waste or overexpenditures under state ownership. State ownership does not necessarily lead to waste, but it is certainly a prospect, and one that only the naive will ignore. More is said about this subject at various points in the book, but especially in Chapter 6.

Voluntary Organizations and Firms as Solutions for "Tragedies of the Commons"

Tragedies of the commons are also problems that can cause people to search earnestly for other solutions. The late Indiana University political science professor Elinor Ostrom shared the 2009 Nobel Prize in Economics for pointing out – to economists steeped in Hardin's dismal view – that people often form voluntary associations to restrict and direct the use of communally owned property, because they can be more cost-effective than private ownership or government control.

She found voluntary associations working well all over the world when forests, fisheries, oil fields, and grazing lands are held communally (Ostrom 1990). The voluntary associations need clear, pre-established rules on how the gains from use of the communal property are to be divided and how conflicts are to be resolved. Even ranchers in the so-called "Wild West" formed cattlemen's associations that solved Hardin's potential tragedy of the commons. The associations effectively laid claim to the communal property, restricting the entry of "outsiders," putting limits on cattle in the common area, and requiring participation in the annual roundups (Anderson and Hill 2004). The tragedy of the commons, played out in the willful poaching of elephants in Namibia, Africa, was partially solved by giving local tribes private ownership rights to the elephant herds in their areas, ensuring that they received some of the gains from tourists coming to see wild elephant herds. The tribes then had greater incentives to control poaching (Henderson 2009).

University of California, Berkeley, economics professor Oliver Williamson shared the 2009 Nobel Prize in Economics for stressing that "firms" are nothing more than voluntary associations of varying numbers of people who organize themselves to achieve economic gains that are shared. Because firm resources are used "communally," there are ever-present prospects for people misusing firm resources for their own private ends (Williamson 1967, 1990, 1998). Part B in each chapter of this text reflects those who have followed Williamson's lead, explaining how firms seek to abate their potential tragedies of the commons through their structure and incentives.

Most microeconomics textbooks treat "firms" as theoretical "black boxes" that magically transform inputs into outputs cost-effectively, so long as their markets are competitive. Such an approach misses a major reason that business students are in their microeconomic classes – to gain insights on how the transformations are orchestrated, which includes avoiding firm-based tragedies of the commons. In the following chapters, we will pay due attention to how markets work, but we will also peel back the sides of the black boxes called firms to gain insights into how they can produce more efficiently.

If common access resources are privatized (turned into private property), then the owners will incur the cost of the property being overused and abused – and will use prices to restrict this deterioration. Such a solution might not be practical, however, when dealing with pollution of the atmosphere or draining aquifers that extend across nations and hundreds of millions of people. Handing over full ownership rights to a single owner raises the prospects of monopoly pricing. If the property rights are distributed to a number of owners, then collective decision-making problems emerge. Then, maybe, the commons tragedy can be mitigated, by privatizing the resource and distributing "extraction limits," which can be sold to individuals (or firms) to extract set quantities of water.

The Tragedy of the Anticommons

The *tragedy of the commons* is a powerful justification for the establishment of private property rights (or, at least, a case for managing a resource so that much of its value is not destroyed with overuse). But the argument for the establishment of property rights must be understood in its proper context, with an eye toward a balance in assigning property rights to decision-makers. For the tragedy of the commons to be a potential threat, the resource must be subject to *rivalry* and must be *exhaustible*, much like the pasture in Garrett Hardin's discussion. There is no reason for establishing property rights, giving owners rights of exclusion, when the resource is inexhaustible, because there can be no rivalry and the resource cannot be subject to overuse.

Numbers (1, 2, 3, etc.), letters (A, B, C, etc.), and musical notes (whether marks on sheet music or sounds from instruments) need not be subject to property rights assignment because they are inexhaustible in supply – anyone can use them without reducing the ability of others to use them – they are *nonrivalrous* in use. When the words you are reading were typed into a computer, the supply of letters available to everyone else in the world was not diminished. Hence, there can be no potential for a "tragedy" of the *overuse* of letters. Privatization in this case would lead to a greater tragedy, a monopoly of letters and words, which in turn could lead to the *underuse* of letters and words – another form of waste (or in economic jargon, "resource misallocation") dubbed the *tragedy of the anticommons* (Heller 1998).

This tragedy of the anticommons would be especially tragic if one person or firm privately owned all letters and words. The tragedy would be even more severe if different people or firms owned individual letters or words, because there could be enormous costs to people engaging in all the transactions required to make letters into words and words into published documents. (Economists call this "transaction costs" – the costs of communication and transportation required to make a trade happen.) The assignment of private rights could, in other words, substitute one tragedy – *overuse* – for another – *underuse* – with no convincing argument that the rights assignment has, on balance, improved welfare.

The tragedy of the anticommons can also be encouraged by the requirement that users seek agreement on *usage rights* from several (or many) agents who control access to the resource. For example, Michael Heller noticed the anticommons tragedy as it played out in the streets of Moscow after the fall of the Soviet Union. The streets were lined with carts of goods outside perfectly good multistory buildings that stood empty. Many buildings remained unused because vendors had to get permission to use the buildings from several government agencies, each of which had exclusion rights but not usage rights. The vendors obviously found it less costly to set up their carts and kiosks than to incur the costs involved in obtaining the required usage rights (Heller 1998).

Lawrence Lessig (2001), a Harvard law professor, stresses that the logic underlying the tragedy of the commons has been so widely accepted that analysts no longer harbor the requisite appreciation for having at least *some* resources – especially those that are nonrivalrous in nature – remain under common ownership, to be exploited with a high degree of freedom by all without the need to get the permission of the property owners (especially multiple owners). As a consequence, we may be suffering a growing tragedy of the anticommons without noticing the damage from underusage that is developing, especially in the use and growth of ideas and technology.

Lessig notes how almost everything used in movie scenes – pictures on the wall, distinctive chairs and couches, computers, place settings, and images of identifiable bystanders, not to mention the images and voices of the actors and actresses in lead and supporting roles – is owned by someone, which means that usage rights from all the various owners must be secured before the movie can be shot. If permission is not secured before the scene is shot, each owner can be expected to bargain strategically (while threatening a lawsuit), trying to secure a price for his or her agreement that extracts close to the full value of the scene. This means, of course, that the scene might not be used, even though it is "in the can." To prevent such strategic bargaining (and waste), the producers can bargain for the rights prior to filming. However, the potential for an anticommons tragedy in the form of fewer films produced still exists, given the multiple resource owners who must give their consent. Again, the transaction costs involved can result in "too few" films being produced.

Similarly, patents and copyrights can give rise to a tragedy of the anticommons. Consider authoring a textbook and imagine copyright protection for quotes used by the author. For example, we're about to use an entire essay by Leonard Read in Perspective 1. In such cases, we ask permission and pay for use if the fee is low enough to justify the cost. But what about shorter quotes? For example, we used a seventeen-word quote from Barringer earlier in the chapter. We cited the publication in the text and the bibliography, giving the author credit, and promoting her work. Should more be done? Should we ask permission to reprint every quote? Should we pay to use every quote?[2] Under the law, "fair use" is allowed if it is a reasonable use of the intellectual property rights that does not harm the owner. But "fair use" is subjective – and in a society that encourages lawsuits, this artificially increases the risks and the costs of producing new material.

The problem can be exponentially worse when products incorporate any number of patented parts held by different owners. The various owners of patented parts

---

[2] We've been told that a chapter's opening epigraph always requires permission and that permission fees are nonnegotiable. If so, these are interesting institutional arrangements that impact how this market functions.

(to an engine or computer program, for example) can hike development costs as they each bargain strategically and seek monopoly profits, which in turn increases transaction costs and the prices of engines, reducing the number of engines produced and sold.

Lessig recognizes that patents and copyrights are devices that have been developed to provide economic incentives for creativity. However, the incentive for creativity does not need to be unlimited – a fact that has historically been recognized by the limited life of patents and copyrights. Lessig notes that we have extended the life of both greatly since the 1950s. These extensions might be required, given the growth in development costs for many products. At the same time, the extensions may have been grounded in special-interest politics, not economics, which can imply that the extensions have unnecessarily increased the monopoly rents that patent holders have realized. The extensions, Lessig argues, have given rise to an extended tragedy of the anticommons in the form of too few technological developments that are available for other creative people to exploit at no cost. He concludes (Lessig 2001, 97):

In essence, the changes in the environment of the Internet that we are observing now alter the balance between control and freedom on the Net. The tilt of these changes is pronounced: Control is increasing. And while one cannot say in the abstract that increased control is a mistake, it is clear that we are expanding this control with no sense of what is lost. The shift is not occurring with the idea of a balance in mind. Instead, the shift proceeds as if control were the only value.

Lessig charts the multiple ways that patent and copyright laws have been changed, with the effect that transaction costs for the development of new ideas and products have been increased – a social cost that should not be ignored.

PERSPECTIVE 1
"I, Pencil," by Leonard E. Read (1983, originally published 1958)[3]

I am a lead pencil – the ordinary wooden pencil familiar to all boys and girls and adults who can read and write. (My official name is "Mongol 482." My many ingredients are assembled, fabricated and finished by Eberhard Faber Pencil Company, Wilkes-Barre, Pennsylvania.)

Writing is both my vocation and my avocation; that's all I do.

---

[3] The late Leonard Read was the founder of the Foundation for Economic Education (FEE). The article was downloaded from http://fee.org/resources/detail/i-pencil-audio-pdf-and-html. Reproduced with permission, Foundation for Economic Education https://creativecommons.org/licenses/by/4.0/.

You may wonder why I should write a genealogy. Well, to begin with, my story is interesting. And, next, I am a mystery – more so than a tree or a sunset or even a flash of lightning. But, sadly, I am taken for granted by those who use me, as if I were a mere incident and without background. This supercilious attitude relegates me to the level of the commonplace. This is a species of the grievous error in which mankind cannot too long persist without peril. For, as a wise man, G. K. Chesterton, observed, "We are perishing for want of wonder, not for want of wonders."

I, Pencil, simple though I appear to be, merit your wonder and awe, a claim I shall attempt to prove. In fact, if you can understand me – no, that's too much to ask of anyone – if you can become aware of the miraculousness that I symbolize, you can help save the freedom mankind is so unhappily losing. I have a profound lesson to teach. And I can teach this lesson better than can an automobile or an airplane or a mechanical dishwasher because – well, because I am seemingly so simple.

Simple? Yet, not a single person on the face of this earth knows how to make me. This sounds fantastic, doesn't it? Especially when you realize that there are about one and one-half billion of my kind produced in the US each year.

Pick me up and look me over. What do you see? Not much meets the eye – there's some wood, lacquer, the printed labeling, graphite lead, a bit of metal, and an eraser.

Innumerable Antecedents

Just as you cannot trace your family tree back very far, so is it impossible for me to name and explain all my antecedents. But I would like to suggest enough of them to impress upon you the richness and complexity of my background.

My family tree begins with what in fact is a tree, a cedar of straight grain that grows in northern California and Oregon. Now contemplate all the saws and trucks and rope and the countless other gear used in harvesting and carting the cedar logs to the railroad siding. Think of all the persons and the numberless skills that went into their fabrication: the mining of ore, the making of steel and its refinement into saws, axes, motors; the growing of hemp and bringing it through all the stages to heavy and strong rope; the logging camps with their beds and mess halls, the cookery and the raising of all the foods. Why, untold thousands of persons had a hand in every cup of coffee the loggers drink!

The logs are shipped to a mill in San Leandro, California. Can you imagine the individuals who make flat cars and rails and railroad engines and who construct and install the communication systems incidental thereto? These legions are among my antecedents.

Consider the millwork in San Leandro. The cedar logs are cut into small, pencil-length slats less than one-fourth of an inch in thickness. These are kiln-dried and then tinted for the same reason women put rouge on their faces. People prefer that I look pretty, not a pallid white. The slats are waxed and kiln-dried again. How many skills went into the making of the tint and kilns, into supplying the heat, the light and power, the belts, motors, and all the other things a mill requires? Are sweepers in the mill among my ancestors? Yes, and also included are the men who poured the concrete for the dam of a Pacific Gas & Electric company hydroplant, which supplies the mill's power. And don't over-look the ancestors present and distant who have a hand in transporting sixty carloads of slats across the nation from California to Wilkes-Barre.

Complicated Machinery

Once in the pencil factory – $4,000,000 in machinery and building, all capital accumulated by thrifty and saving parents of mine – each slat is given eight grooves by a complex machine, after which another machine lays leads in every other slat, applies glue, and places another slat atop – a lead sandwich, so to speak. Seven brothers and I are mechanically carved from this "wood-clinched" sandwich.

My "lead" itself – it contains no lead at all – is complex. The graphite is mined in Ceylon. Consider the miners and those who make their many tools and the makers of the paper sacks in which the graphite is shipped and those who make the string that ties the sacks and those who put them aboard ships and those who make the ships. Even the lighthouse keepers along the way assisted in my birth – and the harbor pilots.

The graphite is mixed with clay from Mississippi in which ammonium hydrox-ide is used in the refining process. Then wetting agents are added such as sul-fonated tallow – animal fats chemically reacted with sulfuric acid. After passing through numerous machines, the mixture finally appears as endless extrusions – as from a sausage grinder – cut to size, dried, and baked for several hours at 1,850 degrees Fahrenheit. To increase their strength and smoothness the leads are then treated with a hot mixture, which includes candelilla wax from Mexico, paraffin wax and hydrogenated natural fats.

My cedar receives six coats of lacquer. Do you know all of the ingredients of lacquer? Who would think that the growers of castor beans and the refiners of castor oil are a part of it? They are. Why, even the processes by which the lac-quer is made a beautiful yellow involves the skills of more persons than one can enumerate!

Observe the labeling. That's a film formed by applying heat to carbon black mixed with resins. How do you make resins and what, pray, is carbon black?

My bit of metal – the ferrule – is brass. Think of all the persons who mine zinc and copper and those who have the skills to make shiny sheet brass from these products of nature. Those black rings on my ferrule are black nickel. What is black nickel and how is it applied? The complete story of why the center of my ferrule has no black nickel on it would take pages to explain.

Then there's my crowning glory, inelegantly referred to in the trade as "the plug," the part man uses to erase the errors he makes with me. An ingredient called "factice" is what does the erasing. It is a rubber-like product made by reacting grape seed oil from the Dutch East Indies with sulfur chloride. Rubber, contrary to the common notion, is only for binding purposes. Then, too, there are numerous vulcanizing and accelerating agents. The pumice comes from Italy; and the pigment which gives "the plug" its color is cadmium sulfide.

Vast Web of Know-How

Does anyone wish to challenge my earlier assertion that no single person on the face of this earth knows how to make me?

Actually, millions of human beings have had a hand in my creation, no one of whom even knows more than a very few of the others. Now, you may say that I go too far in relating the picker of a coffee berry in far-off Brazil and food growers elsewhere to my creation; that this is an extreme position. I shall stand by my claim. There isn't a single person in all these millions, including the president of the pencil company, who contributes more than a tiny, infinitesimal bit of know-how. From the standpoint of know-how the only difference between the miner of graphite in Ceylon and the logger in Oregon is in the type of knowhow. Neither the miner nor the logger can be dispensed with, any more than the chemist at the factory or the worker in the oil field – paraffin being a by-product of petroleum.

Here is an astounding fact: Neither the worker in the oil field nor the chemist nor the digger of graphite or clay nor anyone who mans or makes the ships or trains or trucks nor the one who runs the machine that does the knurling on my bit of metal nor the president of the company performs his singular task because he wants *me*. Each one wants me less, perhaps, than does a child in the first grade. Indeed, there are some among this vast multitude who never saw a pencil nor would they know how to use one. Their motivation is other than me. Perhaps it is something like this: Each of these millions sees that he can thus exchange his tiny know-how for the goods and services he needs or wants. I may or may not be among these items.

No Human Master-Mind

There is a fact still more astounding: The absence of a master-mind, of anyone dictating or forcibly directing these countless actions that bring me into being. No trace of such a person can be found. Instead, we find the Scottish economist and moral philosopher Adam Smith's famous "Invisible Hand" at work in the marketplace. This is the mystery to which I earlier referred.

It has been said that "only God can make a tree." Why do we agree with this? Isn't it because we realize that we ourselves could not make one? Indeed, can we even describe a tree? We cannot, except in superficial terms. We can say, for instance, that a certain molecular configuration manifests itself as a tree. But what mind is there among men that could even record, let alone direct, the constant changes in molecules that transpire in the life span of a tree? Such a feat is utterly unthinkable!

I, Pencil, am a complex combination of miracles: a tree, zinc, copper, graphite, and so on. But to these miracles which manifest themselves in Nature an even more extraordinary miracle has been added: the configuration of creative human energies – millions of tiny bits of know-how configurating naturally and spontaneously in response to human necessity and desire and in the absence of any human master-minding! Since only God can make a tree, I insist that only God could make me. Man can no more direct millions of bits of know-how so as to bring a pencil into being than he can put molecules together to create a tree.

That's what I meant when I wrote earlier, "If you can become aware of the miraculousness that I symbolize, you can help save the freedom mankind is so unhappily losing." For, if one is aware that these bits of know-how will naturally, yes, automatically, arrange themselves into creative and productive patterns in response to human necessity and demand – that is, in the absence of governmental or any other coercive master-minding – then one will possess an absolutely essential ingredient for freedom: a faith in free men. Freedom is impossible without this faith.

Once government has had a monopoly on a creative activity – the delivery of the mail, for instance – most individuals will believe that the mail could not be efficiently delivered by men acting freely. And here is the reason: Each one acknowledges that he himself doesn't know how to do all the things involved in mail delivery. He also recognizes that no other individual could. These assumptions are correct. No individual possesses enough know-how to perform a nation's mail delivery any more than any individual possesses enough know-how to make a pencil. In the absence of a faith in free men – unaware that millions of tiny kinds of know-how would naturally and miraculously form and cooperate to satisfy this necessity – the individual cannot help but reach the erroneous conclusion that the mail can be delivered only by governmental master-minding.

Testimony Galore

If I, Pencil, were the only item that could offer testimony on what men can accomplish when free to try, then those with little faith would have a fair case. However, there is testimony galore; it's all about us on every hand. Mail delivery is exceedingly simple when compared, for instance, to the making of an automobile or a calculating machine or a grain combine or a milling machine, or to tens of thousands of other things.

Delivery? Why, in this age where men have been left free to try, they deliver the human voice around the world in less than one second; they deliver an event visually and in motion to any person's home when it is happening; they deliver 150 passengers from Seattle to Baltimore in less than four hours; they deliver gas from Texas to one's range or furnace in New York at unbelievably low rates and without subsidy; they deliver each four pounds of oil from the Persian Gulf to our Eastern Seaboard – halfway around the world – for less money than the government charges for delivering a one-ounce letter across the street! [*Some things have changed since this essay first ran in 1958 and 1983!*]

Leave Men Free

The lesson I have to teach is this: Leave all creative energies uninhibited. Merely organize society to act in harmony with this lesson. Let society's legal apparatus remove all obstacles the best it can. Permit creative know-how to freely flow. Have faith that free men will respond to the "Invisible Hand." This faith will be confirmed. I, Pencil, seemingly simple though I am, offer the miracle of my creation as testimony that this is a practical faith, as practical as the sun, the rain, a cedar tree, and the good earth.

Part B Organizational Economics and Management

Property Rights (or Not) in the Workplace

The absence of defined and enforceable property rights explains a number of problems in the workplace. Some of these are minor and mostly irritating. Common spaces such as kitchens and bathrooms are often unkempt. Someone takes your food from the refrigerator, while other food is left in there far too long. Someone takes coffee without contributing to the coffee fund or takes the last cup without brewing another batch. The communal candy dish goes empty and Bob eats at the holiday potluck meal without bringing anything. To raise money for an office gift to a co-worker, you have to go door-to-door or only allow donors to sign the card. Or think about the difference between property rights in a locked office instead of a cubicle.

Some omissions of property rights have much more consequence. Budgets tend to expand because we're spending someone else's money. The printer is used for personal use and a variety of office supplies find their way home. Computers and lights are left on overnight. Equipment is misused. In each case, the absence of enforceable property rights creates a tendency toward abuse and inefficiency.

More abstract but perhaps most important: Who gets the intellectual property rights for work that you complete on the job? How do we determine (and enforce) territory for personnel in sales or between franchises? When you leave a company, a noncompete agreement may restrict your property rights, going forward. Or consider what happens in a firm where neither credit nor blame are properly allocated. If I succeed but don't have property rights to receive credit, the incentive to be productive is reduced; if I fail but am not required to "own" the blame, again, the incentives are inefficient.

Managing through Incentives

We noted above that much of this book is concerned with the problem of overcoming a basic condition of life: *scarcity* (in terms of both limited resources in the external world and the limited resources in our brains). Firms are an integral means by which the pressures of scarcity are partially relieved for all who either own or work for firms. How does the tragedy of the commons developed in Part A reveal itself inside firms, especially large ones? Owners and their top managers want to get as much production from their workers as possible for the wages paid. But workers may not want to work as hard as their bosses want. Each worker can figure that if she shirks, her lack of work intensity will not be noticed in terms of the firm's total production. The problem is that if all workers follow suit, then the firm's profitability (if not survivability) and workers' jobs can be jeopardized – a tragedy of the commons that no worker may want. In order to get employees to work diligently for their firms (if they are not internally motivated to do so), managers and line workers must have some reason or purpose – some *incentive* – to do what they are supposed to do.[4] The motivation can come "from within," which underlines the importance of a company's hiring process. But external incentives will be a (large) piece of the puzzle.

A more positive angle: tying compensation to some objective measure of firm performance can cause worker productivity to rise substantially. (We discuss this in greater detail in Chapter 12, but introduce the concept here.) This is because tying pay to performance is a way of giving workers a form of property rights to a portion of the output they produce. In addition, tying pay to performance can change the type of workers who are attracted to pay-for-performance jobs.

---

[4] Students who wish to go beyond the basics of the "organizational economics" discussed in this textbook are advised to consider three important books: Rubin (1990), Milgrom and Roberts (1992), and Roberts (2004).

As such, appropriately structured incentive pay can increase a firm's rate of return and stock price, as well as the income of the affected workers.

When Safelite Auto Glass switched from paying its glass installers by the hour to paying them "piece rates," worker productivity went up by 44 percent, only half of which could be attributable to the motivational effect of the piece-rate pay system. The other half was attributable to the fact that Safelite started attracting people who were willing to work hard and began holding on to its more-motivated and more-productive workers, even as its less-motivated and less-productive workers were leaving the company (Lazear 2000).

One study of managers at large corporations found that adding a 10 percent bonus for good performance could be expected to add 0.3–0.9 percent to the after-tax rate of return on stockholder investment. If managerial bonuses are tied to the market prices of a company's stock, share prices can be expected to rise by 4–12 percent. The study, which covered 16,000 managers in 250 firms, also found that greater sensitivity of management pay to company performance correlates with better performance (Abowd 1990). Another study found that firms don't have to wait around for the incentives to have an impact on the firms' bottom line to get a jump in their stock prices. Merely *announcing* that executive compensation will be more closely tied to performance measures (through stock options or bonuses) increases stock prices and shareholder wealth (Brickley, Bhagat, and Lease 1985).

Naturally, if managers are paid just a straight salary, they have less reason to take on risky investments (Roberts 2004, chapter 4). Managers' potential gain from the higher rates of return associated with risky investments is uncertain and problematic (given that the rise in their future salaries from performance may not be clear and direct). They may shy away from risky investments – but more so than if their pay was clearly tied, in part or in whole, to some measure of firm performance. Accordingly, when managers are given bonuses based on performance, they tend to undertake riskier, higher-paying investments (Holmstrom 1979; Shavell 1979; Amihud and Lev 1981; Smith and Watts 1982). But then, if the bonuses are based on some short-term goal (e.g., this year's earnings) instead of some longer-term goal (e.g., some level for the stock price), managers will tend to sacrifice investments with higher longer-term payoffs for the smaller payoffs that are received within the performance period. The managers' time horizons can be lengthened by tying their compensation to the firm's stock value and then requiring them to hold the firm's stock until some later date – for example, retirement (Jensen and Meckling 1979).

Although incentives have always mattered, they probably have never been more important to businesses competing on a global scale. Greater competition means that producers everywhere must meet the best production standards anywhere on the globe, which requires them to have the best incentive systems anywhere. Incentives will continue to grow in importance as the economy becomes more complex, more global, and more competitive. When structured properly, incentives (both positive and negative) can increase the likelihood that managers, workers, owners, and consumers will prosper.

Like it or not, managers and owners should think about incentives with the same rigor with which they now contemplate their balance sheets and marketing plans. They should justify the incentive structures they devise, implying they will understand why they do what they do. High pay and so-called "golden parachutes" (or generous firing packages) for executives and stock options for workers will need to be used judiciously – rather than used because they seem like nice ideas or "everyone else" is using them. Investors who find it increasingly easy to move their investment funds around the world will be less inclined to allow their capital to be used for "nice ideas." Unless well designed, they can result in suboptimal investments. Incentives matter, so studying them is important to the bottom line.

Perverse Incentives

Unless policies are carefully considered, *perverse incentives* can be an inadvertent consequence, because people can be quite creative in responding to policies. Lincoln Electric is known for achieving high productivity levels among its production workers by tying their pay to measures of how much they produce. But the company has gone too far at times. When it tied the pay of secretaries to "production," with counters installed on typewriters to measure how much was typed, secretaries responded by spending their lunch hours typing useless pages of manuscript to increase their pay, resulting in this incentive being quickly abandoned (Fast and Berg 1971; Roberts 2004, 42).

In seeking to reduce the number of "bugs" in its programs, a software company began paying programmers to find and fix bugs. The goal was noble but the response wasn't: Programmers began creating bugs so that they could find and fix them, with one programmer increasing his pay $1700 through essentially fraudulent means. The company eliminated this incentive pay scheme within a week of its introduction (Adam 1995).

These experiences bring us to a general rule that managers of all companies must keep in mind: Incentives almost always work, but they don't always work well or in the anticipated ways – a fact that has led to harsh criticisms of even the attempt to use incentives, punishments, or rewards.[5] Economic researchers in Israel sought to help ten day-care centers in Haifa reduce the number of times

---

[5] For criticisms of the explicit use of incentives, see Kohn (1993b) and Pearce (1987).

parents picked up their children late (Gneezy and Rustichini 2000). For the first four weeks of their twenty-week research experiment, the researchers did not impose a fine for late pickups and observed that the day-care centers had an average of seven late pickups per week. After the fifth week, they imposed a fee of $3 per late pickup. Contrary to their presumption, late pickups jumped to an average of twenty per week per center. The late pickups could have increased for two reasons that the researchers did not consider, according to Stephen Levitt and Stephen Dubner, who report on the experiment in their best-selling economics book, *Freakonomics*. First, the parents considered the $3 fee to be an approved and cheap form of added babysitting. (Thus, a $20 late fee might have had the expected response, because the fee would then be greater than the cost of babysitting found elsewhere.) Second, the day-care centers had probably lowered, on balance, the true cost for tardiness: The monetary late fee took the place of the "psychic cost" associated with doing something considered "wrong," such as not picking up children on time (Levitt and Dubner 2005, 19–20, 23).

Mitsubishi Motors sought to increase the sales of its cars in 2003 through a promotional campaign dubbed "zero-zero-zero": zero down-payment, zero interest, and zero payments for the first twelve months after sale. According to one automobile industry journalist, "a hefty number [of car buyers] used this promotion to drive a new car without paying anything for a year, after which they let the car get repossessed," resulting in losses of hundreds of millions of dollars for the company (Ingrassia 2005).

One source of the worldwide mortgage market meltdown in the 2000s was that lenders, with the encouragement of the federal government, began making mortgage loans in the 1990s to prospective homeowners with little to no down-payments and "teaser" (below-market) interest rates for two or three years (after which the interest rates and mortgage payments would increase). Many prospective homebuyers (and speculators) snapped up the so-called "subprime" mortgages, figuring that they could reap an increase in their home equity as housing prices continued to rise. The problem: If the housing bubble burst, then the homebuyers had little or nothing to lose. The mortgage lenders bundled their subprime mortgages and sold them to investors around the world, who assumed that the mortgages were a safe investment because of the housing bubble. Few investors recognized that the value of their securities would plummet with the subsequent crash in housing prices, aggravated by many homeowners who walked away from their homes (and mortgage payments) when their payments escalated and the resale prices of their homes fell below their mortgage balances.

With the mortgage market meltdown, bank regulators clamped down on banks' ability to make loans of all kinds, including mortgages. The result? As expected, down-payment and credit-score requirements for all forms of credit went up and homeownership declined significantly from 69 percent in 2006 to 64 percent in 2014 (Gupta 2014). Builders started concentrating on the construction of apartment complexes instead of housing development. In effect, developers began to trade on their relatively greater ability to get credit, with apartment rents rising in the process. Not surprisingly, political operatives saw the personal gains of returning to earlier campaign themes (all people should be able to own a house) and financial regulators began to relax their down-payment demands. The concern is that politics and poor incentives could set the stage for another financial meltdown.

Why Incentives Are Important

Incentive systems can cause managers to manage their earnings. For example, when managers are paid on the basis of *annual* performance targets, research shows that they have been induced to advance the reporting of sales when they expect to be short of the set targets. When they expect to exceed their targets, managers have moved sales to the first quarter of the next year on the grounds that there is no reason for them to "waste" sales (Oyer 1998; Horngren 1999, 937–938). A prominent example: The fact that so many executives at Enron and WorldCom held so much of their companies' stock can go a long way toward explaining the extensive accounting fraud at those companies. By "cooking the books," the managers were able to inflate the value of their stock holdings (Roberts 2004, 156–157), which carries a valuable lesson: beware of tying managers' pay to performance measures that are easily manipulated (Baker 2000).

In the increasingly globalized world economy, business incentives will continue to become ever more commonplace. Getting them right – and not getting them wrong – will be an even greater concern for managers. Such conceptual and factual points beg two critical questions: Why are incentives important within firms? And why do they work?

Admittedly, the answers are many. One important reason is that firms are collections of workers whose interests are not always aligned with the interests of those who employ them. The subsequent problem for owners is how to get workers to do what the owners want them to do. The owners could just issue directives, but, without sufficient incentive to obey them, nothing may happen. Directives may have some value in themselves: People do feel a sense of obligation to do what they were hired to do, and one of the things they may have been hired to do is to obey orders (within limits). However, directives can be costly. Firms may use incentives as a cheaper substitute for giving out orders that can go unheeded.

Firms may also use incentives to clarify firm goals, spelling out in concrete terms to workers what the owners want to accomplish. As every manager knows all too well, it is difficult to establish and write out the firm's strategies to achieve its stated goals. It is an even more difficult task to get workers to appreciate, understand, and remember firm goals – and then work toward them. The communication problem typically escalates with the size of the organization (as will be explained in Chapter 2).

Goals are always imperfectly communicated, especially by emailed memoranda or through employment manuals that may be read once and deleted. Workers do not always know how serious the owners and upper managers are: they can remember many times when widely circulated memos were nothing but "window dressing." Incentives are a means by which owners and upper managers can validate overall company goals and strategies. Reinforced regularly in paychecks and end-of-year bonuses, they can in effect say: "This is what we think is important. This is what we will be working toward. This is what we will be trying to get everyone else to do. And this is where we will put our money." Even if workers are not sensitive to the pecuniary benefits of work, incentives may effectively communicate what their companies want them to do – with a valuable and direct impact on what workers actually do and how long, hard, and smart they work (White 1991; Robins 1996).

But there is a far more fundamental reason that incentives matter: *managers don't always know what orders or directives to give.* No matter how intelligent, hard-working, and well informed, managers seldom know as much about particular jobs as those who are actually doing them. Knowing about the peculiarities of a machine, the difficulties a fellow worker on the production line is experiencing at home, or the personality quirks of a customer are just a few examples of the innumerable particular bits of localized knowledge that are crucial to the success of a firm. And this knowledge is spread over everyone in the firm without the possibility of being fully communicated to, and effectively utilized by, those who are primarily responsible for managerial oversight. The only way a firm can fully benefit from such localized knowledge is to allow those who possess the knowledge – the firm's employees – the freedom to use what they know. To economists, this is what it means to *empower* workers.

But the benefits from participatory management (employee empowerment) can be realized only if employees have the freedom *and* the motivation to use their special knowledge in productive cooperation with each other. The crucial ingredient for bringing about the requisite coordination is incentives that align the otherwise conflicting interests of individual employees with the collective interests of all members of the firm. Without such incentives, there can be no real employee empowerment, because there is no hope that the knowledge dispersed throughout the firm will be used in a coordinated and constructive way. The only practical alternative to a functioning system of incentives is a top-down, command-and-control approach that, unfortunately, never can allow the full potential of a firm's employees to be realized.

Hayek's ageless insight about the dispersion of economically relevant information applies within the firm (Hayek 1960). With the growing complexity and sophistication of production, knowledge becomes ever more widely dispersed among a growing number of workers (many of whom can be scattered around the country and the globe). Hence, the importance of incentives has grown with modern-day leaps in the technological sophistication of production processes. Incentives will continue to grow in importance as production and distribution processes become ever more complex and increasingly spread among workers.

Seen in this light, the problem of the firm is the same as the problem of the general economy. Economists have argued for years that government planners, even if intelligent and dedicated, cannot acquire all the localized knowledge necessary to allocate resources intelligently. The long and painful experiments with socialism and its extreme variant, communism, have confirmed that economists got this argument right. But the freedom for people to use their personalized knowledge must be coupled with incentives that motivate people to use this knowledge in socially cooperative ways – meaning that the best way for individuals to pursue their own objectives is by making decisions that improve the opportunities for others to pursue their objectives. A hidden message in incentives is this: "If you use well your localized information, you will prosper, to a degree. If not, you will share in the firm's added costs or lost profitable opportunities."

In a market economy and across firms, incentives are found primarily in the form of *prices* that emerge from the rules of private property and voluntary exchange. Market prices provide the incentives needed to productively coordinate decisions – thus making it not only possible, but also desirable, for people to have a large measure of freedom to use the localized information and expertise they have. Market-determined prices can be seen as an information system that inspires cooperation among firms and people.

A perfect incentive system would assure that everyone could be given complete freedom because it would be in the interest of each to advance the interests of all. No such system exists – within any firm or any economy. In every economy, there is a combination of market incentives and government controls that would achieve the best overall results. The argument over "the right mix" will no doubt continue indefinitely, but few deny that both incentives and controls (for example, in setting and enforcing property rights) are needed. Similarly, for any firm with more than one worker, there is some mix of incentives and direct managerial control that best promotes the objectives of the firm and the general interests of its members.

Of course, if a given firm doesn't pay attention to its incentives, it may lose more than its lunch; it may be forced out of business by firms that do recognize the importance of incentives. Seen from this perspective, incentives can be a critical component of firm survival – perhaps just as critical as product development or technological sophistication. The problem is in getting the incentives right and using the full range of potential incentives. Unfortunately, we can't say exactly what incentives your firm should employ. The ideal incentives depend on local conditions that can vary greatly across firms. The important point to remember is that incentives must be given careful consideration.

Practical Lessons

An admonition that we'll repeat throughout this book: Envision management as a problem in solving Prisoner's Dilemmas, finding ways to overcome the pursuit of personal interests at the expense of the organization's larger interests. Make sure that you understand how this seemingly simple "game" has wide application in your personal and business lives.

Management self-help books describe management as an extremely complex undertaking. It can be, but the economic way of thinking about management seeks to cut through the complexity with practical pointers. The central task of managers is to provide employees with a set of incentives that encourage them to take the cooperative solution. Too often, managers rely on directives to bring about cooperation among workers. Directives can work well, but only when managers know more about what the workers do than the workers. In complex working environments, this is often not the case. Managers hire workers because managers can't know or do all the things that workers are supposed to do. In such cases, managers should consider replacing directives with incentives that encourage workers to use their specialized and localized knowledge to use firm resources in the most cost-effective manner.

Profits can be made from product development. Profits can also be made from getting incentives right, making sure that workers share in firm gains when workers do things right and in firm losses when workers do things wrong. In effect, getting incentives right can mean making workers in many job categories into *residual claimants*.

One final example: In the midst of a budget "crunch," a university was looking for ways to reduce its expenditures on "large-ticket items" such as electricity. The university was spending $120 per year per computer to keep its computers running overnight. Almost all of the university's 1500 professors were leaving their computers on when they left the office – out of laziness or to tap into their office computers from home through the "Desktop Remote" feature of Windows. At the time, a software program was available that would "wake up" turned-off computers for $68 per computer. Substantial cost savings were obvious, but faculty were not rushing to buy the program. Why? The university paid the electricity bill, but professors would have to pay for the wake-up program out of their discretionary budgets. One potential organizational fix should have been apparent: Give each professor (or his department) an electricity budget that would more than cover the cost of the wake-up software and allow each professor to keep any residual for research purposes.

Further Reading Online

Reading 1.1: The economics of suspense (*The New York Times*, link available on the online resources website www.cambridge.org/mckenzie4)

Reading 1.2: The cost of paying attention (*The New York Times*, link available on the online resources website www.cambridge.org/mckenzie4)

Reading 1.3: Disincentives in poverty relief

Reading 1.4: Game theory says Pete Carroll's call at goal line is defensible (*The New York Times*, link available on the online resources website www.cambridge.org/mckenzie4)

Reading 1.5: In Greek debt puzzle, the game theorists have it (*The New York Times*, link available on the online resources website www.cambridge.org/mckenzie4)

Recommended Videos Online

1   Video course introduction (Richard McKenzie, 17 minutes)

2   Introduction to the economic way of thinking, 1 (Richard McKenzie, 28 minutes)

3   The economic way of thinking, 2 (Richard McKenzie, 29 minutes)

4   Property rights, markets, and tragedies of the commons (Richard McKenzie, 33 minutes)

5   Prisoner's Dilemma (Richard McKenzie, 28 minutes)

6   Comparative advantage (Richard McKenzie, 21 minutes)

7   Tragedies of the anticommons (Richard McKenzie, 18 minutes)

The Bottom Line

The key takeaways from Chapter 1 are the following:

1   Economics is a discipline best described as the study of human interaction in the context of scarcity. It is the study of how people (individually and collectively) use their scarce resources to satisfy as many of their wants as possible. The economic method is founded in a set of presuppositions about human behavior on which economists construct theoretical models.

2   Economics is a way of thinking about virtually everything, including the issues that managers confront daily. Economics is especially applicable to business dealings in markets where economic interests ("What can you do for me and

what can I do for you in financial terms?") are dominant. The ability of economics to explain behavior in personal realms (where a variety of motives, including love and beneficence, can have powerful coordinating effects on behavior) loses some (but not nearly all) of its force.

3 Communally owned property is a common cause of resource misuse and over-use. Private property rights matter because they affect people's incentives to use scarce resources. This is because they affect people's rewards from effectively using scarce resources – and the costs incurred from misusing and abusing scarce resources.

4 Not all potential tragedies of the commons need to be resolved through private property rights and government regulation. Voluntary associations and firms are means by which the overuse of communally owned resources has been abated.

5 Trade must be perceived as mutually beneficial to the trading partners. And trade can be mutually beneficial even when one party to the trades is more efficient (has a comparative advantage) in both goods subject to trade.

6 In general, incentives of all kinds matter in how effectively scarce resources are used. There is obviously profit to be made from developing better goods and ser-vices. Less widely recognized is the fact that there is also profit to be made from developing better, more cost-effective, incentive systems.

7 Overcoming Prisoner's Dilemmas is a pervasive problem in the development of social and management policies.

Review Questions ▶▶

1 In the prison camp described early in this chapter, rations were distributed equally. Why did trade within and among bungalows result?

2 Recall the priest who traded cigarettes for cheese and cheese for cigarettes, so that he ended up with more cigarettes than initially. Did someone else in the camp lose by the priest's activities? How was the priest able to end up better off than when he began? What did his activities do to the price of cheese in the different bungalows?

3 Theories may be defective and are always limited, but economists continue to use them. Why?

4 A microeconomics book designed for business students could include theories more complex than those in this book. What are the trade-offs in using more complex theories?

5 What are the economic consequences of extending the copyright term for a book from fourteen to seventy-five years?

6 What are some examples from your workplace where property rights are handled well or not so well?

7   What is an example where communal property rights (or a lack of personal property rights) works well enough? Why does it work?

8   What are the costs and benefits of people specializing their efforts?

9   Apply the principles of "*I, Pencil*" to your industry.

10 As products become increasingly complex, what does "*I, Pencil*" say about the resulting specialization of efforts? As products become ever more complex, should production become increasingly based on markets?

11 Some restaurants have their bartenders "tip pool" (or divide up their total tips at the end of their shifts). Servers in the rest of the restaurant often do not tip pool. What are the problems of tip pooling? Why do bartenders often tip pool while other servers in the same restaurant do not? How do restaurants overcome the potential problems with tip pooling?

12 Most business students study in "teams." Is there a potential tragedy of the commons within the teams? How have your teams sought to overcome the incentive problems? Why are teams generally small? What would be the consequence of doubling the size of study teams?

2

Principles of Rational Behavior in Society and Business

The combined assumptions of maximizing behavior, market equilibrium, and stable preferences, used relentlessly and unflinchingly, form the heart of the economic approach.

Gary S. Becker[1]

Critics frequently object to the icy rationality of ... . I'm always tempted to ask in reply: "Would you prefer a warm, human error? Do you feel better with a nice emotional mistake?"

Herman Kahn[2]

Our purpose in this chapter is to explain how economists think about people's decision-making and behavior. We recognize that the economic way of thinking is not the only way people think about business and life (through methods used in the hard sciences, psychology, the arts, etc.). Most people operate on several different intellectual plains – simultaneously, shifting from one to another, or with a concentrated focus on one method of thinking. However, be forewarned: with enough work on the economics plain, we expect many students will come to recognize the benefits of shifting to the economics plain more often than you might now expect. We have frequently told our students that "economics is as much a 'discipline' as it is a disease. Once you catch it, it can be terminal, pervading much of your thinking." We think you will be pleasantly surprised at how much markets, business, and the world can be understood through the economic way of thinking.

That said, we do consider alternative disciplinary ways of thinking about observed human behavior. And we understand criticisms of the economic approach coming from other disciplines. (From time to time, we will note these critiques and deal with them briefly.) For example, in Part B of this chapter, we develop the

---

[1] Gary Becker, 1978. *The Economic Approach to Human Behavior*, University of Chicago Press, Chicago (p. 5).

[2] Herman Kahn, 2009. *In Defense of Thinking*, Lexington Books, Blue Ridge Summit, PA (p. 22).

economic logic behind people's *economic* behavior in "small" and "large" groups – mostly in terms of individual calculations of costs and benefits, without reference to group interests. But in Perspective 2, we discuss the evolutionary foundation of cooperation within groups and consider the "common interest theory" of group behavior. Maslow's "Hierarchy of Needs" is used extensively in other business disciplines, especially in marketing. Later, in Perspective 5, we explore differences in analytical predictions coming from the use of Maslow's hierarchy in marketing and economics. We also devote Online Chapter 1 to the concerns and findings of a burgeoning subdiscipline called "behavioral economics," which relies heavily on the analytical methods and findings of psychology.[3]

We make these forays into other disciplinary approaches, because they are important, but also because this will sharpen your use of the economic way of thinking – a useful but partial lens through which we can better understand the people around us and the world we inhabit. All disciplines have their limits, so everyone can benefit from shifts across several intellectual plains.

Part A Theory and Public Policy Applications

With these introductory caveats in mind, we can start by asserting that micro-economics rests on certain assumptions about individual behavior (as is true of all other disciplines). One is that people are capable of envisioning various ways of improving their position in life. Here, we extend the discussion in Chapter 1 about how people cope with scarcity, choosing among alternatives for improved well-being. According to microeconomic theory, people make choices *rationally*, trying to maximize their own welfare ("self-interested" whether their motives are selfish or charitable). This seemingly innocuous premise about human behavior will allow us to deduce an amazing variety of implications for business and other areas of human endeavor. For example, the premise undergirds our study of voluntary, mutually beneficial trade considered in Chapter 1 and the forces of supply and demand to be developed in Chapter 3. The assumption of rationality is at the core of the economic way of thinking about everything.

We understand that rational behavior is not applicable to all behavior under all circumstances. (Economists do not know the exact limits of rational behavior as a theoretical foundation.) We will unabashedly push the economic way

---

[3] In the subdiscipline *behavioral economics*, psychologists and economists have documented a variety of "irrational" behaviors (Thaler and Sunstein 2008; Ariely 2010). We acknowledge and accept the behavioral evidence in a range of studies, although we cover the findings and our problems with the behavioral approach in Online Chapter 1. Both analytical paradigms are imperfect means of ferreting out understandings about human behavior; neither should be jettisoned because they have limits and flaws. It is an important challenge for economists to find some way of integrating the two analytical approaches – a topic far beyond the scope of this book.

of thinking into every nook and cranny of behavior to see where we can gain insights. Still, we will be ever mindful of the limits of rational behavior – on alert for when deductions don't make sense. (Economists insist on empirical testing of their hypotheses to see if they have gone too far – where conclusions are not supported by real-world data, suggesting that behavior has some other non-rational foundations.)[4]

Rationality: a Basis for Exploring Human Behavior

We can never satisfy all our wants. The best we can do is to maximize our satisfaction in the face of scarcity. Economists use the term **utility** to describe our well-being when we buy and sell, achieve a success (small or large), earn a living, drink, eat, have sex, read a good book, have children,

Utility is the satisfaction (pleasure, happiness, joy) a person receives from the consumption of a good or service – or from participation in an activity.

play, or earn an A on a microeconomics exam! When economists talk of "maximizing utility," they mean that people seek to gain as much utility as they can within *all* the constraints they face, in terms of both the limited resources of the external physical world and those internal to us. The ultimate assumption behind this theory is that *people act with a purpose*, at least much of the time. In the words of Ludwig von Mises, they act because they are "dissatisfied with the state of affairs as it prevails" (von Mises 1962, 2–3).

The Acting Individual

If people act in order to satisfy their wants, their behavior must be self-directed rather than externally controlled – at least to some extent. (There is no way to fully prove an assertion about "free will." Economists simply presume that individuals are "agents" who possess some degree of "agency," have "agendas," and make decisions.) It is the individual who has wants and desires, looks for the means to fulfill them, and attempts to render his or her state more satisfying.

For analytical purposes (if for no other reason), group action results from the actions of the individuals in the group (as we shall see in Part B of this chapter). Social values, for instance, draw their meaning from the values that individuals share, while still holding values individually. Economists would even say that group action cannot be separated from individual action, although economists argue that individual actions can lead to outcomes that no member of the group

---

[4] We are not willing to accept some behaviorists' claim that behavior is so irrational that it is "predictably irrational" (Ariely 2010) – if for no other reason than the claim itself draws into question its own validity: If the claim is true, it also has an irrational grounding! If people are so completely irrational, why should we trust the deductions of those who draw such a conclusion? But there are other problems with such claims, which we will consider in Online Chapter 1.

wants. As we began to see in Chapter 1, economists can explain such outcomes as the result of rational individuals responding to incentives that may be improved.

Of course, individuals in a group can impact one another's wants and behavior, but the focus of decision-making will stay on individuals (mainly for methodological reasons). Among other factors, the size and structure of a group can have a dramatic effect on individual behavior. For example, when economists speak of a competitive market, they are describing the influence that other competitors have on individual consumers and firms – and the choice dynamics of the individuals involved.

Rational Behavior

When individuals act to satisfy their wants, they exhibit **rational behavior**. The notion of rational behavior rests on three assumptions:

> **Rational behavior** is consistent behavior that maximizes an individual's satisfaction through comparisons of the costs and benefits of alternative courses of action.

1 The individual has a preference and can identify, within limits, what is wanted.
2 The individual is capable of ordering his or her wants consistently – from most to least preferred (the principle of "transitivity").
3 The individual will choose consistently from these ordered preferences to maximize his or her satisfaction.

Even though the individual cannot fully satisfy all of her wants, when possible, she will always choose more of what she wants rather than less. (The fancy term for this is "monotonicity." Sometimes, less is better – as with pollution and crime – what economists call "economic bads.") In short, the rational individual always stands ready to further her own interests (which do not always have to be strictly selfish; indeed, they can be selfless).

Some readers will find these assertions obvious and acceptable. To others, they may seem narrow and uninspiring. Economists often talk and write *as if* people are perfectly rational – that is, as if they always make decisions with great care and precision and without errors in judgment (other than mistakes in dealing with the risks and uncertainties of life). This is not because economists truly believe that people's decisions are never prone to error, decision-making biases, or "irrationalities." Rather, economists press the founding premise of rationality for two reasons:

1 An assumption of perfect rationality can ease the difficulty (cost) of thinking through the implications of decision-making. If we were to assume that people are imperfectly rational or "quasi-rational," it would become exceedingly difficult to model human thinking and decision-making, in trying to gain insight through the development of logical deductions and testable hypotheses. (This is a goal of all science, including "social sciences" such as economics.) The

frailties and limitations of the brain are all the more reason we need to simplify our models of human decision-making.

2 By developing theory based on a premise of perfect rationality in personal and business decision-making, we can deduce a variety of principles that can lead to improved decision-making for people who are beset with decision-making biases, resulting in enhanced personal welfare and greater firm profits. People might harbor innate imperfections in their rationality, but competitive pressures in markets can encourage them to find ways of improving their thinking and their rationality.

Note that, even with *perfect* rationality, we would *not* observe perfect decision-making. People simply cannot assess with total precision *all* costs and benefits in given decisions. Many costs and benefits can be hidden from decision-makers' purview, maybe not even detectable until decisions have been made. Other costs and benefits might be too varied and inconsequential to consider. It is not worth it for rational people to understand all costs and benefits in decisions, large and small. In fact, to be rational, people must consider the costs and benefits of finely determining costs and benefits!

The punchline is that people are assumed to be generally trying to behave in this manner – maximizing utility subject to their constraints. And cutting through some of these methodological complications can improve analytical progress – our ultimate goal in this book. Later in the chapter, we examine some common objections to the concept of rational behavior, but first we examine a few logical consequences of the rationality premise.

Rational Decisions in a Constrained Environment

Three important conclusions flow from the economist's presumption of rational behavior:

1 The individual makes choices from an array of alternatives.

2 In making each choice, a person must forgo one or more things for something else. Hence, all behavior involves a cost – the value of the most preferred alternative.

3 In striving to maximize welfare, the individual will take those actions whose benefits exceed their costs and will continue to consume any given good (or undertake any given activity) until the additional value of the last unit equals the additional cost incurred.

Choice

We assume that the individual can evaluate the available alternatives and select the one that maximizes her utility. But nothing in the economic definition of rational behavior suggests that the individual is completely free to do as she wishes. Whenever we talk about individual decisions, we are actually talking about *constrained choices* – limited by outside forces and internal limitations. For example, as a student or manager, you are in a particular social and physical environment with certain physical and mental abilities. These environmental and personal factors influence the options open to you. You may not have the money, the time, or the stomach to become a surgeon – and you don't have the time to take all the courses listed in the schedule for your business program.

Although your range of choices may not be wide, you still have many options. At this moment, you could be doing any number of things instead of reading this book. You could be studying some other subject, sharing a meal with a friend, playing with your child, completing a company project, or staring at the Moon. In fact, you not only can make choices; you must make them.

Suppose that you have an exam tomorrow and there are only two things you can do within the next twelve hours: study economics or play golf. These two options are represented in Figure 2.1. Suppose you spend the entire twelve hours studying economics. In our example, the most you could study is four chapters or E_1. At the other extreme, you could do nothing but golf – but again, there is a limit: eight rounds or G_1.

Neither extreme is likely to be acceptable. Assuming that you aim both to pass your exam and to have fun, what combination of rounds of golf and study should you choose? The available options are represented by the straight line E_1G_1, the "production possibilities frontier" (PPF) for study and play, and the area underneath it. If you want to maximize your production, you will choose some point on E_1G_1, such as a: two chapters of economics and four golf rounds.

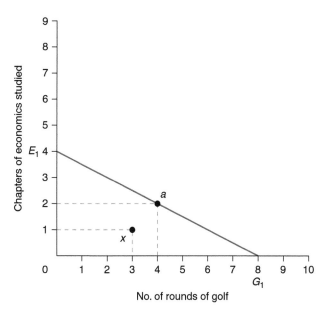

Figure 2.1 Constrained choice With a given amount of time and other resources, you can produce any combination of study and golf along the curve E_1G_1. The particular combination you choose will depend on your personal preferences for those two goods. You will not choose point x, because it represents less than you are capable of achieving – and as a rational person, you will strive to maximize your utility. Because of constraints on your time and resources, you cannot achieve a point beyond E_1G_1.

You might yearn for five rounds and the same amount of study, but that point is above the curve and beyond your capabilities (the "frontier"). If you settle for less – say, one chapter and three golf rounds (at point x) – you will be doing less than you are capable of doing and will not be maximizing your utility. The combination you actually choose will depend on your preferences.

Changes in your environment or your physical capabilities can affect your opportunities and consequently the choices you make. For example, if you improve your study skills, your production rate for chapters studied will rise. You might then be able to study eight units of economics in twelve hours – in which case, your PPF would expand outward. Even if your ability to play golf remained the same, your greater proficiency in studying would enable you to increase the number of rounds of golf played. Your new set of production possibilities would be E_2G_1 in Figure 2.2.

Again, you are able to choose from a range of opportunities; the option you choose is not predetermined. You may decide against further golf rounds and opt instead for four chapters of economics (point c). Or you could move to point b, in which case you would be learning more economics and playing more golf. An improvement in your study skills might show up in your golf game as well as your course performance.

Notice that we assumed the available trade-off between study and golf is consistent. Initially, it was one chapter for every two rounds of golf (on E_1G_1 in Figures 2.1 and 2.2). The result is a linear PPF with a slope of ½ reflecting the 2:1 trade-off. Then, the trade-off changed to 1:1 with a slope of 1. (We see the same linear relationship with "budget constraints" for consumers with respect to

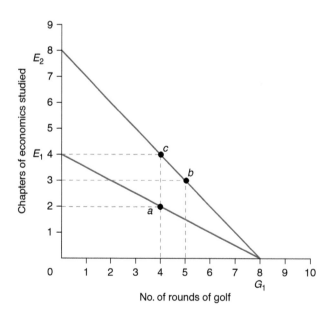

Figure 2.2 Change in constraints
If your study skills improve and your ability at golf remains constant, your PPF curve will shift from E_1G_1 to E_2G_1. Both the number of chapters and the number of rounds of golf may increase. On your old curve, E_1G_1, you could study two chapters and play four rounds of golf (point a). On your new curve E_2G_1, you can study three chapters and play five rounds of golf (point b).

income and the prices they face in the market for two goods. We cover this in the Online Math Appendix.)

In the real world, PPFs are often nonlinear for individuals, firms, and countries (given comparative advantage and specialization from Chapter 1 – and diminishing marginal returns, a concept we'll cover in Chapter 7). The result is a changing trade-off and slope – for example, between points A and B compared to points X and Y in Figure 2.3.

Cost

The fact that choices exist implies that some alternative must be forgone when another is taken. For example, suppose that you have decided to spend an hour watching sitcoms. The two sitcoms you most want to watch are *The Office* and *Stranger Things*. If you choose *The Office*, the cost is the pleasure you sacrifice by not watching *Stranger Things*.

Notice that cost does not require spending money. The cost of watching one TV show instead of another has nothing to do with money. Money can be a useful

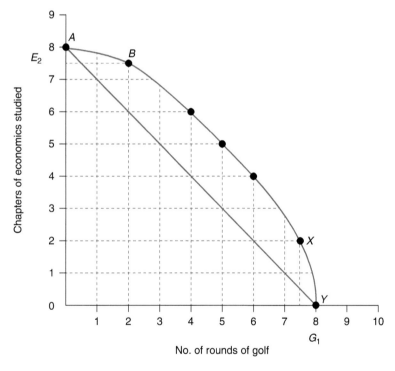

Figure 2.3 Nonlinear constraints
The linear relationship between E_2 and G_1 depicts a constant slope and trade-off between golf played and chapters studied. The nonlinear relationship between E_2 and G_1 shows a slope that changes, reflecting trade-offs that change with diminishing marginal returns. From A to B, you could play two rounds of golf by only giving up a half-chapter of Econ. But from X to Y, you could study two chapters of Econ instead of a half-round of golf.

measure of costs, because it can reduce all costs to one common denominator. But money is not a cost itself. The shoes you are wearing may have cost you $80 (a **money cost**), but the real cost (the **opportunity cost**) is the value of the next best thing you could have purchased with the $80. The real cost is the actual benefits given up from the most preferred alternative not taken when a choice is made.

> **Money cost** is a monetary measure of the benefits forgone when a choice is made.

> **Opportunity cost** is the *value* of the most highly preferred alternative not taken at the time the choice is made – what could have been done instead of what is done.

As long as you have alternative uses for your time and other resources, "there is no such thing as a free lunch" – a pat phrase economists repeat often. Nothing can be free if other opportunities are available. One goal of any economics course is to help you recognize this simple but underrated principle and to train you to search for hidden costs. There is a cost to writing a poem, watching a sunset, and extending a common courtesy of opening a door for someone. Although money is not always involved in choices, the opportunity to do other things is. *A cost is incurred in every choice.*

Economics has often been described as the "dismal science" because of the attention economists give to ferreting out all costs (including opportunity costs) that are not always easy to see. For example, tuition and fees are hardly the full cost of education. Students' time cost is often higher than out-of-pocket expenditures, especially for working business professionals who forgo drawing a salary or don't have time to complete lucrative business deals. When in business, you would be well advised to seek out all the costs of ventures, including the opportunity cost of time and interest. For example, when firms use their own funds to do one venture, they give up the potential interest earnings on other investments. Business ventures vary in the likelihood of failure, which means they carry different and easily overlooked **risk costs**. These should be assessed (at least roughly) to make intelligent business choices – all with an eye on profitability. (We will say more about time and risk costs shortly.)

> **Risk cost** is an assessment of the value of any decision adjusted for the likelihood that the business venture will fail (or not succeed as hoped).

Maximizing Satisfaction: Cost–Benefit Analysis

An individual who behaves rationally will choose an option only when its calculated benefits are greater than or equal to its calculated costs. This is equivalent to choosing the most favorable option available. That is, people will produce or consume those goods and services whose benefits exceed the benefits of the most favored opportunity not taken.

This restatement of the *maximizing principle* explains individual choice in terms of cost. In Figure 2.1, the choices along curve $E_1 G_1$ represent various cost–benefit trade-offs. If you choose point *a*, we assume that you prefer *a* to any other combination because it yields the most favorable ratio of benefits to costs.

A change in cost will produce a change in incentives and perhaps a change in behavior. Suppose you and a friend set a date to play checkers, but at the last moment he receives a lucrative job offer on the day of the match. Most likely, the contest will be rescheduled. The job offer will change your friend's opportunities in such a way that what would have been the rational act (playing checkers) is probably no longer rational. If so, the cost of playing checkers has risen significantly enough to exceed the benefits.

Economists see **cost–benefit analysis** as the basis of much (but certainly not all) of our behavior. Why do you attend classes, for example? The obvious answer is that, at the time you decide to attend class, you expect the benefits of attending to exceed the opportunity costs. The principle applies even to courses you dislike. A particular class may have no intrinsic value, but you may fear missing information that would be useful for the exam. Thus, the benefits of attending are a higher grade than you would otherwise expect. Besides, the other options open to you at 7 o'clock on a Tuesday evening may have so little appeal that the cost of going to class is modest.

> **Cost–benefit analysis** is the careful calculation and comparison of all costs and benefits associated with a given course of action.

Take another example. Americans are known for the amount of waste they accumulate. America's "gross national garbage" (what Americans collectively discard annually) is estimated to be more valuable than the gross national output of many other nations, throwing away many things that people in other parts of the world would be glad to have. However morally reprehensible some people may find such "waste," it can be seen as the result of economically rational behavior. The food wrappings people throw away, for example, add convenience and freshness to the food – the value of which can easily exceed the costs. And in many cases, the cost of transporting our waste to others is prohibitively high.

So does it make sense to say that using and disposing of food wrapping is wasteful (from our disciplinary perspective)? Perhaps sometimes, but only if the person throwing away the trash is able to impose some of the waste disposal costs on others, thereby making a decision in which the personal value of the disposal is less than the total cost incurred by all people. So, litter can be an economic waste of a sort (an inefficiency) because taxpayers cover the cost of litter collection, which encourages excessive littering by all.

How much should people buy or consume of a given product? They should look to the *marginal benefits* and *marginal costs* and try (as best they can) to consume in such a way that, for the last units of goods consumed, their marginal benefit equals their marginal cost. If the marginal benefit of the last unit of any good exceeds its marginal cost (and vice versa), there are welfare gains to be picked up by consuming more (or less). This line of argument has been employed by one of the authors (Lee) in his discussion of "Marriages, mistresses, and marginalism," which can be accessed on the Web through a link embedded in Online Reading 2.1.

The behavior of those in business is not materially different from that of consumers or students (from an economic perspective). People in business are constantly concerned with cost–benefit calculations, except that the comparisons are often (but not always) made in dollar terms. For example, will the cost of a small improvement in the quality of a product be more than matched by the additional (marginal) revenues generated from the improvement? In other words, will consumers value the added benefits enough to pay for them? In assessing the safety of their products, managers and owners must consider how much consumers are willing to pay for the additional safety and how much it costs. It doesn't pay to make products as safe as possible, if providing the additional safety costs more than it is worth to consumers. Automobile manufacturers could build cars like Sherman tanks that would be safe under most driving conditions, but could not sell them at a price necessary to cover the cost of making them. The added safety would drain stockholder wealth over time and discourage investors from providing funding for the companies (except at higher interest rates) – a sure and well-worn route to business failure.

The Effects of Time and Risk on Costs and Benefits

When an individual acts, all the costs and benefits are not necessarily incurred immediately. The decision to have a child is a good example. The cost of raising a child averages $250,000 in the U.S., from birth through college. And the first child of a college-educated couple is much more expensive when the cost of parental time involved is considered (Craig 2003). Fortunately, this high cost is incurred over a relatively long period of time or many people would not become parents!

Benefits received in the future must also be compared with present benefits. If you had a choice between receiving $10,000 now and $10,000 one year from now, you would take it today. You could put the money in a bank (if nothing else) where it would earn interest – or you could avoid the effects of future inflation by spending the money now. In other words, future benefits must be greater than present benefits to be more attractive than present benefits.

To compare future costs and benefits on an equal footing with costs and benefits realized today, we must adjust them to their **present value** (*PV*). The usual procedure for calculating *PV* – a process called *discounting* – involves an adjustment for the interest that could be earned (or would have to be paid) if the money were received (or due) today rather than in the future. A dollar received a year from now is worth less than a

Present value is the value of future costs and benefits in terms of current dollars.

dollar received today. If the rate of interest is 6 percent, then a dollar received a year from now is the same as $0.943 today. A dollar earned two years from now would have a *PV* of just under $0.90 because the amount received today will rise to the value of $1 over the next two years. Accordingly, a dollar to be received fifty years from now would only be worth a few cents.[5]

Discounting a dollar for time may seem like a trivial exercise – and many people might not want to waste their time (incur the cost) of doing the discounting math. But the principle is certainly worth contemplating when millions of dollars (e.g., of a firm's costs and profits) are at stake. The principle of discounting suggests a business strategy you should consider:

1 Postpone costs as long as possible and collect revenues as soon as possible.
2 The higher the interest rate, work all the more diligently to follow the first rule in the strategy.

If there is any uncertainty about whether future benefits or costs will actually be received or paid, further adjustments must be made. Without such adjustments, perfectly rational acts may appear to be quite irrational. Not all business ventures can be expected to succeed; some will be less profitable than expected or may collapse altogether. For example, the *average* fast-food franchise may earn a yearly profit of $1 million, but only nine out of ten franchises may survive their first year (because the *average* profits are distorted by the considerable earnings of one franchise). Thus the estimated profits for such a franchise must be discounted, or multiplied by 0.90. If 10 percent of such ventures can be expected to fail, on average each will earn $900,000 ($1 million × 0.90).

Entrepreneurial Risk-Taking

The entrepreneur who starts a single business venture runs the risk that it may fail. In this case, profit will be zero. To avoid putting all their eggs in one basket, many entrepreneurs prefer to initiate several new ventures, thereby spreading the risk of doing business. In the same way, investors spread their risk by investing in a wide variety of companies – and firms spread their risk by producing a number of products. The principle at stake is a simple and straightforward one: When risks and uncertainties are present, diversify! Diversify your portfolio of stocks and bond holdings, but also diversify your business ventures and product lines. By diversifying, you can play the odds and lower the potential damage of wipeouts. Net gains can rise from diversifying portfolios because risky projects come with "risk premiums," since many people are risk-averse. This means net income across a number of risky ventures can be greater than otherwise.

---

[5] The formula for computing the present value (*PV*) of future costs or benefits received one year from now is $PV = [1/(1 + r)] \times f$, where *r* stands for the rate of interest and *f* for future costs or benefits.

Risk-Taking by Banks and Homeowners

Discounting for time and risk can be applied to many economic decisions. Consider the case of prospective homeowners who seek mortgages from banks. Prospective homeowners vary in their riskiness to banks because people have different income levels, income stabilities, and credit histories. Some prospective homeowners have well-paid government jobs with a very low probability of ever being laid off (e.g., professors); other prospective homeowners have moderate-paying and unstable jobs (e.g., construction workers). When granting mortgages, banks also have to consider that the loan balances will be paid off over time and payments will be more or less secure, depending on general factors such as overall economic activity and the prices of houses. Banks can be expected to charge an interest rate based on four factors:

1 *The mortgage payments will flow in over time.* The total payments for interest and principal in nominal dollars must far exceed the dollars loaned out today. The longer the mortgage term, the greater the interest rate to accommodate the discounting of payments further into the future on longer-term mortgages (and the risk that the borrower will, for a variety of reasons, be unable to make payments along the way).

2 *Inflation can erode the real value of the mortgage payments.* Thus, the higher the *expected* inflation rate, the higher the interest rate. (The "nominal" or market interest rate will tend to reflect the "real" interest rate plus the expected inflation rate.)

3 *The creditworthiness of the borrower can affect the interest rate charged.* Prospective homeowners who have poor credit records will be considered higher risks because they are (as a group) more likely to walk away from their homes and mortgages, leaving the bank with a foreclosed home that may have to be sold at a fire-sale price. The higher the riskiness of borrowers, the greater the banks will discount the value of future payments – which is why such borrowers must suffer a greater interest rate on mortgages.

4 *The interest rate a bank will charge on mortgages can be expected to vary with the down-payment.* The lower the down-payment, the smaller the loss borrowers will incur if housing prices fall and borrowers walk away from their houses. The greater the down-payment, the more assured banks can be that borrowers will not walk away from their homes when housing prices retreat.

Banks will gladly compete for creditworthy borrowers, thus lowering the interest rates of the creditworthy (and improving other terms of mortgages). As the creditworthiness of borrowers goes down, interest rates can be expected to rise, which implies a "risk premium" is tacked on to some base ("prime") interest rate for the most creditworthy borrowers. But given the risks involved, the higher interest rates charged to high-risk borrowers do not make such mortgages more profitable than lower interest rates charged to low-risk borrowers, given the risk premium.

Risk-Taking by Banks and the Mortgage Crisis

Banks can deal with the risks of mortgages because they sell many of them; that is, they diversify their mortgage portfolios across many borrowers. With risks moderated by volume and diversification, banks can then take on more risks. In fact, banks have an incentive to take on risks because of the risk premiums built into the interest rates charged on risky loans. Banks also borrow for short terms from their checking and saving depositors to make long-term mortgage loans.

They can make loans equal to upwards of 90 percent of their checking and saving deposits, which means they are highly leveraged. (In Online Chapter 4, we explain how and why this system usually works quite well.) It also means that if banks take risks on loans and the loans are paid off, the bank owners get all the gains from the risk premium. If many of the loans go bad, causing banks to go bankrupt, then the government will absorb the downside losses because checking and saving deposits are insured by the Federal Deposit Insurance Corporation (FDIC). This suggests that deposit insurance can encourage risk-taking by banks.

If banks bundle their mortgages into "mortgaged-backed securities" and sell them to investors worldwide (who might consider such securities safe because banks have been safe and the securities are seen as a diversified portfolio), banks can use the proceeds from the security sales to originate even more mortgage loans. They can go up the risk ladder, making loans (including subprime mortgages) to less and less creditworthy prospective homeowners whose down-payments can dwindle.

Banks and mortgage-backed security buyers might feel safe in their dealings when housing prices are going up, fueled by easy-money policy, the growth in the volume of investment funds going into housing, government subsidies on home purchases, and the belief that housing prices will continue upward. Higher housing prices can mean growing equity for homebuyers, suggesting to banks and mortgage-backed security buyers that mortgages have lower risks. This is the case so long as a housing price bubble lasts – as it did until some time in 2005 (Coleman, Lacour-Little, and Vandell 2008). Then, housing prices began to level off and turn south, causing a rise in delinquent mortgages and foreclosures. The increased supply of foreclosed housing caused housing prices to tumble farther. In turn, the safety of mortgage-backed securities was jeopardized and their market prices began to fall. With the growth in home foreclosures, many (not all) banks quickly became insolvent, pushing them to the brink of bankruptcy and beyond.

In brief, we have described the key risk elements of the housing and credit crisis that engulfed much of the advanced world economies in 2007, all grounded in the rationality of risk-taking with loanable funds. We will return to the tie between leverage and risk-taking at several junctures in this book. (And we develop these arguments further in Online Chapter 4.) Governments around the world were taught valuable economic lessons in the housing and financial crises and the subsequent "Great Recession":

- First, highly leveraged financial institutions have built-in incentives to take on risks, mainly because they have little "skin in the game" (they lose little of their own wealth if risky investments go bad).
- Second, when highly leveraged financial institutions are encouraged by government (through sticks and carrots) to make loans to people with credit risks (e.g., limited or no documented income or low credit scores), they will do so and put the system at a greater risk of failure in the process.
- Third, when borrowers are encouraged to buy houses with low to no down-payments, they will have little to lose. Many homebuyers will take the bait and buy houses they can't really afford (at least, when housing prices begin to fall).

What Rational Behavior Does *Not* Mean

The concept of rational behavior can be bothersome to noneconomists. Most of the difficulties surrounding this concept arise from a misunderstanding of the economic definition of rationality. Common objections include the following:

1 *People do many things that do not work out to their benefit.* Many examples can be cited: a driver speeds and ends up in the hospital; a student gets caught cheating and is expelled from school; we see a movie that we regret. But people behaving "rationally" does not mean never making mistakes. We can calculate our options with some probability, but we do not have perfect knowledge and cannot fully control the future. We will make mistakes, because we base our choices on what we *expect* to happen, not on what does happen. We speed because we expect not to crash; we cheat because we expect not to be caught; we see the movie because we trusted a friend's recommendation. All can be perfectly rational behaviors from a cost–benefit perspective.

2 *Rational behavior implies that a person is totally self-centered, doing only things that are of direct personal benefit.* Wrong. Rational behavior need not be selfish or narrowly defined. Most of us get pleasure from seeing others happy, particularly when their happiness is the result of our actions. Whether a person's goal is to improve her own well-being or to help others, she has a motivation to act rationally – make decisions that do the most to accomplish her objectives.

3 *People do not necessarily maximize their satisfaction.* For instance, many people do not perform to the limit of their abilities. But satisfaction is a question of personal taste. To some individuals, lounging around is an economic good. By consuming leisure, people can increase their welfare. Criticizing the

decisions others make is often based on the assumption that others have the same preferences and face the same constraints that you do. Anyone who equates rational behavior with what she would do will have no trouble concluding that others are irrational. (And if the other person returns the favor, they'll conclude the same about you!)

4 *People's behavior is subject to psychological quirks, hang-ups, habits, and impulses.* True enough! Can such behavior be considered "rational"? Why not? Human actions are governed by the constraints of our physical and mental makeup. As is true of our intelligence, our inclination toward aberrant or impulsive behavior is one of those constraints. Such constraints make our decision-making less precise and contribute to our mistakes, but they do not prevent our seeking to act as rationally as possible. Moreover, what looks to be impulsive or habitual behavior may actually be the product of some prior rational choice.

5 *People can't make refined cost–benefit calculations for everything.* True enough. As a consequence, they oftentimes use heuristics (rules of thumb) to make decisions, especially those that need to be made quickly. For example, we might make slightly better decisions if we examined all the information available about the cereal selection at the grocery store every time we bought a box. But such scrutiny could cost more than the benefit of the improved choice. Instead, having found a brand of cereal that we enjoy, we tend to stick with it for a long period of time – to buy it out of habit – and use our limited time on making better decisions that yield bigger payoffs. Similarly, we might note that baseball outfielders are incapable of making the complex calculations necessary to be where they should be to catch a fly ball. (They don't have the skills or the time to make the calculations.) But they successfully catch balls routinely all the time – with heuristics developed through practice and experience. Heuristics themselves have a rational foundation in that people use them as cost-saving and welfare-enhancing over a range of decisions.

One financial heuristic we use in our personal finance is "don't play the market, buy the market" (Lee and McKenzie 1998). This means we don't try to pick stocks. We generally buy collections of stocks: mutual funds, "index funds," or "Spydrs" – shares in a trust that buys all 500 stocks in the Standard & Poor's (S&P) Index. We follow this rule of thumb for two main reasons. First, it is a brainless investment strategy; we don't suffer the considerable personal time costs of picking stocks with care. Second, a sizable majority of fund managers, who spend their waking hours trying to pick stocks, can't beat the return (for long) on the S&P Index. And we can attest that our investment strategy has worked well for us over the long haul. (For a brief summary of the financial research on the issue, see McKenzie and Lee (1998, chapter 6).)

PERSPECTIVE 2

The Evolutionary Foundations of Cooperation

Much of our analysis in this book is grounded in rational decision-making, which implies that people might be inclined solely to pursue their own private interest without any innate regard to pursue the common interests of groups (or firms).

In adopting the rationality premise, we are not suggesting that people cannot be motivated by an innate sense of duty or obligation to do "what they are supposed to do" – or that they lack any predisposition to cooperate with others in acknowledged common interests. On the contrary, people seem to have a built-in tendency to cooperate – at least to a degree. It certainly wouldn't be surprising if a Creator God made us this way. Evolutionary narratives face considerable challenges in explaining group dynamics while celebrating "survival of the fittest" among individuals as a key mechanism. But a substantial literature has grown up around theories that evolution has encouraged modern humans to work together (to some degree) for their own survival, through greater prosperity.

Before humans developed agriculture, they were hunter-gatherers in groups of twenty-five to 150, with kinship likely playing an important role in group coherence (Hamilton, Jay, and Madison 1964; Dawkins 1976). Group size was small enough for group members to monitor each other, but large enough for free-riding to emerge (Dunbar 1998; Bowles and Gintis 2001). Hunter-gatherers needed cooperation to hunt game that was too large or dangerous for individuals to kill alone; to defend themselves against the predation of other groups of humans; and to successfully prey upon other bands of humans. Evolutionary theorists believe that human groups with a predisposition to cooperate efficiently (by developing the requisite rules and incentives that engendered cooperation) survived with greater frequency than groups that were not able or willing to cooperate efficiently (Hirshleifer 1999). Consequently, cooperative humans saw their genes (and predisposition for cooperation) passed down through the succeeding generations.

As Paul Rubin (2002, 60–61) observes, summarizing a mountain of research in evolutionary psychology, behavioral biology, and "bioeconomics":

The groups formed by more cooperative players will do better than groups with less cooperative members, and members of the cooperative group will have more offspring. As a result, the degree of cooperativeness can grow in the population over time. This assortment by cooperativeness has another interesting feature. Everyone (cooperator or cheater) would prefer to deal with a cooperator. Therefore, individuals will have an incentive to appear to be cooperators even if they are not.

This ability to pretend undermines the narrative. But the prospect of pretending to cooperate also implies that people should be expected to develop and evolve skills to detect deception and cheating (Trivers 1971; Frank 1988; Cosmides and Tooby 1992). Would these skills be strong enough to allow credible group cooperation? We face similar dilemmas today in our more-sophisticated settings.

The late economist and criminologist James Q. Wilson (1993) argued that most people have evolved a "moral sense," which can show up in their willingness to forgo individual advantage (or opportunities to shirk) for the good of the group. Moreover, many factors – including culture, training, and considerations of equity and fairness – influence the willingness to cooperate (Ostrom 2000; Fehr and Schmidt 2002). People from "collectivistic" societies, such as China, may be more inclined to cooperate than people from "individualistic" societies, such as the United States (Earley 1989). Training in "group values" can affect the extent of cooperation, although evolutionary forces have left all cultures with admixtures of people who exhibit varying degrees of selfishness and nonselfishness (Sethi and Somanathan 1996; Bowles and Gintis 2001; Henrich *et al.* 2001).

Experiments have shown that people will be more likely to cooperate when the shares of whatever is being divided are more or less equal, with women more inclined to favor "equal shares" than men (Knauft 1991; Boehm 1993). People are willing to extend favors in cooperative ventures if they know the favor will be returned (Trivers 1971; Steiner *et al.* 1998; Gintis 2000a, 2000b). They will work harder when they believe that they are not underpaid – that is, when the owner is "cooperating" with them (Fehr and Schmidt 2002). People are more likely to cooperate with close family members and friends than with strangers – and they will be less likely to cooperate with others (whether friends or strangers) when the cost of cooperating is high. Cooperation is more likely when people are allowed to communicate with one another and made to feel as though they are members of the relevant group (Thaler 1992; Ledyard 1995; Hoffman, McCabe, and Smith 1998). And negatively, experiments have shown that some are willing to go a step further and devote some of their own resources to punish shirkers and cheaters (McCabe and Smith 1999).

Why is it that people are inclined to cooperate more or less naturally? Wilson (1993) repeats a favorite example of game theorists to explain why "cooperativeness" might be partially explained as an outcome of natural selection. Consider two people in early times, Trog and Helga, who are subject to attack by sabertoothed tigers. The "game" they must play in the woods is a variant of the Prisoner's Dilemma game. If they both run when they spot the tiger, then the tiger will kill and eat the slower runner.[6] If they both stand their ground – and cooperate in their struggle – then perhaps they can defeat the tiger or scare him

---

[6] There's an old joke here: "Why are you running? You can't outrun a tiger." The reply: "I don't need to outrun the tiger. I just need to outrun you!"

off. However, each has an incentive to run when the other stands his or her ground, leaving the brave soul to be eaten.

What do people do? What *should* they do? Better yet, what do we *expect* them to do? We suspect that different twosomes caught in the woods by tigers over the millennia have tried a number of strategies. In the long run, running is a strategy for possible extinction, given that the tiger can pick off the runners one by one. Societies that have found ways of cooperating have prospered and survived. Those that haven't would languish or retrogress into economic oblivion, leaving the current generation with a disproportionate number of ancestors who behaved cooperatively. Those who didn't cooperate long ago when confronted with attacks by saber-toothed tigers were eaten; those who did cooperate with greater frequency lived to propagate future generations.

Human society is complex, driven by a variety of forces that vary in intensity and that at times conflict. However, there are reasons to expect that people who cooperate will be disproportionately represented in societies that survive and thrive. In any case, today's organizations can exploit – and given the forces of competition, must exploit – people's limited but inherent desire or tendency to work together, to be a part of something that is bigger and better than they are. Organizations should be expected to try to reap the *synergetic consequences* of individual and collective efforts.

If that were the whole story – if all that mattered were people's tendencies to cooperate – then management would hardly be a discipline worthy of much professional reflection. There would be little need or role for managers, beyond communication and training. The problem is that our cooperative tendencies are not sufficient to overcome the temptation of uncooperative behavior. Two people may well be able to work together "naturally," fully capturing their synergetic potential. The same may be said of groups of three and four people, maybe ten, or even thirty. The point that emerges from the economic logic of group behavior is that, as the group size – team or firm – gets progressively larger, the consequences of impaired incentives mount and heterogeneity between group members increases. Both give rise to a growing prospect that people will shirk, taking advantage of the fact that others cannot properly assess what they contribute to the group.[7]

The bottom line is that a tendency to cooperate may be built into the DNA of human beings; however, the size and structure of groups can be a countervailing force toward cooperation – as we will explain in the following section.

---

[7] Wilson (1993) cites experimental evidence that shows people in small towns are, indeed, more helpful than people in larger cities – and the more densely packed the city population, the less helpful people will be. Gary Miller (1992) reports that when people think that their contribution to group goals – for example, pulling on a rope – cannot be measured, then individuals will reduce their effort. When members of a team pulling on a rope were blindfolded and then told that others were pulling with them, the individual members exerted 90 percent of their best individual effort when one other person was supposed to be pulling.

Part B Organizational Economics and Management

The Logic of Group Behavior in Business and Elsewhere

In the following chapters, we introduce the usefulness of markets as a means of generating a form of cooperation through trades, buying, and selling. However, as is evident inside firms, not all human cooperation is through "markets." People often act cooperatively in groups – or of greater interest to us, in "firms." In this section, we make use of the rationality principles developed in Part A, applying them to the organization of groups and firms. The focus of our attention is the viability of groups – such as families, cliques, communes, clubs, unions, professional associations and societies, as well as firms, in which individual participation is voluntary – to cohere and pursue the common interests of the members.

We consider two dominant and conflicting theories of group behavior, both of which take a partial view of complex life and yield insights about groups. They are "the common-interest theory" and "the economic theory" of group behavior, with more focus on the latter because it is founded on the premise of rational behavior developed in Part A. This economic theory of groups helps us understand how firms are organized and why owners and workers alike can benefit when firms employ "tough bosses."

All theories of group behavior begin by recognizing the multiplicity of forces that affect group members and, thus, groups. This is especially true of what we term the *common-interest theory*. Sociologists, political scientists, and psychologists generally share this point of view, which has been prominent at least since the time of Aristotle in the fourth century BC. The determinants of group behavior most often singled out are the "leadership quality" of specific group members and the need among group members for affiliation, security, recognition, social status, or money. Groups such as clubs or unions form so that members can achieve a goal or satisfy a want that they could not accomplish as efficiently through individual action. All these considerations are instrumental in affecting "group cohesion," which, in turn, affects the "strength" of the group and its ability to compete with other groups for the same objectives. From the perspective of this theory, when people join firms, they accept the firm's objective and pursue it because everyone else wants the same thing, leading to self-enforcing group cohesion.

The common-interest theory views the "group" as an organic whole, much like an individual – as opposed to a collection of individuals whose separate actions *appear* to be "group action." According to the theory, the group has a life of its own that is to a degree independent of the individuals who comprise it. Herbert Spencer, a nineteenth-century sociologist, often described the group as a "social organism" or "superorganic" entity (Spencer 1896). It was probably the social-organism view of groups that Karl Marx had in mind when he wrote of the "class struggle" and predicted that the proletariat class would bring down "bourgeois capitalism" and erect a communist society in its place.

Two major reasons are given for viewing groups as social organisms. First, a group consists of a mass of *interdependencies*, which connect the individuals in the group. Without the interdependencies, there would be only isolated individuals and the term "group" would have no meaning. Individuals in groups are like the nodes of a spider's web. The spider's web is constructed on these nodes, and the movements in one part of the web can be transmitted to all other parts. Similar to the process of synergism in biology, the actions of individuals within a group combine to form a force that is greater than the sum of the forces generated by individuals isolated from one another. The group must, so the argument goes, be thought of as more than the sum total of its individuals. This argument is used by union leaders to argue that unions can get higher wage increases for all workers than individual workers can obtain by acting independently. The reason is that union leaders efficiently coordinate the efforts of all. Environmental groups make essentially the same argument: with well-placed lobbyists, they can have a greater political impact than all the individuals they represent could have by writing independent letters to their representatives at different times.

Second, groups tend to emerge because they satisfy some interest shared by all the group's members. Because all share this "common interest," individuals have an intrinsic incentive to work with others to pursue that interest, sharing the costs as they work together. Aristotle (Ethics, 1160a) wrote, "Men journey together with a view to particular advantage." Arthur Bentley, a group theorist who is recognized as an intellectual father of contemporary political sciences, wrote: "There is no group without its interest. ... The group and the interest are not separate. ... If we try to take the group without the interest, we simply have nothing at all" (Bentley 1967, 211–213).

Having observed that a common interest can be shared by all of a group's members, the adherents of this theory of group behavior argue that a group can, with slight modification, be treated as an individual, meaning that the group can maximize its well-being. But an implicit assumption is that this will be true of large as well as small groups. This latter deduction prompts many economists to take issue with this approach to analyzing group behavior.

The Economic Logic of Group Behavior

Economist Mancur Olson, on whose work this section largely rests, agrees that the "common interest" can be influential in motivating behavior – but primarily the behavior of members of small groups. He insists that a group must be looked upon as a composite of rational individuals, as opposed to an anthropomorphic whole – and that the common interest, which can be so effective in motivating members of small groups, can be impotent in motivating members of large groups: "Unless there is coercion in large groups ... *rational self-interested individuals will not act to achieve their common or group interest*" (Olson 1971, 2, emphasis in the original). Further, he contends, "These points hold true when there is unanimous agreement in a group about the common goal and the methods of achieving it" (Olson 1971, 2). To understand this theory, we examine the propositions upon which it is founded, and then consider some qualifications.

Basic Propositions

Using economic analysis, people are assumed to be as rational in their decision to join a group (a firm or a club) as they are toward doing anything else; they will join a group if the expected benefits of doing so are greater than the expected costs they must bear. These costs and benefits, like all others, must be discounted by the going interest rate on borrowed funds (to account for any delay in incurring the costs and receiving any benefits) and by the risks (probabilities that the costs and benefits will be realized).

There are several direct, private benefits of belonging to groups, such as companionship, security, recognition, and social status. For example, a person may belong to a group simply to have contact from the organization – and, in that small way, to feel important. A group may serve as an outlet for our altruistic or charitable feelings. If by "common interest," we mean a collection of these types of *private benefits*, it is easy to see how they can motivate group behavior. Entrepreneurs can emerge to "sell" these types of private benefits – as they do in the case of private golf clubs or Weight Watchers. The group action is then a market phenomenon – that is, a straightforward exchange of **private goods**.

> A strictly **private good** is any good or service the benefits of which are received exclusively by the purchaser.

However, the central concern of this theory is a "common interest" that is separate and detached from the diverse private interests of group members. The problem arises because the public (common) benefits that transcend the entire group cannot be provided by the market, and can be obtained only by some form of *collective action* to obtain a **collective good**. That is, a group of people must band together to change things from what they would otherwise be. Examples include the

> A **collective good** is a good or service the benefits of which are shared by all members of the relevant group if the good is provided or consumed by anyone.

common interest of a Second Amendment group to limit restrictions in gun ownership; farmers to secure higher prices than could be obtained by independent actions; and students to resist tuition increases.

Small Groups

Small groups are not without their problems in pursuing the "common interest" of their members. There are difficulties and costs in becoming organized, holding together, and ensuring that everyone contributes her part to the group's common interest. This point is relevant to Fred and Harry's (or Crusoe and Friday's) problems of setting up a social contract considered in Chapter 1. And it can be understood in terms of the little things we can do with friends and neighbors – that may go undone because of the problems associated with having even two or three people come together for the "common good." For example, it may be in the common interest of three neighbors – Fred, Harry, and now Judy – for all to rid their yards of dandelions. If one person does it, and the other two do not, the person who removes the dandelions may find his yard full of them the next year because of seeds from the other two yards.

Even though Fred, Harry, and Judy may not ever agree to work out their common problem (or interest) cooperatively, there are several things that make it more likely that a small group will cooperate than a large group. In a small group, everyone can know everyone else. What benefits or costs may arise from an individual's action are spread over just a few people and, therefore, the effect felt by any one person can be significant. (Fred knows that there is a reasonably high probability that what he does to eliminate dandelions from the border of his property affects Harry's and Judy's welfare.) If the individual providing the public good is concerned about the welfare of those within his group and receives personal satisfaction from knowing that he has helped them, he has an incentive to contribute to the common good. *Before the common good can be realized, individuals must have some motivation for contributing to it.*

Furthermore, "free-riders" are easily detected in a small group. (Harry can tell with relative ease when Fred has not worked on the dandelions in his yard.) If one person tries to let the others shoulder his share, the absence of his contribution will be detected with a reasonably high probability. Others can then impose social pressure (accompanied by the sting of a cost) to encourage him to fulfill his end of the bargain. The enforcement costs are low because the group is small. There are many ways to let a neighbor know you are displeased with some aspect of his behavior.

Finally, in small groups, an individual shirking her responsibilities can sometimes be excluded from the group if she does not contribute to the common good (although this would be difficult in the dandelion example) and joins the group merely to free-ride on the efforts of others. In larger groups, such as nations, exclusion is usually more difficult (more costly) and, therefore, less likely.

The problem of organizing "group behavior" to serve the common interest has been a problem for almost all groups – even the utopian communities that sprang up during the nineteenth century and in the 1960s. Rosabeth Kanter (1973, 64), in her study of successful nineteenth-century utopian communities, concluded:

The primary issue with which a utopian community must cope in order to have the strength and solidarity to endure is its human organization: how people arrange to do the work that the community needs to survive as a group, and how the group in turn manages to satisfy and involve its members over a long period of time. The idealized version of communal life must be meshed with the reality of the work to be done in the community, involving difficult problems of social organization. In utopia, for instance, who takes out the garbage?

Kanter found that the most successful communities minimized the free-rider problems by restricting entry into the community – requiring potential members to make commitments to the group. Six "commitment mechanisms" distinguished the successful utopias:

1 sacrifice of habits common to the outside world, such as the use of alcohol and tobacco – or, in some cases, sex;
2 assignment of all worldly goods to the community;
3 collective sharing of all property and all communal work;
4 adoption of rules that would minimize the disruptive effects of relationships between members and nonmembers and that would distinguish members from nonmembers (e.g., wearing uniforms);
5 submission to public confession and criticism; and
6 expressed commitment to an identifiable power structure and tradition.

Needless to say, the cost implied in these "commitment mechanisms" would tend to discourage most potential free-riders from joining the society! By identifying the boundaries to societies, these mechanisms made exclusion possible. As Kanter points out, the importance of these commitment mechanisms is illustrated by the fact that their breakdown foreshadowed the end of the community. (All of this also implies the importance of homogeneous preferences, appropriate recruitment into social groups, and the immense value of effective hiring within firms.)

The cattlemen's associations formed during the nineteenth century suggest other means of bringing about collective behavior on the part of group members. At the time, cattle were allowed to run free over the ranges of the West in the U.S. The cattlemen had a common interest in preventing a tragedy of the commons – that is, ensuring that the ranges were not overstocked and overgrazed (as per our discussion in Chapter 1) – and in securing cooperation to round up the cattle. To provide for these common interests, cattlemen formed associations that sent out patrols to keep out intruders and take responsibility for the roundups. Any cattleman who failed to contribute his share toward these ends could be excluded from the association, which generally meant that his cattle were excluded from the roundup or confiscated by the association (Dennen 1975).

The family is a small group which is designed to promote the common interest of its members. The family obviously does not escape difficulties, given the prevalence of divorce and common family feuds. At present, its validity as a viable institution is being challenged by many sources; however, it does have several redeeming features that will cause it to endure as a basic component of the social fabric. Because of the smallness of the group, contributions made toward the common interest of the family can be shared and appreciated directly. Family members are generally able to know what others in the group like and dislike; they can set up an interpersonal cost–benefit structure that guides all members toward the common interest. Most collective decisions are also made with relative ease. However, even with all the advantages of close personal contact, the family as a small group often fails to achieve the common interest. Given this, the failure of much larger groups to achieve their expressed common objectives is not difficult to understand.

Large Groups

In a large-group setting, the problems of individual members contributing toward the development of the common interest are potentially much greater. The direct, personal interface in small groups is usually lacking in larger groups. And because of the size of large groups, the communal good they produce is diffused so that no one sees his actions having a significant effect on anyone, even themselves.

Even when an individual can detect benefits from his actions, he must weigh those benefits against the costs he has to incur to achieve them. For a large group, the costs of providing detectable benefits can be substantial. This can occur because there are more people to be served by the good and because large groups are normally organized to provide communal goods that are rather expensive to begin with – whether public policy, large social groups, or large firms. If all group members contribute to the communal good, the cost to any one person can be slight. But the question confronting the individual is how much he will have to contribute to make his actions detectable, *given what all the others do.*

In the context of a nation (a very large group indeed), suppose there are certain common objectives to which we can all subscribe, such as a specific charitable program. It is, in other words, in our "common interest" to promote this program. Will people be willing to voluntarily contribute to the federal treasury for the purpose of achieving this goal? Some people will, but many may not. A person may reason that, although he agrees with the national objective, his contribution will have no detectable effect in achieving it. This explains why compulsory taxes can be useful and why philanthropic contributions may fall short of accomplishing communal goals (Olson 1971, 13).

This also applies to organizations such as World Vision, a voluntary charitable organization interested mainly in improving the diets of impoverished people around the world. Many are disturbed by scenes of undernourished and malnourished children in TV commercials for World Vision (or any number of other charitable groups seeking donations). But how many people ever contribute so much as a dollar? Many do, but many who are "concerned" never make a contribution. There may be many reasons for this, but we note that the large-group problem is a significant piece of the puzzle.

True, if all members of a large group make a small contribution toward the common interest, there may be sizable benefits to all within the group. But again, the problem that must be overcome is the potential lack of *individual* incentives from which the collective behavior must emerge. In large groups, Prisoner's Dilemma problems (as in our two-member group, Fred and Harry) are ever-present and magnified – because a larger group has less detectable consequences of individual behavior and less monitoring of behavior.

Through appropriate organization of group members, the common interest *may* be achieved, even if the membership is large. But such groups may be prohibitively difficult to establish at all for two reasons. First, there are many people to organize, which means that, even if group members are not resistant to being organized, there will be costs associated with getting them together or having them work at the same time for the same objectives. Second, some individuals may try to free-ride on the efforts of others, which means it will cost more to get people to become members of the group. Further, each free-rider implies a greater burden on the active members of the group. If everyone waits for "the other guy to take the initiative," the group may never be organized.

Organizational costs often prevent students who complain (about the instructional quality of faculty or some other aspect of university life) from doing anything about it. The same costs block people who are disgruntled with the two major political parties from forming a viable party among those who share their views. The probability of getting sufficient support is frequently low, which is another way of saying the expected costs are high.

The free-rider problem may emerge in the workplace as worker absenteeism for a variety of reasons, including sickness, real or feigned (Barham and Begum 2005, 157). The Confederation of British Industry found that the British economy lost 175 million days of work from absenteeism in 2006, well beyond what could be attributable to understandable reasons, such as illness.[8] Another study found that the rate of absences for illness during the survey week was 29 percent higher in private firms with 500 workers than in private firms with fewer than twenty-five workers (Barham and Begum 2005, 154). Not surprisingly, the rate of absence for sickness was higher in the public sector than in the private sector. This is probably attributable, at least in part, to the pressure of private firms to avoid losses and make a profit.

---

[8] As reported by the consulting firm of Smith & Williamson in 2008, with the report accessed on May 14, 2023 from www.mondaq.com/article.asp?articleid=52770.

Economist Stephen Levitt and journalist Stephen Dubner report on their findings from the sales data collected by Paul Feldman, who sold bagels on the "honor plan" for many years in Washington, DC (Levitt and Dubner 2005). Feldman would leave bagels early in the morning at gathering places for office workers. The workers were initially asked to leave their payments in open baskets. Because the money often was taken from the baskets, Feldman made wooden boxes with slits in the top for depositing payments. Initially, in the early 1980s, when he started his bagel business, Feldman suffered a 10 percent loss of bagels (that is, he received no payment for 10 percent of the bagels he left). After 1992, his losses of bagels began a slight but steady rise. By 2001, he reached 13 percent over all companies, only to go back down to 11 percent during the two years following 9/11. (Levitt and Dubner speculate that the 15 percent decline in the nonpayment rate could be attributed to the fact that many of his customers were connected to national security with a heightened sense for doing what was right.) Relevant to the "logic of collective action," Feldman found that honesty measured by payments received for bagels was marginally affected by firm size: "An office with a few dozen employees generally outpays by 3–5 percent an office with a few hundred employees" (Levitt and Dubner 2005, 49). We suspect that the difference in the payment rate between small and large offices might be greater were the required payment higher than the price of a bagel.

California and other parts of the Western United States often suffer through droughts and water shortages. Governors call for greater water conservation. And it's noteworthy that pleas result in reduced water use at all – whether from individual conscience, social pressures, or the threat of serious fines. But voluntary reductions often move to legal restrictions on water use, backed up by cadres of water police to monitor lawn sprinkling, etc. (In Chapter 5, we return to the policy issue of subsidized water which greatly aggravates the problem.)

Of course, because of scarcity, people everywhere share the common interest of ensuring that the available resources are used efficiently. If resources are used efficiently, more wants can be satisfied than otherwise. How do you get large groups of consumers to contribute to this common good? One means of encouraging conservation and smart purchases in large-group settings is the pricing system. As to be discussed in Chapter 3, when electricity or gasoline becomes scarce and the market supply contracts, the prices of those products rise, and consumers are induced to curb their consumption of those goods. If we restrict prices from rising when products become scarcer, consumers will fall into the large-group trap: they will continue to buy as if nothing had happened to the scarcity of the products. Consumers can reason that their continued consumption at old levels will have no impact on the overall availability of the product, which means they will not conserve when the greater scarcity of the good indicates that they should.

Qualifications to the Economic Theory

Obviously, there are many cases in which large groups appear to be trying to accomplish things that are in the common interest of the membership. Early in the civil rights struggle, the League of Women Voters pushed hard for passage of the Equal Rights Amendment to the Constitution; labor unions work for international trade restrictions; the American Medical Association lobbies for legislation that is beneficial to many doctors; and many charitable groups work toward the "public interest." Several of the possible explanations for this observed behavior force us to step outside the standard economic arguments about communal goods.

First, as Immanuel Kant, an eighteenth-century philosopher said, people can place value on the *act* itself as distinguished from the results or consequences of the act (Kant 1999, first published 1781). The *act* of making a charitable contribution, which can be broadly defined to include picking up trash in public areas or holding the door for someone with an armful of packages, may have a value in and of itself. This is true whether the effects of the act are detectable to the individual making the charitable contribution or not. To the extent that people behave in this way, the public good theory loses force. Notice, however, that Olson, in formulating his argument, focused on rational, *economic man* as opposed to the *moral man* envisioned by Kant. We expect that, as the group becomes larger, a greater effort will be made to instill in people the belief that the *act* itself is important.

Second, the contribution that a person makes in group settings is often so slight that, even though the private benefits are small, the contribution to the common interest is also small and can be a rational policy course. This may explain, for example, student membership in a university club. All one has to do in many situations is to show up at an occasional meeting and make a small dues payment. Further, the private benefits of another line on a (lean) résumé and being with others at meetings can be sufficient incentive to motivate limited action in the common interest.

Third, all group members may not share equally the benefits received from promotion of the common interest. One or more persons may receive a sizable portion of the total benefits and thus be willing to provide the public good, at least up to some extent. Many business owners are willing to participate in local politics or to support advertising campaigns to promote their community as a recreational area. Although a restauranteur may believe that the entire community will benefit economically from an influx of tourists, he is surely aware that a significant share of these benefits will accrue to him. Negatively, business owners may also support such community efforts because of the implied threats of being socially ostracized.

Fourth, large organizations can be divided into smaller groups. With the personal contact of smaller units, people end up promoting the common interest in promoting the interest of the small unit to which they belong. The League of Women Voters is broken down into small community clubs. The national Chamber of Commerce has local chapters. The Lions Club promotes programs to prevent blindness and to help the blind, but members do this through a highly decentralized organizational structure. Or think of the change in perception that results from emphasizing participation in small groups within a large church. This approach can lead to viable voluntary cooperative behavior in groups larger than the economic theory of groups would suggest. In fact, quite often, a multiplicity of small groups is actually responsible for what may appear to be the activity of a large group. Large firms almost always divide their operations into divisions and then smaller departments. The decentralization that is prevalent among large, voluntary, and business organizations tends to support the economic view of groups.

Fifth, large groups may be viable because the group organizers sell their members a service and use the profits from sales to promote projects that are in the common interest of the group. The Sierra Club receives voluntary contributions from members and nonmembers alike to research and lobby for environmental issues. However, it also sells a number of publications and offers a variety of environmentally related tours for its members. The American Economic Association (AEA) has several thousand members. However, most economists belong to the AEA not for what they can do for it; they join primarily to receive its journal and to be able to tell others that they belong – both of which are private benefits. The AEA also provides economists with information on employment opportunities.

Sixth, the basic argument for any group is that people can accomplish more through groups than they can through independent action. This means that there are potential benefits to be reaped by anyone who is willing to bear some of the cost of developing and maintaining the organization. A business firm is fundamentally a *group* of workers and stockholders interested in producing a good (a communal good, to them). They have a common interest in seeing a good produced that will sell at a profit. The entrepreneur is essentially a person who organizes a group of people into a production unit; she overcomes the problems associated with trying to get a large number of people to work in their common interest by providing workers with private benefits – that is, she pays them for their contribution to the production of the good. The entrepreneur-manager can be viewed as a person who is responsible for reducing any tendency of workers to avoid their responsibilities to the large-group firm.

The general point that emerges from our discussion of incentives within "small" and "large" groups is that, as a group grows in size, shared values can become progressively inconsequential in motivating people to act cooperatively.

This means that as a group grows, alternative mechanisms – incentives, and organizational and financial structures – must be developed to supplant the power of shared values in achieving the shared goals (including firm profitability, worker job security, social, and environmental ends). Effective management can be construed as finding ways to overcome the large-group problems, which often reduce to Prisoner's Dilemmas.

Of course, *disincentives* that discourage people from doing anything – working or contributing to a group's welfare – can be as important as incentives that encourage people within management and public policies. In Online Reading 2.2, we show how rational-behavior precepts can be used to conceptualize optimum management snooping on workers who may be using work time to play games and shop online. In Online Reading 2.3, we explain how varying preferences for "risk aversion" can help explain why firms tend to be owned by capital investors, not workers.

Overcoming Prisoner's Dilemmas through Tough Bosses

How does the economic theory of group behavior – including the underlying precepts of rationality – relate to business students who seek to run businesses and direct the work of others? In a word, "plenty." Throughout the rest of this book, we demonstrate how the "logic" is central to how competitive markets (and cartels) work (or don't work), and we discuss a multitude of ways to apply the "logic" directly to management problems.

For now, we can stress an inference that emerges from the economic view of group behavior: people often rationally spurn tough jobs, unless compensated for the personal cost and displeasure involved in them. Being a "tough boss" is one such job, but a boss who isn't tough might not be worth much. Because tough, effective bosses are valuable and lenient bosses are not, organizational arrangements are likely to discipline pain-avoiding bosses to encourage them to impose discipline on the workforce. In a word, competition will press firms to hire tough bosses. Workers may not like tough-bossed firms but, as we explain, workers can be better off with tough bosses – and will rationally seek to work in firms that employ them. (We see similar dynamics with coaches, personal trainers, parents, and teachers (Lee 1990).)

Though probably overstated, common wisdom says that workers do not like their bosses, much less tough bosses. The sentiment expressed in Johnny Paycheck's iconic country song, "Take This Job and Shove It," is directed at a boss. Or, as the old quip puts it: boss spelled backward is "Double SOB." If not for an element of truth, such comments would not be funny. Bosses are often unpopular with those they boss. But tough bosses have much in common with foul-tasting medicines for the sick: you don't like them, but you want them anyway, because they are good for you. Workers may not like tough bosses, but they willingly put up with them because tough bosses lead to higher productivity, more job security, and better wages.

The productivity of workers is an important factor in determining their wages. More-productive workers receive higher wages than less-productive workers. Firms would soon go bankrupt in competitive markets if they paid workers more than their productivity is worth. But firms would soon lose workers if they paid them less.

Many things determine how productive workers are – most notably, the amount of physical capital they work with and the amount of human capital (experience and education) they bring to their jobs. But how well the workers function together *as a team* is also important. An individual worker can have all the training, capital, and diligence needed to be highly productive, but productivity will suffer unless other workers pull their weight by properly performing their duties. The productivity of each worker is crucially dependent upon the efforts of *all* workers in the vast majority of firms.

Although each worker wants other workers to work hard to maintain the general productivity of the firm, each worker recognizes that her contribution to the general productivity is small (at least in very large firms). By shirking some responsibilities, she receives all the benefits from the extra leisure, but suffers only a scant portion of the productivity loss, which is spread over everyone in the firm. She suffers, of course, from some of the productivity loss when other workers choose to loaf on the job, but she knows that the decisions others make are independent of whether she shirks or not. And if everyone else shirks, little good will result for her (or for the firm) from diligent effort on her part. So no matter what she believes that other workers will do, the rational thing for her to do is to capture the private benefits from shirking at every opportunity. With all other workers facing the same incentives, the strong tendency is for shirking on the job to reduce the productivity and the wages of all workers in the firm – and, quite possibly, to threaten their jobs by undermining the firm's viability. The situation just described is another example of the general problem with the logic of group behavior – or, more precisely, a form of the Prisoner's Dilemma we considered earlier.

Game Theory: Prisoner's Dilemma Games in the Workplace

Consider a slightly different form of the Prisoner's Dilemma described in Table 2.1, which shows the payoff to Jane for different combinations of shirking by her and her fellow workers. No matter what Jane believes others will do, the biggest payoff to her (in terms of the value of her expected financial compensation and leisure time) comes from shirking. Clearly, she hopes that everyone else works responsibly, so that general labor productivity and the firm's profits will be high despite her lack of effort – in which case, she receives the highest possible payoff of 125. Unfortunately for Jane, all workers face payoff possibilities similar to the

Table 2.1 **The inclination to shirk on the job**

		Other workers		
		None shirk	Some shirk	All shirk
Jane	Don't shirk	100	75	25
	Shirk	125	100	30

ones she faces. (To simplify the discussion, we assume that everyone faces the same payoffs.) So, everyone will shirk, which means that everyone will end up with a payoff of 30, which is the lowest possible collective payoff for workers. Workers are faced with self-destructive incentives when their work environment is described by the shirking version of the Prisoner's Dilemma. It is clearly desirable for workers to extricate themselves from this dilemma. But how?

In an abstract sense, the only way to escape this dilemma is somehow to alter the payoffs for shirking. More concretely, this requires workers to agree to subject themselves collectively to tough penalties that no one individual would unilaterally be willing to accept. Although no one likes being subjected to tough penalties, everyone can benefit from having those penalties imposed on everyone, including themselves.

The situation here is analogous to many others. Remember the problem of controlling pollution that was briefly mentioned in Chapter 1. Although each person would find it convenient to freely pollute the environment, when everyone is free to do so, we each lose more from the pollution of others than we gain from our own freedom to pollute. So, we accept restrictions on our own polluting behavior in return for having restrictions imposed on others. Polluting and shirking are surprisingly analogous: one harms the natural environment; the other harms the work environment.

Workers may not like bosses who carefully monitor their behavior, spot the shirkers, and ruthlessly penalize them. But they want such bosses. The penalties on shirkers must be sufficiently harsh to change the payoffs in Table 2.1 and eliminate the Prisoner's Dilemma. If Jane had a boss tough enough to impose 30 units of cost on her (and everyone else) for shirking, her relevant payoff matrix would be transformed into Table 2.2. Jane may not like her new boss, but she would cease to find advantages in shirking. And with a tough boss monitoring all workers, and unmercifully penalizing those who shirk, Jane will find that she is more than compensated because her fellow workers also have quit shirking. Instead of being in an unproductive firm, surrounded by a bunch of other shirkers, each receiving a payoff of 30, she will find herself as part of a hard-working, cooperative team of workers, each receiving a payoff of 100.

Table 2.2 Shirking in large worker groups

		Other workers		
		None shirk	Some shirk	All shirk
Jane	Don't shirk	100	75	25
	Shirk	95	70	0

The common perception is that bosses hire workers – and in most situations this is what appears to happen. Bosses see benefits that can be realized only by having workers, and so they hire them. But it is also true that workers see benefits that can be realized only from having a boss. So, it is not unreasonable to think of workers hiring a boss – and preferably a tough one.

Actual Tough Bosses

Even highly skilled and disciplined workers can benefit from having a "boss" who helps them overcome the shirking that can be motivated by the Prisoner's Dilemma. Consider the experience related by Gordon E. Moore, a highly regarded scientist and one of the founders of Intel, Inc. Before Intel, Moore and seven other scientists entered a business venture that failed because of what Moore described as "chaos." Because of the inability of the scientists to act as an effective team in this initial venture, Moore said that "The first thing we had to do was to hire our own boss – essentially hire someone to run the company" (Moore 1994).

Pointing to stories and explicit cases where the workers hire their boss is instructive in emphasizing the importance of tough bosses to workers. But the typical situation finds the boss hiring the workers. We will explain later why this is the case, but we can lay the groundwork for such an explanation by recognizing that we have left an important question unanswered. An important job of bosses is to monitor workers and impose penalties on those who shirk. But how do we make sure that the bosses don't shirk themselves? How can you organize a firm to make sure that bosses are tough?

A boss's work is not easy or pleasant. It requires serious effort to keep close tabs on a group of workers. It is not always easy to know when a worker is really shirking or just taking a justifiable break. A certain amount of what appears to be shirking at the moment has to be allowed for workers to be fully productive over the long run. There is always some tension between reasonable flexibility and credible predictability in enforcing the rules – and it is difficult to strike the best balance. Too much flexibility can lead to an undisciplined workforce, and too much rigidity can destroy worker morale. Also, quite apart from the difficulty of knowing when to impose tough penalties on a worker is the unpleasantness of doing so. Few people enjoy disciplining workers by giving them unsatisfactory progress reports, reducing their pay, or dismissing them. The easiest thing for a boss to do is to be easy on shirkers. But the boss who is not tough on shirkers is also a shirker!

Here is a related issue: A boss can also be tempted to form an alliance with a group of workers who provide favors in return for letting them shirk more than other workers. Such a group improves its well-being at the expense of the firm's productivity, but most of this cost can be shifted to those outside the alliance.

Of course, a firm could always hire someone whose job it is to monitor the boss, but two problems with this solution immediately come to mind. First, the additional boss will be even more removed from workers than the initial boss, and so will have an even more difficult time knowing whether the workers are being properly disciplined. Second, and even more important, who is going to monitor the second boss and penalize him or her for shirking? Who is going to monitor the monitor? This approach ends in "infinite regress": it leads nowhere. A solution to the problem lies in the observation that workers should want their bosses to be rewarded for remaining tough in spite of all the temptations to concede in particular circumstances for particular workers.

Jack Welch, the former CEO of General Electric (GE), is an example of the central point of this "organizational economics and management" section, because he surely qualifies as a tough boss. Indeed, *Fortune* once named Welch "America's Toughest Boss" (Tichy and Sherman 1993). Welch earned his reputation by cutting payrolls, closing plants, and demanding more from those that remained open. Needless to say, these decisions were not always popular with workers at GE. But, today, GE is one of America's most profitable companies, creating far more wealth for the economy and opportunities for its workers than it would have if the tough and unpopular decisions had not been made. In Welch's words: "Now people come to work with a different agenda: They want to win against the competition, because they know that ... customers are their only source of job security. They don't like weak managers, because they know that the weak managers of the 1970s and 1980s cost millions of people their jobs" (Tichy and Sherman 1993, 92).

Game Theory: the "Battle of the Sexes"

In the previous section, we pointed out how workers could benefit from tough bosses who help them overcome the Prisoner's Dilemma that workers face. The Prisoner's Dilemma is an example of the type of situation that is analyzed by *game theory* – the study of how people make decisions when the benefit each person realizes from the decision she makes depends on the decisions others make in response. But there are other "games" that also explain how managers can be useful as tough bosses or tough leaders. For example, the "battle of the sexes" illustrates a more general conflict that is best resolved by managers who can make tough decisions.

Let's consider first the conflict between the sexes. Tom and Marsha have just started dating and enjoy each other's company. Both also like going to the movies, preferably together. But they have different tastes in films – Marsha prefers murder mysteries while Tom prefers action films. They are planning to go out on Saturday night, but Marsha wants to see *Knives Out* and Tom wants to see *Star Wars*. The value each receives from going out on Saturday night depends on what movie each sees and whether each sees it with the other or alone. The payoffs for Tom and Marsha are given in Table 2.3, which shows the different possible outcomes, with the first number in each box representing Marsha's payoff and the second number representing Tom's payoff. As shown, if both go to *Knives Out*, Marsha will receive a payoff of 100 and Tom gets a payoff of 75. If both go to *Star Wars*, Marsha receives a payoff of 75 and Tom gets the 100 payoff. If each goes to their choice of movie, but goes alone, then both receive 60. And in the highly unlikely event that they each go alone to the other's favorite movie, each will receive 40.

In the Prisoner's Dilemma game, the best choice for each (the noncooperative choice) is the same *no matter what* the other is expected to do. In the "battle of the sexes" game, the best choice for each varies, *depending on* what the other person is expected to do. For example, if Marsha can convince Tom that she is definitely going to see *Knives Out*, then the best choice for Tom is to see the same movie and get a payoff of 75 instead of 60. But it may be difficult for Marsha to convince Tom that she is going to her preferred movie, come what may. Tom knows that if he can convince Marsha that he is definitely going to see *Star Wars*, then this will be Marsha's best choice. So, making a credible commitment may be difficult for both Marsha and Tom.

Further aggravating the problem is that both may decide that it is worth going to a movie alone (reducing their payoff by 15 this time), rather than acquiescing to the stubbornness of the other. By doing so, each can hope to establish a reputation for making credible threats that will improve the chances of getting their way in the future. The result can be a lot of time and emotion expended negotiating over which movie to attend, when the most important thing is for both to attend the same movie – something that may not happen despite costly negotiation.

Table 2.3 The "battle of the sexes"

	Marsha/Tom	
	Knives Out	*Star Wars*
Knives Out	100/75	60/60
Star Wars	40/40	75/100

Workers routinely confront their own "battle of the sexes" problems on the job. Workplace decisions often have to be made about issues for which workers have different preferences, but yield the greatest payoff to all workers if they all accept the same decision. For example, some workers will prefer to start working at 6:30 a.m., have a one-hour lunch, and leave at 3:30 p.m. Others will prefer to start at 7:00 a.m., take no lunch, and leave at 3:00 p.m. Others will prefer to start at 10:00 a.m., take a two-hour lunch, and leave at 8:00 p.m. Indeed, there will probably be as many different preferences as there are workers, with these preferences changing from day to day. But typically, it is best for everyone to be in the workplace at the same time every workday.

Some may prefer to resolve such individual differences "democratically" with everyone making their case until an agreement emerges in some level of consensus. But agreement may never emerge and, even if it did, the cost would probably far exceed the benefit from a better decision. At some point relatively early in the discussion, the best approach is for a manager to assume leadership and make a decision on the starting time for work that everyone has to accept. There are many characteristics that go into making a good leader. Certainly, one of the first is the ability to make good decisions. But often, the most important thing is not the decision, but getting everyone to accept it. It is hard to argue that the decision to have everyone drive on the right-hand side of the road is better than having everyone drive on the left-hand side. Either decision is fine as long as everyone abides by it. In the workplace, getting everyone to accept a decision can require a tough-minded leader who imposes her will on others. Ideally, leaders will get the job done through gentle persuasion rather than bull-headed arrogance. But if the former doesn't work, it's nice to have the latter in reserve.

The Role of the Residual Claimant in Abating Prisoner's Dilemmas in Large Groups

Every good boss understands that he has to be more than just "tough." A boss needs to be a good leader, coach, midwife, and so on. A good boss can't be a micro-manager. A good boss inspires allegiance to the firm and the commonly shared corporate goals. Every good boss wants workers to seek the cooperative solutions in the various Prisoner's Dilemmas that invariably arise in the workplace. Having said this, a good boss will invariably be called upon to make some tough decisions, mainly because the boss usually stands astride the interests of the owners above and the workers below. The lesson of this section should not be forgotten: "Woe to the boss who simply seeks to be nice." Firms must structure themselves so that bosses will *want* to be tough, but appropriately tough. How can this be done?

In many firms, the boss is also the owner. The owner/boss is someone who pays for the physical capital (e.g., the building, land, machinery, office furniture), provides the raw materials and other supplies used in the business, and hires and supervises the workers necessary to convert those factors of production into goods and services. In return for assuming the responsibility of paying for all of the productive inputs (including labor), the owner earns the right to all of the (net) revenue generated by those inputs.

Economists refer to the owners as *residual claimants*: they have the claim to any (monetary) residual produced. As the boss, the owner is responsible for monitoring the workers to see whether each is properly performing her job, and applying the appropriate penalties (or encouragement) if not. By combining the roles of ownership and boss in the same individual, the residual claimant has a powerful incentive to work hard at being a tough boss. (We are sidestepping the issue of why workers aren't typically residual claimants of their firms. Because of space limitations, we have decided to answer those questions in Online Reading 2.3.)

The employees who have the toughest bosses are likely to be those who work for residual claimants. But the residual claimants probably have the toughest boss of all – themselves. There is a lot of truth to the old saying that when you run your own business, you are the toughest boss you will ever have. Small-business owners commonly work long and hard, because there is a direct and immediate connection between their efforts and their income. When they are able to obtain more output from their workers, they increase the residual they are able to claim for themselves. A residual claimant boss may be uncomfortable disciplining those who work for her or dismissing someone who is not doing the job – and indeed may choose to ignore some shirking. But in this case, the cost of the shirking is concentrated on the boss who allows it, rather than diffused over a large number of people who individually have little control over the shirking and little motivation to do anything about it. With a boss who is also a residual claimant, there is little danger that shirking on the part of workers will be allowed to get out of hand.

When a residual claimant organizes productive activity, all resources – not just labor – tend to be employed more productively than when the decision-makers are not residual claimants. The contrast between government agencies and private firms managed by owner/bosses is instructive. Examples abound of the panic that seizes the managers of public agencies at the end of the budget year if their agencies have not spent all of the year's appropriations. The managers of public agencies are not claimants to the difference between the value their agency creates and the cost of creating the value. This does not imply that public agencies have no incentive to economize on resources, but their incentives to do so are impaired by the absence of direct, close-at-hand residual claimancy. An additional problem is that taxpayers gain little to nothing by incurring the personal costs associated with closely monitoring the public agencies (Tullock 1972, chapter 7).

To make the point differently, assume that, as a result of your management training, you become an expert on maximizing the efficiency of trash collection services. In one nearby town, the trash is picked up by the municipal sanitation department, financed out of tax revenue and headed by a government official on a fixed salary. In another nearby town, the trash is picked up by a private firm, financed by direct consumer charges and operated by a local owner who is proud of her loyal workers and impressive fleet of trucks. By applying linear programming techniques to the routing pattern, you discover that each trash service can continue to provide the same pickup with half the number of trucks and personnel currently being used.

Who is going to be more receptive to your consulting proposal to streamline their trash collection – the bureaucratic manager who never misses an opportunity to tell of his devotion to the tax-paying public, or the proprietor who is devoted to her workers and treasures her trash trucks? The proprietor will hire you as a consultant as soon as she becomes convinced that your ideas will allow her to lay off half of her workers and sell half of her trucks. The manager who is also a residual claimant can be depended on to economize on resources despite her other concerns. The manager who is not a residual claimant will likely waste resources despite her statements to the contrary.

No matter how cheaply a service is produced, resources have to be employed that could have otherwise been used to produce other things of value. The value of the sacrificed alternative has to be known and taken into account to make sure that the right amount of the service is produced. As a residual claimant, a proprietor not only has a strong motivation to produce a service as cheaply as possible, but also has the information and motivation to increase the output of the service – only as long as the *additional value generated is greater than the value forgone elsewhere in the economy.*

Having the residual claimant direct resources is, understandably, an organizational arrangement that workers should applaud. The residual claimant can be expected to press all workers to work diligently so that wages, fringe benefits, and job security can be enhanced. Indeed, the workers would be willing to pay the residual claimants to force all workers to apply themselves diligently; both workers and residual claimants can share in the added productivity from added diligence.

Practical Lessons

One of the more important lessons from the analysis in this chapter is that size matters in business: as firms expand, shirking can be a growing problem. Firms will have to incur more monitoring costs with larger firm size, which means that bosses will have to become progressively tougher or incentives will have to overcome worker inclinations to shirk. To keep the analysis clear in this chapter, we have discussed shirking as if it were all "bad" – always and everywhere a net drain on corporate profits. Hence, the task of managers is, in such a world, relatively simple: eliminate all shirking by monitoring and "cracking the corporate whip."

While our approach has been useful to highlight key points, we need to stress before closing the chapter that shirking on the job, at least up to a point, can be viewed as a worker fringe benefit – something that has intrinsic value to workers. To the extent that this is the case, some shirking can actually increase company profits because it leads to a greater supply of good workers willing to work for the firm that allows some shirking and permits a reduction in the firm's wage rates. The company's lower productivity can (up to a point) be more than offset by its lower total wage bill. Indeed, workers can also be "better off" with some shirking. This is because the intrinsic value of some shirking on the job can afford them more utility than the additional money wages they could receive if some shirking were not allowed. Thus, shirking up to a point can be a win–win for both workers and firm owners. The win–win nature of some shirking is obvious in most offices and plants as workers – even highly respected workers – can be seen relaxing around vending machines, chatting in the hallways, and taking unscheduled breaks.

Further Reading Online

Reading 2.1: Marriages, mistresses, and marginalism (Foundation for Economic Education, link available on the online resources website www.cambridge.org/mckenzie4)
Reading 2.2: Management snooping
Reading 2.3: Risk-taking, risk aversion, and firm ownership

Recommended Videos Online

1 Rational behavior and the law of demand (Richard McKenzie, 31 minutes)
2 Rational behavior, continued (Richard McKenzie, 26 minutes)

The Bottom Line

The key takeaways from Chapter 2 are the following:

1 The concept of rational behavior means that the individual has alternatives, can order those alternatives on the basis of preference, and can act consistently on that basis. The rational individual will also choose those alternatives whose expected benefits exceed their expected costs.
2 Rational behavior implies that people have choices which imply that there is a foregone value or cost to every decision.
3 All choices involve cost–benefit calculations.
4 Traditionally, economics has focused on the activities of firms, and much of this book is devoted to exploring human behavior in a market setting. However, the concept of rational behavior can be applied to other activities, from politics and government to family life and leisure pursuits. Any differences in our behavior can be ascribed to differences in our preferences – and the institutional settings and constraints in which we operate.

5   The timing and riskiness of options will affect their present value. The more distant into the future that benefits will be received (or costs incurred), the lower their present values. The more risky options are, the greater their cost (or the lower their net value).

6   The importance of "common interest" can significantly affect the willingness of group members to cohere and pursue the common interest of the membership. However, a "common interest" can more effectively motivate a "small" group than a "large" group. This suggests that, given other considerations, an increase in group size beyond some point can have an adverse effect on the motivation that group members have to pursue their group's common interest.

7   Appeals to people's public-spiritedness can change behavior of large groups, at least to a limited extent, but they should not be considered a cure-all for major scarcity problems. Prices also have an economic role to play in encouraging people to pursue their "common interests."

8   The logic of collective action can explain the growth in employee shirking and the misuse of resources as firms grow. The logic can also explain why firms divide their operations into small groups, including departments and teams.

9   The basic problem of managers can be construed as one of overcoming the large-group problem that, at its heart, is dealing with Prisoner's Dilemmas.

10 Leadership in the form of setting a course for all to follow can be productive since it can reduce haggling (costs) about what course of action all should take.

11 Residual claimants have powerful incentives to encourage firms to minimize costs and maximize profits since they have claims to any firm resources after all other claims have been fulfilled.

12 Companies are typically controlled by the owners of capital because they would otherwise have to fear that their capital, once deployed in companies, would be subject to appropriation by workers.

13 A boss who is tough on employees can have supporters among employees as well as owners. There is, however, both an optimal amount of toughness on the part of bosses and an optimal amount of shirking on the part of workers.

14 A boss who is not tough on shirkers is also a shirker.

Review Questions ▷▷

1   What are the costs and benefits of taking this course? Develop a theory of how much a student can be expected to study for this course. How might the student's current family and employment status affect his studying time?

2   Some psychologists see people's behavior as determined largely by family history and external environmental conditions. How would "cost" fit into their explanations?

3   Are "rules of thumb" (heuristics) rational? Why? Provide an example.

4   How could drug use and suicide be considered "rational"?

5 What do economists mean by "rationality"? What is its importance in modeling economic behavior and why are economists reluctant to part with this assumption?

6 Radio stations give away "free money" to various listeners. Is the money really "free"?

7 Develop an economic explanation for why professors give examinations at the end of their courses. Would you expect final examinations to be more necessary in undergraduate courses or MBA courses? In which classes – undergraduate or MBA – would you expect more cheating?

8 "Tit-for-tat" is a strategy people adopt in cooperative relationships. This strategy means that people will work with others so long as others work for them. Why is tit-for-tat so widely adopted? What does it imply for management strategy with colleagues in a firm and with buyers and suppliers?

9 The common interest of people who are in a burning theater is to walk out in an orderly fashion and avoid a panic. If so, why do people so frequently panic in such situations? Use rational behavior and the logic of collective action in your answer.

10 Discuss the costs of making collective decisions in large and small groups. What do these costs have to do with the viability of large and small groups? Explain why the "free-rider" problem is likely to be greater in a large group than in a small group.

11 In what ways do firms overcome the free-rider problems discussed in this chapter relating to large groups? How do market pressures affect firm incentives to overcome these problems?

12 Describe the semi-ironic worker incentive to want a "tough" boss. Evaluate your previous bosses in this respect: too tough; not tough enough; or just right. If they have struggled, why do you think this happened?

13 You may have a class in which the professor grades according to a "curve," where she adjusts the grading scale to fit the test results. Assume the class is one in which all the students would prefer *not to* learn as much as they can. In such a situation, the "common interest" of the class members would be for everyone to study less: the same grading distribution with far less effort. Why do class members not collude and reduce their studying? Would you expect collusion against studying to be more likely in undergraduate general education courses or classes in an MBA program?

14 Describe the text's discussion of managerial snooping and "optimal shirking." How does your workplace perform on these two metrics?

3

Competitive Product Markets and Firm Decisions

I am convinced that if [the market system] were the result of deliberate human design … this mechanism would have been acclaimed as one of the greatest triumphs of the human mind.
   Friedrich A. Hayek[1]

In the heart of New York City, Fred Lieberman's small grocery is dwarfed by the tall buildings that surround it. Yet it is remarkable for what it accomplishes. Lieberman's carries thousands of items, most of which are not produced locally and some of which come from other parts of the world. A man of modest means, with little knowledge of the relevant production processes, Lieberman has nevertheless been able to stock his store with many of the foods and toiletries his customers want. Occasionally, he runs out of certain items; but most of the time, the supplies are ample. His store is so dependable that customers tend to take it for granted, forgetting that Lieberman's is one small strand in an extremely complex economic network.

How does Lieberman get the goods he sells – and how does he know which ones to sell and at what price? The simplest answer is that the goods he offers and the prices at which they sell are determined through the *market process* – the interaction of many buyers and sellers trading what they have (their labor or other resources) for what they want. Lieberman stocks his store by appealing to the private interests of suppliers and paying them competitive prices. His customers pay him extra for the convenience of purchasing goods in their neighborhood grocery, appealing to their private interests. To determine what he should buy, Lieberman considers his suppliers' prices. To determine what and how much they should buy, his customers consider the prices he charges compared to other offers. The economist Friedrich Hayek (1945) has suggested that the market

[1] Hayek, F. A. "The Use of Knowledge in Society." *The American Economic Review*, vol. 35, no. 4, 1945, pp. 519–530, used with permission.

process is manageable for people such as Fred Lieberman, his suppliers, and his customers, precisely because prices condense a great deal of information into a useful form, signaling quickly what people want, what goods cost, and what resources are readily available.

Prices guide and coordinate production decisions and consumer purchases. Prices forge a form of generally mutually beneficial cooperation among many people – notably, Lieberman and his workers, the investors and workers at his suppliers, and his customers. (Consider again the innumerable people who must coordinate their efforts to make a product as simple as a pencil available in the market – as per Leonard Read's essay in Perspective 1.)

The role of prices in market economies is as substantial as it is unheralded. The value of prices to human welfare only becomes apparent when they are artificially suppressed or manipulated by people who think they know more about what's better for prices than markets. After all, markets are ephemeral. Prices seem to be just "there" and appear to be set by the people who post them on, say, grocery store shelves or at Amazon. However, prices emerge in highly complex ways from forces that sometimes extend to all corners of the globe, with the prices serving as communication devices on the relative value and scarcity of resources, goods, and services. Prices are to markets what "packets" of electrons (or 1s and 0s) are to the Internet.

How are prices determined? This is an important question for people in business, because understanding this can help them understand the forces that will cause prices to change in the future – a key factor that affects their businesses' bottom lines. There is money to be made in being able to comprehend the dynamics of prices. Our most general answer to the question of price determination is deceptively simple: in competitive markets, supply and demand establish prices. However, there is much to be learned about supply and demand. Many students will find them to be the most useful concepts and tools of analysis developed in this book (and perhaps their entire business program). But to understand supply and demand, you must first understand that market processes and prices emerge everywhere and are usually competitive. (Remember R. A. Radford's account of markets in his POW camp during World War II in Chapter 1. Other examples: Markets for Nobel Prize medallions in Online Reading 3.1; and the (212) Manhattan area code discussed in Online Reading 3.2.

Part A Theory and Public Policy Applications

The Competitive Market Process

So far, our discussion of markets has been rather casual. We started by trying to describe how people behave in broad terms, especially in the context of "markets." Individuals are assumed to be (largely) rational, weighing expected benefits and costs as they make decisions. Many of those decisions involve voluntary, mutually beneficial trades with other parties. The voluntary nature of the trades largely assumes away coercion and fraud.[2] Both parties (at least perceive to) benefit – an attractive outcome, both philosophically and practically. The benefits accrue trade by trade in microeconomic terms – but in aggregate, they feed economic growth in macroeconomic terms.

In the next few sections, we will define "competition," examine how competitive markets work through demand and supply, and learn why markets are generally efficient systems for determining what and how much to produce. Markets, along with the prices that emerge in them, make the problem of scarcity less pressing than it otherwise would be. By looking to prices as summaries of market information, Fred Lieberman can use his scarce brainpower to focus on choosing better, more cost-effective products and providing his customers more cost-effective service than would otherwise be possible – a point central to Hayek's (1945) seminal essay, "The use of knowledge in society" in Online Reading 3.3.

The Market Setting

Most people tend to think of a market as a geographical location – a shopping center, an auction hall, a business district. From an economic perspective, however, it is more useful to think of a market as a *process.* You may recall from Chapter 1 that a market is defined as the process by which buyers and sellers determine what they are willing to buy and sell – and on what terms – whether in a building, at a street corner, or on the Internet. That is, a market is the process by which buyers and sellers decide the prices and quantities of goods and services to be bought and sold.

In this process, individual market participants search for information relevant to their own interests. Buyers ask about models, sizes, colors, quantities available, and the prices sellers will accept. Sellers inquire about the types of goods and services buyers want and the prices they are willing to pay. This market process is *self-correcting.* Buyers and sellers routinely revise their plans on the basis of information and experience. As economist Israel Kirzner has written (Kirzner 1973, 10):

The overly ambitious plans of one period will be replaced by more realistic ones; market opportunities overlooked in one period will be exploited in the next. In other words, even without changes in the basic data of the market, the decision made in one period one time generates systematic alterations in corresponding decisions for the succeeding period.

---

[2] Defining and measuring the extent of coercion and fraud is an interesting and important topic. In economics, fraud is most interesting in contexts where information is highly imperfect (a topic in Chapter 6) and coercion is most relevant in terms of government policy (Chapter 6) and monopoly power (Chapters 10 and 11).

The market consists of people – consumers and entrepreneurs – attempting to buy and sell on the best terms possible. Through a groping process of trial and error, producers move from relative ignorance about consumer wants to a reasonably accurate understanding of how much can be sold at what price. The market functions as an ongoing *information and exchange system*, with the emerging competition in markets leading to, ironically, the *cooperation* of innumerable people on a global scale.

Competition among Buyers and among Sellers

Competition is the process by which market participants, in pursuing their own interests, attempt to outdo, outprice, outproduce, and outmaneuver each other – and avoid being outdone, outpriced, outproduced, or outmaneuvered by others.

Part and parcel of the market process is the concept of **competition**. Competition does not occur so much *between* buyer and seller, but *among* buyers and *among* sellers. Buyers compete with other buyers for the limited number of goods on the market. To compete, they must discover what other buyers are bidding and offer the seller better terms – a higher price or the same price for a lower-quality product. Sellers compete with other sellers for the consumer's dollar. They must learn what their rivals are doing and attempt to do it better – to lower the price or enhance the product's appeal.

This kind of competition stimulates the exchange of information, forcing competitors to reveal their plans to prospective buyers or sellers. The exchange of information can be seen clearly at auctions. Before the bidding begins, buyers look over the merchandise and the other buyers, attempting to determine how high others might be willing to bid for a particular item. During the auction, more information is revealed as buyers call out their bids and others try to top them. From the seller's point of view – say, the auctioneer's – competition among buyers will bring the highest prices possible.

Information exchange is less apparent in department stores, where competition is not as transparent. Even there, comparison shopping by buyers across stores will often reveal some sellers who are offering lower prices in an attempt to attract consumers (Hayek 1948, 97):

In competing with each other, sellers reveal information that is ultimately of use to buyers. Buyers likewise inform sellers. From the consumer's point of view, the function of competition is precisely to teach us who will serve us well: which grocer or travel agent, which department store or hotel, which doctor or solicitor, we can expect to provide the most satisfactory solution for whatever particular personal problem we may have to face.

Competition among sellers can take many forms, including the price, quality, weight, volume, color, texture, durability, and smell of products – as well as the credit terms offered to buyers. Sellers also compete for consumer attention by appealing to their hunger and sex drives or their fear of death, pain, and illness. All these forms of competition can be divided into two basic categories – *price* and *non-price* competition. Price competition is of particular interest to economists, who see price as a crucial source of information for market participants and a coordinating force that brings the quantity produced into line with the quantity consumers are willing to buy. In the following sections, we shall construct a model of the competitive market and use it to explore the process of *price* competition under intense competitive market conditions called **perfect competition**. (Although we will focus on price competition, we will also discuss non-price competition as appropriate.)

> **Perfect competition** is a market composed of numerous independent sellers and buyers of an identical product, such that no one individual seller or buyer has the ability to affect the market price by changing the production level. Entry into and exit from a perfectly competitive market is unrestricted; anyone can enter the market, duplicate the good, and compete for consumer dollars. Since each competitor produces or buys only a small share of the total output, the individual competitor cannot significantly influence the degree of competition or the market price.

We will devote much space to "perfectly competitive markets" – an idealized situation well suited to graphic analysis and helpful to clarify the pricing forces afoot in competitive markets. A fully competitive market is made up of many buyers and sellers searching for opportunities and ready to enter the market when opportunities arise – both actual and potential competitors. A fully competitive market offers freedom of entry: there are no legal or artificial barriers to producing and selling goods in the market. Since each competitor produces or buys only a small share of the total output, the individual competitor cannot significantly influence the degree of competition or the market price.

Although few (if any) markets are "perfect," we will use the model of perfect competition – captured in its basic form of supply and demand curves – because it is simple, well understood, and allows for much analytical progress. (We will take up more "realistic" and more complex market structures in Book III.) Always keep in mind that "models" of markets are what they are intended to be: *devices* for coming to grips with complex reality, expecting insights that would otherwise remain hidden. We also pay attention to the perfectly competitive market model because our analysis of it leads to a powerful point we will develop later: these are market conditions that you, as a business decision-maker and investor, should avoid to the extent possible.

Supply and Demand: a Market Model

Our discussion concentrates on how two groups (buyers and sellers) interact to determine the price of tomatoes – a product Fred Lieberman almost always carries. We will use two curves. The first represents buyer behavior – consumer

> **Demand** is the assumed inverse relationship between the price of a good or service and the quantity consumers are willing and able to buy during a given period, all else constant.

"demand" for the product. To the general public, **demand** is simply what people want to buy. But to economists, demand has a more technical meaning and wider application to everyday life.

Describing Demand

The relationship between price and quantity demanded is *inverse*. That is, when the price of a good rises, the quantity bought (and sold) will decrease, *ceteris paribus* (Latin for "everything else held constant"). Conversely, when the price of a good falls, the quantity bought goes up. Demand is not a single quantity, but is the relationship between price (and other variables) and quantity purchased. A given quantity bought at a particular price is properly called the *quantity demanded*.

Both tables and graphs can be used to describe this inverse relationship between price and quantity. Demand may be seen as a *schedule* of the various quantities of a particular good consumers will buy at various prices. Table 3.1 contains a hypothetical schedule of the demand for tomatoes in the New York area during a typical week. Column (2) shows prices that might be charged. Column (3) shows the number of bushels consumers are willing to buy at those prices. Note that, as the price rises from zero to $11 per bushel, the number of bushels purchased drops from 110,000 to zero.

Table 3.1 **Market demand for tomatoes**

(1) Price–quantity combinations	(2) Price per bushel ($)	(3) No. (000) of bushels
A	0	110
B	1	100
C	2	90
D	3	80
E	4	70
F	5	60
G	6	50
H	7	40
I	8	30
J	9	20
K	10	10
L	11	0

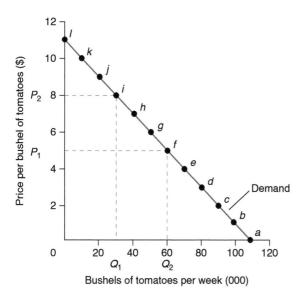

Figure 3.1 Market demand for tomatoes Demand, the inverse relationship between price and quantity purchased, can be represented by a curve that slopes down toward the right. Here, as the price falls from $11 to zero, the number of bushels of tomatoes purchased per week rises from zero to 110,000.

Demand may also be depicted graphically as a *curve*. With price scaled on the vertical axis and quantity on the horizontal axis, the demand curve has a negative slope (downward and to the right), reflecting the inverse relationship between price and quantity demanded. The shape of the market demand curve is shown in Figure 3.1, which is based on the data from Table 3.1. Points *a* through *l* on the graph correspond to the price–quantity combinations A through L in the table. Note that, as the price falls from P_2 ($8) to P_1 ($5), consumers move along their demand curve from a quantity of Q_1 (30,000) to the larger quantity Q_2 (60,000).[3]

The Slope and Determinants of the Demand Relationship between Price and Quantity

Price and quantity demanded are inversely related for two primary reasons. First, as the price of a good decreases (and the prices of all other goods remain the same), the good becomes relatively cheaper, and consumers will substitute it for others. This response is called the "substitution effect." The substitution will most obviously come within product categories. If the price of oranges falls (the price of apples remaining constant), people can be expected to buy more oranges and fewer apples. But the substitutions can also occur across categories, since the lower-priced good has become more attractive compared to all other goods.

---

[3] The demand curve can also be derived with a powerful (but more complicated) form of analysis using budget constraints and indifference/utility curves. We cover this in the Online Math Appendix.

Second, as the price of a good decreases (and the prices of all other goods stay the same – remember *ceteris paribus*), the purchasing power of consumer incomes rises. That is, their *real* incomes increase. Existing consumers are able to buy more and additional customers may now engage with the product. This response is called the "income effect."[4]

The downward-sloping demand curves can reflect large or small behavioral changes among consumers. (This topic is developed in Chapter 4.) For example, the behavioral response to a change in gasoline prices is generally small. However, when the price of gasoline goes up, drivers can still be expected to economize on their uses of gasoline in a variety of ways. Drivers may use more fuel-efficient cars and reduce the number of times they stomp on the accelerator when leaving stoplights – behavioral changes that enable them to buy less gasoline.

Although price is an important component in demand, it is not the only variable influencing how much people want. It may not even be the most important. The major factors that affect market demand are called the *determinants of demand* – for example:

- consumer tastes and preferences;
- the prices of other goods;
- consumer incomes;
- the number of consumers; and
- expectations concerning future prices and incomes.

A change in any of these determinants of demand will cause either an increase or a decrease in the demand schedule's relationship between price and quantity demanded.

- An *increase in demand* is an increase in the quantity demanded at every price. It is represented graphically by a rightward/outward shift of the demand curve.
- A *decrease in demand* is a decrease in the quantity demanded at every price. It is represented graphically by a leftward/inward shift of the demand curve.

Figure 3.2 illustrates the shifts in the demand curve that result from a change in one of the determinants of demand (other than the price of the good). The outward shift from D_1 to D_2 indicates an increase in demand: consumers now want more of a good at every price. For example, they want Q_3 instead of Q_2

---

[4] Thus, the income and substitution effects move consumption in the same direction for the good whose price has changed – for example, providing two reasons why consumption drops when price increases: It tightens the budget constraint and it encourages substitution away from the more-expensive good. These concepts are interesting and useful by their own rights, but also because they are analogous to the scale and substitution effects we will develop in producer theory.

tomatoes at price P_2. Consumers are also now willing to pay a higher price for any quantity. For example, they will pay P_3 instead of P_2 for Q_2 tomatoes. Notice that in Figure 3.1 (and Table 3.1), people bought more *because* the price of the good decreased – a movement along the demand curve with the shift to D_2; in Figure 3.2, people are willing to buy more *despite* a higher price.

Likewise, an inward shift from D_1 to D_3 indicates a decrease in demand: consumers want less of a good at every price – Q_1 instead of Q_2 tomatoes at price P_2. And they are willing to pay less than before for any quantity – P_1 instead of P_2 for Q_2 tomatoes. Again, in Figure 3.1 (and Table 3.1), people bought less *because* the price of the good decreased – a movement along the demand curve. Now, they're buying less *despite* lower prices, because of the change in the price–quantity schedule and the shift in the demand curve.

A change in a determinant of demand will translate into an increase or decrease in current market demand. For example, an increase in market demand can be caused by any of the following:

- *An increase in consumer desire or taste for the good or service.* If people want it more, they will buy more of it at any given price or pay a higher price for any given quantity.
- *An increase in the number of buyers.* If more buyers enter the market, more will be purchased at any given price and the price will be higher for any given quantity.
- *An increase in the price of substitute goods* (which can be used in place of the good in question). If the price of oranges increases, the demand for grapefruit will increase.

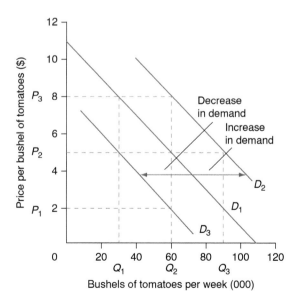

Figure 3.2 Shifts in the demand curve
An increase in demand is represented by a rightward/outward shift in the demand curve from D_1 to D_2. A decrease in demand is represented by a leftward/inward shift in the demand curve from D_1 to D_3.

- *A decrease in the price of complementary goods* (which are used in conjunction with the good in question). If the price of peanut butter falls, the demand for jelly and honey will increase. If the price of gasoline falls, the overall demand for automobiles can increase.[5] (The demand for various models will also rise or fall, depending on their gas consumption: the demand for SUVs would rise while the demand for hybrids would fall.)
- *Generally speaking (but not always), an increase in consumer incomes.* An increase in people's incomes will increase the demand for "normal" goods (e.g., new cars). It may also decrease demand for lower-quality "inferior" goods (e.g., hamburgers or off-brand/generic items) because people can now afford better-quality products (e.g., steak or name-brand items).
- *An expected increase in the future price of the good in question.* If people expect the price of gasoline to rise faster than the prices of other goods, they may buy more gasoline now in trying to avoid an expected additional cost in the future.
- *An expected increase in the future incomes of buyers.* College seniors' demand for cars tends to increase as graduation approaches and they anticipate a rise in income.

We will place much attention on how changes in price affect the quantity demanded with little attention to how changes in "tastes" affect the demand. The differential treatment of price and tastes does not imply that price is more important than tastes in determining the consumption level of any good. Rather, economists concentrate on price because they seek a theory of price determination (not a theory of taste determination – a major interest of psychology). In addition, the effect of price changes on quantity demanded is more predictable, given extensive consumer theory and empirical observation. The inverse relationship between price and quantity consumed is viewed as a "law" (the "law of demand"). "Tastes and preferences," on the other hand, are an amorphous, subjective concept largely outside our interest and expertise.

Describing Supply

On the other side of the market are the producers of goods and services. The average person thinks of supply as the quantity producers are willing to sell. To economists, however, **supply** means something quite different. As with demand, supply is not a "given quantity," but a *relationship between price and quantity supplied.* As the price of a good rises, producers are generally willing to offer a larger quantity. The reverse is equally true: as price decreases, so does quantity supplied. Like demand, supply can be described with a table or a graph.

---

[5] This is akin to the law of demand: since the complementary package of goods is increasing in price, interest in the combination will decrease.

Supply may be described as a *schedule* of the quantity that producers will offer at various prices during a given period of time. Table 3.2 shows such a supply schedule. As the price of tomatoes increases from zero to $11 per

> **Supply** is the relationship between the quantity producers are willing to offer (during a given period) and the price, all else constant. Generally, because additional costs tend to rise with expanded production, this relationship is presumed to be positive (a point that is developed with care in Chapters 7 and 8). In other words, individual producers will often require higher prices to supply more units.

bushel, the quantity offered rises from zero to 110,000, reflecting the positive relationship between price and quantity supplied.

Table 3.2 **Market supply of tomatoes**

(1) Price–quantity combinations	(2) Price per bushel ($)	(3) No. (000) of bushels
A	0	0
B	1	10
C	2	20
D	3	30
E	4	40
F	5	50
G	6	60
H	7	70
I	8	80
J	9	90
K	10	100
L	11	110

Supply may also be depicted as a *curve*. If the quantity producers will offer is scaled on the horizontal axis and the price of the good is scaled on the vertical axis, the supply curve will slope upward to the right, reflecting the positive relationship between price and quantity supplied. In Figure 3.3, points *a* through *l* represent the price–quantity combinations A through L from the data in Table 3.2. Note how a change in the price causes a movement along the supply curve.

The Slope and Determinants of the Supply Relationship between Price and Quantity

The quantity producers will offer depends on their *production costs*. Obviously, the total cost of production will rise when more is produced, because more resources will be required to expand output. The additional cost or **marginal cost** of each additional

> **Marginal cost** is the additional cost of producing an additional unit of output.

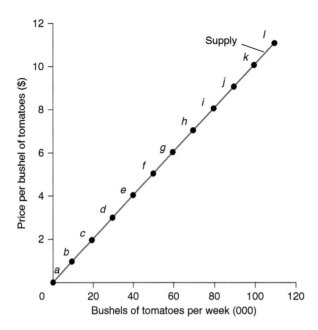

Figure 3.3 Supply of tomatoes Supply, the relationship between price and quantity produced, can be represented by a curve that slopes up toward the right. Here, as the price rises from zero to $11, the number of bushels of tomatoes offered for sale during the course of a week rises from zero to 110,000.

bushel produced also tends to rise as total output expands (beyond some point, which will be explained in Chapters 7 and 8). In other words, when it costs more to produce the second bushel of tomatoes than the first, and more to produce the third than the second, firms will not expand their output unless they can cover their progressively higher marginal costs with a progressively higher price. This is why supply curves typically slope upward.

Anything that affects production costs will influence supply and the position of the supply curve. Such factors, which are called *determinants of supply*, include:

- change in productivity due to a change in technology;
- change in the profitability of producing other goods; and
- change in the scarcity (and prices) of various productive resources ("inputs").

Many other factors, such as expectations of the future or the weather, can also affect production costs and therefore supply. A change in any of these determinants of supply can either increase or decrease supply – that is, shift the entire supply curve/schedule:

- An *increase in supply* is an increase in the quantity producers are willing and able to offer at every price. It is represented graphically by a rightward/outward shift in the supply curve.
- A *decrease in supply* is a decrease in the quantity producers are willing and able to offer at every price. It is represented graphically by a leftward/inward shift in the supply curve.

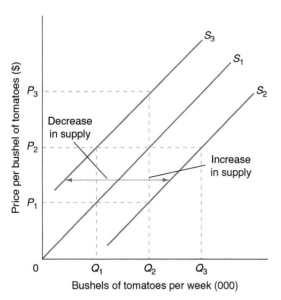

Figure 3.4 Shifts in the supply curve
A rightward/outward shift in the supply curve, from S_1 to S_2, represents an increase in supply. A leftward/inward shift in the supply curve, from S_1 to S_3, represents a decrease in supply.

In Figure 3.4, an increase in supply is represented by the shift from S_1 to S_2. Producers are willing to produce a larger quantity at each price – Q_3 instead of Q_2 at price P_2, for example. They will also accept a lower price for each quantity – P_1 instead of P_2 for quantity Q_2. Conversely, the decrease in supply represented by the shift from S_1 to S_3 means that producers will offer less at each price – Q_1 instead of Q_2 at price P_2. They must also have a higher price for each quantity – P_3 instead of P_2 for quantity Q_2.[6]

A few examples will illustrate the impact of changes in the determinants of supply. If firms learn how to produce more goods with the same or fewer resources, the cost of producing any given quantity will fall. Because of the technological improvement, firms will be able to offer a larger quantity at any given price or the same quantity at a lower price. The supply will increase, shifting the supply curve outward to the right.[7] Similarly, if the profitability of producing oranges increases relative to grapefruit, grapefruit producers will shift their resources to oranges. The supply of oranges will increase, shifting the supply curve to the right. Finally, if lumber (or another input) becomes scarcer,

---

[6] A shift in supply can be confusing, especially if you're trying to memorize rather than think about the shift. An increase in supply looks like an increase since the curve moves to the right, but it looks like a decrease since the curve moves down. Why does an increase in supply "go down"? Because producer costs – and thus market prices – are decreasing.

[7] Here, we're describing a technological advance that allows the same item to be made at lower cost. Technological advance can also result in the creation of a new product or an improved product. But the former requires a new graph (with the new product and the newly created market) and the latter complicates the analysis by changing two things: improved quality and different costs.

its price will rise, increasing the cost of new housing and reducing the supply of new houses coming onto the market. The supply curve of new houses will shift inward to the left.

Many students find this univariate approach – focusing on a change in one variable while holding all other market forces constant – troubling because they can readily see that, in real-world markets, many forces are changing in various combinations during any timeframe. This is a reasonable concern, but there is a "method to our madness." Consider what workers in the hard sciences do in their laboratories. They may isolate any given germ in a Petri dish and then introduce a chemical or organism one at a time. Clearly, any given germ in a natural state is hit by a host of other forces more or less at the same time. But the scientists use Petri dishes to do what we are doing in our conceptual framework. Like the scientist, having excluded changes in other market forces from our analysis, we can gain understanding on how one variable matters – and, then, how other relevant market forces affect prices and sales. This approach allows us to advance the analysis one step at a time – without the debilitating confusion that would emerge if a host of forces changed all at once. If we have trouble understanding how markets work, it is not because we have too little information on what is happening in markets, but rather the opposite: difficulty in cutting through the "fog" created by too much information.

Market Equilibrium

Supply and demand represent the two sides of the market – sellers and buyers. By plotting the supply and demand curves together, as in Figure 3.5, we can explore the conditions under which the decisions of buyers and sellers will be

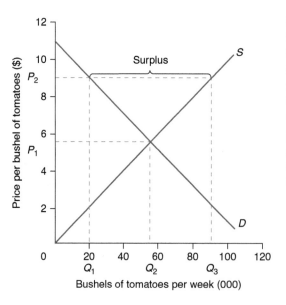

Figure 3.5 Market surplus
If a price is higher than the intersection of the supply and demand curves, a market surplus results: greater quantity supplied (Q_3) than demanded (Q_1). Competitive pressures will push the price down toward the equilibrium price (P_1), the price at which the quantity supplied equals the quantity demanded (Q_2).

incompatible with each other, and why a market surplus or shortage of tomatoes will result. We can also illuminate the competitive market forces at work to push the market price toward the market-clearing price – the price at which the market is said to be in **equilibrium**, where the forces of supply and demand balance one another with no net pressure for the price and output to move up or down.

> **Market equilibrium** occurs when the forces of supply and demand are in balance with no net pressure for the price and output level to change.

Students can get hung up on the concept of equilibrium if they deduce that it really exists "out there" in the marketplace. As we try to talk and write efficiently, it may seem as if this is the case. But the construct of an equilibrium really is designed as a *reference point* – the central tendency toward which competitive pressures will guide price and quantity. "Equilibrium" is only an analytical device or tool. Markets in the real world may never actually get to any given equilibrium, because so many market forces are changing at all times. However, we can come to understand the *directional* movement (up or down) of price and quantity if a market is not at equilibrium. We can also determine the *directional* movements of price and quantity if the supply or demand schedules change.

Market Surpluses

Suppose that the price of a bushel of tomatoes is $9 or P_2 in Figure 3.5. At this price, the quantity demanded by consumers is 20,000 bushels, much less than the quantity offered by producers of 90,000. There is a **market surplus**, or excess supply, of 70,000 bushels. Graphically, an excess quantity supplied occurs at any price above the intersection of the supply and demand curves.

> A **market surplus** is the amount by which the quantity supplied exceeds the quantity demanded at any given price.

What will happen in this situation? Producers who cannot sell their tomatoes will have to compete by offering to sell at a lower price, forcing other producers to follow suit. All producers might agree that holding the price above equilibrium would be in their "common interest," since an above-equilibrium price can generate extra profits for all (even though sales might be hurt). However, in competitive markets, producers are in a large-group setting in which their individual curbs on production to pursue their common interest will have an inconsequential impact on total market supply. They each can reason that they can possibly gain market share by individually lowering their price, if all others hold to the higher price. And each can reason that all others are thinking the same way, which means they can expect other producers to lower their prices. The logic leads the producers to do what is not in their common interest and to act competitively by cutting their prices.

As the competitive process forces the price down, the quantity that consumers are willing to buy will expand, while the quantity that producers are willing to sell will decrease. The result will be a contraction of the surplus, until it is finally eliminated at a price of $5.50 or P_1 (at the intersection of the two curves). At this price, producers will be selling all they want at that price; they will see no reason to lower prices further. Similarly, consumers will see no reason to pay more; they will be buying all they want at that price. This point at which the wants of buyers and sellers intersect is called the *equilibrium*, with the price and quantity at this point called *equilibrium price* and *equilibrium quantity*.

- The *equilibrium price* is the price toward which a competitive market will move, and at which it will remain once there, everything else held constant. It is the price at which the market "clears" – that is, at which the quantity demanded by consumers is matched exactly by the quantity offered by producers.
- The *equilibrium quantity* is the output (or sales) level toward which the market will move, and at which it will remain once there, all else constant.

Market Shortages

Suppose that the price asked is below the equilibrium price, as in Figure 3.6. At the relatively low price of $1 ($P_1$), buyers want to purchase 100,000 bushels – substantially more than the 10,000 bushels producers are willing to offer. The result is a **market shortage**. Graphically, a market

A **market shortage** is the amount by which the quantity demanded exceeds the quantity supplied at any given price.

shortage is the shortfall that occurs at any price below the intersection of the supply and demand curves.

As with a market surplus, competition will correct the discrepancy between the plans of buyers and sellers. Buyers who want tomatoes but are unable to get them at a price of $1 will bid higher prices, as at an auction. They have a

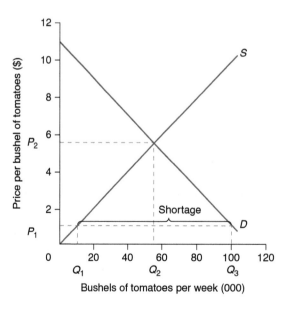

Figure 3.6 Market shortage
A price that is below the intersection of the supply and demand curves will create a shortage – a greater quantity demanded (Q_3) than supplied (Q_1). Competitive pressure will push the price up to the equilibrium price (P_2) – the price at which the quantity supplied equals the quantity demanded (Q_2).

"common interest" to hold the price below the equilibrium price (even with fewer units of the good they can buy). However, as with producers when there was a market surplus, buyers are in a large-group setting, with each individual buyer reasoning that not offering a higher price will not affect the market outcomes, because other buyers will offer a higher price. Each buyer can reason that they might as well offer a higher price to get the units they want.

As the price rises, a larger quantity will be supplied because suppliers will be better able to cover their increasing marginal costs. Simultaneously, the quantity demanded will contract as buyers seek substitutes that are now relatively less expensive compared with tomatoes. At the equilibrium price of $5.50 ($P_2$), the market shortage will be eliminated. Buyers will have no reason to bid prices up further; they will be getting all the tomatoes they want at that price. Sellers will have no reason to expand production further; they will be selling all they want at that price. The equilibrium price will remain the same until some force shifts the position of the supply or the demand curve. If such a shift occurs, the price will move toward a new equilibrium at the new intersection of the supply and demand curves.

In our graphical treatment of supply and demand, movement toward equilibrium can be imagined as instantaneous. But real-world movements in price necessarily take some time, given the limits of competition and available information (topics we will detail later).

The Effect of Changes in Demand and Supply

Figure 3.7 shows the effects of shifts in demand and supply on equilibrium price and quantity. In Figure 3.7(a), an increase in demand from D_1 to D_2 raises the equilibrium price from P_1 to P_2 and quantity from Q_1 to Q_2. The equilibrium price rises because, at the moment the demand curve shifts out to the right, a market shortage develops at the initial price P_1. The quantity demanded at the initial price is Q_3; the quantity supplied is less (still Q_1). Those buyers who want the good but are unable to get it will bid the price up. As the price goes up, producers can justify incurring the higher marginal costs of producing more, but some buyers will retreat on their purchases. The market will clear – quantity supplied and demanded will be equal – at the higher price of P_2.

Figure 3.7(b) shows the effects of a decrease in demand. When the demand initially falls, a market surplus develops at price P_1: quantity demanded is Q_3 while the quantity supplied is still Q_1. Producers who want to sell their output will put downward pressure on the price. As the price falls, buyers increase their purchases while producers curb their output. Equilibrium is re-established at a price of P_2 and quantity Q_2.

With the increase in supply from S_1 to S_2 in Figure 3.7(c), the equilibrium quantity rises from Q_1 to Q_2 and the equilibrium price falls from P_1 to P_2. When supply initially expands, a market surplus emerges at price P_1: quantity demanded is still Q_1 while the quantity supplied increases to Q_3. As producers try to sell what they

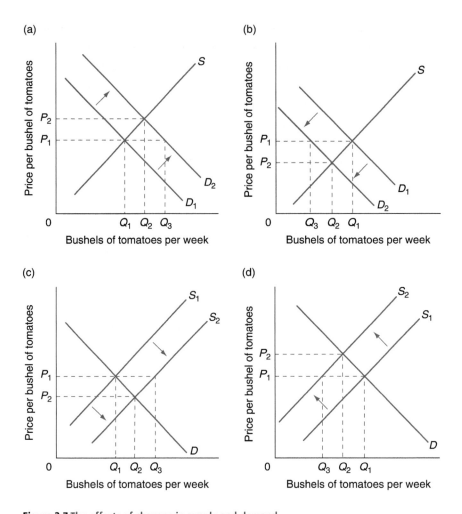

Figure 3.7 The effects of changes in supply and demand
(a) An increase in demand raises both the equilibrium price and the equilibrium quantity. (b) A decrease in demand has the opposite effect: a decrease in the equilibrium price and quantity. (c) An increase in supply causes the equilibrium quantity to rise but the equilibrium price to fall. (d) A decrease in supply has the opposite effect: a rise in the equilibrium price and a fall in the equilibrium quantity.

produce, they put downward pressure on the price. As the price falls toward P_2, the quantity produced contracts from Q_3 to Q_2 and the quantity demanded rises from Q_1 to Q_2.

A decrease in supply from S_1 to S_2 in Figure 3.7(d) causes the opposite effect: equilibrium quantity falls from Q_1 to Q_2; equilibrium price rises from P_1 to P_2. When supply decreases, a shortage develops at the original price with quantity supplied at Q_3 and quantity demanded at Q_1. Buyers who want more units of the good than are available at P_1 will bid the price up. As the price rises from P_1 to P_2, quantity demanded decreases from Q_1 to Q_2 and quantity supplied rises from Q_3 to Q_2.

We have limited the analysis so far to equilibrium in the "short run" – when production occurs within the constraints of a firm's plant size and equipment. This will be developed fully in Book III. For now, Online Reading 3.4 extends the market adjustments to the "long run" – when firms can expand their use of plant and equipment and when new producers can enter the market – with an application to handheld calculators in the 1960s and 1970s.

The Efficiency of the Competitive Market Model

Early in this chapter, we asked how Fred Lieberman knows what prices to charge for the goods he sells. The answer is now apparent: He adjusts his prices until his customers buy the quantities that he wants to sell. If he cannot sell all the fruits and vegetables he has, he lowers his price to attract customers and cuts back on his orders for those goods. If he runs short, he knows that he can raise his prices and increase his orders. His customers then adjust their purchases accordingly. Similar actions by other producers and customers all over the city move the market for produce toward equilibrium. The information provided by the orders, reorders, and cancellations from stores such as Lieberman's eventually reaches the suppliers of goods and then the suppliers of resources. Similarly, wholesale prices give him information on suppliers' costs of production and the relative scarcity and productivity of resources.

The use of the competitive market system to determine what and how much to produce has two advantages. First, it coordinates the decisions of consumers and producers very effectively. Most of the time, the amount produced in a competitive market system is close to the amount consumers want at the prevailing price. Second, the market system maximizes the amount of output that is acceptable to both buyer and seller. In Figure 3.8(a), note that all the price–quantity combinations acceptable to consumers lie either on or below the market demand curve, in the shaded area. (If consumers are willing to pay P_2 for Q_1 in Figure 3.8(a), then they should also be willing to pay less for this quantity – for example, P_1.) Furthermore, all the price–quantity combinations acceptable to producers lie either on or above the supply curve, in the shaded area shown in Figure 3.8(b). (If producers are willing to accept P_1 for quantity Q_1 in Figure 3.8(b), then they should also be willing to accept a higher price – for example, P_2.) When supply and demand curves are combined, as in Figure 3.8(c), we see that all the price–quantity combinations acceptable to both consumers and producers lie in the darker-shaded triangular area. From all of those acceptable output levels, the competitive market produces Q_1 – the maximum output level that can be produced given what producers and consumers are willing to do. In this respect, the competitive market can be said to be *efficient*, or to allocate resources with **efficiency**. The achievement of efficiency means that an expansion or contraction of output will reduce consumer and/or producer welfare.[8]

Efficiency is the maximization of output through careful allocation of resources, given the constraints of supply (producer costs) and demand (consumer preferences).

The producers' total production cost for Q_1 units is the area under the supply curve bounded by $0acQ_1$. The potential net gain from production is the difference between consumers' total value of Q_1 (area $0bcQ_1$) minus the producers' total cost (area $0acQ_1$), or the triangle area bounded by *abc*. In a competitive market, with production at Q_1, all of those net gains are generated and split between producers and consumers by way of the price charged, P_1. If production fell short of Q_1, then some of those potential net gains would not be generated. If production were greater than Q_1, then the cost of the added units to producers would exceed their added value to consumers. The net gains would again fall short of the potential net gains of the triangle *abc*. If more or less is produced than Q_1, the market is said to be **inefficient**.[9]

Market inefficiency is the extent to which potential net gains from trades are not generated.

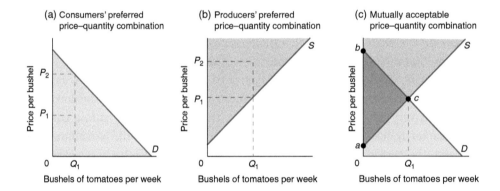

| (a) Consumers' preferred price–quantity combination | (b) Producers' preferred price–quantity combination | (c) Mutually acceptable price–quantity combination |

Figure 3.8 The efficiency of the competitive market
(a) Only those price–quantity combinations on or below the demand curve are acceptable to buyers. (b) Only those price–quantity combinations on or above the supply curve are acceptable to producers. (c) Price–quantity combinations that are acceptable to both buyers and producers are shown in the darker-shaded area. The competitive market is "efficient" in the sense that it results in output Q_1 – the maximum output level acceptable to both buyers and producers. It is inefficient to the extent that the quantity falls short of Q_1 or goes beyond Q_1.

---

[8] The relevant terms here are "consumer surplus" and "producer surplus" – both of which we will develop further in Chapter 9.

[9] From a social perspective, these inefficiencies are called "deadweight losses" or "social welfare costs."

The competitive market exploits all the possible trades between buyers and sellers. Up to the equilibrium quantity, buyers will pay more than suppliers require (those points on the demand curve that lie above the supply curve). Beyond Q_1, buyers will not pay as much as suppliers need to produce more (those points on the supply curve that lie above the demand curve). Again, in this regard, the market can be called efficient. (In the foregoing section, the focus has been on the efficiency of markets – how well they usually operate. Later, we will describe efficiency concerns in markets – for example, pollution, monopoly power, and information problems.)

Non-Price Competition

Markets in which suppliers compete solely in terms of price are relatively rare. In fact, price competition is not always the best method of competition – not only because price reductions mean lower average revenues, but because the reductions can be costly to communicate to consumers. Advertising is expensive; consumers may not notice price reductions as readily as improvements in quality; and quality changes are not as easily duplicated as price changes. Consumer preferences for quality over price should be reflected in the profitability of making such improvements. If consumers prefer a top-of-the-line item to a cheaper basic model, then producing the more sophisticated model could, depending on the cost of the extra features, be more profitable than producing the basic model and communicating its lower price to consumers.

If all consumers had exactly the same preferences on size, color, etc., then producers would make uniform products and compete through price alone. For most products, however, people's preferences differ. To keep the analysis manageable, we will explore non-price competition in terms of just one feature – product size. Suppose that in the market for ultra-HD television sets, consumer preferences are distributed along the continuum shown in Figure 3.9. The curve is bell-shaped,

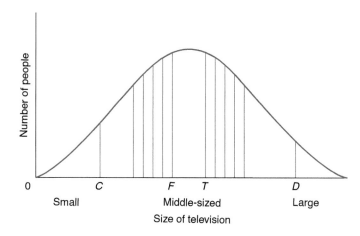

Figure 3.9 Consumer preferences in television size
Consumers differ in their wants, but most desire a medium-sized television. Only a few want a very small or a very large television.

indicating that most consumers are clustered in the middle of the distribution and want a medium-sized television. Fewer consumers want a giant screen or a mini-television.

All else equal, the first producer to enter the market, Alpha TV, will probably offer a product that falls somewhere in the middle of the distribution – for example, at the "hump" in Figure 3.9. In this way, Alpha TV offers a product that reflects the preferences of the largest number of potential buyers. Furthermore, as long as there are no competitors, the firm can expect to pick up customers to the left and right of center. (Alpha TV's product may not satisfy the wants of consumers who prefer a larger or smaller television, but it is the only one available.) The more that Alpha TV can meet the preferences of the greatest number of consumers, all else equal, the higher price it can charge and the greater profit it can make. (Because consumers value the product more highly, they will pay a higher price for it.)

The first few competitors that enter the market may also locate close to the center – in fact, several may virtually duplicate Alpha TV's product. These firms may conclude that they will enjoy a larger market by sharing the center with several competitors than by moving out into the "tails" of the distribution. They are probably right. Although they may be able to charge more (relative to production cost) for a giant screen or a mini-television that closely reflects some consumers' preferences, there are fewer potential customers for those products.

To illustrate, assume that competitor Zeta TV locates at F, close to T. It can then appeal to consumers on the left side of the curve because its product will reflect those consumers' preferences more closely. Alpha TV can still appeal to consumers on the right half of the curve. If Zeta TV had located at C, however, it would have direct appeal only to consumers to the left of C and those between C and T who are closer to C. Alpha TV would have appealed to more of the consumers on the left, between C and T, than in the first case. In short, Zeta TV has a larger potential market at F than at C.

As more competitors enter the market, the center will become so crowded that new competitors will find it advantageous to move away from the center – for example, to C or D. At those points, the market will not be as large as it is in the center, but competition will be less intense. If producers do not have to compete directly with as many competitors, they can charge higher prices. How far they move into the tails of the distribution will depend on the trade-offs they must make between the number of customers they can attract, the costs they face, and the price they can charge. As with price reductions, the movement of competitors into the tails of the distribution benefits consumers whose tastes differ from those of the consumers in the middle. These atypical consumers now have a product that comes closer to, or even directly reflects, their preferences.

Our discussion has assumed free entry into the market. If monopoly of a strategic resource or government regulation restricts entry, the variety of products offered will not be as great as in an open, competitive market. If there are only two or three competitors in a market, everything else being equal, we would expect them to cluster in the middle of a bell-shaped distribution. This tendency is evident in the broadcasting industry, when the Federal Communications Commission (FCC) strictly regulated the number of television stations permitted in a given geographical area in the U.S. Not surprisingly, stations carried programs that appealed predominantly to a mass audience – that is, to the middle of the distribution of television viewers. The U.S. Government organized the Public Broadcasting System (PBS) partly to provide programs with niche appeal to satisfy viewers on the fringes of the distribution. When cable television emerged and programs became more varied, the prior justification for PBS subsidies became even more debatable. (All of this has relevance to "political markets" with two major political parties dominating the system. As such, we discuss a "median-voter model" in Online Chapter 6.)

Even with free market entry, product variety depends on the cost of production and the prices people will pay for variations. Groceries would find it easier (lower cost) to stock only two or three types of cereal. Pizzerias would reduce their costs by only using two or three toppings. For their own reasons, consumers may prefer such a compromise. Although they may desire a product that perfectly reflects their tastes, they may buy a product that is not perfectly suitable if they can get it at a lower price. Producers can offer such a product at a lower price because of the economies (or cost savings) gained from selling to a large market (a topic detailed in Chapter 8). For example, instead of private tutorials, most students take predesigned classes in classrooms or even lecture halls. They do so largely because it is far less expensive, even though less effective. In a market that is open to entry, producers will take advantage of such opportunities.

If producers in one part of a distribution attempt to charge a higher price than necessary, other producers can move into this segment of the market and push the price down (or consumers can switch to other products). In this way, competition in markets can press buyers and sellers to move toward an optimal mix of products. Without freedom of entry, we cannot tell whether it is possible to improve on the existing combination of products. A free, competitive market gives rival firms a chance to better the combination. The case for the (relatively) free market becomes even stronger when we recognize that market conditions – and therefore the *optimal product mix* – are constantly changing.

Changes in Combination of Features

To this point, we have assumed that products bought and sold in competitive markets are given – in the sense that they are of a certain quality with a fixed set of attributes. But many products are upgraded with additional features at what seems to be a progressively rapid pace. Laptop computers have been introduced in succession with faster processors, larger hard drives, and an ever-growing array of features – built-in WiFi connections, cameras, microphones, headphone ports, bigger and brighter screens, etc. Cell phones have followed much the same upgrade paths. Understandably, firms often add many such features to avoid price cuts or being made irrelevant in their markets. But when should firms upgrade product quality and add features? In highly competitive markets (monopoly markets will be considered in Chapters 10 and 11), the straightforward answer is that firms should and must improve their products only when the marginal (added) cost of the improvement is less than the marginal value of the improvement to consumers. Under such a condition, producers can increase their profits because they can increase their prices by more than their costs. Consumers can be better off with the higher prices because the added values of the improvements are higher than the added prices for the improved products. That is, the product improvement is mutually beneficial, for both producers and consumers.

Producers will not consider improvements for which the additional values realized by consumers are less than the additional costs of the improvements to producers. If the added costs were greater than the added values, the improvement would not be mutually beneficial. The improvement would require the producers to increase their prices by more than the added value to consumers (who would reject the improved products). Or the producers could raise the prices by less than the added values to consumers, but the higher prices would not cover the added costs.

Product Improvement with Supply and Demand

To see this central point graphically, consider Figure 3.10, which contains the initial supply and demand curves (S_1 and D_1) for a hypothetical product with equilibrium price and quantity (P_1 and Q_1). Suppose that an upgrade becomes

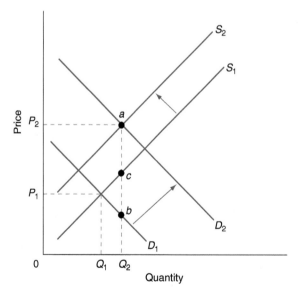

Figure 3.10 Product improvements When a product is improved, demand will rise from D_1 to D_2 while the added costs will push supply from S_1 to S_2. The equilibrium price and quantity will both rise, to P_2 and Q_2, respectively. The price increase ($P_2 - P_1$) is less than the added value to buyers (*ab*), but greater than the added costs incurred by producers (*ac*) .

available for the product through a technological breakthrough which all producers can adopt. The added value of the improvement is greater than the added costs, so it can be mutually beneficial to producers and consumers. The demand curve will shift up and to the right from D_1 to D_2, reflecting the added value to consumers (as measured by the added price consumers are willing to pay for the improved product, indicated by the distance ab). The supply curve shifts up and to the left from S_1 to S_2, reflecting the added production cost (as indicated by the higher price producers must incur to make the improvement, indicated by the distance ac). The new equilibrium price and quantity will be at the intersection a of D_2 and S_2 (P_2 and Q_2). The price will be competed upward because at P_1 there would be a market shortage.

Are consumers and producers better off because of the product improvement? The answer is clearly "yes," as can be seen in the graph. Consumers pay a higher price (P_2), but the increase in the price ($P_2 - P_1$) is less than the increase in value added from the improvement (ab). Producers are also better off because the increase in their price (again, $P_2 - P_1$) is greater than the increase in their costs (ac). Again, both sides of the market gain.

Will the improvement in the product be made in a competitive market? Yes, for offensive and defensive reasons. Producers will offer the improvement because they can make a profit on it and can gain a competitive advantage if other producers don't follow. But other producers must follow suit for a defensive reason; producers who don't can expect to lose sales to the producers who do.

PERSPECTIVE 3
Why Queues?

In the supply and demand models discussed in this chapter, one observation stands out: *markets clear.* That is, price adjusts up or down until the quantity demanded equals the quantity supplied. Here, we ponder issues that might have occurred to alert readers: If this is the case, then why are there so many queues – in grocery stores, at concerts, at theme parks, etc. – suggesting that market shortages abound? Put another way, do queues indicate that markets are not in equilibrium or fail the test of economic efficiency? Does the existence of queues mean that supply and demand models of markets are defective or irrelevant?

Not really. If nothing else, such models facilitate discussions of how prices can be expected to adjust *toward* (but not necessarily *to*) the equilibrium price. Such models allow us to predict the directional changes in prices, given changes in a variety of market forces, including technological and governmental policy changes. There are also several explanations for queues as efficient and mutually beneficial.

First, given how many products are sold in markets, businesses are bound to make mistakes. From time to time, a business will simply set a price that it believes to be the market-clearing price but which turns out to be below equilibrium. The result will be that the quantity demanded exceeds the quantity supplied. Many such "mistakes," which means the firm does not charge as much as it could have, are the calculated costs of doing business. Managers can reason that, as they raise their prices, they run a growing risk of charging too high a price – the result of which is that they are left with unsold goods (or unfilled seats in theaters and airplanes) and lost revenue.

Related, there are solid business reasons for businesses maintaining inventories of the products they sell. They can rarely predict sales during any time period with complete accuracy. Inventories allow firms to limit the costs of constantly missing sales. Similarly, businesses can understandably seek a "stock" or "inventory" of customers because such stocks, in the form of queues, enable businesses to have some customers in reserve – to bring on line, so to speak, if demand varies. In short, businesses might be said to seek optimal stocks of both goods to sell and customers to sell to. Of course, a firm has to consider the strong possibility that, if their customers don't receive as much of the firm's product as they want, they will simply go elsewhere.

Second, in some cases, queues can be devices for screening out less-desirable customers. Consider the challenge faced by concert promoters. Metallica knows that some potential (mainly young) attenders are more rabid about seeing the band than others. (Imagine the difference in concert experiences with an audience of fanatics rather than lawyers clapping politely.) Promoters also can surmise that rabid fans will be more inclined to buy Metallica albums and concert memorabilia. Queues can be a way of discouraging the less enthusiastic (perhaps older and more highly paid) potential attendees from going to the concert given their relatively higher opportunity costs of standing in the ticket line (or buying online immediately as tickets become available).

Third, queues can be mutually beneficial to both buyers and sellers because they may keep down costs and prices. Consider grocery stores where lines at checkout counters are common at almost all times of the day, but especially in late afternoon when many people get off work. Store managers could eliminate the lines by adding checkout counters and hiring more clerks. But reducing queues would add costs. A grocery store knows it can reduce checkout/clerking costs (and hence prices) by reducing service and allowing lines to form at the remaining counters. In short, lines can be profitable. The store's customers might not like incurring the added cost of the time spent standing in line; however, if the efficiency gains to the store are greater than the customers' wait costs, then the store can lower its grocery prices by more than the customer's wait costs, making the customers better off and causing customers to flock to the store with the checkout queues.

Other stores would follow suit to protect their market position and add to their profits. If stores don't take opportunities to increase the lines when their cost savings are greater than the wait costs customers have to incur, their value will suffer. And savvy investors would be expected to buy the stores and operate them more efficiently.

If queues were not mutually beneficial to firms and their customers, we would have to wonder how they could be so prevalent in competitive markets – for example, in the grocery store industry. If queues created losses for firms, then firms should be expected to eliminate them. If customers did not gain *on balance* from standing in line, then we would expect firms to enter their market and serve such customers without lines forming.

How long should stores allow queues to become? Obviously, there is some limit to most queues, given that grocery stores rarely have lines stretching to the backs of their stores. In conceptual terms: To consider allowing even a short queue to form, the cost savings to the store must be greater than the cost to customers of waiting in the queues. Rational (profit-maximizing) store managers should be expected to allow their lines to grow (foot by foot) so long as their additional cost savings for each (foot of) extension of the queues is greater than the added wait costs their customers have to incur. Under this operating rule, with each extension of the line, both customers and stores can be better off. The total value (in profit terms for the stores and lower prices for customers) increases with the length of the line.

However, as the lines are extended, the wait costs that customers incur are likely to grow as these people have to forgo more and more valuable oppor-tunities to do other things with their time.[10] And with each extension, the cost savings for the stores should begin to contract. As the checkout lines grow, less and less profitable goods will be put in the space once occupied by the checkout counters. And as the queues grow, the people standing in line can obstruct more and more of their fellow shoppers. If the queues are extended beyond the opti-mum, then both store owners/managers and customers are worse off than they could be. This means that both "too short" and "too long" lines can give rise to the under-performance of firms and a potential change in management.

The optimum-length queue will vary with different products and services in different markets. As might be imagined, the optimum will depend critically on the opportunity cost of a particular customer's time. Customers with higher wage

---

[10] To spend the first minute standing in line, the customer will forgo the least-valuable other opportunity. The next minute in line means that the next least-valuable opportunity is given up. The growing value of the opportunities given up with more time in line will translate into an increase in the cost of standing in line.

rates (or more valuable opportunities for use of their time) will incur higher *opportunity costs* than customers with lower wage rates. As a general rule, we should expect that lines in low-wage-rate neighborhoods and lower-end stores will tend to be longer than the lines in high-wage-rate neighborhoods and higher-end stores. And if wage rates in a given neighborhood rise, we should expect the length of the lines to contract.

The bottom line is clear: Queues can have an economic foundation. That is, queues can be mutually advantageous to both buyers and sellers, which explains why they are so prevalent and persistent. The economic issue that firms face is developing the optimal length of queues. (Another view of the "upside" of queues is presented in a *New York Times* column available in Online Reading 3.5.)

Part B Organizational Economics and Management

Henry Ford's "Overpayment"

This chapter has been about how markets operate, setting product prices and production levels through the forces of competition. Labor markets behave in the same manner. (We will detail labor demand by firms and labor supply by workers in Chapter 12.) As such, good managers creatively motivate employees – a force within the supply and demand curves in labor markets. When someone develops a more productive payment scheme, others are pressed to follow for fear of losing sales and profits. Henry Ford is remembered for his organizational inventiveness (the assembly line) and his presumption that he could ignore the wishes of customers (the famous statement that consumers could have any color of car as long as it was black). But in 1914, he stunned his board of directors by proposing to raise his workers' wages to $3 per day, one-third higher than the going wage in the Detroit automobile industry at the time ($2.20). When one of his board members wondered aloud why Ford did not consider a wage of $4 or $5 a day, Ford quickly agreed to $5, more than twice the prevailing market wage. Why? He *seemed* to be denying market forces when it came to setting worker wages. But was he?

In the basic, competitive framework illustrated with supply and demand curves, the "market wage" will settle where the market clears – where the number of workers demanded by employers equals the number of workers willing to work. No profit-hungry employer would ever pay above the market wage. For that matter, employers in a competitive labor market are *unable* to pay anything other than the market wage, given competition. If employers ever tried to pay more, they could be underpriced and competed out of business by other producers who paid the lower market wage for their labor. If employers paid below the market wage, they would not be able to hire employees and would be left without products to sell.

There are some obvious limitations with this basic model. First and most pressing, it won't be sufficient to explain Ford's choice to pay more than the prevailing wage! Second, although not the primary factor in this example, it's important to know that markets are not always nearly as competitive as we've described so far. This will be a topic of considerable interest in product markets (Chapters 9–11) and in labor markets (Chapter 12).

Third and most broadly, there are many real-world experiences that do not fit the simple supply and demand model. Granted, the standard model is still highly useful for discussing how wages might change with movements in the forces of supply and demand. For example, from this framework, we can see why wages move up when labor demand rises from increases in productivity or price increases. But many employers have followed Ford's lead and pay more than supposed "market wages." With an open professorship, departments can expect dozens or hundreds of qualified applicants. The U.S. Postal Service receives far more applications for its jobs than it has jobs available. When popular companies announce their intention to hire workers, the queues can be impressive whether in-person or online. These examples cannot be explained by market-clearing wages.[11]

Fourth, we don't want to assume away any relevant business strategies and policy choices. On the contrary, we want to discuss how policies might affect worker productivity and how employers might achieve maximum productivity from workers. We seek a rationale for Ford's dramatic wage move if there is one to be found. In doing so, we don't deny that productivity affects worker wages – a well-established theoretical proposition in economics. But we also insist that the reverse is true – worker wages affect productivity – for good economic reasons.

We also don't pretend to provide a complete explanation for "overpaying" workers here. It may be that employers overpay their workers for psychological reasons: greater loyalty or reducing financial strains, leaving workers with more energy to devote to their jobs. Although these are relevant considerations, we want to focus on improving incentives for workers to do as the employer wants.

As such, Ford was not offering his workers something extra for nothing in return (Halberstam 1986). He "overpaid" his workers primarily because he could then demand more of them. He could work them harder and longer – and he did. He also could expect to lower his training costs and be more selective in the people he hired – a boon to all Ford workers. Workers could reason that they would be working with more highly qualified colleagues, all of whom would be forced

---

[11] Consider the persistence of unemployment in macroeconomics. The traditional view of markets would predict that the wage should be expected to fall until the market clears and the only evident unemployment should be transitory: people who are not working because they are between jobs or are first looking for a job. But "involuntary unemployment" abounds and persists, which must be attributable (at least partially) to employers paying workers "too much" (above the market-clearing wage rate).

to devote themselves to their jobs more energetically and productively, creating a more viable firm and greater job security.

There were other benefits for Ford as well. When workers are paid exactly their market wage, there is little cost to quitting. A worker making his market (or opportunity) wage can simply drop his job and move on to the next job with little loss in income. To note, Ford's workers were quitting with great frequency. In 1913, Ford had an employee turnover rate of 370 percent; the company hired 52,000 workers that year to maintain a workforce of 13,600 workers! At any one time, most workers were new at their jobs. Hiring and training costs were extraordinary.[12]

Before the pay raise, the absentee rate at Ford was 10 percent. Workers could stay home from work, more or less when they wanted, with virtually no threat of penalty. Given that they were only being paid the market wage, the cost of their absenteeism was relatively low to the workers. In effect, workers were buying a lot of absent days from work – and it was a bargain. They could reason that if they were only receiving the "market wage rate," then they could easily replace that wage rate elsewhere should Ford fire them for absenteeism or other misbehavior. Likewise, on-the-job shirking was rampant. Ford complained that "the undirected worker spends more time walking about for tools and material than he does working; he gets small pay because pedestrianism is not a highly paid line" (Halberstam 1986, 94).

In order to control workers, the company had to create some buffer between itself and the fluidity of a "perfectly" functioning labor market. Ford's above-market wage was, in effect, a premium paid to enforce the strict rules for employment eligibility that he imposed. Beyond their work habits on the job, Ford's "Sociology Department" was staffed by investigators who made frequent home visits and checked into workers' savings plans, marital happiness, alcohol use, and moral conduct. Ford was effectively paying for the right to make those checks, which he thought would lead to more productive workers.

Ford was also paying for obedience. He noted: "I have a thousand men who if I say 'Be at the northeast corner of the building at 4 a.m.' will be there at 4 a.m. That's what we want – obedience" (Halberstam 1986, 94). The extent of the obedience and allegiance may be disputed, but he got dramatic results. In 1915, the turnover rate was only 16 percent and productivity increased about 50 percent.

Even if a boss has control over the presence of workers, there must be some way of knowing what employees should be doing to maximize their contribution to the firm. This wasn't a difficult problem for Ford; there was little opportunity

---

[12] Those costs are higher today. The hiring cost to replace an information technology employee in 2015 who earns $60,000 a year can be as much as $150,000 (Greenwood, Beth, and Demand Media, "The average cost to hire a new employee," *Chron*, accessed November 9, 2015, from http://work.chron.com/average-cost-hire=new-employee-13262.html).

for a shirker to prosper. On the assembly line, it was obvious what Ford wanted his workers to do and it was relatively easy to spot shirkers. After the plant was mechanized and the $5-a-day policy was implemented, foremen were chosen largely for physical strength – and "If a worker seemed to be loitering, the foreman simply knocked him down" (Halberstam 1986, 94). Given that the high wage attracted many applicants, Ford's workers simply put up with the discipline and threat of abuse because they didn't want to be replaced. The lines outside the employment office were a strong signal to workers.

This type of heavy-handed control wasn't prevalent in the Ford plants because workers quickly shaped up and responded to the new incentives. And, of course, the threat of physical punishment wouldn't work today – at least in developed economies. Beyond that, when productivity requires workers with specialized knowledge to exercise creativity in response to changing situations, heavy-handed management tactics can easily undermine productivity. How is a manager to know whether a research chemist, a software developer, or a manager is behaving in ways that make the best use of his or her talents in promoting the objectives of the firm? Do you knock workers down if they gaze out the window? Of course not. Managers typically provide more subtle incentives than a high daily salary and a tough foreman. The big problem is controlling employees who have expertise you lack. One way to inspire effort from those who can't be monitored directly on a daily basis is to "overpay" workers, and ensure that they suffer a cost in the event that their performance, as measured over time, is not adequate. The "overpayment" gives workers a reason to avoid being fired or demoted for lack of performance and excessive shirking. Even when shirking is hard to detect, the threat of losing a well-paying job can be sufficient to motivate diligent effort (Lawler 1968; Shapiro and Stiglitz 1984; Bulow and Summers 1986; Roberts 2004).

In 2015, Dan Price, the founding CEO of Gravity Payments (a human resources firm) decided to start workers at $70,000, regardless of skill grade (Maney 2015). The pay increase for his hundred-plus workers was financed partially by cutting his pay from $1 million annually to $70,000. (He would still receive, as a major stockholder, compensation from dividend distributions.) He probably anticipated that a portion of the compensation increase would be offset by reduction in turnover and training costs and by his demanding more output from his workers.

Such a pay increase is a two-edged sword: it can make workers happier and more productive, but it can also reduce firm profits (or turn profits into losses), depending on how much worker productivity rises relative to pay. If a dramatic pay increase cuts into the firm's profit stream, investors will likely shy away from the company, which can depress the firm's stock, creditworthiness, and access to loans. Such a pay move could help the worker in the near term, but then undercut the firm's market survivability and jeopardize their jobs. The minimum annual salary of $70,000 for the newer lowest-skilled recruits could cause resentment among long-term higher-skilled workers who would be paid similarly, which could undercut worker morale and productivity.

To an unheralded degree, the "market" is a laboratory, full of product and pay experiments being tested. Henry Ford's experiment worked in grand style. Gravity Payments struggled during Covid, but the pay experiment seemed to work well enough. When such experiments pay off, especially in grand style, then other firms can be expected to follow with dramatic compensation changes of their own.

Overpayments to Prevent Misuse of Firm Resources

Many workers are in positions of responsibility, meaning they have control over firm resources that they use with discretion but could misuse for their own purposes. Their actions are also difficult to monitor. Misuse of funds may only infrequently be discovered. How should such employees be paid? More than likely, they should be "overpaid." That is, they should be paid more than their market wage as a way of imposing a greater cost on them if their misuse of funds is uncovered. The less likely that employees will be found out, the greater the overpayment must be in order for the cost to be influential.

Why do managers of branch banks make much more than bank tellers? One reason is that the managers' talents are scarcer. This is a common (and correct) point from standard labor market theory. But it can't be the whole story because the pay difference is greater than the skill gap. Two additional factors: First, the manager is in a greater position to misuse (or steal) more firm resources than each individual teller. Second, the manager's actions are less likely to be discovered than the teller's. The manager usually has more discretion than each teller – with one less level of supervision.

Why does pay escalate with rank within organizations? There are myriad reasons, several of which we cover later. We suggest here that, as managers move up the corporate ladder, they typically acquire more responsibility, gain more discretion over more firm resources, and have more opportunities to misuse those resources. In order to deter the misuse of firm resources, the firm needs to increase the threat of penalty for misuse, which implies a greater wage premium for each step on the corporate ladder.

Workers in the bowels of their corporations often feel that the people in the executive suite are drastically "overpaid," given that their pay appears to be out of line with what they do. To a degree, the workers are right. People in the executive suite are often paid a premium simply to deter them from misusing their powers. The workers should not necessarily resent the overpayments. The overpayments may be the most efficient way available for making sure that firm resources are used efficiently. To the extent that the overpayments work, the jobs of people at the bottom of the corporate ladder can be more productive, better paying, and more secure.

The Underpayment and Overpayment of Workers

Should workers accept "overpayment"? Is a greater overpayment always better for workers? The natural tendency is to answer with a strong "Yes!" We think a more cautious answer is in order. Workers would be well advised to carefully assess what is expected of them immediately and down the road. High pay means that employers can make greater demands – in terms of the scope and intensity of work assignments. This is because of the cost employees will bear if they do not consent to the demands.

Clearly, workers should expect that their employers will demand value equal to, if not above, the wage payments, and workers should consider whether they contribute as much to their firms' coffers as they receive. Otherwise, their job tenure may be tenuous. A high-paying job that is lost almost immediately for inadequate performance may be a poor deal for an employee. Similarly, it is common (and acceptable) to bargain over starting compensation with a new job. Any gains here are obvious to the worker. But they also potentially introduce a problem: higher employer expectations associated with the claimed higher value of one's labor. If you ask for more, it probably puts more pressure on you to deliver more.

Firms might also "overpay" their workers because they have "underpaid" their workers early in their careers. The "overpayments" are not so much "excess payments" as they are "repayments" of wages forgone early in the workers' careers. Of course, the workers would not likely forgo wages unless they expected their delayed overpayments to include interest on the wages forgone. So, the delayed overpayments must exceed underpayments by the applicable market interest rate. In such cases, the firms are effectively using their workers as sources of capital. The workers themselves become "venture capitalists" of an important kind. Indeed, compensation in such cases often involves a slice of ownership in the firm.

Why would firms do this? Some new firms must do it just to get started. They don't have access to all of the capital they need in their early years, given that their product or service has not been proven. They must ask their workers to invest "sweat equity" – the difference between what the workers could make in their respective labor markets and what they are paid by their firms. The under-payments not only extend the sources of capital to the firm but also give the workers a strong stake in the future of the firm, which can make the workers work all the harder to make the firm's future prosperous. The up-front underpay-ments can make the firm more profitable and increase its odds of survival, which can be a benefit to workers as well as owners. Of course, this is one reason that many young workers are willing to accept employment in fledgling firms. Young workers often have a limited financial base from which to make investments; they do, however, have their time and energy to invest.

So, we have a creative form of compensation that could be attractive to firms and employees. But two problems remain: Managers must be able to *commit* themselves to the overpayments *and* there must be some end to the overpayments.

Mandatory Retirement

Not too many years ago, firms regularly required their workers to retire at age sixty-five. Retirement was ritualistic for managers. Someone would organize a dinner at which the manager would be given a gold watch, a plaque for venerable service, one last goodbye, and then be shown the door.

Why would a firm impose a mandatory retirement age on its workers? Such a policy seems bizarre, given that most companies are intent on making as much money as they can. Often the workers forced to retire are some of the most productive in the firm, because they have more experience with the firm and its customer and supplier networks. If a worker was productive and profitable at age sixty-five, why not at age sixty-six? And it creates what we'll later describe as a "last-period problem" (in Perspective 8), distorting incentives to upgrade their skills and to be productive toward the end of their careers.

Although mandatory retirement may appear to be a mistake, particularly in the case of highly productive employees, it often makes good business sense – especially when they have been "overpaying" their workers for some time. (Otherwise, we would be hard-pressed to explain why such policies would survive and would need to be outlawed to get rid of them!) To lay out the logic, we must return to our analysis of the way that workers who come under mandatory retirement policies are paid throughout their careers.

Paying market wages, or exactly what workers are worth at every stage in their career, does not always maximize worker incomes. We extend our earlier discussion by showing how the manipulation of a worker's *career* wage structure, or earnings path over time, can actually raise worker productivity and lifetime income. However, as also will be shown, when worker wages diverge from their value over the course of their careers, mandatory retirement is a necessary component of the labor contract (Lazear 1979).

Suppose that a worker goes to work for Apex, Inc. and is paid exactly what she is worth at every point in time. Assume that she can expect to have a modest productivity improvement over the course of a thirty-year career, described by the slightly upward sloping line A in Figure 3.11. If her income follows her productivity, her salary will rise in line with the slope of line A. In year Y_1, the worker's annual income will be I_1; in year Y_2, it will be I_2; and so forth.

Is there a way by which management can restructure the worker's income path and simultaneously enable both the workers and the firm to gain? No matter what else is done, management must clearly pay the worker an amount equal at least to what she is worth *over the course of her career*. Otherwise, the worker

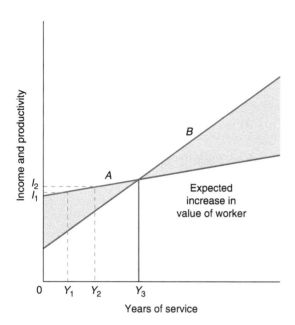

Figure 3.11 Twisted pay scale
The worker expects her productivity to rise along line *A* with years of service. If she starts work with less pay than she could earn elsewhere, then her career pay path could follow line *B*, representing greater increases in pay with time and greater productivity.

would not stay with the company. The worker would exit the firm, moving to secure a higher career income.

However, management could pay the worker less than she is worth for a while, as long as management is willing to compensate by overpaying her later. For example, suppose that management charts a career pay path given by line *B*, which implies that, up until year Y_3, the worker is paid less than she is worth, with the extent of the underpayment equaling the shaded area between the origin and Y_3. However, the worker would be compensated for what amounts to an investment in the firm by an overpayment after year Y_3, with the extent of the overpayment equal to the shaded area above line *A* after Y_3.

Are the firm and worker likely to be better off? Notice that the actual proposed pay line *B* is much steeper than line *A*. The greater angle of line *B* means that the worker is less likely to leave the company after she has been with the firm for a while. This increases the expected payoff realized by the firm from investing in the worker with varied assignments and training – investments that would not make sense if the firm thought the worker was going to take the training (and her improved skills) to another firm. The additional training obviously improves the worker's productivity, which shifts up her productivity curve in Figure 3.11. This can mean more compensation over a worker's entire career and more compensation at every point in time (even early on when she is being "undercompensated").

There is another advantage workers receive from the deferred compensation illustrated in Figure 3.11, especially good workers. When interviewing prospective employees, a firm wants the worker to know the worker's dedication and work ethic. Of course, anyone can claim to be a great employee, but the interviewers are likely to discount self-serving claims which are difficult to verify. It would be to the employer's advantage to convince the firm of those attributes. One of the most credible ways of doing so is to accept a pay arrangement in which he works for something less than he might be worth initially, proving his worth before receiving a more significant salary – that is, a job with a steeper earning profile and more deferred compensation. Good workers can also reason that everyone in the firm will have a greater incentive to work harder and smarter, leading to even greater prospective incomes over the course of their careers.

Normally, commentaries on worker pay implicitly assume that pay structure is imposed by management on workers. But one could just as easily reason that the kind of pay structure represented by line *B* in Figure 3.11 is what workers would encourage management to adopt. The twisting of the pay structure is nothing more than an innovative way for managers to increase the money they make from workers while also increasing the money that workers are able to make from firms. In short, it could be a mutually beneficial trade.

The Role of "Credible Commitments" by Employers

If twisting the pay structure is such a good idea, why isn't it observed more often in industry? One answer is that it is not always recognized, even when it is done. For example, universities are notorious for making assistant professors work harder than full professors who have tenure and far more pay. Large private firms, such as General Motors and IBM, appear to have pay structures that are more like line *B* than line *A* in Figure 3.11. However, many firms appear to be unwilling or unable to move away from a pay structure such as line *A*.

One of the problems with line *B* is that young workers must accept a cut in pay for a promise of greater pay in the future. The future pay must exceed what the workers can get elsewhere *and* be more than what their firm would pay if they simply hired replacement workers at the going market wage. Obviously, the workers take the considerable risk that their firm will not live up to its promise and fail to raise their pay appropriately – or, even worse, to fire them.

Thus, the firm must be able to make a *credible commitment* to its workers that it will live up to its part of the bargain, the *quo* in the *quid pro quo*. Credible commitments require the firm to demonstrate a capacity and inclination to do what it says it will do. Many firms will not be able to twist their pay structures (and thereby gain the productivity improvements) because they have a shaky financial base and an uncertain future. New firms have little history by which workers can assess the value of their firms' commitments. Small firms are often short-lived. Firms in highly fluid and competitive markets are also unlikely candidates for having the ability to twist their pay structures. Their workers will be paid their market worth, or even a premium, to accommodate the risks that workers must accept when the company's future is in doubt.

Which firms are most likely to twist their pay structures? Ones that have been established for some time, have a degree of financial and market stability, have some monopoly power, and have proven (by their actions) that their word is their bond. To prove the latter, firms must be careful about dismissing workers or cutting pay when they can find cheaper replacements. To do so would be to undermine credibility with their workers.

We can't be too precise in identifying the types of firms that can twist their pay structures since there can be extenuating circumstances. For example, we can imagine that some unproven upstart companies would be able to pay their workers below-market wages. As noted, they may have to do so, simply because they do not have the requisite cash flow early in their development. New firms often require their workers to provide "sweat equity" in their firms through the acceptance of below-market wages, but always with the expectation that their investment will pay off. Which new firms are likely to be able to do this?

Firms with new products that represent a substantial improvement over established products would be good candidates. The likely success of the new product gives a form of baseline credibility to owner commitments that they can – and intend to – repay the "sweat equity" later. Indeed, the greater the improvement, the more likely it is that the firm can make the repayment – and in an expeditious manner. This makes it more likely that the workers will accept below-market wages to start. The very fact that the product is a substantial improvement increases the likelihood of the firm's eventual success for two reasons. The first reason is widely recognized: a product that represents a substantial improvement will likely attract considerable consumer attention. The second reason is less obvious: the firm can delay its wage payments, using its scarce cash flow in the initial stages of production for other things, such as quality control, distribution, and promotion. The firm gets capital – sweat equity – from an unheralded source, workers. The workers' investment of sweat equity can enhance the firm's survival chances and even reduce interest rates for loans, since its debt is more secure.

Breaking Commitments

Of course, there are times when firms must break their past commitments. For example, if a firm suddenly faces more cost-effective foreign competitors in domestic markets, then the firm may have to break its commitments to overpay workers late in their careers. The competition will pay people the going market wage and erode the markets of those firms who continue to overpay their older workers. Without question, many older American workers – for example, middle managers in the automobile industry – have hard feelings about the advent of the "global marketplace." They may have suffered through years of hard work at (maybe) below-market wages in the belief that they would be able, later in their careers, to see their wages rise further above the market rate. The advent of global competition, however, has undercut the capacity of many American firms to fulfill their part of an implied bargain with their workers.

Even though they may have hard feelings, it does not follow that the workers would want their firms to try to hold to their prior agreements. Without the reneging, the firm might fold. In a sense, the workers made an investment in the firm through their lower wages, and the investment didn't pay off as much as expected. However, we hasten to add that some American workers have probably been burned by firms that have used changing market conditions as an *excuse* to break with their commitments – or have sold their firms to buyers who felt no compulsion to follow the original owners' commitments.

The answer to the question central to this discussion – "Why does mandatory retirement exist?" – can now be provided, at least partially. Mandatory retirement may be instituted for any number of plausible reasons. It might be introduced simply to move out workers who have become mentally or physically impaired. In an ideal world, the policy would not be applied to everyone. After all, many older workers are in the midst of their more productive years, because of their accumulated experience and wisdom. However, it may still be a reasonable *rule* because its application to *all* workers may mean that, *on average*, the firm is more efficient and profitable than by avoiding the costs of individually scrutinizing workers at retirement time and potentially being accused of discrimination.

However, the *expected* fitness of workers at the time of retirement is not the only issue at stake. Mandatory retirement is one part of what is presumed to be a mutually beneficial employment contract, replete with many other rules. It is a contract provision that helps both the firms that adopt it and their workers who must abide by it. We have spent much of this section exploring the logic of twisting career income paths. If such a twist is productive and profitable, and if workers must be overpaid late in their careers to make the twist possible, then it follows that firms will want, at some point, to cut the overpayments off. In this light, mandatory retirement is a means of cutting off the stream of overpayments at some definite point. This makes it possible, and economically practical, for a firm to use a twisted pay scale and to improve incentives, adding to the firm's productivity and profitability. Continuing overpayments indefinitely would be a choice that courts financial disaster.

Having said all this, the U.S. Congress decided in 1986 that mandatory retirement is bad employment policy. (Only a handful of developed countries have such laws.) As they reasoned, many of the workers who are forced to retire are still quite productive. But what are the consequences? Clearly, older workers with the twisted pay structure would gain from the law. They continue to collect their overpayments until they drop dead or decide that work is something they would prefer not to do. They gain more in overpayments than they could have anticipated (and they get more back from their firms than they paid in terms of their early underpayments). These employees will experience an unexpected wealth gain.

Younger workers lose in a subtle way, having a potentially favorable compensation scheme made illegal. But there is a clear loser. In addition to losing a productive and profitable pay structure, the owners will suffer a wealth loss; they will have to continue with the overpayments. Knowing this, the owners will likely try to minimize their losses. Assuming that the owners can't lower their older workers' wages to market levels and eliminate the overpayment (because of laws against age discrimination), they will try to capitalize the expected stream of losses and buy them out with a lump-sum amount to induce retirement.

In order for the buyout to work, both the owners and the workers will perceive gain by any deal that is struck. To buy the workers out, the owners would not have to pay their workers an amount equal to the current value of their expected discounted future wages. One reason is that leisure has considerable value and the worker may be reasonably content to retire. Another is that the worker can earn a (lower) wage in some other job. Also, workers cannot be sure how long they will be around to collect the overpayments. By taking the payments in lump-sum form, they reduce the risk of collection and increase the security of their heirs. Similarly, workers tend to concentrate their capital in terms of *human capital* which is connected to their jobs. By agreeing to a buyout, workers can diversify their portfolios by scattering the cash among other real and financial assets. Related, some workers may take a (lower) buyout because they expect that their companies will meet with financial difficulty down the road. Workers may also worry about the threat of the firm making work (and life) more difficult for them (by changing work and office assignments, discretionary budgeted items, flexibility in scheduling, and so on). We expect workers' fears to vary across firms and industries – and be related to a host of factors, including the size of the firm.

Workers who work for large firms may not be as fearful as workers for small firms, if large firms are more likely to be sued for any retaliatory use of discretionary employment practices. Moreover, it appears that juries are far more likely to impose much larger penalties on large firms (with lots of equity) than their smaller counterparts. This unequal treatment before the courts suggests that laws abolishing mandatory retirement rules will give small firms a competitive advantage over their larger market rivals.

The broadest points that emerge from this line of discussion are that the reasons for the level and structure of pay are not always obvious. And the reasons for "overpayment" can apply to the purchase of any number of resources other than labor. You may simply want to "overpay" suppliers to encourage them to provide the agreed-upon level of quality and not take opportunities to shirk (Klein and Leffler 1981).

Practical Lessons

Business students and managers are fully aware that firm profits can be enhanced by producing the proverbial "better mousetrap." In highly competitive markets, product improvement can be a business necessity for offensive and defensive reasons. Firms with improved products can charge higher prices, gaining market share and increasing profits. And firms that resist product improvements can lose market share, be urged to charge lower prices, or even be forced to close. In highly competitive environments, cost-effective product improvement is not optional.

But business students and even seasoned managers often fail to fully appreciate that creative compensation and company credibility can also be an important profit source. Managers whose word is their bond can reduce the risk that workers, suppliers, and buyers incur. Such managers (and their firms) will not have to pay a "risk premium" in wages or the prices paid to suppliers – and will obtain price advantages in dealing with buyers. Although ephemeral and never captured on accounting statements, "risk cost" is no less a real cost of doing business than the cost of materials.

Managers who can make credible commitments can achieve a competitive advantage *in lieu* of developing their products or selling their products at lower prices. One of the best ways managers can make credible commitments is to find ways to convey to others how the managers will suffer if they break their commitments. Managers who have established reputations for making credible commitments can be expected to earn a salary premium because of the cost saving they can bring to the firms that hire them.

Further Reading Online

Reading 3.1: Putting a price on Simon Kuznets's Nobel Prize in Economics (*The New York Times*, link available on the online resources website www.cambridge.org/mckenzie4)

Reading 3.2: Manhattan area codes multiply, but the original 212 is still coveted (*The New York Times*, link available on the online resources website www.cambridge.org/mckenzie4)

Reading 3.3: The use of knowledge in society (The Library of Economics and Liberty, link available on the online resources website www.cambridge.org/mckenzie4)

Reading 3.4: Price competition in the short run and the long run

Reading 3.5: The upside of waiting in line (*The New York Times*, link available on the online resources website www.cambridge.org/mckenzie4)

Recommended Videos Online

1 Supply and demand (Richard McKenzie, 33 minutes)

2 Market efficiency (Richard McKenzie, 26 minutes)

3 Adding features to products (Richard McKenzie, 32 minutes)

4 The logic of queues 1 (Richard McKenzie, 24 minutes)

5 The logic of queues 2 (Richard McKenzie, 25 minutes)

6 Executive pay and overpayment (Richard McKenzie, 33 minutes)

7 Both Curves; Shifts in Supply and Demand; Supply; Demand (Marginal Revolution University, link available on the online resources website www.cambridge.org/mckenzie4)

The Bottom Line

The key takeaways from Chapter 3 are the following:

1 The market is a system that provides producers with incentives to deliver goods and services to others. To respond to those incentives, producers must meet the desires of consumers, competing with other producers to deliver their goods and services in the most cost-effective manner.

2 A market implies that sellers and buyers have options and can freely respond to incentives. It does not mean, however, that behavior is totally unconstrained or that producers can choose from unlimited options. What a competitor can do may be severely limited by what rival firms are willing to do.

3 Demand curves for products (and labor or any other input) slope downward, representing an inverse relationship between price and quantity demanded. Supply curves for products and labor slope upward, representing a positive relationship between price and quantity produced. The positions of these curves are determined by a number of market forces.

4 Price and quantity in competitive markets will tend to move toward the intersection of supply and demand, which is the point of maximum efficiency.

5 Equilibrium price and quantity in competitive markets can be expected to change in predictable ways relative to increases and decreases in supply and demand.

6 Market shortages will lead to price increases. Market surpluses will lead to price decreases.

7 Obstructions to price movement upward to equilibrium give rise to market shortages. Obstructions to price movement down toward equilibrium give rise to market surpluses.

8 The market system is not perfect. Producers may have difficulty acquiring enough information to make reliable production decisions. People take time to respond to incentives and producers can make high profits while others are gathering their resources to respond to an opportunity.

9 Queues can arise out of mismanagement or from profit-maximizing combinations of prices and convenience that are palatable to consumers.

10 Wage rates are determined by the interaction of essentially the same market forces that determine the prices of products. The demand for labor is a function of worker productivity and the prices secured for the products which workers help

produce. The supply of labor is determined by the opportunity costs of workers and working conditions.

11 Under certain conditions, firms would be well advised not to match up worker pay with worker "worth" at every moment in time. Current and prospective compensation can be used as a means of increasing worker productivity and rewards over time.

Review Questions ▶▶

1 Can the outcomes of markets result in market participants (buyers and sellers) being more rational than they might otherwise be inclined to be? If so, how?

2 Why does the demand curve have a negative slope and the supply curve a positive slope?

3 Why will the competitive market tend to move toward the price–quantity combination at the intersection of the supply and demand curves? What might keep the market from moving all the way to the equilibrium point?

4 "Pizzas have become more expensive." Draw the two different graphs – each with demand and supply, each shifting demand or supply – which illustrate/cause this sentence. Name one factor for each graph that would cause the shift.

5 Let $QD_x = 50 - 4P_x$ and $QS_x = 1 + 3P_x$. Calculate price (P_x), quantity demanded (QD_x), and quantity supplied (QS_x) at equilibrium. Calculate QD_x and QS_x for a price less than equilibrium. Shortage or surplus of how much?

6 Using the supply curve from the previous question, let demand shift to $QD_x' = 65 - 5P_x$. Calculate equilibrium price and quantity. What would have happened if price had remained the same as your answer in question 5?

7 How does a market adjust from a price that is "too high" (higher than equilibrium price)? Explain from the perspectives of both consumers and producers.

8 Suppose you work for Levi Strauss and the demand for blue jeans suddenly increases. Discuss possible short-run and long-run movements of the market and the consequences for your company. What will tend to happen to worker wage rates?

9 How would you respond to the following: "We know that markets don't always clear since the quantity supplied and the quantity demanded do not always match. Queues can be observed everywhere. Store shelves are often emptied or overstocked. Hence, why pay so much attention to the intersection of supply and demand?"

10 Queues have been considered in Chapter 3 as devices for making money and (ironically) satisfying customers. Why don't grocery stores have one or two checkout counters that have signs at their entrance that read, "Anyone who goes

through this line will have 10 percent added to their total bill"? How have self-checkout lanes evolved for similar reasons?

11 Consider a young seller of pastries at a "farmers' market." He has several products, including extra-large doughnuts and apple fritters, both of which sell for $2.50 each. The market is open 7–12 on Saturdays. He regularly sells out of his apple fritters by 9:00 a.m. and sometimes has doughnuts left when the market closes. Does this entrepreneur have a problem? If so, how can it be resolved? Identify recommendations. If the owner doesn't take your advice, what might he know that you don't see? (Remember he could have local information outside observers don't have.) If his market were highly competitive, how might his production and pricing policies change?

12 Henry Ford more than doubled his workers' wages. Reflecting on the general principles behind Ford's action, when should any firm stop raising the pay of workers in terms of some economic/management principle that you can devise?

4

Consumer Choice and Demand
in Traditional and Network Markets

It is not the province of economics to determine the value of life in "hedonic units" or any other units, but to work out, on the basis of the general principles of conduct and the fundamental facts of social situations, the laws which determine prices of commodities and the direction of the social economic process. It is therefore not quantities, not even intensities, of satisfaction with which we are concerned ... or any other absolute magnitude whatever, but the purely relative judgment of comparative significance of alternatives open to choice.

Frank H. Knight[1]

People adjust to changes in economic conditions with a reasonable degree of predictability. When stores announce lower prices, more customers will come through the doors. The lower the prices, the larger the crowd. When the price of gasoline goes up, drivers will make fewer and shorter trips. If the price stays up, drivers will buy more fuel-efficient cars. Even defense departments will reduce their planned purchases of tanks and bombers when their prices rise.

Behavior not measured in dollars and cents is also predictable. Students who stray from the sidewalks to dirt paths on sunny days stick to concrete on rainy days. Professors who raise their course requirements and grading standards often find their classes shrinking in size. Small children shy away from doing things for which they have recently been punished.

On an intuitive level, these examples of behavior are reasonable. Going one step beyond intuition, the economist would say that such responses are governed by the *law of demand*, a concept we introduced in Chapter 3 and now take up in greater detail, with greater precision, and with more varied applications. In this

[1] Knight, Frank, 1921. *Risk, Uncertainty, and Profit*, Houghton Mifflin (republished 1971, University of Chicago Press).

chapter, we show how our understanding of a firm's strategy can be enhanced by classifying various goods into such categories as "normal" and "inferior," "substitute" and "complementary," "network" and "lagged-demand" – with the nature of the goods affecting their demands. We will also develop the concepts of "elastic" and "inelastic" demands. All of this suggests that the development of profit-maximizing pricing strategies will benefit from students (and firms) knowing more about goods than merely that their demands slope downward.

Part A Theory and Public Policy Applications

The assumptions about rationality described in Chapter 2 provide a useful basis for explaining much behavior. People will tend to do things for which the expected benefits exceed the expected costs. They will avoid doing things for which the opposite is true. The law of demand, which is a logical consequence of the assumption of rationality, allows us to make general predictions about *consumer* behavior.

Our ability to predict is always limited. We cannot specify with precision every choice the individual will make. For instance, without some data, we cannot say much about what a particular person wants or the sensitivity of her desire to changes in prices. But we can predict the general direction of her behavior with the aid of the *law of demand* that we now derive. Our predictive capability rises as we move from an individual to groups. It rises further still when we have data on past behavior that is indicative of future behavior. Nevertheless, we must start with the choice calculus of representative individuals, starting simple for purposes of clarification and then aggregating across individuals who comprise the market demands for goods.

Rational Consumption: the Concept of Marginal Utility

The essence of the economist's notion of rational consumer behavior is that consumers will allocate their incomes over goods and services so as to maximize their satisfaction or happiness – what economists call "utility." This implies that consumers compare the value of consuming an additional unit of various goods with their other uses of scarce resources.

Generally speaking, the value the individual places on any one unit of a good depends on the number of units already consumed. For example, you may be planning to consume two hot dogs and two Cokes for your next meal. The value of the second hot dog is its marginal utility (*MU*): the change in total utility from consuming one more unit. The *MU* of the second hot dog depends on the fact that you have already eaten one. The value you place on the second unit of each good will generally be less than the value realized from the first unit (at least beyond some point as consumption proceeds).[2] This applies to all goods and services – and is known as the *law of diminishing marginal utility*.

Achieving Consumer Equilibrium

Marginal utility helps to determine the variety and the quantity of goods and services you consume. The rule is simple. If the two goods, Cokes and hot dogs, both have the same price (a temporary assumption), you will fully allocate your income so that the marginal utility of the last unit consumed of each will be equal – or come as close to being equal as mental faculties and choice conditions allow. (The point is that buyers will *seek* equality at the margin. If not at equality, they will move toward equality as best they can.) This rule can be stated as:

$$MU_c = MU_h,$$

where MU_c equals the marginal utility of a Coke and MU_h equals the marginal utility of a hot dog. This is to say, if the price of a Coke is the same as the price of a hot dog, the last Coke you drink should give you (approximately) the same amount of enjoyment as the last hot dog you eat. If this is not the case ($MU_c > MU_h$ or $MU_c < MU_h$), you could increase your utility with the same amount of money by reducing your consumption of the good with the lower marginal utility by one unit and buying another unit of the good with the higher marginal utility. According to the law of diminishing marginal utility, as more of a good is consumed, its marginal utility diminishes. Thus, if $MU_h > MU_c$, and MU_h falls relative to MU_c as more hot dogs and fewer Cokes are consumed, sooner or later the result will be $MU_h = MU_c$.

> **Consumer equilibrium** is a state of stability in consumer purchasing patterns in which the individual has maximized her utility.

When the marginal utilities of goods purchased by the consumer are equal, the resulting state is called **consumer equilibrium**. Unless conditions (income, taste, prices, etc.) change, the consumer equilibrium remains the same.

Adjusting for Differences in Price and Unit Size

Different goods are seldom sold at exactly the same price, so we now drop the assumption of equal prices. The condition for choosing the combination of Cokes and hot dogs that maximizes utility becomes

---

[2] We focus on *diminishing* marginal utility because this is the relevant range of consumption for most people consuming most goods. If people experience *increasing* marginal utility for goods, they will continue to consume them (if available) and face choice problems only when diminishing marginal utility sets in. (If they chose the first unit, why wouldn't they consume a more-pleasing second unit at the same price?)

$$\frac{MU_c}{P_c} = \frac{MU_h}{P_h},$$

where MU_c and MU_h are the marginal utilities, P_c is the price of a Coke, and P_h is the price of a hot dog. The consumer will allocate her money so that the last penny spent on each commodity yields (approximately) the same amount of satisfaction. In colloquial terms, we would say that she gets the same "bang for the buck" with the two goods. (We leave it to the reader to consider how the consumer can increase her utility without spending more money if the above equality is not satisfied – and how doing so will result in the equality being satisfied.)

So far, we have been talking in terms of buying whole units of Cokes and hot dogs, but the same principles apply to other kinds of choices as well. Marginal utility is involved when a consumer chooses a 12-ounce can rather than a 20-ounce bottle of Coke – or a regular-size hot dog instead of a foot-long hot dog. The concept can also be applied to the decision of whether to add coleslaw or chili to the hot dog. The pivotal question the consumer faces in these situations is whether the marginal utility of the additional quantity consumed is greater or less than the marginal utility of other goods that can be purchased per penny (or per dollar).

Most consumers do not think in terms of utils when they are buying their lunch, but they are still weighing alternatives (*as if* they were thinking in terms of the utils obtained from each additional unit). Suppose you walk into a snack bar with only five dollars to spend for lunch. You look at the menu and weigh the options offered. If you have 50 cents to spare, do you not find yourself mentally asking whether the difference between a large Coke and a small one is worth more to you than a slice of bacon or avocado on your hamburger? (If not, why do you choose a small Coke instead of a large one?) We become so accustomed to making decisions of this sort that we can be unaware that we are weighing the marginal values of the alternatives.

Consumers do not usually make choices with such conscious precision. Nor can they achieve a perfect equilibrium; the prices, unit sizes, and values of the various products available may not permit it. But they are trying to come as close to equilibrium as possible. The economist's assumption is that the individual will move toward equilibrium – not that he will always achieve it.

To illustrate, suppose your marginal utility for Cokes and hot dogs is as shown in Table 4.1. If a Coke is priced at $0.50 and a hot dog at $1, then $3 will buy you two hot dogs and two Cokes – the best you can do with $3 at those prices. Now suppose the price of Coke rises to $0.75 and the price of hot dogs falls to $0.75. With a budget of $3, you can still buy two hot dogs and two Cokes, but you will no longer be maximizing your utility. Instead, you will be inclined to reduce your consumption of Coke and increase your consumption of hot dogs.

Table 4.1 **Marginal utility for Cokes and hot dogs**		
Unit consumed	Marginal utility of Cokes (utils)	Marginal utility of hot dogs (utils)
First	10	30
Second	9	15
Third	3	12

At the old prices, the original combination (two Cokes and two hot dogs) gave you 64 utils (45 from hot dogs and 19 from Cokes). If you cut back to one Coke and three hot dogs with the new prices, your total utility will rise to 67 utils (57 from hot dogs and 10 from Coke). Your new utility-maximizing combination – the one that best satisfies your preferences given your income constraints and prices – is one Coke and three hot dogs. No other combination of Coke and hot dogs will give you greater satisfaction.

Changes in Price and the Law of Demand

If the price of hot dogs goes down relative to the price of Coke, people will tend to buy more hot dogs. If the price of Coke rises relative to the price of hot dogs, people will tend to buy less Coke. Assume the consumer is in equilibrium to start:[3]

$$\frac{MU_c}{P_c} = \frac{MU_h}{P_h}.$$

When the price of Coke rises and the price of hot dogs falls, then there is a disequilibrium:

$$\frac{MU_c}{P_c} < \frac{MU_h}{P_h}.$$

To re-establish equilibrium, the consumer will shift expenditures from Cokes to hot dogs. This principle will hold true for any good or service: as the relative price of a good falls, the individual will buy more; as the relative price rises, the individual will buy less – the **law of demand**.

The **law of demand** states the assumed inverse relationship between product price and quantity demanded, everything else held constant.

Figure 4.1 shows the demand curve for Coke – that is, the quantity of Coke purchased at different prices. The inverse relationship between price and quantity demanded is reflected in the curve's downward slope. If the price falls from

---

[3] In our example, equilibrium is not perfectly satisfied because we aren't considering fractional amounts of Cokes and hot dogs.

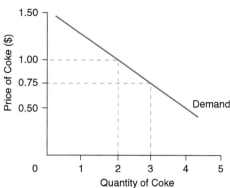

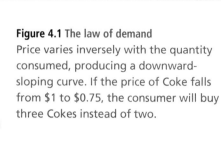

Figure 4.1 The law of demand
Price varies inversely with the quantity consumed, producing a downward-sloping curve. If the price of Coke falls from $1 to $0.75, the consumer will buy three Cokes instead of two.

$1 to $0.75, the consumer will buy three Cokes instead of two. And vice versa. (The law of demand can also be derived using what economists call "indifference/utility curves" – graphical devices for structuring consumer preferences. We develop this tool in the Online Math Appendix. We apply indifference-curve analysis to the issue of how much workers need to be paid when they are relocated to an area with higher housing costs in Online Reading 4.1.)

The assumption of rational behavior, coupled with the consumer's willingness and ability to substitute less-costly goods when prices go up, leads to the law of demand. We cannot say how many Cokes and hot dogs a particular person will buy to maximize his satisfaction. This depends on the individual's income and preferences – which depend in turn on other factors (e.g., how much he likes hot dogs, whether he is on a diet, and how much he worries about the nutritional deficiencies of such a lunch). But we can predict the general response, whether positive or negative, to a change in prices.

Price is the value of whatever a person must give up in exchange for a unit of a good or service. It is a rate of exchange and is typically expressed in dollars per unit. Note that price is not necessarily the same as cost. In an exchange between two people – a buyer and a seller – the *price* at which a good sells can be above or below the *cost* of producing the good. What the buyer gives up to obtain the good does not need to match what the producer gives up in order to provide the good.

Nor is price always stated in money terms. Some people have a desire to watch sunsets – a desire characterized by the same downward-sloping demand curve as the one for Coke. The price of the sunset experience is mostly denominated in time – the lost opportunity to do something else or the added cost and trouble of finding a house that will offer a view of the sunset. (In this case, price and cost are the same because the buyer and the producer are the same.) The law of demand will apply nevertheless. The individual will spend some optimum number of minutes per day watching the sunset and will vary that number of minutes inversely with the price of watching. And the price of pleasant views often takes the form of money when, for example, people pay more for a house that offers a nice view of the ocean than for one that doesn't.

From Individual Demand to Market Demand

Thus far, we have discussed demand in terms of the individual's behavior. The concept is most useful, however, when applied to whole markets or segments of markets – **market demand** interacting with market supply to determine price. To obtain the market demand for a product, we need to *add up* the wants of the individuals who collectively make up the market.

> **Market demand** is the summation of the quantities demanded by all consumers of a good or service at every price during some specified time period.

The market demand can be shown graphically as the horizontal summation of the quantity of a product each individual will buy at each price. Assume that the market for Coke is composed of two individuals, Anna (*A*) and Betty (*B*), who differ in their demand for Coke, as shown in Figure 4.2. The demand of Anna is D_A and the demand of Betty is D_B. To determine the number of Cokes both of them will demand at any price, we simply add together the quantities each will purchase, at each price (as in Table 4.2). At a price of $11, neither person is willing to buy any Coke; consequently, the market demand must begin below $11. At $9, Anna is still unwilling to buy any Coke, but Betty will buy two Cokes per unit of time, say a week. The market quantity demanded is therefore two. If the price falls to $5, Anna wants two Cokes and Betty wants six – a total of eight. If we continue to drop the price and add the quantities bought at each new price, we will obtain a series of market quantities demanded. When plotted on a graph, they will yield curve D_{A+B}, the market demand for Coke. The market demand curves for much larger groups of people are derived in essentially the same way.

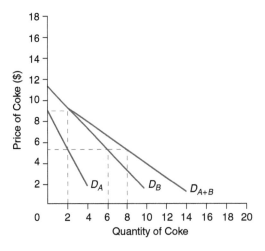

Figure 4.2 Market demand curve
The market demand curve for Coke (D_{A+B}) is obtained by summing the quantities that individuals *A* and *B* are willing to buy at every price (shown by the individual demand curves D_A and D_B).

Table 4.2 **Market demand for Coke**

(1) Price of Coke ($)	(2) Quantity demanded by Anna (D_A)	(3) Quantity demanded by Betty (D_B)	(4) Quantity demanded by both Anna and Betty (D_{A+B})
11	0	0	0
10	0	1	1.0
9	0	2	2.0
8	0.5	3	3.5
7	1.0	4	5.0
6	1.5	5	6.5
5	2.0	6	8.0
4	2.5	7	9.5
3	3.0	8	11.0
2	3.5	9	12.5
1	4.0	10	14.0

Note: The market demand curve (D_{A+B}) in Figure 4.2 is obtained by plotting the quantities in column (4) against their respective prices in column (1).

As more people demand more Coke, the market demand extends further to the right and flattens out.[4]

Elasticity of Demand: Consumer Responsiveness to Price Changes

We often hear claims that a price change will have no effect on purchases. Someone may predict that an increase in the price of prescription drugs will not affect people's use of them. The same remark is heard in connection with other goods and services – from gasoline and public parks, to medical services and salt. What people usually mean is that a price change will have only a *slight* effect on consumption. The law of demand states only that a price change will have an inverse effect on the quantity of a good purchased. It does not specify how much of an effect.

In other words, we have established only that the market demand curve will slope downward. The actual demand curve for a product may be relatively flat, like curve D_1 in Figure 4.3, or relatively steep, like curve D_2. Notice that, at a price of P_1, the quantity of the good or service consumed is the same in both

---

[4] Different preferences (and budget constraints) yield different individual demand curves. Sometimes, firms can segment their markets and charge different prices based on this different willingness to spend. We explore the topic of "price discrimination" in Chapter 10.

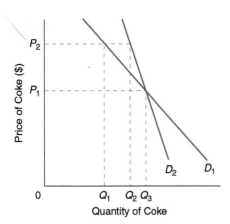

Figure 4.3 Elastic and inelastic demand
Demand curves differ in their relative elasticity. Curve D_1 is more elastic than curve D_2: consumers on curve D_1 are more responsive to a given price change (P_2 to P_1) than consumers on curve D_2.

markets. If the price is raised to P_2, however, the response is substantially greater in market D_1 than in D_2. In D_1, consumers will reduce their purchases all the way to Q_1. In D_2, consumption will drop only to Q_2.

Economists refer to this relative responsiveness of demand curves as the **price elasticity of demand**. (The elasticity of demand with respect to income and other prices is interesting and important. We will focus on own-price elasticity and let students extrapolate from there.) Demand is relatively **elastic** or **inelastic**, depending on the degree of sensitivity to price change. The demand curve D_1 in Figure 4.3 is relatively elastic; D_2 is relatively inelastic.

Price elasticity of demand is a measure of the responsiveness of consumers, in terms of the quantity purchased, to a change in price (all else constant).

Elastic demand is a relatively sensitive consumer response to price changes. If the price goes up or down, consumers will respond with a large decrease or increase in the quantity demanded.

Inelastic demand is a relatively insensitive consumer response to price changes. If the price goes up or down, consumers will respond with a small decrease or increase in the quantity demanded.

The elasticity of demand is a useful concept, but our definitions of elastic and inelastic demands are imprecise. What do we mean by "relatively sensitive" and "relatively insensitive"? Under what circumstances are consumers flexible or inflexible with respect to price change? There are two ways to add precision. One is to determine the effect of a change in price on total consumer expenditures (or its equivalent, producer revenues). The other is to develop a mathematical formula that will calculate values for various levels of elasticity. We now deal with each in turn.

Analyzing Total Consumer Expenditures

An increase in the price of a particular product will cause consumers to buy less. Whether total consumer expenditures (and thus business revenues) rise, fall, or stay the same depends on the extent of the consumer response. Many people assume that businesses will maximize profits by charging the highest price possible. But high prices are not always the best policy. For example, if a firm sells fifty units for $1, its total revenue (consumers' total expenditures) for the product will be $50 (50 × $1). If it raises the price to $1.50 and consumers cut back to forty units, its total revenue would rise to $60 (40 × $1.50). But if consumers are more sensitive to price changes for this particular good, the 50-cent increase may lower the quantity sold to thirty units. In this case, total consumer expenditures would fall to $45 ($1.50 × 30). The price increase (by itself) was good for revenues, but the reduced revenue from the loss of customers overwhelms the gain.

Similarly, lowering price doesn't always decrease revenues. If a firm drops a price from $1.50 to $1, the quantity sold may rise enough to increase revenue. Whether this happens depends on the degree of consumer response. In other words, consumer elasticity helps to determine whether a firm should raise or lower its price. (We shall see later that the firm is generally interested in maximizing profit rather than revenue and must consider costs too.)

We can define a simple rule of thumb for using total consumer expenditures to analyze the elasticity of demand. Demand is *elastic* if:

- total consumer expenditures rise when the price falls; or
- total consumer expenditures fall when the price rises.

Demand is *inelastic* if:

- total consumer expenditures rise when the price rises; or
- total consumer expenditures fall when the price falls.

Demand is *unitary elastic* (a special case) when total revenues remain unchanged with an increase or decrease in the price.

Determining Elasticity Coefficients

Although the previous approach gives us a useful sense about elasticity and its implications, it does not allow us to precisely measure elasticity or inelasticity. Expressed as a formula,[5] the **elasticity coefficient** is

> The **elasticity coefficient of demand** (E_d) is the ratio of the percentage change in the quantity demanded to the percentage change in price.

---

[5] There are actually two formulas for elasticity recognized by economists – one for use at specific points on the curve (*point elasticity*) and one for measuring average elasticity between two points (*arc elasticity*). The formula for point elasticity is used for very small changes in price and quantity. Arc elasticity describes elasticity over a range of prices:

$$E_d = \frac{Q_1 - Q_2}{Q_1} \div \frac{P_1 - P_2}{P_1},$$

where the subscripts 1 and 2 represent the two points on the demand curve, Q is the average quantity between the points, and P is the average price.

$$E_d = \frac{\text{percentage change in quantity}}{\text{percentage change in price}} = \frac{\text{change in } Q}{\text{initial } Q} \div \frac{\text{change in } P}{\text{initial } P}.$$

Of course, since demand curves slope downward (price and quantity are inversely related), the elasticity coefficient must be negative. But, by convention, we don't use the negative sign because it only adds confusion to the analysis.

When the percentage change in quantity is greater than the percentage change in price, the elasticity coefficient is greater than 1.0 and demand is elastic. When the percentage change in quantity is less than the percentage change in price, the elasticity coefficient is less than 1.0 and demand is inelastic. When the percentage change in the price is equal to the percentage change in quantity, the elasticity coefficient is 1.0 and demand is unitary elastic. These are summarized in Table 4.3. Using this result and the "consumer expenditure" approach, an important rule emerges: Pricing a product to maximize profits requires choosing a price on the elastic portion of the demand curve.[6]

Table 4.3 Coefficients for three categories of demand elasticities

Elastic demand	$E_d > 1$
Inelastic demand	$E_d < 1$
Unitary elastic demand	$E_d = 1$

Students often confuse the elasticity of demand with the slope of the demand curve. Elasticity includes (the reciprocal of) the slope, but it also varies with location on the demand curve (P/Q):

---

[6] To prove this result, let's look at marginal revenue MR: the change in total revenue, $P \times Q$, in response to a change in quantity Q (where price P depends on Q). Taking the derivative of $P \times Q$ with respect to Q, we obtain

$$MR = \frac{d[P \times Q]}{dQ} = P + \frac{dP}{dQ} \times Q.$$

Factoring price out of the right-hand side of this equation gives us

$$MR = P\left[1 + \frac{dP}{dQ} \times \frac{Q}{P}\right].$$

Because

$$E_d = -\left(\frac{dQ}{dP}\right)Q/P,$$

we then get

$$MR = P\left[1 - \frac{1}{E_d}\right] \quad \text{so} \quad \begin{cases} MR > 0 \text{ if } E_d > 1, \\ MR = 0 \text{ if } E_d = 1, \\ MR < 0 \text{ if } E_d < 1. \end{cases}$$

Thus, an increase in Q (from a decrease in P) increases total revenue if $E_d > 1$, has no effect on total revenue if $E_d = 1$, and reduces total revenue if $E_d < 1$.

$$E_d = \frac{\text{percentage change in } Q}{\text{percentage change in } P} = \frac{\text{change in } Q}{Q} \div \frac{\text{change in } P}{P} = \frac{\text{change in } Q}{\text{change in } P} \times \frac{P}{Q}.$$

The confusion is understandable. The slope of a demand curve does say some-thing about consumer responsiveness: it shows how much the quantity consumed goes up when the price goes down by a given amount. But slope is an unreliable indicator of consumer responsiveness because it varies with the units of measure-ment for price and quantity. For example, if price rises from $10 to $20 and quan-tity demanded decreases from 100 pounds to 60 pounds, then the slope is −1/4:

$$\text{slope} = \frac{-10}{40} = \frac{-1}{4} = -1/4.$$

But if price is measured in cents instead of dollars (with quantity still measured in pounds), the slope is −25:

$$\text{slope} = \frac{-1000}{40} = \frac{-25}{1} = -25.$$

So, slope alone cannot be sufficient. No matter what units are used to measure price and quantity, the *percentage* changes in price and quantity remain the same and the elasticity of demand will not be affected by changes from one set of units to another. Likewise, with percentage changes, we can compare the elasticities of goods with radically different prices – for example, salt and cars.

Elasticity along a Linear Demand Curve
Since slope and elasticity are different concepts, it should not surprise us that the elasticity coefficient will vary along a linear demand curve. Consider the linear demand curve in Figure 4.4. At every point on the curve, a price reduction of $1

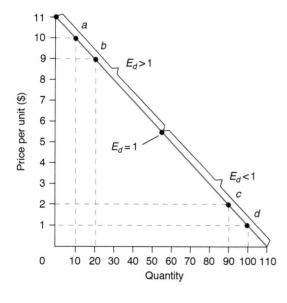

Figure 4.4 Changes in the elasticity coefficient
The elasticity coefficient decreases as a firm moves down a linear demand curve. The upper half is elastic: the elasticity coefficient is greater than one. The lower half is inelastic: the elasticity coefficient is less than one. This means that the middle of the linear demand curve has an elasticity coefficient equal to one.

causes quantity demanded to rise by 10 units, but a $1 decrease in price at the top of the curve is a much smaller *percentage* change than a $1 decrease at the bottom of the curve. Similarly, an increase of units in the quantity demanded is a much larger *percentage* change when the quantity is low than when it is high. Therefore, the elasticity coefficient falls as consumers move down their (linear) demand curve. To be more precise, a straight-line demand curve has an inelastic range for the bottom half, a unitary elastic point in the center, and an elastic range for the top half.[7]

Applications of the Concept of Elasticity

Elasticity of demand is particularly important to producers. Together with the cost of production, it determines the prices they should charge for their products. We have shown that an increase or decrease in price can cause total consumer expenditures to rise, fall, or remain the same – depending on the elasticity of demand. Thus, if a firm lowers its price and incurs greater production costs (because it is producing and selling more units), it may still increase its profits. As long as the demand curve is elastic, revenues can (but will not necessarily) increase more than costs. Companies may lower their prices in response to intense competition, but also in response to highly elastic demand.

Governments, too, should consider the elasticity of demand. If a government raises excise taxes too much, it may end up with lower tax revenues. The higher

---

[7] To prove this, we recognize that the equation for a linear demand curve can be expressed mathematically as

$$P = A - BQ,$$

where P represents price, Q is quantity demanded, and A and B are positive constants. The total revenue associated with this demand curve is given by

$$PQ = AQ - BQ^2.$$

The marginal revenue is obtained by taking the derivative of total revenue with respect to Q, or

$$MR = A - 2BQ.$$

We know that when marginal revenue is equal to zero, elasticity is equal to one. This implies that $E_d = 1$ when

$$A - 2BQ = 0$$

or when

$$Q = \frac{1}{2} \times \frac{A}{B}.$$

We know that when the demand curve intersects the Q axis, $P = 0$ and

$$Q = \frac{A}{B}.$$

Thus, with a linear demand curve, $E_d = 1$ when Q is one-half the distance between $Q = 0$ and the Q value where $P = 0$.

tax, added to the final price of the product, may cause an elastic consumer response. It is no accident that the heaviest excise taxes are imposed on goods where demand is inelastic, such as phones, gasoline, and liquor – as well as broad categories such as income and consumption. The same reasoning applies to property taxes. That said, many large cities have underestimated the elasticity of demand for living space. Indeed, one reason for migration from city to sub-urbs in many metropolitan areas has been a desire to escape rising tax rates. By moving just outside a city's boundaries, people can retain many of the benefits a city provides without paying for them. This lowers the demand for property within the city, undermining property values and the city's tax base. We can also predict that the elasticity of demand for the services of local governments is greater than the elasticity of demand for the services of the national government because people can more easily move from one local government to another ("vote with their feet") than they can change national governments.

Beyond raising tax revenues, a "fat tax" on fatty and sugary foods and drinks could be used to curb the country's growing obesity and related healthcare prob-lems.[8] However, the exact effects of price increases on the consumption of fatty and sugary foods and drinks are unclear – that is, the relevant elasticities are centered around unitary elasticity but vary considerably across studies.[9]

The elasticity of demand for water in drought-plagued areas is important for determining how much the price of water should be increased to achieve conservation goals. In 2015, California Governor Jerry Brown mandated a 25 percent reduction in residential water consumption, to be achieved with reduc-tions in water allocations across the State's 411 water districts, ranging from 10 to 35 percent (depending on a prior water consumption level deemed to be "excessive"). But the Governor never ordered a price increase. The elasticity of demand has been computed between 0.3 and 0.4, which means that every 10 percent increase in the price would lower water consumption by 3–4 percent (Klaiber 2010). If so, his water conservation goal could have been achieved by a 60–80 percent increase in water prices. This would also eliminate the need for

---

[8] Calorie intake *per capita* in the United States from beverages increased by nearly threefold in the last quarter of the twentieth century. By the start of the twenty-first century, beverages accounted for 10-15 percent of calorie intake by children and adolescents, with each extra can of soda drunk per day increasing the chances of becoming obese by 60 percent (Ludwig, Peterson, and Gortmaker 2001). In 1960-62, the average obesity rate for adults was 13.3 per-cent. By 2003-06, the average obesity rate for adults had more than doubled to 34.1 percent, as measured by the National Center for Health Statistics (2009). Thirty-five diseases – including hypertension, heart disease, various cancers, type-2 diabetes, osteoarthritis, gall-bladder disease, and incontinence – have been linked to obesity, according to the National Heart, Lung, and Blood Institute (1998).

[9] See *Beverage Digest* (2008), and Brownell and Frieden (2009). On "fat taxes" and obesity rates, see Gelbach, Klick, and Stratmann (2007), Brownell and Frieden (2009), and Kaplan (2009).

complicated water allocations and a "water police" to enforce water-use rules. Nearly "doubling" water prices might seem severe, but most Californians pay less than a penny per gallon. In any case, as we'll describe in Chapter 5, the policy choice is always whether to let prices work – or not.

Determinants of the Price Elasticity of Demand

Various factors can affect consumer flexibility, such as the number of **substitutes** and the amount of *time* consumers have to respond to a change in price by shifting to other products or producers.

> **Substitutes** allow consumers to respond to a price increase by switching to another good. For example, if the price of orange juice goes up, you can substitute a variety of other drinks, including water, apple juice, wine, or soda.

Substitutes

The existence of a large number and variety of substitutes means that demand will be elastic. That is, if people can switch easily to another product that will yield approximately the same value, many will do so when prices increase. The similarity of substitutes – how well they can satisfy the same basic want – also affects elasticity. Closer substitutes imply more elastic demand. If there are no close substitutes, demand will tend to be inelastic. What we call "necessities" are often things that lack close substitutes.

Few goods have *no substitutes* at all. Because there are many substitutes for orange juice – soda, wine, apple juice, and so on – we would expect the demand for orange juice to be more elastic than the demand for salt, which has fewer viable alternatives. Yet even salt has synthetic substitutes – or, less close, other spices that can provide flavor. Furthermore, although human beings need a certain amount of salt to survive, most of us consume much more than the minimum and can easily cut back if the price of salt rises. The extra flavor that salt adds is a benefit that can be partially recouped by buying other things.[10]

At the other extreme are goods with *perfect substitutes*. Perfect substitutes exist for goods produced by an individual firm engaged in perfect competition. An individual wheat farmer, for example, is only one among thousands who produce essentially the same product. The wheat produced by others is a perfect substitute for the wheat produced by the single farmer. Perfect substitutability can lead to perfect elasticity of demand. The demand curve facing the perfect competitor is horizontal, like the one in Figure 4.5. If the individual competitor raises her price even a minute percentage above the going market price, consumers will

---

[10] Water is a terrific example of the same principle: we "need" water to survive, but most of our uses of water go far beyond those needs. As such, the substitutes for water include fewer flushes, shorter showers, brown lawns, dirty cars, and so on.

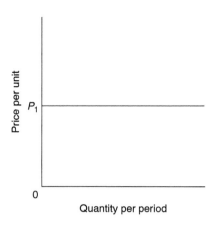

Figure 4.5 Perfectly elastic demand
A firm with many competitors may lose all its sales if it increases its price even slightly. Its customers can simply move to another producer. In this case, its demand curve is horizontal, with an elasticity coefficient of infinity.

switch to other sellers. The elasticity coefficient of a horizontal demand curve is infinite; this demand curve is **perfectly elastic**. (We'll revisit this concept in Chapter 9.)

> A **perfectly elastic demand** is a demand that has an elasticity coefficient of infinity. It is expressed graphically as a curve horizontal to the x axis.

Other Factors in Elasticity

Time: Consumption requires time. Accordingly, a demand curve must describe a particular time period. Over a very short period of time – say, a day – the quantity demanded for a good may not react immediately to a price change. It takes time to find substitutes; alternatively, consumers have more substitutes and more flexibility with more time. With enough time, however, consumers will have more options in responding to a price increase. Thus, a demand curve that covers a long period will tend to be more elastic than one for a shorter period. (The same will be true when we develop short-run and long-run responses of firms in Books II and III.)

Oil and gasoline: These provide a good example of how the elasticity of demand can change over time. When their prices increase markedly, most consumers have little short-term flexibility. They might combine errands or ride a bike to work. But, in particular, they are limited in their ability to reduce consumption because of their current cars and homes. You can change your vehicle and your house location to lessen commuting distance, but you probably won't do either right away. (More moderate examples: adding insulation or upgrading windows.) Again, the long-term demand curve for gasoline is much more elastic than the short-term demand curve.

Individuals versus the market: Preferences can differ between people in a manner that leads to elastic or inelastic responses. If one person strongly prefers Brand X over Brand Y, then they will not see Y as a close substitute for X and will be willing to pay much higher prices for X. Another person may be indifferent between the two – and thus elastic, unwilling to pay anything more for X than Y. Because market demand is the aggregation of individuals, market demand is always more elastic than individual demand (as per Figure 4.2). And, under certain conditions, firms may be able to take advantage of those with inelastic demand – a topic called "price discrimination" in Chapter 10.

Importance in consumer budgets: Another reason for the inelasticity of salt is that it is such a minor part of our budgets. If the price of salt doubles, it doesn't bother us. But if our rent doubles, then we're much more likely to make adjustments – to be elastic in our responses.

Broad versus narrow categories: Again, gasoline is a helpful example here. The demand for gasoline is highly inelastic because most consumers have few substitutes for gasoline: walking, biking, car-pooling, mass transit, etc. But the demand for gasoline at any given gas station is highly *elastic*, since there are many locations where consumers can buy gas. Likewise, the demand for meat is far less elastic than the demand for any given type of meat. And the demand for a brand is far more elastic than the overall demand for the good.

Changes in Income and the Prices of Related Goods (Revisited)

Some variables are consistent in impacting demand in a certain direction. But a change in consumer income is more complicated. The demand for most goods, called normal goods, increases with income. Beans are an example of what many people would consider inferior goods. People with low incomes may rely on beans as a staple or filler food but substitute meat and other higher-priced foods when their incomes rise.

Whereas economists can confidently predict the directional movement of consumption when prices change, they cannot say what will happen to the demand for a particular good when income changes, because each individual determines whether a particular good is a normal or inferior good. Beans may be an inferior good to most low-income consumers but a normal good to many others.

For example, how do you think a change in income affects the demand for low-, medium-, and high-quality liquor? During past recessions, the demand for both low- and high-quality liquor has increased. Some consumers may have switched to high-quality liquor to impress their friends and suggest that they have been unaffected by the economic malaise. Others may have tried to maintain their old level of consumption by switching to a low-quality brand. More broadly, during a recession, companies that specialize in inferior goods will be in a relatively strong position. But as the recession ends, they may want to reposition toward normal goods.

The effect of a change in the price of other goods is similarly complicated. Here, the important factor is the relationship of one good – say, ice cream – to other commodities. Are the goods in question substitutes for ice cream, such as frozen yogurt? Are they complements, such as waffle cones? Are they used independently of ice cream? Demand for ice cream is unlikely to be affected by a drop in the price of baby rattles, but it may well decline if the price of frozen yogurt drops or the price of waffle cones skyrockets.

Two products are considered *substitutes* if the demand for one goes up when the price of the other rises. Zippers are substitutes for buttons in clothing construction. If the price of zippers goes down, the demand for buttons can be expected to fall as consumers and clothing companies shift from buttons to zippers.

Note that the price of a product does not have to rise above the price of its substitute before the demand for the substitute is affected. Assume that the price of sirloin steak is $12 per pound and the price of hamburger is $4 per pound. The price difference reflects the general consumer belief that the two meats differ substantially in quality. If the price of hamburgers rises to $6 per pound while the price of sirloin remains constant at $12, many buyers will substitute from hamburger to steak. For them, the perceived difference in quality now outweighs the difference in price.

Because *complementary* products – razors and razor blades, oil and oil filters, tickets and concessions – are consumed *jointly*, an increase in the price of one will cause a decrease in the demand for both products simultaneously. An increase in the price of razor blades, for instance, will induce some people to switch to electric razors, causing a decrease in the quantity of razor blades demanded and a decrease in the demand for safety razors. Again, economists cannot predict how many people will decide that the switch is worthwhile; they can merely predict from theory the direction in which demand for the product will move.

Acquisition and Transaction Utility

Behavioral economist Richard Thaler (2015b) has forcefully argued that consumers get two sources of utility from the goods they buy: **acquisition utility** (pleasure from the consumption of a good or service) and **transaction utility** (pleasure from the transaction itself – what consumers perceive as "good/bad deals," with prices below/above expected levels).

> **Acquisition utility** is the pleasure consumers get from the consumption of a good or service, which is equivalent to what conventional economists mean by "utility."

> **Transaction utility** is the pleasure consumers get from what they perceive as "good deals," which carry prices below expected levels, and the displeasure they experience from "bad deals" or "rip offs," brought about by higher-than-expected prices.

The demand curves covered so far have been derived with only acquisition utility in mind. It turns out that goods subject to transaction utility can have a higher elasticity than the demand for goods based only on acquisition utility. The inclusion of transaction utility can mean that, as the price rises, the displeasure from bad deals can go progressively negative, depressing total utility more so with higher prices.

Recognition of transaction utility has little to no effect on most of our discussion about the nature and elasticity of demand. However, the concept can help explain why sellers often prominently display the "normal price" in a large font size and add the "new lower sale price" in a smaller font size (or vice versa): the display can increase consumer perception of getting a good deal, with added utility, which means that sellers can sell more of the good at higher prices than they might otherwise be able to do. It might also explain why many consumers have closets full of goods they rarely or never use: they bought the good when they received high acquisition utility. (Much more will be said about "behavioral economics" in Online Chapter 1.)

Objections to Demand Theory

From years of teaching, we have learned that students often question aspects of demand theory, pointing out that:

- consumers are not as rational as the law of demand presumes;
- consumers exhibit some randomness in their buying decisions; and/or
- consumers often buy goods even as prices rise, because higher prices convey a message to others whom the consumers want to impress.

These objections are discussed further in Perspective 4, which largely reinforces the basic conclusion: demand curves slope downward. When economists note this principle, they are not trying to suggest that the contrary *never* happens. They are saying it is a widely applicable heuristic. University of Chicago economist and philosopher Frank Knight used to insist with his students that there are no absolutes in this world (aside from that statement), but there are more tenable "relatively absolute absolutes." These are principles which have proven so reliable in such a broad range of situations that they are about as close to absolute in our world as we are likely to find – and the law of demand should be treated as such. It might not be applicable in every situation, but we should hold to the principle until presented with overwhelming evidence that the principle needs to be revised.

PERSPECTIVE 4
Common Concerns Relating to the Law of Demand

Many business students harbor understandable concerns about the claim that all demand curves slope downward – or that price and quantity are always and everywhere inversely related. We readily concede that such a claim seems too absolute. With the billions of goods and services in the world, there may well be some goods that violate the law of demand. Nevertheless, given the frequency with which the law of demand appears to apply, it still can be a sound rule for firms to adopt, until they are given strong reasons to assume otherwise.

Sometimes, students note that consumers seem to buy more of some good when the price rises *because the price rose*. It turns out that standard economic theory can accommodate this when a good's price indicates something about the good's relative value. Alternatively, many consumers are thought to be "irrational" (or "nonrational") – here, that they cannot be expected to respond to price changes in the standard (rational) way. Indeed, irrational consumers might ignore price in their purchases and hence not respond at all to a price change. We consider each of these concerns in turn.

Conspicuous Consumption and the Law of Demand

Sociologist Thorstein Veblen (1902, 68–101) argued in his well-known book *The Theory of the Leisure Class* that many high-income and "high-bred" people engage in "conspicuous consumption." That is, they often buy high-price goods in order to put their income and wealth on display. This means that high-price goods have value, apart from their intrinsic worth, because of the not-so-hidden messages such purchases convey to others. An all-too-easy deduction is that the demand curves for "conspicuous consumption goods" are upward-sloping, supposedly clear violations of the law of demand.

For purposes of argument, we might agree that prices can convey messages and that they can indicate goods' relative worth to a degree and at certain times. Higher-price goods can indicate greater value, which can mean that some increase in price from an initial low price can lead to greater purchases. In Figure 4.6(a), an increase in price from P_1 to P_2 will lead to an increase in quantity from Q_1 to Q_2. Why? People deduce from the higher price that the value of the good is greater – because others have been willing to pay the higher price or its purchase conveys to other relevant people that the buyers have done well in life. For example, by raising its prices, Mercedes-Benz might be able to sell more cars.

But after making such a concession, we must insist that sales will contract at some price. Beyond some very high price, many buyers will not be able (or willing) to afford the good, resulting in a backward-bending demand curve, as illustrated in Figure 4.6(b). Above a price of P_3, sales drop and continue to decrease with higher prices. Moreover, the seller would raise the price above P_3, given that the demand curve above P_3 will likely be inelastic for some distance (which means that revenues will rise with a higher price) and production costs will fall with the cutback in sales, leading to greater profits. More simply, if the seller was operating on the upward sloping portion of the demand curve (for example, point *b*) then a higher combination (*d*) would be preferable. This is because the

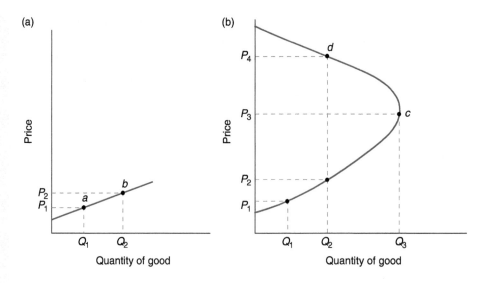

Figure 4.6 Upward-sloping demand?

(a) A good might have an upward-sloping range, as depicted, if a price increase conveys greater value to consumers. However, there must be some higher price that will cause sales to contract, since many consumers will no longer be able (or willing) to buy the good. (b) This means that the demand curve must bend backwards at some point, such as at price P_3, as shown, and thus must have a downward-sloping range. The downward sloping range of the curve in panel (b) is the relevant range. If the seller is at combination b, then there is some combination such as d in the downward-sloping range of the entire demand curve that is more profitable.

same quantity Q_2 can be sold at a higher price, P_4, which necessarily means that combination d is more profitable than combination b. Hence, the relevant portion of the demand curve is the downward portion because this is where sellers would maximize profits.

Our point here is that, even *if* there is an upward-sloping range for a demand curve for some "conspicuous consumption good" (and we have serious doubts), the upward-sloping portion of the entire demand curve would not be the relevant range of the complete demand curve – as in Figure 4.6(b). The relevant portion or range would be the downward-sloping portion, because that is where profit-maximizing sellers would operate, if given a choice in the matter.

Irrationality and the Law of Demand

So far, we have been discussing demand in terms of rational behavior. Suppose there were some people who did not act rationally – and, therefore, were not inclined to respond to price. Even if some consumers behave irrationally, the law of demand could easily apply at the market level. As long as enough people in the market respond rationally, the amount demanded would still decrease (increase) with an increase (decrease) in price.

For instance, many people buy cigarettes because they are addicted to them. For the sake of argument, let's assume that habitual smokers do not consider price in making their purchases at all; therefore, the quantity they buy will not vary with price. But if occasional smokers take price into consideration when they buy, their demand for cigarettes will produce the normal downward-sloping curve. If we add the quantity of cigarettes that addicted smokers buy to the quantity that occasional smokers buy, the total market demand curve will still slope downward (see Figure 4.7). At a price of P_1, Q_1 cigarettes will be bought by addicted consumers, and $Q_3 - Q_1$ cigarettes will be bought by occasional consumers. If the price then rises to P_2, the total quantity bought will fall to Q_2, reflecting a predictable drop in the quantity purchased by occasional consumers.

This kind of reasoning can be extended to "impulse buying." Some people respond more to the packaging and display of products than to their price. *Their* demand may not slope downward. But as long as some people check prices and resist advertising, the total demand for any good will slope downward. Store managers must therefore assume that changes in price will affect the quantity demanded. The fact that some people may behave irrationally reduces the elasticity of demand but does not invalidate the concept of downward-sloping demand for a market.

In fact, the standard theory has already provided two concepts that help us explain these scenarios. First, we've distinguished between individuals and markets. When prices change, we're confident that markets will exhibit changes in behavior, but far less confident that any given individual will change behavior.

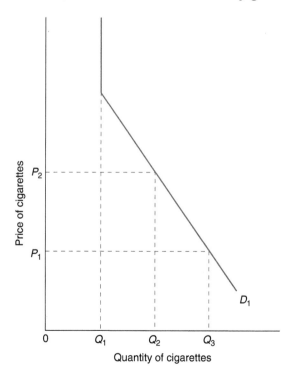

Figure 4.7 Demand including irrational behavior
If irrational consumers demand Q_1 cigarettes no matter the price and rational consumers take price into consideration, then market demand will be D_1. The quantity purchased will still vary inversely with the price in the relevant range of the demand curve.

A change in prices always causes a change in incentives, but it only results in behavioral change if the costs or benefits are impacted enough at the margin for a given individual. Second, we described how elasticity is relevant at a price or over a small range of prices. It is likely that demand is perfectly inelastic for individuals over small ranges of prices; again, their purchases would be unaffected by modest increases in price. But this is a far cry from a perfectly inelastic demand curve for a market over any substantive range of prices.

Random Behavior and Demand

Critics of demand curve theory might still complain: "The demand *curve* (drawn as a thin line on the graphs throughout this chapter) presumes that buyers know exactly how much they want to buy at any given price. Buyers are not always this well informed about their own preferences for particular goods. There is certainly a degree of randomness in how much people are willing and able to buy at various prices."

The broadest answer deals with imperfect information – a topic we'll develop in Chapter 5. For now, this concern can be addressed in two ways. First, Gary Becker (1971, 29–31) has noted that, even if buyers behaved totally randomly in their purchases, scarcity would ensure downward-sloping demand curves when relative prices change. Consider Figure 4.8, in which there are many buyers with identical budget lines, A_1B_1, for two goods A and B. (Consumer budget constraints are analogous to the production constraints of the production possibilities frontiers (PPFs) from Chapter 2. See the Online Math Appendix for more on the construction of budget lines.) If buyers are faced with such a budget constraint and randomly buy combinations of A and B along A_1B_1, then buyers will be spread out along A_1B_1 in a normal, bell-shaped distribution. The *mean* quantities of A and B purchased along A_1B_1 will be in the middle of this line: combination *a* with quantities A_2 and B_2. If the price of A is raised and the price of B is lowered such that consumers

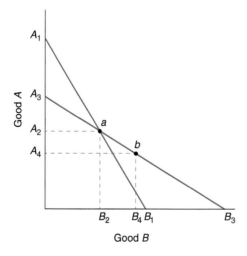

Figure 4.8 Random behavior, budget lines, and downward-sloping demand curves

If buyers are faced initially with budget line A_1B_1 and behave randomly, they will buy average quantities of A_2 and B_2. If the price of A increases while the price of B decreases, the budget line pivots on *a*, causing buyers to purchase on average more of B (B_4) and less of A (A_4). Thus, quantity still changes in the direction predicted by the law of demand despite the absence of rational behavior.

can still buy combination *a*, then the buyers' budget line will pivot on *a* to A_3B_3. Buying randomly along the new budget line means that buyers on average will then buy combination *b* with quantities A_4 and B_4. The drop in the price of B leads to more B being bought; and the increase in the price of A leads to less of A being bought. Hence, the overall market demand curves for A and B are downward-sloping even though individuals are acting randomly.

Second, suppose that the market demand curve is not a thin downward-sloping line, but a downward-sloping "band," as in Figure 4.9. The "band" indicates some randomness in the quantity buyers will purchase at any given price. At P_1, buyers can be expected to buy anywhere from Q_1 to Q_2 of good A. At P_2, they will buy anywhere from Q_2 to Q_3. Exactly how much individual buyers consume is uncertain, but if the "band" indicates true randomness among buyer purchases, then we know that, when faced with a price of P_1, buyers can be expected to buy on average Q_4 (the middle quantity between Q_1 and Q_2). When the price falls to P_2, they can be expected to buy on average Q_5 (or the middle of Q_2 and Q_3). This means that, even in markets where individuals' preferences exhibit a degree of randomness (or uncertainty), price and quantity purchased in the market will tend to be inversely related and follow the law of demand.

"Free" and Irrationality

Behavioral psychologist Daniel Ariely argues that the law of demand is really unsettled when the price of a good becomes "free." A price of free presses an "emotional hot button" and elicits a form of "irrational excitement" (back to "transaction utility") among consumers which, in turn, can dramatically change consumption choices at prices above zero. He made this point by first offering MIT students a 30-cent Lindt truffle for 15 cents and a 2-cent Kiss for 1 cent: 73 percent of the students bought the truffle. When the price of each chocolate was lowered one more

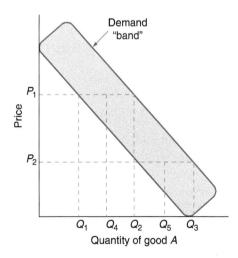

Figure 4.9 Random behavior and the demand curve as a "band"

If buyers randomly purchase anywhere from Q_1 to Q_2 when the price is P_1 and anywhere from Q_2 to Q_3 when the price is P_2, then they will tend to increase their *average* quantity purchased from Q_4 to Q_5 when the price falls from P_1 to P_2.

cent (14 cents for the truffle and 0 cents for the Kiss), the consumption distribution almost reversed: 69 percent of the students chose Kisses (Ariely 2010, 51–53).

According to Ariely, the students were freely grabbing the Kisses "not because they had made reasoned cost–benefit analysis before elbowing their way in, but simply because the Kisses were FREE!" (Ariely 2010, 53). The word and concept of "free" has an "emotional charge" to people "because we humans are afraid of loss." One doesn't have to fear loss when something is free (Ariely 2010, 54) – a line of argument that suggests people can engage in a constrained form of rationality where they are weighing the subjective damage from a loss.

This is an interesting result, but Ariely's experiment should be considered with some skepticism. In his report, Ariely doesn't say whether the two sets of prices were offered to the same group of students – or whether the number of customers was greater when the two prices were lowered (with the possibility that the greater percentage emerged from additional students taking the Kisses, not from buyers switching from the truffle to the Kiss). A more likely factor: the importance of transaction costs involved in any full discussion of product prices. To take something that is free, subjects in an experiment need not go to the trouble of getting out the necessary change to make a purchase or of waiting to receive change from the transaction. They can simply grab the Kisses as they pass the experimenter's table. "Loss aversion" may indeed motivate behavior, as Ariely and others suggest, but the effective price decrease for the Kiss could simply have been much greater than the suggested 1 cent drop in money prices, which suggests that the elasticity of demand for Kisses between 1 cent and zero may not be as great as the experiment suggests.[11] (In Online Reading 4.2, we explore an experiment by the *New York Times* to use a price equal to zero.)

The lesson? Exceptions to the law of demand are likely rare. The rule that price and quantity vary inversely (everything else held constant) is one that managers and owners should take seriously.

Part B Organizational Economics and Management

Pricing Strategies and Demand Characteristics

All microeconomics textbooks provide a lengthy discussion of the demand for "standard" goods, as we have done in Chapter 3 and Part A of this chapter: the quantity of a good purchased will be related to the price of the good in question

---

[11] A similar result obtains in labor markets with the psychology of work moving from unpaid (voluntary with intrinsic rewards) to paid (with extrinsic rewards).

and a number of other considerations (such as weather, income, and the prices of other goods). For example, the lower the price of a candy bar, the greater the quantity purchased: the "law of demand." The general rule deduced is that the more scarce the good, the greater the (marginal) value and price.

However, little is said in most textbooks about our coverage in Perspective 4 and this chapter's Part B. Here, we cover two additional categories of demand: first, when the consumption level of a good today might affect its demand in the future; and second, how the benefits (and demand) can depend upon how many other people have bought the good. These are uncommon categories. Taking candy bars as an example: their benefit in one time period does not materially affect the benefits of eating another later – and is not materially affected by how many other people are eating them.

This is not true for **lagged-demand** goods and **network** goods. A lagged-demand good has one defining feature: the greater the quantity purchased today, the greater the demand tomorrow. Good examples include cigarettes, alcohol, and drugs, since they tend to be addictive. (As we shall show, this is similar to the theory of "rational addiction" – the view that, before consumption begins, people can rationally weigh the long-term costs and benefits of consuming goods that can be physically compelling in consumption.)

> A **lagged-demand good** is one in which consumption today affects consumption tomorrow (or in future time periods).

> A **network good** is a product or service whose value to consumers depends on how many other people buy the good.

A network good has one defining feature: the greater the number of buyers, the greater the benefits to most buyers. These goods are said to exhibit a "network effect" (sometimes called "network externalities"), which means that the attractiveness or value of a product to buyers will increase with others' use of the product. Good examples include telephones and computer software. One person's telephone is useless unless someone else owns a phone – and more people with phones implies a greater value of a phone to those who own a phone, because more people can be called.

As you can see, lagged-demand goods and network goods have something in common – the potential *interconnectedness of consumption*. This commonality has important implications for pricing strategy.

Lagged Demands

One of the authors of this book (Lee) was involved in the development of the theory of lagged demands (Lee and Kreutzer 1982). They argued that the future demands for some goods can be dependent on the current demand. From this perspective, a lagged-demand good is one in which the future good is a complement to the current good; they go together. According to Lee and Kreutzer (1982, 580):

The crucial assumption behind our analysis is that lags exist in the demand for the resource; future demands are influenced by current availability. The demand for petroleum is clearly an example of such a lagged demand structure, with future demand for petroleum significantly influenced by investment decisions made in response to current availability.

Behind such an obvious point is an insight that might otherwise go unrecognized: the *future* demand for a product depends on the *current* price for the good. As a consequence of the complementarity in consumption over time, firms faced with lagged demand have an incentive to lower their *current* price in order to stimulate *future* sales. They might even charge a price in the inelastic range of their current demand curves – despite losing current revenues (and profits) from doing so – to stimulate a greater future demand, which will permit them to raise future prices and generate greater profits in the future.

We see one prominent version of this with entry into a market by new firms. Trying to gain the attention of customers who have some brand loyalty to existing firms, challengers are likely to try lower prices to stimulate both current and future demand – and develop brand loyalty to their goods and services.

One surprising application: under conditions of lagged demand, a cartel of firms (considered in detail in Chapter 11) may form – not with the intent of raising the group's current price, but rather to lower the current price (below) and expand current output (above) the levels that would exist under competition. But this is easier said than done. The standard angle on cartels is that they increase their prices above the level that would be possible under competition, and that cartels tend to break down because individual firms will cheat on the cartel agreement by lowering price to gain customers at the expense of the other cartel firms. Here, a cartel could dissolve because of rampant cheating involving price *increases*, with firms seeking to benefit from the greater demand stimulated by the lower prices charged by other cartel members.

All of this is true as long as the producers' rights to exploit future profits are not threatened. The conventional treatment of demand predicts that threats to the future stability of property rights will lead to "overproduction" during the current time period. If a firm (e.g., an oil company) fears losing the property rights to its reserves, then it has an incentive to increase production and expand sales today. Never mind that the added supply of oil might depress the current price. The oil firm can reason that if it doesn't pump the oil out of the ground soon, it may not have rights to the oil in the future. But for goods subject to the lagged-demand phenomenon, any looming threat to property rights can cause firms to do the opposite: reduce the production of oil, hike the current price, and extract whatever profits remain. When its property rights are threatened, the firm no longer has an incentive to artificially suppress its current price in order to cultivate future demand.

Rational Addiction

Gary Becker and Kevin Murphy (1988) developed a similar argument to develop an economic theory of "addiction" – a general concept that suggests a connection between current and future consumption of a good or activity. People's future demand for smokes can be tied to their current consumption because of the body's chemical dependency on nicotine. As in the case of lagged-demand goods, producers of addictive goods have an incentive to suppress the current price of their good in order to stimulate future demand. The lower the current price, the greater the future demand and future consumption.

This complementarity in consumption for an addictive (and lagged-demand) good is illustrated in Figure 4.10. At price P_3, the consumption will be Q_1 in the current time period. Because of the current consumption level, the demand in the future rises to D_2. At a price of P_2, current consumption rises to Q_2, but the future demand rises to D_3. At even lower prices (P_1), an even higher demand curve will occur in the future. Figure 4.10 shows why firms have an incentive to lower the current price: future demand rises. With other complementary goods, if the price of one complement goes down and more of it is sold, then the demand for the other complement goes up, with its price rising. The same thing happens in this case, but the complements are the same good consumed in different time periods.

The current demand for one addictive good (cigarettes) might be highly inelastic, but this does not mean that long-run demand is necessarily inelastic. As illustrated in Figure 4.10, each of the short-term demand curves are inelastic, but the long-term (long-run) demand curves (Dlr_1 and Dlr_2) are rather elastic. Indeed, Becker and Murphy (1988, 695) maintain that, the more addictive the good, the more elastic will be the long-term demand. This is the case because a reduction in the *current* time period might not stimulate *current* sales very much. However, for

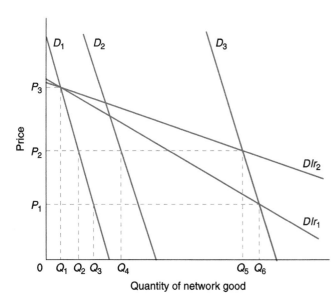

Figure 4.10 Rational addiction, network effects, and demand
As the price falls from P_3 to P_2, the quantity demanded in the short run rises from Q_1 to Q_2. However, sales build on sales in this case, causing the demand in the future to expand outward to, say, D_2. The lower the price in the current time period, the greater the expansion of demand in the future. The more the demand expands over time in response to greater sales in the current time period, the more elastic is the long-run demand.

highly addictive goods, current consumption can give an even greater increase in the future demand because the buyers "have to have more of it," resulting in even more future consumption than would be the case for less addictive goods.

Hence, it is altogether understandable why cigarette firms in the 1960s used "cigarette girls" in short skirts to give away small packs of cigarettes – and why many drug dealers give away the first "hits" to their potential customers. Indeed, it seems reasonable to conclude that, the more addictive the good, the lower the current price for first-time users. In fact, we might expect producers to "sell" their goods at below-zero prices, paying customers to take the good.

This theory of rational addiction suggests explanations for a variety of behaviors – most notably, the observed differences in the consumption behavior of young and old, the tendency of overweight people to go on "crash diets" even when they may want to lose only a modest amount of weight, or alcoholics who become "teetotalers" when they want to curtail their drinking. Older people may be less concerned about addictive behavior, all else constant, than the young. They have less to lose over time from addictions than do younger people (given older people's shorter remaining life expectancies). People who are addicted to food may rationally choose to drastically reduce their intake of food, even though they may need to lose only a few pounds because their intake of food compels them to "overconsume." Similarly, alcoholics may "get on the wagon" in order to temper their future demand for booze, because even a modest consumption level can have a snowballing effect – with a little consumption leading to more and more drinks.

Network Effects

The theory of "network effects" shares a key construct with the theory of lagged demand: the interconnectedness of demands (Arthur 1996; Farrell and Klemperer 2007). In the theory of lagged demand, interconnectedness is formed through time; in the theory of network effects, it is formed across people and markets. The theory of network effects is analogous to telephone systems that form "networks" tied together with telephone lines (as well as microwave disks and satellites). No one would want to own a phone or buy a telephone service if he was the only phone owner. There would be nobody to call! However, if two people – A and B – buy phones, then there are two pair-wise calls that can be made: A can call B, and B can call A. As more and more people buy phones, the benefits of phone ownership escalate geometrically; there are progressively more people to call and even more possible pair-wise calls.[12] The benefits that buyers garner from others

---

[12] If there are three phone owners – A, B, and C – then calls can be made in six pair-wise ways: A can call B or C; B can call A or C; and C can call A or B. If there are four phone owners, then there are twelve potential pair-wise calls; five phone owners, twenty potential pair-wise calls; twenty phone owners, 380 calls; and so forth – where the number of calls is $N \times (N - 1)$ with N phones. If the network allows for conference calls, the count quickly accelerates through the proverbial roof.

who join the network can rise simply from the *potential* to call others; they need not ever call all the additional joiners.

Accordingly, the demand for phones can be expected to rise with phone ownership. That is to say, the benefits from ownership go up as more people join the network. Hence, people should be willing to pay more for phones as phone ownership increases. Some of the benefits of phone ownership are said to be "external" to the buyers of phones because people other than those who buy phones gain by the purchases (as we will see in our study of "public goods" and external benefits in Chapter 6). For that matter, everyone who has a phone gains more opportunities to call as other people buy phones and the network expands – what are called "network externalities."

Thus, network effects can be discussed with the same graph that was developed for rational addiction in Figure 4.10. Under both market conditions – rational addiction and network effects – short-term prices of zero and even below zero are potential market-development strategies. Low prices can encourage current consumption, which can elevate future demand and future prices. Indeed, the prospects of higher prices (and profits) in the future are a key motivation for short-term price reductions – even to zero or beyond.

Networks and network goods turn one basic economic proposition on its head: as any good becomes scarcer, it becomes more valuable. In the case of network goods, the opposite is true: as a good becomes more abundant, its value goes up (Kelly 1998, chapter 3). This does not mean, however, that the demand curve for a network good slopes upward. Given the number of phones that others have, people can still be expected to buy more phones at a low price than a high price.

A phone company faces two basic problems in building its network. First, the company has the initial problem of getting people to buy phones, since the benefits will be low at the start. Second, if some of the benefits of buying a phone are "external" to the buyer, then each buyer's willingness to buy a phone can be impaired. How does the phone company build the network? One obvious solution is for the phone company to emulate producers in the theory of lagged demand: "underprice" (or subsidize) their products – or, at the extreme, give them away or even pay people to install phones in their homes and offices.

Software Networks

The network effects in the software industry – for example, operating systems – are similar. But the software developer may face more difficult problems, given that the software development must somehow get the computer users on one side of the market and application developers on the other side to join the network more or less together.

Few people are likely to buy an operating system without applications (for example, word processing programs or games) being available. If a producer of an operating system is able to get only a few consumers to buy and use its product, the demand for the operating system will be highly restricted. A major problem is that few software firms will write applications for an operating system with few users because the software firms will have few opportunities to sell their products – which in turn keeps demand for the operating system low. However, if the firm producing the operating system can motivate more consumers to purchase it, a cycle of increased demand can result as the number of applications written for the operating system grows, stimulating yet more demand for the system, more applications written for it, and so on.

As in the case of telephones, some of the benefits of purchasing the operating system (and applications) are "external" to the people who buy them. People who join the operating system network increase the benefits to all previous joiners because they have more people with whom they can share computers or files. All joiners have the additional benefit of knowing that, as the network increases, they are likely to have a greater number of applications from which to choose. However, as in phone purchases, when the benefits are "external," potential users have an impaired demand for buying into the network. The greater the "external benefits," the greater the initial buying resistance.

The network may grow slowly at the start because people (both computer users and programmers) may be initially skeptical that any given operating system will be able to become a sizable network (and provide the "external benefits" that a large network can provide). But if the network for a given operating system continues to grow, more and more people will begin to believe that the operating system will become sizable (if not dominant), which means that the network can grow at an escalating pace.

In short, such network growth can reach a "tipping point," beyond which the growth in the market for the operating system will take on a life of its own – at an ever-faster pace *because* it has grown at an ever-faster pace (Gladwell 2000). People will buy the operating system because everyone else is using it, which can mean that the accelerating growth of one operating system causes a contraction in the market share for other operating systems. After the "tipping point" has been reached, the firm's eventual market dominance and monopoly power (according to the U.S. Department of Justice; Klein *et al.* 1998) is practically assured.

This discussion is relevant to the history of the Apple and Microsoft operating systems. Before the introduction of the IBM personal computer, Apple was the dominant personal computer (PC), running the ProDOS operating system; however, IBM and Microsoft jointly developed their respective operating systems, PC-DOS and MS-DOS, in 1981. At that time, 90 percent of programs ran under some version of the CP/M operating system. Two important factors likely undermined CP/M's market dominance. First, CP/M was selling at the time for $240 a copy; DOS was introduced at $40. Second, IBM's dominance of the mainframe computer market no doubt convinced many buyers that some version of DOS would eventually be the dominant operating system. In addition, Apple refused to "unbundle" its computer system: it insisted on selling its own operating system with the Macintosh (and later-generation models) – and at a price inflated by the restricted availability of Apple machines and operating systems (Evans, Nichols, and Reddy 1999, 4).

Microsoft took a radically different approach: It got IBM to allow it to license MS-DOS to other computer manufacturers – with the expectation that competition among non-Apple computer manufacturers would spread the use of their computers (and not incidentally, Microsoft's operating system). This expectation was realized and the "abundance" of MS-DOS systems led to an even greater demand for such systems and a lower demand for Apple systems. Many people started joining the Microsoft network, not necessarily because they thought that MS-DOS or Windows was a superior operating system to Apple's, but because of the benefits of the larger network. There was a "tipping point" for Microsoft some time in the late 1980s or early 1990s (possibly with the release of Windows 3.1) that caused Windows to take off, sending Apple into a market-share tailspin.

In 1998, the Justice Department took Microsoft to court for violation of anti-trust laws. Among other charges, the Government maintained that Microsoft was a monopolist because it held more than 90 percent of the market share in operating systems and it was engaging in "predatory" pricing of its browser, Internet Explorer. Microsoft had been giving away Internet Explorer with Windows 95 and had integrated it into Windows 98. The Justice Department claimed that Microsoft offered Internet Explorer to eliminate Netscape Navigator from the market. We can't settle these issues here (see McKenzie 2000), but we can point out that the Justice Department started its case against Microsoft with the admission that the operating system and software markets are full of "network effects."

Although it may be true that Microsoft engaged in pricing designed to eliminate competition, it may also be true that Microsoft was responding to the dictates of "network effects," underpricing its product to build future demand. The company had another reason for its actions: if Microsoft lowered its price on Internet Explorer (or lowered its *effective* price for Windows by including Internet Explorer), then more computers could be sold – which means that more copies of Windows would be sold *and* more copies of Microsoft's applications (Word, Excel, etc.) would be sold. In a word, a lower price for Internet Explorer or Windows could give rise to higher sales, prices, and profits on their other applications. (More discussion of antitrust in general – and the 1998 Microsoft antitrust case in particular – will be provided in Chapter 11.)

The Justice Department was convinced in the 1990s that Microsoft had locked itself into a long-term dominant market position in operating systems for PCs. But within two years of the lawsuit, Larry Page and Sergey Brin began to work on creating a "better mousetrap" through a search engine that was called BackRub and then Google. Little did the Justice Department expect that a search engine company could, in less than a decade, threaten Microsoft's dominance of the operating systems for "computers" – broadly defined as extending beyond the desktop and into music players, smartphones, and tablets. Moreover, Apple came back from its corporate deathbed in the 1990s to become the world's most valuable company by 2015, mainly because of the introduction of its iPod, iPad, and iPhone, in addition to a series of new models of desktops and laptops that acquired a "cool factor" and a cult following. As a result, Microsoft's share of the operating system market (broadly defined) has been shrinking relentlessly. It has, at this writing, been unable to find a significant sales footing in the mobile-device market. As a consequence, Google's Android system was, as early as 2014, running on close to 50 percent of all computing devices, while Microsoft's Windows was running on only 14 percent (Wikipedia 2015).

Practical Lessons

As Frank Knight noted, managers and owners should treat the law of demand for what it is: a *relatively absolute* absolute. The law of demand is a principle that has been tested and validated so often that economists have come to think of it as true, bordering on a law of nature. The law of demand holds with such frequency and durability that business students would be well advised to presume the law of demand holds for whatever pricing problem they are considering until strong evidence proves otherwise. Unless their firms operate in a perfectly competitive market where firms have little or no control over price, managers should develop their pricing policy on the presumption that price and quantity are inversely related.

Having adopted the law of demand as a key pricing principle, managers assess the elasticity of their market demand. If their demands are inelastic (or unitary elastic) within the relevant range of market sales, then they should definitely consider raising their prices to improve their profitability. If demand is inelastic, a higher price will lead to slightly fewer units sold, but lower costs and greater revenues. If the demand is unitary elastic, then revenues will remain the same when the price is raised, while costs will fall with lower sales.

But a firm producing a good that has network effects should ponder a radically different pricing strategy. The firm should consider pricing its product below cost (or even zero or negative) with an eye toward boosting current sales. The increase in current sales in and of itself can add to consumer value and boost future demand and sales even at elevated future prices. Pricing among initial producers of a network good can be expected to be especially aggressive because more than current sales will be at stake. The prospects of future market dominance can drive initial prices below production costs because of the potential for elevated profits from future market dominance.

Further Reading Online

Reading 4.1: Covering relocation costs of new hires
Reading 4.2: For *New York Times*, a gamble on giveaways (*The Wall Street Journal*, link available on the online resources website www.cambridge.org/ mckenzie4)

Recommended Videos Online

1 Elasticity of demand (Richard McKenzie, 29 minutes)
2 Rational addiction (Richard McKenzie, 21 minutes)
3 Network effects (Richard McKenzie, 27 minutes)
4 Trust Me (Freakonomics, link available on the online resources website www.cambridge.org/mckenzie4)
5 Joe Gebbia: How Airbnb designs for trust (TED, link available on the online resources website www.cambridge.org/mckenzie4)

The Bottom Line

The key takeaways from Chapter 4 are the following:

1 Rational consumers will equate at the margins. That is to say, they will allocate their expenditures so that the marginal utility of the last unit of every good is equal to every other.

2 The law of demand is a natural consequence of rational behavior. Although economists do not have complete confidence in all applications of the law of demand, they consider the relationship between price and quantity to be so firmly established, both theoretically and empirically, that they call it a law.

3 Demand does not consist of what people would like to have or are willing to buy at a given price; rather, it represents the inverse relationship between price and quantity demanded – a relationship described by a downward-sloping curve.

4 When the price of a good goes down, the quantity purchased may fall rather than rise. In such cases, economists assume (until strong evidence is presented to the contrary) that some other variable has changed, offsetting the positive effects of the reduction in price.

5 The market demand curve is obtained by horizontally summing individual demand curves.

6 Not all downward-sloping demand curves are alike. They differ radically in terms of the price elasticity of demand – the responsiveness of consumers to a price change. The elasticity of demand can heavily influence business pricing strategies. Total revenue will rise when demand is elastic and the price is reduced; total revenue will fall when demand is inelastic and the price is reduced.

7 The slope and elasticity of a demand curve are not the same. The slope of a linear demand curve is the same at all points along the demand curve. The elasticity of demand, as measured by the elasticity coefficient, is based on percentage changes and will increase as a firm moves up a linear demand curve.

8 When the price of a network good is lowered, the current and future demand for the good will increase as the value of the good rises with the increase in the number of consumers. Producers of the network good can (depending on the extent of the network effects) have an incentive to charge zero and negative prices.

Review Questions ▷▷

1 What role does the law of demand play in economic analysis?

2 If the price of jeans rises and the quantity sold goes up, does this mean that the demand curve slopes upward? Why or why not?

3 If the prices of most goods are rising by an average of 15 percent per year, but the price of gasoline rises just 10 percent per year, what is happening to the real, or relative, price of gasoline? How do you expect consumers to react?

4 Suppose that a producer raises the price of a good from $4 to $7, and the quantity sold drops from 250 to 200 units. Is demand for the good elastic or inelastic?

5 Draw a relatively elastic demand D_1 and a relatively inelastic demand D_2 on the same graph. Illustrate and explain why one is more elastic than the other.

6 Using a graph or one version of the elasticity equation, illustrate why the elasticity of demand varies along a linear demand curve.

7 Suppose that the (own-price/demand) elasticity for cigarettes is 2.0. If the elasticity for Camel cigarettes is 6.0, must there be some cigarette brands with an elasticity less than 2.0? Why or why not?

8 All things equal, would a politician rather tax a good whose demand is elastic or inelastic? Explain. How does this relate to an example of tax policy?

9 Why is gas competitively priced at gas stations – while snacks inside the gas station's store are so expensive? Use the concepts of transaction costs and elasticity in your answer.

10 If the campus police force is expanded and officers are instructed to increase the number of parking tickets they give out, why might the initial effect of this policy

increase revenues from fines more than the long-run effect? What does your answer have to do with the elasticity of demand for illegal parking?

11   If some consumers (Group A) were price-sensitive (their demand curve slopes downward) and some consumers (Group B) were totally price-insensitive (their demand curve is vertical), would you charge the two groups of consumers different prices? If the good could be freely resold across Groups A and B, would you charge different prices?

12   Suppose consumers believe that higher prices translate into higher quality. What would consumers' demand curves look like? When would producers be able to exploit consumers who equate higher quality with higher prices in competitive product markets?

13   Many computer programs – for example, operating systems and word processors – are said to be "network goods." Software piracy is often relatively easy because of the digital nature of software. Should software developers oppose all piracy?

14   Consider two markets, one in which the market has a "tipping point" and another in which it does not. Compare the incentives of firms in the two markets to lower their prices before the market "tips."

15   Assume network effects in two markets. In one market, there are no "switching costs" – the cost of switching from one provider to another. In the other, there are substantial switching costs. How do switching costs affect the initial price competition in the two markets?

16   Why would any firm ever pay consumers to take their products? Can you think of examples of such a pricing strategy?

5

Applications of Demand and Supply to Government and Management Policies

Painting is easy when you don't know how, but very difficult when you do.
  Edgar Degas

The real and effectual discipline which is exercised over a workman is that of his customers. It is the fear of losing their employment which restrains his frauds and corrects his negligence.
  Adam Smith

Chapters 1–4 showed how the models of mutually beneficial trade, budget and production constraints, demand and supply, and competitive markets are fundamental to the economic way of thinking. With such models, we can illuminate the economic effects of changes on incentives and outcomes for buyers and sellers – as individuals and in markets. This chapter examines how government policies and management practices can affect the operation of markets, product prices, output levels, worker wages, and employment levels. In Part A, we apply the supply and demand curve analysis developed in Chapters 3 and 4 to five types of government intervention: excise taxes, price regulations (floors and ceilings), minimum-wage laws, and mandated fringe benefits. These policies inspire (if not force) management reactions that negate some of the desired effects of the regulations. Throughout the chapter, we consider how management decisions about work demands, fringe benefits, and honesty affect wage rates and the efficiency of firm operations in competitive markets given imperfect information. Our goal is to demonstrate how the application of a few economic principles and the economic way of thinking can generate useful insights and testable predictions for policy-makers and managers to consider before choosing various policies.

The approach taken by economists to analyze human satisfaction stands in contrast to the approach taken in psychology and other social sciences. Business students will probably work with Maslow's "Hierarchy of Needs," which psychologists (and business school professors in organizational behavior and marketing) use to explain the way people satisfy their various wants. In Perspective 5, we lay out Maslow's hierarchy with two goals in mind. First, we want to clarify the distinguishing characteristics of the economic approach to human-want satisfaction. Second, we want to use demand curves to better understand why Maslow found the structure of his hierarchy and how the structure might have been different if prices had been different when he formulated it.

In Part B, we examine how the economic way of thinking, founded on rational behavior and market analysis, can be used to understand "information problems" and the role of honesty and morality in business – in particular, the unheralded role of trust in affecting profitability and market competition. We use our earlier game-theoretic models to understand how trust can overcome Prisoner's Dilemma games and how business can inspire greater trust with their workers, buyers, and suppliers. Throughout the chapter, we are confident that the economic way of thinking, supported by graphical analysis, will generate unexpected insights.

Part A Theory and Public Policy Applications

Who Pays the Tax?

Many people believe that companies bear the burden of taxes imposed on business. They don't understand market processes or political economy, imagining that these taxes are paid by passive producers with immeasurably deep pockets. Others are convinced that consumers bear the full burden of excise taxes. They believe that producers simply pass the tax to consumers through higher prices. Yet, new (or increased) excise taxes are often opposed by producers. If excise taxes could be fully passed to consumers, firms would have little reason to spend resources opposing them. Fortunately, we have analytical tools to help us discern who bears the costs under what conditions.

Figure 5.1 shows the margarine industry's original supply and demand curves, S_1 and D. In a competitive market, the price will tend toward P_2 and the quantity sold toward Q_1. If the state imposes a $0.25 tax on each pound of margarine sold and collects the tax from producers, it effectively raises the cost of production. The producer must now pay a price for the right to use resources (e.g., equipment and raw materials) and for the right to continue production legally. The supply curve, reflecting the added tax, shifts to S_2. The vertical difference between the two curves, P_1 and P_3, represents the $0.25 added tax – an added cost of doing business.

Given the shift in supply (and some elasticity in demand), the quantity of margarine produced falls (to Q_2) and the price rises (to P_3). Note, however, that the equilibrium price increase (P_2 to P_3) is less than the vertical distance between the two supply curves (P_1 to P_3). That is, the price increases by less than the amount

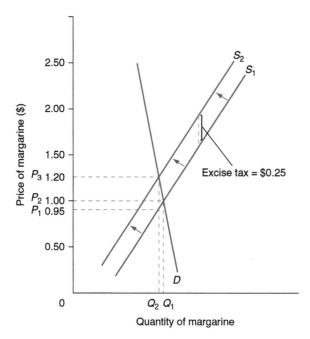

Figure 5.1 The economic effect of an excise tax
An excise tax of $0.25 will shift the supply curve for margarine up and to the left by $0.25 from S_1 to S_2. The quantity produced will fall from Q_1 to Q_2; the price will rise from P_2 to P_3. However, the increase in price ($0.20) will not cover the added tax to the producer ($0.25).

of the tax that caused the shift in supply – and so the producer's net (after-tax) price has fallen. If the tax is $0.25, but the price paid by consumers rises only $0.20 ($1.20 minus $1.00), the producer loses $0.05 per unit sold. The tax not only reduces the quantity of margarine producers can sell, but also lowers the after-tax price to the margarine producers – both of which are good reasons for them to oppose such taxes.

The $0.25 tax in Figure 5.1 is divided between consumers and producers, but most of it ($0.20) is paid by consumers in this case, because they are relatively unresponsive to the price change (inelastic). If consumers were more responsive to the price change, their demand curve would be flatter (more "elastic") and a greater share of the tax burden would fall on producers. As can be seen in Figure 5.2, when consumers are more responsive to a price change, the price rises from $1 to $1.05. The after-tax price received by producers falls from $1 to $0.80, meaning that the producers pay 80 percent of the tax in this case. This suggests that, when consumers are more responsive to price changes, producers will more aggressively oppose an excise tax on their products.

As it turns out, taxes on elastic goods are rare for two reasons. First, as we discussed in Chapter 4, tax revenues will drop – not usually a goal for higher tax rates! Second, the greater impact on quantity translates into painful and obvious costs imposed on the industry (its owners, workers, and suppliers). Even when it's difficult to see the particulars, we know that taxes are always borne by people – whether consumers, owners, or workers (depending on the relevant elasticities). And for reasons we'll discuss in Chapter 6, politicians usually prefer

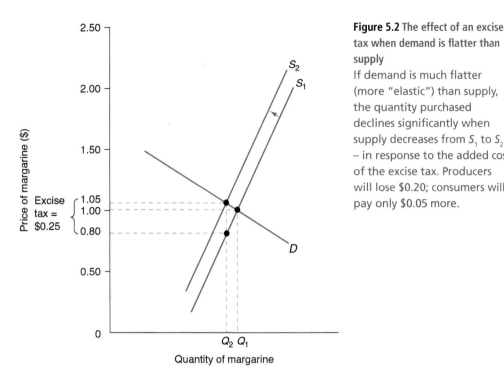

Figure 5.2 The effect of an excise tax when demand is flatter than supply
If demand is much flatter (more "elastic") than supply, the quantity purchased declines significantly when supply decreases from S_1 to S_2 – in response to the added cost of the excise tax. Producers will lose $0.20; consumers will pay only $0.05 more.

the costs of policies to be as subtle as possible (as with taxes on inelastic goods imposed on firms).

All government decision-makers – federal, state, and local – have a management problem not unlike the pricing choices that managers face in private firms: they must choose their excise tax rates carefully when seeking to maximize revenue collection, win re-election, limit damage to the economy, etc. The general rule that follows from this illustration is important to remember: the more responsive consumers (or workers or owners of capital) are to a price increase, the lower the tax must be to maximize tax revenues, limit economic damage, and avoid political fall-out.

If the burden of the tax is typically borne by consumers, why not impose the tax directly on consumers? There are two primary reasons. First, it is often politically expedient to let people believe the fiction that the tax is not only collected and paid by the firm, but borne by the firm. Second, it is practically efficient to use firms as the low-cost tax collector for the government. For example, imagine how difficult (costly) it would be to collect a gas tax from tens of millions of consumers, rather than from a handful of companies that sell gasoline.

Note also that, in our example, butter producers have a clear incentive to support a tax on margarine. When the price of margarine increases, consumers will seek substitutes. The demand for butter will rise, and producers will be able to sell more butter and charge more. Broadly, this points to a potential political strategy: seek legislation that increases costs (disproportionately) for your competitors. (We'll return to this point in Part B of this chapter.)

Finally, note that this analysis applies to any tax increase, any regulatory burden, or even any market factors that cause a leftward/upward shift of the supply curve. Higher corporate income taxes are borne by owners, workers, and consumers. Despite being imposed half on employers and half on employees, federal payroll taxes (FICA, Federal Insurance Contributions Act) on income are mostly shifted to workers because the elasticity of labor supply is so low. And so on. Raising taxes and imposing regulations on business may ultimately be good ideas, but they should not be embraced under the illusion that they will be paid completely or even mostly by business.

Price Controls

Price controls are not a modern invention. The first recorded legal code, the 4000-year-old Code of Hammurabi, included regulations governing the maximum wage, housing prices, and rents on property such as boats, animals, and tools. In AD 301, the Roman Emperor Diocletian issued an edict specifying maximum prices for everything from poultry to gold, and maximum wages for everyone from lawyers to the cleaners of sewer systems. The penalty for violating the law was death. More recently, in the United States, wage and price controls have been used in wartime (during World War II and the Korean War), during crises (after natural disasters like hurricanes), and in peacetime (e.g., when Richard Nixon imposed an across-the-board wage-price freeze in 1971).

Producers always want higher prices for what they sell; consumers always want lower prices for what they buy; and politicians may respond to dissatisfaction with market outcomes. If buyers or sellers are able to petition government effectively, they may get their wish through political markets. But wage and price controls often create more problems than they solve. For example, when Jimmy Carter controlled energy prices in 1977, the result was long lines at gas pumps everywhere – an outcome completely consistent with economic theory.

Price Ceilings

In a competitive market, restrictions on the upward movement of prices can lead to shortages. Consider Figure 5.3, which shows supply and demand curves for gasoline. Initially, the supply and demand curves are S_1 and D, with an equilibrium price of P_1. Suppose the supply of gasoline shifts to S_2 and government officials, believing the new equilibrium price is unjust, freeze the price at P_1. What will happen to the market if the government imposes a price ceiling? At the same price P_1 (which is now below equilibrium),

A **price ceiling** is a government-determined legal maximum price above which a specified good or service cannot be bought or sold.

the number of gallons demanded by consumers is still Q_2, but the number of gallons supplied is now much lower, Q_1. A shortage of $Q_2 - Q_1$ gallons has developed. As a result, some consumers will not get all the gasoline they want and some may not get any.

Because of the shortage, consumers will have to wait in line to get whatever gasoline they can. To avoid a long line, consumers may arrive at the pumps before the station opens. Ironically, in winter, waiting in line will waste gas to keep warm. Although the pump price of gasoline may be held constant at P_1, the effective price – the sum of the pump price and the value of time lost waiting in line – will rise. Shortages can raise the effective price of a product in other ways. A service station owner can afford to lower the quality of services provided and allow stations to become less clean. In the 1970s, some service station owners started closing on weekends and at night. A few required customers to sign long-term contracts and pay in advance for their gasoline. The added interest cost of advance payment raised the price of gasoline even higher.

Controls on apartment rents have been tried in the name of fairness to low-income tenants. The effect of rent controls is similar to gasoline price controls (Tucker 1997). If the rent is kept below the equilibrium price, the result will again be a shortage. Faced with this, landlords can be expected to respond in many ways. First, if the rent controls only apply to "low-income housing," some landlords will upgrade their apartments to escape the controls, sell their apartments as condominiums, or migrate their business to Airbnb or Vrbo. (And, of course, developers have a strong incentive to avoid rent controls by

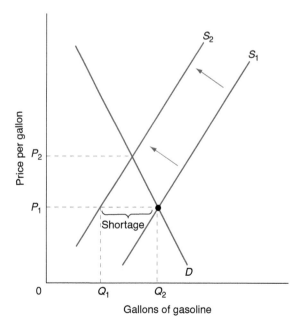

Figure 5.3 The effect of price controls
If the supply of gasoline is reduced from S_1 to S_2, but the price is controlled at P_1, a shortage equal to the difference between Q_1 and Q_2 will emerge.

building nicer housing.) Second, landlords can be selective within the queue for apartments – for example, renting to higher-income tenants who are more likely to pay their rent (on time) and shifting the benefits of the rent controls away from the targeted low-income tenant group.

Third, landlords can reduce their costs by lowering maintenance and improvements to their units. In the absence of rent controls, landlords can be expected to upgrade quality and amenities (e.g., appliances) when tenants value the improvements by more than the cost of the improvements. But if rents are controlled, landlords are likely to reduce their costs by lowering the quality of their units and shifting maintenance costs to tenants. Tenant demand will fall from the reduction in the rent tenants are willing to pay for lower-quality units. But the subsequently reduced demand is of no consequence to the landlords, since they have an excess of prospective tenants to accommodate. The landlords can offset some (but not all) of the effect of the suppressed rent with lower costs. But with lower-quality apartments, both tenants and landlords can be worse off.[1]

In addition to legal maneuvers to evade price controls, some businesses may engage in fraud or "black markets." During the 1970s, many gasoline station owners filled their premium tanks with regular gasoline and sold it at premium prices. Suppliers can tie the sale of the controlled good to the sale of an uncontrolled good. With rent control, apartment rates are regulated, but landlords can mandate furniture rental at artificially high prices. Indeed, the ways of circumventing price controls are limited only by creativity.

To distribute goods with scarcity, markets use prices. Without prices, some means of *rationing* is needed. In the 1970s, some States only allowed odd/even-numbered license plates to buy gas on odd/even-numbered days. If no formal system is adopted, supplies will be distributed on a first-come, first-serve basis – in effect, rationing by congestion. Lotteries and issuing coupons are more efficient to avoid lines. Coupons entitle people to buy specific quantities of the rationed good at the prevailing price. By limiting the number of coupons, the government reduces the demand for the product to match the available supply, thereby eliminating the shortage and relieving the congestion in the marketplace. In Figure 5.4, for example, (legal) demand is reduced from D_1 to D_2.

The coupon system may appear to be fair and simple, but how are the coupons to be distributed? Clearly the government will not want to auction off coupons since this would let consumers bid up the price. Should coupons be distributed equally among all consumers? Should the distribution of coupons be based on the distance traveled or perceived need? (And if such a system is adopted, will people lie about their "needs"?) Not everyone lives the same distance from work

---

[1] Increasing legal difficulties to evict, especially during and after the Covid-19 pandemic, is another example of similar dynamics.

or school. Salespeople travel much more than others. Should a commuter receive more gas than a retired person? If so, how much more? These are formidable questions that must be answered if a coupon system is to be reasonably equitable and efficient. By comparison, the pricing system inherently allows people to reflect the intensity of their needs in their purchases.

After the coupons have been distributed, should the recipients be allowed to sell them? That is, should legal markets for coupons be permitted to spring up? If voluntary, both parties to the exchange will benefit. The person who buys coupons values gasoline more than money; the person who sells coupons values the money more than the coupons. The positive (and often high) market value of coupons indicates that price controls have not really eliminated the shortage. And if the coupons have a value, the price per gallon of gasoline has not really been held constant.

Perhaps the most damaging aspect of a rationing system is that the benefits of such a price increase are received not by producers – oil companies, refineries, and service stations – but rather by those fortunate enough to get coupons. Thus, the price increase does not provide producers with an incentive to supply more gasoline.

In the market for water, California is famous for its shortages. This seems odd. California has never experienced a crisis in Snickers candy bars or Mercedes-Benz cars. How can this be? Snickers and Mercedes have never rained from the skies, but water does: trillions of gallons, even in drought years. Californians have historically paid very low prices for water and prices have not been allowed to rise

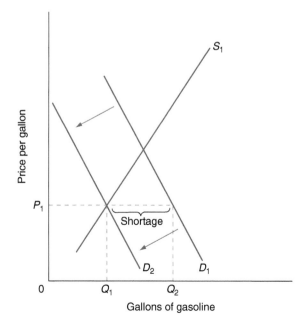

Figure 5.4 The effect of rationing on (legal) demand

Price controls can create a shortage. For instance, at the controlled price P_1, a shortage of $Q_2 - Q_1$ gallons will develop. By issuing a limited number of coupons to purchase a product, the government can reduce (legal) demand and eliminate the shortage. Here, rationing reduces demand from D_1 to D_2, where demand intersects the supply curve at the controlled price.

as droughts have persisted. During an "historic" drought in 2015, Californians paid a mere $1.55 per hundred cubic feet of water (748 gallons): $0.002 (two-tenths of a cent) per gallon. While the obvious effect of extremely low prices is to encourage people to use more water, the less obvious effect is to discourage people from incurring even modest costs to curb water use – through more-efficient toilets, washers, and sprinkler systems (McKenzie 2015).[2]

This connects back to principles developed in Chapter 1. Because water drawn from underground is not priced and drilling wells in the State is uncontrolled, farmers and other major commercial water users are doing what should be expected: drilling ever deeper into the State's aquifers (a common-access resource), with each party reasoning that the water they obtain will have little if any impact on the State's dwindling water resources. As should have been expected, a tragedy of the commons has emerged: the aquifers are drying up, causing drillers to drill ever deeper and the ground surface to collapse, as much as a foot in some parts of the State (Howard 2014). (See the *New York Times* article on the average American's "contribution to the California drought" in Online Reading 5.1.)

In 2014, when tiered water pricing was introduced in Riverside County, California, water consumption fell by 10–15 percent, and the distribution of the cutbacks were as expected: water users who had used little water reduced their consumption by 5 percent, while those considered "guzzlers" lowered their consumption by 25 percent. People were not willing to pay more for extra water for their lawns (Schwartz 2015). Some demand for water is highly *inelastic* since some of its uses are vital to consumers. But most uses of water are more optional – and at low prices, consumption of water comprises only a small part of the average budget.

Other examples? Because we don't allow the buying and selling of vital organs (and because charitable donations are insufficient to meet demand), we end up with a shortage – and thus thousands of additional people dying every year. And in the realm of business, this concept ably describes what happens when prices are too low or nonexistent. For example, if people can print with no cost to themselves or their department, it's not surprising that there would be "too much" printing. If there is no cost to an individual or a department to using IT services, non-price rationing (usually, lines and delays) should not be a surprising outcome. Sometimes, prices are too difficult (costly) to impose; but other times, some experimentation with prices may be helpful to deal with costly wait times. (In Online Reading 5.2, Michael Munger describes the odd reaction to government-created shortages after a natural disaster.)

---

[2] Environmentalists work to restrict pumps and dams that would allow California to capture rain before it flows back to the ocean.

Price Floors

When producers can get politicians to control prices in their favor, the result is a **price floor** that sets a minimum price above equilibrium, elevating price beyond competitive levels. The result is a surplus – where will-

> A **price floor** is a government-determined, legal minimum price (or wage) below which a specified good or service cannot be bought or sold.

ingness to supply exceeds willingness to purchase. And the usual mechanism of market adjustment (lower prices) is ruled out (at least legally). Although producers are excited about higher prices, they will not enjoy the reduced quantity demanded or the hassles (costs) of dealing with the surplus. But as it turns out, if producers are powerful enough to get their way with prices, they are also able to lobby for complementary policies that resolve the surplus in ways favorable to them.

American farm policy provides a set of classic examples. Price floors in agriculture began during the "New Deal" of the 1930s. And they are accompanied by policies that either increase demand or reduce supply to benefit politically connected producers while eliminating the surpluses. For example, the government purchases the surplus of some crops to store, sell at subsidized rates, or destroy. They pay farmers not to produce ("conservation programs"). They restrict imports from foreign suppliers or they require domestic producers to have a license to sell a crop (tobacco, marijuana, hemp, and peanuts). Of course, all of these policies are harmful to consumers and/or taxpayers – and to the economy in general. (In Chapter 6, we will explain why interest groups are so effective at advocating for their own interests at the expense of others and the country as a whole.)

In the business world, the equivalents of price floors are less common than price ceilings. But, in any context where prices are higher than equilibrium and firms are unable or unwilling to lower the price, the effect is the same. For example, if a firm wants its workers to be healthier than they are choosing to be – for their own good or to lower health insurance premiums – they could lower the cost of being healthy by providing a gym or a cafeteria, or subsidizing gym memberships or healthy food. Setting lower "prices" for these may be helpful to the firm's bottom line.

Sometimes, union-negotiated contracts have the same impact as price controls. As fixed wages, they can act the same as a price floor, a price ceiling, or both at the same time. The wages are set through collective bargaining, but often in a rigid manner that causes surpluses or shortages. For example, in the United States, it is common to read stories about a shortage of K-12 teachers in three fields: Math, Science, and Special Education. As a budding young economist, you know how to fix a shortage – through higher wages – and there is no law preventing wages from rising. K-12 also generally has a surplus of teachers in other fields: say, English, History, and Physical Education. So, the budget implications could be neutral if we had higher wages for Math, Science, and Special Ed. – with lower wages for English, Science, and Phys Ed. Why don't we observe this wage structure? Because the union wants all teachers to be paid the same, regardless of demand and supply in particular fields. We see a similar thing in union shops where everyone gets the same percentage raise, but productivity rises more in some fields, resulting in a surplus in some areas and/or a shortage in others.

Something similar may occur with certain fringe benefits. It's a common problem for workers to want to use vacation (weeks or days) at popular times – and not to use vacation time at less-popular times. The root problem is that the "price" is the same to the employee for using the vacation on any given day. How do firms allocate vacation when they can't offer it to everyone at the same time? Usually by seniority or first come, first serve. An alternative system would involve prices: more vacation offered during less-popular times (perhaps two days for every one "day" of vacation). Again, firms may find it beneficial (and profitable) to experiment with prices and markets.

Minimum Wages

Minimum wages imposed by federal, state, and local levels of government are another popular example of price (wage) floors. The U.S. minimum wage has been raised in a series of nineteen steps from 25 cents per hour when the first federal minimum wage took effect in 1938 to its last increase to $7.25 per hour in 2009. Some states have floors more than double the federal level; five states have no minimum at all, but are still bound by the federal law; most but not all developed countries have minimum wages. Recognizing differences in cost of living, some cities have floors that are still higher; and some states have floors that differ between urban and rural areas.[3] Many policies are "indexed" (adjusted) for the effects of inflation (e.g., income taxes, Social Security payments), but the federal minimum and two-thirds of state floors are not. As such, in constant 2023 dollars, the federal minimum wage rose irregularly from $5.22 per hour in 1938 to an all-time high of $13.55 per hour in 1968 before falling irregularly to its 2023 level of $7.25.

As with other price controls, minimum wages disable the market's ability to clear – and have consequences for employees and employers. In this section,

---

[3] Puerto Rico's history with the minimum wage is noteworthy in this regard. When the federal minimum was first passed, it exceeded Puerto Rico's *average* wage. Recognizing the negative labor market outcomes that would follow, they were given an exemption. With amendments to the 1938 Fair Labor Standards Act, the gap shrunk until it was eliminated in 1987 (Castillo-Freeman and Freeman 1992).

we start with a basic analysis on the effects of the minimum wage on covered labor markets. Then we move to a more sophisticated analysis with employers adjusting compensation, work demands, and the prices of the goods and services they sell.

Consider Figure 5.5, which depicts demand and supply for low-skilled labor. The upward-sloping curve that represents the supply of labor implies that the wage must be raised in order to attract additional workers. The downward-sloping demand curve implies that employers will hire more workers (everything else remaining constant) at a lower wage. There are several reasons for this. First, profit-maximizing employers will tend to expand production until the marginal contribution of additional workers begins to diminish, which implies that their worth (in terms of productivity) will become progressively less.[4] When the wage rate falls, employers can hire more of these workers. Second, lower wages can inspire substitution of low-skilled workers for other resources used in production, such as higher-skilled workers and equipment. Third, a decline in the wage rate implies lower costs – and thus prices – for the goods and services produced by the firms. This can inspire more sales and lead to a greater need for workers to satisfy the additional quantity demanded.

If the market is competitive and free of government intervention, the wage rate will settle at the intersection of the supply and demand curves (W_0). A wage above W_0 would indicate that there are more workers seeking jobs than jobs available, so competition would push the wage down. A wage below W_0 would imply that there are more jobs than workers willing to work, causing upward pressure on the wage.

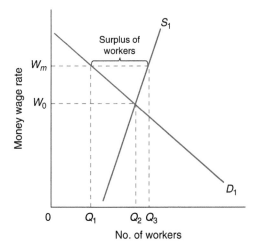

Figure 5.5 The standard view of the impact of the minimum wage

When the minimum wage is set at W_m (above the market-clearing wage of W_0), employment will fall from Q_2 to Q_1; simultaneously, the number of workers who are willing to work in this labor market will expand from Q_2 to Q_3. The market surplus (unemployment) is then $Q_3 - Q_1$.

---

[4] This is called the "law of diminishing marginal returns" – a cousin of the "law of diminished marginal utility" (from Chapter 4) – which we will develop in Chapter 7.

Suppose, however, that politicians consider W_0 too low to provide a decent living and pass a law requiring employers to pay no less than W_m. The policy is often promoted as helping people without any mention of job loss. (It's telling that the law is not usually described as "making it more costly to hire less-skilled workers.") But the law reduces employment because, in the face of limited worker productivity and higher costs, employers cannot afford to employ as many people. The quantity of labor demanded falls from Q_2 to Q_1. Those who manage to keep their jobs will be better off. But others will no longer have jobs or will work in legal or illegal labor markets not covered by the minimum. With a higher minimum wage, more workers enter the labor force and are willing to work. (Labor supply turns out to be inelastic, so this effect is relatively small.) Workers who had jobs paying W_0 now have fewer opportunities at W_m and must compete with an influx of other workers.

Economists also anticipate several other effects. By increasing unemployment, minimum-wage laws increase the number of people receiving public assistance and unemployment compensation. The laws may also account for increases in some criminal activity, because the unemployed who lack opportunities in the legitimate labor market may see crime as an alternative form of employment. With the larger labor pool that develops when the minimum wage increases, competition for jobs is also likely to increase discrimination (on the basis of sex, race, religion, etc.) by artificially creating a labor surplus that lowers the effective cost of discrimination (Williams 2005).

There are other troubling costs of the minimum wage. Its harms are often imposed on struggling people, when public policy usually tries to help them. Its harms are imposed on the stated beneficiaries; the policy helps some people in group X by harming other people in group X. Any unemployment is a reduced opportunity to obtain experience and training that would be a common avenue to higher future productivity and earnings. And the policy is poorly targeted – aiming at the relative handful of workers trying to raise a family on the minimum wage, but imposing costs and benefits on the far-wider range of workers who earn the minimum (e.g., teenagers). In contrast, a policy like the Earned Income Credit gets additional resources to the targeted population without making it more expensive to hire them.

Political Support

Why do minimum-wage laws attract so much political support? Part of the reason may be that the general public is largely unaware of their negative effects. Many forces operate on labor markets, making it almost impossible for the average person to single out the effects of one law. The people who retain their jobs at the higher wage are visible members of the workforce; those who lose their jobs are less visible. Those who bear most of the burden of these laws – young, relatively unproductive workers – are perhaps least likely to understand the negative effects and many are not old enough to vote.

Another reason is that many people benefit from the laws – most notably, those who retain their jobs and receive higher paychecks. College students are generally more productive than less-educated members of their generation and less likely to lose entry-level jobs because of the minimum wage. Labor unions also have an incentive to support wage floors since they put them in a better bargaining position when the government raises wages in nonunion sectors of the economy. Union wage demands are not as likely to prompt employers to move into nonunionized sectors of the economy, as nonunion and less-skilled workers may substitute (at some ratio) for union workers.

Interestingly, the *New York Times* editorial board has reversed itself several times since the first federal minimum wage was enacted in the late 1930s. The *New York Times* board was solidly against the initial proposal because they feared it was a means to put down "Blacks," especially in the South, who would not be able to compete with "Whites" if their wages were equalized.[5] In the 1950s, the editorial board endorsed minimum-wage increases, a position they reversed in 1987 with a dramatic editorial title: "The right minimum wage: $0.00." (See Online Reading 5.3 for a link to the editorial.) Since the turn of the twenty-first century, the editors have strongly favored minimum-wage hikes at all levels of government, making a strong plea for a hike in 2015. (See Online Reading 5.4 for a link to the editorial.)

Beyond the Basic Analysis

Because it focuses on only one variable (wages), the basic analysis misses several important points. The upshot of a more sophisticated analysis is that modest increases in the minimum wage will not help the targeted workers much or lead to substantial adverse employment effects in most low-skilled labor markets, because firms will make adjustments in other variables. This helps to explain why empirical studies have generally found only a modest impact on unemployment in the relevant labor markets.[6]

---

[5] As was argued by the editors of the *New York Times* in 1937, the first minimum wage retarded the exodus of firms and jobs to the nonunionized South from the unionized North. The introduction of the minimum wage reduced the net benefit of moving south (McKenzie 1994). This was an *explicit* aim of wage floors in some trades for public works projects – called the Davis-Bacon Act at the federal level and "prevailing-wage laws" at the state level – also starting in the 1930s (U.S. Congressional Record, 1931).

[6] For a survey of the literature, see: Peterson and Stewart (1969, 151–155); Kosters and Welch (1972); Ragan (1977); Brown, Gilroy, and Kohen (1982); Card and Krueger (1995); and Neumark and Wascher (2008).

First, consider that the minimum wage is often irrelevant to market conditions. It does not cover every sector of the labor market. And, often, it is set below market equilibrium. In markets for more-skilled labor (e.g., doctors, engineers, professors), it is not meant to be relevant. But even with less-skilled labor, the wage control may still not be above market wages. This happens because inflation, productivity gains, and market conditions all serve to increase nominal wages above the floor. (The federal minimum has been the same since 2009 and costs of living vary widely within the U.S.) When this is the case, the minimum wage is "ineffective" – having no effect (for good or for ill) on a labor market. (That said, we've been assuming – and will continue to assume – an *effective* minimum wage for the rest of this discussion.)

Second, it turns out to be difficult to measure the impact of a higher minimum wage on employment; the cause/effect is much more convoluted than would be ideal. If the minimum wage increases on April 1, firms don't fire a bunch of workers that day. They would let them go before/after the increase and they would reduce their hiring over many months. And many variables impact labor markets all the time. Our ability to estimate the impact of one variable in a complex system is limited. Finally, firms might reduce hours instead of workers, increasing *underemployment* but not unemployment – and unemployed workers might leave the labor force (and thus not be counted as unemployed).

Third, firms may adjust by increasing prices in the face of higher costs. If costs are higher across an industry that has relatively few substitutes (consumers have inelastic demand), then firms could pass most of their higher costs to consumers in the form of higher prices – and not need to reduce output or release workers. This is akin to our analysis of the burden of taxation in Figures 5.1 and 5.2 – not surprising, since the minimum wage is, in essence, a tax on less-skilled workers.

Fourth, minimum-wage laws establish a legal floor for *money wages*; they do not, however, suppress competitive pressures outside of money wages. More to the point, they do not set a legal minimum for the *effective wage* paid to workers (including the money and nonmoney benefits of employment). The basic analysis of minimum-wage laws, in many economics textbooks, implicitly assumes that money wages are the only form of labor compensation. But the employer may adjust the nonmoney conditions of work or fringe benefits in response to a mandated pay hike.[7] Employers can be expected to reduce their labor costs in these

---

[7] Few minimum-wage jobs have prominent fringe benefits such as medical insurance and retirement plans. However, most firms offer some fringe benefits: conditions in the work environment, attitudes of bosses, breaks, frequency and promptness of pay, variety of work, uniforms, use of company tools and supplies, meals and drinks, flexible hours, discounts on company goods and services, and greater precautions against accidents. These fringe benefits are subject to withdrawal when minimum wages are mandated.

ways until the worker surplus vanishes.[8] (The basic analysis may still be fully applicable to labor markets in which money is the only form of compensation and employers can do little to change production demands on workers.) Further, employers in competitive product markets *must* adjust to survive. Otherwise, other firms will lower their labor costs and prices, eliminating employers who retain fringe benefits and continue to pay the higher wage rate.[9]

The net effect – pushing pay from nonmonetary compensation to wages – would be expected to be negative, since it takes markets away from an equilibrium that workers and firms were choosing voluntarily. All of this leads to the conclusion that the effective wage rate of *all* workers decreases, including those who retain their jobs despite minimum wages; they are worse off to the extent that employers can adjust working conditions and fringe benefits. For this reason, minimum wages appear patently unfair to those who are covered by them – even by the standards of many of those who promote the laws.

Key econometric studies on the effects of the minimum wage are briefly reviewed in Online Reading 5.5. These studies have been trying to assess the consequences of relatively modest minimum-wage increases – not the major increases recently passed in some cities and states. Inflation and Covid-inspired labor market changes may mitigate the effects of these laws as well. But the employment effects of major minimum-wage hikes could be far greater for three reasons. First, they would affect a greater range of workers within a community. Second, since they are only local or state laws, employers could adjust by moving out of the city or state. Third, it's possible that employers will have already exhausted the nonmoney ways to offset the money-wage increases, so the only remaining avenue may be reduced employment.

Fringe Benefits, Incentives, and Profits

Varying the form of pay is a way for firms to motivate workers and overcome the Prisoner's Dilemma problems described earlier. Worker pay can range from simple cash to deferred compensation and an assortment of fringe benefits. But it is noteworthy that workers tend to think and talk about fringe benefits in remarkably different terms than their wages: They "earn" their wages, but often talk about fringe benefits as if employers "give" them. "Our bosses *give* us three

---

[8] More precisely, the labor markets should, after adjustments, clear more or less to the same extent as they did before the minimum-wage law was imposed. Of course, employers are not directly concerned with ensuring that their labor market clears. But they are interested in minimizing their labor costs – a motivation that drives them to adjust the conditions of work until the market clears.

[9] It is possible that a labor market is not competitive – a topic we will detail in Chapter 12.

weeks of paid vacation per year, 30 minutes of coffee breaks per day, flexible schedules, and discounts on purchases of company goods. And we pay for some of it, but they also give us medical and dental insurance." Wages are the result of hard work, but fringe benefits are thought to be a matter of employer generosity. Wages come from the revenues that workers add to the bottom line, but fringe benefits are implicitly assumed to come from a different source.

Employers use some of the same language and their answers are also misleading. They inevitably talk in terms of the cost of their fringe benefits. "Would you believe that the annual cost of health insurance to our firm is $21,000 per employee? We spend millions each year for employee health insurance. Our total fringe benefit package is 36.4 percent of our total wage bill!" The point (often left unstated) seems to be: "Aren't we nice?"

Our argument here will require readers to set aside any preconceived view that fringe benefits are a gift. We will use *marginal* analysis of fringe benefits – the marginal (or added) cost and the marginal (or added) value of successive units provided. As before, employer profits and employee well-being can be increased as long as the marginal value of doing something is greater than the marginal cost. This principle implies that a decrease in the cost of any fringe benefit to firms or an increase in its value to workers can lead to more of it being provided.

Workers as Profit Centers

We don't want to be overly crass in our view of business, but we want to be realistic. As such, we surmise that most firms provide their workers with fringe benefits for the same reason they hire workers: *to add more to their profits than if they didn't*. Like it or not, most firms are in the business of making money off their employees – in all kinds of ways – and employees are trying to maximize utility (including compensation) through their work. If firms don't provide their workers with a given fringe benefit, it's because they can't add to profits by doing so and workers don't value it enough.

When making decisions on fringe benefits, employers face two unavoidable *economic* realities. First, fringe benefits are costly (and some, such as health insurance, are extraordinarily expensive). Second, there are limits to the value that workers place on such benefits. Workers value many things – and what they buy, whether directly from vendors or indirectly through their employers, is largely dependent on cost.

Workers will *buy* fringe benefits from an employer when the value they place on the benefits exceeds their cost to the firm. When this condition holds, firms can make money by "selling" benefits (e.g., health insurance) to their workers. Of course, most firms don't send salespeople around the office to sell health insurance or weeks of vacation to their employees as they sell food in the company cafeteria (another benefit). But they nevertheless engage in trade with employees. How? If workers value a particular benefit, then firms that provide it will see an increase in the supply of labor available to them. They will be able to hire more workers at a lower wage and/or be able to increase the "quality" (productivity) of the workers hired.

The Supply and Demand for Fringe Benefits

A simple graph using supply and demand displays the labor market effects of fringe benefits with greater clarity. In Figure 5.6, D_1 and S_1 reflect a circumstance in which no fringe benefit is provided. Without the fringe benefit, the workers will receive a wage rate of W_1, where the market clears. Now consider the simplest case: The firm's cost of providing a fringe benefit is a uniform amount for each worker; each worker values the benefit equally; and its provision has no impact on worker productivity. Adding a fringe benefit, the demand curve drops down vertically by the per-worker cost of the benefit from D_1 to D_2; the vertical drop (*ab*) equals the added cost of the fringe. Firms are not willing to pay as high a wage if they cover the cost of the benefit. On the other hand, the supply of workers shifts outward, from S_1 to S_2, because the firm is now more attractive to workers because of the benefit, leading more workers to apply. The vertical difference between S_1 and S_2 (*cd*) represents how much each worker values the benefit and is willing to reduce her wage rate to obtain it; this vertical difference is a money measure of the benefit's value to workers.

What happens, given these shifts in supply and demand? The wage falls from W_1 to W_2, but nonwage compensation is higher. Are workers and firms better off? Figure 5.6 shows that more workers are employed (Q_2 instead of Q_1), suggesting something good has happened. (Otherwise, we must wonder why firms would want to hire more workers and why more workers would be willing

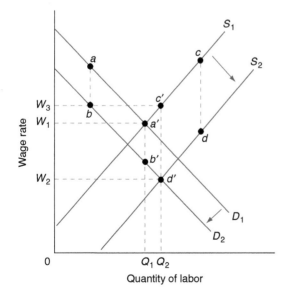

Figure 5.6 Fringe benefits and the labor market
If fringe benefits are more valuable to workers than the cost to an employer, the supply of labor will increase from S_1 to S_2 while the demand curve falls from D_1 to D_2. The wage rate falls from W_1 to W_2, but the workers get fringe benefits with a value of $c'd'$, which means their overall payment goes up from W_1 to W_3.

to be employed!) Firms and workers are better off when both sides agree to more work.

Notice that the total cost of the benefit, the vertical distance between the two demand curves ($a'b'$), is less than the reductions in the wage ($W_1 - W_2$). So, we can draw two inferences. First, the firm's total cost per worker falls ($W_2 + a'b'$), which explains why the firm is willing to expand its hires. Second, while workers accept a lower wage rate (W_2 instead of W_1), they gain the value of the benefit (the vertical distance cd). The sum of the new lower wage and the value of the benefit is W_3, which is higher than the wage without the benefit. Both sides gain.

Finally, extending this from an employer to the market: if providing desirable and inexpensive fringe benefits is advantageous to one firm in a competitive market, it will be advantageous to all firms. All firms in the market can be expected to provide benefits for offensive and defensive reasons: offensive because firms can add to their profits; and defensive because failure will put them at a competitive disadvantage in attracting workers and containing labor costs. The converse is true as well. If the cost of a benefit to firms is greater than its value to workers (ab would be greater than cd in Figure 5.6), the benefit should not be provided since both sides (workers and owners) would lose. (To see this point, try drawing a graph with the vertical drop in the demand greater than the outward shift of the supply.)[10]

Optimum Fringe Benefits

How much of the fringe benefit should be provided? Given the variation of business and market circumstances, we can only use a generally applicable rule: expand the benefit as long as the *marginal cost is less than the marginal reduction in their wage bill and the workers' evaluation of the marginal increase in the benefit.* For example, the number of paid vacation days should be extended as long as the value that workers place on additional vacation days is greater than the marginal cost to the employer of providing the additional days. As additional

---

[10] Firms that persist in providing such benefits will have difficulty competing because their cost structure will be higher. Such firms would be subject to friendly takeovers because those bidding for the firm would be able to pay a higher price for the stock than the going market price (depressed because the fringe benefits were not profitable). After acquiring control, the new owners could eliminate the excessively costly benefits (or reduce them to profitable levels), enhance the firm's profitability and competitive position, and then sell the firm's stock at a price higher than the purchase price. Workers would support such a takeover because they could see two advantages: They could have a benefit eliminated that is not worth what they pay in terms of lower wages. They could also gain employment security, given the improved competitive position of their firm. Of course, a firm is unlikely to be taken over because of its failure to provide one efficiency-enhancing fringe benefit. But when enough of these mistakes are made, the inefficiency mounts, increasing the chance that the firm will be a takeover target. (We will expand our discussion of takeovers in Part B of Chapter 11.)

vacation days are added, worker value of each additional day will fall and costs to the firm will likely rise. A point will be reached beyond which the additional cost of the next vacation day will exceed its marginal value (the possible reduction in the wage bill). At this point, employers have maximized their profit from "selling" the benefit to their workers.

Of course, tax rules affect the ideal amounts (and types) of benefits. Since most fringe benefits (most notably, health insurance) are not subject to taxation, employees will often want firms to provide more of them than otherwise, simply because a reduction in worker taxes will partially cover the cost of the benefit.[11] (We show this using indifference curves and budget constraints in the Online Math Appendix.) And some benefits can be less expensive when bought in bulk by firms, achieving economies of scale. (Again, health insurance is an excellent example.) The result may well be that workers actually get more of the benefit than they could if they were covering the cost themselves. Employers must provide such benefits; otherwise, they will lose employees or fail to keep their compensation costs competitive with those of rival companies.

Another consideration is the use of specific fringe benefits to act as (legal and inexpensive) screening devices to attract certain types of employees or to influence employee behavior on matters related to costs and productivity. For example, a discount on pet store products will attract pet owners to work for you. Tuition reimbursement will attract younger workers who are interested in improvement through education. Firms may provide amenities that are generally attractive to families. Firms may offer gym memberships or healthy food options at work – attractive to more-active people and a way to encourage healthy lifestyles. And so on.

Managers are well advised to search earnestly for the optimal combination (likely through some experimentation), even though the process of finding an optimum is never precise. One example is seeking ways to eliminate redundancy in health insurance coverage for employees when both spouses work and have insurance as a fringe benefit. The redundancy is an unfortunate drag on their wage earnings. Firms that can address this problem will be more attractive to employees. Another example: One local company (to Schansberg) offers first-class airline seats on international trips. This is itself a fringe benefit, but they also offer the additional benefit of a sizable cash payment if the employee switches to coach. The cash is cheaper to the employer and offers an opportunity for an employee to make more money. Think creatively – and as in Chapter 1, provide "property rights" to decision-making and resources when you can.

---

[11] The subsidy of health insurance causes profound distortions in the markets for healthcare and health insurance. For discussion of this and many other government policies that impact these markets, see: Schansberg (2011, 2014).

Firms that come closest to an optimum will provide their employees the greatest compensation for the money spent, will have the lowest cost structure, and be the most competitive. By trying to make as much money as possible *with* their employees, firms stay more competitive and also benefit their workers.

Fringe Benefits Provided by Large and Small Firms

We can now understand why many large firms provide their employees with health insurance and many small firms do not. For example, large firms can buy/ sell a large number of health insurance policies, achieving economies associated with scale and spreading risks. This is a widely recognized answer.

At another level, the answer is more complicated and obscure. "Small" and "large" firms do not generally hire from the same labor markets. Small firms tend to provide lower-paying jobs. Workers in lower-paying jobs within small firms don't have the means to buy many things that workers in larger firms have, including health insurance. Given their limited income, workers don't think insurance is a good deal and prefer to buy other things with higher monetary compensation. One of the reasons that low-income workers may gravitate to small firms is that they want to avoid giving up wages to buy insurance because of company policies that apply to all workers.

Of course, the analysis gets even trickier considering that lower-income workers, many of whom work for small firms, tend to be younger people – who also tend to be healthier and prefer a different combination of fringe benefits than older workers. The young can appreciate that the price they would have to pay for health insurance through firms is inflated by older workers. (We'll discuss this further in Online Reading 7.2.)

In any case, this section has led to a clear conclusion: workers pay for what they get. They may not hand over a check for fringe benefits, but they give up the money nonetheless through a reduction in pay. If workers didn't give up anything for the fringe benefit, we would have to conclude that it was not worth anything to the workers. This would mean that employers would cover the full cost of the fringe benefit, adding to their costs without getting anything for it. Workers should not want that to happen – if for no other reason than that the company's future and their job security would be threatened.

Critics might argue that managers don't know that certain fringe benefits are "good" for business and their workers. This is often the case, and the history of business is strewn with the corpses of firms that failed to serve the interests of their workers and customers – who were forced into bankruptcy by other firms who were better at finding the best way to increase value at lower cost, including the right combination of fringe benefits. The market is a powerful, though imperfect, educational system. If the critics really know better than existing firms, they can make tons of money by doing it better themselves.

We think that workers and owners should talk as frankly about fringe benefits as they do about their wages. Workers earn their wages. The same is true for fringe benefits. No gift is involved. As long as it's voluntary, both wages and fringe benefits represent mutually beneficial exchanges between workers and their firms.

PERSPECTIVE 5
Maslow's "Hierarchy of Needs" and Contrasting Views on Human (and Economic) Choices

Business students rarely make it through their programs without encountering Maslow's "Hierarchy of Needs" in several of their courses, most notably in marketing.[12] A. H. Maslow, a psychologist, argued that basic human needs can be specified with reasonable clarity and can be ranked according to their importance in providing motivation and influencing behavior (Maslow 1954, primarily chapter 5). Embedded in Maslow's hierarchy is a theory of human behavior that is somewhat foreign to the economist's way of thinking. In this Perspective, we will see how to apply supply and demand curve analysis to the development of any "hierarchy of needs." This analysis will help us understand differences between economic and psychological approaches to welfare enhancement.

Maslow's "Hierarchy of Needs"
Maslow's hierarchy is shown in Figure 5.7. The importance of "needs" – in terms of how powerful they are in affecting human behavior – ascends as one moves downward through the pyramid. The most fundamental (physiological) needs are at the bottom, including all attempts by the body to maintain basic chemical balances (such as water, oxygen, and hydrogen ion levels) – and beyond that, desires for food, sex, sleep, sensory pleasures, etc. Next in importance, the need for safety may include the desires of the individual for security, order, protection, and family stability. The next category (belongingness and love) includes desires for companionship, acceptance, affection, etc. Under the heading of esteem, Maslow lists the desire for achievement, adequacy, reputation, dominance, recognition, attention, appreciation, and importance. Finally, he argues that self-actualization "refers to man's desire for self-fulfillment, namely, to the tendency that might be phrased as the desire to become more and more what one is, to become everything that one is capable of becoming" (Maslow 1954, 90–92).

---

[12] AIDA (attention, interest, desire, action) is a prominent model in marketing related to Maslow's hierarchy. At the least, it is implicit that marketing efforts should be tailored to the (perceived) needs of consumers and that consumers and goods/services can be segmented accordingly.

Figure 5.7 Maslow's "Hierarchy of Needs"
The pyramid orders human needs using broad categories from the most important needs on the bottom through to less important needs at the top. According to Maslow, an individual can be expected to satisfy her needs in order of importance, moving from the bottom of the pyramid through the various levels to the top, subject to the individual's resource constraints.

Maslow specifies this particular ranking because it appeared to be descriptive of his associates, in line with his survey of a few dozen people, and generally applicable to human motivation.[13] Although he qualifies his argument, the core proposition in Maslow's theory of human behavior is that a person will first satisfy her most basic (physiological) needs before she attempts to satisfy higher-order needs.[14]

If all the needs are unsatisfied, the organism is then dominated by the physiological needs, all other needs may become simply nonexistent or be pushed into the background. It is then fair to characterize the whole organism by saying simply it is hungry, for consciousness is almost completely preempted by hunger. All capacities are put into the service of hunger satisfaction, and the organization of these capacities is almost entirely determined by the one purpose of satisfying hunger .... Capacities that are not useful for this purpose lie dormant, or are pushed into the background (Maslow 1954, 92).

---

[13] Maslow does not hold rigidly to this ordering of needs. Because of cultural or environmental factors – or because, for example, love has been denied in the past – some people may place more emphasis on esteem needs than the need for love. Maslow also reasons that: "There are other apparently innately creative people in whom the drive to creativeness seems to be more important than any other counter-determinant" (Maslow 1954, 98). He also imagines needs beyond the five categories (e.g., to understand or for aesthetic quality), which can be handled by adding more tiers. In addition, Maslow argues that certain preconditions, such as the freedom to express oneself, are necessary before basic needs can be satisfied.

[14] Maslow argues that an individual may indicate she is striving for one need when in fact she is pursuing something else. For example, the individual may express hunger to acquire companionship, affection, and attention – because she may find it useful to deceive another person or she does not consciously know her true motivation.

If the most basic needs are satisfied, "At once other (and higher) needs emerge and these, rather than physiological hungers, dominate the organism. And when these in turn are satisfied, again new (and still higher) needs emerge, and so on" (Maslow 1954, 92). One often gets the impression in reading Maslow that the individual will not attempt to satisfy a higher need until the more-important (lower) need has been satisfied – or at least, "fairly well gratified" (Maslow 1954, 89). In any case, he does not explain why this would be the case – what would keep the individual from fully satisfying any given need level before moving to a higher tier or why a person would not fully satisfy the higher needs before he moves to the next tier.[15]

Economics and Maslow's Hierarchy

Maslow's approach to human motivation and behavior resembles the approach of economists in several respects. First, at the foundation of both theories is an assumption that the individual is able to rank all of her wants (or needs) according to their importance to her. In the Maslow system, needs are ranked according to how close they are to a basic need. The economist starts with the simpler assumption that the individual knows what she wants and can rank all possible goods and services that can satisfy her wants.

The two approaches are dissimilar when it comes to specifying the ranking. Maslow argues that the basic needs and their ranking can generally be identified; that is, he can say what *all* individuals need and is willing to venture a statement about their relative importance. Economists take the position that the relative importance of needs varies so much from person to person that a hierarchy of needs does not take us very far in our understanding of human behavior. Economists assume that more of an economic good is preferred to less, but are unwilling to say exactly where the good may lie on some relative scale. Maslow saw this specificity as a useful basis to predict human behavior. Economists believe they can say a great deal about human behavior without specifying the relative importance of the things people want.

---

[15] Or the explanations are *ad hoc*: "So far, our theoretical discussions may have given the impression that these five sets of needs are somehow in such terms as the following: if one need is satisfied, then another emerges. This statement might give the false impression that a need must be satisfied 100 percent before the next need emerges. In actual *fact*, most members of our society who are normal are partially satisfied in all their basic needs and partially unsatisfied in all their basic needs at the same time. A more realistic description of the hierarchy would be in terms of decreasing percentages of satisfaction as we go up the hierarchy of prepotency. For instance ... it is as if the average citizen is satisfied 85 percent in his physiological needs, 70 percent in his safety needs, 50 percent in his love needs, 40 percent in his self-esteem needs, and 10 percent in his self-actualization needs (Maslow 1954, 100–101, emphasis in the original). Maslow also allows that tiers can be skipped entirely, given insurmountable environmental or physiological barriers.

The two systems are similar to the extent that they view the individual as consuming those things that provide the most satisfaction. The Maslow system lacks a direct statement to this effect, but there is the implicit assumption that the individual is a *utility maximizer*. Maslow also implicitly assumes "diminishing marginal utility" as more of the need is consumed; this explains how the individual can become satisfied ("fairly well gratified") at each tier.

The two systems are different because of their views on the constraints that impinge on the individual's ability to maximize her utility. The constraints in the Maslow hierarchy include environmental and cultural factors and the individual's character (her beliefs about right and wrong). There is no mention in Maslow of the individual's productive ability, income, or the costs attached to fulfilling her basic needs. By not considering cost, Maslow implicitly assumes no cost to need gratification or that cost is irrelevant (the demand curve for any need is vertical and perfectly inelastic).[16] In contrast, these considerations are crucial constraints in the economist's view of human behavior.

The Relevance of Demand

An economist might concede for purposes of argument that the demand for a physiological need is greater (and the demand less responsive to price changes) than a safety need, a love need, and so on. But it does not follow that the love need will be less fulfilled than safety or physiological needs. The extent to which different needs are gratified also depends on the costs (prices) of the means for satisfying needs and how people respond to changes in prices.

If the cost of satisfying each need is the same, the individual will consume more of the means of satisfying his physiological need. But if there are more physiological needs to be met, the *percentage* of the needs gratified may not be greater. Moreover, it is doubtful that the costs of satisfying the different needs are the same. The availability and costs of the resources required to satisfy the different needs can easily be different. If the costs of fulfilling the physiological needs are substantially greater, the percentage of the physiological needs fulfilled would be even less.

Maslow claimed that people fulfill a higher percentage of their physiological needs than of other needs. Our line of argument suggests that this could be the case because the price of physiological need fulfillment is lower than the prices of fulfilling the other needs. In any case, the point to make is that a change in prices (costs) can bring about a change in the extent of need gratification at each level. In such an event, a good definition of what may be considered "normal"

---

[16] An implied assumption of the vertical demand curve is that the needs are independent of one another; they cannot be substitutes. For example, in the Maslow system, a unit of an esteem need fulfilled does not seem to take the place of even a small fraction of a physiological need.

in terms of need gratification should be reconsidered. People's behavior need not have changed in any fundamental sense; they may merely be responding to different prices while their preferences remain the same.

To summarize, from the economist's way of thinking, people don't move up some consumption pyramid in the manner described by Maslow's hierarchy. Rather, they weigh the relative marginal values of all sorts of goods and services. How satiated people are in the consumption of *any* set of goods (wants, needs) is dependent on preferences for the goods, income, *and* relative prices.

Part B Organizational Economics and Management

In Part A of this chapter, we used supply and demand curves to gain insights about various government and firm policies. In this Part B, we apply concepts from "organizational economics" to show how markets and incentives can promote "values" – morality, honesty, integrity, etc. – that are normally considered to be matters of ethics and philosophy, not economics. As we will see, honesty and trust can affect business costs and market share, which means they can affect supply and demand, the intensity of competition, and the efficiency of markets. (Food for thought: Why are people typically nice and helpful to us in markets? Among other reasons, such behaviors could be driven by love of others or a desire to make money.)

How Honesty Can Pay in Business

It is a popular perception that business is full of dishonest scoundrels – especially high-ranking executives – who lie, cheat, and steal to increase profits. This perception is reflected and reinforced by the way people in business are depicted in the media and movies. No one can deny that people in business have done all kinds of nasty things for a buck, but the impression of pervasive dishonesty is probably exaggerated. If people in business are about as dishonest as other people, they might *behave* more dishonestly because there's more to gain (at least in some contexts). Or they might behave *more* honestly because they find it profitable to engage in (and "sell") honest behavior.

We have no keen insights into the virtue of those in business (or anyone else). But we do know one simple but powerful fact about human behavior: people respond to incentives in predictable ways. In particular, as the personal cost of dishonesty decreases, we expect more dishonesty. If people in business act honestly to an unusual degree, it is probably because they expect to pay a high price for behaving dishonestly. In fact, people in business have often found, somewhat paradoxically, that they can increase profits by accepting institutional and contractual arrangements that impose large losses on them if they are dishonest.

Those in business who attempt to profit from dishonest dealing face the fact that few people are naively trusting, certainly when you have taken advantage of their trust. Perhaps it is possible to profit from dishonesty in the short run, but it will be increasingly difficult to get people to deal with you in the long run. People in business, therefore, have an incentive to act with integrity – and a strong motivation to put themselves in situations in which their own dishonest behavior would be penalized. Only by doing so can they provide *potential* customers, workers, and investors with the assurance of the honest dealing required for those people to become *actual* customers, workers, and investors.

Consider this illustration: Mary has a well-maintained older-model Honda Accord that she is willing to sell for as little as $7000. If interested buyers know the car is well maintained, they will be willing to pay as much as $8000 for it. Therefore, a wealth-increasing exchange is likely, because any price between $7000 and $8000 will result in the car being transferred to someone who values it more than the existing owner. But there is a wrinkle here: asymmetric information and the so-called "lemon problem."

Many owners are selling their cars *because* their cars have not been well maintained and are at risk of serious mechanical problems. Let's assume that 75 percent of the used Honda Accords being sold are in such poor condition that a fully informed buyer would only be willing to pay $4000. The remaining 25 percent of these cars on the market (those that can be trusted) are worth $8000. This means that a buyer with no information on the condition of a car for sale would expect a same-year Honda Accord to be worth, on average, only $5000 (0.75 × $4000 + 0.25 × $8000). But if buyers are willing to pay only $5000, the sellers whose cars are in good condition will refuse to sell, such as Mary.

So, the mix of used Accords for sale will tilt more in the direction of poorly maintained cars; their expected value will decline further; and even fewer well-maintained Accords will be sold. This situation is often described as a market for "lemons" (the dominance of low-quality goods in a market) and illustrates the value of sellers being able to commit themselves to honesty (Akerlof 1970). Interestingly, the lack of trust is a problem for both buyers and (good) sellers. If Mary could somehow convince potential buyers of her honesty (and her Accord's good condition), she would be better off, along with those looking for a good used car. The advantage of being able to commit to honesty in business extends to any situation in which it is difficult for buyers to determine the quality of what they are buying.

The "lemon problem" is also an opportunity to profit for entrepreneurs who can solve it: Good cars are being undervalued and bad cars are being fraudulently bought. In our example, the amount of money (and value) on the table from the development of solutions is impressive. Mary might not receive the full price of $8000, but even $7500 would make her and the buyer happy.[17]

In fact, various entrepreneurs have largely solved the "lemon problem" in the market for cars (Lott 2007). Car manufacturers and new car dealers offer multiyear warranties, the balance of which can be transferred to used-car buyers. Used-car dealers may offer warranties – for an added price, of course. Nationwide used-car dealers, such as CarMax, carefully scrutinize the cars they buy and offer warranties. The reputation of these sellers is another check on poor behavior. Those who buy from individuals often check on the trustworthiness of car sellers (giving preference to friends and family who will bear personal costs if their promises don't pan out) and check the car's records through CarFax. Prospective buyers can have cars evaluated by mechanics. Lott found that "new" used cars (less than a year old with an average of 3340 miles) sold for practically the same as the Kelley Blue Book prices for new cars. For cars with fewer than 15,000 miles and less than a year old, the depreciation in price was no more than 4 percent. Older cars sold for much less, but the depreciation in prices can easily be chalked up to – well, depreciation. (For more discussion of this, see Online Reading 5.6.)

Game Theory (Again): Games of Trust

The advantages of honesty in business and the problem of trying to provide credible assurances of honesty can also be illustrated as a game. In Table 5.1, we present a payoff matrix for a buyer and a seller, giving the consequences from different choice combinations. The first number in each cell of the bracket is the payoff to the seller; the second number is the payoff to the buyer. If the seller is honest (the quality of the product is as high as he claims) and the buyer trusts the seller (she pays the high-quality price), then both realize a payoff of 100. If the seller is honest but the buyer does not trust him, then no exchange takes place and both receive a payoff of zero. If the seller is dishonest while the buyer is trusting, then the seller captures a payoff of 150, while the buyer gets the sucker's payoff of –50. Finally, if the seller is dishonest and the buyer does not trust him, then an exchange takes place with the buyer paying a price that reflects the lower quality of the product – with both seller and buyer receiving a payoff of 25.

---

[17] The value gained from the market's perspective is $3000. For example, with a price of $7500, Mary gains $2500 over what she could sell in the market struggling with the lemon problem. And the buyer would have paid as much as $8000. Only paying $7500 results in a $500 gain in "consumer surplus."

Table 5.1 **The problem of trust in business**

		Buyer	
		Trust	Doesn't trust
Seller	Honest	(100, 100)	(0, 0)
	Dishonest	(150, −50)	(25, 25)

Table 5.2 **The problem of trust in business (again)**

		Buyer	
		Trust	Doesn't trust
Seller	Honest	(100, 100)	(0, 0)
	Dishonest	(50, −50)	(25, 25)

From a joint perspective, honesty and trust are the best choices because this combination results in more wealth for the two to share. But this will not likely be the outcome, given the incentives created by the payoffs in Table 5.1. The buyer will not trust the seller. The buyer knows that if her trust of the seller is taken for granted by the seller, he will attempt to capture the largest possible payoff by acting dishonestly. On the other hand, if the seller believes that the buyer does not trust him, his highest payoff is still realized by acting dishonestly. So the buyer will reasonably expect the seller to act dishonestly. This is a *self-fulfilling expectation*: when the seller doesn't expect to be trusted, his best response is to act dishonestly.

The seller (and buyer) would clearly be better off in this situation if he created an arrangement that reduced the payoff from acting dishonestly. If, for example, the seller only received a payoff of 50 from acting dishonestly when the buyer trusted him, as shown in Table 5.2, then the buyer (assuming she knows of the arrangement) can trust the seller to respond honestly to her commitment to buy. The seller's commitment to honesty allows both seller and buyer to realize a payoff of 100 rather than the 25 they each receive without the commitment. But how can a seller commit himself to honesty in a way that is convincing to buyers? What kinds of arrangements can sellers establish that penalize them if they attempt to profit through dishonesty at the expense of customers?

As one would expect, business practices that can cause sellers to commit to honest dealing are varied, because the ways a seller can profit from dishonest activity also vary. Notice that our discussion of the situation described in

Table 5.1 implicitly assumes that the buyer and seller deal with each other only once. This is clearly a situation in which the temptation for the seller to cheat the buyer is the strongest, because the immediate gain from dishonesty will not be offset by a loss of future business from a mistreated buyer. If a significant amount of repeat business is possible, then the temptation to cheat decreases and may disappear altogether. One answer is to promote repeat business where somewhat-frequent purchases are feasible.

If this is not possible, one way for sellers to attempt to move from the situation described in Table 5.1 to the one described in Table 5.2 is by demonstrating that they are in business for the long run. For example, selling out of a permanent building with the seller's name or logo on it, rather than on a street corner, informs potential customers that the seller has been (or plans on being) around for a long time. Sellers commonly advertise how long they have been in business (for example, "Since 1982" under the business name) to inform people that they have a history of honest dealing (or otherwise they would have been out of business long ago) and plan on remaining in business.

However, the advantages motivated by repeated encounters tend to break down if it is known that the encounters will come to an end at a specified date. (This is a version of the "last-period problem" which we will detail in Perspective 8.) For this reason, firms will attempt to maintain continuity beyond what would seem to be a natural end period. For example, single proprietorships would seem to be less trustworthy when the owner is about to retire or sell. A common way of reducing this problem is for the owner's offspring to join the business ("Samson and Sons" or "Delilah and Daughters") and ensure continuity after their parents' retirement.

The Role of "Hostages" in Business

Another way that businesses may create trust is to provide their customers with a **hostage** – something of value to the seller that customers can destroy by taking their business elsewhere and harming the company's reputation

> A **hostage** is something of value to the seller that customers can destroy by taking their business elsewhere if the seller does not keep his promises.

if the seller does not keep his promises. For example, when an owner publicizes that his family members are involved in the business, he is sending the message that the firm is planning to be in business a long time. This suggests that the owner has something to lose – potential future business – if he engages in dishonest dealing. In effect, such a firm is providing potential customers with a hostage.

The best hostage is one that the firm values highly and the consumer doesn't value at all; therefore, the best hostage serves no purpose other than to motivate the seller to keep his promise. A firm's reputation is a substantial hostage because it is valuable to the firm as a nonsalvageable investment (what we will call a "sunk cost" in Chapter 7). But it has no value to customers apart from its ability to ensure honesty. A firm has a motivation to remain honest in order to prevent its reputation from being tarnished or destroyed by customer dissatisfaction, but customers cannot capture the value of the reputation for themselves.

Storefronts and Fixtures

Businesses use a range of nonsalvageable investments to penalize themselves if they engage in dishonest dealing. Such investments are particularly common when the quality of the product is difficult for consumers to determine. For example, the products sold in jewelry stores can vary tremendously and few consumers can judge the value themselves. Expensive jewelry stores want to be convincing when they tell customers that those products are worth the prices being charged. One way to do this is to install expensive fixtures that would be difficult to use elsewhere: ornate chandeliers, unusual display cases, and expensive countertops. What could the store do with this stuff if it went out of business? Not much, and this tells the customers that the store has a lot to lose by misrepresenting its merchandise to capture short-run profits. In contrast, street vendors are less credible because they have no hostages and can be "here today, gone tomorrow."

Firm Logos

Consider the value of a logo to a firm. Companies commonly spend what seems an enormous amount of money for logos to identify themselves to the public. Well-known artists are paid handsomely to produce designs that do not seem any more attractive than those that could be rendered by lesser-known artists. Furthermore, companies are seldom shy about publicizing the high costs of their logos.

It may seem wasteful for a company to spend so much for a logo – and silly to let consumers know about it (the cost of which ends up in the price of its products). But expensive logos make sense when we recognize that much of a logo's value *depends on* its cost. A more expensive logo implies that the company loses more if it engages in business practices that harm its reputation with consumers – a reputation embodied in the company logo. The company that spends a lot on its logo is effectively giving consumers a hostage that is, in turn, valuable to the company. Consumers have no interest in the logo except as an indication of the company's commitment to honest dealing, but will not hesitate to damage the value of the logo by no longer buying the company's products (and sharing their bad experiences with the company) if it fails to live up to a commitment.

Firm Profitability and Advertising

Another rather subtle way that sellers use "hostages" to provide assurances of honesty is to let consumers know that they (the sellers) are making lots of money. If it is known that a business is making impressive profits, consumers will have more confidence that the business won't risk that profit with misleading claims. The extra profits of the business are a hostage that consumers can harm or destroy if the business begins employing dishonest practices. In this sense, expensive logos and nonsalvageable capital are not only hostages, but also inform consumers that the firm is making enough money to afford such extravagances. Expensive advertising campaigns, often using well-known celebrities, serve the same purpose. Through expensive advertising, a company is doing more than informing potential customers about the availability and attributes of the product; it is letting them know that it has a lot of profits to lose by misrepresenting the quality of the product.

The Ironic Value of Creating Competition

The importance that people attach to committing themselves to honesty sometimes leads them to put their profits in jeopardy from competition with other firms. Consider the situation of a firm with a patent on a high-quality product that consumers would like to purchase at the advertised price, but its use requires costly long-term commitments. Potential buyers may fear that the seller will exploit the long-term patent monopoly on the product by raising the price after the buyer commits to it at the attractive initial price. The seller may promise not to raise the price, but the buyer will be taking an expensive risk to trust the seller's honesty. A long-term contract is possible, but it is difficult to specify all the contingencies under which a price increase would be justified. Also, such a contract can reduce the flexibility of the buyer as well as the seller – and legal action to enforce the contract is expensive.

Another possibility is for the seller to give up her monopoly position by licensing other firms to sell the product. By doing so, the seller makes credible the promise to charge a reasonable price in the future, because breaking the promise allows the buyer to turn to an alternative seller. Giving up a monopoly position is a costly and unorthodox move, but it is exactly what semiconductor firms have done with their patented chips. To make credible their promise of a reliable and competitively priced supply of a new proprietary chip (the use of which requires costly commitments by the user), semiconductor firms have licensed such chips to competitive firms.[18] Such a licensing arrangement is another example of a firm giving up a hostage to encourage honesty.

---

[18] When Intel developed its 286 microprocessor in the late 1970s, it gave up its monopoly by licensing other firms to produce it (Brandenburger and Nalebuff 1996, 105–106).

Joint Ownership

The more difficult it is for consumers to determine the quality of a product or service, the more advantageous hostage arrangements become. Consider the case of repair work. When people purchase repair work on their cars, they can generally tell whether the work eliminates a problem: the car is running again; the rattle is gone; the front wheels now turn in the same direction as the steering wheel. But few people know whether the repair shop charged them for unnecessary repairs – parts and hours of labor unrelated to the problem. One way for repair shops to reduce the payoff to dishonest repair charges is through joint ownership with the dealership selling the cars being repaired. In this way, the owner of the dealership makes future car sales a hostage to honest repair work. Dealerships depend on repeat sales from satisfied customers, and an important factor in customer satisfaction is the prevalence and cost of upkeep and repairs. The gains that a dealership could realize from unnecessary repair work could be offset by reductions in both repair business and car sales. Of course, we would expect part of this quality assurance to be reflected in higher prices for any given service.

Guarantees

Automobiles are not the only products in which it is common to find repairs and sales tied together in ways that provide incentives for honest dealing. Many products come with guarantees entitling the buyer to repairs and replacement of defective parts for a specified period of time. These guarantees also serve as hostages against poor quality and high repair costs. Of course, guarantees provide not only indirect assurance of quality, but also direct protection against the failure of the assurance. Sellers often offer extra assurance – and the opportunity to reduce risks – by selling warranties that extend the coverage of the standard guarantee.

But firms should be careful with guarantees, given the signals that are being sent. If I buy a Maytag washer with a one-year warranty, it indicates that the washer might be expected to have trouble shortly after one year. Buyers are likely to expect a trouble-free washer for far more than twelve months. Is this the signal Maytag wants to send? Moreover, required repairs within the warranty period are likely to worry the consumer even more. If repairs are needed, the company should consider aggressive steps to placate customers and reduce fears about quality commitments.

Adverse Selection and the "Moral Hazard" Problem

The root problem throughout Part B is "incomplete information" – or, more precisely, "asymmetric information," where one party has a significant information advantage over the other. If people had complete information, they wouldn't have to worry much about honesty, credibility, and morality. Why don't we have (anything close to) complete information? Because it is costly to obtain. So we engage in a cost–benefit calculus for the accumulation of information with varying degrees of accuracy.

So far, we've emphasized cases where the seller knows more than the buyer. The buyer is obviously at a disadvantage, but as long as the buyer *knows* about the asymmetry, they can take defensive measures, trying to assess credibility and honesty. This is called a "known unknown" – a common outcome in markets that doesn't lead to much trouble. (Think about how little you know about most of the goods and services you purchase.) An "unknown unknown" is a much worse level of ignorance; when I don't know that I don't know, I'm much more likely to be abused.

The potential for opportunistic behavior – from buyers or sellers, in the face of asymmetric information – is a risk cost that can undercut firm profitability. (We'll talk about these principles in the vital context of labor markets in Chapter 12.) Hostages are means that businesses can use to assure their workers, customers, and suppliers that they will hold to their commitments. Although guarantees and warranties reduce the incentive of sellers to act dishonestly, they simultaneously create opportunities for *buyers* to benefit from dishonest behavior. Two separate problems arise: **adverse selection** and **moral hazard**.

> **Adverse selection** is the tendency of people with characteristics undesirable to sellers to buy a good or service from those sellers.

First, consider the problem of adverse selection. In the case of warranties, the buyer has crucial information that is difficult for the seller to obtain: Some buyers are harder on the product than others.

> A **moral hazard** is the tendency of behavior to change after contracts are signed, resulting in unfavorable outcomes from the use of a good or service.

For example, some people drive in ways that greatly increase the probability that their cars will need expensive repair work. If a car manufacturer offers a warranty at a price equal to the average cost of repairs, only those who know that their driving causes greater-than-average repair costs will purchase the warranty, which is therefore being sold at a loss. If the car manufacturer attempts to increase the price of the warranty to cover the higher-than-expected repair costs, then more people will drop out of the market, leaving only the worst drivers buying the warranty – another version of the "lemon problem."

Even though people would like to be able to reduce their risks by purchasing warranties at prices that accurately reflect their expected repair bills, the market for these warranties can obviously collapse unless sellers can somehow obtain information on the driving behavior of different drivers. If all buyers were honest in revealing this information, they would be better off collectively. But because individual buyers have a strong motivation to claim they are easy on their cars, sellers of warranties try to find indirect ways of securing honest information on the driving behavior of customers. For example, warranties on "muscle" cars that appeal to young males are either more expensive (buried in the price of the car) or provide less coverage than warranties on station wagons.

The second problem is that having a product under guarantee or warranty can tempt buyers to use the product improperly and then blame the seller for the consequences. With this "moral hazard" in mind, sellers put restrictions on guarantees that leave buyers responsible for problems that they are in the best position to prevent. For example, refrigerator manufacturers insure against defects in the motor but not against damage to the shelves or finish. Automobile manufacturers insure against problems in the engine and drivetrain (if the car has been properly serviced) but not against damage to the body and the seat covers. Although such restrictions obviously serve the sellers' interests, they also serve the buyers. When a buyer takes advantage of a guarantee through misrepresentation of the cause, all consumers pay because of higher costs to the seller. Buyers are in a Prisoner's Dilemma in which they are better off collectively using the product with care and not exploiting a guarantee for problems they could have avoided. But without restrictions on the guarantee, each individual is tempted to shift the cost of careless behavior to others.

Moral hazard was also at the root of the world financial and economic crisis that emerged in 2008 and stifled economic recovery well into the next decade. Banks originate many long-term mortgages and hold them until the balances are paid off in fifteen or thirty years. Bank loan officers had a strong incentive to scrutinize borrowers for creditworthiness. But in recent decades, banks began to bundle many mortgages into securities and sell them to Wall Street investors, reducing the incentive to scrutinize borrower creditworthiness. Banks obtained more funds to lend and were able to originate riskier mortgages with less oversight and scrutiny.

Moreover, bank deposits are insured by the federal government. When bank deposits are not insured, depositors have strong reasons to monitor the financial health of banks – and banks are incentivized to maintain strong financial positions through conservative lending practices to ward off bank runs by depositors. When the government insures depositors, neither depositors nor banks will be as concerned. Beyond that, the government decided during the crisis that banks were "too big to fail." (Additional bailouts and the extension of federally insured deposits in 2023 have extended this concern.) So, successful risky investments were profitable and failed risky investments were subsidized by the government – an ideal (and terrible) recipe for the moral hazard problem.

Adverse selection and moral hazard are quite evident in the markets for insurance. Those who are riskier are more likely to seek (more) insurance – and, once they have insurance, they're more likely to engage in risky behavior. Insurance companies do their best to screen applicants, write contracts carefully, and monitor fraudulent behavior. But these are challenging (and costly) tasks.

Adverse selection and moral hazard play an important role in rental housing. An extra month of rent up front and a security deposit are a helpful corrective to misusing the resources. And landlords are wise to investigate the creditworthiness of prospective tenants. Finally, apartment complex owners who include utilities in a fixed rental payment can expect to attract renters who will make heavy use of those services. Moreover, any renter can be expected to increase their use of the utilities. Because of the high rental payments when utilities are included in apartment rents, renters who expect to use little of the included utilities should try to select other apartment complexes.

Likewise, adverse selection and moral hazard are useful for understanding why insurance for cell phones is usually a bad investment. Who tends to purchase the insurance? Adverse selection indicates that it will be those who tend to be careless with their devices. And once anyone has the insurance? The moral hazard problem tells us that they're even more likely to mistreat the device. The insurance company knows this and must accommodate those risks (and the relevant costs) into the insurance premiums. Unless you are terribly careless with your phone, such insurance is probably not a good investment.

Practical Lessons

An important lesson from this chapter is that owners and managers should seek mutually beneficial deals with workers (as well as their suppliers and customers). Employers pay their workers for two reasons. First, they must make payments in line with offers workers can get from other firms. Second, they can make a profit from paying workers, at least up to a point.

We are confident that many employers would like to *overpay* their workers so they can better support their families and friends. But such warm-hearted employers have a problem: worker wages feed into product costs and thus prices. Overpayments can undermine a firm's competitive position, causing the firm to lose market share, if not close down. Consequently, even workers have an economic interest in not being overpaid.

In addition to money wages, workers typically want their firms to provide fringe benefits of various kinds and are willing to forgo wages for these nonmonetary benefits (especially as a nontaxed form of compensation). That is, workers are willing to pay for benefits through wage reductions. Employers would be well advised to treat workers as buyers of fringe benefits and to search out a "payment bundle" (money wages and nonmonetary benefits) that minimizes their labor costs. To do this, extend the provision of each fringe benefit so long as workers are willing to give up more in money wages than each fringe benefit costs the firm.

Most business students understand that firms should seek competitive advantage in their final product markets through product development and marketing. We suggest here that firms should also seek competitive advantage through cost savings that can come with the development of improved payment bundles that are mutually beneficial to firms and their workers. And if government policy dictates that workers be paid a higher money wage (as in the case of a minimum wage or other employer mandates), then firms should reconstruct their payment bundles to mitigate the higher costs and remain competitive.

Further Reading Online

Reading 5.1: Your contribution to the California drought (*The New York Times*, link available on the online resources website www.cambridge.org/mckenzie4)

Reading 5.2: They clapped: Can price-gouging laws prohibit scarcity? (The Library of Economics and Liberty, link available on the online resources website www.cambridge.org/mckenzie4)

Reading 5.3: The right minimum wage: $0.00 (*The New York Times*, link available on the online resources website www.cambridge.org/mckenzie4)

Reading 5.4: A $15 minimum wage bombshell in Los Angeles (*The New York Times*, link available on the online resources website www.cambridge.org/mckenzie4)

Reading 5.5: Key econometric findings on the effects of the minimum wage

Reading 5.6: Driving the lemon myth off the lot (Fox News, link available on the online resources website www.cambridge.org/mckenzie4)

Recommended Videos Online

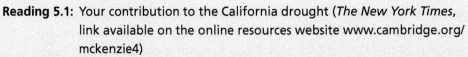

1   Taxes, subsidies, and prostitution (Richard McKenzie, 30 minutes)
2   Rent controls (Richard McKenzie, 25 minutes)
3   Minimum wages (Richard McKenzie, 27 minutes)
4   Adding fringe benefits (Richard McKenzie, 29 minutes)
5   Maslow's "Hierarchy of Needs" (Richard McKenzie, 21 minutes)
6   Incentives, trust, and welfare (Richard McKenzie, 25 minutes)
7   Leverage and moral hazard (Richard McKenzie, 16 minutes)
8   The lemon problem (Richard McKenzie, 19 minutes)
9   The true story of the minimum-wage fight (Freakonomics, link available on the online resources website www.cambridge.org/mckenzie4)
10   What you don't know about online dating (Freakonomics, link available on the online resources website www.cambridge.org/mckenzie4)
11   Price Ceilings; Price Floors (Marginal Revolution University, link available on the online resources website www.cambridge.org/mckenzie4)

The Bottom Line

The key takeaways from Chapter 5 are the following:

1 The market system can perform the exceedingly valuable service of rationing scarce resources among those who want them; however, markets are not always permitted to operate unobstructed. Government has objectives of its own that are determined through a different process. This has important implications for the types of public policies selected (a topic we develop in Chapter 6).

2 Excise taxes tend to be passed in large part to consumers, but producers still pay a portion of the tax in the form of a lower after-tax price. How the tax is shared between buyers and sellers depends upon the elasticities of supply and demand.

3 Effective price ceilings result in shortages. They also tend to result in costs being passed along to buyers in other ways – for example, a reduction in the quality of the good.

4 Effective price floors result in surpluses and are usually accompanied by other policies that mitigate the impact of the surplus on producers.

5 As a wage floor, minimum-wage laws tend to result in a surplus (for less-skilled workers) called "unemployment." However, such surpluses enable employers to offset at least partially the employment effects of minimum wages by reducing fringe benefits, increasing work demands, and/or increasing product prices.

6 When a minimum wage is imposed, both workers and employers can be worse off. Employers can be worse off because the higher wage exceeds the possible cost reductions from fringe benefits being taken away and/or the productivity gains from the imposition of greater work demands. Workers can be worse off because the value of the reduced fringe benefits and the greater work demands imposed can exceed the higher wage rate.

7 Firms offer fringe benefits because it is profitable. Fringe benefits should not be offered unless they are mutually beneficial to workers and employers. An increase in worker nonwage benefits can be expected to lead to a reduction in workers' wage rates in competitive labor markets. They increase costs, but they can also increase productivity and the supply of labor wanting to work where fringe benefits are offered, resulting in lower labor costs overall.

8 With a fringe benefit, workers can be better off despite a lower wage rate because the value of the benefit to workers exceeds the value of the lost money wages. The employers can be better off because the wage reduction caused by the increase in the worker supply can be greater than the cost of the benefit to employers.

9 The provision of fringe benefits will be extended until the additional value to employees of the last unit equals the additional cost of the fringe benefit to employers.

10 Honesty in business has both a moral and an economic dimension. Honesty is an economic force because it can be profitable.

11 "Hostages" (or "assets" bought by firms that increase the credibility of commitments) can be profitable when they reduce the transaction costs of making and fulfilling business deals.

12 "Adverse selection" and "moral hazard" offer challenges and opportunities for buyers and sellers. Firms who handle them well can earn greater profits.

Review Questions ▸▸

1 Is a tax on margarine "efficient"? Why might margarine or butter producers prefer to have an excise tax imposed on both butter and margarine? Would such a tax be more or less efficient than a tax on margarine alone?

2 Using $QD_x = 100 - 1P_x$ and $QS_x = -20 + 4P_x$, solve for equilibrium price (P_x), quantity demanded (QD_x), and quantity supplied (QS_x). With a tax of $5 (per unit) on firms, the supply becomes $QS_x' = -20 + 4(P_x - 5)$. Calculate the new equilibrium and draw a graph with the information you have so far. Illustrate and calculate the tax burden for consumers and producers.

3 Are politicians more likely to tax inelastic or elastic goods? Why?

4 Federal payroll taxes on income (FICA) are imposed half on employers and half on employees. But the burden is determined by the elasticities of labor demand and labor supply. The elasticity of labor supply is determined by substitutes for workers: how can they avoid the payroll tax? The elasticity of labor demand is determined by the firm's substitutes: how can they avoid the payroll tax? Because firms generally have more options than workers, employees typically bear most of the burden of payroll taxes. How do firms shift their burden to workers?

5 In a competitive market, if prices are held below market equilibrium by government controls, what will be the effect on output? How might managers be expected to react to the laws?

6 Why might some producers want price controls? Why wouldn't they get together and control prices themselves (if such price controls were legal)?

7 How could price controls affect a firm's incentive to innovate? Explain.

8 "Price controls can be more effective in the short run than in the long run." Explain.

9 Workers and their employers often talk as if workers "earn" their wages, but firms "give" their workers health insurance (or any other fringe benefit). Should these different methods of pay be discussed in different terms?

10 Suppose the government requires employers to provide health (or dental) insurance. How might the requirement affect the supply of and demand for labor in competitive markets?

11 How might the construction of Maslow's hierarchy be different if it were constructed today? Would there be additional levels to the hierarchy? Would the

levels be moved? How might the modern problems of weight gain and obesity and weight control be illuminated by Maslow's hierarchy? How can price changes be used to explore those modern problems?

12   Explain how a reputation for "honest dealing" on the part of executives can elevate a company's stock.

13   Why do many consumers pay extra for goods with "brand names"? Conceptually speaking, how much should firms spend on "branding" their products?

14   What hostages does your firm use?

15   Would you expect hostages to be used more by new or established firms?

16   Name an example where buyers have more information than sellers – and vice versa. Why is this a problem for both parties? What does the market do to address the information asymmetries?

17   Where do you see important information asymmetries in your workplace with consumers, suppliers, or investors? What could your firm do to minimize the relevant risk costs?

6

Principles of Political Economy for Public Policy and Business

If you take away from government its specialists in force – the police officers and soldiers – you don't have government. You would have an organization that might be respected in the way a conclave of religious figures or a group of scientists are respected, but it would not be feared – and probably not be widely obeyed. Here's the definition of government, then: government is the organization that directs the regular, public use of physical force in a territory and makes rules upheld with the threat of force.

James Payne[1]

Why talk about political economy in a microeconomics course for business students? As we've seen, you can't talk about economics for long without talking about public policy. Markets rarely operate without government regulation – and markets always operate within an environment which is largely established by government policy. Since we're referring to public policy so often, it makes sense to spend time thinking about how people are incentivized (and how they behave) in "political markets." In a word, how can we talk about public policy at any length *without* talking about political economy?

Once we start into this discussion, many other questions emerge. Why do voters, politicians, and bureaucrats do what they do? By what criteria do we judge government activism? How do we weigh trade-offs between these criteria? When is the use of government an ethical and practical means to various ends? What levels of government (federal, state, county, city, township, neighborhood) are best positioned to deliver the most effective policies in any given context? What are the policy tools at their disposal? Can the government use the private sector to help them provide goods and services? And so on.

In his terrific book on public policy, *In Pursuit of Happiness and Good Government*, Charles Murray (1988) helps readers think about what we're trying to achieve with public policy, developing principles and parameters to best

---

[1] Payne, James, 2018. "The government nobody knows – nor wants to know," *The Independent Review* 22 (3): 444.

achieve our goals. Notably, Murray relies on Maslow's "Hierarchy of Needs" to detail policy goals from material needs to self-actualization. Material and safety needs are not just the most important, but also the easiest for government to accomplish. But Murray asks what we should do when pursuing lower-tier goals militates against higher-tier goals – for example, if giving people material goods serves to undermine their ability to self-actualize (short-term and/or long-term)?[2]

Another reason for us to discuss political economy is that the prevalence of government intervention into business implies that political activity is a potential "input" to production. There are times when political activism – defensive or offensive – may be worth considering. We'll want to explore the conditions under which political activity makes sense for the profit-maximizing firm. Along the way, we'll see that political markets are quite different from economic markets – in terms of both process and outcomes. But it turns out that some of the most popular models in political economy can be applied to the "politics" and bureaucratic machinery within (larger) companies. As we grow to understand politics, we'll gain surprising insights into the workings of firms.

Part A Political Economy, Public Policy, and the Role of Government

Efficiency, Equity, and Paternalism

Why do people advocate different public policies? Some people passionately oppose policies that are avidly endorsed by others. So far, we've talked mostly about efficiency as a criterion to judge economic markets and public policy – and found many policies that are inefficient. Why are these popular enough to become law? There must be other criteria driving politicians and voters – what we'll call "equity" and "paternalism." Before we turn to those, let's review efficiency.

Efficiency is a familiar concept at this point. Outcomes will be efficient when (1) rational agents are (2) engaging in voluntary trade with (3) reasonable levels of information in (4) relatively competitive markets that are (5) largely unregulated by government. In such circumstances, exchange will be mutually beneficial and resources will be allocated by the market to their highest-valued uses in a socially efficient manner.

---

[2] Murray asks his readers to engage in provocative thought experiments. For example, he asks whether you would want your children raised by peasants in a foreign land with the same values as you or people in your country with values that are polar opposite to yours. And he asks how much money it would take for you to move your family to live in the South Bronx. The questions illustrate the trade-offs between the tiers in Maslow's hierarchy and makes policy analysis much more complex (and valuable).

Moving away from any one of these assumptions will likely result in inefficiencies – what are called "deadweight losses" or "social welfare costs." If agents in the marketplace are not "rational," if trade is coerced or fraudulent, or if one participant has significant market power over the other, then efficiency is far from assured. Further, if an otherwise efficient market is regulated by the government, then economic activity will be artificially decreased or increased away from the socially efficient level. (In cases where markets are inefficient, it is possible for government to intervene in a way that enhances efficiency. We will discuss this in the next section.)

A continued focus on efficiency still leaves us with the question of why political markets would promote inefficiency in policies ranging from farm price supports to minimum wages. As long as the costs of inefficiency are recognized (at least in part), there must be some benefits that make the costs worthwhile in the eyes of voters and policy-makers. These benefits can be classified into the categories of equity and paternalism.

"Equity" in terms of public policy is a sense of "fairness" applied to process, outcomes, or both. For example, you might find the current distribution of income or wealth in your country to be fair or unfair. Or you might find the redistribution of income from taxpayers and consumers to wealthy farmers to be fair or unfair. Obviously, "fairness" is in the eyes of the beholder – a subjective matter, but also a crucial factor in determining policy preferences.

For processes and outcomes that are viewed as equitable and efficient, there will be little substantive debate on government involvement. For example, stop signs are a form of government intervention that mostly help with traffic and accidents – and are viewed as equitable.[3] For policies that are efficient but considered *inequitable*, the debate becomes more interesting. Some people are willing to sacrifice considerable efficiency to reach solutions they consider equitable; others do not want to make the same trade-off. Thus, even well-informed people of goodwill can come to different policy conclusions given their tastes and preferences about equity. (Of course, many people don't know much about the inefficiencies of policies – and thus largely base their positions, by default, on equity considerations.)

"Paternalism" in terms of policy is government activism to prevent people from making "the wrong decisions" or to urge them to make "the right decisions." In this sense, government can act as a "father" – or, more broadly, as a parent – to paternalistically "encourage" us to make good choices. Again, a preference for paternalism is highly subjective. The concept also questions a founding assumption in economics – that market participants are "rational" (people try to weigh benefits and costs effectively and make decisions that will maximize utility subject to their constraints). People often assume that *other* people are not

---

[3] There are still interesting and important debates on the ideal form of intervention in certain intersections – whether stop signs, stop lights, or traffic circles ("roundabouts").

rational. (They rarely assume this about their own decisions!) But beyond this, some people are fond of using government to mandate or subsidize good decisions and prohibit or tax bad decisions.

Can you think of some examples where paternalism is a key criterion in advocating a public policy? The government only allows young people to do certain things at certain ages (e.g., to drive, work, drink alcohol, or vote). The government gives poor people "food stamps" instead of cash, because they don't trust at least some of the recipients to spend the resources appropriately. (In the Online Math Appendix, we show why cash leads to greater utility than in-kind transfers – as long as decision-makers are rational.) The government tells us to buckle our seat belts and to wear motorcycle helmets for our own good. Fireworks are illegal in many U.S. states – and in New Jersey you're not allowed to pump your own gas. The government can use prohibition or taxation to discourage us from ingesting certain things (e.g., illegal drugs, cigarettes, large soft drinks in convenience stores). And the U.S. Government forces most workers to "contribute" much of their income into an investment vehicle with painful taxes and a 0 percent average rate of return – in large part, because some of us are not trusted to save for our own retirements.

Do people always make the best decisions, even with adequate information? Of course not. But when should government force be used to encourage people to make the best decisions? Will the use of government force make them more or less capable to make good decisions in the future? Will government force be used on me someday to regulate *my* "bad" decisions? The answers to these questions are debatable and subjective – and thus a matter of "tastes and preferences." But views on these questions clearly affect the public debate on optimal policy. Even with the same assessment of an individual's ability to make decisions, people differ considerably on whether government policy should be invoked.

As should be clear from the examples, support for or opposition to policy can be based on different knowledge of the costs and benefits of the policy, different views about equity in weighing those costs and benefits, preferences about paternalism, and different weights on the importance of equity and efficiency. At the end of the day, the economist's primary job is to teach critical and creative thinking about the costs and benefits of personal choices, business decisions, and public policies. But even if this task is done well, people will still disagree about policy as a function of their preferences for efficiency, equity, and paternalism.

Government Intervention on Efficiency Grounds

The policy debate is cleaner in the five areas where markets struggle to be efficient. In such cases – at least in theory – government intervention may improve efficiency (and is less likely to run into equity concerns). First, the macroeconomy struggles with business cycles. During a recession, resources are unemployed and thus allocated inefficiently. At least in theory, government activism can regulate the business cycle and reduce inefficiency. Proponents of activism believe that market processes (the market's "self-correcting mechanism") is too slow when trying to recover from a recession – and that government activism is relatively effective in fixing the problem. A lengthy discussion of this is beyond the scope of this book, but in Online Chapter 4, we discuss market struggles in macroeconomics and the possibilities of government activism through fiscal and monetary policy.[4]

Second, in Chapter 11, we'll talk about natural monopoly power and the potential for government to regulate it through antitrust law and price regulations. Third, in Chapter 5, we described information asymmetries, impressive market responses, and a potential role for government through small claims courts and "lemon laws." Another example: In cases where weights and measures are in play, consumers are not in a low-cost position to monitor their accuracy. (How do you *know* that you got 14.2 gallons of gas?) The market provides discipline through reputation. (Imagine if a gas station was caught skimming 1 percent from each gallon of gas.) But the government may be able to provide credible inspections at low cost that improve the efficiency of markets in the face of this information asymmetry. Now, we add the other two categories to finish the list: "public goods" and externalities.

"Public Goods"

We've already developed many of the concepts behind "public goods" in our discussion of "communal goods" in Chapter 1. Unfortunately, the term "public good" sounds like a product that is available to the public or produced in the public sector, but economists mean something quite particular by the term. For one thing, "public goods" can be goods or services. Beyond this, they are "nonexcludable" and "nonrival" in consumption. If a good or service is nonexcludable, then consumers cannot be excluded, *even if they do not pay*. This leads to the "free-rider problem" we described earlier with communal goods. Consumers are incentivized to "free-ride" against the efforts, contributions, and resources of others. "Nonrival" is a second consideration that flavors the first – the idea that my consumption does not "rival" or impact yours. When this is the case, there is even less ability to collect monies for the goods or services being provided.

A classic example is "asteroid abatement." Imagine that I have the technology to destroy an asteroid approaching the Earth and consumers believe I will honor

---

[4] Government policy also impacts social efficiency (and economic growth) through its choice of legal "institutions," strongly influencing the "environment" in which economic activity takes place – for example, protecting property rights, enforcing contracts, an effective judicial system, a stable monetary system, low marginal tax rates, free international trade and investment, etc.

my commitment to do so.[5] It is still unlikely that I will collect enough money to outweigh the costs. Consumers are likely to free-ride against the payments of other consumers and my efforts to provide this service. They will reason that they cannot be excluded if the service is provided, whether they pay or not. They know that their consumption of the service does not impact other consumers. And since this is a large-group setting, they can reason that their decision to contribute is unlikely to make a difference in the provision. This is a "pure" public good – perfectly nonexcludable and perfectly nonrival. The problem is that consumers have two goals in this regard: avoid being hit by the asteroid, and keep as much of their money as possible.

The extent to which a good or service falls under this category is obviously relevant to business practice and profitability – a topic in Part B of this chapter. Because markets struggle to provide public goods that are socially valuable, we expect market participants to look for creative ways to provide (and collect revenues) for these goods and services. And if markets struggle too much, there is a potential role for government to provide these socially valuable goods through taxation, despite the various inefficiencies of government provision. It turns out that there is no simple relationship between the degree of "public good-ness," the ability of businesses and the market to provide it, and the ability of government to improve on market outcomes.

Externalities

When exchanges between buyers and sellers significantly affect people who are not directly involved in the trades, they generate **externalities**. When such effects are pleasurable, the positive externalities create *external benefits*. When unpleasant, imposing a cost on people other than the buyers or sellers, the negative externalities create *external costs*. The effects of external costs and benefits on production and market efficiency can be seen with supply and demand curves.

Externalities are the positive or negative effects that exchanges may have on people who are not directly in the market. They are also called third-party or spillover effects.

External Costs

Figure 6.1 represents the market for a paper product. The market demand curve *D* indicates the benefits that consumers receive from the product. To make paper, the producers must pay the costs of labor, chemicals, and pulpwood – as reflected by the supply curve S_1. In a competitive market, the quantity bought

---

[5] On September 26, 2022, NASA used a 1260-pound Double Asteroid Redirection Test (DART) spacecraft to practice their skills on this by deflecting an 11-billion-pound, 520-foot-long asteroid called Dimorphos.

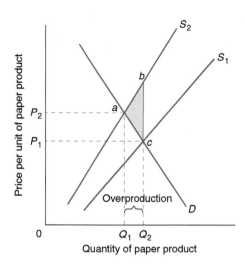

Figure 6.1 External costs
Ignoring the external costs associated with the manufacture of paper products, firms will base their production and pricing decisions on the supply curve S_1. If they consider external costs, such as the cost of pollution, they will operate on the basis of the supply curve S_2, producing Q_1 instead of Q_2 units. The shaded area abc shows the amount by which the (private and social) marginal cost of production of $Q_2 - Q_1$ units exceeds the marginal benefits to consumers. It indicates the social inefficiency of the private market when external costs are not borne by producers or consumers.

will be Q_2 and the price paid will be P_1. At point c, the marginal cost of the last unit produced will equal its marginal benefit to consumers – a point of productive efficiency.[6]

Producers may not bear all the costs associated with production. A byproduct of the production process may be waste dumped into rivers or emitted into the atmosphere. The stench of production may pervade the surrounding community. Towns located downstream may have to clean up the water. People paint their houses more frequently or seek medical attention for eye irritation. Homeowners may have to accept lower prices than usual for their property. All these costs are imposed on people not directly involved in the production, consumption, or exchange of the paper product. Nonetheless, these external costs are part of the *total cost of production to society* (or to all affected parties).

The supply curve S_2 in Figure 6.1 incorporates both the private production costs borne by firms and the external production costs of pollution borne by society. The *full* marginal cost of each unit of paper between Q_1 and Q_2 is greater than the marginal benefit to consumers. The marginal cost of those units exceeds their marginal benefit by the shaded triangular area bounded by abc – a measure of market or social inefficiency. (Pollution that gives rise to the overproduction of paper also gives rise to an underproduction of other goods, as well as an underproduction of a higher-quality environment.) But if producers (or consumers) bear these costs, the price of the product will be higher (P_2 rather than P_1) and consumers will buy a smaller quantity (Q_1 rather than Q_2).

It's easy to think that the culprits in the pollution problem are the producers, but a competitive market can easily put them in a Prisoner's Dilemma. An

---

[6] For a review of why Q_2 is the efficient, welfare-maximizing output level in the absence of externalities, review the discussion on market efficiency around Figure 3.8.

individual producer who voluntarily installs equipment to clean up pollution will incur higher costs than its competitors and will not be able to match prices. In the long run, it may be out of business. When all participants act independently, survival may *require* that a producer impose external costs on others. Other producers may not care whether they harm others by polluting the environment. Even if they do, they cannot easily organize themselves to curb production and pollution, resulting in an undesirable but inevitable level of environmental degradation.

Consumers can also be seen as culprits, since they are buying "too much" at prices that are "too low." They could solve the pollution problem, but they are also in a Prisoner's Dilemma and can't organize themselves to curb their excessive purchases. In fact, consumers implicitly ask producers to pollute on their behalf. When you buy a car or a refrigerator, you know that pollution is part of the production process – and are implicitly OK with it. Or consider other consumer examples of pollution: Did you think about the pollution of your driving or consuming mass transit services this week? Did you fret over the carbon footprint of the texts and emails you sent today?

There are too many producers and consumers to organize a reduction in production to socially optimal levels (voluntarily and at low cost). So, there is a potential role for government to work toward an effective coercive response to the externality. (We leave detailed discussion of this to Part B and Online Chapter 2.) Other examples of external costs that encourage overproduction are highway congestion and the noise around airports. If government does not penalize such behaviors, the market will overproduce them at a high external cost to others. Adult bookstores, street drugs, and brothels can impose costs on neighboring businesses and drive away consumers who would patronize the more-reputable businesses. Zoning laws can be used to limit this damage. Cell phones are a significant distraction to many drivers, causing more accidents and deaths on highways – as users impose external costs on those around them. Governments have responded by prohibiting drivers from using cell phones while driving.

The most prominent recent example is Covid-19. Our troubles with the virus can be understood through the lens of negative externalities. Individuals mostly worry about personal costs and benefits, and are far less likely to consider their impact on others. If someone feels "under the weather," they may still go shopping, even though they could impose costs on others through contagion. Lockdown orders and mandates to wear a mask (of some quality) were government attempts to mitigate negative externalities.[7]

---

[7] "Self-control problems" – such as eating/drinking too much (or the wrong things) and failing to exercise properly – are examples where people seem to have trouble in making decisions rationally (weighing costs and benefits in their self-interests). This is a topic for "behavioral economics" in Online Chapter 1. But, here, they can be modeled as our "current self" imposing negative externalities on our "future self."

External Benefits

Sometimes market inefficiencies are created by external benefits. Market demand does not always reflect all the benefits received from a good. Instead, people not directly involved in the production, consumption, or exchange of the good receive some of its benefits. A voluntary decision to get vaccinated will involve weighing personal costs and benefits. But if I get a vaccine, others benefit as well, since they are less likely to catch the contagion from me. To see the effects of external benefits on the allocation of resources, consider the market for vaccines. The cost of producing a vaccine includes labor, research and production equipment, materials, and transportation. The resulting market supply curve is S in Figure 6.2.

The fact that many millions of people pay for flu shots every year shows there is a demand, as illustrated by D_1. In getting shots, people receive important personal benefits, but also provide external benefits for others. By protecting themselves, they reduce the probability that contagion will spread. Those benefits are not captured in D_1; they are realized in the higher societal demand curve D_2. Left to itself, the market will produce at the intersection of market supply S and demand D_1 at point c. If external benefits are considered in the production decision, the *full* marginal benefit of flu shots between Q_1 and Q_2 (shown by demand curve D_2) will exceed the marginal cost of production (shown by S). If all benefits (private and external) are considered, Q_2 shots would be produced and purchased at a price of P_2. At Q_2, the marginal cost of the last shot would equal its marginal benefit. Social welfare would rise by an amount equal to the triangular shaded area abc in Figure 6.2. Because a free market can fail to capture such external benefits, government action to subsidize vaccines may be justified.

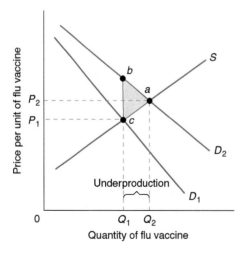

Figure 6.2 External benefits
Ignoring the external benefits of getting a vaccine, consumers will base their purchases on demand curve D_1 instead of D_2. Fewer shots will be purchased than would be justified economically, i.e., Q_1 instead of Q_2. Because the marginal benefit of each shot between Q_1 and Q_2 (as shown by demand curve D_2) exceeds its marginal cost of production, external benefits are not being realized. The shaded area abc indicates market inefficiency.

The external benefits argument has also been used to justify some government support for education, medical research, mass transit, and other public services.[8] One last example: Shock-absorbing bumpers are a benefit to the person who buys a car, but also to those who may be involved in a collision with the buyer. If John collides with Mary's car, which is protected by shock-absorbing bumpers, he may sustain less damage than he would have otherwise, without having paid for the protection received. He free-rides on Mary's purchase. Because of the externality, the quantity of shock-absorbing bumpers purchased in an unregulated market will fall short of the economic optimum. Hence, the potential usefulness of requiring safety equipment such as shock-absorbing bumpers, headlights, and mud flaps on trucks to prevent rocks from being propelled through windshields.

The Pros and Cons of Government Action

Most exchanges between buyers and sellers affect others to some extent. People buy clothes for their comfort and protection, but most people value their appearance as well. In part, we choose clothing because we want others to be pleased or impressed (or perhaps irritated). The same can be said about the cars we drive, the places we go to eat, the haircuts and styling we get, and the universities we select. We impose external effects through our actions, deliberately as well as accidentally, with almost every decision.

The presence of externalities in economic transactions does not necessarily mean that government should intervene. First, the economic distortions created by externalities are often quite small. If so, little can be gained by government intervention. This limited benefit must be weighed against the cost of government action. If the cost of government intervention exceeds the cost of the market's inefficiencies, government action will *increase* inefficiency, even if the government action corrects the market inefficiencies.

A second reason for limiting government action is that it (ironically) generates substantial external costs. When government intervenes, agencies are set up, employees are hired, papers are shuffled, and reports are filed. Almost invariably, lawsuits are brought against firms and individuals who have violated government rules that are often obscure and sometimes silly. When government dictates construction methods for building homes, the way in which firms must reduce pollution, and who has the qualifications to cut hair, this creates regulation costs for producers and consumers. In short, significant costs can be incurred in trying to correct modest market inefficiencies.

---

[8] The ratio of public to private benefits varies by educational level. Elementary school education develops crucial social and communication skills; its private benefits (or those benefits received by the people who are educated) are largely side effects. At the college level, however, the private benefits to students dominate the public benefits. Thus, on efficiency grounds, it is appropriate that elementary education is supported almost entirely by public sources, whereas college education is only partially subsidized.

Third, in certain markets over the long run, some external costs and benefits may be *internalized*. That is, they become private costs and benefits. Suppose the development of a park would generate external benefits for all businesses in a shopping district, attracting more customers and increasing sales. An alert entrepreneur could internalize those benefits by building a shopping mall with a park in the middle. Because the mall may attract more customers than other shopping areas, the owner would benefit from higher rents. When shopping centers can internalize such externalities, economic efficiency will be enhanced – without government intervention.

When Walt Disney built Disneyland on a small plot of land in Orange County, California, he conferred benefits on merchants in the surrounding Anaheim area. Other businesses quickly moved in to take advantage of the external benefits – the crowds of visitors – spilling over from the amusement park. Disney did not make the same mistake twice. When he built Disney World in Orlando, Florida, he bought enough land so that most of the benefits of the amusement park would stay within the Disney domain. Inside the more than 6000 acres of Disney-owned land in Florida, development has been controlled and profits captured by the Disney Corporation. Although other businesses have established themselves on the perimeters of Disney World, their distance from its center makes it more difficult for them to capture the benefits spilling over from the Disney amusement park.

What Sort of Government Intervention Should We Choose?

If one believes that government should be involved for some reason (efficiency, equity, paternalism) and in some way, there are still questions about exactly what should be done – choices to be made among collective decision-making rules. Government action can take several forms: attempts at persuasion; assignment of communal property rights to individuals; regulation of production, distribution and consumption; regulating prices directly or influencing prices through taxes, fines, and subsidies; and government production of goods and services. Economists generally argue that, if government is going to intervene, it should choose the least costly means sufficient for the task at hand.

Two key concepts here are decentralization and privatization. Decentralization refers to the level of government to be used – whether federal, state, or one of many local options. Privatization alludes to the degree of private involvement within the public provision. We might all agree that "government should do something," but disagree vehemently over either or both of these considerations.

For example, given social efficiency concerns, government is involved with regulating the externality of trash, but the involvement of government can range considerably. Trash could be regulated by the federal, state, or local governments.

But unless there is an inter-state component to the trash, local governments are probably most effective. From there, citizens of a town or city might be told to take care of trash appropriately (under penalty of law), dealing with any number of private providers. Or the government could use taxpayer dollars to contract with a particular private producer which is given monopoly rights to provide the service. Or the government could operate the trash trucks themselves, hiring the workers and running it as a bureaucracy. In each case, government is intervening in the marketplace, but the scope of the involvement is radically different.

Consider how we get food to poor people. The government takes money from taxpayers and provides financial resources to the indigent to obtain food. "Food stamp" recipients are not given cash, but are allowed to mostly buy what they want (a modest degree of paternalism). They can use the stamps at any number of privately run stores, purchasing privately produced food. Another way to get them food would be to have the government produce the food and run the grocery stores – and perhaps to make indigents go to the store closest to where they live. This would be quite different!

Finally, consider government's involvement with K-12 education. To what extent should funding, regulation, curriculum, and testing be handled by the federal, state, and local governments – and to what extent should the private sector be involved? The most prevalent method is to take money from taxpayers so that a local government can operate schools, often forcing its students to attend the school closest to their homes. These schools are also regulated by state and federal governments. Another option would be to give parents "education stamps" (known as "vouchers" or "backpack funding") that would allow them to purchase education services at the private or public school of their choice. Even within public provision of schooling, note that schools don't write their own books; and they often contract out to the private sector to provide food and transportation. What should government-run schools outsource to private firms?

Knowledge and Motives in Economic versus Political Markets

To be effective, markets and governments must get around the knowledge and motive problems. We've already discussed this in the context of markets. Markets generally do an amazing job with knowledge, bringing together an unimaginable amount of information about consumer preferences and constraints (as modeled by the demand curve) and an equally staggering amount of knowledge in terms of producer costs, input prices, and technology (as modeled by the supply curve). Markets coordinate these two groups – as prices, profit, interest rates, and labor market compensation send signals to market participants – to buy more/less and to provide more/less. (This is a key topic in the field of "Austrian economics.")

Markets are also generally impressive in how they handle an array of motives. Why do people do what they do in the context of markets? They are motivated by a wide range of self-interests which are typically harnessed by incentives to cooperate in the marketplace, satisfy others, and strive to improve in this ability. There are certainly notable exceptions, especially information asymmetries and monopoly power. But the record of markets to provide productive outcomes, despite decidedly mixed motives is certainly impressive.

What about knowledge and motives in political markets? If we believe that government is generally effective (or will be effective in any given realm), then we also believe that government knows enough and will be motivated well enough to deliver outcomes that are an improvement over what the market offers. Working through the counterexamples, we can see why this is so. If government agents are motivated well enough (sufficient integrity, selflessness, kindness, etc.) but don't have sufficient knowledge, then we will usually end up with ineffective policy. We may give credit for "good intentions," but the result will not be good policy. In contrast, if government agents know enough but are motivated "poorly" (dishonest, unethical, corrupt), then they will be effective at helping themselves but probably won't choose policies that are socially optimal. Finally, if government lacks sufficient motives *and* knowledge, we can't expect its choices to be impressive!

How much knowledge is necessary to be effective? Let's start with a relatively simple example: What you need to know to fix potholes in your local community. Where are the potholes? (What's the best way to gain this information?) How to fix potholes, including ideal combinations of capital and labor, how many workers to use, types of machines to use, materials to use, etc. Does optimal pothole maintenance vary with time of day, time of year, climate, underlying road composition, etc.? When should we fix the potholes – during the day or overnight? How do we prioritize the various potholes? What is the price of the inputs and how should we compensate workers? The list goes on and on. What seems simple is in fact surprisingly complex. (One of the authors (Schansberg) has written an essay called "*I, Pothole*" available on EconLib!)

Now for a more daunting example: How much knowledge is required to run the healthcare system of the United States or even a smaller country like the United Kingdom? From allergy shots to cancer treatments, from Birmingham to Manchester, from individual service providers to hospitals and researchers, there is a staggering amount of knowledge in play. For government to ably run the nation's entire healthcare system, they would need an unimaginable level of information. (In Online Reading 6.1, we consider the surprising and subtle environmental costs of walking rather than driving to work, making environmental regulations of driving less impressive than usually imagined. And in Online Reading 6.2, Richard McKenzie and Kathryn Shelton discuss the well-intentioned but surprisingly costly regulations to address the threat of pedophiles in childcare settings.)

Ultimately, our interest is not in what government *could* do in some ideal world, but how well it's likely to do – as a supplement or replacement for market activity. This is the distinction between theory and practice – or, more precisely, sophisticated and naive theories of how government will work in practice. Whether in government or markets, concerns about outcomes can be reduced to a few key questions about decision-makers: Did they have the knowledge, the motives, and the incentives to do well? If not, then wisdom dictates changing the decision-maker, the flow of information, and/or the incentives.

"Public Choice" Economics and the Inefficiencies of Democracy

There's an old saying that democracy is the worst form of government, except for all of the others. Or putting it another way: the best form of government is a benevolent and knowledgeable dictator, except for the problem of finding a good and wise leader. Whatever democracy's strengths, they are relative not absolute, and they are contingent on context: the people being governed, the people governing, and the underlying institutions (Schansberg 2021).

As a form of government, democracy has some important advantages. It disperses the power of decision-making among many people, reducing the influence of individual whim and personal interest. Thus, it provides some protection for individual liberties. Democracy also gives political candidates some incentive to seek out and represent a broad sector of public opinion and interests. Competition for votes forces candidates to reveal what they are willing to do for various interest groups. As with any system, the democratic system has drawbacks as well. In particular, democracy is inefficient as a producer of many goods and services.

The inefficiency of a democratic form of government in some respects does not mean that we should replace it with another decision-making process – any more than we should replace the market system, which is also less than perfectly efficient. Instead, we should measure the costs of one type of production against others. Neither system is perfect, so we must choose carefully between them – and consider when to use democracy, markets, or some other process.

Political Ignorance in the General Public and the Passion of Special-Interest Groups

"Public Choice" economists point to the foibles of political markets in general and democracy in particular – for example, the disproportionate power of interest groups in some contexts ("tyranny of the minority"); the unjust exercise of power by the general public ("tyranny of the majority"); the problems caused by any system of government where people are fond of using power to take others' resources; and so on. In a word, it turns out to be difficult to have an optimistic view of the general public, elected (and unelected) leaders, or those who work diligently to influence the political process.

The lack of an informed citizenry may be the most severe problem in a democratic system. If voters were better informed on legislative proposals and their implications, then government might make better decisions. If so, political information is a "public good" that benefits everyone, but individuals have little incentive to contribute anything toward its production. Their individual efforts simply have little effect on the outcome and each implicitly free-rides against the contribution of others. The result: exceedingly few voters are well informed about political issues and candidates – and they usually cast their votes based on impressions received from headlines or commercials which are carefully created by advertisers and press secretaries.[9]

One of the most powerful observations from "Public Choice" economics is that political activity often features concentrated benefits and diffuse costs. Even when the costs are much larger than the benefits in *aggregate*, the costs are much smaller *per person*. The subtlety of the costs makes their occurrence much more likely. Voters have little to offer in political markets: a modest voice, a single vote, and perhaps a bit of money. So, it is "rational" to be ignorant and apathetic about policy and politics, tolerating the diffuse costs.[10]

Benefits of political activity are often spread unevenly; subgroups of voters (e.g., farmers, labor unions, government workers) receive a highly disproportionate share. Interest groups will passionately pursue such laws and engage in mutually beneficial trade with politicians and bureaucrats. Members of these "interest groups" have a special incentive to acquire and disseminate information on the legislative proposals that affect them. Likewise, congressional representatives, knowing they are being watched by special-interest groups, will tend to cater to their wishes. Those engaging in political activity are further motivated to tell "good stories" for government intervention: rationales for why benefiting themselves at the expense of others is (supposedly) good for the country and the

---

[9] It is possible that the media can serve a "watchdog" function or be manipulated by the government (Besley and Prat 2006; Coyne and Leeson 2009). One might hope that low-cost media would be helpful in enhancing information. But given the constraints we've described, consumers are prone to choosing "news and opinions that affirm confirmation biases or media delivery that lampoons an opposing view" (Mullainathan and Schleifer 2005; Gentzkow and Shapiro 2006; Schansberg 2021). Munger (2008) labels this the market for "truthiness."

[10] See: Somin (2003). Brennan (2016) notes the stability of political ignorance despite greater education and lower-cost information over time. Citizens are more likely to know more about civics and politics when they don't get most of their information from social media (Mitchell *et al.* 2020). As knowledge increases, citizens are pro-market/liberty (Caplan 2007). Citizens are more likely to vote with higher income, education, and age (Caplan 2007, 157). But relatively impressive knowledge (compared to other people) does not imply objectively impressive levels of insight. And none of this lends itself toward much optimism about governance in a democracy.

economy. (We share a satirical version of one such rationale in Perspective 6.) This is especially true when voters are "politically ignorant." As a result, government programs are often designed to serve the interest of groups with political clout rather than the public as a whole. It's easy to imagine and document the misuse of government power to enrich some at the expense of others.

Imagine a government program that takes $1 from 300 million people and redistributes the money in $30,000 bundles to 10,000 people. Even if they noticed, the 300 million may find it annoying, but it's "only a buck" – not worth much if any time to learn about the program or to oppose it. The general public is *rationally* ignorant and apathetic since the benefits of taking action are far outweighed by the costs, particularly the opportunity costs of time. How can they influence the process? It's a classic Prisoner's Dilemma where almost everyone has an incentive to oppose the legislation, but it's in no one person's interest to oppose it.

In contrast, the recipients are *especially* interested in this legislation, more than any other policy. In fact, we call them members of a "special-interest group." (What matters more than whether one receives a check for $30,000 or not?!) This will determine their vote and they'll be willing to devote financial resources (e.g., campaign contributions) to influence the process. Even though the 300 million should overwhelm the 10,000 in a democratic process, the latter will often win because they're actively involved and the general public is not paying attention – busy working, mowing their lawns, raising their kids, and watching TV.

Imagine going to dinner with 534 other people and splitting the bill. To order an appetizer or a dessert on the menu for $5.35 will only cost you a penny. This dramatically changes the cost–benefit calculus for those ordering food. In fact, ordering food now constitutes a negative externality, since others will be forced to pick up $5.34 of the $5.35 total cost. With 435 members of the U.S. House and 100 members in the U.S. Senate, the federal budget is equivalent to a huge dinner tab, with all paying for everyone's subsidized and inflated appetites.

Related, any given person has less clout in political markets – especially as we move from local to state to federal – than a consumer or shareholder in the marketplace. In Chapter 7, we'll cover the "agency problems" that plague firms – when the agendas of workers, managers, and owners are not in alignment. But the gap between politicians and voters with little knowledge or power is far greater. Paraphrasing James Madison to describe the dilemma: we aren't angels, so we need to be governed – but we're also being governed by non-angels.

There are exceptions to the "diffuse costs/concentrated benefits" formula – when costs are borne by unsympathetic parties (e.g., "the rich," business in general, and coal companies in particular) or benefits go to sympathetic parties (e.g., the poor). But the norm is redistribution to the *non*-poor since the costs are diffuse and the benefits go to the politically organized who have resources in hand and an incentive to use them.

Caplan (2007) extends the usual "Public Choice" framework by arguing that voters also practice "*irrational* ignorance." Voters are generally ignorant – and rationally so – not knowing much about politics and public policy. But they can also be "irrational" in their ignorance – not knowing, but thinking that they know (more than they do). Rational ignorance implies random errors that are corrected through aggregating over many voters. But systemic errors by voters on policy often emerge from misunderstanding and not knowing that one is wrong.[11]

Rent-Seeking

Rent-seeking is epitomized by the various companies, non-profits (including colleges and K-12 education), and trade associations in the capitals of the world, whose lobbyists are constantly knocking on the doors of key politicians. But this activity is not restricted to private businesses. When Congress began considering various bailout and stimulus plans in 2008 to rectify the financial market meltdown, the National Conference of Mayors sent its lobbyists to Washington, D.C., to lobby for the inclusion of more than 11,000 municipal projects in any orchestrated federal government relief programs. The list included a duck-pond park for one small California town and a senior citizen center for a small town in Texas (Poole 2008). Since the 1980s, universities in the United States have engaged in rent-seeking, lobbying for so-called federal "legislative earmarks" or special appropriations for university projects (buildings and curriculum development) that are attached to (and buried in) budget bills.[12]

> **Rent-seeking** is the pursuit of monopoly profits through market restrictions and subsidies provided by the political process.

---

[11] Caplan (2007) points to four common biases: anti-market, anti-foreign, make-work, and pessimism. He notes that students routinely enter economics classes with these systemic errors and it is difficult to correct them. Or as Brennan (2016, 121) describes his five-year-old: "He is merely ignorant, while they're mistaken. Keaton might not understand much about economics, yet at least he's not a mercantilist like almost everyone in the U.S." Hersh (2020) describes "educated" people thinking they're deeply engaged, while getting their information by scrolling through Twitter feeds. This sort of ignorance can easily lead to dogmatism – when politics are practiced as a casual hobby or a type of tribalism, with an emphasis on the abstract merits of a few policies, an attraction to politicians who pay lip service, and a greater value placed on voting and talking over knowing and doing. Related: it's strange and troubling when people combine ignorance with certainty and passion. Irrational ignorance explains this overreaction. Or from another angle: if the unwashed are more aware of their ignorance, they will have more "known unknowns," while the elites may have more "unknown unknowns." In a word, ignorant people may not be (nearly) as bad as stupid "smart people."

[12] In fiscal year 2003, the *Chronicle of Higher Education* found that 716 U.S. colleges and universities benefited from 1964 "legislative earmarks" worth $2 billion (Krueger 2005). Economists from UCLA and the University of Toronto found that a $1 increase in lobbying expenditures can be expected to lead to a $1.56 increase in "earmarks." However, for those universities who have a member of Congress on either the House or Senate Appropriation Committee, a $1 increase in lobbying leads to a $4.50 increase in "earmarks." This means that university fortunes rise and fall with changes in the membership of appropriation committees (Krueger 2005).

This tendency is not restricted to direct income redistribution. Interest groups can also benefit through legislation that restricts their competitors – allowing them to charge higher prices, sell more product, and deal with less competition. Another angle is to impose costs on all producers in an industry, but costs that are disproportionately painful for competitors. For example, as we'll discuss in Chapter 11, greater regulation compliance leads to higher fixed costs, which imposes a greater burden on smaller businesses. Ironically, large businesses can benefit, on net, by increasing their own regulation costs.

As long as there are monopoly rents to be garnered from market-entry restrictions or government subsidies, political entrepreneurs can be expected to compete for the rents through lobbying (e.g., providing political decision-makers with lavish dinners and junkets to exotic locations for "working vacations"), campaign contributions, and outright bribes (Tullock 1967; Krueger 1974; McChesney 1997). Rent seekers can be expected to assess their rent-seeking expenditures as investments, aiming for rates of return that are no less than their other investments.

Almost every economic activity is subject to some type of regulation at one stage or another. The list of federal regulatory agencies virtually spans the alphabet – to say nothing of various state utilities commissions, licensing boards, health departments, and consumer protection agencies. Here, we can only review the two major lines of explanation for the existence of so much regulation: the public-interest theory and the economic theory of regulation.

The public-interest theory of regulation starts with the idea that regulation can improve market efficiency. In this chapter, we have discussed how externalities can cause market inefficiencies – and, in response, how tax or regulatory regimes can increase the efficiency of markets. In Chapter 10, we will stress the extent to which monopoly power can generate inefficiency in the allocation of resources – and in Chapter 11, we will see how government regulation of monopoly power might enhance consumer welfare and efficiency. But we have also noted how the cost of regulation can restrict its efficacy. We've wondered whether government regulators have the knowledge and the motives to implement effective policy. If regulation is truly to serve the public interest, it must increase the efficiency of the entire social system. That is, its benefits must exceed its costs.

Unfortunately, regulation often seems to serve the interests of the regulated industry, not the broader "public interest." Starting in the 1960s, many economists became skeptical of this theory in favor of an industry-centered view. Instead of seeing regulation as something thrust on firms, they began to view it as a government-provided service frequently sought by those who are regulated – a market for politically provided benefits (Stigler 1971; Breyer 1985). Government can be a supplier of regulatory services to industry – for example, price fixing, restrictions on market entry, subsidies, suppression of substitutes, promotion of complementary goods, and so on. For example, commercial television stations successfully petitioned the Federal Communication Commission (FCC) to delay the introduction of cable television.

These regulatory services can be "sold" to industries willing to pay. In the political world, the price of regulatory services may be campaign contributions or lucrative consulting jobs, votes and volunteer work for political campaigns, and so on. Regulators and politicians allocate the benefits among all the various private-interest groups to equate political support and opposition at the margin. Not surprisingly, firms are often interested in regulation that serves their private interest. The view that certain forms of regulation emerge from the interaction of government suppliers and industry demanders seems to square with much historical evidence. As Richard Posner has observed (Posner 1974, 337):

The railroads supported the enactment of the first Interstate Commerce Act, which was designed to prevent railroads from price discrimination because discrimination was undermining the railroad's cartels. American Telephone and Telegraph pressed for state regulation of telephone service because it wanted to end competition among telephone companies. Truckers and airlines supported extension of common carrier regulation to their industries because they considered unregulated competition excessive.

Likewise, Gabriel Kolko provides a useful example of this flaw in democracy, arguing that business leaders, rather than "reformers," were the chief catalysts behind the Progressive Era's regulation of business. Instead of a "progressive" period of "populist" reform, it "was really an era of conservatism ... a conservative triumph" (Kolko 1963, 2). In sum, "It is business control over politics rather than political regulation of the economy that is the significant phenomenon of the Progressive Era. ... It was not a coincidence that the results of progressivism were precisely what many major business interests desired" (Kolko 1963, 3, 280).

Other examples? Barbers, beauticians, lawyers, and other specialists have all sought mandatory occupational licensing to limit entry into their professions. Farmers support regulation of the supply of commodities produced. Whenever deregulation is proposed, the industry in question almost always opposes it. Gasoline retailers in North Carolina (and a dozen other states) got a state statute passed that restricts gas stations from selling gasoline below their "wholesale price" (except for ten days during the grand opening of a new station). The law places a lower bound on price competition and restrains the creative efforts of convenience stores from using gasoline pricing as a means of bringing in customers who buy higher-margin nongasoline products on their refueling stops (Associated Press

2005).[13] (In Online Reading 6.3, Jim Payne defines government as the legitimate use of force and wrestles with why people don't want to see government through this lens. In Online Reading 6.4, Dwight Lee discusses why people in business are more honest than those in religion, politics, and higher education.)

The Central Tendency of a Two-Party System: Median Voter Preferences

In a two-party democratic system, elected officials typically take middle-of-the-road positions. Winning candidates tend to represent the relatively moderate views of most voters who are rarely strongly liberal or strongly conservative on a range of issues. For this reason, there is often not much difference between Republican and Democratic candidates. Even where they differ noticeably, they tend to move closer together as a campaign progresses. Likewise, voters might expect the fiscal records of presidents to be radically different. But, by the presidential records on federal government expenditures as a percentage of gross domestic product (GDP), this quick-and-easy assessment is not supported.[14]

This also explains why we see more political disparity between districts and more homogeneity within districts. It explains why candidates adjust between primary and general elections – trying to please members of their own party to win the primary and appealing to a broader array of voters in the general election. In fact, "flip-flopping" is to be expected if not inevitable. Broadly, this model implies both mediocrity and moderation, with niches at the tails/extremes. We saw something similar with emerging markets in Chapter 3. Entrepreneurs will often aim for the middle and appeal to the masses – and not move to the tails until the middle gets "crowded." In politics, with only two major parties, the tails will be served by niche political parties (if at all).

All of this can be chalked up to the political incentive to move closer to the middle of the spectrum in Figure 6.3. The bell-shaped curve shows the

---

[13] To the extent that regulation benefits all regulated firms, whether they have contributed to the cost of procuring it, industries may consider regulation a public good. It is useful to organize, but costly to establish and enforce. Some firms will try to free-ride on others' efforts to secure regulation. But if enough firms free-ride, the collective benefits of regulation will be lost. Large groups may have the advantage of established trade associations which can push for protective legislation at low cost (Olson 1971, chapters 1 and 2).

[14] Of course, there are differences – stated and real – on issues like abortion, guns, free speech, immigration, regulations, judges, etc. Republicans are supposedly much more inclined to favor defense over social program spending, but again the data don't indicate as much difference as the rhetoric. Of course, every president must negotiate with Congress and thus should not receive full blame (or credit) for what happens to federal spending (or any other policy where they work together). There may be a dime's worth of difference in the fiscal inclinations of elected Democrats and Republicans, but not more than a dime.

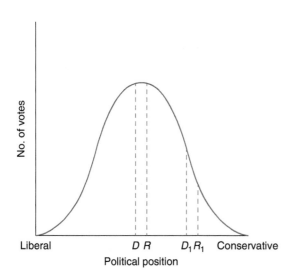

No. of votes

Liberal   D R $D_1 R_1$ Conservative

Political position

Figure 6.3 The political spectrum
A political candidate who takes a position in the "tails" of a voter distribution, such as D_1 or R_1, will win fewer votes than a candidate who moves toward the middle of the distribution. In a two-party election, both candidates will tend to take middle-of-the-road positions, such as D and R.

approximate distribution of voters along the political spectrum from very liberal to very conservative on fiscal matters. A few voters have views that place them in the "tails" of the distribution, but most cluster near the center. Assuming that citizens will vote for the candidate who most closely approximates their own political position, a politician who wants to win the election will not choose a fringe position from his constituency's perspective.

Suppose, for instance, that the Republican candidate chooses a position at R_1. The Democratic candidate can easily win the election by taking a position slightly to the left, at D_1. Although the Republican will take all the votes to the right of R_1 and roughly half the votes between R_1 and D_1, the Democrat will take all the votes to the left. Clearly, the Democrat will win an overwhelming majority. A pragmatic politician will therefore choose a position near the middle. Then the opposing candidate must also move to the middle or accept likely defeat.

In short, candidates would improve their vote total by moving toward the middle of the distribution. Does this mean that both candidates will always choose the middle – or even end up exactly in the middle of the distribution? Probably not – for at least two reasons. First, principles matter to some extent. And even when pragmatism dominates, politicians can misinterpret the political climate. Just as producers find the optimal production level through trial and error, so might politicians lose voters (consumers) by misestimating public opinion. Still, political competition will tend to drive politicians toward the middle of the distribution, where the median voter group resides. Second, politicians can influence public opinion as well as simply respond to it. Ronald Reagan was known as "The Great Communicator" and was no doubt able to pull the median voter in his direction. But it was also probably true that world and domestic events were causing public opinion to shift in a more conservative direction – and Reagan was better positioned politically to take advantage of this shift.

The Simple-Majority Voting Rule

When you buy ice cream in the marketplace, you can decide how much you want, based on your individual preferences and ability to pay. However, if you join with your neighbors to purchase a communal good, you must accept whatever quantity of service the collective decision-making process yields. (Think of buying pizza on your own – in contrast to buying it with a group and the compromises this may necessitate. Or beyond this, imagine the compromise that would go with one set of pizza toppings chosen by democracy and majority rule, especially for those with niche preferences.) How much (and what type) of a government expenditure depends not only on citizen preferences but also on the voting rule used.

Consider police protection. Perhaps you would prefer to pay higher taxes in return for a larger police force and lower crime rate. Your neighbors might prefer a lower tax rate, a smaller police force, and a higher crime rate. If these services are purchased collectively and if preferences differ, each cannot have his own way. In a democracy, the preferences of the median voter group will tend to determine the types and quantities of goods and services produced by government. If you are not a member of this group, the compromise necessary in a democracy inflicts a cost on you.

Any decision that is made less than unanimously can benefit some people at the expense of others – ironically imposing negative externalities on them. Because government expenses are shared by all taxpayers, the majority who vote for a project impose an external cost on the minority who vote against it. Consider a democratic community composed of only five people, each of whom would benefit to some degree from a proposed public park. If the $500 cost of the park is divided evenly among the five, each will pay a tax of $100. The costs and benefits to each taxpayer are shown in Table 6.1. Because the total benefits of the project ($550) exceed its total cost ($500), society will benefit as a whole. Because the measure is beneficial to a majority of voters, it will pass, with the majority imposing net costs of $50 and $75 on taxpayers D and E.

Table 6.1 Costs and benefits of a public park for five people, case I

(1) Individuals	(2) Dollar value of benefits to each person ($)	(3) Tax levied on each person ($)	(4) Net benefit (+) or net cost (−), (2) − (3) ($)	(5) Vote for or against
A	200	100	+100	For
B	150	100	+50	For
C	125	100	+25	For
D	50	100	-50	Against
E	25	100	-75	Against
Total	550	500		

Table 6.2 **Costs and benefits of a public park for five people, case II**

(1) Individuals	(2) Dollar value of benefits to each person ($)	(3) Tax levied on each person ($)	(4) Net benefit (+) or net cost (−), (2) − (3) ($)	(5) Vote for or against
A	140	100	+40	For
B	130	100	+30	For
C	110	100	+10	For
D	50	100	−50	Against
E	0	100	−100	Against
Total	**430**	**500**		

When total benefits exceed total costs, decision by majority rule is relatively easy to tolerate. But projects can easily pass even though their cost exceeds benefits. Table 6.2 illustrates such a situation. Again, the $500 cost of a proposed park is shared equally by five people. Total benefits are only $430, but again they are unevenly distributed. Taxpayers A, B, and C each receive benefits that outweigh a $100 tax cost. Thus A, B, and C will pass the project, even though it cannot be justified on economic grounds.

It is conceivable that many different measures, each of whose cost exceeds its benefits, could be passed by separate votes. If all of the measures were considered together, however, the package will more likely be defeated. If voters are knowledgeable, then the various minority groups can use "logrolling" (vote trading) to defeat some projects that might otherwise pass. But if voters are ignorant or apathetic about the political process, then logrolling may further obscure the aims of legislation. Context, voting rules, and assumptions about voters all matter, as we've seen. Our purpose here is simply to demonstrate that the democratic process should be expected to be inefficient in many cases (Keech and Munger 2015).[15]

---

[15] Most issues that confront civic bodies are determined by simple-majority rule. But some decisions are too trivial for (costly) group consideration and others are too important to be decided by a simple majority (e.g., impeachment, murder cases decided by juries). More broadly, the voting rule helps to determine the size and scope of government activities. Under a voting rule that requires unanimous agreement, few proposals will be implemented. But a unanimity rule can be exploited by small groups of voters. If everyone's vote is critically important, then everyone is in a strategic bargaining position, threatening to veto the proposed legislation unless given special treatment. Such tactics increase the cost of decision-making. If only 51 percent need to agree, proposals can pass more easily, expanding the scope of government activity. But the 49 percent may feel resentment when unwanted costs are foisted on them. In companies and non-profits, even if "majority rule" is the policy, seeking consensus is still important when possible.

The Economics of Government Bureaucracy

Bureaucracy is not limited to government. Large corporations such as General Motors and Walmart employ more people than major departments of the federal government and the entire government of some nations. Corporate bureaucracies have their problems, but they tend to work more efficiently than government bureaucracy. The primary reason is that firms pursue one simple objective – profit – that can be easily measured in dollars and cents. Governments usually have a multiplicity of ill-defined objectives.

It's not that stockholders are better informed than voters. Most stockholders are "rationally ignorant" of their companies' doings, for the same reason that voters are rationally ignorant of government policy – the personal costs of becoming informed outweigh the personal benefits. But even in large corporations, some individuals hold enough stock to make the acquisition of information a rational act. Often, such stockholders sit on the company's board of directors, where their interest in increasing the value of their own shares makes them good representatives of the other stockholders. And this informed stockholder has one relatively simple objective (profit) and can determine (relatively easily) whether the corporation is meeting it. The voter, on the other hand, must do considerable digging to find out whether the various, ill-defined objectives are being met.

Because most corporations face competition, the stockholder's drive toward profit is reinforced. General Motors knows that its customers may switch to Toyota if it offers them a better deal. In fact, stockholders can sell their General Motors stock and buy stock in Toyota. Corporate executives thus have a strong incentive to make decisions on the basis of the consumer's well-being – not necessarily because they want to serve the common good, but because they want to keep their jobs and make money.

Government bureaucracies, however, tend to produce goods and services for which there is no competition; there are no built-in efficiencies to guard the taxpayer's interests. Both government bureaucrats and corporate executives base their decisions on their own interests, not those of society. But competition ensures that the interests of corporate decision-makers coincide with those of consumers; no such safeguards govern the operations of government bureaucracies. Bureaucracies are constrained by political, as opposed to market, forces.

Although some owners pursue other goals – for example, personal income, power, respect – their behavior can generally be explained quite well in terms of a single objective: profit. No single goal such as profit drives a government bureaucracy. We do not have time or space to consider all the possible objectives of

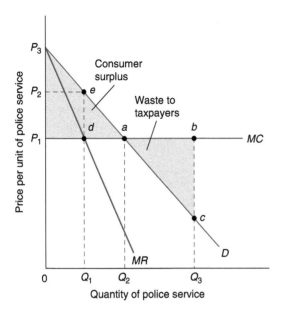

Figure 6.4 Bureaucratic maximization
Given the demand *D* for police service and the marginal cost *MC* of providing it, the optimum quantity of police service is Q_2. A monopolistic police department interested in maximizing its profits will supply only Q_1 service at a price of P_2. A monopolistic bureaucracy interested in maximizing its size would expand police service to Q_3.

bureaucracy, but we will touch on two: a type of profit maximization and size/budget maximization.[16]

Assume that police protection can be produced at a constant marginal cost, as shown in Figure 6.4. The demand for police protection is shown by the downward-sloping demand curve *D*. If individuals could purchase police service competitively at a constant price of P_1, the optimum amount of police service would be Q_2, the amount at which the marginal cost of the last unit of police service equals its marginal benefit. The total cost would be $P_1 \times Q_2$, leaving consumer surplus equal to the triangular area P_1P_3a and no economic profit realized by the police.

However, police protection is usually delivered by regional monopolies that have their own goals and their own decision-making process, which do not necessarily match those of individual taxpayers. If police service must be purchased from a profit-maximizing monopoly, service will be produced to the point at which the marginal cost of the last unit produced equals its marginal revenue (Q_1). The monopolist will set this quantity, allowing a profit equal to the rectangular area P_1P_2ed.

At the monopolized production level, there is still some surplus left for consumers (the triangular area P_3P_2e), but they are worse off than under competitive market conditions. They get less police protection (Q_1 instead of Q_2) for a higher price (P_2 instead of P_1). This analysis presumes that the police can conceal

---

[16] Another key incentive is risk aversion. For example, bureaucrats generally have much less to lose from delaying a health treatment, rather than even the miniscule probability that a likely-effective treatment will cause significant problems.

their costs. If taxpayers know that P_2 is an unnecessarily high price, the outcome might be the same as with competition – if they can use political or social pressure to produce Q_2 protection for a price of P_1. But not having other sources of supply with which to compare costs, taxpayers may not know that costs are inflated or that the efficient output level is Q_2.

That said, a government bureaucracy is unlikely to make profit its overriding objective, since bureaucrats do not pocket the profit. Instead, government monopolies may try to maximize the size of their operations, because employees will have more chance of promotion; their power, influence, and public standing will improve; and they will likely get nicer offices and better equipment.

What level of protection will a police department produce under such conditions? Instead of providing Q_1 service and misrepresenting its cost at P_2, it will probably provide Q_3 service – more than taxpayers desire – at the true price of P_1. The bill will be the area $P_1 \times Q_3$ in Figure 6.4. Note that the net waste to taxpayers, shown by the shaded area abc, exactly equals the consumer surplus, P_1P_3a. By extending service to Q_3, the police have squeezed out the entire consumer surplus and spent it on themselves.

Fortunately, government bureaucracies do not usually achieve perfect size maximization and the waste that would result. Most legislatures have at least some information about the production costs of various services, and bureaucrats may not be willing to do the hard work necessary to exploit their position fully. Either way, if the bureaucracy does not manage to capture the entire consumer surplus, citizens will realize some net benefit from their investment.

What can be done to make government bureaucracy more efficient? First, the development of managerial expertise by the legislative and executive branches would encourage more accurate measurement of the costs and benefits of government programs. Cost–benefit analysis alone, however, will not necessarily help. Given the clout of special-interest groups (including those of government employees), the potential for waste can be substantial.

Second, we could work to increase competition in the public sector. Any monopoly makes this task difficult, but the existence of even one competitor for a government bureaucracy's services would allow some comparison of costs. With more sources of a service, the demand curve becomes flatter and encourages greater efficiency to stay in business. How exactly can competition be introduced into government bureaucracy?

One way is to contract with private producers; "publicly financed" need not imply "publicly produced." In the United States, highways are usually built by private companies but repaired and maintained by government. Competitive provision of maintenance as well as construction might reduce costs. Other services that might be "privatized" are fire protection, garbage collection, and jails – and, if not fully privatized, then at least aspects of the services provided.

With jails, food and healthcare can be outsourced. With K-12 education, transportation, books, food, janitorial and payroll services, etc., can be handled by private firms.

Competition can also be increased by dividing a bureaucracy into smaller departments with separate budgets, thus increasing competition. Such a change would eliminate a dissatisfied consumer of a government service from having to move to a different political jurisdiction to get better or cheaper government services. The consumer/taxpayer could simply switch to a different government provider of a service in the same jurisdiction. The loss (or threat of loss) of customers can put pressure on a government agency to improve its performance.

It follows that proposals to consolidate departments should be carefully scrutinized. Just as in private industry, large governments can realize economies of scale in the production of services. Garbage, road, and sewage service can, up to a point, be provided at a lower cost on a larger scale. But what appears to be wasteful duplication may actually be a source of competition in the provision of service. In the private sector, we would not expect the consolidation of General Motors, Ford, and Daimler-Chrysler to improve the efficiency of the auto industry. If anything, we would favor the break-up of the large firms into separate, competing companies. As such, why should we necessarily merge the sanitation departments of three separate cities?

The Efficiency of Competition among Governments

In the private sector, competition among producers keeps prices down and productivity up. Any one producer knows that any independent attempt to raise prices or lower quality will fail. Customers will switch to other products or buy from other producers – and sales will fall sharply. Only a producer who has no competition – that is, a monopolist – can hope to raise the price of a product (or lower quality) without fear of losing profits. (In Chapter 11, we'll describe how competition can be helpful to deal with monopoly power *within* firms through outsourcing and takeovers.)

These points also apply to the public sector. In fact, the framers of the U.S. Constitution bore them in mind when they set up the federal government. Recognizing the benefits of competition, they established a system of competing state governments loosely joined in a national "federation." As James Madison described in *The Federalist* papers, "In a single republic, all the power surrendered by the people is submitted to the administration of a single government: and the usurpations are guarded against by a division of the government into distinct and separate departments" (Hamilton, Jay, and Madison 1964).

Under the federal system, the power of local governments is checked by the ability to vote and the ability to move somewhere else. If a city government raises its taxes or lowers the quality of its services, residents and businesses can go elsewhere, taking with them part of the city's tax base. Of course, many are reluctant to move, so government has a measure of market power. But competition among governments affords at least some protection against the abuses of this power. It may not take many people and businesses to "vote with their feet" and send a strong signal to the political authorities that they must be more competitive.

It is often argued that local governments should consolidate to avoid duplication and achieve economies of scale. But consolidation is a mixed blessing if it reduces competition among governments. A large government restricts the number and variety of alternatives open to citizens and increases the cost of moving to another locale by increasing the geographical size of its jurisdiction. Consolidation, in other words, can increase the government's monopoly power. So, the potential for achieving greater efficiency through consolidation could easily be lost in increased monopoly power, bureaucratic expansion, and red tape. Studies of consolidation in government are inconclusive, so consolidation proposals should be examined carefully (Faulk and Schansberg 2009).

PERSPECTIVE 6

"A PETITION From the Manufacturers of Candles, ... and Generally of Everything Connected with Lighting," by Frédéric Bastiat (1845)

Gentlemen, You are on the right track. You reject abstract theories and have little regard for abundance and low prices. You concern yourselves mainly with the fate of the producer. You wish to free him from foreign competition, that is, to reserve the *domestic market* for *domestic industry.*

We come to offer you a wonderful opportunity for your – what shall we call it? Your theory? No, nothing is more deceptive than theory. Your doctrine? Your system? Your principle? But you dislike doctrines, you have a horror of systems, as for principles, you deny that there are any in political economy; therefore we shall call it your practice – your practice without theory and without principle.

We are suffering from the ruinous competition of a rival who apparently works under conditions so far superior to our own for the production of light that he is *flooding* the *domestic market* with it at an incredibly low price; for the moment he appears, our sales cease, all the consumers turn to him, and a branch of French industry whose ramifications are innumerable is all at once reduced to complete stagnation. This rival, which is none other than the sun, is waging war on us so mercilessly we suspect he is being stirred up against us by perfidious Albion (excellent diplomacy nowadays!), particularly because he has for that haughty island a respect that he does not show for us.

We ask you to be so good as to pass a law requiring the closing of all windows, dormers, skylights, inside and outside shutters, curtains, casements, bull's-eyes, deadlights, and blinds – in short, all openings, holes, chinks, and fissures through which the light of the sun is wont to enter houses, to the detriment of the fair industries with which, we are proud to say, we have endowed the country, a country that cannot, without betraying ingratitude, abandon us today to so unequal a combat.

Be good enough, honourable deputies, to take our request seriously, and do not reject it without at least hearing the reasons that we have to advance in its support.

First, if you shut off as much as possible all access to natural light, and thereby create a need for artificial light, what industry in France will not ultimately be encouraged?

If France consumes more tallow, there will have to be more cattle and sheep, and, consequently, we shall see an increase in cleared fields, meat, wool, leather, and especially manure, the basis of all agricultural wealth.

If France consumes more oil, we shall see an expansion in the cultivation of the poppy, the olive, and rapeseed. These rich yet soil-exhausting plants will come at just the right time to enable us to put to profitable use the increased fertility that the breeding of cattle will impart to the land.

Our moors will be covered with resinous trees. Numerous swarms of bees will gather from our mountains the perfumed treasures that today waste their fragrance, like the flowers from which they emanate. Thus, there is not one branch of agriculture that would not undergo a great expansion.

The same holds true of shipping. Thousands of vessels will engage in whaling, and in a short time we shall have a fleet capable of upholding the honour of France and of gratifying the patriotic aspirations of the undersigned petitioners, chandlers, etc.

But what shall we say of the *specialities* of *Parisian manufacture*? Henceforth you will behold gilding, bronze, and crystal in candlesticks, in lamps, in chandeliers, in candelabra sparkling in spacious emporia compared with which those of today are but stalls.

There is no needy resin-collector on the heights of his sand dunes, no poor miner in the depths of his black pit, who will not receive higher wages and enjoy increased prosperity.

It needs but a little reflection, gentlemen, to be convinced that there is perhaps not one Frenchman, from the wealthy stockholder of the Anzin Company to the humblest vendor of matches, whose condition would not be improved by the success of our petition.

We anticipate your objections, gentlemen; but there is not a single one of them that you have not picked up from the musty old books of the advocates of free trade. We defy you to utter a word against us that will not instantly rebound against yourselves and the principle behind all your policy.

Will you tell us that, though we may gain by this protection, France will not gain at all, because the consumer will bear the expense?

We have our answer ready. You no longer have the right to invoke the interests of the consumer. You have sacrificed him whenever you have found his interests opposed to those of the producer. You have done so in order *to encourage industry and to increase employment*. For the same reason you ought to do so this time too.

Indeed, you yourselves have anticipated this objection. When told that the consumer has a stake in the free entry of iron, coal, sesame, wheat, and textiles, "Yes," you reply, "but the producer has a stake in their exclusion." Very well, surely if consumers have a stake in the admission of natural light, producers have a stake in its interdiction.

"But," you may still say, "the producer and the consumer are one and the same person. If the manufacturer profits by protection, he will make the farmer prosperous. Contrariwise, if agriculture is prosperous, it will open markets for manufactured goods." Very well, if you grant us a monopoly over the production of lighting during the day, first of all we shall buy large amounts of tallow, charcoal, oil, resin, wax, alcohol, silver, iron, bronze, and crystal, to supply our industry; and, moreover, we and our numerous suppliers, having become rich, will consume a great deal and spread prosperity into all areas of domestic industry.

Will you say that the light of the sun is a gratuitous gift of Nature, and that to reject such gifts would be to reject wealth itself under the pretext of encouraging the means of acquiring it?

But if you take this position, you strike a mortal blow at your own policy; remember that up to now you have always excluded foreign goods *because* and *in proportion* as they approximate gratuitous gifts. You have only *half* as good a reason for complying with the demands of other monopolists as you have for granting our petition, which is in *complete* accord with your established policy; and to reject our demands precisely because they are *better founded* than anyone else's would be tantamount to accepting the equation: $+ \times + = -$; in other words, it would be to heap *absurdity* upon *absurdity*.

Labour and Nature collaborate in varying proportions, depending upon the country and the climate, in the production of a commodity. The part that Nature contributes is always free of charge; it is the part contributed by human labour that constitutes value and is paid for.

If an orange from Lisbon sells for half the price of an orange from Paris, it is because the natural heat of the sun, which is, of course, free of charge, does for the former what the latter owes to artificial heating, which necessarily has to be paid for in the market.

Thus, when an orange reaches us from Portugal, one can say that it is given to us half free of charge, or, in other words, at *half price* as compared with those from Paris.

Now, it is precisely on the basis of its being *semigratuitous* (pardon the word) that you maintain it should be barred. You ask: "How can French labour withstand the competition of foreign labour when the former has to do all the work, whereas the latter has to do only half, the sun taking care of the rest?" But if the fact that a product is *half* free of charge leads you to exclude it from competition, how can its being *totally* free of charge induce you to admit it into competition? Either you are not consistent, or you should, after excluding what is half free of charge as harmful to our domestic industry, exclude what is totally gratuitous with all the more reason and with twice the zeal.

To take another example: When a product – coal, iron, wheat, or textiles – comes to us from abroad, and when we can acquire it for less labour than if we produced it ourselves, the difference is a *gratuitous gift* that is conferred upon us. The size of this gift is proportionate to the extent of this difference. It is a quarter, a half, or three-quarters of the value of the product if the foreigner asks of us only three-quarters, one-half, or one-quarter as high a price. It is as complete as it can be when the donor, like the sun in providing us with light, asks nothing from us. The question, and we pose it formally, is whether what you desire for France is the benefit of consumption free of charge or the alleged advantages of onerous production. Make your choice, but be logical; for as long as you ban, as you do, foreign coal, iron, wheat, and textiles, *in proportion* as their price approaches zero, how inconsistent it would be to admit the light of the sun, whose price is *zero* all day long!

Part B Organizational Economics and Management

Applying Political Models to the Workplace

The median voter model in politics illustrates how the middle of the spectrum of policy preferences impacts political outcomes. A similar principle holds in many aspects of business. Mass marketing appeals to the vast middle. Firms establishing a new market will typically produce items with broad appeal until the middle becomes crowded and there is a greater incentive to address niche audiences in the tails of the distribution of preferences. Firms offer employees compensation packages and implement policies that appeal to most workers. The preferences of those in the tails of these distributions will often be overlooked. A firm's tendency to play it safe, to implement modest changes in policy, to rely heavily on "rules of thumb," to innovate carefully, etc. – these are all connected to the weight of the median "voter" in the markets for goods, services, labor, and investment. In each of these cases, the "majority rules" in that they have a large (and, beyond that, a disproportionate) impact on outcomes.

In contrast, our discussion about the "inefficiencies of democracy" was primarily about the weight of small groups – minority preferences gaining power over the majority. In politics, this manifests through the power of special-interest groups which benefit themselves at the expense of a general public which isn't paying much attention. In some contexts within business, we see similar outcomes where "the tail wags the dog." Policies are established to deal with rare cases. Squeaky wheels get the attention and the resources. Some companies focus on market niches, appealing to the tails of the distribution of preferences on goods and services. And, as we'll discuss in Chapter 11, small departments within firms can achieve monopoly power, gaining excessive leverage and benefits from their position.

Finally, governments are famous for their political and bureaucratic tendencies. But as firms grow, they also deal with increasing challenges from the costs of bureaucracy. Department heads tend to value size over productivity and efficiency – more employees and larger budgets, even at the expense of the company's profitability as a whole. In everyday life, cultivating "political" connections within a firm can accelerate progress in one's career. And the risk aversion that dominates in government bureaucracies (wanting to avoid noticeable mistakes of commission, while putting less weight on subtle, abstract mistakes of omission) can be a feature of business and the non-profit sector as well.

Examples of "Public Goods" in Business

In Part A, we described "public goods" in the context of market inefficiencies and the prospects for government provision as an improvement over market outcomes, using asteroid abatement as an example. The two challenges of public goods – the nonexcludability and nonrivalry of consumption – cause difficulties for collecting the revenues necessary to offset costs and earn a level of profit that makes provision desirable for producers. If consumers can "free-ride" against the contributions of other consumers and the producers, market provision will be somewhere between less than ideal and prohibitively costly – even though the social benefits of provision outweigh the cost of the resources required to provide those benefits.

Consider broadcast radio. Like asteroid abatement, it is a pure public good – completely nonexcludable (the radio station cannot prevent you from consuming the service even if you don't pay them) and completely nonrival (you listening to a certain station has no impact on me listening to the same station).[17] Despite these inherent challenges, broadcast radio is a $20 billion industry in the United States. Why is the market utterly unable to provide one pure public good and able to impressively provide another? Let's start with the incentives: With so much social value being produced, the ability to monetize those consumer preferences would produce impressive revenue and hopefully, profit. In the case of broadcast radio, companies have been able to use advertising to generate revenues while allowing consumers to use their services for "free" (no direct monetary cost).[18]

Newspapers are in a similar spot. At least until recent market innovations greatly increased their competition, newspapers have been able to get around significant aspects of the free-rider problem with admirable success. If I subscribe to the newspaper, a few other people could read the paper at the same time as me – each reading a different section of the paper, reading over another person's shoulder, etc. And in short order, dozens of people could read the newspaper after I finish with it and lay it down in a public place. None of these other consumers would be required to pay for using the service – a terrific problem for the newspaper, which is incurring costs to provide the service but capturing only a fraction of the relevant revenues. Given the low cost of a newspaper subscription and the relatively high transaction costs of sharing a newspaper, these problems have *not* been prohibitively painful for newspapers. And again, advertising is part of the story: even if many people read the paper for free, advertisers are excited to get in front of more readers and willing to pay higher rates.

In Louisville, two weeks before the Kentucky Derby, the city has "Thunder Over Louisville" – a huge fireworks show. This service is mostly nonexcludable and nonrival in consumption. (In theory, you could exclude people from watching if they didn't pay, but the costs of collecting the revenue are generally too high to be profitable. That said, access is limited by market prices to see the fireworks up close – either on the ground or on top of nearby buildings.) The city government could argue that the social benefits of the fireworks exceed the social costs – and use taxes to put on the show. But it turns out that the private sector has been able to get around the free-rider problem and raise adequate revenue, especially through sponsorships and advertisements.

Finally, consider the dilemmas of some prominent non-profit service providers. Churches could be excludable, but they choose not to be; they could charge an entry fee (like a theater), but, instead, they have an open-door policy. Thus, people can consume church services without paying anything, creating a

---

[17] In contrast, satellite radio has little trouble with nonexcludability, charging subscription rates to those who consume the service. (It has been less successful as an industry because it emerged on the market later and its costs are much higher.)

[18] Interestingly, radio stations often pay their listeners through offers of "free money" to motivate listening.

classic free-rider problem. Churches incur costs and have no guaranteed revenue stream – and yet churches abound. The problem is particularly acute in large churches, where anonymity is greater and the peer pressure of contributing is less. Yet, churches are impressive in their ability to get around the free-rider problem, getting members to cooperate with the church's mission.

In the arts sector, service providers raise revenues through ticket sales, grants, advertisements, and donations. When you see a production at Actors Theater or Kentucky Center for the Arts in Louisville, they sell tickets (no free-rider problem there!) and they hand you a program, using advertising to generate revenue. There is also a long list of donors in the back, categorized by the amount of money they've given. Why are the names listed – and why are they divided into groups by donation levels? Economists call this "purchasing prestige": people enjoy having their names (positively) in print – and larger (publicly acknowledged) donations usually generate even more satisfaction. (Some people would rather give anonymously.) In fact, one would expect non-profits to choose categories that encourage donors to move up to the next level. For example, if $5000 is a common donation choice, they might choose $6000 as the lower bound of a donation category. Then, a donor will weigh the benefits of moving up to a more prestigious category by giving another $1000.

Spam: an Example of Negative Externalities in Business

Ironically, email spam is an internet scourge that spammers hate as much as their victims. For one thing, spammers are also greeted daily with dozens of unwanted emails, pitching everything from herbal enhancements for body parts to petitions by exiled foreign princes. For another, spammers don't want competition from other spammers or the reputation problems that dominate their market.

In Chapter 1, we developed "the tragedy of the commons" – and, in this chapter, we've described negative externalities – both of which are relevant to the spam plague. Akin to ranchers using open pasture lands, the dominant incentives are to overuse the resource and to impose costs on others who seek to use the same resource. Unabated, the spam problem would be expected to worsen, as spammers escalate the "spam arms race," with each spammer trying to compensate for their own spam's growing ineffectiveness by hiking their volume – a process that undermines the credibility of all broadcast email messages, including their own. The easiest solution, at least in theory, is to privatize the commons, establishing property rights for the common good. In this context, we can think of people's email boxes (or their attention spans) as a "commons." Seen in this light, we can understand the tragedy from the spammee's perspective – and from the view of spammers as well.

Spammees experience the tragedy since, like grass in the commons, their time is overused as they waste it deleting unwanted emails. The tragedy faced by spammers is that their emails are largely ignored because of the overwhelming flow of spam. Notice that this is true whether the spam is a scam (e.g., Nigerian princes) or merely something that will be attractive only to a small percentage of the spam recipients (e.g., an offer to receive or buy a book). Only gullible people pay attention to "scam spam" – and because they do, they share some blame for the scam spam scourge. (If no spammees responded to spam, then spammers would not waste their time concocting their scams.) And if the offer is legitimate, there is another interesting problem: 99 percent are annoyed, but 1 percent value it, so the spammer and the 1 percent both want the email to be sent.

A partial solution may come from a legislated or court-ordained assertion that email box "owners" have rights of exclusion and the right to charge for entry. Barring an imposed solution, private solutions remain. Given the social benefits at hand, market providers have been incentivized to produce and sell anti-spam programs. Beyond this, providers might charge for the right to spam targeted audiences – to the benefit of the spammers as well as the spammees. The software developers can turn a profit by charging spammers for the right to spam people who, in turn, have been paid for the right of "safe passage" to their email boxes. Or the software developers can sell to email box holders who then charge spammers directly for not blocking their spam. With the charges, spammers also benefit from the greater effectiveness of the reduced flow of spam through the anti-spam gates of email box owners.

Similarly, internet service providers have good reason to seek improved solutions to this tragedy of the commons. And Microsoft wants effective approaches to spam, since it impacts the value of Outlook and undercuts the company's stock value. Unfortunately, many of the worst spammers are workplace colleagues who can't resist clicking the "everyone" email list and distributing their banal jokes or invective against political leaders. Firms can assert control through policy, regulation, or social pressures. Another option would be to allocate employees an email (or discretionary) budget and then charge a per-recipient fee for each email distributed. The price placed on emails would cause workers to think twice about how many emails to write and who should receive them. Without this kind of arrangement, the cost that a worker places on sending an email to additional colleagues is zero. With a positive price, the worker would have to ask whether the value of the email being sent to an additional person is more than the price, leading to fewer emails sent to fewer people.

The bottom line: there is money to be made in spam and anti-spam, especially if property rights are well defined and prices are greater than zero. Individual spammers would provide relatively useful information and deals in their emails. And all spammers would benefit from an increased willingness of people to open emails from unknown parties. As in the case of polluters wanting controls on everyone's pollution, spammers might even welcome restrictions on spam, just to raise the probability that the distributed emails are considered.

Choosing the Most Efficient Remedy for Reducing External Costs of Pollution

Selecting the most efficient method of minimizing externalities can be a complicated process. To illustrate, we compare the costs of two approaches to controlling pollution: government standards versus property rights. Suppose five firms are emitting sulfur dioxide (SO_2) – a pollutant that causes acid rain. The reduction of the unwanted emissions can be thought of as an *economic good* whose production involves a cost. We can assume that the marginal cost of reducing SO_2 emissions will rise as more units are eliminated. We can also assume that such costs will differ from firm to firm. Table 6.3 incorporates these assumptions.

Table 6.3 lists costs for abating marginal units of pollution; these can be aggregated to a total cost. For example, the cost to firm A of eliminating 3 units is $700: $100 for the first unit; $200 for the second; and $400 for the third.

Table 6.3 **Costs of reducing SO$_2$ emissions**

Firms	Marginal cost of eliminating each unit of pollution ($)				
	A	B	C	D	E
First unit	100	200	200	600	1000
Second unit	200	600	400	1000	2000
Third unit	400	1800	600	1400	3000
Fourth unit	800	5400	800	1800	4000
Fifth unit	1600	16200	1000	2200	5000

Cost of reducing pollution by establishment of government standards		Cost of reducing pollution by sale of pollution rights	
Cost to A of eliminating 3 units	700	Cost to A of eliminating 4 units	1500
Cost to B of eliminating 3 units	2600	Cost to B of eliminating 2 units	800
Cost to C of eliminating 3 units	1200	Cost to C of eliminating 5 units	3000
Cost to D of eliminating 3 units	3000	Cost to D of eliminating 3 units	3000
Cost to E of eliminating 3 units	6000	Cost to E of eliminating 1 unit	1000
Total cost for all five firms' units	13500	**Total cost** for all five firms' units	9300

Although the information in Table 6.3 is hypothetical, it reflects the structure of real-world pollution cleanup costs. Firms face increasing marginal costs when they clean up the air as well as when they produce goods and services.

Suppose the Environmental Protection Agency (EPA) decides that the maximum acceptable level of SO_2 is 10 units. To achieve this level, the EPA prohibits firms from emitting more than 2 units of SO_2 each. If each firm was emitting 5 units, each would have to reduce its emissions by 3 units. The total cost of meeting the limit of 2 units is shown in the lower half of Table 6.3. Firm A incurs the relatively modest cost of $700 ($100 + $200 + $400). But firm B must pay $2600 ($200 + $600 + $1800). The total cost to all firms is $13,500.

What if the EPA adopts a different strategy and sells the rights to pollute? Such rights can be imagined as tickets that authorize firms to dump a unit of waste into the atmosphere. The more tickets a firm purchases, the more waste it can dump, and the more cleanup costs it can avoid. With this approach, the EPA can control the number of tickets it sells – here, selling ten to limit pollution to the maximum acceptable level of 10 units. Here, the pollution rights method allows firms that want to avoid the cost of a cleanup to bid for tickets.

The conventional supply and demand curves in Figure 6.5 illustrate the potential market for such rights. EPA policy-makers limit the number of tickets to ten, resulting in a vertical (perfectly inelastic) supply curve; whatever the price, the number of pollution rights remains the same. The demand curve reflects the willingness of firms to buy the permits and is derived from the costs to clean up their emissions. Higher cleanup costs imply more attractive pollution rights. As with all demand curves, price and quantity are inversely related. The lower the price of pollution rights, the higher the quantity demanded.

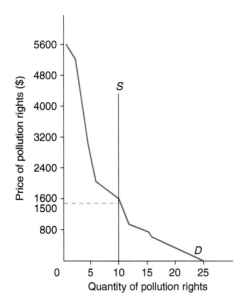

Figure 6.5 Market for pollution rights
Reducing pollution is costly (see Table 6.3). It adds to the costs of production, increasing product prices and reducing the quantities demanded. Therefore, firms have a demand for the right to avoid pollution abatement costs. At lower prices for such rights, the quantity of rights demanded will increase. If the government fixes the supply of pollution rights at ten and sells those ten rights to the highest bidders, the price of the rights will settle at the intersection of the supply and demand curves – here, about $1500.

Table 6.4 shows the total quantity demanded by the firms at various prices. At a price of zero, the firms want twenty-five rights (five each). At a price of $201, they demand only twenty-one. Firm A wants only three, because the cost to clean up its first 2 units (at costs of $100 and $200) is less than to buy rights to emit them at a price of $201. Firm B wants four rights since its cleanup costs are higher. The market-clearing price (the price at which the quantity of property rights demanded exactly equals the number of rights for sale) will be something over $1400 (say $1500, as shown in Figure 6.5). Who will buy those rights and what will the cost of the program be?

At a price of $1500 per ticket, firm A will buy only one permit. At this price, it is cheaper for the firm to clean up its first 4 units (the cost of the cleanup is $100 + $200 + $400 + $800). Only the fifth unit, which would cost $1600 to clean up, makes the purchase of a $1500 permit worthwhile. Similarly, firm B will buy three tickets, firm C none, firm D two, and firm E four. The cost of any cleanup must be measured by the value of the resources going into it. The value of the resources is approximated by firm expenditures on the cleanup – not by expenditures on pollution tickets. (The tickets do not represent real resources, but a transfer of purchasing power from the firms to the government.) Accordingly, the economic cost of reducing pollution to 10 units is $9300: $1500 for firm A; $800 for B; $3000 each for C and D; and $1000 for E. This is significantly less than the $13,500 cost of the cleanup when each firm is required to eliminate 3 units of pollution. Yet in each case, 15 units are eliminated. In short, the pricing system is more cost-effective (efficient) than setting standards. Alternatively, more pollution could be abated at the same cost to society. With more resources going into production and fewer into cleanup, it's better for the economy and/ or the environment.

Table 6.4 Demand for pollution rights

Price ($)	Quantity	Price ($)	Quantity
0	25	1601	9
101	24	1801	7
201	21	2001	6
401	19	2201	5
601	16	3001	4
801	14	4001	3
1001	11	5001	2
1401	10	5601	0

The idea of selling rights to pollute may not sound attractive, but it makes sense economically. When the government sets standards, it is actually *giving away* rights to pollute. In our example, telling each firm that it must reduce its SO_2 emissions by 3 units is effectively giving each company *permission* to dump 2 units into the atmosphere. One might ask whether the government should be giving away rights to the atmosphere, which has many other uses besides the absorption of pollution! Though some pollution may be necessary to continued production, this is no argument for giving away pollution rights. Land is needed in many production processes, but the Forest Service does not give away the rights to public lands. When pollution rights are sold, on the other hand, potential users can express the relative values they place on the right to pollute. In this way, rights can be assigned to their most valuable and productive uses. (For those who want more content on the environment, we have Online Chapter 2.)

International Trade: There's Always an Incentive to Restrict Your Competition

The term "international trade" can be misleading: nations don't trade; people do. This is important because it allows us to approach international trade as an extension of supply–demand models, the concept of voluntary mutually beneficial trade, and the economic way of thinking. This also prevents us from overlooking the distributional effects of international commerce – the gains and losses to individual companies (their workers and owners) and individual consumers. Even though international trade necessarily increases a *nation's* total income, its impact on individuals will vary. These individual gains and losses are important to any discussion of free trade among nations and to understand political support for trade restrictions.

International trade lowers import prices and raises export prices in the domestic nation. The net impact is expanded *total* available output and consumption opportunities for people in *both* trading countries – as before, the fruit of expanding comparative advantage, specialization, and voluntary, mutually beneficial trade. But domestic firms, their employees, and their suppliers still lose. Because the price is lower, domestic producers must move down their supply curve S_1 to the lower quantity Q_1 in Figure 6.6.

Their revenues fall from $P_2 \times Q_2$ to $P_1 \times Q_1$. In other words, the revenues in the shaded L-shaped area bounded by $P_2aQ_2Q_1bP_1$ are lost. Of this total loss in revenues, owners of domestic firms lose, on balance, the area above the supply curve, P_2abP_1, representing profits. Workers and suppliers of raw materials lose the area below the supply curve, Q_2abQ_1. This is the cost domestic firms no longer incur when they reduce domestic production from Q_2 to Q_1 – the payments that would be made to domestic workers and suppliers in the absence of foreign

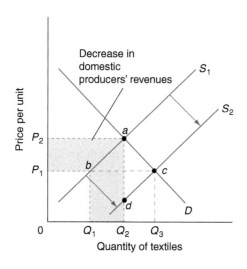

Figure 6.6 Losses from competition with imported products

Opening up the market to foreign trade increases the supply of textiles from S_1 to S_2. As a result, the price of textiles falls (from P_2 to P_1) and domestic producers sell a lower quantity (Q_1 at P_1 on their supply curve S_1, instead of Q_2 at P_2.) Consumers benefit from the lower price and the higher quantity of textiles they are able to buy, but domestic producers (owners, workers, and suppliers) lose. Producer revenues drop by an amount equal to the shaded area $P_2aQ_2Q_1bP_1$. Payments to workers and suppliers drop by an amount equal to the shaded area Q_2abQ_1. Alternatively, with free trade starting at point c, a tariff or tax equal to ad could be levied, shifting the supply curve from S_2 to S_1 and reversing the benefits and costs above – as well as imposing efficiency costs on the economy as a whole.

competition. If workers and other resources are employed in textiles because it is their best possible employment, the introduction of foreign products harms the employment opportunities of some workers – and political activity becomes attractive.

An examination of the impact of **tariffs** can illustrate the distributional impact of various forms of trade protection. (We'll focus on tariffs here, but **import quotas** have similar effects.) If tariffs are imposed on a foreign good such as textiles, the supply of textiles will decrease – say, from S_2 to S_1 in Figure 6.6 – and the price of imports will rise. (A lower tariff would have a more modest effect, shifting the supply curve only part

> A **tariff** is a tax or duty on imported goods that can be a percentage of the price (*ad valorem* duty) or a specific amount per unit of the product (specific duty).

> An **import quota** is a limit on the number of units of a good (or a dollar-value limit) that can be imported from a given country.

way toward S_1, reducing all of the above effects.[19]) As domestic demand shifts from the higher-priced imported textiles to domestic sources, domestic producers will be able to raise their prices and domestic production will go up (from b to a, moving along their supply curve S_1).

---

[19] The price of textiles will rise and domestic producers will expand their production, but imports will continue to come into the country. How much the price rises and the quantity falls after the imposition of the tariff depends on the level of the tariff and how much consumers respond to a price increase. With more price-responsive consumers, the quantity of textiles consumed domestically falls more and price rises less.

In sum, tariffs and quotas reduce the market supply in the country where they are imposed, raise domestic market prices, and encourage domestic production – helping domestic producers, harming domestic consumers, and hurting the economy overall. Domestic restrictions on international trade undercut economic gains that result when countries (and the people in them) exploit the benefits of trading according to the law of comparative advantage. Restrictions also narrow markets. Thus, they can undercut economies of specialization and scale in both resources and production. For these reasons, from the days of Adam Smith, most economists have favored the reduction, if not elimination, of tariffs and quotas. (The cases for and against protectionism have been extended in Online Reading 6.5. In Online Reading 6.6, we recount how the production of cotton has moved around the globe over the past few centuries.)

Tariffs promote a less efficient allocation of the world's scarce resources, but, because domestic producers stand to gain private benefits from them, we should expect those producers to seek tariffs as long as the benefits to them exceed the political cost of acquiring protection. Politicians are likely to expect votes and campaign contributions in return for tariff legislation that generates highly visible benefits to special interests. Producers (and labor) usually will make the necessary contributions because the elimination of foreign competition promises increased revenues in the protected industries. The difference between the increase in profits caused by import restrictions and the amount spent on political activity can be seen as a kind of profit in itself. That is, the potential for the imposition of tariffs can be expected to lead to lobbying efforts and "rent-seeking." Because lobbying for protection soaks up resources that would otherwise have a productive use, the aggregate economic costs and inefficiencies from protectionist policies are extended even further.

In contrast to producers, consumers have reason to oppose tariffs or quotas on imported products. Such legislation inevitably causes prices to rise and competition to decline. But consumers rarely offer any resistance, since the financial burden that any one consumer bears is slight – particularly if the tariff in question is small (as most tariffs are). The benefits of a tariff accrue principally to a relatively small group of firms, whose lobbyists may already be well entrenched in Washington. These firms have a strong incentive to be fully informed on the issue, make campaign contributions, and craft enticing rationales for why government intervention is supposedly good for the economy. (Bastiat's essay in Perspective 6 lampoons this approach.) The political influence of the producers can, at times, be offset partially by the political activism of large retailers, who bear some of the burden of protectionist policies through higher prices of imported goods and through lower sales to

American buyers.[20] But generally, the political calculus here leans heavily in favor of politically connected interest groups using government to restrict their competition. (There is much more to say about the economics and politics of international trade and finance. Interested parties are encouraged to read Online Chapter 3.)

Practical Lessons

If your firm faces foreign competition, it can increase its profits by producing a better product, cutting costs, or developing an effective marketing campaign. But your firm may also look to influence politicians to impose tariffs on imports that compete with your firm's products, which will allow your firm to increase both its prices and sales. If you can't secure tariff protection, your best bet could be to shift production to the countries with a comparative cost advantage in your product. You can shift production for offensive and defensive reasons: a production-location shift can increase your firm's profitability – and if you don't make the shift, firms willing to move their capital can outcompete you in your product markets.

On the other hand, your firm might seek the elimination of tariffs imposed on the parts and materials you use in your production processes. You can then reduce your production costs and increase sales as you lower your prices. If your firm exports products to foreign countries, you should even consider seeking the elimination of import restrictions on products you do *not* produce. Such import restrictions reduce sales by firms in foreign countries, cramping the ability of people in those countries to buy imports, including the goods your firm exports. Your firm should consider being "anti-protectionist" to improve your firm's profitability by increasing foreign sales.

Students of business also need to understand the economics of externalities, both benefits and costs. Externalities are seen by economists and policy-makers as a major

---

[20] Trade restrictions also cause economic harm in other ways. First, they harm the market for trade itself – for example, the shipping industry. Second, through the "balance of payments," if foreigners have fewer dollars (from domestic consumers buying goods and services from other countries), they will have fewer dollars to spend and invest in our economy. Third, foreign countries may retaliate with protective tariffs of their own to increase employment in their own industries or to impose economic costs with the hope that countries will reduce tariffs. The Smoot–Hawley Tariff Protection Act at the start of the Great Depression is a classic example. Its higher tariffs (averaging 62 percent on some 60,000 agricultural and industrial goods) led to higher tariffs on American goods and contributed to the early stages of a global Great Depression. Trade restrictions pose a global Prisoner's Dilemma. Every nation has strong domestic political incentives to impose protectionist measures, but, if many nations impose tariffs, then everyone can be worse off. Related, there is good reason to be suspicious of free-trade "negotiation" and "deals." Politicians will want to seem supportive of free trade while actually invoking protectionism.

source of so-called "market failures," both real and imagined. The consequences of environmental externalities will drive policies at all levels of government for the foreseeable future, probably leading to greater governmental regulation of business.

Likewise, business students should understand the relative efficiency of various government policies to correct for externalities. They should always be alert to the prospects of "government failures" that can come from the adoption of proposed policies. The consequences can result in net welfare gains for your firm, your industry, and the rest of the country. But they can also come with economic costs that exceed the expected benefits – for example, a corrective tax so high that its projected welfare loss is greater than the inefficiency of the external costs that are the focus of the corrective tax.

Of course, political dynamics can cause some corrective policies to be proposed by some firms for no higher purpose than to hobble competitors (for example, toy regulations designed to throttle competition from low-quality toy imports). Then there are the proposed corrective policies that can worsen environmental problems while benefiting politically powerful interest groups. For example, farmers understand that a requirement to add ethanol to gasoline can raise corn prices and sales. Producers of electric-powered cars have lobbied politicians for buyer subsidies, understanding that they will boost prices and sales. Business students should carefully scrutinize the claims of advocates that their proposed "green" remedies will actually improve the environment in cost-effective ways.

Further Reading Online

Reading 6.1: Why walking to work can be more polluting than driving to work

Reading 6.2: Pedophiles and the regulation of hugging

Reading 6.3: The government nobody knows – nor wants to know (*The Independent Review*, link available on the online resources website www.cambridge .org/mckenzie4)

Reading 6.4: Why businessmen are more honest than preachers, politicians, and professors (*The Independent Review*, link available on the online resources website www.cambridge.org/mckenzie4)

Reading 6.5: The cases for and against free trade

Reading 6.6: The travels of a T-shirt in a global economy

Recommended Videos Online

1 External costs and pollution rights (Richard McKenzie, 37 minutes)

2 External benefits (Richard McKenzie, 24 minutes)

3 International trade and protection (Richard McKenzie, 32 minutes)

4 Government employees gone wild (Freakonomics, link available on the online resources website www.cambridge.org/mckenzie4)

5 Tariffs; Trade; Winners And Losers (Marginal Revolution University, link available on the online resources website www.cambridge.org/mckenzie4)

6 Katherine Mangu-Ward: What capitalism gets right – and governments get wrong (TED, link available on the online resources website www.cambridge.org/mckenzie4)

7 San Francisco's Happy Meal ban (*The Daily Show*, link available on the online resources website www.cambridge.org/mckenzie4)

8 Traffic (*The Guardian*, link available on the online resources website www.cambridge.org/mckenzie4)

The Bottom Line

The key takeaways from Chapter 6 are the following:

1 People have preferences for government policies on the basis of efficiency, equity, and paternalism. Equity and paternalism are important considerations, but highly subjective.

2 Markets struggle to be efficient in five key areas: macroeconomics, natural monopoly power, information problems, "public goods," and externalities. In such cases, government intervention can be efficiency-enhancing, if done well.

3 A market economy will overproduce goods and services that impose external costs on society. It will underproduce goods and services that confer external benefits.

4 Sometimes, government intervention can be justified to correct for externalities. To be worthwhile, the benefits of action must outweigh the costs. Some ways of dealing with external costs and benefits are more efficient than others.

5 Some critics of markets suggest that markets are bound to fail because of the gains to business from being dishonest, which implies a form of "externality." Nevertheless, markets have built-in incentives for people to be more honest than they might otherwise be.

6 Economists use models to understand political activity – of greatest interest to business students, redistribution from the general public to special-interest groups (emphasizing the power of small groups), the median voter model (emphasizing the power of majorities), and bureaucracy.

7 Political parties in two-party systems will tend to gravitate toward the middle of the voter distribution – aiming to represent the views of the "median voter."

8 Voters in large electorates are impaired by incentives to become informed about political issues. Special-interest groups often exert disproportionate influence on political markets, since voters are "rationally ignorant and apathetic" about public policy and political philosophy.

9 In the private and public sectors, actors will look to obtain, extend, and exploit monopoly power. Interest groups often attempt to use government to this end and bureaucracies often take advantage of monopoly power to expand budgets.

10　Tariffs and quotas reduce the aggregate real incomes of countries that impose them and countries that are subject to them, because they reduce mutually beneficial trades.

11　Those industries protected by tariffs and quotas can gain from them, but only at the (greater) expense of consumers who must pay higher prices for the protected goods and exporters who are not able to export as much.

12　The growth in capital mobility on a global scale has provided businesses with cost-saving opportunities, but it has also tightened competitive constraints on businesses. Capital mobility has also imposed competitive constraints on governments as they seek to determine their tax and regulatory policies.

Review Questions ▸▸

1　Define "public goods" and explain why markets struggle in dealing with them.

2　Define externalities and explain why markets struggle in dealing with them.

3　Graph a positive or negative externality. Detail equilibrium in the absence of government intervention in contrast to the socially efficient equilibrium level.

4　How are public goods and externalities different from income redistribution?

5　When is it desirable, in your opinion, for government to adopt policies to please the median voter? What criteria are you using to form your opinion?

6　Think of a good or service provided by government. What would it look like for it to be provided by the private sector? How could the government continue to provide the good but increase or decrease the extent of the private sector in this provision?

7　In some detail, describe the mechanism by which income is typically redistributed within political markets. Why do the losers tolerate these schemes?

8　When would workers want democratic governance in the workplace?

9　Apply the concept of externalities to decisions and solutions in your workplace.

10　Using supply and demand curves, show how a U.S. tariff on a foreign-made good will affect the price and quantity sold in the country that imports the good and in the country that exports the good.

11　"Tariffs on imported textiles increase the employment opportunities and incomes of domestic textiles workers. They therefore increase aggregate employment and income." Evaluate this statement.

12　What are the costs and benefits of allowing U.S. consumers (the producers who use it as an input to production) the ability to buy steel produced and subsidized by foreigners.

13　How much would a business spend to get a tariff? What economic considerations will have an impact on the amount spent?

14　How can greater capital mobility across national boundaries affect governments' tax policies? Why must businesses pay attention to the tax rates and regulations in different countries?

Book II
Producer Theory

In Chapters 1–6, we provided a broad overview of the forces of supply and demand, with an emphasis on the application of those analytical devices to a variety of management and public policies. In Chapters 3 and 4, we developed the theoretical underpinnings of demand. Now, in Book II (Chapters 7 and 8), we do the same for supply. We then use these concepts in Book III (Chapters 9–12) to explore firm production and organizational strategies under different market structures, ranging from competitive to monopolistic.

7

Production, Costs, and the Theory of the Firm

It is not from the benevolence of the butcher, the brewer, or the baker, that we expect our dinner, but from their regard to their own.

Adam Smith

We may not recognize it, but cost pervades our everyday thought and conversation. Although money is the most frequent measure of cost, it is not cost itself. When we say "this course is difficult," or "the sermon seemed endless," or "changes to the product design at this stage can't be made," we are indicating something about the costs involved. Complaints about excessive costs sometimes indicate an absolute limitation, but more often they merely indicate that the benefits of the activity are too small to justify the cost. Managers (and everyone else) are constantly forced to make choices in the face of the universal "scarcity" we described in Chapter 1 – to do one thing and not another.

This chapter explores the meaning of cost for human behavior in general and for business in particular. Many people who "can't afford" a vacation have the money, but do not want to spend it on travel; most students who find a course "difficult" are simply not willing to make the necessary effort; and a marketing plan that we choose to pursue or eschew is a function of its expected costs and benefits.

In conventional economic discussions of production costs, incentives are nowhere considered, because the "firm" is mostly a theoretical "black box" in which things happen mysteriously. Textbooks typically acknowledge the firm as the basic production unit, but little or nothing is said about what the firm *is* or why it came into existence. As a consequence, we are told little about why firms do what they do (and don't do) – and there is little about the role of real people in a firm.

How are firms to be distinguished from the markets they inhabit, especially in terms of the incentives faced by people in firms and markets? This question is seldom addressed – other than specifying that firms can be one of several legal forms (proprietorships, partnerships, professional associations, or corporations). In standard discussions of the "theory of the firm," firms maximize their profits – sometimes their only specified *raison d'être*. But students are not told how or why firms do what they are supposed to do.

The owners, presumably, devise ways to ensure that everyone in the organization follows instructions – all of which exist to squeeze every ounce of profit from every opportunity. Students are never told what the instructions are or what is done to ensure that workers follow them. The structure of incentives inside the firm never comes up, because their purpose is effectively assumed away: people do what they are supposed to do – naturally or by some unspecified process.

For people in business (and business students), this approach to the "firm" must appear strange indeed, given that owners and managers spend much of their working day trying to coax people to do what they are supposed to do. Nothing is more problematic in business than getting employees to consistently devote their efforts to increasing firm profits instead of devoting themselves to more personal concerns. (In Online Reading 7.1, we discuss the challenges of finding and being an effective manager.)

In Part A of this chapter, we begin by describing deviations from profit maximization. Then, largely assuming profit maximization, we show how the hidden costs of a choice often explain seemingly irrational behavior. We then develop further the concept of marginal cost, which, together with the related concepts of demand and supply, defines the limits of rational behavior in business, including how much should be produced. Our development of a firm's cost structure will continue in Chapter 8. Then, we will use this cost structure in Chapters 9–11 to determine how much firms in different markets facing different competitive pressures will produce to maximize profits.

In Part B of this chapter, we address the issue of *why firms exist*, which, believe it or not, has been debated for a long time by economists. This is not just an interesting academic question. Rather, the answer can help us understand why the existence of firms and incentives go hand-in-hand – and how production costs connect to the size and organization of firms. Costs and profitability depend critically upon how well production is coordinated both inside and outside the firm. As we will see, firm size will affect its overall coordinating costs and its organizational structure. We also want to provide practical guidance on how firms can minimize their cost structures. (In Online Reading 7.2, we discuss cost control on a big-ticket item in many firms' cost structure – health insurance.)

And related to this, in Perspective 7, we take up an issue that often perplexes people, especially in business: Why do professors have tenure and others (generally) do not? We submit that professor tenure, in most cases, has little to do with protecting freedom of speech in their lectures and writings from religious and political forces external to their universities. It has far more to do with the fact that professors work often in "labor-managed firms," which means their colleagues are constantly judging their work in merit and promotion reviews.

Part A Theory and Public Policy Applications

Deviations from Profit Maximization

Aside from profit-maximizing firms, there are other entities that produce goods and services – government agencies and non-profit organizations. Government is different enough that we treated it separately in Chapter 6. Government agencies operate in political markets which are often dominated by budget maximization and bureaucratic incentives that vary considerably from what we see in profit-seeking firms. Non-profits have considerable over-lap with for-profits. (If you've served on the board of a smaller non-profit, you may have experienced an impressive determination to raise revenue and efficiently use resources.) But at least their explicit goals are different, so it is safer to evaluate them differently – albeit perhaps still using the tools we'll develop here.

Focusing on profit-maximizing firms, this does not imply that every action within those firms will be profit-maximizing. Employees and managers have their own agendas – what we will soon describe as "agency costs" – that deviate from an owner's desire to maximize profit. And sometimes, owners at least seem to have a variety of other agendas – with a willingness to sacrifice some profit to accomplish other goals. Owners might overpay some workers to be compassionate. They might donate some of their profits to charitable efforts. They might allow their workers to be paid by the firm while volunteering in the community once per quarter.

Then again, such expenditures may be "goodwill investments" that actually enhance profits. If I give away resources, this may enhance the firm's goodwill in the community, providing me with additional customers, more passionate workers, sympathetic investors, or greater political influence – with some positive "return on investment." At the end of the day, it's difficult if not impossible to discern why firms spend money in these ways. But even if the results are not profitable, the presence of relatively minor expenditures of this type do not constitute a significant deviation from our standard assumption of profit maximization.

Finally, profit maximization does not imply that every item sold will be, itself, profit-maximizing. "Loss leaders" are items purposefully sold at prices below marginal cost – to attract people to the business and enhance profits overall. Consider Best Buy selling big-screen televisions. It's possible that they lose money on televisions, while making money on accessories, service, extended warranties, delivery, installation, and/or financing – again, profit-maximizing overall.

Various Cost Conceptions

Now we begin to model the cost *structure* of firms. We are not simply concerned with a firm's costs for a given output level and time period in the past; a firm's accounting statements provide this vital historical information. We seek to develop the conceptual structure for a firm's costs over a wide range of output levels in different time periods, which can help managers think about what output level they should choose and how they should expand/contract production now and in the future. You and your classmates work in a variety of industries with different production costs. Our goal here is to devise a cost structure that is generally applicable to all industries, providing tools that can help us consider production decisions for any firm. (Ultimately, we will determine production decision rules that arise from merging our development of a firm's cost structure with the structure of demand from Chapters 3 and 4.) For purposes of effective communication, if nothing else, economists have identified key cost concepts that play important roles in a firm's cost structure.

Explicit and Implicit Costs

An out-of-pocket expenditure is an obvious cost – for example, the cost of a movie ticket and popcorn. These are **explicit costs**. Other costs are less immediately apparent – for example, the time spent at the movie and the risk of a car crash in transit. These are **implicit costs**. Together, they acknowledge the value of what you could have done instead. Although implicit costs are not always recognized, they are often much larger than the more obvious explicit costs of an action.

> An **explicit cost** is the money expenditure required to obtain a resource, product, or service.

> An **implicit cost** is the forgone opportunity to do or acquire something else – or to put one's resources to another use that doesn't require a monetary payment.

The cost of a college education is a good illustration of implicit costs. Suppose an MBA student takes a course and pays $2000 for tuition and $300 for books. The money cost of the course is $2300, but this does not include the implicit costs. To take a course, the student must study for the course, attend class, complete assignments, and study for tests. Let's say the total number of hours spent on any one course is 120 hours. The business student could have spent this time doing other things, including working for a money wage. If the student's time is valued at $40 per hour, the time cost of the course is $4800 (120 h × $40/h). Moreover, if she experiences some anxiety because of taking the course, this psychic or risk cost must be added to the total as well. If she would be willing to pay $500 to avoid the anxiety, the total implicit cost of taking the course climbs to $5300. The implicit costs represent the largest component of the total cost of the course ($7600).

The value of one's time varies from person to person.[1] The time cost also explains the popularity of executive MBA programs, which allow working students to do more of their course work online and on weekends. Likewise, few CEOs of major corporations can be found in graduate, much less undergraduate, business programs of any type. Their explicit costs are the same, but their implicit (time) costs are far higher – so much so that they have little hope of recovering their education investments. This is especially true since many CEOs may have only a few years left in their careers. And when we recognize the opportunity costs, it is not surprising that applications to graduate business programs run somewhat countercyclically, increasing when the economy goes into a recession and decreasing in the recovery phase of macroeconomic business cycles. During an economic downturn, people's opportunity costs go down with a decrease in business opportunities (or even unemployment) and increase with a recovery.[2]

Why "Sunk Costs" Don't Matter

Some "costs" on accounting statements should not be considered in making business decisions. If current decisions cannot alter costs that have already been incurred and cannot be recouped, they are beyond the realm of choice. These costs are called **sunk costs**.

> A **sunk cost** is a past cost. It has already been incurred and cannot be recouped; it cannot be changed and hence is irrelevant to current decisions.

An example can help illustrate the irrelevance of sunk costs. Suppose an oil exploration firm purchases the mineral rights to a particular piece of property for $1 million with no resale market. After several months of drilling, the firm concludes that the land contains no oil. Will the firm reason that, having spent $1 million for the mineral rights, it should continue to look for oil on the land? If the chances of finding oil are nonexistent, the rational firm will cease drilling on the land and try somewhere else. The $1 million is a sunk cost, which should not influence the decision to continue or cease exploration. Indeed, the firm may begin drilling on land for which it paid far less for the mineral rights, if management believes the chances of finding oil there are higher than on the $1 million property.

In fact, the term "sunk cost" itself is misleading, since they are no longer costs at all. The opportunity cost of an activity is the value of the best alternative

---

[1] For students who are unable to find work or have few productive skills, the time costs of taking a course may be quite small. This is why most college students are young. Their time cost is generally lower than that of experienced workers, who would forfeit the opportunity to earn a better wage to attend classes full time. There is also the question of the value of business education for someone with business experience. The relationship is probably U-shaped: most valuable with a few years of experience – to more fully understand and apply the classroom education.

[2] The analysis must be qualified because people's incomes tend to fall (rise) with an economic downturn (upturn), which means that an income effect can mute the opportunity-cost effect of the business cycle.

not chosen. In the case of an historical cost, however, there are no longer any alternatives. Although the oil exploration firm could have chosen an alternative way to spend the $1 million, this alternative has ceased to be available. Nor can the firm resell the mineral rights for $1 million; those rights are now worth far less because of accumulated evidence that the land contains no oil. Sunk costs, however painful the memory of them might be, are gone and best forgotten. Profits are made by looking forward, not backward. To complete the example: If the land can be sold, there is a cost of using it or just holding onto it – not the $1 million purchase price, but its (far lower) resale price.

The Cost of Bargains

Every week, most supermarkets advertise weekly specials. Generally, only a few items are offered at especially low prices, since store managers know that most bargain seekers can be attracted to the store with just a few carefully selected specials. After the customer has gone to the store, he would incur a travel (transaction) cost to buy other items in a different store. Even though peanut butter may be on sale elsewhere, the sum of the sale price and the travel cost exceed the regular price in the first store. Through attractive displays and packaging, customers can be persuaded to buy many other goods not on sale – particularly toiletries, which tend to have high markups. If done well, stores more than recoup the revenues lost on sale items with higher prices on other goods. In other words, the cost of a bargain on sirloin steak may be a high price for toothpaste.

Some shoppers make the rounds of the grocery stores when sales are announced. For such people, time and transportation are cheap. A person who values his time at $40 per hour is not going to spend an hour trying to save a dollar or two. The cost of gas alone can make it prohibitively expensive to visit several stores. Because of the costs of acquiring information, many shoppers do not even bother to look for sales. The expected benefits are simply not great enough to justify the information cost. As we saw with voters in Chapter 6, these consumers enter the market "rationally ignorant."

Normal Profit as a Cost

In accounting, profit is the "bottom line" of profit and loss (P&L) or income statements – the difference between recorded revenues and recorded expenses. However, some costs of doing business are never reported on a company's books – for example:

1 the opportunity cost of the firm's owner/manager (the salary the owner/manager could have received elsewhere);
2 the opportunity cost of capital (the earnings that would have been received had the firm's owner invested his finance in some risk-free investment – for example, a government bond); and
3 the risk cost of doing business (or the expected losses from firm failure).

Even though these costs may not be recognized on a firm's books, they must be recovered in order for the firm to continue "profitably" in business. These costs are called **normal profits** by economists. The "profits" reported by a firm on its P&L statement are called **book (accounting) profits** by economists.

> **Normal profits** are the opportunity and risk costs of doing business not reported on firms' P&L statements. They must be covered or the owners will not redeploy firm resources.

If book profits are less than normal profits, the firm incurs an **economic loss**. If book profits are greater than normal profits, the firm earns **economic profits**. The amount by which book profits exceed normal profits is economic profit. Economic profit is a return that is more than

> **Book (accounting) profits** are the profits reported on the "bottom lines" of firm P&L statements.

> **Economic loss** occurs when *total* costs, including unrecorded opportunity and risk costs, exceed total revenues.

> **Economic profits** are realized when *total* costs, including unrecorded opportunity and risk costs, are less than total revenues.

necessary to keep resources employed where they are. A simple example: If the risk-free return on investment is 8 percent and you earn a 3 percent book profit, then you're forfeiting 5 percent – an accounting profit, but an economic loss.

Peter Drucker once quipped that: "Few U.S. businesses have been profitable since World War II" (Drucker 2001, 117). Most may find this hard to accept – and those who do believe it may interpret Drucker as talking about business failure. But he was commenting about *economic profits* and, once understood, his statement can be seen as a comment on the *success* of the U.S. economy. As Drucker wrote, "Until a business returns a profit that is greater than its cost of capital [opportunity cost], it operates at a loss. … The enterprise … returns less to the economy than it uses up in resources" (Drucker 2001, 117). On the other hand, if many firms made large economic profits, it would also be a sign of inefficiency in the economy – a failure to reallocate resources to more profitable endeavors.

The Special Significance of Marginal Cost

The rational person weighs the cost of an action against its benefits and comes to a decision: whether to invest in an education, to shop around for a bargain, to learn how to fly. So far, we have been considering cost as the determining factor in the decision to undertake a particular course of action – or in business, how much of a given good or service to produce. A key part of the answer relies on the concept of **marginal cost**. (We emphasize marginal cost in this chapter, but marginal benefits are also critical to production and consumption decisions – as will be detailed in Chapter 9.)

> **Marginal cost** is the additional cost incurred by producing one additional unit of a good or service.

Rational Behavior and Marginal Cost

Marginal cost is the cost incurred by reading one additional page, watching one more movie, giving one additional gift, or going one additional mile. Depending on the activity in question, marginal cost can stay the same or vary as additional units are produced. For example, imagine that Jan wants to give Halloween candy to ten of her friends. In a sense, she is producing gifts by procuring bags of candy. If she can buy as many bags as she wants at a unit price of 50 cents, the marginal cost of each additional unit is the same: 50 cents. The marginal cost is constant over the range of production.

However, marginal cost can vary with the level of output for two reasons. First, the opportunity cost of time must be considered. Suppose Jan wants to give each friend a miniature watercolor, which she will paint over the course of the day. To make time for painting, Jan can forgo any of the various activities that usually make up her day – for example, recreational activities, gardening chores, or time spent at work or study. If she behaves rationally, she will give up the activities she values least. To do the first painting, she may forgo laying soil on a bare spot in her lawn. The marginal cost of her first watercolor is therefore a lawn eyesore. To paint the second watercolor, Jan will give up the next most valuable item on her list of activities. As she produces more and more paintings, Jan will forgo more and more valuable alternatives. Hence, the marginal cost of her paintings will rise with her output. If the marginal cost of each new painting is plotted against the quantity of paintings produced, a curve like that in Figure 7.1 will result. Because the marginal cost of each additional painting is higher than the marginal cost of the last one, the curve slopes upward to the right.

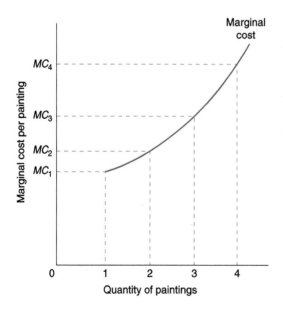

Figure 7.1 Rising marginal cost
To produce each new watercolor, Jan must give up an opportunity more valuable than the previous. Thus, the marginal cost of her paintings rises with each new work of art.

The Law of Diminishing Marginal Returns

The second reason that marginal cost may vary with output involves a technological relationship known as the **law of diminishing marginal returns**: beyond some point, less output is received from each added

> The **law of diminishing marginal returns** states that, as more units of one resource (labor, fertilizer, etc.) are applied to a fixed quantity of another resource (e.g., land), the additional output gained from each additional unit of the variable resource will eventually begin to diminish.

unit of a resource. Alternatively stated, more of the resource will be required to produce the same amount of output as before. And thus, after some level of production, the marginal cost of additional units of output rises.

Although the law of diminishing marginal returns applies to any production process, its meaning can be easily grasped in the context of agricultural production. Assume that you are producing tomatoes. You have a fixed amount of land (an acre), but you can vary the quantity of labor applied to it. If you try to do the planting by yourself – dig the holes, pour the water, insert the plants, and cover up the roots – you will waste time when you change tools and you will engage in aspects of production where you are not as proficient. If a friend helps you, you can divide the tasks and specialize. Less time will be wasted in changing tools, and production will be enhanced by focusing on each person's areas of comparative advantage.

At first, output may expand faster than the labor force. That is, one laborer may be able to plant 100 tomatoes per hour; two working together may be able to plant 250 per hour. Thus, the marginal cost of planting the additional 150 plants is lower than the cost of the initial 100. Up to a point, the more workers, the greater their efficiency and the lower the marginal cost. At some point, however, the addition of another laborer will not contribute as much to production as the previous one – if only because workers begin bumping into one another. The point of diminishing marginal returns has been reached and the marginal cost of putting plants into the ground will begin to rise.

Diminishing marginal returns are an inescapable fact of life. If marginal returns did not diminish at some point (and eventually become negative – adding another laborer actually *reduces* output), output would expand indefinitely and the world's food supply could be grown on just one acre of land! The point at which output begins to diminish varies from one production process to the next, but eventually all marginal cost curves will slope upward to the right, as in Figure 7.1.

Table 7.1 shows the marginal cost of producing tomatoes with various numbers of workers, assuming each worker is paid $5 and production is limited to one acre. Working alone, one worker can produce a quarter of a bushel; two can produce a full bushel, and so on [columns (1) and (2)]. Column (3) shows the

Table 7.1 **Marginal costs of producing tomatoes**

(1) No. of workers employed	(2) Total no. of bushels	(3) Contribution of each worker to production (marginal product)	(4) No. of workers required to produce each additional bushel at this rate	(5) Marginal cost of each bushel, at this production rate, assuming $5 per worker ($)
1	0.25	0.25	4	20
2	1.00	0.75	1.33	6.67
3	2.00	1.00	1	5
Point at which diminishing marginal returns emerge				
4	2.60	0.60	1.67	8.33
5	3.00	0.40	2.5	12.50
6	3.30	0.30	3.33	16.67
7	3.55	0.25	4	20
8	3.75	0.20	5	25
9	3.90	0.15	6.67	33.33
10	4.00	0.10	10	50

marginal product. The first worker contributed 0.25 (one quarter) of a bushel; the second worker, an additional 0.75 of a bushel, and so on. These are the marginal productivity of successive units of labor.

> **Marginal product** is the increase in total output that results when one additional unit of a resource – for example, labor, fertilizer, and land – is added to the production process, all else constant.

Although two workers are needed to produce the first bushel, the efficiencies of specialization require only one additional worker to produce the second bushel. Beyond this point, however, marginal returns diminish. Each additional worker contributes less, so two more workers are needed to produce the third bushel and five more to produce the fourth. If Table 7.1 were extended, each bushel beyond the fourth would require a progressively larger number of workers – and, eventually, additional workers would begin to reduce output.

Column (4) norms column (3) to the number of workers required to produce one additional bushel at the same marginal rate. Column (5) shows that if all of these workers are paid $5, the marginal cost of a bushel of tomatoes will decline from $10 for the first bushel to $5 for the second, before rising to $10 again for the third bushel. That is, increasing marginal costs (or diminishing returns) emerge with the addition of the third worker and beyond (to $25 for the fourth

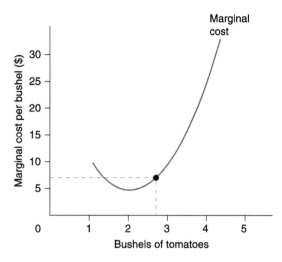

Figure 7.2 The law of diminishing marginal returns

As production expands with the addition of new workers, efficiencies of specialization initially cause marginal cost to fall. At some point, however – here, just beyond two bushels – marginal cost will begin to rise again. At this point, marginal productivity will begin to diminish and marginal costs will begin to rise.

bushel). If the marginal cost of each bushel [column (5)] is plotted against the number of bushels harvested [column (2)], the curve in Figure 7.2 will result.

Although the curve slopes downward at first, the relevant segment of the curve is usually the upward-sloping portion of a U-shaped marginal cost curve. In Chapters 8 and 9, we will note that profit-maximizing firms tend to produce in the output range where diminishing returns are experienced with increases in output levels – and thus where marginal cost of production is increasing. This explains why market supply curves in competitive markets tend to be upward-sloping. It also means that, outside of insufficient demand, firms should take advantage of all efficiencies of production and expand output at least until increasing marginal costs set in. (We have more work to do before this will become clear, but we introduce it here to emphasize that the analysis has a purpose in the workplace.)

The Cost–Benefit Trade-Off

A marginal cost schedule shows the increasing marginal cost for producers to supply more goods. As explained earlier, the demand curve shows the decreasing marginal value or marginal benefit of those goods to consumers. Together, marginal costs and benefits determine the amount of production and consumption that creates the greatest net value. Producers and consumers gain from both producing and consuming more of a good as long as the marginal cost of producing it is less than the marginal value of consuming it. That is, there are additional gains to be had from increasing production and consumption, until the marginal cost curve intersects the marginal benefit curve. Going beyond this, the costs outweigh the benefits. Thus, the intersection of the two curves represents the point where welfare is maximized.

To demonstrate this point, we consider the costs and benefits of fishing for Gary. What he does with the fish he catches is of no consequence to our discussion; he can make them into trophies, give them away, or store them in a freezer. Even if Gary places no money value on the fish, we can use dollars to illustrate the marginal costs and benefits of fishing to Gary, since money is a convenient way to indicate relative value. How many fish will he catch? From our earlier analysis of Jan's desire to paint, we know that the cost of catching each additional fish will be higher than the cost of the one before. Gary will confront an upward-sloping marginal cost curve as in Figure 7.2. Gary's demand curve for fishing will slope downward (see Figure 7.3) because, as he catches more fish over some period of time (say, a day), the marginal value he receives from catching fish will eventually start declining.

From the positions of the two curves in Figure 7.3, we can see that Gary will catch up to five fish before he heads home. He places a relatively high value of $4.67 on the first fish (point a) and figures that the first fish caught has a relatively low marginal cost of $1 (point b) – the value of the forgone opportunities. In other words, he gets $3.67 more value from using his time, energy, and other resources to catch the first fish than he would receive from his next best alternative. The marginal benefit of the second fish also exceeds its marginal cost, although by a smaller amount (say, $4.25 – $1.50 = $2.75). Gary continues to gain with the third and fourth fishes, but the fifth fish is a matter of indifference to him. Its marginal value equals its marginal cost (point c). Although we cannot say that Gary will actually bother to catch a fifth fish, we do know that five is the limit toward which he will aim. He will not catch a sixth (during the period of time offered by the graph), because it would cost him more than he would receive in benefits.[3]

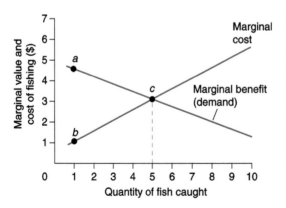

Figure 7.3 Costs and benefits of fishing For each fish up to the fifth, Gary receives more in benefits than he pays in costs. The first fish gives him $4.67 in benefits (point a) and costs him only $1 (point b). The fifth yields equal costs and benefits (point c), but the sixth costs more than it is worth. Therefore, Gary will catch no more than five fish.

---

[3] More precisely, Gary is weighing his expectation of costs against expected benefits as he fishes. But the principles play out the same way.

The Costs and Benefits of Preventing Accidents

All of us would prefer to avoid accidents. In this sense, we have a demand for accident prevention which slopes downward as all other demand curves. We benefit more from trying to prevent the most likely and harmful accidents, before trying to prevent those that are less likely and harmful. However, preventing accidents also entails costs – whether in time, forgone opportunities, or money. Should we attempt to prevent all accidents? No. Eventually the cost of preventing an accident is greater than the expected benefit. Would you spend $10,000 to prevent an occasional paper cut from opening the mail?

As with the question of how long to fish, marginal cost and benefit curves can help illustrate the point at which preventing accidents ceases to be cost-effective. Suppose that Bob's experience indicates that he can expect to have ten accidents over the course of the year. If he tries to prevent all of them, the value of preventing the last one, as indicated by the demand curve in Figure 7.4, will be only $1 (point *a*). The marginal cost of preventing it will be much greater: approximately $6 (point *b*). If Bob is rational, he will not try to prevent the last accident. As a matter of fact, he will try to prevent only five accidents (point *c*). As with the tenth accident, it will cost more than it is worth to Bob to prevent the sixth through ninth accidents. He would try to prevent all ten accidents only if his demand for accident prevention were so great that his demand curve intersected, or passed over, the marginal cost curve at point *b*. The same principle applies to loss prevention for retail companies: the optimal level of shoplifting is not zero.

Some accidents may be unavoidable. In this case, the marginal cost curve will eventually become vertical. But most accidents are "avoidable" in the sense that it is physically possible to take measures to prevent them – although the rational course may be to allow them to happen.

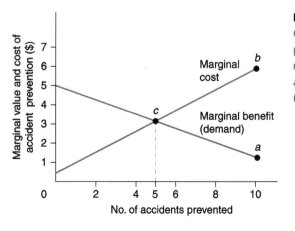

Figure 7.4 Accident prevention
Given the increasing marginal cost of preventing accidents and the decreasing marginal value of preventing the accidents, five accidents will be prevented (point *c*).

Price and Marginal Cost: Producing to Maximize Profits

Production is not generally an end to itself in business. Granted, many people derive intrinsic reward from their work. They may value the satisfaction of producing a product that meets a human need as much as they value profits. Some owners may even accept lower profits so that their products can sell at lower prices and serve more people. But most firms seek to make a profit. And for most of those, the profit generated by sales is the major motivation for doing business. So it is useful as a first approximation to assume that firms maximize profits. In fact, firms that do not maximize profits will be subject to takeover by entrepreneurs seeking to buy firms at depressed prices, institute profit-making policies, and then sell the firms at a higher price.

We can usefully consider how firms go about the task of trying to maximize profits by converting the total and marginal product curves into *cost curves*. By doing so, we can engage in familiar analysis of marginal cost and marginal benefit. How much will a profit-maximizing firm produce? Assume that its marginal cost curve is represented in Figure 7.5(a) and the owners can sell as many units as they want at the same price (P_1). Thus, the firm's **marginal revenue** is also P_1, since

Marginal revenue is the additional revenue that a firm receives by selling another unit of output.

its total revenue will increase by P_1 when the firm produces and sells an additional unit.

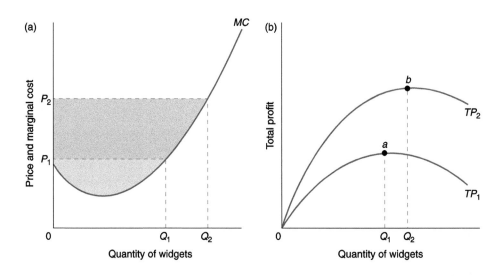

Figure 7.5 Marginal costs and maximization of profit
At price P_1 [panel (a)], the firm's marginal revenue (represented by P_1), exceeds its marginal cost (*MC*) up to the output level of Q_1. At this point, total profit [shown in panel (b)] peaks at point *a*. At price P_2, marginal revenue exceeds marginal cost up to an output level of Q_2. The increase in price shifts the profit curve in panel (b) upward – from TP_1 to TP_2 – and profits peak at *b*.

Clearly, a profit-maximizing firm will produce and sell any unit for which the marginal revenue (*MR*) exceeds the marginal cost (*MC*). (Profits are the difference between *total* costs and *total* revenues; therefore, a firm's profits rise whenever an increase in its revenues exceeds the increase in its costs.) At a price of P_1, this firm will produce Q_1 units. For every unit up to Q_1, price (marginal revenue) is greater than marginal cost; for every unit beyond Q_1, the marginal revenue is less than marginal cost.

The vertical distance between P_1 and the marginal cost of each unit – as shown by the *MC* curve in Figure 7.5(a) – is the additional profit obtained from each additional unit produced. By taking the difference between the vertical distance P_1 and the *MC* curve for all units up to Q_1, we can obtain the firm's total profits from producing Q_1 – the shaded area below P_1 in Figure 7.5(a). Total profit at various levels of output can also be represented as TP_1 in Figure 7.5(b). Notice that the curve peaks at Q_1, the point at which the firm chooses to stop producing. Beyond Q_1, marginal cost is greater than marginal revenue, so total profits would fall, as shown by the downward slope of the total profits curve.

What will the firm do if the price of its product rises from P_1 to P_2? For the firm that can sell all it wants at a constant price, a rise in price means a rise in marginal revenue. After the price rises to P_2, the marginal revenue of an additional $Q_2 - Q_1$ units exceeds their marginal cost. At the higher price, a larger number of units can be profitably produced and sold. The firm will seek to produce up to the point at which marginal cost equals the new, higher marginal revenue (P_2) – at output level Q_2 in Figure 7.5(a). As before, profit is equal to the vertical distance between the price line (P_2) and the *MC* curve – the two shaded areas below P_2 in Figure 7.5(a). The total profit curve shifts to the position of the line TP_2 in Figure 7.5(b).

From Individual Supply to Market Supply

The upward-sloping portion of the firm's *MC* curve is its supply curve; for each price, the amount the firm will supply is given by the firm's marginal cost at each price. (More will be said about this in Chapter 8.) If the *market* supply is the amount *all* producers are willing to produce at various prices, we can obtain the market supply curve by adding together the upward-sloping portions of the individual firms' *MC* curves. (This procedure is akin to how we determined the market demand curve in Chapter 4.)

Figure 7.6 shows the supply curves S_A and S_B, derived from the *MC* curves of two producers, *A* and *B*. At a price of P_1, only producer *B* is willing to produce anything – and it is willing to offer only Q_1. The total quantity supplied to the market at P_1 is therefore Q_1. At the higher prices of P_2, both producers are willing to compete. Producer *A* offers Q_1 whereas producer *B* offers more, Q_2. The total quantity supplied is therefore Q_3 – the sum of Q_1 and Q_2.

The market supply curve (S_{A+B}) is obtained by adding the amounts that *A* and *B* are willing to sell at each price. Note that the market supply curve lies further

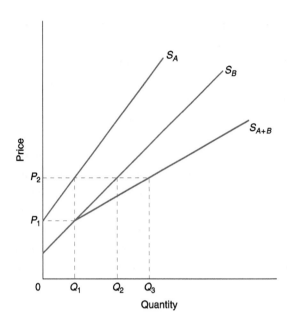

Figure 7.6 Market supply curve
The market supply curve (S_{A+B}) is obtained by adding together the amount producers A and B are willing to offer at every price, as shown by the individual supply curves S_A and S_B. (The individual supply curves are obtained from the upward-sloping portions of the firms' MC curves.)

from the origin and is flatter (more elastic) than the individual producers' supply curves. The entry of more producers will shift the market supply curve further out and lower its slope even more. (More will be said about this in Chapter 8.)

PERSPECTIVE 7
Why Professors Have Tenure and Business People Don't

Tenure is nothing short of the Holy Grail for newly employed assistant professors in colleges and universities. Without tenure, faculty members must, as a general rule, be dismissed after seven years of service, which means they must seek other academic employment or retreat from academic life. With tenure, professors have the equivalent of lifetime employment. Rarely are they fired by their academies, even if they cease to meet adequately performance norms as teachers, researchers, or service providers.

   Professors do not have complete protection from dismissal, and the potential for being fired is greater than is reflected in the number of actual firings. Moreover, a university may not be able to fire a faculty member quickly, but it can repeatedly deny salary increases and gradually increase teaching loads until the faculty member "chooses" to leave.[4] When professors are fired, it is generally for causes unrelated to their professional competence: "moral turpitude" (academic code for sexual indiscretions with students), financial exigencies (where

---

[4] Accordingly, the degree of protection that tenure affords is a function of such variables as the inflation rate. That is, the higher the inflation rate, the more quickly the real value of the professor's salary will erode each time an increase is denied.

whole departments are eliminated), and outright scholarly fraud (which generally involves plagiarism or bogus empirical findings).

Most opponents and supporters of academic tenure express their views in emotional terms: "Tenure is sloth" or "Tenure protects academic freedom." We suggest that tenure should be considered as one part of an employment relationship. It amounts to an employment contract provision specifying that the holder cannot easily be fired. People in business seldom, if ever, have this type of tenure protection. Why the different treatment? Perhaps universities are stupid, bureaucratic organizations in which professors are able to obtain special treatment. Maybe so, but we would like to think not. (Indeed, we think our universities have shown great wisdom in granting us tenure in our current positions!) We suggest that our explanation for why professors have tenure will help us understand why some form of tenure will gradually find its way into businesses that have begun to rely progressively more on "participatory management" – with low-ranking managers and line workers having a greater say in how the business is conducted (McKenzie 1996).

The Costs and Benefits of Tenure to Universities, Professors, and Students

Clearly, tenure has costs that the university's various constituencies must bear. Some professors exploit tenure by shirking their duties in the classroom, their research, and their service to the university. However, tenure is not the only contract provision with a cost. Other fringe benefits for professors impose costs directly on colleges or universities – and indirectly on students. Nonetheless, universities continue to cover health insurance costs because the benefits of doing so exceed those costs. On balance, this is a mutually beneficial trade for the various constituencies of the university. Universities can buy group insurance policies more cheaply than can individual faculty members – and health insurance through employers is subsidized by taxpayers as a nontaxed form of compensation. So, professors and universities are willing (if not excited) to trade additional wages for health insurance.

Likewise, professors "pay for" tenure; presumably, tenure is worth more to them than the value of the forgone wages. Why tenure? Any reasonable answer must start with the recognition that academic labor markets are reasonably competitive – with thousands of employers, hundreds of thousands of professors, and compensation packages that respond relatively well to market conditions. If tenure was not a mutually beneficial trade between employers and employees, universities and/or professors would seek to alter the employment contract, modify the tenure provision, increase other forms of payment, lower overall university costs, and increase worker well-being.[5]

---

[5] Granted, tenure may be required by accrediting associations; however, there is no reason that groups of universities could not operate outside accrediting associations or organize their own accrediting associations without the tenure provision – if tenure were, on balance, a significant impairment to academic goals. In many respects, the accrediting association rules can be defended on the same competitive grounds that recruiting rules of the National Collegiate Athletic Association (NCAA) are defended. See McKenzie and Sullivan (1987).

The analysis continues with the recognition that jobs vary in difficulty, required time and skills, and satisfaction. "Boss" can define many jobs, and bosses are generally quite capable of evaluating the performance of those they hire. For example, in response to sales, supervisors in fast-food restaurants can determine how many hamburgers to cook and how many employees are needed to flip and assemble those hamburgers. Where work is relatively simple and routine, we would expect it to be defined and evaluated within a hierarchical governance structure, as is generally true in the fast-food industry.

Academic work is substantially different. Many forms of the work are highly sophisticated and cannot be observed directly and easily (given the reliance on thinking skills). Academic work also involves a search for new knowledge that, when found, is transmitted to professional and student audiences. (Academic work is not the only form of work that is heavily weighted with these attributes – a point that is further considered later.) Academic supervisors may know in broad terms what a "degree" should consist of and roughly what courses should be required for a major in particular subjects. But academic supervisors must rely extensively on their workers/professors to define their own specific research and classroom curricula – and to change the content of degrees and majors as knowledge in each field evolves. Academic administrators employ people to conduct research and explore uncharted avenues of knowledge that the administrators themselves cannot conduct or explore, because they lack knowledge of the various academic fields they supervise, and have insufficient time and even competence to investigate.

Fast-food restaurants can be governed extensively (but not exclusively) by commands from supervisors – and there is an obvious reason why this is possible. The goods and services produced are easily valued and sold, with little delay between the time they are produced and the time the value is realized and evaluated. Workers in such market environments would be inclined to see supervisors as people who increase the income of stockholders *and* workers primarily by reducing the extent to which workers shirk their agreed-upon duties, because the supervisors are easily able to assess the productivity of their workers. This is not the case in the university, where teaching and especially research are challenging to assess.

Worker-Managed Universities and Academic Politics

Academe, however, is a type of business that tends to be worker-managed and controlled, at least in many significant ways. This aspect of the academic marketplace solves many decision-making problems. But it also introduces serious problems alleviated by providing contractual job security (tenure). Professors are extensively called upon to determine what their firms (universities) produce (what research will be done, what courses will be required, and what the contents of the various courses will be). In addition, they help to determine who is hired to teach identified courses and undertake related research, how workers are evaluated, and whether a worker/professor is competent enough to have her employment continued.

Our argument begins with the plausible view that the more sophisticated, esoteric, and varied the job to be done, the more likely that decision-making will be democratic – and managerial control will be shifted to the workers (professors) who are the experts in "good performance."[6] This supports the view that universities have reason to "supply" tenure because existing professors are called upon to select who is hired to be a professor, which stands in sharp contrast to the way hiring decisions are usually made in business (Carmichael 1988).

For example, in baseball, the owners through their agents (managers) determine who plays in what position on the team. Baseball is, in this sense, "owner-managed." In academe, the incumbent professors select the team members and determine which positions they play. Academe is, in this sense, "labor-managed." In baseball, the owners' positions are improved when they select "better players." On the other hand, in academe, without tenure, the position of the incumbent decision-makers (professors) could be undermined by their selection of "better professors," those who could teach better and undertake more and higher-quality research for publication in higher-ranking journals.[7] Weaker department members would reasonably fear that their future livelihoods (as well as prestige) would be undermined if they support prospective hires who may be better teachers and researchers. Thus, tenure can be construed as a means used by university administrators and board members – who want the most promising professors to be hired, but must delegate decision-making authority to the faculty – to induce faculty members to honestly judge the potential of the new recruits. In effect, university officials and board members strike a credible bargain with their professors/decision-makers: if you select new recruits who are better than you are, you will not be fired.

Universities have reason to *supply* tenure, but what reason do professors have to *demand* it? Some faculty members could worry that their freedom to pursue research will be violated by public opinion (religious, political, and ideological forces external to universities). But few faculty members go public with their work or say anything controversial enough in their classes for them to trade up

---

[6] Of course, not all academic environments share the same goals or face the same constraints. Some universities view pushing back the frontiers of knowledge as central to their mission, whereas others are intent on transmitting the received and accepted wisdom of the times, if not the ages. Some universities are concerned mainly with promoting the pursuit of usable (private goods) knowledge, that which has a reasonable probability of being turned into saleable products, whereas other universities are interested in promoting research, the benefits of which are truly public, if any value at all can be ascertained.

[7] "[T]enure is necessary," Carmichael concludes, "because without it incumbents would never be willing to hire people who turn out to be better than themselves" (Carmichael 1988, 454).

much pay for protection from these external forces. (In recent decades, external ideological forces have increasingly monitored research and classroom practices, looking for violations of a growing array of group sensitivities, which has increased some professors' demand for tenure.)

Rather, we believe that, to a much greater degree, tenure is designed to protect professors from their *colleagues* in a labor-managed work environment, operating under the rules of academic democracy. That is, the greater worry is that one's research and teaching will prompt a hostile reaction from colleagues (who may have attachments to ideologies shared by groups external to their universities) – rather than from politicians or the public. Academic work is often full of strife, and the reasons are embedded in the nature of the work and the way work is evaluated and rewarded – a point discussed by one of the authors in detail elsewhere (McKenzie 1996). Suffice it to say here that tenure is a means of putting some minimum limits on political infighting. It increases the costs that predatory faculty members must incur to be successful in having more productive colleagues dismissed.

In addition, professors understand that the relative standing of their positions and ranking of their research can vary over time with changes in the cast of decision-makers, who are likely to adjust their assessments from time to time. The ranking of their research can also change with shifts in the relative merit that department members assign to different types and forms of academic work. When the decision-making unit is multidisciplinary, shifts in the relative assessments of the worth of individual professors' work in different disciplines can fluctuate even more dramatically, given that each professor is likely to have allegiance first to her own discipline – and then to other, closely related disciplines.

Within schools of business, for example, accounting faculty members may have, on the margin, an incentive to deprecate the work of marketing professors, given that such deprecation may shift faculty positions to accounting – and vice versa. Even more fundamentally, organizational theorists in the management department steeped in behavioral psychology may have an incentive to depreciate the work of professors in finance whose work is grounded in economics – given that negative shifts in the relative evaluation of economics-based work can marginally improve the chances of faculty positions being shifted to the management department. From time to time, like-minded faculty members can be expected to coalesce to increase their political effectiveness in shaping decisions that can, in turn, inspire the formation of other coalitions – thus, motivating all coalitions to increase their efforts. The inherent instability of coalitions can, of course, jeopardize anyone's job security and long-term gains.

Universities also realize, given the nature of academic democracy and the threat it poses, that faculty members have inherent reasons for demanding tenure, and these make it possible to recoup the cost of tenure by reducing professorial wages to less than what they would have to be if the professors did not share a need for job security.

Of course, this line of analysis leads to other deductions:

- If the work of professors were less specialized, professors would be less inclined to demand tenure. For example, in colleges in which the emphasis is on teaching rather than research, tenure would likely be less prevalent and/or less protective. So, we would expect that any pressure to eliminate tenure would be stronger in teaching colleges than in research universities. We would also expect for-profit colleges to be less likely to offer tenure, because they have a far clearer measure of the value of professors: their bottom lines.
- As a group of decision-makers or a discipline becomes more stable, we would expect faculty to consider tenure less important and to be less willing to forgo wages and other fringe benefits to obtain tenure.
- If there is a close-to-even split on democratic decisions related to employment, merit raises, and even tenure, faculty members will assign more value to tenure, given that vote outcomes may change dramatically with slight shifts in the composition of the decision-making group.
- With below-market wages during the probation period and above-market wages afterwards, tenure will be more valuable to faculty members.
- As the diversity within a decision-making unit increases (e.g., more disciplines included with more divergent views on how analyses should be organized and pursued), the demand for tenure will increase.
- When political and religious forces inside and outside universities rise (along with their use of media and social media influence), we would expect an increased demand for tenure. This will translate into an increased willingness to forfeit wages for tenure.

Why People in Business Don't Have Tenure

Why don't other sorts of employees have provision for the same kind of job security? The quick answer to this question is that businesses, in contrast to universities, are not typically labor-managed. As already noted, goals in business are usually well defined. Perhaps more important, success can usually be identified with relative ease by using an agreed-upon measure – that is, profit. The owners, who are residual claimants, have an interest in maintaining the firm's focus on profits. Moreover, people who work for businesses tend to have a stake in honest evaluations of potential employees, given that their decisions on "better" recruits can increase firm profits as well as the incomes and job security of all parties.

Admittedly, real-world businesses do not always adhere to the process as described. They use, to a greater or lesser degree, participatory forms of management – and, for some businesses, profit is not always the sole or highest-priority goal. "Office politics" is a nontrivial concern in many firms. But the point is *in business, the usefulness of tenure is not nearly as great as it is within academe.* Employees in business do not have as much incentive to demand tenure, primarily because business employees do not experience the problems inherent in democratic management that derive from imprecise and shifting goals – or from esoteric and often ill-defined research projects. Tenure is seldom found in firms, for the simple reason that granting tenure to employees in business is less likely to be done in a way that is mutually beneficial to both employees and employers.

But in some cases, for-profit businesses are similar enough to labor-managed universities to make tenure-type arrangements beneficial to employees and the firm. Consider firms in law, accounting, and consulting. These businesses are often organized as partnerships, which are in effect worker/partner-managed firms, with the existing partners choosing new hires just as existing professors choose new hires in universities. In these partnerships, much as in universities, employees who are judged not to have the dedication and ability to contribute significantly to the firm are dismissed after a few years (or relegated to low-status and low-paid employment). Those judged worthy are made a partner in the firm, which comes with higher income and greatly increased job security – something akin to university tenure.

Tenure as a Tournament

The granting of tenure can also be seen as a "tournament" to determine who can beat other competitors for some prize – in this case, a lifetime employment contract (Lazear and Rosen 1981). Tenure decisions are a way of allowing faculty members to reveal their skills. An employer cannot depend on a potential employee to be fully objective or honest in presenting her qualifications. The graduate school records of new doctorates provide useful information on which to base judgments of potential recruits for success as university teachers and researchers. However, such records are of limited worth in instances when a professor's research is at the frontier of knowledge in her discipline. The correlation between a person's performance as a student, prospective professor, teacher, and researcher is, at best, highly imperfect.

To induce promising faculty members to accurately assess their abilities and confess their limits, the competitors (new assistant professors) are effectively told that only some among them will be promoted and retained. Because standards for tenure differ from one university to another, universities offer prospective faculty members an opportunity to, in effect, self-select and go to a university where they think they are likely to make the tenure grade. The prospects of being denied tenure will encourage weak candidates to avoid universities with tough tenure standards, given the probability that they would have to accept wages below the market during the probation period. The lost wages amount to an investment that probably will not be repaid with interest (in terms of wages above the market after the probation period when tenure is acquired). Thus, the tenure tournaments can reduce the costs that universities incur in gathering information and making decisions, because they force recruits to be somewhat more honest in their claims.

Competition for the limited number of "prized positions" often will drive new faculty members to exert a level of effort and produce a level of output that exceeds the value of their current compensation. To induce prospective faculty to exert the amount of effort necessary to be ability-revealing, universities must offer a "prize" that potential recruits consider worth the effort. That is, the recruits must expect the future (discounted) reward to compensate them for the extra effort they expend in the tournament and for the risk associated with not "winning" – some combination of greater compensation and greater job security. In this sense, tenure can be offered as a "prize."[8]

Tenure is a contract provision that faculty members value, universities provide, and just about everyone else criticizes. Tenure for professors can be viewed as a fringe benefit (job security) that has the effect of lowering money wages. Tenure can be seen as a form of job protection from internal political forces inside the labor-managed firm. In theory, any employee could also have tenure. All they would have to do is "pay" for it in terms of lost wages. However, few workers have the same strong reasons for wanting tenure as do professors and universities. Tenure survives in academe because faculty members aggressively demand it (even those who believe strongly in the value of markets) and because universities voluntarily negotiate it. Tenure's long-term survival and the competitiveness of university labor markets suggest that the trade is mutually beneficial.

Part B Organizational Economics and Management

Production Costs, Firm Size, and Organizational Structure

In Part A, we assumed the existence of firms with the primary intent to economize on resources and to maximize profits (which leads them to equate marginal cost with marginal benefit/revenue). Given alternative ways of organizing production, there must be efficiency advantages to production through firms – or

---

[8] After tenure is awarded, faculty efforts should be expected to decline while their pay simultaneously rises. In the midst of the tournament, the new faculty members will exert unduly high amounts of effort, simply because of the prospect of being rewarded in the future by higher pay and greater job security. Also, the rise in compensation and fall in effort that accompany tenure may correlate with the fact that the added money makes it possible for faculty members to buy more of most things, including greater leisure (or leisure-time activities). If we did not expect new faculty members to anticipate relaxing somewhat after attaining tenure and enjoying, to a degree, being "overpaid," we could not expect the tenure tournament to be effective as a means to an end, which is disclosure of the limits of the new faculty members' true abilities.

they would not arise and survive in a market economy. In other words, firms must enable owners to press their cost curves down as far as possible. There is far more to say here.

The management of firms to contain production costs is not as simple as it might seem. Owners must consider how their organizational structures affect costs. To contain costs, firms face decisions to make products inside or to outsource. Inside the firm, there are ever-present problems associated with "principal–agent conflicts" for managers to control. They must figure out how best to contain the opportunistic behavior of workers, suppliers, and buyers. And in Online Reading 7.2, we explore how firms can affect their overall labor cost structure by adjusting the structure of their health insurance plans. First, however, we must address the seemingly innocuous but important question of why "firms" exist in the first place.

Firms and Market Efficiency

In "The nature of the firm," the classic 1937 article that earned him a Nobel Prize, Ronald Coase defined a *firm* as any organization that supersedes the pricing system, in which hierarchy and methods of command and control are substituted for exchanges. In his words: "A firm, therefore, consists of the system of relationships which comes into existence when the direction of resources is dependent on an entrepreneur" (see Coase 1988, 41–42).

But why and how do firms add to the efficiency of markets? This is an intriguing question, especially given how much standard economic theory trumpets the efficiency of markets. Students might rightfully wonder: if markets are so efficient, why do so many entrepreneurs go to the trouble of organizing firms? Why not just have everything done by way of markets, with little or nothing actually done inside firms? All firm inputs could be bought instead by individuals – with each individual adding value to the inputs she purchases and then selling this result to another individual, who adds more value, and so on – until a final product is produced and the completed product is sold to consumers.

Individuals, as producers relying exclusively on markets, could always take the least costly bid. They could keep their options open, including the options of immediately switching to new suppliers who propose better deals. Nobody would be tied down to internal sources of supply for their production needs. They would not incur the considerable costs of organizing themselves into production teams, departments, and various levels of management. They would avoid the costs of internal management and the Prisoner's Dilemma of shirking workers. In a word, there are many costs (inefficiencies) that go with organizing production into firms.

So, why do firms exist? More to the point, if markets are so efficient in getting things done, why do less than 30 percent of all transactions in the United States occur through markets, which means that more than 70 percent of transactions are made through firms (McMillan 2002, 168–169)? There must be sizable benefits of firms to offset these costs.[9] Some economists have speculated that firms exist because of the *economies of specialization* of resources – in particular, labor. Adam Smith was correct when he observed that, by dividing tasks among workers, they become more proficient. He began his classic *The Wealth of Nations* by describing how specialization of labor increased "pin" (really, nail) production (Smith 1937, 4–12). By specializing, workers also avoid the waste of changing tasks, leaving more time for production and promoting efficiency.

Although improvements can certainly result from specialization of any resource, Smith was wrong to conclude that firms were *necessary* to coordinate workers in their separate tasks. The pricing system within markets could coordinate workers. Conceivably, markets could exist even within the stages of production that are held together by assembly lines. The person who produces soles in a shoe factory could buy the leather and then sell the completed soles to the shoe assemblers. The bookkeeping services provided to a shoe factory by its accounting department could easily be bought on the market (as many firms do this with accounting firms). Similarly, all the intermediate goods involved in Smith's pin production could be bought and sold until the completed pins were sold to those who want them.

Another explanation is variance in preferences about risk and uncertainty – and the comparative advantage of some people (entrepreneurs) in embracing these risks (at higher rates of return) for other people (workers).[10] The most common answer relates to **economies of scale**: as more of all resources are added to production within a given firm, output can expand in

> **Economies of scale** are the cost savings that emerge when all resource inputs – labor, land, and capital – are increased together.

percentage terms by more than the use of resources. For example, if all resource use expands by 10 percent and output expands by 15 percent, then the firm experiences economies of scale – as the long-run average cost of production declines. Why does this happen? And why does it happen in some industries (steel and automobile) much more than others (beauty shops and music composition)? We'll have more to say about this in the next chapter.

---

[9] A similar question arises in noticing that labor markets are rarely "spot markets," where wages are determined "on the spot" – for example, on a daily basis. Instead, there are greater efficiencies from employees and employers binding themselves into explicit or implicit contracts where compensation is visited irregularly – for example, on an annual basis.

[10] Knight (1921) argued that, if business were conducted in a totally certain world, there would be no need for firms. Workers would know their pattern of rewards, so there would be no need for anyone to specialize in the acceptance of the costs of the risks and uncertainties that abound in the real world of business. As it is, workers accept a reduction in their expected pay in order to reduce the variability and uncertainty of their pay. Entrepreneurs are willing to make such a bargain with their workers because their workers effectively pay them to do so (by accepting a reduction in pay).

How did Coase explain the existence of firms?[11] Simply put, he observed that there are costs of dealing in markets. He dubbed these *marketing costs* – what most economists now call *transaction costs*. These costs include the time and resources that must be devoted to organizing economic activity through markets. Transaction costs include the real economic costs of discovering the best deals as evaluated in terms of prices and attributes of products, negotiating contracts, and enforcing the terms of the contract. One could imagine the terribly time-consuming process of organizing shoe production through markets, especially if the suppliers and producers at the various stages were constantly looking for new people to deal with, negotiating new agreements, and vulnerable to replacement by competitors.

Once the transaction costs of market activity are recognized, the reason for the emergence of the firm is transparent: firms substitute internal direction for markets because they *decrease the need for making (costly) market transactions* and reduce the attendant costs. If internal direction is not more cost-effective than markets, then nobody would have an incentive to create a firm. Although firms will never eliminate the need for markets, neither will markets eliminate the need for the internal direction of firms.

In sum, entrepreneurs and their hired workers essentially substitute one long-term contract for a series of short-term contracts: The workers agree to accept directions from the entrepreneurs (or their agents/managers) within certain broad limits (varying between firms) in exchange for security and a level of welfare (including pay) that is higher than the workers would be able to receive in the market without firms. Similarly, the entrepreneurs (or their agents) agree to share with the workers some of the efficiency gains obtained from reducing transaction costs.[12] Again, we have a form of voluntary, mutually beneficial trade, as owners and workers look to cooperate in pleasing consumers and making money.

---

[11] There are many reasons people think firms exist, several of which Coase dismisses for being wrongheaded or unimportant. For example, Coase concedes that some people might prefer to be directed in their work, accepting lower pay just to be told what to do. But he dismisses this explanation as unlikely to be important because "it would rather seem that the opposite tendency is operating if one judges from the stress normally laid on the advantage of 'being one's own master'" (Coase 1988, 38). Alternatively, some people might like to control others, meaning they would give up a portion of their pay to direct other people. Coase also finds this explanation lacking, saying it could not possibly be true "in the majority of the cases" (Coase 1988, 38), since we observe that people who direct the work of others are frequently paid a premium for their efforts.

[12] Coase recognizes that entrepreneurs could overcome some of the costs of repeatedly negotiating and enforcing short-term contracts by devising one long-term contract. However, as the time period of a contract is extended, more unknowns are covered, implying that the contract must allow for progressively greater flexibility. In essence, a firm is a substitute for such a long-term contract by covering an indefinite future and providing flexibility. The firm is a legal institution which permits workers to exit (more or less at will) and gives managers the authority (within bounds) to change the directives given to workers.

The firm is a viable economic institution because *both sides to the contract* – owners and workers – gain. Thus, firms can be expected to proliferate in markets because of the mutually beneficial deals that can be made.

Costs that Limit Firm Size: "Agency Problems"

Given all of these benefits, does it follow that it would be most efficient for one giant firm to span the entire economy? Beyond our intuitions that say "no," sound reasons exist for limiting the size of firms. Clearly, by organizing activities under the "umbrella" of firms, entrepreneurs give up some of the benefits of markets, which provide competitively delivered goods and services. Managers suffer from their own limited organizational skills and skilled managers are scarce, as evidenced by the relatively high salaries they command. Communication problems within firms expand as firms grow, encompassing more activities, more levels of production, and more diverse products.

In short, there are limits to what can be done efficiently through organizations. These limits cannot always be overcome, except at costs that exceed the benefits of doing so. Even with the application of the best organizational techniques, whether through the establishment of teams, the empowerment of employees, or the creation of new business and departmental structures (e.g., relying on top-down, bottom-up, or participatory decision-making), firms are limited in their ability to reduce organizational costs.

Firms are restricted in their size because they suffer from what are called **agency problems** (or **principal–agent problems**) – conflicts of interests between individuals and groups within firms. The entrepreneurs or owners of firms (the *principals*) organize firms to pursue their interest, which is often (but not always) seeking greater profits. To pursue profits, the entrepreneurs (or shareholders) hire managers who then hire workers (all of whom are *agents*). However, the interests of the worker/agents are not always compatible with the interests of the owner/principals; indeed, they are often in direct conflict.

> The **agency problem** or **principal–agent problem** inside firms is the conflicts of interest between the owners (principals) of firms and their hired employees (agents) that emerge because both want to maximize their own gain from the use of firm resources.

Principals face the problem of getting the agents to work diligently to serve the principals' interests – the business problem that Adam Smith recognized in the 1770s (Smith 1937, 700). Needless to say, agents often resist doing the principals' bidding – a fact that makes it difficult (costly) for the principals to achieve their goals. Many of these conflicts can be resolved through contracts. However, as with all business arrangements, contracts have serious limitations – not the least of which is that they cannot be all-inclusive, covering all aspects of even simple business relationships. Contracts simply cannot anticipate and cover all the possible ways that the parties to the contract can get around specific provisions, if they are so inclined. Enforcing contracts can be problematic, and represents an added cost, even when both parties know that provisions have been violated. Each party will recognize these enforcement costs and may be tempted to exploit them. Ideally, contracts will be *self-enforcing* – that is, their provisions encourage each party to live up to the letter and spirit of the contract, because it is in each party's interest to do so. This is where incentives come in, making contracts as self-enforcing as possible. Good incentives can encourage all parties to follow more faithfully the intent of contracts.

Competition serves as a powerful force in minimizing agency costs. Firms in competitive markets that struggle to control agency costs are not likely to survive for long, given the "market for corporate control" (Manne 1963) – failure or takeover by way of proxy fights, tender offers, or mergers. In Chapters 8–11, we discuss how managers can solve agency problems, including controlling their own behavior as agents for shareholders. At the same time, market pressures compel managers to solve such problems, even if they are not naturally inclined to do so. More broadly, if corporations are not able to adequately solve agency problems, this corporate form of doing business will be eclipsed as new forms of business emerge (Jensen 1989). Of course, this means that obstructions in the market for corporate control (for example, legal impediments to takeovers) can translate into greater agency costs and less-efficient corporate governance.

Why are firms the sizes they are? Coase and his followers have focused on the difficulties managers face as they seek to expand the scale and scope of the firm. They posit that, as a firm expands, *agency costs* increase. This happens primarily because workers (including managers) have more and more opportunities to engage in *opportunistic behavior*, taking advantage of their position for personal gain at the expense of the firm's profits (and its owners). *Shirking* (not working with due diligence) is one form of opportunistic behavior that is known to all employees. Theft of firm resources is another. Employees politicking their bosses for advancement or choice assignments – selectively using firm and market information to make their case – can drive up agency costs and the need for more monitoring costs.[13] As the firm grows, the contributions of the individual worker become less detectable, which means that workers have progressively fewer incentives to work diligently on behalf of firm objectives or to do what they are told by their superiors. They can more easily hide.

The tendency for larger size to undercut the incentives of participants in any group is not just theoretical speculation; it has been observed in closely

---

[13] One way firms have attempted to control employee politicking (or internal "rent-seeking") has been to develop well-defined rules and procedures for salary increases and promotions, relying on measures (e.g., seniority) that may have little connection to workers' relative productivity. Having seniority determining outcome may impair employee incentives to work harder and smarter for the firm, but seniority can also reduce the incentive for workers to waste resources on internal politicking (Roberts 2004, chapter 3).

monitored experiments. In a still-relevant experiment conducted more than a half-century ago, a German scientist asked workers to pull on a rope connected to a meter that would measure the effort expended. Total effort for *all* workers increased as workers were added to the group. Simultaneously, the *individual* efforts of the workers declined. When three workers pulled on the rope, the individual effort averaged 84 percent of the effort expended by one worker. With eight workers pulling, the average individual effort was half the effort of the one worker (Furnham 1993). Hence, group size and individual effort were – as in most group circumstances – inversely related.

The problem is that each worker's incentive to expend effort deteriorates as the group expands. Each person's effort counts for less in the context of the larger group – a point from Mancur Olson (1971) that we developed in Chapter 2. The "common objectives" of the group become less and less compelling in directing individual efforts. Such a finding means that, if each worker added to the group must be paid the same as all others, the cost of additional production obviously rises with the size of the working group. This also implies that to get a constant increase in effort with the additional workers, all workers must be given a greater incentive to hold to their previous level of effort.[14]

Optimally Sized Firms

The optimal size of a firm depends on more than technology-based economies of scale. Technology determines what *can* be done, but not what *is* done. What is done depends on firm policies and practices that minimize shirking and maximize worker use of technology and inputs. The size of the firm obviously depends on the extent to which owners must incur greater monitoring costs and additional layers of hierarchy as the firm's size increases (a point well developed by Williamson (1967) in his classic article in organizational economics).

Management information system theorists Vijay Gurbaxani and Seungjin Whang (1991) have devised a graphical means of illustrating optimal firm size as the consequence of two opposing forces: "internal coordinating costs" and "external coordinating costs." As a firm expands, its internal coordinating costs are likely to increase. This is because the firm's hierarchical pyramid will likely become larger, with more and more decisions made at the top by managers who are further and further removed from the local information available to workers at the bottom of the pyramid. There is a need to process information up and down the pyramid. When the information travels up, there are unavoidable problems and hence, costs – costs of communication, costs of miscommunication,

---

[14] Workers can also reason that if the residual from their added effort goes to the firm owners, they can possibly garner some of the residual by collusively (by explicit or tacit means) restricting their effort and hiking their rate of pay, which means that the incentive system must seek to undermine such collusive agreements (FitzRoy and Kraft 1987).

and opportunity costs associated with delays in communication – all of which can lead to suboptimal decisions. These "decision information costs" become progressively greater as decision rights are moved up the pyramid.

Attempts to rectify the decision costs by delegating decision-making to the lower ranks may help, but this will introduce greater agency costs. These include the cost of monitoring (managers watching employees or checking their production), "bonding" (workers bonding themselves through assurances that the tasks will be done as the agreement requires), and the loss of residual gains (profits) through worker shirking, which we covered in Chapter 2.

Managers must balance the decision information costs with the agency costs to find the decision rights that minimize the two costs combined. From this perspective, the ideal location of decision rights will depend heavily on the amount of information flow per unit of time. When upward flow of information is high, decision rights will tend to be located toward the floor of the firm, since the costs of suboptimal decisions by those higher up the hierarchy can be considerable. In other words, the firm can afford to tolerate agency costs because the costs of avoiding them, via centralized decisions, are even higher. Nevertheless, as the firm expands, we should expect the internal coordinating costs (both the decision information cost and the agency cost) along with the cost of operations to increase. The upward-sloping line in Figure 7.7(a) depicts this relationship.

But internal costs are not all that matter to a firm contemplating an expansion. It must also consider the cost of the market, or what Gurbaxani and Whang (1991) call "external coordination costs." If the firm remains "small" and buys many of its parts, supplies, and services (such as accounting, legal, and advertising services) from outside vendors, then it must consider the resulting "transaction costs." These include the costs of transportation, inventory holding, communication and contract writing, monitoring, and enforcing. However, as the firm

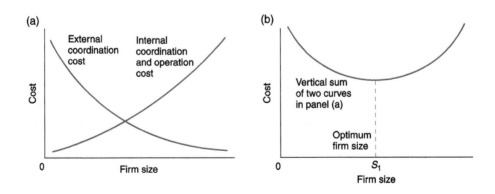

Figure 7.7 External and internal coordinating costs
(a) As the firm expands, the internal coordinating costs increase as the external coordinating costs fall. (b) The optimum firm size is determined by summing these two cost structures.

expands in size, these transaction costs should be expected to diminish. After all, as a firm becomes larger, it will have eliminated those market transactions with the highest transaction costs. The downward-sloping line in Figure 7.7(a) depicts this inverse relationship between firm size and transaction costs.

Again, how large should a firm be? If a firm vertically integrates, it will engage in fewer market transactions, lowering its transaction costs. It can also benefit from technical economies of scale (increases in productivity that lead to lower average costs when all factors of production are increased). However, in the process of expanding, it will confront growing internal coordination costs – the problems of trying to move information up the decision-making chain, getting the "right" decisions, and preventing people from exploiting their decision-making authority to their own advantage. The firm should stop expanding in scale when the total of the two types of costs – external and internal coordinating costs – are minimized. This minimum can be shown graphically by summing the two curves in Figure 7.7(a) to obtain the U-shaped curve in Figure 7.7(b). The *optimal* (or most efficient/cost-effective) firm size is at S_1.

This way of thinking about firm size would have only limited interest if it did not lend itself to additional observations about the location, shape, and changes in the curve. First, the exact location of the bottom will, of course, vary by firm and by industry. Firms differ in capacity to coordinate activities through markets and hierarchies. Second, firm size will also vary according to the changing abilities of firms to coordinate activities internally and externally.

Knowing that owners recognize that managers/agents can exploit their positions to their own benefit, managers will see advantages in "bonding" themselves against this possibility. Managers have an interest in communicating (to owners) that they will suffer some loss if exploitation occurs. Devices such as audits of the company are clearly in the interest of stockholders. But they are also in the interest of managers because reducing the scope for managerial misdeeds increases the market value of the company – and the market value of its managers. By buying (or being compensated with) company stock, managers can also bond themselves, assuring stockholders that they will incur at least some losses from agency costs. To the extent that managers/agents can bond themselves convincingly, the firm can grow from expanded sources of external investment funds. By bonding themselves, managers can demand higher compensation. Firms can be expected to expand and contract with reductions and increases in the costs of developing effective managerial bonds (Jensen and Meckling 1976).

Changes in Organizational Costs

The size of the firm can be expected to change with fluctuations in the relative costs of organizing a given set of activities by way of markets and hierarchies. For example, suppose that the costs of engaging in market transactions are lowered and markets become relatively more economical than firms. Entrepreneurs should be expected to organize more of their activities through markets and fewer through firms. Firms that more fully exploit markets and rely less on internal direction should be able to reduce their costs without sacrificing output by "downsizing" and becoming smaller.

A well-worn and widely appreciated explanation for downsizing is that modern technology has enabled firms to produce more with less. Personal computers, with their ever-escalating power, have enabled firms to lay off workers (or hire fewer workers). Banks no longer need as many tellers given the advent of the ATM. And so on. A less-recognized explanation is that markets have become cheaper, so there is less incentive to use hierarchical structures and more incentive to use markets. One good reason that firms have found markets relatively more attractive is rapidly developing computer and communication technology, which has reduced the costs of entrepreneurs operating in markets. The new technology has lowered the costs of locating suitable trading partners and suppliers, as well as negotiating, consummating, and monitoring market-based deals (and the contracts that go with them). In terms of Figure 7.7(a), the downward-sloping transaction costs curve has dropped down and to the left, causing the bottom of the U to move leftward.

"Outsourcing" became a management buzzword in the 1980s because the growing efficiency of markets, through technology, made it more economical to use markets, often on a global scale. Outsourcing has continued apace into this century, contributing significantly to the relatively faster pace of manufacturing productivity growth since the 1990s, spurred upward by cloud computing technology which has eased teamwork for people in different locations (Bureau of Labor Statistics 2004; Kvochko 2013).

But modern technology has also improved the monitoring of employees, reducing the costs of providing employee incentives and encouraging cooperation among workers – thereby reducing agency costs and enabling the expansion of firms (Roberts 2004, chapter 3; Kvochko 2013). This is because firms have been able to use technology to garner more of the gains from economies of scale.

The optical scanners at grocery store checkout counters are valuable because they can speed up the flow of customers through the checkout counters, but they also can be used for other purposes, such as inventory control and restocking. Each sale is immediately transmitted to warehouse computers that determine daily shipments to stores. The scanners also can be used to monitor the work of clerks, a factor that can diminish agency costs and increase the size of the firm. In Figure 7.7(a), the upward-sloping curve moves down and to the right, while the U-shaped curve in Figure 7.7(b) moves to the right.

Companies as diverse as FedEx and Frito-Lay have issued hand scanners to their salespeople, which are connected by satellite to their offices – to increase the reliability of information to company distribution centers and to track employee work.

The company can obtain data on each employee's start and stop time, the time spent on trips between stores, and the number of returns. Accordingly, the salespeople are asked to account for more of their time and activities while they are on the job.

Obviously, we have not covered the full spectrum of explanations for the various sizes of firms in the "real world" of business. We also have left the net impact of technology somewhat up in the air, given that it is pressing some firms to expand and others to downsize. The reason is simple: technology is having a multitude of impacts that firms in different situations can exploit in various ways.

Overcoming Prisoner's Dilemma Problems in Larger Firms

The discussion to this point reduces to a relatively simple message: *firms exist to bring about cost savings through effective cooperation.* Firms enable owners to optimize their marginal cost of production (and other cost curves to be covered in Chapter 8), pushing the *MC* curve down as far as it can go, which is needed to meet the competition. However, cooperation within firms is not always "natural" (especially as the group of cooperators expands). The problem is that people often realize personal gains by "cheating" – not doing what they are supposed to do – often because of the powerful incentives toward noncooperation that are built into many business environments.

An illustration of the tendency toward noncooperative behavior, despite the general advantage from cooperation, is a **conditional-sum game**, also known as the Prisoner's Dilemma (which we introduced in Chapter 2). Motivating cooperative behavior to overcome a Prisoner's Dilemma in a large group

> **Conditional-sum games** are games in which the value available to the participants is dependent on how the game is played.

is difficult but not impossible. The best hope *is to agree ahead of time to certain rules, restrictions, or arrangements that will punish those who choose the noncooperative option.* For example, those who are jointly engaging in criminal activity will see advantages in forming gangs whose members are committed to punishing non-cooperative behavior. The gang members who are confronted with the Prisoner's Dilemma orchestrated by the police will seriously consider the possibility that the shorter sentence received for confessing will hasten the time when the gang will impose a far harsher punishment for "squealing" on a fellow gang member.

Many areas of business are fertile ground for the conditional-sum game situations represented by the Prisoner's Dilemma. Several business-related examples are discussed in subsequent chapters because it is important for managers to identify and resolve these dilemmas as they arise with suppliers, customers, and employees. Indeed, we see the task of "management" as being largely concerned with finding resolutions of Prisoners' Dilemmas. Good managers constantly seek to remind employees about the benefits of cooperation and the costs that can be imposed on people who insist on taking the noncooperative course.

Consider the issue of corporate travel – a major business expense for some companies. If a business can economize on travel costs, it would realize significant gains. Some of these gains would be captured by traveling employees who would earn higher incomes as their net value to the firm increased. But employees are often in a Prisoner's Dilemma, because each recognizes that she is personally better off by flying first-class, staying at hotels with multiple stars, and dining at elegant restaurants (behaving noncooperatively) than by making less-expensive travel plans (behaving cooperatively) – regardless of what the other employees do. Each employee would be best off if *all* other employees economized. But if others make more expensive travel arrangements, an individual would be foolish not to do so as well, because the sacrifice would not noticeably increase her salary. Management of travel is a problem of making cooperative solutions pay for individual workers.

Of course, airlines have an interest in excessive business travel and recognize the "games" people play with their bosses and other workers. They have played along by making the travel game more rewarding to business travelers, more costly to firms, and more profitable to the airlines – through "frequent-flyer" programs. As a result, managers are more than incidentally concerned about employee use of such programs. When American Airlines initiated its AAdvantage frequent-flyer program in 1981, the company was intent on staving off the fierce price competition that had broken out among established and new airlines after fares and routes were deregulated in 1978. The airline wanted to enhance "customer loyalty" by offering its best, most regular customers free or reduced-price flights after they had built up their mileage accounts. Greater customer loyalty can mean that customers are less responsive to price increases, which could translate into actual higher prices than could otherwise be charged (Brandenburger and Nalebuff 1996).

At the same time, there is more to the issue than "customer loyalty." No doubt, American Airlines figured that it could benefit from the Prisoner's Dilemma for business travel. By setting up the frequent-flyer program, American Airlines (and others that followed suit) increased the individual payoff to business travelers for noncooperative behavior. Frequent-flyer programs allowed travelers to benefit from free flights and first-class upgrades when they chose more expensive and sometimes less direct flights. They encouraged business travelers to act opportunistically, to use their discretion for their own benefit at the expense of everyone else in their firms. The Prisoner's Dilemma problem for workers and their companies has also prompted rental-car companies, hotels, and restaurants to begin granting frequent-buyer points in conjunction with selected airlines for the travel services people buy with them, again encouraging higher travel costs.

Inefficient use of frequent-flyer miles might actually lower worker wages, because of the added cost to their firms. Still, workers have an incentive to exploit the program. They are in a Prisoner's Dilemma under which the cooperative strategy might be best for all, but the noncooperative strategy dominates the choice each individual faces. These problems are significant for many businesses, and we expect that, the bigger the firm, the greater the problem, given the greater opportunity for opportunistic behavior in large firms (Stephenson and Fox 1992; Dahl 1994). In an effort to cut these costs, managers are also in a game with the airlines, which respond to cost-cutting measures with new wrinkles designed to intensify the Prisoner's Dilemma faced by business travelers. The resulting costly airfares, particularly for business travelers, are being countered by low-cost airlines such as Southwest, Spirit, and Frontier – whose low-fare, no-frills service is capturing an increasing share of the market.

"Make-or-Buy" Decisions

What should firms make inside their organizations and what should they buy from an outside vendor? At one time, the answer to the "make-or-buy" problem would have focused on technological considerations: firms often produce more than one product because of what economists call **economies of scope**. But even firms with diverse product lines are actually quite spe-

> **Economies of scope** emerge when the skills developed in the production, distribution, and sale of one product lower the cost of producing other products.

cialized in that they purchase most of their inputs in the market rather than produce them in-house. General Motors, for example, does not produce its own steel, tires, plastic, or carpeting. Instead, it is cheaper for automobile manufacturers to concentrate on the assembly of automobiles and purchase inputs from firms which specialize in them. Likewise, few restaurants grow their own vegetables, raise their own beef, catch their own fish, or produce their own toothpicks.

Given the advantages of specialization and the ability to buy most of the necessary inputs in the marketplace, why do firms do as much as they do internally? Why don't firms buy almost all the inputs they need from others? Instead of having employees in the typical sense, a firm could hire workers on an hourly or daily basis at a market-determined wage. Instead of owning and maintaining a fleet of trucks, a transport company could rent trucks, paying only for the time they were in use. Loading and unloading the trucks could be contracted out to firms which specialize in this work, and the transport firm would specialize in transporting products. Similarly, the paperwork required for such things as internal control, payroll, and taxes could be contracted out to those who specialize in providing these services. Indeed, taking this concept to the limit would eliminate firms as we typically think of them.

The problem with total reliance on the market should now be familiar: significant costs – transaction costs – are associated with making market exchanges. In general, the higher the cost of transacting through markets, the more a firm will make for itself with its own employees rather than buying from other firms.

The reason that restaurants don't make their own toothpicks is that the cost of transactions is extremely low. It is difficult to imagine the transaction costs of acquiring toothpicks getting so high that restaurants would make their own.

"Dedicated" Investments

Negotiating an agreement between two parties can be expensive, including attempts to avoid opportunistic behavior. This is an especial challenge when one party needs to make investments in plant and equipment that are expensive and specific to a narrow productive activity. After the investment is made, the plant and equipment have little if any value for other uses – a sunk cost. Thus, these investments are often risky and unattractive. The problem is that, once someone commits to an investment in specific capital to provide services, the other party can take advantage of the investor's inflexibility by paying less than the original agreement called for, creating a "hostage" situation akin to what we described in Chapter 5. There are so-called "quasi-rents" that can be appropriated – taken by another party through unscrupulous, opportunistic dealing.[15]

Consider the example of a pipeline to transport natural gas to an electric generating plant. Such a pipeline is expensive to construct, but it can lower the cost of producing electricity by more than enough to provide an attractive return on investment. To be more specific, assume construction costs of $1 billion; an interest rate of 8 percent so that the annual capital cost is $80 million; and annual maintenance and operating costs of $20 million. Obviously, it would not pay investors to build the pipeline for less than the $100 million in annual costs. If the pipeline lowers the cost of producing electricity by $150 million per year, it is a good investment. But would you invest your money to build it?

Any price between $100 million and $150 million per year would be attractive to investors in the pipeline and the electric generating plant. If the generating plant agrees to pay investors $125 million each year to build and operate the pipeline, both parties would realize annual profits of $25 million from the project. But the investors would be taking a serious risk because they lack flexibility *after* the pipeline is built. Since the pipeline is a *dedicated* investment, there is a big difference in the return needed to make the pipeline worth building and the return needed to make it worth operating after it is built. Although it takes at least $100 million per year to motivate the building of the pipeline, the firm will find that any payment over $20 million will be a paying proposition *after* building the pipeline. Why? Because this is the *marginal* cost of production – what it takes to operate the line each year. The pipeline investment itself is a sunk cost (literally and figuratively) that cannot be recaptured once it has been made. After

---

[15] The available quasi-rents are the differences between the purchase and subsequent selling price of an asset, given the limited resale market for the asset (Klein, Crawford, and Alchian 1978).

investors have made the commitment to construct the pipeline, the generating plant would be in a position to capture almost the entire value of initial pipeline investment by repudiating the original agreement and offering to pay only slightly more than $20 million per year.

Of course, our example is too extreme. The generating plant is not likely to risk its reputation by overtly repudiating a contract. And even if it did, the pipeline investors would have legal recourse with a good chance of recovering much of their loss. Furthermore, as the example is constructed, the generating plant has more to lose from opportunistic behavior by the pipeline owners than vice versa. If the pipeline refuses service to the plant, the cost of producing electricity increases by $150 million per year. So, the pipeline owners could act opportunistically by threatening to cut off the supply of natural gas unless they receive an annual payment of almost $150 million per year.

Opportunistic behavior will seldom be so blatant. But cost-minimizing and profit-maximizing owners and managers dare not overlook our main point: when a transaction requires a large investment in dedicated capital (limited in use to a particular project), there is potential for costly problems in negotiating and enforcing agreements. In contracts involving long-term capital commitments, unforeseen changes in circumstances (higher costs, interrupted supplies, stricter government regulations, etc.) can justify changes in prices or other terms of the contract. Typically, contracts will anticipate some of these changes and incorporate them into the agreed-upon terms. But it is impossible to anticipate and specify appropriate responses to all possible changes in relevant conditions. Ambiguities in long-term contractual arrangements, therefore, can open the door for opportunistic behavior, which can be resolved only through protracted and expensive legal action.

Committing to investments in dedicated capital carries great risk without some assurance that such opportunistic behavior will not pay. The threat of hold-ups invariably converts to risk costs, which must be covered one way or another, undermining a firm's profitability. One way to avoid this is for the firm to merge with the supplier. Another way is for the investment to be made by the same firm that will be using the output it produces. Each party can reduce the risks of being "held up" when the purchaser buys the equipment and rents it to the supplier. The supplier is not on the hook for the investment. And if the supplier attempts to take advantage of the crucial nature of the input, the firm can move the specialized equipment to another supplier. This is exactly the arrangement that Ford and other automobile companies have with some of their suppliers. They buy components from many small and specialized companies, but often own the specialized equipment and rent it to the contracting firms (Cooter and Ulen 1988, 245–246; Roberts 2004, 204–206).

Another angle is developing a reputation among suppliers for not acting opportunistically. To increase supplier confidence, Toyota encourages its suppliers to talk with one another through an association of suppliers. Each supplier can reason that such ongoing interactions among them can increase the costs that Toyota would incur from taking advantage of any one supplier, thus reducing the probability that Toyota will engage in forms of opportunistic behavior, especially hold-ups. Toyota's formal and informal contracts with suppliers are thus *self-enforcing* to a greater degree than otherwise. Toyota's reputation for fair dealing translates into lower risk costs throughout its supply chain, which, in turn, translates into lower production costs for suppliers and lower prices for Toyota's parts. The economies of reputation then reveal themselves to consumers in the relatively lower prices of the company's cars.

Company Towns

An arrangement that reduced the threat of opportunistic behavior by firms against their workers has been the much-criticized "company town." In the past, it was common for mining companies to set up operations in remote locations. In the company towns, the company owned the stores in which employees shopped and the houses in which they lived. The popular view is that these company towns allowed the companies to exploit their workers with outrageous prices and rents, often charging them more for basic necessities than they earned from back-breaking work in the mines. (Tennessee Ernie Ford captured this popular view in his cover of the classic song, "Sixteen Tons.")

Without denying that nineteenth-century miners had difficult lives, company stores and houses can actually be seen as a way for the companies to *reduce* (but not totally eliminate) their ability to exploit workers through opportunistic behavior. To note, workers would be reluctant to purchase a house in a remote location with only one employer. The worker who made such an investment would be far more vulnerable to the employer's opportunistic wage reductions than a worker who rented company housing. Similarly, few merchants would be willing to establish a store in such a location, knowing that they would be vulnerable to opportunistic demands for price reductions that just covered their variable costs, leaving no return on their capital cost.

Again, in an ideal world without transaction costs – and without opportunistic behavior – mining companies would have specialized in extracting ore and would have let suppliers of labor buy their housing and other provisions through other specialists. But in the real world of transaction costs (including the temptations of opportunistic behavior), it was better for mining companies to provide basic services for their employees. This is not to deny that there was exploitation. But the exploitation was surely less under the company town arrangement than if, for example, workers had bought their own houses (Fishback 1992, chapters 8 and 9).

Franchising

If a firm wants to expand, should it own and operate – or should it franchise to outside investors? The own-or-franchise decision is similar to the make-or-buy decision because both decisions involve problems of monitoring, risk-sharing, and opportunistic behavior. As such, franchising is a type of firm expansion with special contractual features and all the attendant problems. Franchise contracts between the "franchisor" (franchise seller) and the "franchisee" (franchise buyer) typically have several key features:

- The franchisee generally makes an up-front payment and pays a royalty from a percentage of monthly sales for the right to use a brand name and/or trademark (e.g., the name "McDonald's" and the "golden arches").
- The franchisee agrees to conduct business along the lines specified by the franchisor, including the nature and quality of the good or service, operating hours, sources for purchasing key inputs in the production process, and prices to be charged.
- The franchisor agrees to provide managerial advice, undertake national advertising, provide training, and ensure that quality standards are maintained across all franchisees.
- The franchisor typically retains the right to terminate a franchise agreement for specified reasons (if not at will).

At one time, scholars believed that firms expanded by franchising as a means of raising additional capital through tapping the franchisee's creditworthiness. If the firm owned the additional outlet, it would need more investors (lenders) at higher capital costs. Supposedly, franchisees could raise the money more cheaply than could the franchisor (Thompson 1971). Paul Rubin (1978) argued that franchising reduces the cost of capital in a less direct manner. For example, a firm in the restaurant business can expand through franchising only if it has a successful anchor store. It can establish another outlet through the sale of its own securities, equities, or bonds – in which case, the investors will have an interest in both the successful anchor restaurant and the new one. Investment in a proven franchised restaurant is likely to be less risky than an investment in a totally independent restaurant. Hence, the cost of capital for the franchisee, all else constant, is likely to be higher than it is for the franchisor.

Why franchise at all? Rubin argues that the primary reason for franchising is that the agency costs are reduced. The manager of a company-owned restaurant will likely be paid a salary plus some commission or bonus related to revenues. But the manager's incentives are still only somewhat related to the interests of the owners, so the manager must be closely monitored. In contrast, a franchisee becomes the residual claimant on the new business with a stronger incentive not to shirk himself – and to reduce shirking and opportunistic behavior by employees.

Monitoring costs are certainly not eliminated through franchising. The franchisee has some reason to shirk, even though he is a residual claimant to the profits generated by his outlet. Customers often go to franchised outlets because they have high confidence in the consistent quality of the goods and services offered. McDonald's customers know they may not get the best burger in town, but they have strong expectations on the size, taste, and price of the burgers and the cleanliness of the restaurant. McDonald's has a strong incentive to build and maintain a reputation for its stores. But each franchisee, especially with limited repeat business, can "cheat" (or "free-ride") on McDonald's overall reputation by reducing the size of the burgers or letting the restaurant deteriorate. The cost savings for the individual cheating store can translate into a reduced demand for other McDonald's restaurants. This is a Prisoner's Dilemma in which all stores can be worse off if noncooperative behavior becomes a widespread problem. So, McDonald's has a strong incentive to set production and cleanliness standards – and then to back them up with inspections and fines, if not outright termination of the franchise contract.

McDonald's controls quality by requiring franchisees to buy its ingredients (e.g., burgers and buns) from McDonald's or approved suppliers. McDonald's has good reason to want its franchisees to buy the ingredients from McDonald's – not because (contrary to legal opinion) it gives them monopoly power, but because it is prohibitively costly for them to monitor outside suppliers (Rubin 1978, 254).[16] Outside suppliers have an incentive to shirk on the quality standards with the consent of the franchisees that, individually, have an interest in cutting corners and reducing their costs. Moreover, by selling key ingredients, the franchisor has an indirect way of determining whether its royalties are being accurately computed. These "tie-in sales" are simply a means of reducing monitoring costs and enhancing credibility. Of course, the franchisees also have an interest in their franchisor having the lowest possible monitoring costs: it minimizes the chances of free-riding by other franchisees and maintains the value of their franchise.

The chances for opportunistic behavior can be lowered through franchising, but not eliminated (Brickley and Dark 1987). If the franchisee buys the rights to the franchise and then invests in a store with limited resale value, the franchisor can appropriate the rents simply by demanding higher franchise payments or failing to enforce production and quality standards with the franchisees, increasing the take of the franchisor but curbing the resale value of the franchise. On the other hand, the franchisee can, after the fact, demand lower franchise fees and special treatment (given the costs incurred by the franchisor in locating another franchisee).

---

[16] For a review of legal opinion on "tie-in sales" within franchise relationships, see Klein and Saft (1985).

This helps to explain the up-front payment and royalty provisions in franchise contracts. The value of the franchise (the maximum that a franchisee will pay for the franchise) is equal to the expected present value of the difference between two income streams – the income that could be earned with and without the franchise. The greater the difference, the greater the up-front payment the franchisee is willing to make. However, the franchisee will not want to pay the full difference up-front. This is because the franchisor would then have little incentive to live up to the contract (to maintain the flow of business and to police all franchisees). The franchisor could run off with all the gains and no costs. As a consequence, both the franchisor and the franchisee will likely agree to an up-front payment (less than the difference in the two income streams identified above) and a royalty payment. The royalty payment is something that both will want in the contract simply because the franchisor will then have a stake in maintaining the franchisee's business. The combination of up-front payment and royalty is likely to maximize the gains to both franchisee and franchisor.

Franchising also involves risk, no matter how carefully the contract may be drawn. Typically, franchisees invest heavily in their franchise, which means that they have a risky investment portfolio if they are not highly diversified. This can make the franchisee reluctant to engage in additional capital investments in the franchise. As a consequence, franchisors will tend to favor franchisees who own multiple outlets or have wealth from other sources. A franchisee with multiple outlets can spread the risk of its investments and internalize the benefits of its investments in store quality (since customers are more likely to patronize another of the owner's outlets). And with greater and more diversified wealth, the franchisee will also be able to spread the financial risks of the relevant investments.

Obviously, both ownership and franchising have costs and benefits as expansion options for investors. We can't determine whether a firm should expand by ownership or franchising additional outlets. But we can note that franchising will not be as important when markets are "local." Thus, it should not be a surprise that franchising grew rapidly in the 1950s with the spread of television and the development of the interstate highway system, which reduced communication and transportation (transaction) costs, allowing people to move around the country much more easily (Mathewson and Winter 1985, 504).

Franchising will tend to be favored when there is a low investment risk for the franchisee and when there are few incentives for free-riding by both the franchisee and franchisor. We should expect franchises to grow in favor as monitoring costs increase, implying greater distance from the franchisor will encourage expansion through franchising – a conclusion that has been supported by empirical work (Brickley and Dark 1987, 411–416). Also, we would expect that, with fewer repeat customers in a given location, the store will more likely be company-owned, since the incentive for the franchisee to cheat is strong and the franchisor will have higher costs to monitor cheating.[17] The bottom line: franchises exist not so much to increase capital available to franchisors, but to increase the incentives of franchise operators to produce cost-effectively.

Practical Lessons

This chapter is full of practical advice for business students in developing production and organizational strategies. We also recommend two widely read books in "behavioral economics," an emerging subdiscipline in economics: Richard Thaler and Cass Sunstein's *Nudge: Improving Decisions about Health, Wealth, and Happiness* (2008) and Dan Ariely's *Predictably Irrational: The Hidden Forces that Shape Our Decisions* (2010). These authors report findings from laboratory and classroom research that show people are subject to a variety of "decision-making biases" and outright "irrationalities." People (including those in business) do not always discount costs and benefits appropriately, treat opportunity costs and out-of-pocket expenditures differently, value what they possess more than what they don't have, fail to consider marginal costs and benefits, and often fail to ignore sunk costs. To be productive, managers must recognize their potential decision-making biases and think more rationally.

While we have serious concerns with many of the conclusions drawn from behavioral research conducted by economists and psychologists (which are considered in Online Chapter 1), we still think business students should recognize that not all people behave at all times with the level of rationality often assumed in microeconomic theory. Somewhat paradoxically, recognition of human rational limitations and failures make the analytics in this chapter all the more important. This chapter explains how managers can make decisions more rationally, giving them a potential competitive advantage. How? They should:

- discount costs and benefits for time and risk;
- treat all marginal costs the same – whether opportunity costs or out-of-pocket expenditures;
- ignore sunk costs; and
- ferret out marginal cost and marginal value with an eye toward equating at the margin.

---

[17] Unfortunately, the only available study on the relationship between the extent of such business and the likelihood of franchising does not confirm the theory. Brickley and Dark (1987) investigated how the location of outlets near freeways affected the likelihood that they would be franchised. They assumed that locations near freeways would have limited repeat business and hence would tend to be company-owned. But they found the exact opposite; outlets near freeways tended to be franchised. The theory could be wrong or locations near freeways may not be a good measure of repeat business.

And they should follow many of the other production and organizational strategies developed in this book for offensive and defensive reasons. The offensive reason is that these rules can make firms more profitable – precisely because people in firms may fall prey to decision-making biases and irrationalities if they are not guided by the production and organizational rules we have deduced. The defensive reason is that, if managers don't follow these rules, firms will have higher cost structures and be at a competitive disadvantage in the pricing of their products and in securing financial resources to continue and expand their operations.

Further Reading Online

Reading 7.1: Why good managers are so rare (*Harvard Business Review*, link available on the online resources website www.cambridge.org/mckenzie4)
Reading 7.2: Cutting health insurance costs through medical savings accounts

Recommended Videos Online

1 Principal–agent problems (Richard McKenzie, 35 minutes)

2 Academic tenure (Richard McKenzie, 12 minutes)

3 Firms and coordinating costs (Richard McKenzie, 27 minutes)

4 Make-or-buy decisions (Richard McKenzie, 27 minutes)

5 Franchising (Richard McKenzie, 16 minutes)

6 How much does a good boss really matter? (Freakonomics, link available on the online resources website www.cambridge.org/mckenzie4)

7 Why are there so many bad bosses? (Freakonomics, link available on the online resources website www.cambridge.org/mckenzie4)

8 TED-Ed: These companies with no CEO are thriving (TED, link available on the online resources website www.cambridge.org/mckenzie4)

The Bottom Line

The key takeaways from Chapter 7 are the following:

1 Cost plays a pivotal role in producer choices. Costs change with the quantity produced. The pattern of those changes determines the limits of a producer's activity.

2 All costs – explicit and implicit – must be considered when deciding how much of anything should be produced if profits are to be maximized.

3 Costs will not affect an individual's behavior unless she perceives them as costs. For this reason, managers can often improve incentives, firm profits, and employee well-being by looking for hidden/implicit costs in choices and making the changes necessary to ensure that they and their workers account for those costs.

4   "Sunk costs" are not a cost in the present or future. Since they cannot be changed or recouped, they should not matter in production decisions.

5   Normal profit is a cost of doing business.

6   The maximizing individual will produce a good or service (or engage in an activity) until marginal cost equals marginal benefit/revenue. At this point, although additional benefits might be obtained by producing additional units, the additional costs are sufficient to discourage further production.

7   The market supply curve in a competitive goods market is the horizontal summation of individual firms' supply curves.

8   Firm size is limited by economies of scale and agency costs.

9   Firms exist because they tend to reduce the overall cost of doing business – most prominently, external coordinating (or transaction) costs.

10 Firm size, profitability, and survival are crucially dependent on balancing internal and external coordinating costs. Firms can be expected to contract in size if market transactions costs are lowered, everything else equal.

11 Firms are advised to buy inputs from competitive sources of supply. But they often make their own inputs because of the potential for opportunistic behavior in dealing with outside suppliers, especially when investments in firm-specific resources must be made before payments for the produced good are made.

12 People often behave opportunistically. However, it is wrong to conclude that *all* people are *always* willing to behave opportunistically, which is also contradicted by everyday experience. The business world is full of saints and sinners – and most people are some combination. Opportunistic behavior has been emphasized because it is the threat to protect against. People in business don't have to worry about the Mother Teresas of the world; they do need to worry about less than saintly people, including those who pretend to be like Mother Teresa. They need to understand the consequences of opportunistic behavior in order to appropriately structure their contracts and embedded incentives.

Review Questions ▶▶

1   Evaluate the old adages "haste makes waste" and "a stitch in time saves nine" from an economic point of view.

2   When cell phones were first introduced, the price of a one-minute long-distance call was several times the cost of a call on a landline phone. Does this mean that cell phones were increasing the cost of long-distance calling?

3   People take measures to avoid becoming victims of crime. Can the probability of becoming a victim be reduced to (virtually) zero? If so, why don't people eliminate this probability? What does the underlying logic of your answer suggest about the cost of committing crimes and the crime rate?

4   Why do construction contracts usually have provisions for installment payments as the work proceeds? Why do they usually have a provision for a major share (say,

20 percent) of the total cost to be paid only after the project has been completed and approved? Why isn't it 0 percent or 100 percent?

5 What are some examples of "sunk costs" in your business environment?

6 How does the corporate form of business organization overcome the last-period problem?

7 Identify an example of the "last-period problem" in your workplace. Does your firm do anything useful to combat it? Do you have ideas how to address it better?

8 Calculate the marginal product of labor (MP_L) and the average product of labor (AP_L) when the output produced is 40, 100, 150, 180, 200, 210, 210, and 200 units for the first eight workers hired.

9 Would you expect tenure to be of greater concern at major research universities or liberal arts and teaching colleges? How might students be affected if tenure for professors were eliminated?

10 Can you think of employment situations, other than those discussed in this chapter, in which there exists some form of tenure (granted to employees who perform well over some initial probation period)? Does the tenure granted in these situations provide as much job security as does university tenure for professors? Why or why not?

11 Why are some firms "large" and other firms "small"? Use the concept of "coordinating costs" in your answer.

12 If worker monitoring costs go down, what will happen to the size of the firm?

13 What have been the various effects of the computer/telecommunications revolution on the sizes of firms?

14 Could you, or any of your classmates, successfully run a large corporation? Does your answer, and the answers of your classmates, help explain the fantastic, multimillion-dollar salaries of executives at the pinnacle of corporate America? What are the economic reasons for executives' high pay? Why have executive pay rates risen in recent decades faster than line-worker pay rates?

15 If your firm fears being "held up" by an outside supplier of a critical part to your production process, what can your firm do to reduce the probability of such a hold-up?

16 Authors typically receive a percentage of revenues as a royalty. Why do authors typically get only a minor fraction (say, 15 percent) of the revenue stream? What are the economic advantages of large "advances" (payments by publishers to authors before books are published)?

17 How is it that a firm can increase its profitability by franchising its extended operations rather than owning the extended operations outright?

8

Production Costs in the Short Run and Long Run

In economics, the cost of an event is the highest-valued opportunity necessarily forsaken. The usefulness of the concept of cost is a logical implication of choice among available options. Only if no alternatives were possible or if amounts of all resources were available beyond everyone's desires, so that all goods were free, would the concepts of cost and of choice be irrelevant.

Armen Alchian[1]

The individual firm plays a critical role both in theory and in the real world. The firm straddles two basic economic institutions: the markets for resources (labor, capital, and land) and the markets for goods and services (everything from trucks to truffles). The firm must be able to identify what people want to buy, at what price, and to organize a variety of available resources into an efficient production process. It must sell its product at a price that covers the cost of its resources (including the opportunity cost of capital) – if not generate an *economic* profit for its owners. And it must accomplish those objectives while competing firms are seeking to meet the same goals.

How does the firm do all this? Clearly, firms do not all operate in exactly the same way. They differ in organizational structure and management style, in the resources they use, and in the products they sell. This chapter cannot possibly cover the diversity of business management techniques. Rather, our purpose is to develop the broad principles that guide most firms' production decisions. In the process, we develop an alternative explanation for firm size that complements the theory in Chapter 7.

As with individuals, firms are beset by the necessity of choice which, as Armen Alchian reminds us in the chapter epigraph, implies a cost. Costs are both the result of having to make choices and the obstacles to those choices; they restrict us in what we do. Thus, a firm's cost structure (the way cost varies with

[1] Used with permission of Macmillan, from *International Encyclopaedia of the Social Sciences*, 9780028957500, 1972.

production) reflects how firms deal with the obstacles of making a profitable production decision in both the short and the long run. Business students should understand a firm's *cost structure*, because "firms" don't do anything on their own. Managers are a key force behind the firm's activities and the decisions that ultimately determine profitability.

As noted in Chapter 7, the economic analysis of a firm's "cost structure" is different from the costs on accounting statements. Accounting statements provide only a snapshot of costs incurred in a given time period and for a given output level. In this chapter, we devise a cost structure that relates production costs to many different output levels and different time periods. The reason is simple: we want to use this structure to determine which among many possible output levels will enable the firm to maximize profits in the short run and the long run. More importantly, we want to draw out *principles* of firm production decisions that cut across a wide variety of real-world cost structures.

As we did in Chapter 7, we use Part B to explain ways in which firms can contain their costs – to lower their cost structures as much as is economical – and remain competitive. Accordingly, we develop the ways in which the firm's *financial* structure – its combination of debt and equity – can affect manager incentives to economize on firm resources and thus contain its cost structure. This line of explanation will help you understand the Savings and Loan (S&L) debacle of the 1980s and 1990s – and the more recent "mortgage meltdown," which was largely founded on risk-taking encouraged by mortgages that required little to no down-payment from new homebuyers. In taking up these financial debacles, we intend not so much to teach history, but to draw out lessons that go beyond the particulars of the crises covered.

In Perspective 8, we describe another potentially costly issue – the prospect of opportunistic behavior as business (and other) arrangements come to an end. In sum, we will use this chapter to finalize our development of a firm's cost-curve structure and then describe two often-overlooked but important ways to minimize those costs.

Part A Theory and Public Policy Applications

Fixed, Variable, and Total Costs in the Short Run

Time is required to produce any good or service; therefore, any output level must be founded on some recognized time period. Moreover, the types and amounts of costs incurred by firms will vary over time. To think about costs clearly, we must identify the time period during which they apply. For reasons that will become apparent, economists speak of costs in terms of *the extent to which they can*

> The **short run** is the period during which one or more resources (and thus one or more costs of production) cannot be changed – either increased or decreased. (The **long run** is the period in which all resources – and thus all costs – can be changed.)

> A **fixed cost** is any cost that does not vary with the level of output. A **variable cost** is any cost that changes with the level of output.

be varied, rather than the number of months or years required to pay them. In the **long run**, all costs can be varied. In the **short run**, firms face some costs that cannot be varied; thus, short-run costs can be either a **fixed cost** or a **variable cost.**[2]

Total variable costs (*TVC*) increase with the level of output. Total fixed costs (*TFC*) remain the same whether the firm's factories are standing idle or producing at capacity. As long as the firm faces even one fixed cost, it is operating in the short run. Fixed costs (*FC*) include overhead expenditures that extend over a period of months or years – for example, insurance premiums, leasing and rental payments, land and equipment purchases, and interest on loans. Variable costs (*VC*) include wages (workers can be hired or laid off on relatively short notice), material, utilities, and office supplies. In sum, *TFC* are independent of output; *TVC* are dependent on output. Together, total fixed and total variable costs equal total cost (*TC*). Thus *TC* is the sum of fixed costs and variable costs at each output level:

$$TC = TFC + TVC.$$

Columns (1) through (4) of Table 8.1 show fixed, variable, and total costs at various production levels. Total fixed costs are constant at $100 for all output levels. Total variable costs increase gradually, from $30 to $395, as output expands from one to twelve widgets. Total cost, the sum of all fixed and variable costs at each output level – obtained by adding columns (2) and (3) horizontally – increases gradually as well.

Graphically, total fixed cost can be represented by a horizontal line, as in Figure 8.1. The total cost curve starts at the same point as the total fixed cost curve (since there are no variable costs without output) and rises from this point. The vertical distance (difference) between the total cost and the total fixed cost curves shows the total variable cost at each level of production.

Marginal and Average Costs in the Short Run

The central issue of this chapter through Chapter 11 is how to determine the *profit-maximizing level of production*. In other words, we want to know what output a firm will choose to produce. Although fixed, variable, and total costs are important measures, they are not sufficient to determine the firm's profit-maximizing

---

[2] Note that we use the words "cost" and "costs" interchangeably throughout.

Table 8.1 **Total, marginal and average costs of production**

(1) Production level (no. of widgets)	(2) Total fixed costs ($)	(3) Total variable costs ($)	(4) Total cost (2) + (3) ($)	(5) Marginal cost (change in (3) or (4)) ($)	(6) Average fixed cost ((2)/(1)) ($)	(7) Average variable cost ((3)/(1)) ($)	(8) Average total cost ((4)/(1)) or ((6) + (7)) ($)
1	100	30	130	30	100.00	30.00	130.00
2	100	50	150	20	50.00	25.00	75.00
3	100	60	160	10	33.33	20.00	53.33
4	100	65	165	5	25.00	16.25	41.25
5	100	75	175	10	20.00	15.00	35.00
6	100	90	190	15	16.67	15.00	31.67
7	100	110	210	20	14.29	15.71	30.00
8	100	140	240	30	12.50	17.50	30.00
9	100	180	280	40	11.11	20.00	31.11
10	100	230	330	50	10.00	23.00	33.00
11	100	300	400	70	9.09	27.27	36.36
12	100	395	495	95	8.33	32.92	41.25

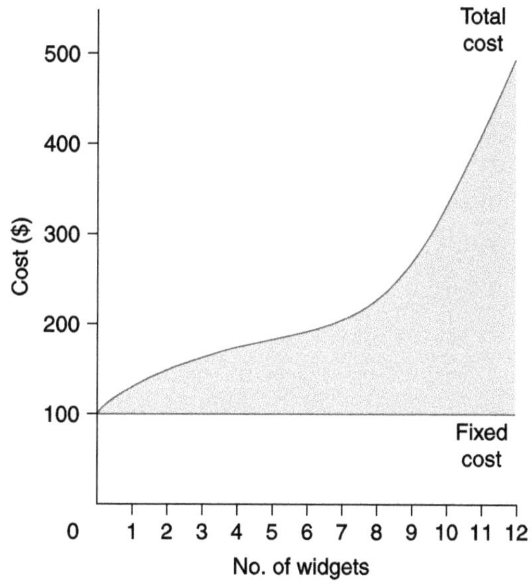

Figure 8.1 Total fixed costs, total variable costs, and total cost in the short run Total fixed cost does not vary with production; therefore, it is drawn as a horizontal line. Total variable cost rises with production. Here, it is represented by the distance between the total cost and total fixed cost curves for any given level of production.

(or loss-minimizing) output. To arrive at this, as well as to estimate profits or losses, we will need information on revenues (to be developed in Chapters 9 and 10) and four additional measures of cost: (1) marginal cost, (2) average fixed cost, (3) average variable cost, and (4) average total cost. When graphed, those four measures represent the firm's cost structure, which covers all costs associated with production, including risk cost and opportunity cost.

We have defined marginal cost (*MC*) as the additional cost of producing one additional unit – that is, the change in total cost (*TC*). Because the change in *TC* must be due solely to the change in total variable cost (*TVC*), *MC* can also be defined as the change in *TVC* per unit:

$$MC = \frac{\text{change in } TC}{\text{change in quantity}} = \frac{\text{change in } TVC}{\text{change in quantity}}.$$

As you can see from Table 8.1, marginal cost declines as output expands from one to four widgets and then rises – as predicted by the law of diminishing marginal returns. This increasing marginal cost reflects the diminishing marginal productivity of extra workers and other variable resources that the firm must employ in order to expand output beyond four widgets. The *MC* curve is shown in Figure 8.2. The bottom of the curve (four units) is the point at which marginal returns begin to diminish.

Average Fixed Cost

Average fixed cost (*AFC*) is total fixed cost (*TFC*) divided by the number of units produced (*Q*):

$$AFC = \frac{TFC}{Q}.$$

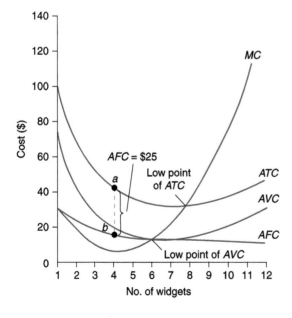

Figure 8.2 Marginal and average costs in the short run
The average fixed cost curve (*AFC*) slopes downward and approaches, but never touches, the horizontal axis. The average variable cost curve (*AVC*) and the average total cost curve (*ATC*) are mathematically related to the marginal cost curve (*MC*); both intersect with *MC* at their lowest point. The vertical distance (difference) between *ATC* and *AVC* equals *AFC* at any given output level. There is no relationship between the *MC* and *AFC* curves.

In Table 8.1, total fixed costs are constant at $100. As output expands, therefore, the average fixed cost per unit must decline – what is meant by "spreading the overhead costs." As production expands, the average fixed cost declines.

In Figure 8.2, the *AFC* curve slopes downward to the right, approaching, but never touching, the horizontal axis. This is because average fixed cost is a ratio of positive numbers (*TFC/Q*), which can never reduce to zero, no matter how large the denominator (*Q*).

Average Variable Cost

Average variable cost (*AVC*) is total variable cost (*TVC*) divided by the number of units produced (*Q*):

$$AVC = \frac{TVC}{Q}.$$

At an output level of one unit, average variable cost necessarily equals marginal cost. Beyond the first unit, marginal and average variable costs diverge, although they are mathematically related. When marginal cost declines, as it does initially in Figure 8.2, average variable cost must also decline: the low marginal value pulls the average value down. For instance, a basketball player who scores fewer points in each successive game will find her scoring average falling, although not as rapidly as her marginal scoring.

Beyond the point of diminishing marginal returns, marginal cost rises, but average variable cost continues to fall for a range of output (as in Figure 8.2). As long as the *MC* curve is below the *AVC* curve, *AVC* must continue to decline. (The two curves meet at an output level of six widgets.) Beyond this point, *AVC* must rise because the average value will be pulled up by the greater marginal value. (After a game in which she scores more points than her previous average, the basketball player's scoring average must rise.) The point at which *MC* and *AVC* intersect is, therefore, the low point of the *AVC* curve. Before this intersection, *AVC* must fall; after it, *AVC* must rise. For the same reason, the intersection of *MC* and *ATC* must be the low point of the *ATC* curve.

Average Total Cost

Average total cost (*ATC*) is the sum of total fixed costs (*TFC*) and total variable costs (*TVC*) divided by the number of units produced (*Q*):

$$ATC = \frac{TFC + TVC}{Q} = \frac{TC}{Q}.$$

Average total cost can also be found by summing the average fixed and average variable costs, if they are known:

$$ATC = AFC + AVC.$$

Graphically, the *ATC* curve is the vertical summation of the *AFC* and *AVC* curves (as in Figure 8.2). Similarly, the average fixed cost can be obtained by subtracting average variable cost from average total cost:

$$AFC = ATC - AVC.$$

So, graphically, *AFC* is the vertical distance (difference) between the *ATC* curve and the *AVC* curve. For instance, in Figure 8.2 at an output level of four widgets, average fixed cost is the vertical distance *ab*, or $25 ($41.25 – $16.25) or column (8) minus column (7) in Table 8.1. (From here, we do not show the *AFC* curve on a graph because doing so complicates the presentation without adding new information. The value for average fixed cost is simply indicated by the vertical distance between the *ATC* and *AVC* curves at any given output.) Cost curves can also be calculated and manipulated using algebra and simple calculus. (This is covered in the Online Math Appendix.)

Marginal and Average Costs in the Long Run

So far, our discussion has been restricted to time periods during which at least one resource is fixed. This assumption is behind the concept of fixed cost. Fortunately, all resources used in production can be changed over the long run. By definition, there are no fixed costs in the long run; all long-run costs are variable.

Our short-run analysis is still useful in analyzing a firm's long-run cost structure. In the long run, the average total cost curve (*ATC* in Figure 8.2) represents one possible scale of operation, with one given quantity of plant and equipment (in Table 8.1, $100 worth). A change in plant and equipment will change the firm's cost structure, increasing or decreasing its productive capacity.

Economies of Scale

Figure 8.3 illustrates the long-run production choices facing a typical firm. The curve labeled ATC_1 is what we developed in Figure 8.2. Additional plant and equipment would change the relationship between average total cost and output, resulting in ATC_2 in Figure 8.3. Because of the additional fixed costs, at low output levels (up to q_1), the average total costs will be higher: ATC_2 will lie above ATC_1. But, in this case, the additional plant and equipment also allow **economies of scale** (or increasing returns to scale) to be

> **Economies of scale** (increasing returns to scale) are cost savings that technology allows when all resource inputs are increased together.

realized beyond q_1, resulting in lower *average* total costs than are possible with the plant and equipment associated with ATC_1.

Economies of scale can occur for several reasons. Expanded operation generally permits greater specialization of resources. Technologically advanced equipment, e.g., supercomputers and management information systems (MIS),

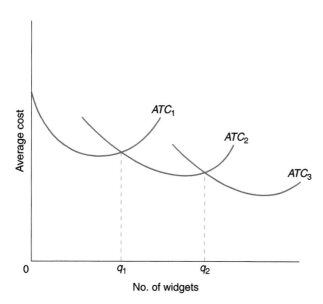

Figure 8.3 Economies of scale
Economies of scale are (average/per-unit) cost savings associated with the expanded use of resources. To realize such savings, however, a firm must expand its output. Here, the firm can lower its costs by expanding production from q_1 to q_2 – a scale of operation that places it on a lower short-run average total cost curve (ATC_2 or ATC_3 instead of ATC_1).

combined with telecommunication systems can be used and more highly skilled workers can be employed. Expansion may also permit improvements in organization, as with assembly-line production. And, by expanding production, the firm can spread the higher cost of additional plant and equipment over a larger output level, reducing its average cost of production.

As long as economies of scale remain in force, the average total costs can be reduced over larger output levels by increasing plant and equipment. Just as curve ATC_2 in Figure 8.3 cuts curve ATC_1 and then dips down to a lower minimum average total cost at a higher output level, so does curve ATC_3 with respect to curve ATC_2, indicating that economies of scale haven't been exhausted with the plant and equipment associated with curve ATC_2.

But at some point the firm will encounter **diseconomies of scale** (or decreasing returns to scale).[3] Related to our earlier discussion of agency costs, the advantages of a growing firm are always limited,

> **Diseconomies of scale** are increased average costs that, beyond some point, accompany the expansion of production through the increased use of *all* inputs in the *long run*. (This is distinct from diminishing marginal returns, which indicates less additional productivity, in the short run, from the addition of variable inputs to fixed inputs.)

---

[3] Another consideration is the change in input usage from the change in the price of an input. For example, if the price of labor rises, costs will increase, causing some combination of higher prices (as consumers are willing to pay, dependent on their elasticity of demand) and reduced output (and therefore reduced use of all inputs). This is a "scale effect," since it tends to impact the *scale* of operations and the use of *all* inputs. There is also a "substitution effect" – here, from more expensive labor toward relatively less-expensive capital, *substituting* from labor to capital as production technology allows. (Such concepts can be illustrated with isoquants and isocost curves – analogous to the utility/indifference curves and budget constraints of consumer theory. These are developed in the Online Math Appendix.)

with average costs eventually rising as output increases from increased plant and equipment. For example, as more people are hired to work with the additional plant and equipment, the problem of free-riders becomes increasingly troublesome.[4] When this occurs, diseconomies of scale have become operative.

Diseconomies of scale are evident in Figure 8.4 as firms consider moving the scale of production from ATC_4 to ATC_5 and ATC_6. In some lines of production, diseconomies of scale are encountered at very small output levels independently of free-rider problems. For example, the production of original works of art, cutting hair, repairing shoes, and writing books are typically done by individuals working alone or by firms with little capital and few workers.

When a firm has enough time to change the amount of all inputs it is using – changing its scale of operation – it is interested in its long-run cost curves. The firm can minimize its overall cost of operation by expanding along the envelope portion of curve ATC_2, pushing its average costs down to the lowest point by expanding its scale to ATC_4 and its output to q_1. Assuming there are many possible scales of operation, the firm's expansion path can be seen as a single overall curve that envelops all of its short-run average total cost curves. Such a curve is shown in Figure 8.4 as the long-run average cost curve ($LRAC$) – and then simply

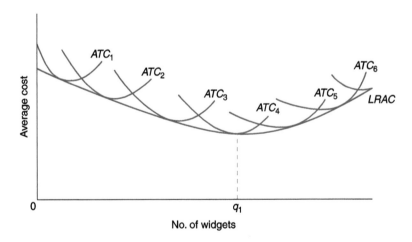

Figure 8.4 Diseconomies of scale

At some level of output, diseconomies of scale will occur because of increasing agency problems in larger firms. Here, the firm realizes economies of scale through its first four short-run *ATC* curves. The *LRAC* (long-run average cost) curve begins to turn up at an output level of q_1, beyond which diseconomies of scale set in.

---

[4] To some extent, a firm may be able to avoid diseconomies of scale by increasing the number of its plants. But management's ability to supervise a growing number of plants is also limited – and eventually diseconomies of scale will emerge at the level of the firm, if not the plant itself. If diseconomies of scale did not exist, in the long run, each industry would have only one firm.

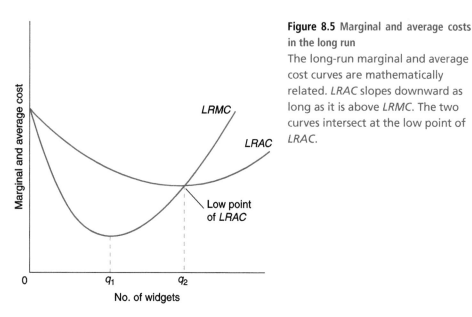

Figure 8.5 Marginal and average costs in the long run

The long-run marginal and average cost curves are mathematically related. *LRAC* slopes downward as long as it is above *LRMC*. The two curves intersect at the low point of *LRAC*.

reproduced in Figure 8.5, along with its accompanying long-run marginal cost curve (*LRMC*).

Revisiting the necessary relationship between average and marginal: If long-run average cost is falling, as it does initially in Figure 8.5, it must be because long-run marginal cost is pulling it down. If long-run average cost is rising, as it does beyond q_2 in Figure 8.5, then long-run marginal cost must be pulling it up. Hence, at some point, long-run marginal cost must turn upward, intersecting *LRAC* at its lowest point, q_2. (In our development of a firm's cost-curve structure, for reasons of space, we have sidestepped the issue of how a firm actually goes about choosing the most efficient combination of resources. We cover such technical details in the Online Math Appendix.)

Industry Differences in Average Cost

Not all firms experience economies and diseconomies of scale to the same degree or at the same levels of production. Their *LRAC* curves, in other words, are somewhat different; Figure 8.6 shows several possible shapes. The curve in Figure 8.6(a) belongs to a firm in an industry with few economies of scale and significant diseconomies at relatively low output levels. (This curve might belong to a small firm in a service industry, such as a shoe repair business.) We would not expect firms in this industry to be large because firms with an output level beyond q_1 can easily be underpriced by smaller, lower-cost firms.

Figure 8.6(b) shows the *LRAC* curve for a firm in an industry with modest economies of scale at low output levels and no diseconomies of scale until the firm reaches a relatively high output level. In such an industry – perhaps

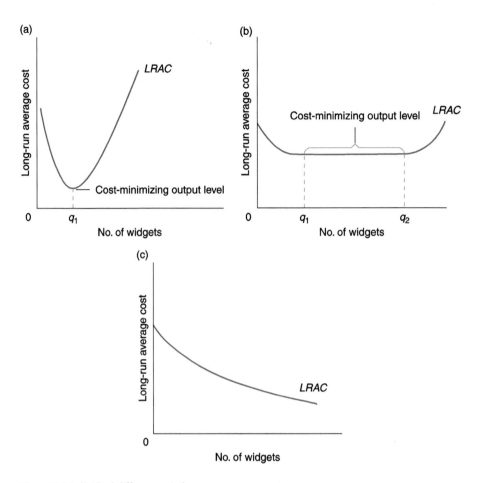

Figure 8.6 Individual differences in long-run average cost curves
The shape of the *LRAC* curve varies according to the extent and persistence of economies and diseconomies of scale. Firms in industries with few economies of scale will have an *LRAC* curve as in panel (a). Firms in industries with persistent economies of scale will have an *LRAC* curve as in panel (b). Firms in industries with extensive economies of scale may find that their *LRAC* curve slopes continually downward as in panel (c).

apparel manufacturing – we would expect to find firms of various sizes, some small and some large. As long as firms are producing between q_1 and q_2, larger firms do not have a cost advantage over smaller firms. In this case, there are "constant" returns to scale, resulting in the same per-unit costs over a range of output levels.

Figure 8.6(c) illustrates the average costs for a firm in an industry that enjoys extensive economies of scale – for example, an electric power company. No matter how far this firm extends its scale, long-run average costs continue to fall. Diseconomies of scale may exist, but, if so, they occur at output levels beyond the effective market for the firm's product. This type of industry tends toward a single seller – a **natural monopoly**. Given the industry's cost structure, one firm can expand its scale, lower average costs, and underprice other firms that attempt to produce on a smaller, higher-cost scale. Natural monopolies are often the subject of regulation – a subject to which we return in Chapter 11.

> A **natural monopoly** is an industry in which long-run marginal and average costs generally decline with increases in production within the relevant range of the market demand for a good or service.

Changes in Input Prices

The average cost curves we have just described all assume that the prices for resources remain constant. This is a critical assumption. If those prices change, so will the average cost curves. The *MC* curve may shift as well, depending on the type of cost (variable or fixed) that changes.

Because a shift in average fixed cost leaves marginal cost unaffected, the firm's profit-maximizing output level remains the same. The firm may make lower profits because of its higher fixed cost, but it cannot increase profits by either expanding or reducing output. This analysis only applies to the short run. In the long run, all costs are variable – and changes in the price of any resource will affect a firm's production decisions. Long-run changes in the output levels of firms, of course, change the market price of the final product, as well as consumer purchases. More will be said on all of these points, especially in the next two chapters.

If the price of a variable input rises (e.g., the wage rate of labor), the firm's average total costs will rise along with its average variable costs, shifting the *ATC* curve upward. The firm's *MC* curve will also shift because the additional cost of producing an additional unit must rise with the higher labor cost, as in Figure 8.7(a). If a fixed cost (e.g., insurance premiums) rises, then average total costs will also rise, shifting the *ATC* curve upward, as in Figure 8.7(b). But the short-run *MC* curve will not shift, because marginal cost is unaffected by fixed cost; the *MC* curve is derived only from variable costs.

Because changes in variable cost affect a firm's marginal cost, they influence its production decisions. As first noted in Chapter 7, the profit-maximizing firm selling at a constant price will produce up to the point at which marginal cost equals price and marginal revenue ($MC = P = MR$). At a price of P_1 in Figure 8.7(a), the firm will produce q_2 widgets. With an increase in variable costs and an upward shift in the *MC* curve, the firm will cut back to q_1 widgets. At q_1 widgets, price again equals marginal cost. The reduction in output has occurred because the marginal cost of producing widgets from q_1 to q_2 now exceeds the price. In other words, an increase in variable cost results in a reduction in a firm's output.

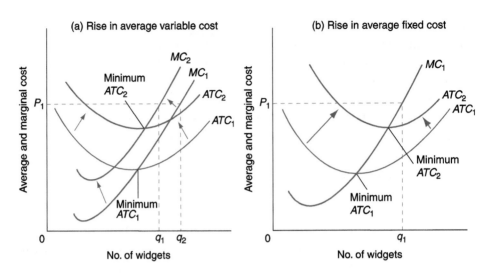

Figure 8.7 Shifts in average and marginal cost curves
An increase in a firm's variable cost, as in panel (a), will shift the firm's ATC curve up – from ATC_1 to ATC_2. It will also shift the MC curve – from MC_1 to MC_2. Production will fall because of the increase in marginal cost. By contrast, an increase in a firm's fixed cost, as in panel (b), will shift the ATC curve upward from ATC_1 to ATC_2, but will not affect the MC curve. (Marginal cost is unaffected by fixed cost.) Thus, the firm's level of production will not change.

The Very Long Run

Economic analysis tends to be restricted to either the short run or the long run for one major reason: for both periods, costs are known with reasonable precision and choices can be made with the attendant costs and benefits.[5] In the *short run*, firms know that, beyond some point, increases in the use of *a* resource (for example, fertilizer) will bring diminishing marginal returns and rising marginal costs. They also know that, with increased use of *all* resources, certain economies and diseconomies of scale can be expected over the *long run*. Given what is known about the technology of production and the availability of resources, economists can draw certain conclusions about a firm's behavior and the consequences of its actions.

However, as economists look further and further into the future, they can predict less and less about a firm's behavior and the consequences in the marketplace. Less is known about the technology and resources of the distant future. In the **very long run**, everything is subject to change – resources themselves, their availability, and the technology for using them.

> The **very long run** is the time period during which production can change because of invention, innovation, and the discovery of new technologies and resources.

---

[5] One might consider a time period called "the immediate run," where all inputs are fixed – or, at least, unable to respond sufficiently to a higher demand by consumers. But such a time frame is of limited interest since no choices can be made to alter input choices, production, and profit.

By definition, the very long run is, to a significant degree, unpredictable. Firms cannot know today how to make use of unspecified future advances in technology. One hundred years ago, firms had little idea about the importance of lasers, satellites, airplanes, and computers to today's economy. Indeed, many products taken for granted today were invented or discovered quite by accident. Edison developed the phonograph while attempting to invent the light bulb. John Rock developed the birth control pill while studying penicillin. Charles Goodyear's development of vulcanization and Wilhelm Roentgen's discovery of X-rays were both accidents. And even if these could have been predicted, they all had unpredictable economic consequences.

That said, not all inventions, innovations, or discoveries are accidental, so we can know something about the very long run. Firms understand the value of investments in research and development (R&D). Research on substitute resources can yield improvements in productivity that translate into cost reductions. Research on new product designs will yield more attractive and useful products. There will be failures as well – research projects that accomplish little or nothing – but, over time, the rewards of research and development can exceed the costs.

Because of the risks involved in R&D, some firms may be expected to fail. In the very long run, they will not be able to keep up with the competition in product design and productivity. They will not adjust sufficiently to changes in the market and will suffer losses. The computer industry provides many examples of firms that have tried to build a better machine, but could not keep pace with the rapid technological advances of competitors.

Proponents of a planned economy see the uncertainty of the very long run as an argument for government direction of the nation's development. They stress that competitors often do not know what other firms are doing and thus need guidance in the form of government subsidies and tax penalties to ensure that the nation's long-term goals are achieved. Proponents of the market system agree that it is difficult to look ahead to the very long run, but they see the uncertainties as an argument for keeping production decisions in the hands of firms. Private firms have the economic incentive of profit to stay alert to changes in market conditions and to respond quickly to changes in technology and resources. Government control might easily slow the adjustment process or focus on helping interest-group cronies.

PERSPECTIVE 8
The Last-Period Problem

Much of the book has been concerned with how people behave rationally. Through agency costs in Chapter 7, we described opportunistic behavior – a form of rational behavior for managers and owners to anticipate and defend against. Here, we suggest another way in which parties to business deals can take advantage of other parties – and how managers can structure their organizational and pay policies to minimize such opportunistic behavior.

More specifically, the goal of this Perspective is to explain how business deals can be structured to maximize their durability and profitability. To do this, business relationships must be ongoing – or, at least, have no clearly defined last period which can inspire opportunistic behavior among rational suppliers and creditors, reducing profits. Related to our discussion of honesty and trust in Chapter 5: a reputation for continuing in business has *economic value*, which explains why managers should work hard to create such a reputation.

Problems with the End of Contracts

A terrific advantage of dealing with outside suppliers is that the relationship is constantly up for renewal and can easily be terminated if it is not satisfactory to both parties. But therein lies an important *disadvantage*: The relationship lacks the permanence or confidence that any given buyer–supplier relationship will be renewed. The supplier must attribute some probability that the end of the contract will be the end of the relationship, given that she might not be the low bidder next time – a conclusion that the astute manager will recognize as posing possibly profound effects on the relationship. When a relationship is known to be coming to an end on a certain date, serious problems can arise. The basic problem is that, during the last period of any business relationship, there is less penalty for cheating, which implies a maximum incentive to cheat. As a consequence, cheating on deals is more likely in the last period than at any other time in the relationship.

Consider a simple business deal. Suppose that you want 1000 widgets of a given quality delivered every month this year and you have agreed to make a fixed payment to the supplier when the delivery is made. If you discover after you have made payment that your supplier sent fewer than 1000 units or sent an inferior quality, you can withhold future checks until the supplier makes good on her end of the bargain. Indeed, you can terminate the contract, which can impose a substantial penalty for any cheating early in the contract. Knowing that, the supplier will have a strong incentive early in the contract period to do what she has agreed to do.

As the year unfolds, however, the supplier's incentive to uphold her end of the bargain begins to fade, since there is less of a penalty that can be imposed in terms of ending the relationship. The supplier might go so far as to reason that during the last period (December), the penalty for cheating is very low, if not zero. The supplier can cut the quantity or quality of the widgets delivered during December and cash the check before you know what happened. You may be able to get the supplier to increase the quantity or quality somewhat with inspection, but you should expect her to be somewhat more difficult to deal with. And you should not *expect* the same level of performance or quality.

Alternatively, you might draw up a contract with a new supplier for December, refusing shipment from your original supplier and imposing costs on *her*. In either case, the problem is that both of you have lost a great deal of your bargaining power during the last month – what is called the **last-period problem**. However, it is a problem that can be mitigated in several ways.

> The **last-period problem** (or **end-period problem**) refers to the costs that can be incurred from opportunistic behavior as the end of a working relationship approaches.

Solutions to the Last-Period Problem

The simplest (and most common) way to solve a last-period problem is to avoid it and maintain continuing relationships. If you constantly jump from one supplier to another, you might save a few bucks, but you might also raise your costs in terms of unfulfilled promises during the last period of the supplier's association with you. In other words, "working relationships" have an economic value apart from what the relationship actually involves – for example, the delivery of so many widgets. This is one important reason for businesses to spend time cultivating their relationships – and why they may stick with suppliers and customers through temporary difficulties.

Nothing works to solve the last-period problem like success. Greater success – greater rates of growth for the firm and its industry – translates into recognizing that the firm will likely continue in business for some time into the future. The opposite is also true: failure can feed on itself as suppliers, buyers, and workers begin to think that the last period is near. Firms understand these facts of business life. Executives tend to stress their successes and downplay their failures. Their intent may not be totally unethical, given how bad business news can cause the news to get worse. But outsiders understand these tendencies. So, investors pay special attention to whether executives are buying or selling their stock in the company. The executives may have access to (accurate) insider information unknown to the public.

Another simple way of dealing with the last-period problem in new relationships is to leave open the prospect of future business, in which case the potential penalty is elevated (in a probabilistic sense) in the mind of the supplier. When there is no prospect of future business, the *expected* cost from cheating is only what can be lost during the last period. When there is some prospect of future business, the cost to an under-performing supplier is greater – and so the rational supplier is more likely to maintain the quality and quantity of his product. For example, when contracting for remodeling or advertising, you can suggest that you might extend the contract or expand the scope of the relationship if the work is done well. In the case of remodeling, you might note other repairs that you are contemplating. In the case of advertising, you could suggest other ad campaigns that you are considering.

How much the compliance is improved can be related to how well you can convince your supplier that you mean business (and a lot of it) for some time into the future. (We are not suggesting that you lie outright about uncertain future business. One problem with lying is that it can, when discovered, undercut the value of your suggestions of further business and inflame the last-period problem!) In other words, you need to be prepared to extend working relationships when they work reasonably well.

If you are not able to develop the impression that future work may be in the offing, the last period can come sooner than you might think. That is, the contractual relationship can unravel because of the way you and the supplier begin to *think* about what the other is thinking and how the other might act as a result. If you or your supplier are inclined to cheat on the contract during the last period, then December becomes irrelevant; November becomes the last period; and the incentive to cheat moves to November. But now, November is the last period and you can imagine what your supplier is thinking: cheating in November before you cheat. Ah, but you can beat the other party by cheating in October. And so on. The possibility of "backward unraveling" suggests that, *before the contract is signed*, you or the supplier might decide that *January* is the (relevant) last period, which means the deal will never be consummated. In this way, the last-period problem becomes a *first-period problem* in setting the terms of the contract.

As we explained in Chapter 7, there are multiple reasons that **firms**, as organizational structures, exist (and production is not carried on strictly through a sequence of market transactions). The last-period problem is one of them. The last-period problem is also a significant reason that the **corporation** is such an important form of doing business. Given that ownership is in shares, the corporation makes for a relatively easy and seamless transfer of ownership, which means that, in an expectational sense, the life of the company is longer as a corporation than as a partnership or proprietorship – two organizational forms that can die with the current owners. This means that the corporate charter should be prized simply because it adds value to the company by muting (though not always eliminating) the last-period problem.

> **Firms** are collections of departments (and people) who have continuing relationships that are not always up for re-bidding, which means that the parties can figure that they will probably be continued, with no clear last period.

> The **corporation** is a legal entity whose existence is independent of the life of the owner or owners; the corporation typically lives on beyond the owner's death.

Firing, Retiring, and Transferring Workers

The last-period problem can surface with a vengeance when an employee who has access to easily destroyed records and equipment is fired. The firm must worry that the employee will use his remaining time in the plant or office to impose costs on the firm – to "get back" at it. As a result, firings are often a surprise and done quickly, with the employee only given enough time to collect his personal things from the office – to minimize damage to the firm. The firm may even hand the employee a paycheck for hours of work not done, simply to make the break as quickly as possible and discourage fired workers from imposing even greater costs through damage to records and equipment. Indeed, when the potential for serious damage is present and likely, firms may hire a security guard to be with the fired employee until he is escorted to the door for the last time.

The last-period problem can also show up in the greater incentives people have to shirk as they approach retirement. To limit worker shirking, firms can use deferred compensation (as discussed in Chapter 3) and withdraw some compensation if shirking occurs. A variation of this solution is to tie executive compensation to stock that they cannot sell without penalty until some time after retirement. If executives shirk toward the end of their career, causing their companies to do poorly, then the executives lose more than any remaining salary they are due for the duration of their tenure: they lose the decline in the value of the stock they own from their pre-retirement shirking. Apparently, corporations' executive compensation committees are aware of the last-period problem. Economists Robert Gibbons and Kevin Murphy have found from their econometric studies that, as CEOs get closer to retirement age, their compensation tends to become more closely tied to their firm's stock market performance (Gibbons and Murphy 1992).

There is a similar last-period problem with military personnel. When officers or enlisted personnel are given their transfer orders, they can sit back and relax, since the penalties that can be imposed on them have been severely limited by the orders. The problem becomes especially severe when personnel are about to leave the military altogether. Military people have a favorite expression for what we call shirking during the last period: "FIGMO." ("F**k you, I've got my orders.") We are sure the military has devised some ways to mute the impact of FIGMO, but it is equally clear that the problem of shirking as they approach the end of their assignment remains pressing. Sometimes you just have to accept some costs of shirking; otherwise, you might conclude that people should be fired the moment they enlist, which can be even more costly.

The Ability to Sell and Transfer a Business

The fact that an older owner of a business can sell to a younger owner also enhances the incentive of the old owner to maintain the reputation of the firm. However, after the firm is sold, there is an incentive for the old owner to allow the firm's reputation to decline, a prospect that encourages a speedy transfer of a business when the deal is closed. If the new owner can't take over the business in a timely fashion, then he might overcome the last-period problem by arranging for the old owner to receive some of the profits in the business after he retires. If the old owner retains some interest in the firm, then he also has an incentive to work with the new owner, giving her time to develop the required reputation for honest dealing with employees and customers and to take control of one of the more elusive business assets – the network of contacts. The practice of retaining the old owner after the sale is common among businesses such as medical offices. Doctors form a firm that looks and operates like a partnership, after which they finalize the sale. In all of these cases, the old owners will want to work with the new owners to make the transfer as seamless as possible, simply because the sale price will be higher and the chance will be greater for the new owners to establish a reputation for honest dealing and take charge of the contacts.

Back in 1983, Scott Cook developed the widely used home-finance software package called "Quicken," the major product of Cook's firm, Intuit, Inc., which was courted for a buyout in the early 1990s by Microsoft. Cook eventually agreed to sell Intuit to Microsoft for $1.5 billion in Microsoft stock, 40 percent above Intuit's market price at the time. Microsoft agreed to pay a premium price for two reasons. First, Bill Gates, the CEO of Microsoft at the time, saw a need to have a dominant personal-finance program that could be integrated into his Microsoft Office line, allowing him to pursue his goal of transforming the way people managed their money. The value of Intuit was greater as an integrated part of Microsoft than by itself. Second, and more relevant to the purposes of this discussion, Cook agreed to become a vice president of Microsoft and to retain an interest in the future development and use of Quicken. This way, Cook could minimize the impact of the last-period problem and the sale of Intuit meant that Quicken might continue to develop. The Justice Department eventually terminated the proposed buyout, threatening to sue Microsoft for antitrust violation. However, the example is still good – not only because it involves prominent business personalities and their successful firms, but also because of the lesson it illustrates: sometimes, by selling only a part of the company, an owner can increase the value of the part that is sold and the part that is retained.

The last-period problem also helps to explain why parents are so anxious for their children to go into their business as retirement age approaches. It extends the life of the business. But it also increases the amount of business that can be done as retirement age is approached, since the elevation of the child to partner/owner extends the last period until some time in the future. The usual answer is that the parent is proud to announce that a child has joined the business. This is probably the case, but it also assures customers and suppliers that the original owner, the parent, will not soon begin to take advantage of them.

Economists have found that the rate of occupational following within families with a self-employed proprietor is three times greater than within other families, suggesting proprietors have good reason – measured in continuing the value of their companies – to bring their children into the business (Laband and Lentz 1990). Caterpillar, the manufacturer of farm equipment and heavy machinery, depends on its dealers to maintain customer trust and goodwill. One way in which Caterpillar has attempted to enhance customer trust has been to set up a school to help children of dealers learn about and pursue careers in Caterpillar dealerships (Davidow and Malone 1992, 234).

Solving Last-Period Problems as an Opportunity for Profit

Bankruptcy laws can be explained in part as a means of reducing end-period problems (Gibbons and Murphy 1992). These laws extend the potential end of the firm and can give the firm a new lease on life and set back the last-period problem indefinitely. Similarly, nervous bondholders may press a financially troubled firm into liquidation, a fact that can exacerbate the last-period problem. In such a situation, suppliers would have to worry that the nervous bondholders will encourage firms to deliver shoddy merchandise, causing customers to be reluctant to deal with the financially strapped firm. Bankruptcy laws allow financially troubled firms to continue operations, making it more likely that the firms will keep up the quality of the products and providing more motivation for suppliers to keep up honest dealing.

Another way of solving the last-period problem is through *performance payments*, which means that payments are made as a project is completed. For example, separate payments (stage payments) can be made for constructing a house when the house is framed, when the roof is on, and when the wiring is in and the interior walls have been finished. A significant portion of the total amount due is withheld until the project is completed and the results are approved. For example, 20 percent of the entire construction cost is often not paid until after the final inspection.

The "last-period" problem is nothing more than what we have tagged it – a "problem" that businesses must consider and handle. It implies costs. At the same time, firms can enhance profit by finding creative ways to make customers and suppliers believe that the "last period" will occur at some reasonable and uncertain future time. Failing firms have a tough time doing this, which is one explanation why the pace of failure quickens when the prospects of failure are recognized, given that customers and suppliers can be expected to withdraw their dealings as a likely end-period approaches.

Firms have an obvious interest in making sure there is a resale market for their company – not just a market for its separate assets. The owners and workers can then capture the long-run value of their efforts to build the firm. By highlighting the last-period problem, we are suggesting that the firm can boost the long-term value of its assets simply by alerting people to the fact that the firm can continue for some time into the future. This means that brokers who operate in the market for buying and selling companies add value in a way not commonly recognized – by giving firms the prospect of longevity. When a firm is expected to remain profitable, it is more likely that rational people will respond in ways that enhance its profitability.

Part B Organizational Economics and Management

Debt/Equity Structures and Executive Incentives

The cost structure developed in Part A helps us conceptualize the problems a firm faces in deciding how much to produce. But production decisions could be among the least of its concerns. The exact placement of the cost structure that a firm faces is not *given* to the firm by some divine being. It emerges from manager decisions, which depend critically on the incentives they face, along with many other factors. Here, we stress the importance of a firm's financial structure – the combination of equity and debt – in shaping manager incentives, the firm's cost structure, and thus its competitive market position.

The *ideal* firm has a single owner and produces a lot of stuff with no resources, including labor. (This firm would be infinitely productive!) But this ideal cannot possibly exist. Resources are always required in the productive process, leading to internal or external coordinating costs. When more than a few people are involved, agency costs arise. And firms often need more funds for investment than one person can generate from her own savings (or would want to commit to a single enterprise). Thus, a successful owner may want to encourage others to join the firm as owners or lenders (including bondholders, stockholders, banks, and trade creditors).

A firm's growth can increase agency costs, as managers and workers use the expanding size of the firm as a screen for their shirking. The addition of equity owners can further dilute the incentive of any one owner to monitor what the agents do. Hence, the greater agency costs can erode (if not negate or overwhelm) any economies of scale achieved through firm expansion (Jensen and Meckling 1976).

Two of the more important questions that a growing firm must face are: How will the method of financing growth – debt or equity – affect the extent of my agency costs? How can the combination of debt and equity be varied to minimize the costs of shirking and opportunism? These questions are really one dimension of a more fundamental question: How does financial structure affect the firm's costs and competitiveness – in particular, its short-run and long-run cost structure?

Here, our focus is on debt, but this is only a matter of convenience in exposition, given that any discussion of debt must be juxtaposed with some discussion of equity as a matter of comparison. In fact, debt and equity are simply two alternative categories of finance (subject to greater variation than we can consider here) available to owners. Owners need to search for an "optimal combination," given the advantages and disadvantages of both in reducing production costs.

Debt and Equity as Alternative Investment Vehicles

By debt, we mean the borrowed funds that must be fully repaid by some agreed-upon time – with regular interest payments made in the interim. If a firm gets into deep financial problems, the lenders have *first* claim on the firm's remaining assets (after worker claims have been paid). By equity (or stock), we mean the funds that people provide in return for control over the disposition of firm resources as residual claimants – a (variable) return on investment paid after all other claims on the firm have been satisfied. The owners (stockholders) will not receive dividends until all required interest payments have been met; they are not guaranteed repayment of their initial investments. Obviously, owners (stockholders) accept more risk on their investment than lenders (bondholders).[6]

Does it matter whether a firm finances its investments by debt or equity? (If not, we would wonder why the two broad categories of finance exist!) With debt, the payments – both the payoff sum and the interest payments – are fixed, which is important for two reasons. First, these fixed payments enable firms to attract funds from people who want security and certainty in their investments. With less risk, the lower costs of investment funds – and thus production costs – allows for more growth and competitiveness. Second, beyond the required interest payments on a given investment project, any residual goes to the equity owners. If the company fails because of investments gone sour and it is liquidated for less than the amount owed to lenders, then stockholders will get nothing. Stockholders can only claim the residual that remains after all expenses and lenders have been paid.

Clearly, the nature of debt biases, to a degree, the decision-making of the owners (and their agents/managers) toward seeking risky investments that will likely carry higher rates of return. These higher rates can tempt equity owners to take unduly high risks. If a firm borrows funds at a 10 percent interest rate and invests those funds in projects with an expected rate of return of 12 percent, the residual left for the equity owners will be the difference of 2 percent. If the funds are invested in a much riskier project with an expected rate of return of 18 percent, then the residual claimed by the equity owners is 8 percent – four times greater.

Granted, the project with the higher rate has a risk premium built into it. However, notice that much of this additional risk is imposed on the lenders. They are the ones who must fear that the risk incurred will translate into failed investments (which is what risk implies). But they are not compensated for the assumed risk they are bearing. Indeed, after a lender has made a loan for a specified rate

---

[6] We recognize that debt and equity come in many forms. Common and preferred stock are the two major divisions of equity. Debt can take a form that has the "look and feel" of equity. For example, much-maligned "junk bonds" often carry with them rights of control over firm decisions and may be about as risky as common stock.

of interest, the managers can increase the risk imposed on the original lenders by pursuing much riskier projects than those lenders anticipated or by increasing the firm's indebtedness with more borrowing.

As a general rule, greater indebtedness provides greater incentives for managers to engage in risky investments. Again, this is because much of the risk is imposed on the lenders – and the benefits, if they materialize, are garnered by the equity owners. When a firm has no debt, then the equity owners incur all the downside risks of risky investment projects. If projects fail, then owners lose whatever was invested. If the firm is 100 percent leveraged, then lenders will suffer the losses from risky investments, but owners will garner all of the risk premium embodied in their investment successes.

As a firm takes on more debt, lenders will become progressively more concerned about losing some or all of their investments. As a consequence, lenders will demand compensation in the form of higher interest payments, which reflect a risk premium. To keep interest costs under control, managers will want to make commitments about how much indebtedness the firm will incur – and the commitments must be credible. Again, we return to a recurring theme: manager reputations for credibility have an *economic value* – in this case, through lower interest payments.

Lenders, of course, will seek to protect themselves from risky managerial decisions in other ways. They may specify the collateral to be committed – and will be most interested in assets that are resaleable ("general capital"), which means lenders can potentially recover their invested funds.[7] They may also seek to obtain rights to monitor and even constrain the indebtedness of the firms to whom they make loans. Managers also have an interest in making such concessions – even though their freedom of action is restricted – because they can be compensated for the restrictions through lower interest rates. Firm managers are granted greater freedom of action in another respect: they control a greater residual, which they can add to their salary and perks (if they have the discretion), extend the investments of the firm, or increase the dividends for stockholders.

Investors will also have a preference for lending to firms with a stable future income stream that can be easily monitored. The more stable the future income, the lower the risk of nonpayments of interest. The more easily the firm can be monitored, the less likely managers will be able to leave creditors with uncompensated risks. The more willing lenders are to lend to firms, the greater the likely indebtedness.

---

[7] Lenders will not be interested in "firm-specific capital" as collateral, since it has little, if any, resale market. Managers should understand that a more firm-specific asset (narrowing the resale market) will lead to a greater risk premium tacked onto the firm's interest rate and reduced residual for the equity owners to control.

Electric utility companies have been good candidates for heavy indebtedness, because: their markets have been protected from entry by economies of scale and government regulations; what they do can be measured relatively well; and their future income stream should be relatively stable. Accordingly, their interest rates should be relatively low, which encourages managers to take on additional debt so equity owners can claim the residual for themselves. (Deregulation of electric power production would allow entry into the generation of electricity. This should lead to a higher-risk premium in interest rates. But the price of electricity can be expected to fall for consumers with increased competition for power sales.)

Destructive Incentives in the Financial Sector and Housing Markets

The incentives of indebtedness are dramatically illustrated by one of the biggest financial debacles of modern times – the Savings and Loan (S&L) crisis in the 1980s. The S&L industry blossomed after the 1932 Federal Home Loan Bank Act to ensure that the savings of individuals were channeled to the housing industry. S&Ls could not diversify their portfolios by buying stock in other companies or even by making other loans. This concentrated focus in their investment portfolios added an element of risk, especially because they were highly exposed to the ups and downs of local housing markets.

Under such market and regulatory conditions, S&Ls understandably sought to mitigate their exposure to risky loans by carefully scrutinizing mortgage borrowers, taking great care to ensure borrowers could make a substantial down-payment and then 30 years of monthly payments. (In the 1920s and before, S&Ls sought to contain their risks further by making mortgage loans for 15 years or fewer.) The government also offset some of their investment risk by limiting competition of S&Ls through strict limits on entry into the savings and mortgage business.

But because S&Ls derived 97 percent of their funding from depositors (and thus only 3 percent from S&L owners), at the margin, owners were more eager to pursue high-risk/high-return projects. They could claim residuals that were inflated because interest rates on deposits were kept low by a federal ceiling. Of course, depositors might be concerned about these risks. But the federal government insured deposits up to $10,000, so concerns about (and a desire to monitor) S&L risk-taking were muted. In 1982, the incentive for risky investment was heightened when the federal insurance on S&L accounts was increased to $100,000, effectively assuring that most depositors would lose nothing if their S&L went under.

With rising inflation in the late 1970s, S&Ls struggled with low, fixed, long-term nominal interest rates (that often resulted in negative *real* interest rates).

Other forms of saving became available (e.g., money market and mutual funds), which were unrestricted in the rates of return they could offer. As a result, S&Ls began to lose lenders and bleed money. To compensate, the federal government gave them greater investment freedom (including the ability to pay out higher interest rates) and tried to closely monitor and regulate their investments. To attract lenders, S&Ls hiked interest rates on deposits and pursued more profitable investments that were riskier. The hope was that greater investment freedom for S&Ls and more insurance for lenders would stave off a crisis.

The result should have been predictable, based on the simple idea that people respond to incentives. S&Ls that made risky investments were able to pay high interest rates, drawing funds from more conservative S&Ls. The incentives were a moral hazard problem: "heads they won; tails the taxpayer lost." To protect their deposit base, conservative S&Ls had to raise their interest rates, which meant they also had to seek riskier investments – all of which led to a shock wave of risky investments spreading through the industry. Unfortunately, many of those investments did what should have been expected given their risky nature: they failed. The government (taxpayers) absorbed the losses and then returned to doing what it had done before 1982 – closely monitoring what was left of the industry and restricting the riskiness of its investments. (The government was unwilling to lower the size of deposits that were subject to federal deposit insurance, which would have given depositors greater incentives to monitor their S&Ls.)

An array of similar policies and incentive problems led to the housing bubble that burst in 2008. "Mortgage-backed securities" were sold in "bundles" to far-removed investors, obscuring what was in the investments. The infusion of funds from optimistic investors encouraged banks to pursue riskier loans and to become creative in their mortgage contracts, offering subprime loans and delayed "balloon payments" to questionable borrowers. It was conventional wisdom that growing scarcity of land available for development was indefinitely feeding the demand for and price of housing. Indeed, the housing bubble led to greater equity for homeowners and greater profitability for lenders in the short term, because the inflated housing prices made their loans look more secured. But eventually, it all unraveled. (We explore this complicated topic in greater detail in Online Chapter 4.)

Clearly, fraud and poor policy contributed much to these debacles in the financial sector. Crooks were attracted to the S&L industry (Black, Calavita, and Pontell 1995; Wauzzinski 2003). Public policy repeatedly subsidized inefficient decisions by banks, investors, and marginal homeowners. However, all of this is a grand illustration of how debt can affect management decisions. It also enables us to draw out a financial/management principle: if owners want to control the riskiness of firm investments, they should watch the debt their firms accumulate. Debt can encourage risk-taking, which can be good or bad, depending on whether the costs are considered and evaluated against the expected return.

Spreading Risks

Why, then, would the original equity owners be willing to issue more shares of stock, attract more equity owners, and share the residual? Sometimes, of course, the original owners are unable to provide the additional funds that a firm may need to pursue what are known (in an expectation sense) to be profitable investment projects. The original owners can figure that their *share* of firm profits will go down, but the *absolute level* of the residual will go up. A 60 percent share of $100,000 in profits is better than 100 percent of $50,000 in profits.

In situations where a firm is involved in new ventures with high risks and bondholders (lenders) have no protection against losses, the firm will have to pay high interest rates to borrow money. This doesn't mean that firms in high-risk businesses will not borrow any money, but most of their financing will come from equity holders. Only when most of the financing comes from equity will lenders see their risks as low enough to loan money at reasonable rates. (If the firm fails, bondholders can be fully paid from the sale of assets.) So, additional equity investment means that the equity owners can claim a greater residual (if the firm is successful) because the firm's interest payments decrease with the reduction in the risk premium to bondholders.

Investment projects often require a combination of firm-specific and general capital. For example, consider the predicament of a remodeling firm that uses specially designed pieces of flooring equipment (which may have little or no market value outside the firm), as well as trucks that can easily be sold in well-established used-truck markets. The investment projects can be divided according to the interests of the two types of investors. The equity owners can be called upon to take the risk associated with the flooring equipment, while the lenders are called upon to provide the funds for the trucks. Of course, it is better for the lenders if the firm profitably uses the trucks and other general equipment rather than selling its assets. So, lenders might not even make the loan for the general investment without equity owners first making the firm-specific investment, precisely because the general investment is less valuable to the firm without the firm-specific capital investment. (The trucks will not be useful to the firm without the output produced by the flooring equipment.)

The original owners can also have an interest in selling a portion of their ownership share because they can then reinvest among other firms and reduce the overall risk within their full portfolio of investments. If the original owners held their full investments in the firm and refused to sell off a portion, then they might be "too cautious" in the choice of investments – not making riskier investments that yield a higher expected profit than more conservative investments. Once the original owners have spread their ownership over a number of firms, they will find the riskier investments more attractive, since diversification has made them collectively less risky. Again, the financial structure of the firm is important – and it can matter to both management policies and the bottom line.

Industry Maturity and the Misuse of Cash

Michael Jensen gives another reason for some firms to stay in debt: it mitigates the problems executives may have with the "free-cash-flow problem." Interest payments on debt can tie the hands (reduce the discretionary authority) of managers who might otherwise engage in opportunism with their firms' residual (Jensen 1989). If a firm has little debt, then managers have a great deal of funds to use as they please – for example, providing themselves with greater compensation; contributing to charities with little impact on their business; and expanding the scope and scale of their firm without the usual degree of scrutiny (again, justifying greater compensation since firm size and executive compensation tend to go together). Even if the investment projects are somewhat profitable, stockholders might find more profitable investments and more worthy charitable causes.

How can the firm be made to disgorge the residual? Jensen suggests that indebtedness is a good way to accomplish this: greater indebtedness reduces the residual and the waste that can go up in the smoke of managerial opportunism. Jensen argues that one of the reasons for firm takeovers through "leveraged buyouts" (i.e., heavy indebtedness) is that the firm is forced to give up the residual through higher interest payments. Again, the hands of the agents/managers are tied; their ability to misuse firm funds is curbed. Indebtedness can enhance the firm's value mainly because it reduces the discretion of managers who have been misusing the funds.

Experience teaches that indebtedness is not necessarily the only or easiest way that firms can disgorge such cash: they can also pay dividends. Moreover, experience also teaches that what a firm should do with "free cash flow" is not always obvious and can prompt strong disagreements among board members and top executives, primarily because of the limited available information on the riskiness and rates of returns on alternative corporate strategies.

The thorny issue of what to do with free cash emerged in 2005 when Carl Icahn, renowned for "raiding" (taking over) faltering corporations, became the biggest stockholder in Blockbuster – at the time, the largest brick-and-mortar video rental retailer in the United States. According to reports, Icahn believed that Blockbuster's management had gone on a "spending spree" and, in the process, had begun to "gamble" away "shareholders' money" on risky investments (Peers 2005). As a new board member, Icahn began insisting that management disgorge its accumulating cash with large dividend payments to stockholders, a strategy that would restrict the ability of top management to engage in investment misadventures, including the company's efforts to "reinvent" itself by moving away from rentals at retail stores and toward rentals over the Internet. Seeing that the retail rental business was dying, Icahn wanted management to use its retail outlets as "cash cows," continuing to operate them for as long as the growing competition from mail-order video rental companies would allow.

On the other hand, John Antioco, the chairman of Blockbuster, believed that the company had to reinvent itself and use its cash flow to undertake a "corporate makeover" to fend off erosion of Blockbuster's market from internet-based movie rental companies such as Netflix and Walmart (Peers 2005).

Who was right? The answer is unclear and dependent upon information about rates of return and risk on alternative investment strategies that can be known only to corporate insiders. However, in hindsight, there is at least one strong argument to think that Icahn's strategy of paying dividends was more compelling. Having disgorged its free cash flow, Blockbuster's top executives would be required to convince outside investors and Blockbuster's own shareholders that Antioco's proposed strategy of reinventing the company could provide them with a greater rate of return than they could achieve by sticking with its brick-and-mortar rental model or through other companies.

The very act of paying out the dividends would have been a sign of considerable confidence on the part of management that they had a solid case for reinventing the company – and, hence, could easily fund their new investment plans. Of course, critics could argue that dividend payouts, along with the issue of new investment instruments, would impose crippling time delays on management's efforts to reposition the company in a highly competitive market. In any case, by 2010, Blockbuster rental revenues at its brick-and-mortar stores were in full retreat from internet rental companies such as Netflix, cable companies offering movie rentals on demand, and growing competition from downloads over the Internet. The number of Blockbuster outlets fell from 9000 in 2004 to 300 in 2012 – with the remaining stores closing in 2015, when sales revenues from downloads of movies and television programs already exceeded DVD sales (Synder 2015).

Similarly, as industries mature (or reach the limits of profitable expansion), the risk of managers "misusing" firm funds increases. Few opportunities may be available for managers to reinvest the earnings in their own industry. This all leads to an interesting proposition: We should expect firm indebtedness to increase with the maturity of its industry. Firms in a mature industry have more stable future income streams than those in fledgling industries and can be monitored more easily. People gain experience working with established firms – and learn how the firms operate and when they may be inclined to misappropriate funds. Also, by taking on more debt, firms in mature industries can alert the market to their intentions to rid themselves of their residual, conveying the message to the market that manager discretion to use and misuse firm financial resources will be constricted – all of which can increase the price of the firm's stock.

Of course, if firms in mature industries don't take on relatively more debt and managers continue to misuse the funds by reinvesting the residual in the mature industry or other industries, then the firm can be ripe for a takeover. An outside "raider" may see an opportunity to buy the stock at a depressed price, paying for the stock with debt. The increase in indebtedness can, by itself, raise the price of the stock, making the takeover a profitable venture. If the takeover target is a disparate collection of production units that do not fit well together because of past management indiscretions in investment, the profit potential for the raider is even greater. The firm should be worth more in pieces than as a single firm. The raider can buy the stock at a depressed price, take charge, and break the company apart – selling off the parts for more than the purchase price. In the process, the market value of the "core business" can be enhanced.

The moral of this section should now be self-evident: *the financial structure of firms matters a great deal.* By choosing the best combination of debt and equity in financing the firm's productive activities, managers can keep its cost curves as low as possible. Keeping those cost curves low is a crucial factor determining how effective a firm is at producing wealth and remaining viable in a competitive market. This also means that choice on debt and equity financing can determine whether the firm will be subject to a takeover. The one great antidote for a takeover should be obvious to managers: firms should be structured, in terms of both their financial *and* other policies, *to create incentives to use their resources to produce as much wealth as possible, which will maximize the stock price.* In this case, potential raiders will have nothing to gain by trying to take over the firm. One of the primary functions of a board of directors is to monitor executives and the policies they implement with an eye toward maximizing stockholder value. As we will show in Chapter 11, executives and their boards that do not maximize the price of their stocks have something to fear from corporate raiders who will look to profit from the firm's inefficiencies.

Practical Lessons

Business students are familiar with accounting documents such as balance sheets and income statements. But such documents are of little help in conceptualizing the larger issue at the heart of the cost curves developed in this chapter: How much should a firm produce if it wants to maximize profits? To answer this question properly, all costs must be considered in a firm's cost structure, including two key numbers that accounting statements do not capture – risk cost and normal profits. Even though such costs are elusive, they are no less real and important than payments to workers and suppliers. Managers must make rough estimates of such costs. Otherwise, the firm can underestimate its costs and overextend production.

The extent that a firm's ventures are leveraged can affect risk costs. Generally, the higher the leverage, the greater the risk costs a firm will incur. When a firm's business ventures are 100 percent leveraged, the firm stands to collect the extra gains that come with successful ventures while creditors will suffer all of the losses from failed ventures. Accordingly, managers can be expected to undertake more risky ventures when they know the projects are highly leveraged, especially since risky ventures usually carry a risk premium that can lead to above-normal profits when successful.

Understandably, creditors will demand progressively higher interest rates from firms as their indebtedness escalates, and those progressively higher interest rates affect a firm's cost structure. This suggests that minimizing the cost curves drawn in this chapter is far more complicated than might be thought, requiring a delicate balancing of a firm's debt and equity. By adding equity, firm owners can push down the interest rates they pay on borrowed funds, but they also incur greater risk costs as more of their own capital can evaporate with failed projects. Clearly, a firm's financial structure and cost structures are inextricably intertwined and interdependent. Managers do indeed need to understand basic finance to contain their costs and obtain competitive advantages in the pricing of their products.

Recommended Videos Online

1　Short-run cost structures (Richard McKenzie, 33 minutes)
2　Long-run cost structures (Richard McKenzie, 27 minutes)

The Bottom Line

The key takeaways from Chapter 8 are the following:

1　Cost structures for firms (made up of average fixed, average variable, average total, and marginal cost curves) are a graphical device designed to yield insights on how much a firm should produce to maximize profits over various time periods for a range of output levels. Such structures help managers go beyond the limitations on thinking presented by a firm's accounting statements, which report the costs incurred in the past for a given output level.

2　The law of diminishing marginal returns determines a firm's short-run *MC* curve and ultimately imposes a constraint on how much a firm can produce in the short run if it intends to maximize profits.

3　In the short run, a firm should not seek to produce where its average cost is at a minimum. It should produce where marginal costs and marginal revenue (price in the case of a perfect competitor) are equal.

4　Fixed costs should be ignored in short-run production decisions since they are sunk.

5　Economies and diseconomies of scale will shape a firm's long-run cost structure.

6   The "last-period problem" can cause trouble at the end of a relationship – or prevent a relationship from starting if at least one party can anticipate the problem.

7   The build-up of equity in a firm can lower the firm's interest rates on borrowed funds for two reasons. First, the firm's lenders stand to lose less in the case of default on interest payments. Second, firms with a lot of equity and few borrowed funds will be inclined to restrain the riskiness of their business ventures.

8   Indebtedness can inhibit executive inclination to waste firm resources by reducing the available cash that can be misused.

9   The maturing of a firm can lead to more indebtedness because mature firms have proven records and tend to have more stable earnings prospects.

10 Leverage can increase the riskiness of investments undertaken because equity owners gain from the risk premium on risky investment projects while the losses that go with failures can be imposed on lenders.

11 In Chapters 9 and 10, we will extend our analysis of firms' production decisions by combining the average and marginal cost curves described in this chapter with the demand curves developed in Chapters 3 and 4. Within that theoretical framework, we can compare the relative efficiency of competitive and monopolistic markets, as well as the role of profits in directing the production decisions of private firms.

Review Questions ▶▶

1   For output levels $Q = 0$–10, total costs are 200, 260, 310, 350, 380, 400, 430, 480, 550, 660, and 790. Construct a table with Q, FC, VC, TC, MC, AFC, AVC, and ATC. Draw a rough graph for AFC. Draw another rough graph for AVC, ATC, and MC.

2   Explain why the intersection of the AVC curve and the MC curve is the minimum point on the AVC curve.

3   Derive the short-run cost curves from the law of diminishing marginal returns.

4   Suppose that no economies or diseconomies of scale exist in a given industry. What will the firm's long-run average and marginal cost curves look like? Would you expect firms of different sizes to be able to compete successfully in such an industry?

5   Why would you expect all firms to eventually encounter diseconomies of scale at some size?

6   Suppose that the government imposes a $100 tax on all businesses, regardless of how much they produce. How will the tax affect a firm's short-run cost curves? Its short-run production? Its long-run costs and production?

7   Suppose that the government imposes a $1 tax on every unit of a good sold. How will the tax affect a firm's short-run cost curves? Its short-run production? Its long-run costs and production?

8 What is the relation between *ATC*, *AFC* and *AVC*? Graph *ATC* and *AVC*.

9 Let $TC = 3000 + 100Q - 12Q^2 + Q^3$. Determine the general equations for *AFC*, *AVC*, *ATC*, and *MC* – and then calculate their values for $Q = 10$. (*MC* is the derivative of *TC* with respect to *Q*.) On the graph, note *Q'* where *AVC* = *MC*.

10 What is the difference between decreasing returns to scale and the law of diminishing marginal returns?

11 What are some examples of the "last-period problem" in your workplace? What has your firm done to address it? What could your firm do to mitigate the problem?

12 Suppose that interest rates fall. How will manager incentives be affected and how will the firm's cost structure be affected?

Book III
Competitive and Monopoly
Market Structures

In Chapters 9–11, we use demand theory (developed in Chapters 3 and 4) and cost structures (developed in Chapters 7 and 8) to examine organizational structure, production decisions, and outcomes for firms and society under four market structures: perfect competition, pure monopoly, monopolistic competition, and oligopoly. In Chapter 12, we will develop our understanding of the market for labor – a critical resource input – by extending our demand and supply analysis from Chapter 3 to see how wage rates are determined in competitive and noncompetitive labor markets.

9

Firm Production under Idealized Competitive Conditions

Economists understand by the term market, not any particular market place in which things are bought and sold, but the whole of any region in which buyers and sellers are in such free intercourse with one another that the prices of the same goods tend to equality, easily and quickly.

Augustin Cournot

After our introductory discussion of markets in Chapter 3, we provided more detail about demand in Chapter 4 and then developed supply in Chapters 7 and 8. In Part A of this chapter, we return to market analysis, bringing demand and cost together in a way that allows us to examine how individual firms react to consumer demand in competitive markets. We do not attempt to give a full description of real-world competitive market settings. Markets are too diverse for this to be of much use. Rather, our aim is to devise a theoretical framework that can enable us to *think* about how competitive markets work in general, as a constructive behavioral force. This will provide a basis for predicting the general direction of changes in market prices and output. And we will see how the absence of restrictions on entry can impose tremendous pressure on existing producers to contain their costs or be replaced.

At the end of Part A, we explain how "perfect competition" is neither as perfect nor as efficient as basic microeconomic theory suggests. We wrestle with the extent to which competitive markets contribute to consumer welfare and market efficiency. And we describe the role of the entrepreneur in the real-world origins (and evolution) of markets. (Similarly, in Chapter 10, contrary to much conventional wisdom, we will explain how "monopoly market power" can be "less bad" than standard theory suggests. Monopoly pricing power can, within limits, be a creative force for entrepreneurs in product development that is under-appreciated in antitrust law.)

In Part B, we explain how getting the sizes of teams and their pay incentives right can be crucial to firm survivability when they face intense competitive pressures. In Perspective 9, of particular interest to entrepreneurs, we explore the popular myth of "the first-mover advantage" – the idea that a company which creates a market ("the first mover") has advantages that will likely extend indefinitely. It turns out that this premise misunderstands market processes, underestimating the costs of being the first mover and the likelihood of sustaining any advantage they may have. In fact, being a "first mover" can be a decided disadvantage. Second, third, and subsequent movers for given products often come to dominate their markets because of cost advantages that go with not having to develop products and the markets for them. Imitation does have its cost rewards, which can add to firm competitiveness.

The competitive market structure considered in this chapter is only one of four basic market structures. (The other three – and their deviations from competition – will be developed in Chapters 10 and 11.) However, an unexpected lesson falls out of our discussion of "perfect competition." This market structure is perfectly efficient when the product subject to competition is a given – when it has already been created (in some unspecified way). But as an entrepreneur, an owner or a manager, you would be wise not to spend scarce firm resources on the development of a product for a market that has the conditions of perfect competition.

Part A Theory and Public Policy Applications

How a firm decides to price its product and how much it decides to produce are functions of many considerations (labor and material costs, weather, macroeconomic conditions, etc.). But one of the more important factors is the *nature of its market* – or what economists call its "market structure," which is really about the extent of the competition that a firm faces. In this chapter and Chapter 10, we will see how a firm's pricing and production strategies will vary with the competitiveness of their markets. We'll start by going through the conventional treatment of perfect competition and briefly comparing its market outcomes with those in the other three market structures.

An Introduction to Pricing and Production Strategies under the Four Basic Market Structures

Markets can be divided into four basic categories, based on the degree of competition that prevails within them – that is, on how strenuously participants attempt to outdo their rivals and avoid being outdone. The four categories are described below and their characteristics are summarized in Table 9.1. The most competitive of the four market structures is perfect competition.

Table 9.1 **Characteristics of the four basic market structures**

	Number of firms	Freedom of entry	Type of product	Example
Perfect competition	Many	Very easy (or costless)	Homogeneous	Wheat, gold, computer chips
Pure monopoly	One	Illegal or prohibitively costly	Single product	Public utilities, postal services
Monopolistic competition	Many	Relatively easy	Differentiated	Pens, fast food, clothing
Oligopoly	Few	Difficult	Either standardized or differentiated	Steel, light bulbs, cereals, autos

Perfect Competition

As discussed earlier, **perfect compe-tition** represents an idealized degree of competition, recognized by the following list of characteristics.

> **Perfect competition** is a market structure in which price competition is so intense that maximum efficiency in the allocation of resources is obtained.

1 There are *many producers* in the market. Thus, no single firm is large enough to affect the going market price for the product. All producers are "price tak-ers" as opposed to the "price searchers" we will describe in Chapters 10 and 11. (We also assume *many consumers* in the market. Thus, no single consumer is powerful enough to affect the market price of the product. As with producers, consumers are "price takers." We will relax this assumption in the context of labor markets in Chapter 12.)

2 All producers sell a *homogeneous product*, meaning that the goods of one pro-ducer are indistinguishable from all others.

3 Consumers are fully knowledgeable about their options and are indifferent about which producer they buy from. (We described the relevance of imperfect information – and especially asymmetric information – in Chapter 5.)

4 Producers enjoy complete *freedom of entry into and exit from* the market – that is, entry and exit costs are minimal.

As we showed in Chapter 4, the demand curve facing each competitor is dif-ferent from the demand curve faced by all producers in aggregate. The *market* demand curve slopes downward, as shown in Figure 9.1(a). (As per our discus-sion in Chapter 4, market demand can be elastic or inelastic.) But the demand curve facing an *individual* producer in a competitive market is horizontal, as in Figure 9.1(b). The firm's demand curve is *perfectly elastic* – that is, the individual firm cannot raise its price even slightly above the market price without losing all its customers to the numerous other producers in the market. But the individual firm can sell all it wishes at the going market price. Hence, it has no reason to offer its output at a lower price. It is a "price taker" – taking the price as given from the interaction of market demand and supply. The markets for wheat and for integrated computer circuits ("computer chips") are good examples of real-world markets that come close to perfect competition.

The extreme conditions of the perfect competition model allow economists to make precise predictions when key variables change under such market conditions. For example, under perfect competition, we will develop the principles below that price will equal the marginal cost of producing the last unit and firms will earn only normal profits (not economic profits) in the long run. This does not mean such conclusions are inapplicable to less than perfectly competitive markets. If individual producers (no matter how few producers there are) *see themselves* as price takers (assess their demand curves to be perfectly elastic at the market-determined price), the outcomes will be equivalent. Even in so-called "contestable markets," in which entry is relatively open, producers can *act as if* they are price takers (above some price) because they fear entry by other competitors. (Contestable markets are considered in Online Reading 9.1.) Experimental research has shown that subjects in laboratory settings can perceive themselves as price takers even when there are as few as a dozen other producers (Smith 1962). Hence, the model of perfect competition can have broader application to

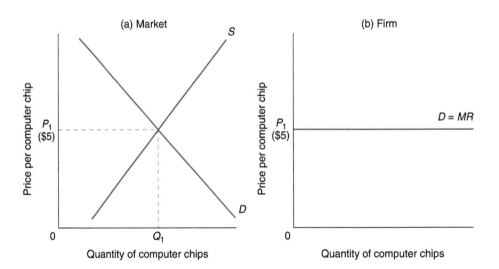

Figure 9.1 Demand curve faced by perfect competitors
(a) The market demand for a product is always downward-sloping. (b) But the perfect competitor faces a horizontal (perfectly elastic) demand curve. It cannot raise its price above the market price even slightly without losing its customers to other producers.

real-world markets than might be surmised from the extreme competitive conditions we have specified.

Another prediction in a perfectly competitive market is that, because of open entry into markets and the resulting intense price competition, consumers will receive much of the "surplus value" available from goods – over and above the prices they pay. Such an outcome is self-evident in many markets, but especially with technology markets. Personal computers have grown ever more powerful as their prices have collapsed during the last four decades, enabling consumers to buy laptops and netbooks as powerful as mainframe computers two decades ago for a few hundred dollars. Similarly, the prices of increasingly feature-rich cell phones have become affordable even to low-income workers. But this observation extends to many other markets. For example, quality all-cotton or silk shirts that were once expensive can now be bought at big-box stores for a few dollars.

Pure Monopoly

Pure monopoly is the polar opposite of perfect competition. Under a pure monopoly, there is no price competition because the only producer in

A **pure monopoly** consists of a single seller of a product where there are no close substitutes and it is protected from competition by barriers to entry into the market.

the market is protected by prohibitively costly entry barriers. (These barriers to entry are detailed in Chapter 10.) Without competitors to undercut its price, the monopolistic firm can raise prices without fear that customers will move to other producers of the same or similar products. The monopolist only worries about losing some customers to firms with distantly related products.

Because the monopolist is the only producer of a particular good, the downward-sloping market demand curve in Figure 9.1(a) is its individual demand curve. In contrast to the perfect competitor, the monopolist can raise its price and sell less – or lower its price and sell more. As will be discussed in Chapter 10, the critical task of the pure monopolist – and, more broadly, firms with some monopoly power – is to determine the price–quantity combination (of all possibilities on its demand curve) that maximizes its economic profits. As such, these firms are "price searchers."[1]

The best (but not perfect) real-world examples of a pure monopoly are electric power companies (which dominate in given geographical areas) and the government's monopoly on "first-class" postal service. (Much more will be said here. To note, electric companies have their prices regulated by government. And the U.S.

---

[1] It is *really* tempting to use the term "price maker" here, since it rhymes with "price taker." But "maker" implies too much power – as if the firm can set whatever price it wants with no consequence. And "searcher" is a far better description of the process at hand: the mysteries of a trial-and-error search to find the optimal price with limited real-world information about the relevant demand curve for the firm's goods and services.

Postal Service is losing more of its monopoly power every year, as technology reduces the costs of alternative ways for people to communicate – for example, by email.)

While our discussion of pure monopoly is couched in terms of a *sole* producer, the model has far broader application. The key consideration is that the producer (no matter how many producers there are) perceives itself as a price searcher. The number of producers in a market often will affect the elasticity of demand for individual producers. Seeking to raise its price and profits, a firm with monopoly power will restrict output below the output level chosen in a competitive market. This general conclusion applies whenever a firm acts on some degree of monopoly power – that is, when it faces a downward-sloping demand curve and is searching for the ideal price–quantity combination.

Apple is hardly a pure monopolist in the smartphone market since other producers abound. But Apple has resurrected itself (from the depths of its financial troubles in the early 1990s) through "cool" designs for those devices, enabling it to charge premium prices over other producers. Despite the economic inefficiencies of monopoly power, the above-normal profits of Apple (and other firms with monopoly power) are a necessary motivation for taking the risks to create, develop, and make their products in the first place. The *prospect* of earning above-normal profits is a strong motivation for other firms to create and develop an array of new products that will give them a measure of monopoly power, but also give consumers value that they might not otherwise have.[2]

Monopolistic Competition

Monopolistic competition is more descriptive of most real-world markets than perfect competition and pure monopoly – and can be recognized by the following characteristics:

> **Monopolistic competition** is a market composed of firms whose products are differentiated – and which face highly (but not perfectly) elastic demand curves.

1 Competitors are producing slightly different products.
2 Advertising and other forms of non-price competition are prevalent.
3 Entry into the market is not barred, but is somewhat restricted by modest entry costs, primarily from overhead.
4 Because of the existence of close substitutes, customers can turn to other producers if a monopolistically competitive firm raises its price too much or declines in some other way (e.g., quality of the good or service). Because of brand loyalty, the monopolistic competitor's demand curve still slopes downward but is relatively elastic (as in Figure 9.2).

---

[2] For an extended discussion of the positive sides of monopoly power, see a book by two of the authors of this textbook (McKenzie and Lee 2008).

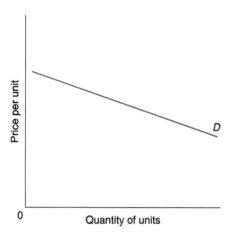

Figure 9.2 Demand curve faced by a monopolistic competitor
Because the product sold by the monopolistically competitive firm is slightly different from the products sold by competing producers, the firm faces a highly (but not perfectly) elastic demand curve.

The market for textbooks is a good example of monopolistic competition. Most subjects are covered by two- or three-dozen textbooks, differing from one another in content, style of presentation, and design. (See Chapter 11 for a more in-depth discussion.)

Oligopoly

Oligopoly is a real-world market structure with monopoly and competitive characteristics. Oligopolists may produce an identical product (e.g., steel) or highly differentiated products (e.g., pickup trucks). There are relatively few producers, generally with barriers to entry significant enough to restrict new producers. But the critical characteristic of oligopolistic firms is their *interdependence*: that is, the deci-

> An **oligopoly** is a market composed of a handful of dominant producers – as few as two and generally no more than a dozen – whose pricing (and other) decisions are interdependent.

sions of any one firm – on pricing, quality, advertising, etc. – can substantially affect other firms. Therefore, each firm must monitor and respond to the pricing and production decisions of the other firms in the industry. (The importance of this characteristic will become clear in Chapter 11.)

The Perfect Competitor's Production Decision

As developed in Chapter 3 and shown again in Figure 9.3(a), the intersection of the supply and demand curves determines the price in a perfectly competitive market. (If the price is above the equilibrium price level, a *surplus* will develop, forcing competitors to lower their prices. If the price is below equilibrium, a *shortage* will emerge, pushing the price upward.) But how much will the individual perfect competitor produce when it has no control over the market price?

The Production Rule: $MC = MR$

Suppose the price in the perfectly competitive market for computer chips is $5 ($P_1$ in Figure 9.3). For each individual competitor, the market price is given; it must be accepted or rejected. If the firm rejects the price, however, it must shut down. If it raises its price even slightly above the market level, its customers will move to other competitors. Its demand, then, is horizontal at $5. The firm's perfectly elastic horizontal demand curve is illustrated in Figure 9.3(b). This is also the firm's marginal revenue (MR) curve. Because each computer chip can be sold at a constant price of $5, the additional (marginal) revenue acquired from selling an additional unit is constant at $5.

The profit-maximizing firm will produce any unit for which marginal revenue exceeds marginal cost. Thus, the profit-maximizing firm in Figure 9.3(b) will produce and sell q_1 units – the quantity at which marginal revenue equals marginal cost ($MR = MC$). Up to q_1, marginal revenue is greater than marginal cost. Beyond q_1, all additional computer chips are unprofitable. The additional cost of producing them is greater than the additional revenue acquired. (We're using a small "q" to remind you that the output of the individual producer in Figure 9.3(b) is a small fraction of market output, designated by a capital "Q" in Figure 9.3(a).)

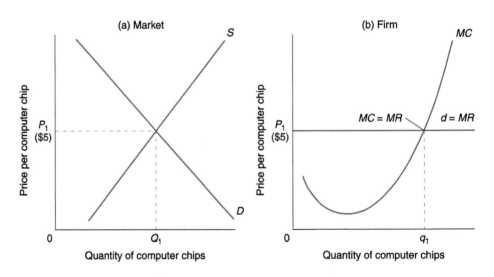

Figure 9.3 The perfect competitor's production decision
The perfect competitor's price is determined by market supply and demand, as in panel (a). As long as marginal revenue (MR) – which equals market price for the price taker – exceeds marginal cost (MC), the perfect competitor will expand production, as in panel (b). The profit-maximizing production level (q_1) is the point at which marginal cost equals marginal revenue (price).

Changes in Market Price

The perfectly competitive firm produces at $MC = MR$, where MR is equal to the price at which the firm can sell its product. Thus, the amount the firm produces depends on market price. As long as market demand and supply remain constant, the individual firm's demand (based on the steady price) will also remain constant – assuming the costs of production remain constant and the cost curves don't shift. But, for example, if market demand and price increase, the individual firm's demand and price also will increase.

Figure 9.4 shows how the shift occurs. The original market demand of D_1 leads to a market price of P_1 in Figure 9.4(a), which is translated into the individual firm's demand: d_1 in Figure 9.4(b). Again, the firm maximizes profit by equating marginal cost with marginal revenue, which is equal to d_1, at an output level of q_1.

An increase in market demand to D_2 leads to the higher price P_2 and a higher individual firm demand curve, d_2. At this higher price, which again equals marginal revenue, the perfect competitor can support a higher marginal cost. The firm will expand production from q_1 to q_2. In the same way, an even greater market demand (D_3) will lead to even higher output (q_3) by the individual competitor.

Why does the market supply curve slope upward and to the right? The answer lies in the upward-sloping marginal cost (MC) curves on which each individual firm operates. The firm will never operate where the MC curve is sloping

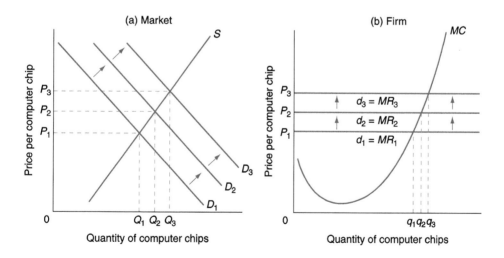

Figure 9.4 Change in the perfect competitor's market price
In panel (a), if market demand rises from D_1 to D_3, the price will rise with it, from P_1 to P_3. As a result, the perfectly competitive firm's demand curve will rise, from d_1 to d_3 in panel (b) – and output will rise from q_1 to q_3 for the firm and from Q_1 to Q_3 in the market.

downward. (If MC = price and the marginal cost is getting smaller, the firm could increase profits by increasing output, which would reduce MC below price – and would continue increasing output until MC started increasing and eventually equals price again.) Since the upward-sloping portion of the MC curve shows us how much output each firm will produce at every price, the market supply curve is obtained by horizontally adding the firms' upward-sloping MC curves (as we showed in Chapter 8).

Maximizing Short-Run Profits

Can perfect competitors make an economic profit? One might think the answer is obviously "Yes," but it is only "Yes" in the short run. To see this, we must incorporate the average and marginal cost curves developed in Chapters 7 and 8 into our graph of the perfect competitor's demand curve, as in Figure 9.5(b).

As before, the producer maximizes profits by equating marginal cost with marginal revenue (which is price in perfect competition), rather than by looking at average cost. This is exactly what the perfect competitor does. The firm produces q_2 computer chips because it is the point at which the MR curve (which equals the firm's demand curve) crosses the MC curve. At this intersection, the marginal revenue of the last unit sold equals its marginal cost. If less were produced than q_1, the marginal cost would be less than the marginal revenue, and profits would be lost. Similarly, by producing anything more than q_2, the firm incurs more

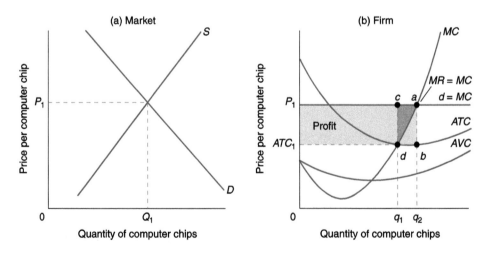

Figure 9.5 The profit-maximizing perfect competitor
The perfect competitor's demand curve is established by the market-clearing price of P_1 in panel (a). The profit-maximizing perfect competitor will extend production up to the point at which marginal cost equals marginal revenue (price): point a in panel (b). At this output level (q_2), the firm will earn a short-run economic profit equal to the shaded area ATC_1P_1ab.

additional costs (as indicated by the *MC* curve) than it receives in additional revenue (as indicated by the demand curve, which is below the *MC* curve beyond q_2).

At q_2, the firm's profit equals total revenue minus total cost (*TR − TC*). To find total revenue at q_2, we multiply the price (P_1, which also equals average revenue) by the quantity produced (q_2) so that $TR = P_1 q_2$. Graphically, total revenue is therefore equal to the area of the rectangle bounded by the price and quantity: $OP_1 a q_2$.[3]

Similarly, total cost can be found by multiplying the average total cost of production (*ATC*) by the quantity produced. The *ATC* curve shows that the average total cost of producing q_2 computer chips is ATC_1. Therefore, total cost is $ATC_1 \times q_2$ or the rectangular area bounded by $OATC_1 b q_2$. The profits of the company are therefore $P_1 q_2 − ATC_1 q_2$, which is the same, mathematically, as $q_2(P_1 − ATC_1)$. Likewise, it is the area representing total revenue ($OP_1 a q_2$) minus the area representing total cost ($OATC_1 b q_2$). Profit is the shaded rectangle bounded by $ATC_1 P_1 ab$. Remember that this profit is *economic profit*, since all costs of production (including opportunity and risk costs) are captured in the *ATC* curve. This means that the firm is earning more from its deployment of resources in the production of this good or service than could be earned elsewhere.

The perfect competitor does not seek to produce the quantity that results in the lowest average total cost. This is q_1, which is defined by the intersection of the *MC* curve and the *ATC* curve. If it produced only q_1, the firm would forfeit some of its profits – on units for which *MR* is greater than *MC*. (If drawn to scale, the resulting rectangle will be smaller than $ATC_1 P_1 ab$.)

Naturally, profit-maximizing firms will attempt to minimize their costs of production. But this does not mean they will produce at the minimum point on their *ATC* curve. They will try to employ the most efficient technology available and minimize their payments for resources. That is, they will attempt to keep their cost curves as low as possible. But, given those curves, the firm will produce where *MC = MR*, not where the *ATC* curve is at its lowest level. Managers who cannot distinguish between those two objectives will probably operate their businesses on a less profitable basis than they could – and will risk being run out of business.

Minimizing Short-Run Losses

In the foregoing analysis, the market-determined price was higher than the firm's average total cost, allowing it to make a profit. Perfect competitors are not guaranteed profits, however. The market price may not be high enough to cover all

---

[3] The area of any rectangle is one side times the other side – often remembered as "length times width" or "base times height." Here, one side of the rectangle is price (P_1); the other is the quantity (q_2). So, the area of the rectangle ($P_1 \times q_2$) represents total revenue at q_2.

the costs. Suppose, for example, that the market price is P_1, below the firm's ATC curve as in Figure 9.6(b). Should the firm still produce where marginal cost equals marginal revenue (price)? The answer, for the short run, is "Yes." It turns out that, as long as the firm can cover its variable cost, it should produce q_1 computer chips. (Fixed costs are sunk and irrelevant to short-run decision-making.)

It is true that the firm will lose money. Its total revenues are only $P_1 q_1$ (the area bounded by $OP_1 bq_1$), whereas its total costs are $ATC_1 \times q_1$ (the area $OATC_1 aq_1$). On the graph, its total (economic) losses equal the difference between those two rectangular areas – the shaded area bounded by $P_1 ATC_1 ab$. But does the firm lose more money by shutting down or by operating and producing q_1 chips?

In the short run, the firm will continue to incur fixed costs even if it shuts down. Since it would not earn any revenues, its losses will equal its total fixed costs. In Chapter 8, we showed that the average fixed cost of production is the vertical distance/difference between the average variable cost and average total cost. Here, this vertical distance (ac) is greater than the average loss (ab). Hence, the firm's total fixed cost, or loss from shutdown, is greater than the loss from operating.

In sum, as long as the price is higher than average variable cost – that is, if the price more than covers the cost associated directly with production – the firm minimizes its short-run losses by producing where marginal cost equals

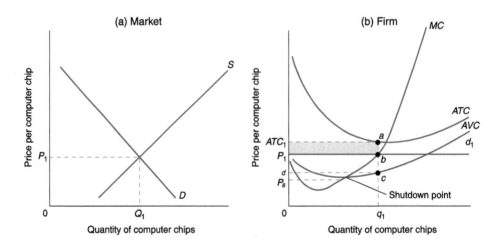

Figure 9.6 The loss-minimizing perfect competitor
The market-clearing price in panel (a) establishes the perfect competitor's demand curve in panel (b). Because the price is below the ATC curve, this firm is losing money. But as long as the price is above the minimum point of the AVC curve, the firm should minimize its short-run losses by continuing to produce where marginal cost equals marginal revenue: at point b in panel (b). This perfect competitor should produce q_1 units, incurring losses equal to the shaded area $P_1 ATC_1 ab$. (But this is better than the alternative: shut down and lose its fixed costs.)

marginal revenue. By earning revenue in excess of its variable costs, the firm loses less than its fixed cost. Hence, we have two production rules that profit-maximizing firms should always keep in mind in the short run: ignore fixed costs, and produce as long as you can cover variable costs.

Only if the price dips below the minimum of the *AVC* curve – where the *MC* and *AVC* curves intersect – will the firm add to its losses by operating. The firm will shut down when price is below this point (P_s in Figure 9.6) – when it cannot cover its variable costs. At prices above this point, the firm simply follows its *MC* curve to determine its production level. Thus, above the *AVC* curve, the *MC* curve is in effect the firm's supply curve. Therefore, if a perfect competitor produces in the short run, it produces in a range of increasing marginal cost (and diminishing marginal returns).

Our analysis has shown why, in the short run, fixed costs should be ignored. The relevant question is whether a given productive activity will add more to the firm's revenues than to its costs – those affected by its *current* decisions. Understanding this principle, businesses may undertake activities that superficially appear to be quite unprofitable. Some grocery stores stay open all night, even though the owners know they will attract few customers. If all costs, including fixed costs, are considered, the decision to operate in the early hours may seem misguided. But the only relevant question facing the store manager is whether the *additional* sales generated are greater than the *additional* costs of light, labor, and goods sold. Similarly, many businesses that are obviously failing continue to operate. But, by operating, they can cover their variable costs and a portion of their fixed costs (e.g., rent) that is still due if they shut down. They stay open until their leases expire or until they can sell out.

Any business that opens and closes at a certain hour is wrestling with a similar decision. Could ALDI sell more groceries if they opened at 8:00 a.m. instead of 9:00 a.m. – or closed at 9:00 p.m. instead of 8:00 p.m.? Certainly, but will the gain in revenues offset the increase in variable costs? The fixed costs are the same, so those are irrelevant. And much of the demand may be satisfied during shorter operating hours, so that its choice of hours makes more financial sense than being open for two additional hours. Likewise, should parking garages, restaurants, and retail stores remain open (and charge fees) before/after a certain hour?

Seasonal businesses are in a similar position. When should ski resorts and golf courses open and close for the year? What about small ice cream shops in climates with four seasons? What about specialty stores for Christmas, Halloween, fireworks, and income tax preparation? At what times of year should state parks have an attendant in the booth at the entrance to collect entry fees? The fixed costs are fixed; the key consideration is whether the available (marginal) revenues exceed – or are exceeded by – additional variable (marginal) costs.

Producing over the Long Run

In the long run, businesses have an opportunity to change their fixed costs. If the market price remains too low to permit profitable operation, a firm can eliminate its fixed costs, sell its plant and equipment, and terminate its contracts for insurance and office space. If the market price is above average total cost, new firms can enter the market and existing firms can expand their scale of operation. In turn, such long-run adjustments affect market supply – which then affects price and subsequent short-run production decisions. To facilitate the discussion, we will examine long-run adjustments in two stages. First, we discuss the effects of market entry and exit, assuming a constant scale of operation. Second, we add adjustments made in response to economies of scale.

The Long-Run Effect of Short-Run Profits and Losses

When profits encourage new firms to enter an industry and existing firms to expand, the result is an increase in market supply (the supply curve shifts out to the right), a decrease in market price, and a decrease in profitability. For example, in Figure 9.7(a), the existence of economic profits (which equal revenues minus *opportunity* costs) in the computer chip market would mean that investors can

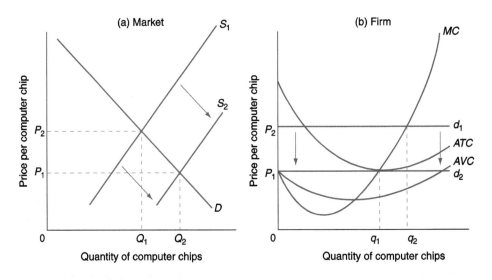

Figure 9.7 The long-run effects of short-run profits

If perfect competitors are making short-run profits, other producers will enter the market (and/or existing producers will expand), increasing the market supply from S_1 to S_2 and lowering the market price from P_2 to P_1 in panel (a). The individual firm's demand curve, which is determined by market price, will shift down, from d_1 to d_2 in panel (b). The firm will reduce its output from q_2 to q_1 – the new intersection of marginal revenue (price) and marginal cost. Long-run equilibrium will be achieved when the price falls to the minimum point of the firm's *ATC* curve, eliminating *economic* profit at price P_1 in panel (b).

earn more in this industry than in the most profitable alternative industry. Some investors will move resources to the computer chip industry. Because the number of producers increases, the market supply curve shifts outward, expanding total production from Q_1 to Q_2 and depressing the market price from P_2 to P_1.

The expansion of industry supply and the resulting reduction in market price make the computer chip business less profitable for individual firms. The lower market price is reflected in a downward shift of the firm's horizontal demand curve, from d_1 to d_2 in Figure 9.7(b). The individual firm reduces its output from q_2 to q_1 – the intersection of the new marginal revenue (price/demand) curve with the MC curve. Note that q_1 is also the low point of the ATC curve. Here price equals average total cost, meaning that *economic* profit is zero. The firm is making just enough to cover its opportunity and risk costs, but no more. If there were still economic profits being made in the computer chip industry, firms would continue to move into the industry until the price equals the minimum point on the ATC curve and economic profits are zero.

Losses have the opposite effect on long-run industry supply. In the long run, firms that are losing money will move out of the industry, because their resources can be employed more profitably elsewhere. When firms drop out of the industry, supply contracts and total production falls – from Q_2 to Q_1 in Figure 9.8(a). As a result, the price of the product rises, permitting some firms to break even and stay in the business. Long-run equilibrium occurs when the price reaches P_2 – where the individual firm's demand curve is tangent to the minimum point of the ATC curve in Figure 9.8(b). The output of each remaining individual firm expands (from q_1 to q_2) to take up some of the slack left by the firms that have withdrawn, but the expansion of the remaining firms is not enough to completely offset the reduction. Again, price and average total cost are equal – and thus economic profit is zero.[4]

The Effect of Economies of Scale

In the long run, competition forces firms to take advantage of economies of scale *if they exist* and to do so as quickly as possible. If expanding the use of resources reduces costs, the perfect competitor has two reasons for taking advantage of scale economies. First, if the firm expands before other firms, its lower average total cost will allow it to make greater economic profits (for a short period of time). Second, the firm *must* expand its scale for self-preservation. Other firms will expand their scales of operation, lowering their cost structures, increasing

---

[4] An irony of (long-run) zero economic profits is that we started our discussion of voluntary, mutually beneficial trades in markets with the view that both parties receive net gains. Here, producers receive no net gains in the long run – other than "normal profits," which is only covering the cost of doing business (e.g., risk costs and the opportunity costs of capital).

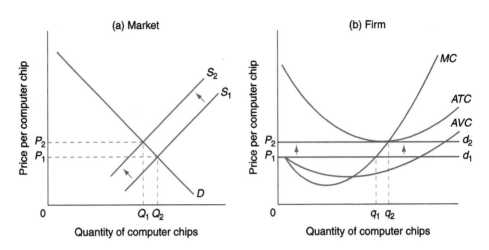

Figure 9.8 The long-run effects of short-run losses
If perfect competitors are suffering short-run losses, some firms will leave the industry, causing the market supply to shift back from S_1 to S_2 – and the price to rise from P_1 to P_2 in panel (a). The individual firm's demand curve will shift up with price, from d_1 to d_2 in panel (b). The remaining firms will expand from q_1 to q_2, and equilibrium will be reached when price (P_2) equals the minimum point of average total cost, eliminating their short-run losses.

market supply, and forcing the market price down below the minimum average cost of any firm that doesn't expand its scale.

In Figure 9.9(a), the market is initially in short-run equilibrium at a price of P_2. The individual firm is on cost curve ATC_1, producing q_1 chips and breaking even in Figure 9.9(b). If the firm expands its scale of operation and produces where its demand curve d_1 intersects the long-run MC curve, it will make a profit equal graphically to the shaded area ATC_1P_2ab. This is the firm's incentive for expansion.

If the firm does not expand and take advantage of these economies, some other firm surely will. Then, any firm still producing on a scale of ATC_1 will lose money. That's because, when the market supply expands, the price will tumble toward P_1, the point at which the long-run ATC curve (and the short-run curve ATC_m) are at a minimum – and both industry and firm economic profits are zero. Because of rising diseconomies of scale, firms will not be able to expand further. Any firm that tries to produce on a smaller or larger scale – for example, ATC_2 or ATC_3 – will incur average total costs higher than the market price and will lose money. Ultimately, it will be driven out of the market or be forced to expand or contract its scale. Hence, each individual firm will look to the long-run average and marginal costs curves and expand as quickly as possible (each firm must respond immediately under the idealized conditions of perfect competition).

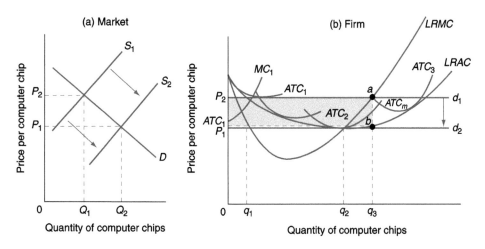

Figure 9.9 The long-run effects of economies of scale
If the market is in equilibrium at price P_1, as in panel (a), and the individual firm is producing q_1 units on ATC_1 in panel (b), firms will be just breaking even. Because of the profit potential represented by the shaded area ATC_1P_2ab, firms can be expected to expand production to q_3, where the $LRMC$ curve intersects the demand curve (d_1). As they expand production to take advantage of economies of scale, supply will expand from S_1 to S_2 in panel (a), pushing the market price down toward P_1, the low point of the $LRAC$ in panel (b). Economic profit will fall to zero. Because of diseconomies of scale, firms will not expand further.

Marginal Benefit versus Marginal Cost

Time lags and temporary disequilibria notwithstanding, the competitive market can produce efficient results in one important sense: the marginal benefit of the last unit produced equals its marginal cost ($MB = MC$). In Figure 9.10(a), for every computer chip up to Q_1, consumers are willing to pay a price (as indicated by the demand curve D) greater than its marginal cost (as indicated by the industry supply curve S). The difference between the price that consumers are willing to pay – an objective indication of the product's marginal benefits – and the marginal cost of production is a kind of "surplus value," or net gain, received from the production of each unit. The net gain is composed of **consumer surplus** and **producer surplus**. In Figure 9.10(a), consumer surplus is the triangular area below the demand curve and above the dotted price line, P_1; producer surplus is the triangular area above the supply curve and below P_1. By producing Q_1 units, the industry exploits all potential gains from production, shown graphically by

Consumer surplus is the difference between the total willingness of consumers to pay for a good and the total amount actually spent.

Producer surplus is the difference between the total willingness of producers to accept various prices and the price they actually receive.

the shaded triangular area in Figure 9.10(a). This net gain is brought about by the price charged (P_1), which induces individual firms to produce where the marginal cost of production equals the price and consumers' marginal benefit.

The marginal cost of production for each individual firm is also P_1, a fact that results in the production of Q_1 units at the minimum total cost. Figures 9.10(b) and (c) show the cost curves of two firms, X and Y. In competitive equilibrium,

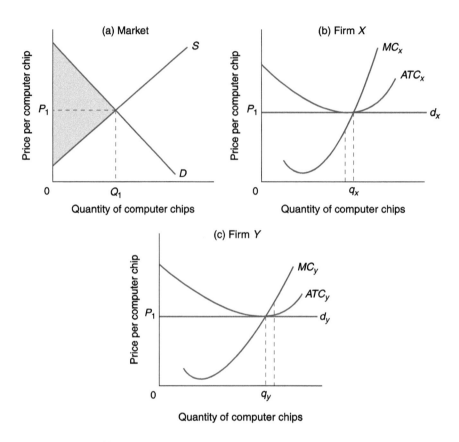

Figure 9.10 The efficiency of the competitive market
Perfectly competitive markets are efficient in the sense that they equate marginal benefit (shown by the demand curve in panel (a)) with marginal cost (shown by the supply curve in panel (a)). At market output level Q_1, the marginal benefit of the last unit produced equals the marginal cost of production. The gains generated by the production of Q_1 units – that is, the difference between cost and benefits – are shown by the shaded area in panel (a). The perfectly competitive market is also efficient in the sense that the marginal cost of production is the same for all firms (panels (b) and (c)). If firm X were to produce fewer than its efficient number of units (q_x), firm Y would have to produce more than its efficient number (q_y) to meet market demand. Firm Y would be pushed up its MC curve, to a point at which the cost of the last unit would exceed its benefits. But competition forces the two firms to produce where marginal cost equals marginal benefit, minimizing the cost of production.

firm X produces q_x units and firm Y produces at q_y. Suppose the market output were distributed between the firms differently – for example, that firm X produced one computer chip fewer than q_x. To maintain a constant market output of Q_1, firm Y would then have to expand production by one unit. The additional chip would force firm Y up its MC curve. To Y, the marginal cost of the additional chip is greater than P_1 and X's marginal cost to produce it. Competition forces firms to produce at a cost-effective output level, minimizing the cost of producing at any given level of output.

Thus, perfectly competitive markets are attractive for another reason. In the long run, competition forces each firm to produce at the lowest point on its ATC curve. Firms must either produce at this point, achieving whatever economies of scale are available – or get out of the market, leaving production to some other firm that will minimize average total cost.

Critiques of the Efficiency of Perfect Competition

Our discussion of perfect competition has been highly theoretical. In real life, the competitive market system is not as efficient as this analysis suggests. From this perspective, several aspects of the competitive market deserve further comment.

The Market's Tendency toward Equilibrium

Market forces are stabilizing: they tend to push the market toward a central point of equilibrium. As such, the market is somewhat predictable. But in the real world, price does not always move as easily toward equilibrium as it appears to do in supply and demand models. A smooth, direct move to equilibrium will happen in markets in which all participants, both buyers and sellers, know exactly what everyone else is doing. Often, however, market participants have only imperfect knowledge of what others intend to do. Indeed, an important function of the market is to generate the pricing and output information that people need to coordinate their actions with one another.

In a world of imperfect information, then, prices probably will not move immediately to equilibrium. Those who compete in the market will continually grope for the "best" price from their own individual perspectives. At times, sellers will produce too little and reap unusually high profits; at other times, they will produce too much and suffer losses. But the advantage of markets is that, when mistakes are made, market prices (and profits and losses) provide information on those mistakes and how to correct them.

This process of groping toward equilibrium can be represented graphically by a supply and demand "cobweb" (as in Figure 9.11). Most firms must plan their production at least several months ahead on the basis of prices received then or during the past production period. Farmers, for instance, may plant for

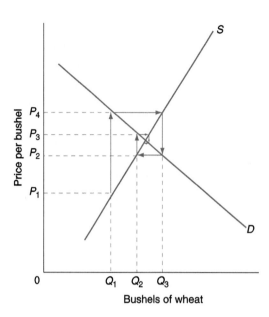

Figure 9.11 Supply and demand cobweb
Markets do not always move smoothly toward equilibrium. If current production decisions are based on past prices, price may adjust to supply in the "cobweb pattern" shown here. Having received price P_1 in the past, farmers will plan to supply only Q_1 bushels of wheat. This amount will not meet market demand, so the price will rise to P_4, inducing farmers to plan for a harvest of Q_3 bushels. But at price P_4, Q_3 bushels will not clear the market. So the price will fall to P_2, encouraging farmers to cut production back to Q_2. Only after several tries do farmers find the equilibrium price–quantity combination.

summer harvest on the basis of the previous summer's prices. Suppose farmers received price P_1 for a bushel of wheat last year. Their planning supply curve, S, will encourage them to work for a harvest of only Q_1 bushels this year. Given the limited output and the rather high demand at price P_1, the price farmers actually receive is P_4. In turn, the price of P_4 may induce farmers to plan for a much larger production level, Q_3, the following year. But the market will not clear for Q_3 bushels until the price falls to P_2. The next year, farmers plan for a price of P_2 and reduce their production to Q_2, which causes the price to rise to P_3. As you can see from the graph, instead of moving in a straight line, the market may move toward the intersection of supply and demand in a web-like pattern.

We hasten to add that, while the "cobweb" is helpful in explaining gyrations in price, actual gyrations likely will be dampened over time with *learning* on the part of market participants, since so much is at stake. Farmers will learn that high prices one year can lead to "oversupply" the following year and can, accordingly, temper their planting response to high prices in any given year, thereby dampening the drop in prices the following year. Labor markets that require substantial human capital investments may be the strongest examples. Sensing a "strong demand" for skills in a certain field, more people will seek education and training to fill this demand. But by the time they complete the training, market conditions may have changed or too many people may have sought the same training. Wages might decrease and workers may slide into different but related fields. Even so, we expect people to be strongly motivated to carefully weigh the personal costs and benefits of such a large investment.

Surpluses and Shortages

Some critics complain that the market system creates wasteful surpluses and shortages. Although all resources are limited in quantity ("scarcity"), a shortage can exist only if the going price is below equilibrium. Thus, shortages can be eliminated by a price increase. How much of an increase, theory alone cannot say. But we do know that market forces, if allowed free play, will work to boost the price and eliminate the shortage. This means, of course, that people of limited financial resources will be more adversely affected than those with larger incomes – a concern that some use to justify government-imposed market restrictions (not all of which actually help the poor, as we saw in our discussion of rent controls and minimum wages in Chapter 5).

Similarly, all surpluses exist because the going price is above equilibrium. Competition will reduce the price, eliminating the surplus. In the process, some firms will be driven out of the market and into other activities where they can produce more value. In the transition, this can result in unemployed workers. A frequent criticism of the market system is that, when this happens, workers have difficulty finding new employment. Part of the problem, however, is that labor contracts, community custom, and minimum-wage laws can limit the ability of wages to adjust downward.

Even acknowledging these concerns, we must compare market outcomes to what government intervention will yield in practice. As we developed in Chapter 5, if government controls prices – that is, if prices are not permitted to respond to market conditions – surpluses and shortages will persist indefinitely.

Externalities (Again)

Critics stress that supply is based only on the costs that firms bear privately. As discussed in Chapter 6, external costs such as air, noise, and water pollution are not counted as part of the cost of production. If the external costs of pollution were counted, the firm's supply curve would be lower (S_2 instead of S_1 in Figure 6.1). If producers and consumers had to pay all the costs of production, fewer units would be bought and sold. In this sense, competition leads to over-production and a market inefficiency (a *social welfare cost* or *deadweight loss*) equal to the shaded triangular area *abc* in Figure 6.1). Indeed, perfect competition will maximize the externalization of costs, because firms that don't externalize all of these costs will be driven from business by those that have lower cost structures by doing so.

Income and Wealth Differences

The cost efficiencies of the market system are achieved within a specific distribution of wealth that depends on the existing distribution of property rights. Moreover, market outcomes have implications for the distribution of income and wealth. Critics worry that this process and/or these outcomes are inequitable, even if efficient. Then again, markets create wealth over time, which means that many people today (even those with little wealth) could have more wealth and purchase better goods and services than would have been possible had redistributive policies constrained markets through time. And government redistributive efforts to remedy perceived inequities must themselves be equitable and actually accomplish the desired ends. In practice, this is quite difficult to do.[5]

The Unreal Nature of Perfect Competition

It is worth noting that most real-world markets are not perfectly competitive. Demanders and suppliers are rarely as well informed as the model suggests. Few markets come close to having numerous firms with identical products and complete freedom of entry and exit. Markets for gold, stocks, bonds, agricultural commodities, and some computer chips are probably the closest markets we have to perfect competition. But even these products are not *completely* identical. Wheat sold by a Kansas farmer is not always viewed the same as wheat sold by a Texas farmer. And even if the products are identical, the customer service attached to the products provides some degree of differentiation.

Actual markets are not inhabited by numerous firms producing standard commodities that can be easily duplicated by anyone who would like to enter the market. Indeed, many markets are inhabited by a few large, powerful firms that do not take price as a given and have a high degree of monopoly power through substantial barriers to entry. More broadly, entry and exit costs always exist – and even abound – in many "competitive" markets.

Thus, the assumptions of the perfect competition model are so extreme that students may be concerned about its relevance: "If there are few market structures that closely approximate perfect competition, why bother to study it?" Remember that the model of perfect competition was never meant to represent all, or even most, markets. It is merely a tool economists use to think about markets and the consequences of changes in market conditions and government policy.

We know that, under the conditions of competition specified, certain results follow. We can logically (with some help from graphs and mathematics) derive these results, as we have done in this chapter. For example, in perfect competition, each firm will extend production until the marginal cost of producing the

---

[5] On government's efforts to help the poor and the inherent dilemmas, see chapters 12–17 of Schansberg's book, *Poor Policy* (Schansberg 1996).

last unit equals the price paid by the consumer. This conclusion *necessarily* follows from the assumptions made.

Granted, the demanding conditions for perfect competition are rarely met. Still, even *under less-demanding conditions, competitive results are often observed*. It may be that the number of producers is not "numerous"; the products sold by all producers are not strictly "identical"; and there are costs to moving in to and out of markets. Nonetheless, individual producers may *act as if* the conditions of perfect competition are met – that they have no control over market price in competition with other actual or potential producers. (We look at such "contestable markets" in Online Reading 9.1.) If so, it is best to think of the other producers as numerous "enough" – in which case, many of the predicted results of perfect competition will still be observed in less than perfect markets.

For these reasons, many economists often talk about **price takers** rather than *perfect competitors.* These producers simply observe the market price and either accept it (and accordingly produce to the point at

> **Price takers** are sellers who do not believe they can influence the market price significantly by varying their own production levels.

which marginal cost and price are equal) or reject it (and go into some other business). Hence, the price taker is one who acts *as if* her demand curve is horizontal (perfectly elastic, more or less). She is therefore someone who assumes that the marginal revenue on each unit sold is constant (and equal to the price) – and that the *MR* curve is horizontal and equivalent to the firm's demand curve.

In contrast, **price searchers** are sellers who have some control over the market price. Price searchers

> **Price searchers** are sellers who can influence the market price by varying their production levels.

have (and act on) some degree of monopoly power, because they can alter production (and thereby market supply) sufficiently to change the price. The individual price searcher's task is not simply to accept or reject the current market price, but to "search" through the various price–quantity combinations on her downward-sloping demand curve with the intent of maximizing profits. As we will demonstrate and detail in Chapter 10, the marginal revenue and demand curves of the price searcher are no longer equivalent.

Finally, the perfectly competitive market can help us gain insight about production decisions precisely because its required conditions are "unreal." The model of market competition simplifies the analysis, giving us clarity about the essential features of competitive markets and showing us how managers can improve their thinking about the complex tasks of achieving maximum survivability and profitability. Behavioral economists have argued that people in general and managers in particular have an array of "decision-making biases" which we fully acknowledge. For example, people might not be naturally inclined to ignore sunk costs and they might harbor a bias toward projects with opportunity costs rather than projects with out-of-pocket expenditures (Thaler and Sunstein 2008; Ariely 2010; Thaler 2015b). But the unreal model of perfect competition helps us drive home the point that managers must consider thinking in terms of equating at the margin (producing where marginal cost and marginal revenue are equal) and ignoring fixed costs in short-run production decisions. Moreover, the analysis can remind managers to treat all costs the same (the explicit costs that are recorded on income statements and the opportunity costs that never see the light of accounting statements). Firms in highly competitive markets who ignore such heuristics might very well see themselves replaced by managers who take "principles of economics" seriously.

The Role of Innovation and Entrepreneurship

Note how our analysis of perfect competition assumed that the "product" already exists and the market for the product has been developed. A demand curve couldn't be placed on a graph if the product's market had not already been identified and developed. In our model, the product and its market effectively emerged out of the "thin air" of theory disconnected from real-world markets. Ironically, economists generally ignore the role of entrepreneurs who make markets possible. (We attempt to address this deficiency in this section, by providing Online Readings 9.2 and 9.3, and by encouraging you to watch the Acton Institute movie, *The Call of the Entrepreneur*.)

These presumptions of zero product and market development costs are crucial to any deduction that perfect competition is perfectly efficient – or far more efficient than other market structures where producers have some degree of monopoly power. Would anyone develop products for perfectly competitive markets or seek to develop such markets? Probably not – *if* the products and their markets require development costs, which is surely the case for real-world markets. If there are development costs at all, who would cover them? Again, very likely, nobody. Under conditions of perfect competition, anyone who incurred the development costs could not get them back. This is the case because, once the development costs are incurred, other competitors would immediately sweep into the market and press the product's price downward. Since new entrants don't have to incur the development costs, they could seek prices below what the product/market developer would need to cover the development costs.

The most practical lesson to be drawn from our analysis of perfect competition may be counterintuitive: don't make up-front investments in markets that come close to the conditions of perfect competition. Avoid investing in markets (or developing products for markets) in which there are many producers or where entry costs are low. If you do incur product and market development costs, you can expect the investments to yield no net gains of economic profits, because of the speed with which competitors can be expected to swoop in the market and depress the price to the minimum average cost. Rather, look to invest in markets where there is some form of entry barrier (or some "friction" in resource movement) so that development costs may be recovered. Such entry restrictions (or market frictions) can have a hidden social welfare benefit not conventionally discussed in microeconomic theory: they can reduce the risk cost of incurring up-front product and market development costs. This means that the average cost (AC) curve under perfectively competitive market conditions can be *higher* than that in other less competitive market conditions where economic profits have a chance of persisting, at least for a time.

"Shark Tank" is a long-standing, popular television program. Entrepreneurs seek to persuade savvy, rich, demanding investors – "sharks" – to invest their own funds in innovative product ideas presented or already developed products that have been market-tested. They turn down most of the products they see but compete with proposed investment terms to partner with some of the budding entrepreneurs. If you watch several of the programs, you will see that the sharks understand the points made here on the limitations of perfect competition: invariably, the sharks ask the entrepreneurs for evidence of the market's potential size and the profitability of their products. They also inevitably ask for evidence of entry barriers (patents, copyrights, market leadership, brand, etc.). They tend to avoid products where there are no entry barriers, or that seem to face the prospects of having competitors in short order, which will undercut the sharks' ability to recover their investment.

While perfect competition enables us to understand some features of market competition and some rules of profit maximization (e.g., "equate at the margin"), it also enables us to see the end results of intensely competitive markets, with economic profits being undercut in the process. This leads to the powerful conclusion introduced above: Avoid such markets if you can; be cautious of entering markets with many producers or where the entry costs are minimal.

Back in the 1990s, the age of emerging internet commerce, many entrepreneurs lost sight of these lessons. Any number of entrepreneurs (and commentators) argued in the early and mid-1990s that the Internet was a "new economy" that harbored the prospects of a new "gold rush." Many entrepreneurs reasoned: To get into e-commerce, just buy a computer with an internet connection and develop a website – all with very little cost (or far lower costs than would be required to set up a brick-and-mortar retail outlet). Their own argument often proved to be self-contradictory. If market entry was as low as claimed and as profitable as argued, the new economy would be overrun with new entrants, making profit elusive. For many unwary internet investors, e-commerce became a financial sinkhole, outcomes that were at the foundation of the bursting e-commerce bubble in the late 1990s.

PERSPECTIVE 9
The Myth of the First-Mover Advantage

One of the most widely believed tenets in management theory and practice is the so-called "first-mover advantage" – the idea that the first firm to market with a product will not only have the market to itself, but will be able to fend off late-comers and dominate the market for some time to come.

The theory holds that the first mover will realize cost advantages from economies of scale (lowering its long-term cost curves), develop brand loyalty (increasing its demand and/or reducing its elasticity of demand), achieve name recognition, and garner the benefits of "network effects" (its demand will build with expanded consumption). Beyond some ill-defined point, the first mover can expect its market expansion to reach a "tipping point," beyond which consumers will move to the first mover because everyone else is moving in this direction (Gladwell 2000). The first mover can expect to have its market locked up because consumers will be locked in, since they face high switching costs to move to potential competitors. Hence, investors should flock to first movers, because they will achieve a long-term stream of monopoly prices and profits (as we will develop in Chapters 10 and 11).

The first-mover advantage sounds good, but it appears to be dead wrong as a generality – according to management professors Gerald Tellis and Peter Golder, whose extensive research is reported in *Will and Vision: How Late Comers Grow to Dominate Markets* (Tellis and Golder 2002). They offer many telling examples, but consider this short list of firms that now dominate their markets but were not first movers:

- Gillette is widely believed to have pioneered safety razors because it has dominated the safety razor market for so long. (It has faced increasingly sharp competition in the U.S. over the past decade.) But the concept of safety razors was proposed a century before Gillette introduced its first razor and several firms introduced safety razors two decades before Gillette.
- Oreo now leads the cookie market, but it wasn't even the original "sandwich" cookie. Hydrox debuted from Sunshine Biscuits in 1908, with Nabisco introducing the Oreo in 1912.
- Pampers now dominates the disposable diaper market – why many people think Procter & Gamble was the first mover in this market in the mid-1960s. They have forgotten that Chux diapers, produced by Johnson & Johnson, were on the market as early as 1932.
- Hewlett-Packard (HP) is assumed to have created the first laser printer, since it has a commanding share of laser printer sales. However, both Xerox and IBM commercialized laser printers years before HP, using engines developed by Canon.

- Many people think Netscape produced the first internet browser. Few remember that Mosaic hit the browser market years prior. Even fewer know that web browsers such as Viola, Erwise, and Midas inspired the development of Mosaic at the University of Illinois.
- People often assume that Apple initially dominated the early market because it created the product category. However, Micro Instrumentation & Telemetry Systems pioneered personal computing with its Altair machine in 1975.
- The first-mover advantage was hardly an advantage for the CPM personal computer operating system or the Mac operating system – both of which dominated the market in their time before Microsoft took over with MS-DOS and, later, Windows (ten years after the advent of CPM).
- There was no obvious first-mover advantage in search engines by first movers. Google is now the dominant internet search engine, responsible for upwards of 80 percent of searches in the world on a daily basis. It was created in 1996 by two Stanford graduate students, Larry Page and Sergey Brin – and was initially called BackRub before being renamed Google in 1997. However, several search engines had already been created: Excite (in 1993) and Infoseek, Altavista, WebCrawler, and Yahoo! (in 1994). Google overwhelmed the competition in part because the founders recognized a serious flaw in existing search engines: they reported "hits" with no concern for their relevance to specified searches.

The case against the first-mover advantage goes beyond the mountain of case histories that led Tellis and Golder to their central conclusion – in all but six of the sixty-six industry groups they studied during the 1990s. The failure rate of pioneers was quite high: 64 percent overall; 71 percent for the forty-two traditional industries; and 50 percent for high-tech industries. Moreover, almost all pioneers only dominated their markets when sales were well below mass-market proportions, indicating some of the challenges of fostering growth and sustaining success. Indeed, the first movers in their analysis only had an average market share of 6 percent.

Secret of Market Leadership

How did the first-mover advantage become such a popular idea? The answer is relatively simple: Many researchers didn't do their historical homework. They often assumed that market leaders today developed their product's category because the dominant firms themselves now claim to be the pioneers and because the first-mover failures have been lost to a history that is all too rarely studied with the care taken by Tellis and Golder.

Market pioneers rarely endure as leaders; most have low market shares or fail completely. In fact, market pioneering is neither necessary nor sufficient for enduring success. So, what is the real secret of market leadership? Tellis and Golder draw an unsurprising old lesson that managers would be well advised to remember: The chief causes of enduring market leadership are vision and will. Enduring market leaders have a revolutionary and inspiring vision of the mass market, and they exhibit an indomitable will to realize this vision. They persist under adversity, innovate relentlessly, commit financial resources, and leverage assets to realize their vision (Tellis and Golder 2002, 41).

Beyond the data and the research, there are strong theoretical advantages to being a second (and later) mover. There is no need to bear the costs of establishing a market. It is often less expensive to establish and maintain supply chains. And they can learn (otherwise costly) lessons from early entrants, avoiding key mistakes and studying first-mover products for ways to improve them. Finally, all of this implies lessons for potential first movers as well: Be cautious with fixed and sunk costs; be careful to avoid costly mistakes; and be nimble in making adjustments if you are initially successful.

Part B Organizational Economics and Management

Competing Cost-Effectively through Efficient Teams

Competitive market conditions put intense pressure on producers to produce cost-effectively. Producers who don't find the most efficient means of production are doomed under perfectly competitive market conditions and will suffer in terms of market share and profitability under intense (but less extreme) competitive market conditions. As such, producers in competitive markets must form firms when such organizational structures are more efficient than market exchanges – and then must break down their organization into cohesive and effective working groups. Otherwise, competitive pressures on prices (via the lower cost curves employed in Part A of this chapter) will cause the demise of firms that fail to identify and implement lower-cost means of production.

In Part A, we implicitly assumed that the firm would organize in a way that minimized its costs. In Part B, we suggest that accomplishing the goal of cost-effectiveness requires managers to understand how the sizes of teams and the system of payments to team members can have profound effects on the firm's cost structure. In other words, we continue to develop why producing cost-effectively is easier said than done. A perfectly competitive firm (or one facing market conditions approximating perfect competition) must produce cost-effectively, matching the cost-effectiveness of the most cost-effective producer in the market. The cost curves drawn in Part A represent the curves of the most cost-effective producers because producers who do not match the standard will not last long in a perfectly competitive market (or a market that approaches perfect competition).

As noted in Chapter 7, the central reason firms exist is that people are often more productive when they work together – in "teams" – than when they work in isolation from one another but are tied together by markets. Teams are no passing and facile management fad; firms have always used them. Indeed, in a broad sense, a firm *is* a team or a collection of teams. Economies can be garnered from assigning complex tasks to relatively small teams of workers – those within departments and, for larger projects, across departments – that can result in substantial productivity improvements.[6] However, teams also present opportunities for shirking – as should be self-evident to many business students who form their own study and project groups to complete class assignments. A central problem that managers face is constructing teams to minimize shirking and maximize production.

Team Production

What do we mean by "team production"? If Mary and Jim could each produce 100 widgets independently of one another and could together produce only 200 widgets, there would be no basis for team production – or for the two to form a firm with all of the trappings of a hierarchy. The added cost of their organization would, no doubt, make them uncompetitive *vis-à-vis* other producers who worked independently of one another. However, if Mary and Jim could produce 250 widgets when working together, then team production might be profitable (depending on the additional costs associated with operating their two-person organization). Hence, we would define "team production" as work in which results are highly interactive: the output of any one member of the group is dependent on what the other group members do. A simple and clear form of effective teamwork is when Mary and Jim move objects together that neither can handle alone. The work of people on an assembly line or an advertising project are more complicated forms of teamwork.

Granted, finding business endeavors with the potential for expanding output by more than the growth in costs is a major problem for businesses. But finding such opportunities leads to another significant problem – making sure the synergetic *potential* of the workers who are brought together into a team is *realized*.

We often think of firms failing for purely financial reasons – when they incur financial losses. Such firms are said to be illiquid and insolvent. This view of failure is instructive, but the matter can also be seen in a different light – as

---

[6] Researchers have found recently that the adoption of teams in garment plants increased annual productivity by 14 percent, partially because the more productive workers were initial movers to teams, sometimes with a net reduction in pay – possibly because of the improvement to their work environment and the potential for collaborative work (Hamilton, Nickerson, and Owan 2003).

an organizational problem with a failure in organizational incentives. A poorly run organization can mean that the value of the 50 "extra" widgets produced by Mary and Jim together are lost in unnecessary expenditures and impaired productivity, because of the problems inherent in team production. If the organizational costs exceed the equivalent of 50 widgets, then we can say that Mary and Jim have incurred a loss that would force them to adjust their practices as a firm or dissolve the partnership.

Many firms do fail and break apart, not because the potential for expanded output does not exist, but because their collective potential is not realized. Why don't people in a team always realize their collective potential? There are many answers to this question. Firms may not have a good product design or a well-thought-out business strategy to promote the products. Some people just can't get along; they rub each other the wrong way when they try to cooperate. Personal conflicts, which deflect people's energies at work into interpersonal defensive and predatory actions, can be so common that production potentials are missed.

While respecting many noneconomic explanations for organizational problems, we reiterate one of our primary themes: managers are unable to find ways to properly align the interests of the workers with those of other workers and the owners. People in firms don't cooperate as cost-effectively as they can and should. This problem only exists in teams; for obvious reasons, it doesn't exist in a one-person firm.

In our simple example, Mary and Jim each have a strong *personal* incentive (quite apart from an altruistic motivation) to work with the other. After all, each can readily tell when the other person is not contributing what is expected (or agreed upon). Accordingly, when Mary shirks, Jim can "punish" Mary by also shirking (and vice versa), ensuring both will be worse off than if they never sought to cooperate at all. In this sense, their agreement can be *self-enforcing*, with each checking the other – and each effectively threatening the other with reprisal in kind. The threat of added cost is especially powerful when Mary and Jim are also the owners of the firm. The two of them fully bear the cost of the shirking and any "tit-for-tat" consequences. There is no prospect for shifting costs to a third party.

Two-person firms are, conceptually, the easiest business ventures to organize and manage (with the exception of one-person firms), because the incentives are so obvious, strong, and well-aligned. But organizational and management problems begin to mount as the number of people in the firm or "team" increases. As discussed under the "The logic of group behavior in business and elsewhere" in Chapter 2, incentives begin to change with growth in group size. Each individual's contribution to the totality of firm output becomes less – and less obvious – as the number of people increases. This is especially true when the firm is organized to take advantage of people's specialties. Employees often don't know what their colleagues do and are unable to assess their work.

When Mary is one of two people in a firm, she is responsible for half of the output (assuming equal contributions). But when she is one of a thousand people, her contribution is only one-tenth of 1 percent. Beyond this, if she is a clerk in the advertising department assigned to sending payment for ads, she might not be able to tell that she is responsible for much in terms of output, income, and profits.

Admittedly, if no one else contributes anything to production, the work of any one person is material – in fact, everything. The point is that, in large groups, and as output expands, each worker has an *impaired* incentive to do that which is in all of their interests to do – to make their small contribution to the sum total of what the firm does. A central lesson of this discussion is *not* that workers never cooperate, but, rather, that countervailing incentives can undercut the power of people's natural tendencies to cooperate and achieve their synergetic potential. Consequently, managers must pay attention to the details of firm organization to counteract these forces.

If all people were "angels" (always inclined to do as they are told or as they said they would do), then the manager's role would be much less important. Even if most people were inclined to do as each was told or had committed to doing, managers would still want to implement policies and an organizational structure that create incentives for people to behave in the firm's best interest. Without such incentives – rewarding cooperative behavior and punishing uncooperative behavior – a few "bad" people can seriously damage the firm. Even employees who forgo opportunities to shirk their responsibilities may soon cease to do so if they see others undermining their efforts and shirking their duties. As more employees shift from responsible to irresponsible behavior, the greater the incentive for the remaining employees to shift as well – and a culture of cooperation can unravel.

Why are large firms divided into departments? Although the administrative overhead of department structures may seem unnecessary, they are a means to reduce the size of the groups within the firm. The purpose is not only to ensure that bosses can more closely monitor individual actions, but also to allow individuals within the department to more easily recognize their own and others' contributions to output.

One good reason for the ongoing interest in teams is that departments are often too large, meaning that people's individual contributions within departments are still too small to detect and monitor. Teams can be ways of reducing the size of the relevant group of workers. Managers have now begun to realize that reducing group size can increase worker productivity and ensure that workers (who often know most about what needs to be done in their specialty) can monitor each other. This reduces the need of managers to "micromanage" employees, leaving them more latitude to make the best use of their knowledge for themselves and for the firm.

Team Size

How large should teams be? How many members should they have? We obviously can't say exactly, given the many factors that explain the great variety of firms. However, we can make several general observations, the most important of which is that managers must acknowledge that shirking will *tend to rise along with group size*, all else constant.

But there are key mitigating factors. The more alike the members, the larger the team can be. People who have more knowledge of what their teammates are doing tend to cooperate. People whose values are similar tend to understand each other better and work harder toward a common goal. With more training on cooperation, teams can be larger. Thus, training can be valuable because it makes workers more productive by increasing the value of their direct contribution – and it can reduce the added overhead of a larger number of smaller departments.[7] The more that workers are imbued with a corporate culture and accept the firm's goals, the larger the team can be. Thus, expenditures on efforts to define the firm's purpose can be self-financing, given that the resulting larger departments can free up resources. The more that team members can detect or measure the outputs of fellow team members, the larger the team can be. Firms, therefore, have an economic interest in developing ways to make work more objective to evaluate. Finally, the greater the importance of quality, the smaller teams should be.

No matter how it is done, the size of the teams within a firm can affect the overall size of the firm. Firms with teams that are "too large" or "too small" can have unnecessarily high cost structures that restrict market share and overall size, as well as the incomes of the workers and owners.

Paying Teams

Recognizing that teams can add to firm output is only half the struggle to get workers to perform as they should. The other key question is: How are the workers on the team to be paid? If workers are rewarded only for the output

---

[7] That said, much depends on the type of training given to workers. Researchers have found that in single-play experimental games designed to test the tendency of people to free-ride on the group's efforts, not everyone contributed to group output. However, they also found that the average group produced 40–60 percent of the "optimal output," except groups comprised of graduate students in economics who provided only 20 percent of the optimal output (Marwell and Ames 1981). Perhaps this is to be expected, given that economics students are more aware than most people of how to capture private benefits in such games. Other researchers found that the explanation is less about what economics students learn and more about less-cooperative students being more likely to major in economics (Frank, Gilgorich, and Regan 1996). As a consequence, it probably follows that teams of economists (and other people with similar conceptual leanings) should be smaller than teams of people from other disciplines. And although we don't intend it, we worry that people who read this book may become less disposed to cooperate!

of the team, then individual workers again have incentives to free-ride on the work of others (to the extent they can get away with it), which can be realized in shirking and absenteeism. But if team members are rewarded exclusively for their own individual contributions, then the incentive for actual teamwork is reduced.

Generally, managers effectively "punt" on compensation issues, not knowing exactly how to structure rewards – and offer compensation that is based partly on team output and partly on individual contributions to the team. Team output is generally the easier of the two compensation variables to measure, as teams are organized along functional lines with some measurable objective in mind. Peer evaluation may play a partial role in how individual contributions are determined, because team members have localized knowledge of how much their co-workers are contributing to team output. But here again, the compensation problem is not completely solved. Team members can reason that how they work – and how they and their co-workers are evaluated – can affect their slice of the "compensation pie." Each can figure that the more highly other members of the team are evaluated, the lower their own relative evaluation – a consideration that can lead team members to underrate the work of other members. Team discord can result, as has been experienced at jeans maker Levi Strauss, where supervisors reportedly spend a nontrivial amount of time refereeing team member conflicts. To ameliorate (but not totally quell) the discord, Levi Strauss resorted to giving employees training in group dynamics and methods of getting along (Mitchell 1994).

How can managers best motivate workers through pay to contribute to team output? Four identifiable pay methods are worth considering:

1 The workers can simply share in the revenues generated by the team (or firm). With revenue sharing, the gain to each worker is the added revenue received minus the cost to the worker of the added effort expended. Under this method of reward, each worker has the maximum incentive to free-ride, especially when the "team" is large.

2 The workers can be assigned target production or revenue levels and be given what are called *forcing contracts* – a guarantee of a high (reward) wage (significantly above their market wage) if the target is achieved and a lower (penalty) wage if the target is not achieved. Under this system, each worker suffers a personal income loss from the failure of the team to work effectively to meet the target.

3 The workers can also be given an opportunity to share in the team or firm profits. *Profit sharing* (or "gain sharing") is another type of forcing contract because the worker receives one income if the firm makes a profit (above some target level) and a lower income if the profit (above a target level) is zero.

4 The workers within different teams also can be rewarded, according to how well they do relative to other teams. These are akin to *tournaments*, in which the members of the "winning team" are given a bonus or higher rates of pay than the members of other teams.[8]

All the pay systems just outlined may have a positive impact on worker input and thus on worker output. Many studies show that profit-sharing and worker stock ownership plans do seem to have a positive impact on worker productivity (Howard and Dietz 1969; Metzger 1975; FitzRoy and Kraft 1986; Wagner, Rubin, and Callahan 1988; Weisman and Kruse 1990; U.S. Department of Labor 1993). One study of fifty-two firms in the engineering industry in the United Kingdom (40 percent of which had some form of profit-sharing plans) found that profit-sharing could add 3–8 percent to firm productivity (Cable and Wilson 1989). With a more "participatory" decision-making process, when more information is shared, when job assignments are more flexible, and with greater profit-sharing, worker performance increased relative to more traditional organizational structures (Husled 1995; Ichniowski, Shaw, and Prennushi 1996).

To pay team members appropriately, managers must know how well teams are doing – not just how many "widgets" the team produces, but also in terms of team contributions to firm profitability. CMC, a computer service company, assigns responsibility to individual teams for a major client or a collection of smaller clients and then develops profit and loss (P&L) statements for each team. Managers recognize that team members have ground-level information on clients that managers can never know (except in screened forms). It wants to give teams the ability to respond to information received, but it also wants team members to know that their decisions will be monitored through the bottom line of their P&L statements. Of course, managers can't rely totally on P&L statements of individual teams to maximize firm profits, simply because they often need teams to cooperate when the teams face the now-familiar Prisoner's Dilemmas.

Experimental Evidence on the Effectiveness of Team Pay

A key question now emerges: Which method of worker compensation is *more* effective in overcoming shirking and causing workers to apply themselves? One of the more interesting studies to address this question uses an experimental/laboratory approach to develop a tentative assessment of the absolute and relative value of the different pay methods on worker effort. Experimental economists Haig Nalbantian and Andrew Schotter (1997) used two groups of six university

---

[8] Ironically, winners may receive a lower net wage, since they may work harder, longer, and smarter in order to win the tournament "prize." Hence, the pay per hour of the winners could be lower.

economics students in a highly stylized experiment in which student pay would be determined by the "profitability" of their respective teams in achieving maximum "output."

The students did their "work" on computers that were isolated from one another. The students indicated how much "work" they would do in the twenty-five rounds of the experiment by selecting a number from 0 to 100. The higher the number selected, the higher the cost to the student, just as rising effort tends to impose an escalating cost on workers. The students in each of the two teams always knew two pieces of important information: how much they "worked" (the number they submitted) in each round, and how much the "team" as a total "worked." They did not know the "effort levels" of other individual students.[9]

The researchers were able to draw conclusions that generally confirmed expectations from the theory at the heart of this textbook. They found that, when the revenue-sharing method of pay was used, the median "effort level" for each of the two teams started at a mere 30. But because the students were then told how little effort other team members were expending in total, the students began to cut their own effort in each of the successive rounds. The median effort level in both teams trended downward until the twenty-fifth round, when the median effort level was under 13. They also were able to deduce that the *history of the team performance* matters: the higher the team performance at the start, the greater the team performance thereafter.

Nalbantian and Schotter (1997) found that forcing contracts and profit-sharing could increase the initial level of effort to 40 or above – one-third higher than the initial effort level under revenue-sharing. But, still, the effort level under forcing contracts and profit-sharing trended downward with succeeding rounds of the experiment. They also found that tournaments encouraged team members to think competitively, with median initial effort levels on par with the initial effort under forcing contracts. However, the effort level tended to increase in the first few rounds and then held more or less constant through the rest of the twenty-five rounds. At the end, the teams had a median effort level of 40 to 50 – four times the final effort level under the revenue-sharing incentive system. Understandably, the authors concluded that "a little competition goes a very long, long way" (Nalbantian and Schotter 1997, 315).

Finally, the authors concluded that monitoring works (no surprise), but the extent to which monitoring hiked the effort level is noteworthy. No monitoring system works perfectly. So the authors evaluated how the teams would

---

[9] Granted, the experiment leaves much to be desired (which the authors fully concede). The experimental setting did not reflect the full complexity of the typical workplace. For example, direct communication among workers can have an important impact on the effort levels of individual workers. The complexity of the workplace is why it is so difficult to determine how pay systems affect worker performance, especially relative to alternative compensation schemes.

perform with a competitive team pay system under two experimental conditions: the probability of team members being caught shirking was 70 percent or 30 percent – with a stiff penalty: the loss of their "jobs."

Obviously, monitoring of team members can have a dramatic impact on team performance. But, in practice, the cost of the monitoring system can be high. Researchers cannot say whether the improvement in team performance is worth the cost of the relevant monitoring system in any given context. But managers must find ways of minimizing their monitoring and shirking costs. One of the great cost-saving advantages of teams, which is not reflected in the way the experiments were run, is that teamwork tends to be self-monitoring – with team members monitoring one another. In the experiment, the team members could not monitor and penalize each other. If self-monitoring were imposed in an experiment, we would expect effort level to increase.

Should all firms adopt the competitive team approach? The evidence suggests a strong "Yes." But we hasten to add a caveat that managers of some firms must keep in mind: greater effort to produce more output is desirable as long as it does not come with a sacrifice in "quality" (or some other important dimension of production). Competitive team production may be shunned in industries such as pharmaceuticals and banking that can't tolerate concessions in their quality standards because of the importance of reputation and liability concerns. The competition of tournaments can drive up output but drive down "quality." Such firms would want to use reward systems that keep competition under control and quality standards up. They would also want to rely on close monitoring, despite the cost, because of the higher costs that they might suffer with defects. This leads to the obvious conclusion that the greater the cost of mistakes, the greater the cost that can be endured from relaxed competition and from monitoring.

Practical Lessons

Costs matter – and marginal costs matter especially. This needs to be drilled home to business students because of how much attention is given to total cost and average cost in workplace business discussions. *Marginal cost* (along with marginal revenue) – not total or average cost – is key to determining a firm's profit-maximizing output level, how much a product should be upgraded (or downgraded), and even how many different products a firm produces.

There is a good reason for the scant attention to marginal cost: estimating a firm's marginal costs is not easy, especially for firms that produce several products. However, without a rough estimate of the structure of marginal cost, a firm can easily overproduce or underproduce, making less than maximum achievable profit. There is money to be made by incurring the cost of product development – a maxim that business students widely appreciate. There is also money to be made by incurring the costs of estimating a firm's marginal cost function and then thinking about production decisions with the cost structures of this chapter in mind. At the least, when managers are in discussions of whether to produce more, they should ask for an estimate of the marginal cost of producing more or less, with the derived figure stripped of any fixed costs.

Research in behavioral economics reveals that many people in business allow sunk costs to affect their production decisions. Why? The historical costs are fully evident in readily available accounting statements. Managers sometimes feel a commitment to cover costs incurred long ago, which means they make many pricing and production decisions with an eye toward (more than) recovering the "costs" reported on accounting statements. An important admonition of this chapter is that such costs are simply not relevant to current production and product development decisions. They can be lamented but should be ignored for current decisions; absolutely nothing can be done about them. The only relevant costs for today's production and product development decisions are those costs that can be incurred (or not). Retail stores may stay open into the wee hours of the morning for one reason: most of the costs on their accounting books are irrelevant to the decision of how long stores should stay open. The only relevant costs are the marginal costs – those that rise with the added hours. The relevant decision of when to close involves comparing the relevant marginal costs with the marginal revenues from adding hours.

There are two other key lessons to be learned from the analytics in this chapter. First, in competitive markets, in the short run, firms should produce in an output range where marginal cost is on the rise (the firm is experiencing diminishing returns). If a firm is experiencing increasing returns (and falling marginal costs), it should consider the prospect that it is producing too little. Second, managers who see their firms operating under market conditions approaching perfectly competitive markets and recognize the cost advantages of economies of scale should expand their operations. The only viable options are to expand or close. Competitors will expand their scales of operation, driving the market price of the good below the minimum production costs of those firms that hesitate to expand.

Firms can obviously improve their bottom lines by creating and developing better products than those available on the market. They can negotiate well, making sure to pay no more for their resources (including labor) than other producers. But also embedded in this chapter's analysis is the suggestion that firms can improve their profitability by simply getting their incentives right – or, more realistically, improving their incentives – so employees are motivated to work more cooperatively in the teams that handle complex tasks within modern businesses. Managers need to look diligently for incentive systems with perverse effects and those that can better overcome problems of free-riding, shirking, and Prisoner's Dilemmas – all of which are concerned with the thorny problem of getting people in large-group settings to seek cooperative solutions, despite the inclination to do otherwise.

Further Reading Online

Reading 9.1: Contestable markets

Reading 9.2: Wanted: entrepreneurs (Federal Reserve Bank of Minneapolis, link available on the online resources website www.cambridge.org/mckenzie4)

Reading 9.3: Political entrepreneurs are crowding out the entrepreneurs (RealClear Markets, link available on the online resources website www.cambridge .org/mckenzie4)

Recommended Videos Online

1   Production under perfect competition (Richard McKenzie, 31 minutes)

2   Contestable markets (Richard McKenzie, 8 minutes)

3   The first-mover advantage? (Richard McKenzie, 12 minutes)

4   *The Call of the Entrepreneur* (The Acton Institute, link available on the online resources website www.cambridge.org/mckenzie4)

The Bottom Line

The key takeaways from Chapter 9 are the following:

1   The demand curve facing a perfect competitor is horizontal (or perfectly elastic), meaning the firm is a price taker – that is, it cannot affect market price by changing its output.

2   All firms maximize profits by producing where marginal cost equals marginal revenue. For a perfect competitor, marginal revenue is equal to market price.

3   If price is below the perfect competitor's average total cost but above its average variable cost, the firm will not shut down in the short run. It is more than covering its fixed costs and therefore is minimizing its losses (compared to the losses if the firm ceased to operate). Such a firm may exit in the long run when it can get out from under its fixed costs.

4   In perfectly competitive markets, any economic profits will be reduced to zero in the long run, due to entry and the resulting increase in market supply and decrease in market price.

5   Perfect competition is an idealized market structure that can never be fully attained in the real world. Nonetheless, the model illuminates the influence of competition in the marketplace – just as the idealized models of the physical sciences help to illustrate the workings of the natural world. Physicists deal with the concept of gravity by talking about the acceleration of a falling body in a vacuum. Vacuums do not exist naturally in the world, but are useful as theoretical constructs to isolate and emphasize the directional power of gravitational pull. In a similar fashion, the theoretical construct of perfect competition helps to highlight the directional influence and consequences of competition in "the real world."

6   The model of perfect competition provides a benchmark for comparing the relative efficiency of real-world markets. The perfectly competitive model clarifies the rules of efficient production and suggests that free movement of resources is essential. Without this, new firms cannot move into profitable production lines, increase market supply, push prices down, and force other firms to minimize their production costs.

7   The prices firms pay for labor and other resources do not solely determine a firm's cost structures. Organizational structures have a large influence on production costs. Managers must pay attention to how they make use of teams as a means of tapping into the specialized knowledge of workers and increasing their incentives to do what they are hired to do.

8   Cost-effective teamwork can be in the interest of principals/owners and all team members, since teamwork can reduce shirking, lower the firm's cost structure, and increase the pay and job security of team members. The more competitive the product markets, the more important it is that managers organize teams and structure their pay in the most efficient way.

9   Research has not substantiated the so-called "first-mover advantage." (There are some cases in which first movers achieve and retain a dominant position in their markets, but don't count on it as a business investor.) Indeed, researchers have found market advantages for second and later movers.

Review Questions ▷▷

1   Draw the short-run AC and MC curves, plus the demand curve, for a perfect competitor. Identify the short-run production level for a profit-maximizing firm and the profits or losses. If losses, should the firm operate or shut down?

2   On your graph for question 1, label P_m as the minimum price the firm requires to continue short-run operations.

3   On your graph for question 1, darken the firm's MC curve above its intersection with the AVC curve. Explain why this portion of the MC curve is the firm's supply curve.

4   Why does a perfectly competitive firm seek to equate marginal cost with marginal revenue, rather than produce where average total cost is at a minimum?

5   If perfectly competitive firms are making a profit in the short run, what will happen to the industry's equilibrium price and quantity in the long run?

6   Suppose the market demand for a product rises. In the short run, how will a perfect competitor react to the higher market price? Draw a graph to illustrate your answer. What will happen to the market price in the long run? Why?

7   Suppose that you know nothing about price and cost in a particular competitive industry. How could you nevertheless determine whether the typical firm in the industry was making economic profits or losses?

8 Other than expecting market conditions to improve in the future (or anticipating other firms leaving in the long run), explain why firms might lose money but continue to operate in the short run.

9 Suppose a manager refuses to provide a fringe benefit that would lower the wages of their workers, but benefit them on balance. How has this manager prevented the firm's *AC* curves from being as low as possible?

10 When should a firm reduce or eliminate fringe benefits?

11 From our discussion of teams, what is applicable to your study teams at school? Does your university allow students to move among teams? Why or why not? How might the prospects of switching teams affect team performances? Should students be able to make monetary side payments to students to switch teams?

12 What have you seen with teams at work in terms of size and pay? What is effective? How might process and outcomes be improved?

10

Monopoly Power and Firm Pricing Decisions

If monopoly persists, monopoly will always sit at the helm of government … its bigness is an unwholesome inflation created by privileges and exemptions which it ought not to enjoy. If there are men in this country big enough to own the government of the United States, they are going to own it.

Woodrow Wilson

At the bottom of most arguments against the free market is a deep-seated concern about the distorting and corrupting influence of private-sector monopolies.[1] People who are suspicious of the free market fear that too many producers are unchecked by the forces of competition and hold considerable "monopoly power" (a term defined below) over market outcomes.[2] Conventional wisdom about government's antitrust efforts is that, unless it intervenes, these firms will routinely exploit this power for their own selfish benefit. The influential economist John Kenneth Galbraith expressed this sentiment well (Galbraith 1967, 6):

The initiative in deciding what is produced comes not from the sovereign consumer who, through the market, issues instructions that bend the productive mechanism to his or her ultimate will. Rather it comes from the great producing organization that reaches forward to control the markets that it is presumed to serve and, beyond, to bend the customers to its needs.

In this view, monopolies are common, inevitable, powerful, and long-lasting – and monopoly has little or no redeeming virtue. Accordingly, we will examine

---

[1] It is odd and telling that many of those concerned with private-sector monopolies have little or no concern about public-sector monopolies.

[2] As we'll cover in Chapter 12, most concerns about labor market outcomes are at least implicitly based on the assumption of significant "monopsony power": a firm's monopoly power over inputs – most notably, labor.

the dynamics of monopoly power and place its consequences in an accurate perspective of its mixed social blessings. In Chapter 11, we extend this model of monopoly power to two other market structures: monopolistic competition and oligopoly. And we consider the usefulness of antitrust laws and price regulations in controlling monopoly and stimulating (or simulating) competition.

Market models with some degree of monopoly power are especially relevant to business students in firms that should consider devising creative pricing strategies. A theme of this chapter and Chapter 11 is that, while firms can surely increase their profitability by producing better mousetraps, they may also have opportunities to increase their profitability through creative pricing, which does not necessarily carry the high product development costs of better mousetraps. However, in order to innovate through pricing strategies, the firm must be able to distinguish its mousetrap from all others in the minds of consumers. While competition has efficiency attributes for society, most business students will spend the bulk of their working hours trying to develop products that offer monopoly pricing power (for reasons initially discussed in Chapter 9).

In Part A, we develop conventional monopoly theory for three reasons. First, it has value in helping us understand markets where producers have impressive levels of monopoly power. Second, it gives insight into how people often *imagine* markets working. For example, in terms of public policy, much antitrust theory and enforcement is guided by this view. Third, we cover it to explain its weaknesses, including its omission of a key social blessing of monopoly power and how it can misguide antitrust enforcement.

In Part B, we develop a theory of monopoly pricing that allows for creative pricing strategies. And we lay out a variety of ways firms have been able to use the theory to develop real-world pricing strategies, allowing them to generate additional revenue through "price discrimination" among different groups of buyers.

Over the last three decades, economists have developed an explanation for a source of monopoly pricing power called "lock-in" – where consumers can be trapped (within limits) by producers who sell products (primarily network goods) that cannot be easily jettisoned by consumers without significant "switching costs." This affords their producers some monopoly power, because consumers will often prefer to accept some price increase rather than incur the switching costs. In Perspective 10, we cover the case of the QWERTY keyboard developed initially for typewriters and then computer keyboards. Supposedly, more efficient keyboard layouts have been developed over the past century or so – only to fail in the market, because people didn't want to incur the switching costs involved in learning the new keyboard. (This turns out to be a myth, but it's still a story worth exploring.)

Part A Theory and Public Policy Applications

The Origins of Monopoly Power

We have defined the competitive market as the process by which market rivals, each pursuing their own private interests, strive to outdo one another. This competitive process has many benefits. It enables producers to obtain information about what consumers and other producers are willing to do. It promotes higher production levels, lower prices, and a greater variety of goods and services than would be achieved otherwise.

Monopoly power is the conceptual opposite of competition. Monopoly power implies the ability of a firm to raise the market price of its good or service by reducing production and hence market supply. The demand curve of the competitive firm is horizontal (see Chapter 9); the firm is a "price taker," taking price as a given from the market. A firm with monopoly power faces a downward-sloping demand curve – with the elasticity of demand inversely related to the *extent* or *degree* of monopoly power. To maximize its profits (or minimize its losses), such a firm will search through the price–quantity combinations on its demand curve. As such, a firm with monopoly power is a *price searcher*. While monopoly power is attractive to the firm, a monopolized market is rougher on consumers and produces fewer social benefits than perfect competition.

Businesses vary considerably in the extent of their monopoly power – and it can change over time. The postal service and your local telephone company both *had* significant monopoly power, until the advent of overnight delivery, email, cell phones, internet telephony, and local Uber-type delivery services. They had few competitors, as entry into their markets was barred by law. Communication technology has rendered those barriers largely irrelevant. Their monopoly positions have also been compromised by package delivery companies (e.g., FedEx and UPS) and may soon be threatened by drone-based delivery services. Since the 1960s, IBM has had far less monopoly power in mainframe computing. Although IBM can expand or contract its sales to affect the price it charges for its computers and business services, it has been restrained by the *possibility* that other firms will enter its market and progressively constrained since the 1970s by the development of personal desktop computers, laptops, and smartphones. On a smaller scale, grocery stores face the same threat. They have competitors already and must be concerned about additional stores entering the market. Nevertheless, a grocery store still retains *some* power to restrict sales and raise its prices by virtue of its location or other features that appeal to some consumers.

How does a monopoly arise? To answer this question clearly, we must reflect once again on the basis for competition. Competition occurs when rivals can enter markets in which profits exist and production technology allows many firms to produce at low costs (economies of scale are not significant for any firm). In the extreme case of (idealized) perfect competition, there are no barriers to entry and competitors are numerous. Entrepreneurs are always on the lookout for opportunities to enter such markets in pursuit of profit. Individual competitors cannot raise their prices – for, if they do, rivals may move in, cut prices, and take away their customers. If a wheat farmer, for example, asks more than the market price, customers can buy from others at the market price. For this reason, perfect competitors are called *price takers*; they have no control over the price they charge.

So, the essential condition for competition is freedom of market entry. In *perfect* competition, entry is assumed to be completely *free* (costless). Conversely, the essential condition for monopoly power is the presence of barriers to entry. (Barriers to *exit* are also relevant, but a relatively small piece of the puzzle.) Those with monopoly power can manipulate price because sufficiently large barriers protect them from being undercut by rivals. Barriers can arise from several sources – some of them "natural" (or economic); and some of them "artificial" (from government activism):

- First, production may be best conducted on a large scale, requiring huge plants and large amounts of equipment. The enormous financial resources needed to take advantage of economies of scale can act as a barrier to entry, because the costs of production for a new entrant operating on a small scale would be too high to compete effectively with the dominant firm.
- Second, the monopolist may own the rights to a well-known brand name with a highly loyal group of customers. Beyond production, impressive resources may be necessary for establishing supply chains, advertising, distribution, etc. In this case, the barrier to entry is the costly process of getting customers to try a new product.
- Third, the monopolist may have sole (or dominant) ownership of a strategic resource, such as bauxite (from which aluminum is extracted) or an advantageous location.
- Fourth, the monopolist may have an exclusive franchise to sell a given product in a specific geographical area. Consider the government-granted franchise of the local electric utility or cable TV provider – and the market's contractual arrangements between franchisors and franchisees.
- Fifth, in labor markets, substantial investments in human capital are often required by law – or, at least, are quite useful for having credibility in a labor market. Such investments act as a barrier to entry into various professions. Government may artificially enhance these natural barriers with legal requirements – for example, mandatory occupational licensing.
- Sixth, the monopolist may have a patent or copyright on the product, which prevents other producers from duplicating it.

- Seventh, a firm might be able to develop a monopoly by keeping essential features of its product as a "trade secret." Coca-Cola has been able to retain some monopoly control over Coke for more than 100 years (well beyond the patent term), because its formula has been closely guarded by the company. It has refused to seek a patent on its secret formula, because the formula would be revealed in its patent application and the government would protect it from competition for only seventeen years. Of course, its monopoly power has still been limited, because other firms (e.g., Pepsi Cola) have sought to imitate the taste of Coke.
- Eighth, government officials often sell monopoly power to benefit themselves and interest groups (as described in Chapter 6). Universities typically have one vendor for food services. K-12 schools use one provider for graduation gowns and senior rings. Airports sell the ability to provide services inside. Local governments may contract with a monopoly provider of trash services. And so on. Related, government often restricts competition to benefit politically connected producers. Tariffs and quotas are particularly prevalent, but examples abound in domestic contexts as well.
- Ninth, government can subsidize certain producers, which makes it more difficult to compete against those receiving the taxpayer resources. Its own provision of K-12 education is a classic and important example. By contrast, vouchers (or "backpack funding") allow lower- and middle-income parents to select between various private and public schools. This promotes competition, efficiency, quality, and flexibility on the delivery of educational services, including some highly contentious social issues.
- Finally, as noted in Chapter 4 and as detailed in Perspective 10, firms can acquire monopoly power through network effects and high "switching costs" – a barrier to *exit* for consumers who are unable to move (easily) to similar products and are said to be "locked in."

The barriers to entry are costs that potential competitors must bear before they can compete. (Barriers to exit can prevent customers from leaving.) Such barriers may be "low," which means that monopoly power may be quite limited, but they can also be prohibitively high. The extent of the barriers to entry will permit those with monopoly power to raise their prices and sustain economic profits.

The Limits of Monopoly Power

A monopolist's market power is restricted in two important ways. First, the monopolist's control over the market is never complete. The consumer can still choose a *substitute*. For instance, until the late 1970s in most parts of the United States, only one firm was permitted to provide a local telephone service. Yet people could communicate in other ways. They could talk directly with one another; they could write letters or send telegrams; they could use their children as messengers. Obviously, none of these alternatives are *close* substitutes for a telephone, but people could also choose to use less of their incomes on telephone services and more on rugs, bicycles, or other goods and services. Demand curves for all goods are downward-sloping, reflecting the fact that not even a monopolist can force consumers to buy its product. As Friedrich Hayek has written (Hayek 1960, 136):

> If, for instance, I would very much like to be painted by a famous artist [one who has monopoly power] and if he refuses to paint me for less than a very high fee, it would clearly be absurd to say that I am coerced. The same is true of any other commodity or service that I can do without. So long as the services of a particular person are not crucial to my existence or the preservation of what I most value, the conditions he exacts for rendering these services cannot be called "coercion."

This is not to say that monopoly power is not harmful. If monopoly means that one firm has few if any rivals providing the same product, then monopoly does reduce consumer choice. It puts less pressure on firms to produce efficiently. In reducing production to increase prices, the firm will not allocate resources in a socially efficient manner. And if the barriers are caused by government intervention, the firm may expend resources to pursue monopoly power instead of production.

But monopoly power can also reflect beneficial considerations for consumers. A firm may gain monopoly power because it has built a better mousetrap or developed a good that was previously unavailable. In other words, a firm may be the only producer because it is the first producer – and no one has yet been able to figure out how to duplicate its product. Although monopolized, a new product results in an expansion of consumer choice. Furthermore, the monopoly may well be temporary, for other competitors are likely to break into the market eventually (if not quickly).

As Micklethwait and Wooldridge observed, when Henry Ford started his car company, he "was devoted to handcrafting toys for the super-rich," but it wasn't long before more than a million Americans were driving Model Ts. George Eastman bought his first (very difficult to use) camera in 1877 for $49.58 (which would be equal to about $500 in today's prices). By 1900, Eastman was selling Brownies for $1 under the slogan "You push the button and we do the rest" (Micklethwait and Wooldridge 2003, 77).

Of course, Kodak became a household brand that was a dominant player in cameras and film. It made a healthy return for its investors and provided substantial consumer surplus for its buyers – until digital photography emerged, along with miniaturized cameras that could be inserted in smartphones and tablet computers. Now, Kodak is a shadow of its former self, with few people knowing what it does in whatever market share it has left. Likewise, for years,

Polaroid had a patent monopoly on the instant-photograph market. Now, digital photography has eclipsed any remaining monopoly Polaroid had in instant pictures.

Ford Global Technologies has filed for a patent on technology that would impose consequences on customers who are delinquent on loan payments – from the sound system playing unpleasant noises to using self-driving technology that would return cars to the bank with the loan (Dawson 2023). Such a technological advance would allow lower prices on cars and lower interest rates on car loans, since the risk of selling cars would be reduced. In the short-term, Ford would earn monopoly profits until the technology could be emulated by others. But it's the at-least-temporary monopoly power that makes the innovation worth attempting.

The point here is that innovation resulted in large companies and products where there was monopoly power. But those companies "improved the living standards of ordinary people, putting the luxuries of the rich within reach of the man in the street" (Micklethwait and Wooldridge 2003, 77). Competition increased those living standards further, but this process often begins with monopoly or at least monopoly power.

Market conditions – the cost of production and the downward-sloping demand curve for the good – also restrict the monopolist's market power. If the monopolistic firm raises its price, it must be prepared to sell less. How much less depends on the available substitutes for consumers – again, the importance of demand elasticity. The monopolist must also consider the costs of expanding production and of trying to prevent competitors from entering the market.

In an open market, monopoly power is typically dissolved in the long run; with time, competitors can invade the monopolist's domain. The Reynolds International Pen Company had a patent monopoly on the first ballpoint pen that it introduced in 1945. Within two years, other pen companies had found ways to circumvent the patent and produce a similar product. The price of ballpoint pens fell from $12.50 (or about $208 in 2023 purchasing power) to the low prices we see today. Many other products that are competitively produced today – calculators, video games, cell phones, and cellophane tape, to name a few – were first sold by companies that enjoyed temporary monopolies.

When Apple introduced its highly successful iPhone in 2007, it had this segment of the cell phone market to itself and charged $600. (Even then, it could not meet market demand.) Apple sold millions of iPhones and made billions in profits. Its next-generation iPhone was introduced in mid-2008 with upgrades in software features, improved performance, and a price reduction of one-third. By the start of 2009, Blackberry and Samsung released iPhone clones; Apple responded by introducing a model that sold at Walmart for $99. This limit on monopoly power is crucial: in the long run, excessively high prices, restricted supply, and high profits give potential competitors a strong incentive to find ways to circumvent the monopolist's power and benefit consumers. At the same time, firms can retain pricing power through advancing their products faster than the competition. Apple has responded to entry of competitors in its markets by developing ever-more-creative and -powerful versions of its products – at the same time, creating an elusive "wow factor" that has given it a loyal and expanding fan base. Even in maintaining its monopoly power, competition (and its threat) has served to benefit consumers.

One of the more effective ways for a monopoly to retain its market power is to enlist the coercive power of government to prevent or limit competition. (We detailed how and why in Chapter 6.) This strategy has been used effectively for decades in the electric utilities industry, the cable television market, insurance industries, and the medical profession. One of the best examples is the distribution of alcoholic beverages at the State level. Many U.S. states require out-of-state alcoholic beverages to be distributed by in-state wholesale distributors. Moreover, the distributors must charge all retailers the same price. In Ohio, beer wholesalers are guaranteed a markup of 25 percent, while wine distributors are guaranteed a markup of 33 percent. The Wines & Spirits Wholesalers of America has supported such market restrictions on the grounds that "alcohol has to be treated as a special product because when it is misused it causes devastating social consequences" (Hirsch 2005).

But even the power of the State may not be enough to shield an industry from competition forever. Consumer tastes and the technology of production and delivery can change dramatically over the very long run. The railroad industry's market, which enjoyed governmental protection from price competition for almost a century, has been gradually eroded by the emergence of new competitors – principally, airlines, buses, and trucks. And the U.S. Postal Service's monopoly on first-class mail continues to be eroded by a host of package and overnight delivery firms, as well as by technological advance (fax machines, email, scanning technology, and cooperative work among far-flung team members on documents in the "Cloud").

Equating Marginal Cost with Marginal Revenue (Again)

Here, we present the conventional theory of pricing for a monopolist. As before, a firm will produce another unit of a good if the additional (marginal) revenue it brings is greater than the additional cost of its production – in other words, if it increases the firm's profits. The firm will therefore expand production to the point where marginal cost equals marginal revenue ($MC = MR$). This is a fundamental rule that all profit-maximizing firms follow; monopolies are no exception.

Suppose you are in the yo-yo business. You have a patent on edible yo-yos which come in three flavors – vanilla, chocolate, and strawberry. (We will assume there is a demand for these products!) If you were a price taker in a competitive market, marginal revenue would be constant and equal to price. But as a monopolist, your marginal revenue does not remain constant; instead, it decreases over the range of production since its price must be reduced to entice consumers to buy more.

Consider the demand schedule in columns (1) and (2) of Table 10.1. Price and quantity are inversely related, reflecting the assumption that a monopolist faces a downward-sloping demand curve. As the price falls from $10 to $6, the number sold rises from one to five. If the firm wishes to sell only one yo-yo, it can charge as much as $10. Total revenue at this level of production is then $10 (in column (3)). To sell two yo-yos, the monopolist must reduce the price for each to $9. Total revenue then rises to $18.

By multiplying columns (1) and (2), we can fill in the rest of column (3). As the price is lowered and the quantity sold rises, total revenue rises from $10 for one unit to $30 for five units. With each unit increase in quantity sold, total revenue does not rise by an equal amount. Instead, it rises in declining amounts – first by $10, then $8, $6, $4, and $2. These amounts are the marginal revenue from the sale of each unit (column (4)), which the monopolist must compare with the marginal cost of each unit. (As you can imagine, extending the table would result in marginal revenues below zero. Of course, a firm would never willingly choose these price–quantity combinations, but they might stumble into this unfortunate outcome.)

At an output level of one yo-yo, marginal revenue equals price, but at every other output, level marginal revenue is less than price. Because of the monopolist's downward-sloping demand curve, the second yo-yo cannot be sold unless the price of *both* units is reduced from $10 to $9. If we account for the $1 in revenue lost on the first yo-yo in order to sell the second, the net revenue from the second yo-yo is $8 (the selling price of $9 minus the $1 lost on the first

Table 10.1 The monopolist's declining marginal revenue

(1) Quantity of yo-yos sold	(2) Price of yo-yos ($)	(3) Total revenue ((1) × (2)) ($)	(4) Marginal revenue (change in (3)) ($)
0	11	0	—
1	10	10	10
2	9	18	8
3	8	24	6
4	7	28	4
5	6	30	2

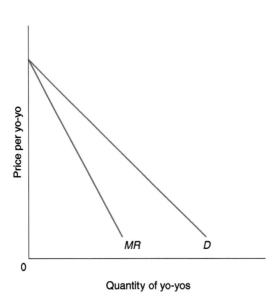

yo-yo). For the third yo-yo to be sold, the price on the first two must be reduced by another dollar each. The loss in revenue on them is therefore $2 – and so the marginal revenue for the third yo-yo is $6 (its $8 selling price less the $2 loss on the first two units).

Thus, the monopolist's *MR* curve (columns (1) and (4)) is derived directly from the market demand curve (columns (1) and (2)). Graphically, the *MR* curve lies below the demand curve – and its distance from the demand curve increases as the price falls, as in Figure 10.1.[3] (More details on the derivation of the *MR* curve can be found in the Online Math Appendix.)

Figure 10.2 adds the monopolist's *MC* curve to the demand and *MR* curves from Figure 10.1. Because a firm should always produce to the point where marginal cost equals marginal revenue, our yo-yo maker will produce Q_2 units. At this quantity, the *MC* and *MR* curves intersect. If the yo-yo maker produces fewer than Q_2 yo-yos – say, Q_1 – profits are lost unnecessarily. The marginal revenue acquired from selling unit Q_1 (MR_1) is greater than the marginal cost of producing it (MC_1). Furthermore, for all units between Q_1 and Q_2, marginal revenue exceeds marginal cost. In other words, by expanding production from Q_1 to Q_2, the monopolist can add more to total revenue than to total cost. Up to an output level of Q_2, the firm's profits will rise.

---

[3] Prove this to yourself by plotting the numbers in columns (1) and (2) versus the numbers in columns (1) and (4). In fact, for a linear demand curve, marginal revenue will always be twice as steep as demand. (Draw a linear demand curve that intersects both the vertical and horizontal axes. Then, draw the *MR* curve starting from the demand curve's point of intersection with the vertical axis to a point midway between the origin and the intersection of the demand curve with the horizontal axis.)

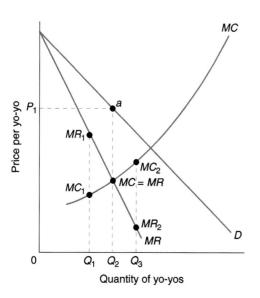

Figure 10.2 Equating marginal cost with marginal revenue
The monopolist will move toward production level Q_2, the level at which marginal cost equals marginal revenue. At production levels below Q_2, marginal revenue will exceed marginal cost; the monopolist will miss an opportunity to increase profits. At production levels greater than Q_2, marginal cost will exceed marginal revenue; the monopolist will lose money on the extra units.

Why does the monopolist produce no more than Q_2? Because the marginal cost of all additional units beyond Q_2 is greater than the marginal revenue they bring. Beyond Q_2 units, profits will fall. If it produces Q_3 yo-yos, for instance, the firm may still make a profit, but not the greatest profit possible. The marginal cost of unit Q_3 (MC_2) is greater than the marginal revenue received from its sale (MR_2). By producing Q_3 units, the monopolist adds more to cost than to revenues. The result is lower profits.

After the monopolistic firm selects the output at which to produce, the market price of the good is determined. In Figure 10.2, the price that can be charged for Q_2 yo-yos is P_1. (Remember, the demand curve indicates the price that can be charged for any given quantity.) Of all the possible price–quantity combinations on the demand curve, the monopolist will choose combination a.

How much profit will a monopolist make by producing at the point where marginal cost equals marginal revenue – and when producing under the cost curves developed in Chapter 8? The answer can be found by adding the ATC curve to the monopolist's demand and MR curves discussed in this chapter, as in Figure 10.3. As we have shown, the monopolist will produce at the point where the marginal cost and revenue curves intersect (Q_1) and will charge what the market will bear for the quantity (P_1). We also know that profit equals total revenue minus total cost ($profit = TR - TC$). Total revenue of $P_1 \times Q_1$ is the rectangular area bounded by OP_1aQ_1. Total cost is the average total cost times quantity ($ATC_1 \times Q_1$) or the rectangular area bounded by $OATC_1bQ_1$. Subtracting total cost from total revenue, we find that the monopolist's profit is equal to the shaded rectangular area ATC_1P_1ab. Mathematically, the expression $profit = P_1Q_1 - ATC_1Q_1$ can be

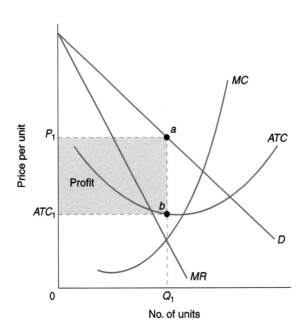

Figure 10.3 The monopolist's profits
The profit-maximizing monopoly will produce at the level defined by the intersection of the MC and MR curves: Q_1. It will charge a price of P_1 – as high as market demand will bear – for this quantity. Because the average total cost of producing Q_1 units is ATC_1, the firm's profit is the shaded area ATC_1P_1ab.

converted to the simpler form, $profit = Q_1(P_1 - ATC_1)$, where we see units sold and profit per unit.

As with perfectly competitive firms, monopolies are not guaranteed a profit. If market demand does not allow them to charge a price which covers the cost of production, they will lose money. Figure 10.4 depicts a monopoly with an economic loss, since it cannot meet its direct and opportunity costs. The monopolist's losses are obtained in the same way as that of profits, by subtracting total cost from total revenue. The maximum price the monopolist can charge for its profit-maximizing (or loss-minimizing) output level is P_1, which yields total revenues of $P_1 \times Q_1$ or OP_1bQ_1. But total cost is higher: $OATC_1aQ_1$. Thus, the monopolist's loss is equal to the shaded rectangular area bounded by P_1ATC_1ab.

In the long run (assuming market conditions are not expected to improve), when the monopolist can extricate itself from its fixed costs, it will exit the industry. Why doesn't it shut down in the short run? Because it follows the same rule as the perfect competitor. Both will continue to produce if price exceeds average variable cost – that is, as long as production will help to defray fixed costs. In Figure 10.4, average fixed cost is equal to the difference between average total cost (ATC_1) and average variable cost (AVC_1) – the vertical distance ac. Total fixed cost is therefore $ac \times Q_1$, or the area bounded by AVC_1ATC_1ac. Because the firm will suffer a greater loss if it shuts down (AVC_1ATC_1ac) than if it operates (P_1ATC_1ab), it chooses to operate and minimize its losses.

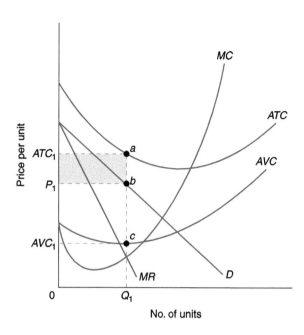

Figure 10.4 The monopolist's short-run losses
Not all monopolists make a profit. With a demand curve which lies below its *ATC* curve, this monopoly will minimize its short-run losses by continuing to produce at the point where marginal cost equals marginal revenue (Q_1 units). It will charge P_1, a price that covers its variable costs, and will sustain short-run losses equal to the shaded area P_1ATC_1ab.

The Comparative Inefficiency of Monopoly

Chapter 9 concluded that, in a perfectly competitive market, firms tend to produce at the intersection of the market supply and demand curves (point *b* in Figure 10.5). This is the most efficient production level, since the marginal benefit to the consumer of the last unit equals its marginal cost to the producer. No units whose marginal costs exceed their marginal benefits are produced – and all units are produced when marginal benefits exceed the marginal costs. All possible net benefits to the consumer have been extracted from production.

For each unit between Q_m and Q_c, the marginal benefits to the consumer (as illustrated by the market demand curve) are greater than the marginal costs of production. These are the net benefits that consumers would like to have, but are not delivered by the monopolistic firm, which is interested in maximizing profits rather than consumer well-being and social welfare. The resources not used in the production of the monopoly good will remain idle or be used in a less-valuable line of production. (Remember, the cost of doing anything is the value of the next-best alternative forgone.) In this sense, economists say that resources are *misallocated by monopoly*. Too few resources are used in the monopolistic industry – and too many elsewhere.

On balance, then, the inefficiency of monopoly (conventionally developed) consists of the benefits lost minus the cost not incurred when output is restricted. When compared to the outcome under perfect competition, monopoly price is too high and output is too low. In Figure 10.5, the gross benefit to consumers of the $Q_c - Q_m$ units is equal to the area under the demand curve (Q_mabQ_c). The

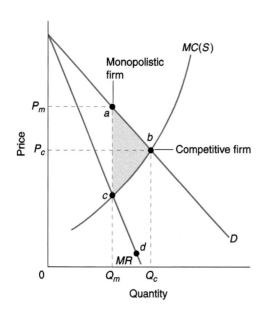

Figure 10.5 The comparative efficiency of monopoly and competition
Firms in a competitive market will tend to produce at point *b*, the intersection of the marginal cost and demand curves (with the marginal benefit given by the height of the demand curve). Monopolists will tend to produce at point *c*, the intersection of marginal cost and marginal revenue, charging the highest price the market will bear at this output level (P_m). In a competitive market, the price will tend to be lower (P_c) and the quantity produced greater (Q_c) than in a monopolistic market. The social inefficiency of monopoly is shown by the shaded triangular area *abc*, the amount by which the benefits of producing $Q_c - Q_m$ units (shown by the demand curve) exceed their marginal cost of production.

cost of those additional units is equal to the area under the *MC* curve ($Q_m cbQ_c$). Therefore, the net benefit of the units not produced is equal to the shaded triangular area *abc*. This area represents the inefficiency of monopoly – sometimes called the "deadweight loss" or "social welfare cost" of monopoly. To put it another way, area *abc* represents the gain in consumer welfare that could be achieved by dissolving the monopoly and expanding production from Q_m to Q_c. This area helps to explain why consumers prefer Q_c and producers prefer Q_m.

Figure 10.6(a) shows the additional benefits that consumers would receive from the $Q_c - Q_m$ units, the area under the demand curve, $Q_m abQ_c$. The additional money that consumers must pay producers for $Q_c - Q_m$ units, shown by the area under the *MR* curve, is a much smaller amount: only $Q_m cdQ_c$. That is, the additional benefits of $Q_c - Q_m$ units exceed the cost to consumers by the area *abdc*. Consumers would obviously gain from an increase in production.

Yet for virtually the same reason, the monopolistic firm is not interested in providing the $Q_c - Q_m$ units. It must incur an additional cost (the area $Q_m cbQ_c$ in Figure 10.6(b)), while it can expect to receive only $Q_m cdQ_c$ in additional revenues. The extra cost incurred by expanding production from Q_m to Q_c exceeds the additional revenue acquired by the shaded area *cbd*. Thus, an increase in production will reduce the monopolistic firm's profits (or increase its losses). Notice that consumers would gain more from an increase in production than the monopolist would lose; the shaded area in Figure 10.6(a) is larger than the shaded area in Figure 10.6(b). As in Figure 10.5, the difference is the triangular area *abc*.[4]

---

[4] If transaction costs were zero, or low enough, consumers would benefit by getting together and agreeing to "bribe" the monopolist to expand output to the competitive level. But the cost of this type of collective action is too high to make it an attractive option for consumers.

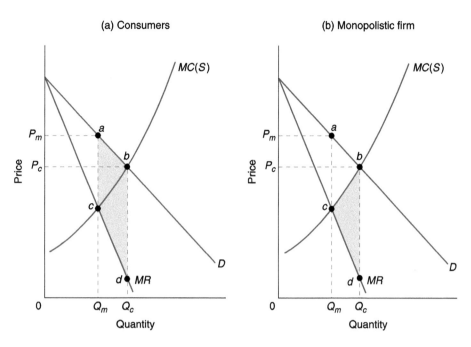

Figure 10.6 The costs and benefits of expanded production
If the monopolist expands production from Q_m to Q_c in panel (a), consumers will receive additional benefits equal to the area bounded by $Q_m abQ_c$. They will pay an additional amount equal to the area $Q_m cdQ_c$ for those benefits, leaving a net benefit equal to the shaded area *abdc*. To expand production, the monopoly must incur additional production costs equal to the area $Q_m cbQ_c$ in panel (b). It gains additional revenues equal to the area $Q_m cdQ_c$, leaving a net loss equal to the shaded area *cbd*. Thus, expanded production would help the consumer but hurt the monopolist.

Monopoly Profits

A key concern of a monopoly is the maximization of its *long-run* economic profits. In the short run, perfectly competitive firms and monopoly firms can make economic profits – for example, from a sudden rise in demand. In competitive markets, the economic profits will be eroded by new entrants in the long run, increasing market supply and pushing the price down to where price equals the marginal cost and minimum average total cost of each firm. The monopolist, on the other hand, can often earn profits into the long run, because barriers to entry protect its market position. Hence, the monopolist can continue to constrict production and market supply into the long run, keeping its price above competitive levels and above-normal profits into the future.

The persistence of monopoly profits into the long run is what makes monopoly ventures attractive for firms, but not for consumers, who pay higher-than-competitive prices. Accordingly, here we focus on a monopolist's long-run production decisions. (Recall that all costs are variable in the long run, which means there is no need to distinguish between fixed and variable costs).

To show monopoly profits in the long run, we could use the bowed long-run AC curve from Chapter 9 in a graph with the monopolist's demand and MR curves. However, in the interest of simplifying and clarifying our analysis, we will assume that marginal cost is constant at all production levels, which means the MC curve is horizontal. More important, the assumption of constant marginal cost means that the average cost of production is also constant and always equals the marginal cost of production. If the long-run marginal cost of producing units is $5 for each unit, then the long-run average cost of production is always $5 per unit. This means that the MC and AC curves are the same horizontal line in Figure 10.7 labeled $MC = AC$. (For those who are interested, we rely on the standard cost curves given in the Online Math Appendix.)

As in our previous discussion, the monopolist will produce where $MC = MR$, which means it will produce Q_m. The monopoly price will be P_m. (As a matter of reference, the competitive output and price levels will be Q_c and P_c, which means the inefficiency triangle abc in Figure 10.7 corresponds to the inefficiency triangle abc in Figure 10.5.) Monopoly revenues are price times quantity, $P_m \times Q_m$, or the area bounded by $OP_m aQ_m$. The total cost incurred to produce Q_m will be average cost times quantity, $AC \times Q_m$, or the area bounded by $OP_c cQ_m$. The monopoly (economic) profits will be total revenues minus total cost – the shaded area bounded by $P_c P_m ac$.

So long as the barriers to entry hold and demand stays where it is, the monopolist can expect to earn the identified monopoly profits. However, many things can change in the long run. Demand can dissipate because of a shift in consumer tastes. Microsoft might have a monopoly in the operating system market, but its market demand can be undermined because people start using their MP3/MP4

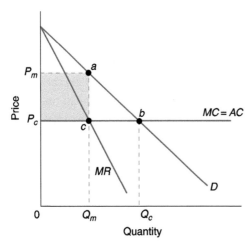

Figure 10.7 Monopoly profit maximization
Assuming constant marginal cost means that the long-run MC and AC curves are the same. A profit-maximizing monopolist will produce where $MC = MR$, restricting production (Q_m instead of Q_c) in order to charge a higher price (P_m instead of P_c). The monopolist will make an economic profit equal to the shaded area $P_c P_m ac$. The inefficiency of monopoly will equal the area bounded by abc – the difference between the area under the demand curve between Q_m and Q_c (consumer valuation of those units) and the area under the MC curve between Q_m and Q_c (what it would cost to produce those units).

players and cell phones for work instead of a personal computer. Technology is ever-moving – and technological developments can be spurred by the monopoly price and profits identified in Figure 10.7.

Price Discrimination

Charging a fixed price for a good (for example, P_m in Figure 10.7) can be profitable, but there can be more-profitable pricing strategies since buyers are willing to pay even higher prices for Q_m units than P_m. As a result, some businesses have become quite creative in developing means of charging different prices for different units sold.

A grocery store may advertise that it will sell one can of beans for $0.30, but two cans for $0.55. Is the store trying to give customers a break? Sometimes, this kind of pricing may simply mean that the cost of producing additional cans decreases as more are sold. At other times, it may indicate that customers' demand curves for beans are downward-sloping and the store can make more profits by offering a volume discount than by selling beans at a constant price. In other words, the store may be exploiting its *limited monopoly power* to enhance profits.

Consider Figure 10.8, where the demand curve represents your demand for beans and the supply curve represents the store's marginal cost of offering the beans for sale. If the store charges the same price for each can of beans, it will have to offer them at $0.25 each to induce you to buy two. Its total revenues will be $0.50. But, as Figure 10.8 shows, you are actually willing to pay more for the first can ($0.30). If the store offers one can for $0.30 and two cans for

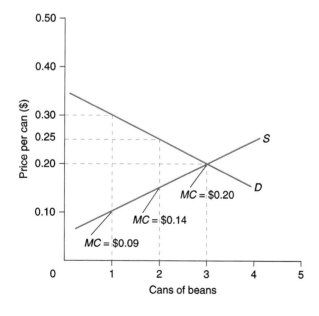

Figure 10.8 Price discrimination
By offering customers one can of beans for $0.30, two cans for $0.55, and three cans for $0.75, a grocery store collects more revenues than if it offers three cans for $0.20 each. In either case, the consumer buys three cans. But by making the special offer, the store earns $0.15 more in revenue per customer.

$0.55, you will still buy two cans, but its revenues from the sale will be $0.55 instead of $0.50. Similarly, to entice you to buy three cans, the store could offer to sell one for $0.30, two for $0.55, and three for $0.75 – and its profits will rise further. The deal does not change the marginal cost of providing each can, which is below the selling price for the first two units and equal to the selling price for the third. The marginal cost of the first can is $0.09; the second, $0.14; and the third, $0.20. The total cost of the three cans to the store is $0.43, regardless of how the cans are priced.[5]

A firm can discriminate in this way as long as its customers do not resell what they buy for a higher price – and as long as other firms are unable to move into the market and challenge its monopoly power by lowering the price. In the case of canned beans, resale is not practical. The person who buys three cans has little incentive to seek out someone who is willing to pay $0.25 instead of $0.20 for one can. The profit potential – $0.05 – is not great enough to bother. But suppose a car dealer has two identical automobiles (with a transferable warranty) carrying a book price of $25,000 each. If the dealer offered one car for $25,000 and a second car for $20,000, many people would be willing to buy the two cars for $45,000 and spend the time needed to find a buyer for one of them at $25,000. The $5000 gain they stand to make would compensate them for their time and effort in searching out a resale. (In Part B of this chapter, we will discuss creative ways in which firms can prevent consumers in the low-price market segment from reselling to consumers in the high-price market segment.)

> **Price discrimination** is the practice of varying the price of a given good or service according to how much is bought and who buys it, supposing that marginal costs do not differ across buyers.

Thus, **price discrimination** is much more frequently found in grocery stores than in car dealerships. But car dealers also discriminate with regard to price. The salesperson who in casual conversation asks a customer's age, income, place of work, etc., is actually trying to estimate the customer's demand curve, to get as high a price as possible. Similarly, many doctors and lawyers quietly adjust their fees to fit client incomes, using information they obtain from client questionnaires. Whatever the case, the important point is that the products or services involved are typically difficult, if not impossible, to resell.

Some monopolies' products are not difficult to resell, so they cannot engage in price discrimination. For example, copyright law gives the publishers of economics textbooks some monopoly power, but textbooks are easily resold – both through a network of used-book dealers and among students. Thus, although textbook

---

[5] The underlying principle is still the same. But with the numbers given, the firm is indifferent between selling two and three cans, since the profit is $0.32 either way. This is an artifact of our graph, since we're using a continuous line to depict discrete choices.

publishers can alter their sales by changing the price, they rarely engage in price discrimination. Nor do they encourage college bookstores to price-discriminate in their sales to students. The discounts that publishers give bookstores on large sales reflect the cost differences in handling large and small orders, not the downward-sloping demand curves of students or professors for books. The same can be said about a host of other products protected by patents and copyrights.

One final consideration: the price discrimination must be "socially acceptable" – either because consumers are completely unaware that prices differ, unaware of the potentially offensive particulars, or the strategy is known but the lower prices are charged to sympathetic parties. (Imagine how *higher* prices for veterans or the elderly would be perceived.)

Perfect Price Discrimination

The monopolist represented in Figure 10.9 can charge a different price for every unit sold. This firm has the power of **perfect price discrimination** ("perfect" from the standpoint of the *producer*, not the consumer). Under perfect price discrimination, the seller's *MR* curve is identical to the seller's demand curve (because the marginal revenue of each unit sold equals the

> **Perfect price discrimination** is the practice of selling each unit of a given good or service for the maximum possible price.

price of that unit). This is shown in Figure 10.9, where the firm's *MR* curve is not separate and distinct from its demand curve, as in Figure 10.6. Its demand curve is its *MR* curve. If the first unit can be sold for a price of $20, the marginal revenue from this unit is equal to the price, $20. If the next unit can be sold for $19.95, the marginal revenue is again the same as the price, since selling the second unit doesn't require lowering the price on the first unit, and so on. In short, the seller monetizes and extracts the *entire consumer surplus*.

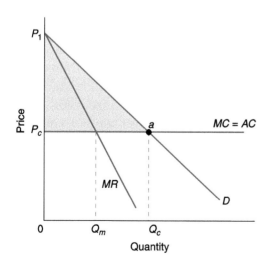

Figure 10.9 Perfect price discrimination
The perfect-price-discriminating monopolist will produce at the point where marginal cost and marginal revenue are equal (point a). Its output level, Q_c, is therefore the same as under perfect competition. But, because the monopolist charges as much as the market will bear for each unit, its profits (the shaded area $P_c P_1 a$) are higher than the competitive firm's. The inefficiency of monopoly is eliminated by perfect price discrimination, but the monopolist monetizes and pockets all of the consumer surplus.

As in Figure 10.7, the perfect-price-discriminating monopolist in Figure 10.9 equates marginal revenue with marginal cost. Equality occurs this time at point *a*, the intersection of the demand curve (now the monopolist's *MR* curve) with the *MC* curve. Thus, the perfect-price-discriminating monopolist achieves the same output level as the industry involved in perfect competition. In this sense, the perfect-price-discriminating firm is an efficient producer. As before, profit is found by subtracting total cost from total revenue. Total revenue here is the area under the demand curve up to the monopolist's output level – the area bounded by OP_1aQ_c. Total cost is the area bounded by OP_caQ_c (found by multiplying average total cost times quantity). Profit is therefore the shaded area above the *AC* curve and below the demand curve, bounded by P_cP_1a.

Through price discrimination, the monopolist increases profits (compare Figure 10.7 with Figure 10.9). Consumers also get more of what they want, although not at the price they want. In the strict economic sense, perfect price discrimination increases the efficiency of a monopolized industry. Consumers would be still better off if they could pay one constant price (P_c) for the quantity Q_c, as under perfect competition. This, however, is a choice the price-discriminating monopolist does not allow.

Discrimination by Market Segment

Charging a different price for each and every unit sold to each and every buyer is improbable, if not impossible. The best that most producers can do is to engage in **imperfect price discrimination** – that is, to charge a few different prices,

> **Imperfect price discrimination** is the practice of charging a few different prices for different consumption levels or different market segments (based on location, age, income, or some other identifiable characteristic) that is unrelated to cost differences.

as the grocery store that sold beans at different rates. The practice is somewhat common. Electric power and telephone companies engage in imperfect price discrimination when they charge different rates for different levels of use, measured in watts or minutes. Universities do the same when they charge more for the first course taken in a semester than for additional courses – or charge different tuition rates based on income. Drugstores price-discriminate when they give discounts to senior citizens and students. Theaters price-discriminate by charging children and senior citizens less than other adults. In those cases, discrimination is based on *market segment* – by age or other criteria. By treating different market segments as having distinctly different demand curves, the firm with monopoly power can charge different prices in each market. (More examples of creative price discrimination will be discussed in Part B of this chapter.)

Figure 10.10 shows how discrimination by market segment works. Two submarkets, each with its own demand curve, are represented in Figure 10.10(a)

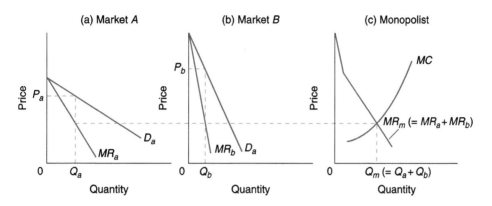

Figure 10.10 Imperfect price discrimination by market segments

The monopolist that cannot perfectly price-discriminate may elect to charge a few different prices by segmenting its market. To do so, it divides its market by income, location, or some other factor – and finds the demand and *MR* curves in each segment (panels (a) and (b)). Then it adds those *MR* curves horizontally to obtain its combined *MR* curve for all market segments (MR_m in panel (c)). By equating marginal revenue with marginal cost, it selects its output level, Q_m. Then it divides this quantity between the two market segments by equating the marginal cost of the last unit produced (panel (c)) with marginal revenue in each market (panels (a) and (b)). It sells Q_a in market *A* and Q_b in market *B*, charging different prices in each segment. Generally, the price will be higher in the market segment with the lower elastic demand (panel (b)).

and (b). Each also has its own *MR* curve. To price its product, the firm must first decide on its output level. To do so, it adds its two *MR* curves horizontally. The combined *MR* curve is shown in Figure 10.10(c). The firm must then equate this aggregate *MR* curve with its marginal cost of production, which is accomplished at the output level Q_m in Figure 10.10(c).

Finally, the firm must divide the resulting output (Q_m) between markets *A* and *B*. The division that maximizes the firm's profits is found by equating the marginal revenue in each market (in Figure 10.10(a) and (b)) with the marginal cost of the last unit produced (in Figure 10.10(c)). That is, the firm equates the marginal cost of producing the last unit of Q_m (Figure 10.10(c)) with the marginal revenue from the last unit sold in each market segment. Then, for maximum profits, output Q_m must be divided into Q_a for market *A* and Q_b for market *B*.

Why does this result in maximum profit? Suppose that MR_a were greater than MR_b. Then, by selling one more unit in market *A* and one fewer unit in market *B*, the firm could increase its revenues. Thus, the profit-maximizing firm can be expected to shift sales to market *A* from market *B* until the marginal revenue of the last unit sold in *A* exactly equals the marginal revenue of the last unit sold in *B*. And unless the common marginal revenue is equal to the marginal cost, the firm can increase its profit by adjusting output until it is.

Having established the output level for each market segment, the firm will charge whatever price each segment will bear. In market A, quantity Q_a will bring a price of P_a. In market B, quantity Q_b will bring a price of P_b. (Note that the price-discriminating monopolist charges a higher price in a market with the less elastic demand – market B.) To find total profit, add the revenue collected in each market segment (Figure 10.10(a) and (b)) and subtract the total variable cost of production (the area under the MC curve in Figure 10.10(c)) and the fixed cost.

Applications of Monopoly Theory

Economics is a fascinating course of study – in part, because it often leads to counterintuitive conclusions. This is the case with monopoly theory, as we can show by considering several policy issues.

Price Controls under Monopoly

Theory suggests that price controls *reducing* price can cause monopolistic firms to *increase* their output. Figure 10.11 shows the pricing and production of a monopolistic electric utility that is not engaged in price discrimination. Without price controls, the utility will produce Q_m kilowatts and sell them at P_m. If the government declares this price to be too high, it can force the firm to sell at a lower price – for example, P_1. At this price, the firm can sell as many as Q_1 kilowatts. With the price controlled at P_1, the firm's MR curve for Q_1 units becomes horizontal at P_1 – akin to the "price taker" of Chapter 9, which is fitting since the producer is "taking" the price as given by the government regulators. Every

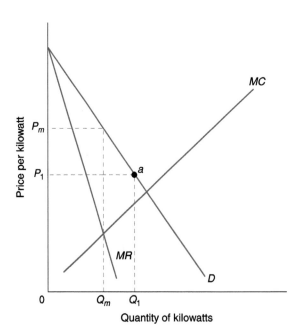

Figure 10.11 The effect of price controls on the monopolistic production decision

In an unregulated market, a monopolistic utility will produce Q_m kilowatts and sell them for P_m. However, if the firm's price is regulated at P_1, its MR curve is horizontal at P_1 (until Q_1, when it drops down discontinuously to the original MR). The firm will produce Q_1 – more than the amount it would normally produce.

time it sells an additional kilowatt, its total revenues rise by the amount of the price, since it doesn't have to lower the price on the previous kilowatts sold. If the government sets the price at the point where the demand curve and the *MC* curve intersect (as in Figure 10.11), then the profit-maximizing monopolist will increase output to the efficient level – where the value consumers place on another unit of output equals the marginal cost of production.

Taxing Monopoly Profits

Some people imagine that the economic profits of monopoly can be taxed with no loss in economic efficiency. By definition, economic profit represents a reward to the resources in a monopolized industry that is greater than is necessary to keep those resources employed where they are. It also represents *a transfer of income* from consumers to the owners of the monopoly. Therefore, a tax extracted solely from a monopoly's *economic* profits should not affect the distribution of resources and would fall exclusively on monopoly owners.

The reasoning behind this position is straightforward. In Figure 10.12, when marginal cost is MC_1, this monopoly produces Q_{m2}, charges P_{m1}, and makes an economic profit equal to the shaded area $P_cP_{m1}ac$. Because marginal cost and marginal revenue are equal at Q_{m2}, the firm is earning its maximum possible profit. Expansion or contraction of production will not increase its profit. Even if the government were to take away 25, 50, or 90 percent of its economic profit, the firm would not change its production plans or its price (90 percent of the *maximum* profit is more than 90 percent of a smaller profit). Nor would it raise prices to pass the profits tax on to consumers. The monopolist price-quantity combination, P_{m1} and Q_{m2}, leaves the monopolist with the largest after-tax profit – regardless of the tax rate.

There is a practical problem with this, however. The economic profit shown in Figure 10.12 is not the same as the firm's book (or accounting) profit. Book

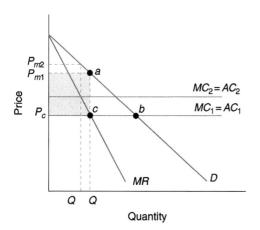

Figure 10.12 Taxing monopoly profits
Theoretically, a tax on the *economic* profit of monopoly will not be passed on to the consumer. But taxes are levied on book profit, not economic profit. As a result, a tax shifts the *MC* curve up, from MC_1 to MC_2, further raising the price to the consumer and lowering the production level.

profit exceeds economic profit by the sum of the owner's opportunity cost and risk cost. For practical reasons, government must impose its tax on book profit, not economic profit. As a result, the tax falls partly on the costs of doing business, shifting the firm's MC curve upward, from MC_1 to MC_2 in Figure 10.12. The monopolist, in turn, will reduce the quantity produced from Q_{m2} to Q_{m1}, and raise the price from P_{m1} to P_{m2}. Thus, part of the government tax on profits is passed along to consumers as a price increase. Consumers are doubly penalized – first through the monopoly price, which exceeds the competitive price, and second through the surcharge, $P_{m2} - P_{m1}$, added by the profits tax.

Monopolies in "Goods" and "Bads"

Because monopolies restrict output, raise prices, and misallocate resources, students and policy-makers tend to view them as market failures that should be corrected by antitrust action. If a monopolized product or service is an economic good – something that gives consumers positive utility – restricted sales will necessarily mean a loss in welfare.

Large portions of the citizenry, however, may view some products and services as "bads." Drugs, prostitution, contract murder, and pornography may be economic goods to their buyers, but represent negative utility to others in the community. Thus, monopolies in the production of such goods may be socially desirable. If a drug monopoly attempted to increase its profits by holding the supply of drugs below competitive levels, most citizens would probably consider themselves better off.

But the question is not quite this simple. A heroin monopoly may restrict the sale of heroin in a given market. Yet, because the demand for heroin is highly inelastic (given drug addiction), higher prices may only increase buyer expenditures, raising the number of crimes they must commit to support their habit. Paradoxically, then, reducing heroin supplies (for example, by drug enforcement agents wiping out some producers in Colombia) could lead addicts to commit more burglaries, muggings, and bank hold-ups. Likewise, the existence of above-normal profits will attract more entrepreneurs who will likely use extra-legal means to increase market share (e.g., Mafia or gang wars). If they are eliminated through legal or extra-legal methods, still other entrepreneurs will find it quite tempting to replace them.

Of course, drugs and other underground services are not subject to antitrust action or price regulation since they are illegal! But the analogy may also be applied to legal goods and services, such as liquor. Given the negative consequences of drinking, many people consider alcoholic beverages an economic bad. As such, a state-run liquor monopoly could provide a social service. By reducing liquor sales through monopoly pricing or higher excise taxes, government would reduce drunk driving, limiting the external costs associated with drinking.

The Total Cost of Monopoly Power

This chapter closes the loop on our earlier discussions of "market struggles." (We have already detailed "public goods," externalities, and information problems in the text – and referred you to Online Chapter 4 about macroeconomics and the business cycle.) Here, monopoly power can cause inefficiencies and inequities through restricted production, which results in higher prices for consumers and deadweight losses for society. But the social costs are actually greater than is shown by the supply and demand model in Figure 10.5.

The Costs of Entry Barriers

Many firms erect barriers to entry in their markets to pursue the benefits of monopoly power. The resources invested in building barriers are diverted from the production of other goods, which could benefit consumers and society. The total social cost of monopoly also includes the time and effort that the Antitrust Division of the Department of Justice, the Federal Trade Commission (FTC), state attorneys-general, and various harmed private parties devote to thwarting attempts to gain monopoly power and to breaking it up when it is acquired.

Monopoly Inefficiency from "Rent-Seeking"

As we discussed in Chapter 6, the actual economic inefficiency from monopoly can be greater when we consider how monopolies can be created – and monopoly power can be extended – through the political process. If there are monopoly profits ("rents") to be garnered from market-entry restrictions or government subsidies, political entrepreneurs can be expected to compete for the rents through lobbying, campaign contributions, and outright bribes. Rent seekers should assess their efforts as investments, aiming for rates of return that are no less than their investments on other business ventures.

In the process of seeking rents through government protections and subsidies, the rent seekers can *collectively* devote more resources to rent-seeking than the expected monopoly profit is worth. In such cases, the inefficiency of monopoly is greater than the inefficiency triangle identified in Figure 10.5. At the extreme, the net welfare loss from monopoly (or a subsidy) can include the deadweight loss triangle and the profit rectangle (Tullock 1967). Such lobbying expenditures can soak up real resources, which would result in lost production of other goods.

The Redistributional Effects of Monopoly

Another, more subtle, social cost of monopoly is its *redistributional effect*. Because of monopoly power, consumers pay higher prices than under perfect competition (P_m instead of P_c in Figure 10.5). The real purchasing power of consumer incomes is thus decreased, while the incomes of monopoly owners go up. To the extent that monopoly increases the price of a good to consumers and profits for producers, then it will often redistribute income from lower-income consumers to higher-income entrepreneurs. Many consider this redistributional effect inequitable and socially undesirable.

In addition, when we measure the inefficiency of monopoly by the triangular area *abc* in Figure 10.5, we are assuming that the redistribution of income from consumers to monopoly owners does not affect demand for all other goods. This may be a reasonable assumption if the monopolist is a maker of musical toothpicks, but is less reasonable for more-consequential monopolies, such as postal and electric power services. Those firms, which are a significant part of the entire economy, can shift the demand for many products, causing further misallocation of resources.

Monopoly Effects on Cost-Saving Incentives

Our analysis has assumed that a monopoly will seek to minimize its cost structure, just as perfect competitors do. This may not be a realistic assumption because the monopolist does not face as much competitive pressure. In addition, principal–agent problems (and added costs) can increase when a market is totally controlled by one producer instead of divided among many producers. In a larger firm, as we saw in Chapter 8, all agents can have less incentive to work diligently because monitoring can become more difficult (costly). And, as we'll develop in Chapter 12, labor unions are much more likely to form in the profitable soil of monopoly power within the private and public sector. If a monopoly relaxes its attentiveness to costs, the result can be inefficient employment of resources over and above the triangular deadweight loss area.

Durable Goods Monopoly

If prohibitive barriers to entry are in place, can a monopolist always charge the monopoly price indicated? Ronald Coase wrote a famous article in which he pointed out that even a monopolistic producer of a durable good would charge a competitive price for its product (Coase 1972).

Why? Because no sane person would buy all or any portion of the durable good at a price above the competitive level. Coase used the example of a monopoly owner of a plot of land. If the owner tried to sell the land all at one time, he would have to lower the price on each parcel until all the land was bought – where the downward-sloping demand for land crossed the fixed vertical supply of land – which means that the owner would have to charge the competitive price (where the demand for the land and the supply of the land come together).

You might think that the sole/monopoly owner of land would be able to restrict sales and get more than the competitive price. However, buyers would reason that the monopoly owner would eventually want to sell the remaining land, but that land could be sold only at less than the price the owner is trying to charge for the first few parcels. Buyers would rationally wait to buy until the price came down, which means that the owner would sell nothing at the monopoly price and would be able to sell the land only at the competitive price.

The analysis works out this way only because the land is *durable*. Monopolies can charge monopoly prices for nondurable goods because they have control over production. Thus, one way a monopoly can elevate its price above the competitive level is to make the product less durable, needing sooner replacement. This may explain why many software producers are constantly bringing out new, updated, and upgraded versions of their programs – to make their programs less than durable in the minds of consumers.

Still, computer programs must remain "durable" to some degree and for some time, which ultimately imposes a competitive check on dominant software producers – for example, Microsoft. The Justice Department seems to believe that Microsoft doesn't have competitors. But one of Microsoft's biggest competitors is Microsoft itself. Any new version of Windows must compete head-to-head with the existing stock of old versions, which consumers can continue using at zero price. This very low price on old versions of Windows imposes a check on the prices that Microsoft can charge on any new version. Microsoft faced a major challenge from its own Windows XP when the company introduced Windows Vista in late 2006 to highly critical reviews (primarily for the new operating system's sluggishness), which encouraged consumers and personal computer manufacturers to stay with Windows XP. Similarly, when Microsoft's Windows 10 appeared, it faced stiff competition from all other versions of Windows installed on people's personal computers. We cover the Microsoft monopoly and antitrust case in some depth in Online Reading 10.1 for this chapter, which is drawn from a book by one of the authors (McKenzie 2000).

Firms with monopoly power in a durable good face the problem of yielding to the temptation to attract more buyers. To overcome the desire (and impatience) to achieve market share, a firm can negotiate contracts with buyers that include "most-favored-customer clauses." Such clauses would require the seller to extend future price concessions to past buyers. The customer signing the contract can reason that other customers will be less likely to get a cost advantage by waiting to buy. So, the most-favored-customer clause raises the cost of price concessions to the seller. Hence, consumers can be expected to be more willing to buy at the higher price currently being charged.

The monopoly seller also can rent (or lease) the good for short periods of time. If the rent is lowered to future customers, then the lower rent will soon be extended to other customers renewing their rental contracts, increasing the cost of the price/rent concession and increasing buyer confidence that the rent will not be lowered to others.

Monopoly in Government and Inside Firms

It is easy to think of monopolies in the production of final goods and services in the private sector. But monopoly theory can also be used to explore the organization of governments and departments within firms. Indeed, the monopoly model might be best applied to these entities because governments are often the sole-source suppliers of goods and services to the public – as departments are the sole-source suppliers of services within their firms. In the private sector, competition among producers keeps prices down and productivity up. A producer who is one among many knows that any independent attempt to raise prices or lower quality will fail. Customers will switch to other products or buy from other producers – and sales will fall sharply. To avoid being undersold, the individual producer must strive continually to keep its production cost as low as (or lower than) that of other producers striving to do the same. Only a producer who has no competition – that is, a monopolist – can hope to raise the price of a product without fear of losing profits.

These points concerning the production and pricing decisions of monopolies apply to the public sector as well. As we discussed in Chapter 6, the framers of the Constitution understood this as they set up our national government, establishing a system of *competing* state governments loosely joined in a federation. Under this system, the power of local governments is somewhat checked by the ability to vote and to move elsewhere – in the face of high taxes, low-quality services, or a mix of services undesirable to a citizen. Unfortunately, the shift of power to the federal government since the 1930s represents an increase in monopoly power for government at all levels, with citizens less able to respond.

When firms create departments to provide their accounting or legal services and do not look outside the firm for alternative sources of supply, they have effectively created internal departmental monopolies, handing sole-source monopoly status to the department. Firms should at least consider the prospects that their own internal departments will act like monopolies. That is, internal departments will restrict their outputs in order to raise their "prices" or reduce quantity (or quality) for whatever services (or inputs) the departments provide. The higher "prices" can show up in departmental budgets that are greater than necessary. Remember the principal–agent problem is potentially everywhere present. Departments can thus siphon off economic profits that would otherwise go to the owners. The problem can be especially acute if managers do not compare the prospective costs of internal departments with those of obtaining the same services (or inputs) from outside suppliers. Consequently, to contain their costs, managers are wise to let internal departments understand that their costs of delivery are regularly compared with those from outside suppliers. Of course, the competitive threat to internal suppliers (departments) is enhanced when top managers actually outsource a service or input on occasion. Internal departments may then seek to contain their costs, recognizing that they, too, can be replaced.

PERSPECTIVE 10
The QWERTY Keyboard: a Case of "Lock-in"?

The "lock-in" theory suggests that markets are "path-dependent," evolving based on how the initial product was developed. It has gained wide support among academics and policy-makers, partially because economists and historians have found two concrete examples of the supposed problems with path dependency and lock-ins. The classic, widely cited, example is the QWERTY keyboard, which gets its name from the first six letters on the top row of the alphabet keys.

According to economic historian Paul David (1985), the QWERTY arrangement was first developed in the 1860s for the typewriter because it minimized the prospect for the keys jamming ("locking up") as their arms moved toward the paper. The original keyboard was supposedly adopted by one typewriter manufacturer after another – not because it was potentially the most productive arrangement of keys, but because it was established as "the standard." Manufacturers became further "locked-in" to the QWERTY keyboard when touch-typing was developed in the 1880s and then widely taught thereafter. David writes, "The occurrence of this 'lock-in' as early as the mid-1890s does appear to have owed something also to the high costs of software 'conversion' and the resulting *quasi-irreversibility of investments* in specific touch-typing skills" (David 1985, 335–336, emphasis in the original). As a result, "competition in the absence of perfect future markets drove the industry permanently into standardization *on the wrong system* – where decentralized decision-making subsequently has sufficed to hold it" (David 1985, 336, emphasis in the original).

August Dvorak and W. L. Dealey developed the Dvorak (or DSK) keyboard in 1932. David claimed (what is now known to be a myth) that the Dvorak "long held most of the world's records for speed typing" (David 1985, 332). Moreover, experiments by the U.S. Navy purportedly showed that the greater productivity from the Dvorak keyboard could more than cover the cost of the required retraining (David 1985, 332).

However, the Dvorak keyboard has never gained a toehold (or should it be "fingerhold"?) in the keyboard market. Why? The advocates of lock-ins argue that there are high switching costs for typists who are used to the QWERTY keyboard and would have to learn another key arrangement. Typewriter manufacturers have never switched to Dvorak because it did not make good business sense, given that they needed to appeal to existing typists. Computer keyboard manufacturers adopted the QWERTY key arrangement because their potential customers were not likely to buy keyboards with the new key arrangement despite its supposed superiority. The authors of the QWERTY story have imagined that "there are many more QWERTY worlds [in which an inferior standard is adopted by historical accident] lying out there in the past, on the very edges of the modern economic analyst's tidy universe; worlds we do not yet fully perceive or understand, but whose influence, like that of dark stars, extends nonetheless to shape the visible orbits of our contemporary economic affairs" (David 1985, 336).

The implication for the Justice Department's antitrust case against Microsoft is obvious. If the QWERTY story is true, then it is plausible that the Windows operating systems might be one of those "dark stars" influencing the visible world of tens of millions of computer users, even though there might be a superior operating system waiting in the wings to be adopted. But any superior system doesn't have a chance of making it in the market because each Windows user does not, by herself, have the requisite incentive to make the switch. Unless large numbers of people make the switch more or less together, then any new user may have a technically superior system but with few applications written for it.

Fortunately for consumers – and unfortunately for the Justice Department's case, which is built partially on the theory of path dependency – the QWERTY story is merely a legend that has taken on a life of its own but is not grounded in the facts of keyboard history. Economists Stan Liebowitz and Stephen Margolis did what a lot of QWERTY storytellers should have done long ago: They went back and researched the history of keyboards and found that much of the evidence on the supposed superiority of the Dvorak keyboard was from Dvorak's own poorly designed evaluations. Even then, Dvorak's own "evidence was mixed as to whether students, as they progress, retain an advantage when using the Dvorak keyboard because the differences seem to diminish as typing speed increases" (Liebowitz and Margolis 1999, II-30). The claimed benefits from the Navy study are similarly disputable, and other studies found substantial retraining costs, leading Liebowitz and Margolis to conclude that "the claims for the superiority of the Dvorak keyboard are suspect" (Liebowitz and Margolis 1999, II-45).

Even if it were proven that the Dvorak keyboard is superior to the QWERTY keyboard, the future gains from making the switch (in present discounted value terms) must be greater than the current costs incurred before it can be said that the "wrong" keyboard continued in use. If the cost of switching were greater than the gains to be obtained from the switch, switching would constitute a net societal loss (as well as a loss for employers and/or typists). Liebowitz and Margolis argue that David made provocative claims but never proved his point.

The Liebowitz–Margolis finding is quite plausible. If a keyboard were substantially more efficient than the established keyboard, it would be hard to see why the new keyboard wouldn't be adopted. Granted, some individual typists might be resistant to making the switch without some outside help. But if the keyboard were substantially superior, then it follows that the manufacturer should have an ample incentive to cover some of the typists' switching costs – through, perhaps, the provision of retraining courses. Companies that hire large numbers of typists or computer users also would have an ample incentive to buy the new keyboard.

Companies could pro-rate the retraining costs over many employees from whom they could garner substantial productivity improvements. Their investment in retraining could be expected to have an immediate upward impact on their company's stock price, given that observant investors would expect the productivity increase to improve the company's long-term profit stream.[6]

Markets for a variety of goods and services have switching costs that new entrants must overcome – a barrier to exit for consumers as they consider (prospective) suppliers. New hamburger restaurants must overcome customer inertia caused by the new restaurant's lack of reputation for good food, clean restrooms, and the small number of convenient locations when getting started. Banks that wish to operate online have the problem of overcoming people's resistance to doing their banking on a computer. But businesses have been creative in finding new ways to cover switching costs. New restaurants will often cut their prices below cost or give out coupons with the same effect. A variety of businesses have offered cash payments or discounts for each online transaction made. In the late 1990s, Chase Bank advertised that it would pay online customers $25 for each of the first five online transactions they made. If there are efficiency improvements with another product that lead to greater profits for new firms, "network externalities" may be "external" to buyers, but entrepreneurial firms can "internalize" them. Such firms can have ample motivation to make it easy for consumers to switch when a better product is available.

The important lesson to draw from the Perspective is this: When consumers are said to be "locked-in" to a particular product, it is usually the case that their "switching costs" are unusually high. But rarely are switching costs so prohibitively high that no amount of gains from switching products can cause consumers to switch. The QWERTY keyboard is supposed be an unchallengeable example in which consumers and manufacturers have been locked-in since typewriters were invented. But this turns out to be a far more questionable claim than originally thought.[7]

---

[6] There is a similar legend about how the VHS format for videocassette tapes and recorders came to dominate the Betamax format, which was supposedly the markedly superior format. The Betamax format may be technically superior to the VHS format (we are unwilling to judge). But the VHS format has always had one big advantage over Betamax: an entire movie could be recorded on a VHS tape, which was not possible on the Betamax. VHS became the adopted format because it better met the needs of the growing home movie rental and sales business (Liebowitz and Margolis 1995).

[7] The width between railroad tracks/gauges is another classic example. But again, even if they're not ideal, the relevant questions are about the net gains and the replacement costs. Goldberg (2022) notes that habits, convention, traditions, and customs are personal and cultural versions of the same principles. There are times to replace each, but not without an accurate assessment of the costs and benefits: "A little respect and humility for the cultural costs – replacement costs, sunk costs, etc. – of treating society like an Etch A Sketch is not merely prudent and not merely moral, but rational."

Part B Organizational Economics and Management

Profits from Creative Pricing

For a price searcher to be successful, it must choose a "good" price (and, ideally, the "right" price) given the demand. But choosing the "right" price is easier said than done. For example, managers can never be completely sure about the demand for their company's product. A company's demand is not given from on high, but is influenced by good management decisions, such as improving product quality, which may increase product credibility, building a reputation for honesty and fair dealing. Other factors also affect demand, many of which are beyond their abilities to control or predict. There are statistical techniques for estimating product demand (a discussion which goes beyond the scope of this book) that can help managers move from *mere* guesses to *educated* guesses. But firms will always have to make guesses about the demands for their products – how much they can sell at different quantities and prices.

Beyond this, there may be opportunities for creative pricing. And such creativity can be profitable. Throughout this book, we have discussed how firms compete on many margins. Certainly, better products at lower prices are a long-run consequence of firms struggling against each other for more consumer dollars. But here, we concentrate on how managers can increase firm profitability through more creative pricing strategies. Managers can often do as much or more for their firms (and their careers) by coming up with better pricing approaches than by coming up with better products. And, as with everything else in business, it's helpful if managers have incentives to be creative in their pricing strategies.

Price Discrimination in Practice

Real-world managers are not limited to charging only one price for a product. For example, several prices are charged for a coach seat (or a first-class seat) on most flights. Passengers who book their flights weeks in advance usually pay less (often several hundred dollars less) than those who book just days before their departure. By charging different prices for the same product, firms can earn higher profits than are possible with only one price.

There is a joke based on the pricing creativity of optometrists. When a customer inquires about the price of a pair of glasses, the optometrist answers, "Seventy-five dollars," and then pays close attention to the customer's expression. If he doesn't cringe, the optometrist quickly adds, "for the lenses." If the customer still doesn't cringe, the optometrist says, "for each one" (Friedman 1996, 134). Beyond the humor, prices are often puzzles – and the price discrimination theory described in Part A of this chapter can be used to unravel them.[8]

Hardback and Paperback Books

There are better (and less devious) ways of charging different prices than the above joke may suggest. Book publishers cannot differentiate between every potential buyer of a book and charge each a different price. But they can separate the market into two broad categories of buyers – those who are most impatient to read the latest novel by J. K. Rowling and those who want to read it but do not mind waiting a while. If publishers can separate (or *segment*) these groups, they can charge a different price to each group. But how so?

One method is to sell hardback and paperback (and now ebook) editions of the same book. Hardback books are issued first and are sold at a significantly higher price than the paperback edition ("significantly" meaning higher than the modest cost difference in producing a hardback and a paperback edition) that will not be available until months later. In this way, the seller charges those customers who are less sensitive to price (who have an *inelastic* demand) a higher price than those who are sensitive to price (who have an *elastic* demand). There is no problem with arbitrage in this case, because those who pay the low price do so long after the high-price customers have made their purchases.

Price Discrimination through Time

Sellers don't always have to package their products differently to distinguish between buyers who have inelastic demands and those who have elastic demands. Just after new electronic gadgets are introduced, their prices can be quite high – only to fall later. Many chalk up the falling prices to reductions in production costs, which may be true. However, we suggest an additional explanation: the sellers are using *time* to segment their markets, charging those who are eager to get the new models a higher price and charging those who are less eager (as evidenced by their willingness to wait) a lower price.

After-Christmas Sales

Department stores almost always have storewide sales after Christmas. Commonly, the explanation for after-Christmas sales is that stores want to get rid of excess inventories. There is a measure of truth to this explanation; stores cannot always judge correctly what will sell in December. However, it is also clear that shoppers have more inelastic demands before Christmas than they have after Christmas. Hence, the stores are often doing nothing more than segmenting their markets.

---

[8] One of the authors has published extended explanations of many such pricing puzzles in his book *Why Popcorn Costs So Much at the Movies and Other Pricing Puzzles* (McKenzie 2008).

They *plan* to hold after-Christmas sales and order accordingly. They are not losing money with the sales. They are making more money because they can charge different prices in the two time periods, attracting customers they otherwise would have lost without lowering the price for consumers who are less price-sensitive.

Coupons

Grocery stores and their suppliers have found a creative way of getting customers to reveal their sensitivity to price, which allows those who are less price-sensitive to be charged more than those who are more price-sensitive. In newspapers, the mail, and along with some of your receipts, there are coupons that allow you to save on a host of products. No coupons, no savings.

Those who go to the trouble of sorting the coupons and carrying them to the store are revealing themselves to be relatively price-sensitive. When you fail to present coupons at the checkout line, you are telling the cashier that you are not especially sensitive to price – that your demand is relatively inelastic. The cashier responds by charging you more for the same products than he charged the coupon-laden customer ahead of you. The problem of arbitrage is averted since few people are tempted by the opportunity to buy a bottle of shampoo for 50 cents off and then resell it for 25 cents more to someone in the parking lot who doesn't have a coupon. The cost of creating the secondary market for something as cheap as shampoo is surely greater than the price differential, especially when few units can be bought at the favorable price and sold at a higher price.

Theater Pricing

Sometimes a firm can profit by charging different prices to different customers without appearing to do so. This can be accomplished by putting the same price on two products that are consumed together by some customers but not by others. Consider the owner of a theater who realizes that some customers are willing to pay more to go to the movies than others. Obviously, the owner would like to charge these customers more. But the owner has no way to determine the price-insensitive customers when they pay for their tickets. So how does the manager charge the price-insensitive customers more without losing the remaining customers?

We have all observed this, but probably didn't think of it as an example of price discrimination. Assume the theater owner believes that customers who are willing to pay the most to watch a movie are generally the ones who most enjoy snacking while watching. If this assumption is correct (and we will argue in a moment that it probably is), the theater owner can take advantage of the inelastic demand of the enthusiastic movie watchers by charging a moderate price for the tickets to the movie and high prices for the snacks sold in the theater lobby. By keeping the ticket prices moderate, the customers with a high demand elasticity for the movie will still buy a ticket because they are not going to do much snacking anyway. Although the low-elasticity demanders will surely complain about the high prices on all the snacks they eat, they still consider the total cost of their movie experience acceptable, because they were willing to pay more for their ticket than they were charged.

If it is not generally true that those who are willing to pay the most to watch a movie also enjoy snacking the most, then it is unlikely that we would observe such high prices for snacks at the movies.[9] For example, assume that the opposite is true: those who are not willing to pay much to watch a movie are the ones who enjoy snacking the most when watching the movie. If this is the case, the theater owner would find that charging moderate prices for the tickets and high prices for the snacks was not a profitable strategy. Because the avid movie watchers are not snacking much, they would be willing to pay more than the moderate price to get into the theater. And because the other customers care more about snacking than seeing the movie, they would see little advantage in paying the moderate price for the movie when the snacks are so expensive. In this case, the most profitable pricing strategy would be high ticket prices and low snack prices. The enthusiastic movie watchers would still come despite the high ticket price. And the snackers would now be willing to pay the high ticket prices for the opportunity to eat lots of cheap snacks.[10] The fact that we do not see such pricing in theaters suggests that, at least for most consumers, our assumption is correct.

Prices and Functionality

Any time a price searcher can identify consumers on the basis of their sensitivity to price, it is in a position to vary its price for different groups in ways that increase the incentive to purchase its product. The advantage of being able to separate customers willing to pay high prices (relatively inelastic) from those

---

[9] The high price for snacks at movie theaters also reflects the higher cost of supplying them to movie theaters than food stores. The snack shop in a movie theater is open for only a limited amount of time, so the overhead cost is spread over less time and fewer sales (Lott and Roberts 1991). And the theater sells fewer items and cannot realize as many economies of scale. We do not quarrel with these reasons, but believe that creative price discrimination also provides part of the explanation for the high price of movie snacks.

[10] Determining the exact combination of prices that maximizes profits depends on the relative differences in demand for the two types of customers. If, for example, the avid movie fans were willing to pay a tremendously high price to see the movie, and snackers couldn't care less about the movie but went into frenzies of delight at the mere thought of a Snickers bar, then the best pricing policy would be an extremely high ticket price with extremely low-priced (maybe free) snacks. In this case, the theater owner would probably stipulate that snack customers would have to eat the snacks in the theater to prevent them from filling large takeaway sacks with popcorn and candy bars. This would be no different than the policy of all-you-can-eat restaurants.

who are more price-sensitive (relatively elastic) is so great in some cases that it explains why some firms will incur costs to reduce the quality of their products so they can sell them for less.

For example, soon after Intel introduced the 486 microprocessor, it renamed it the 486DX and introduced a modified version, which it named the 486SX. Intel disabled the internal math co-processor in the original 486 – a modification that was costly and reduced the performance of the 486SX. Intel then, in 1991, sold the 486SX for less – $333 as compared to $588 for the 486DX. Why would Intel spend money to damage a microprocessor and then sell it for less?[11] The answer is to separate out customers who are willing to pay a lot for a microprocessor from those whose demand is more sensitive to price. Intel could sell the 486DX to the former at a price that would have driven the latter to competitive firms. Yet it managed to keep the business of the latter customers by lowering the price to them without worrying that this would drive the price down for the high-end customers. There was no way for the lower-price consumers to buy the lower-price product and sell it to the high-end consumers, because its performance had been reduced.

Similarly, with the emergence of netbook computers (lightweight but cheap laptops with limited functionality), Microsoft faced a challenge to the dominance of its Windows operating system. Netbook manufacturers used the Linux operating system because it was free, which enabled manufacturers to hold the price of their netbooks under $300. Microsoft initially responded by allowing manufacturers to install the then-dated Windows XP system (the version that pre-dated Windows Vista) at a cut-rate price. With the advent of Windows 7 (a now-dated version of Windows that corrected problems with Windows Vista), Microsoft met the netbook/Linux challenge by introducing Windows 7-Starter, which is a strategically crippled version of the full Windows 7 operating system, designed for netbooks and other low-market personal computers. Starter, which was sold to computer manufacturers at cut-rate prices so they could price their machines competitively with systems using Linux, only permitted three applications running at the same time. However, owners of netbooks with Starter were given the option of buying the full version of Windows 7 – not by downloading the full version, but by buying a code that allowed them to access the already-installed full version (Wingfield and Clark 2009).

When IBM introduced its LaserPrinter E at the start of the 1990s, it set the price lower than the price for its earlier model, the LaserPrinter. The LaserPrinter E was almost exactly the same as the LaserPrinter, except that the newer model

---

[11] It was cheaper to make the 486DX and then reduce its quality than it was to produce the lower-quality 486SX directly. This example, the following example, and several other cases of firms intentionally reducing the quality of their products are found in Deneckere and McAfee (1996).

printed at a slower rate. The LaserPrinter E was slower because IBM went to the expense of adding chips that had no purpose other than to cause the printer to pause. Why would IBM do this? Again, to separate its market between consumers with inelastic demand and those with elastic demand, so that less could be charged to the latter without having to reduce the price to the former.

Now, a host of computers, smartphones, and tablets use Google's Android operating system, working to further differentiate computers and increase the dispersion of prices. Still, Intel continues to bring to market ever-more powerful (i5, i7, i9) microprocessors – in part, to stay ahead of competitor chip-makers and partly to maintain an ability to price-discriminate among computer buyers who differ on price sensitivity. Similarly, computer (and video game) manufacturers price-discriminate by offering computers with and without touch screens.

Golf Balls

One of the authors (Lee) enjoys playing golf. He buys brand-name golf balls that have been labeled with XXX to indicate they have some flaw and are sold at a discount. Many golfers are willing to pay the extra money for regular brand-name balls, which supposedly travel farther than the XXX balls. Lee, on the other hand, sees no advantage in hitting his balls farther into the woods. And he is not convinced that there really is any difference between the regular high-priced balls and the XXX balls, except that the manufacturer went to the extra expense of adding the XXXs. Although we have no documentation, we suspect that manufacturers simply put XXXs on a certain percentage of their balls so that they can separate their market between golfers like Lee (who are quite sensitive to price) and golfers who (because they have a reasonable idea where their balls are going) are not as sensitive to price.

Unadvertised Prices

Another technique firms can use to separate price-sensitive consumers is to make unadvertised price discounts available, but only to those who search them out and ask for them. Obviously, those who go to the trouble to find out about a discount (and ask for it) are more concerned over price than those who do not. AT&T used this approach to identifying customers for discounts on long-distance calls in the 1990s. AT&T responded to Sprint Corporation's 10 cents per minute for calls during weekends and evening hours by offering a flat rate of 15 cents any time – a plan they called One Rate (Keller 1997). But AT&T really had two rates – one of which they did not advertise. The unadvertised rate, available only to those who asked for it, allowed AT&T customers to call around the clock for 10 cents per minute. As reported in the article by Keller, "AT&T customers can get dime-a-minute calling 24 hours a day, seven days a week – if they know to ask for it. That is the hardest part, for AT&T has been uncharacteristically quiet about the new offer. The company hasn't advertised the 10-cent rate; it hasn't sent out press releases heralding the latest effort to one-up the folks at Sprint" (Keller 1997, B1). The old adage about oiling only what squeaks certainly applies in this case. (We suspect that AT&T was not all that pleased with the article simply because the publicity reduced AT&T's ability to segment its market by decreasing the "search costs" that AT&T customers otherwise faced.)

The more competition and price rivalry in an industry, the smaller the gain for a firm charging different prices to different customers. Even relatively price-insensitive customers will be bid away by rival firms when price competition is intense – if one firm tries to charge those customers much more than its more price-sensitive customers. Nevertheless, when firms can segment their market and buffer the price competition among them, the greater the scope for creative pricing strategies.

Implied Cartels

Firms in an industry can simply get together and agree not to compete for consumers through price reductions. This will allow them to keep prices (and their collective profits) higher than will be possible if all firms make a futile attempt to increase their market shares by charging lower prices. But there are two problems with this approach to reducing price competition. The first problem is that any agreement to restrict competition can be illegal – and firms and their managers who enter into such an agreement risk harsh antitrust penalties.

As discussed in Part A of the next chapter, the second problem is that, even if agreements to restrict price competition were legal, they would still be almost impossible to maintain. Members of industry cartels that have agreed to set prices above competitive levels are in another Prisoner's Dilemma. Although they are collectively better off when everyone abides by the agreement, each individual sees the advantage in reducing price below the agreed-upon amount. If other firms maintain the high price, then the firm that cheats on the agreement can capture lots of additional (highly profitable) business with a relatively small decrease in its price. On the other hand, if the other firms are expected to cheat on the agreement, it would be foolish for a firm to continue with the high price, because it would find most of its customers competed away. Only if all firms ignore Prisoner's Dilemma temptations, and take the risk of making the cooperative choice, can cartel price agreements be maintained. Not surprisingly, such agreements tend to break down.

Meet-the-Competition Pricing Policy

Some pricing policies, however, can moderate price competition between rival firms without the need for a cooperative agreement. Ironically, these strategies reduce competition, when competition motivates most firms in an industry to implement them, especially when one firm does.

Consider a pricing policy that would seem to protect your consumers against high prices, but is actually a clever policy that makes higher prices possible. The strategy is quite simple, involving an unqualified pledge: "We will meet or beat any competitor's price." This "meet-the-competition" pricing policy tells your customers that you will match a competitor's lower price – a policy commonly advertised as "guaranteed lowest prices." To implement such a policy, you inform your customers that if they can find a lower price on a product within 30 days of purchasing it from you, they will receive a rebate equal to the difference. Such price guarantees appear to benefit customers, but if they are offered by all or most competitors, they allow all firms to charge higher prices. How so? One straightforward explanation is that the price assurance gives customers some assurance and increases their demand, leading to higher prices.[12]

Another explanation: if you want to charge higher prices, there is an obvious advantage in discouraging competitors from reducing their prices to compete your customers away. This is exactly what a meet-the-competition policy does. Your competitors are probably not all that anxious to initiate a price-cutting campaign. Attempting to compete customers away from another firm through lower prices is always costly. If successful, the new business is likely to be worth less to the price-cutting firm than to the firm that loses it because the price is now lower. Existing customers will want to receive a lower price as well, which can cut deeper into profits. Of course, if a price-cutting campaign aimed at capturing new customers fails to do so, the campaign is all cost and no benefit. Bottom line: if your competitors know that you have a meet-the-competition agreement with your customers, they will have less (and likely nothing) to gain from cutting prices to try to attract those customers.

A meet-the-competition pricing policy can be good for you and your competitors. By allowing you to keep your prices higher than otherwise, it gives your competitors more room to keep their prices high. As opposed to most competitive strategies that become less effective when mimicked by the competition, this becomes more profitable when other firms in the industry implement the same policy. Just as your competitors are better off when you do not have to worry about the competitive consequences of keeping your prices high, so you are better off when your competitors are relieved of the same worry (Brandenburger and Nalebuff 1996, chapter 6).

---

[12] The assurance is not as impressive as it first seems. It reduces to you doing the work to shop for prices – and, then, the supplier merely matching the price. More impressive: giving you an even lower price by X percent or giving it to you for free. Why do customers seem to value this, implied by firms offering it? One answer may be "rational ignorance" – that consumers have rationally low levels of information, even about consumer prices – and are impressed by weak signals about low prices.

Most-Favored-Customer Pricing Policy

A related pricing policy is to offer some of your customers a "most-favored" status, which entitles them to the best price offered to anyone else. (Again, this policy must be checked with lawyers, given that such policies might be construed as illegal in some circumstances.) If you lower your price to any customer under this policy, you are obligated to lower it for all of your most-favored customers. As with the meet-the-competition policy, what at first glance appears to favor your customers can actually give you an advantage. A most-favored-customer policy increases the cost of trying to compete customers away from rival firms by reducing price. And when one firm has such a policy, its reluctance to engage in price competition makes it easy for other firms to keep their prices high. And, as with meet-the-competition policy, the advantage is greater when all the firms in an industry have such a policy (Brandenburger and Nalebuff 1996).

If the idea that a policy of being quick to reduce prices for your customers can result in higher prices seems counterproductive, you are in good company. In their book *Co-Opetition*, Brandenburger and Nalebuff (1996) relate how Congress, in an effort to control the cost of campaigning, required television broadcasters to make candidates for Congress most-favored customers. In the 1971 Federal Election Campaign Act, Congress made it against the law for television broadcasters to lower their rates for an ad to any commercial customer without also lowering their rates to candidates. The result was that television broadcasters found it extremely costly to reduce rates for *anyone* – and networks made more money than ever before. Politicians had the satisfaction of knowing that they did not pay more for airtime than anyone else, but they likely ended up paying more (as commercial advertisers did also).

Congress made a similar mistake in 1990, when it attempted to reduce government reimbursements for drugs by stipulating that Medicaid would pay only 88 percent of the average wholesale price for branded drugs – or, if lower, the lowest price granted anyone in the retail trade drug business. Instead of lowering prices, the law actually raised them. By making itself a most-favored customer, the federal government gave the drug companies a strong incentive to raise prices for everyone. Indeed, this is exactly what happened. According to a study cited by Brandenburger and Nalebuff (1996, 104–105), prices on branded drugs increased by 5–9 percent because of the 1990 rule changes. The advantage realized by keeping its price down to 88 percent of the average wholesale price was probably more than offset (it was often receiving a discount anyway) by the higher average prices. And, certainly, non-Medicare patients ended up paying higher drug prices.

Frequent-Flyer Programs

Another pricing strategy that allows firms in an industry to reduce price competition has been common since the 1980s. This strategy involves a creative way of identifying customers who are most likely to buy from your firm anyway and then lowering their price. At first glance, such a strategy would appear counter-productive. Why would you lower the price for those who are likely to buy from you? The answer is that, by making what appear to be price concessions to your most loyal customers, you can end up charging them higher prices.

A good way of explaining this seemingly paradoxical possibility is by considering the frequent-flyer programs of airlines. In the early 1980s, these programs were initially motivated by American Airlines' desire to compete business away from other airlines by effectively lowering ticket prices. The rapidity with which other airlines countered with their own frequent-flyer programs suggests intense competition between the airlines. But, intended or not, the proliferation of these programs has had the effect of reducing the direct price competition between airlines – and, as a result, may be allowing them to maintain higher prices than otherwise possible. An airline's frequent-flyer program reduces the effective (if not the explicit) price it charges its most loyal customers, reinforcing their loyalty.[13] By increasing the motivation of an airline's frequent flyers to concentrate their flying on this airline, it decreases the payoff other airlines can expect from trying to compete those customers away with fare reductions. This allows an airline with a frequent-flyer program to keep its explicit fares higher than if other airlines were aggressively reducing theirs.[14] This decreased motivation to engage in price competition becomes mutually reinforcing as more airlines implement frequent-flyer programs.

From the perspective of each airline, it would be good to compete away customers from other airlines with lower fares, but collectively the airlines are better off by reducing this ability. And this is exactly what the spread of frequent-flyer programs has done to some degree – by segmenting the airline market. There is now less competitive advantage in reducing airfares and less competitive disadvantage in raising them. The effect has been to *reduce the elasticity of demand* facing each airline, which allows all airlines to charge higher prices than would otherwise be sustainable.[15]

---

[13] Even when a person is a member of more than one frequent-flyer program, there is an advantage in concentrating patronage on one airline because the programs are designed to increase benefits more than proportionally with accumulated mileage.

[14] You may be thinking that keeping the explicit fares higher does not mean much if, because of the frequent-flyer programs, the actual fares to customers are lower because of the value of their mileage awards. But one of the big advantages of frequent-flyer programs is that they do not cost the airlines as much as they benefit the customer. Flights are seldom sold out, so most of the free flights awarded are filling unsold seats. Of course, frequent flyers use their mileage for flights they would have otherwise bought. But by allowing frequent flyers to transfer their mileage awards to others (e.g., a spouse or child), the airlines increase the probability that those who would not have otherwise bought a ticket will use the awards.

[15] Another way of seeing the advantage of segmenting the market is by recognizing that reducing the elasticity of demand facing each airline also reduces the marginal revenue of each airline and brings it more in line with the marginal revenue for the industry. The closer each firm's marginal revenue is to the industry's marginal revenue, the closer the independent pricing decisions of each firm will come to maximizing their collective profits.

A pricing strategy similar to frequent-flyer programs has spread to other industries. In 1992, General Motors joined with MasterCard and issued the GM credit card. By using the GM card, a consumer earned a credit equal to 5 percent of his charges that could be applied to the purchase or lease of any new GM vehicle. (The original arrangement had a yearly cap; the current card provides 7 percent with no cap.) Just like frequent-flyer programs, automobile credit cards allow a car company to focus implicit price reductions on its most loyal customers. An individual is not likely to be using a GM credit card unless she is planning to buy a GM car or truck. As the number of car companies that issue their own credit card increases, the auto market becomes more segmented and the advantage from price competition is diminished. Again, a pricing policy that allows a firm to target its more loyal customers and favor them with price cuts can have the effect of increasing the prices being charged.

Why do companies like Starbucks have loyalty programs? They would likely say: "We want to be nice to our loyal customers" – as if their attempt to be nice is a drain on the company's profits. We doubt this. Starbucks is probably engaging in price discrimination between customers who buy coffee at Starbucks occasionally and those who buy frequently. Starbucks understands that frequent (loyal) customers are likely to have a more elastic demand than occasional customers. Frequent customers have more reason to watch the relative prices of coffee at Starbucks and its competitors. Hence, giving frequent customers a price break (without extending the break to occasional customers) can increase firm revenues and profits. Starbucks effectively lowers the prices to frequent customers by giving them "rewards."

The economic discussions of pricing strategies have mushroomed in recent years for two reasons. First, firms have found that they can make a lot of money by varying their prices. Because of the ongoing digital communication revolution, firms now have the technology to change pricing with ease (at low cost) through their linked cash registers and in response to the data they collect through scanners in checkout lines. Second, behavioral economists have adopted the research methodologies of psychologists and neuroscientists, conducting many classroom and laboratory experiments about how people shop and how they react to prices. (We cover some of these applications in Online Reading 10.2 and Online Chapter 1.)

Practical Lessons

Much conventional analysis of pricing and production decisions under competitive and monopoly market structures is focused on their comparative *efficiency*. The central conclusion is that competitive markets are more efficient than monopoly markets. Perfectly competitive markets maximize output, given cost and demand constraints;

pure monopoly maximizes *inefficiency* (or loss in welfare attributable to monopoly's reduction in output below the competitive output level). The policy implication is that a shift from monopoly to competitive markets makes for greater social welfare – a conclusion that drives antitrust policy enforcement in countries around the globe.

Business students should understand such points, but many will surely draw another deduction: One of the last things a firm should do is get involved in any market that comes even close to perfectly competitive market conditions. In such markets, the best a firm can hope for is fleeting profits because they will be eroded by intense price competition among existing producers and new entrants entering the competitive fray at little cost. Under competitive market conditions, firms have little incentive to innovate in product and market development, because they have little chance to recover these costs.

Monopoly power may result in inefficiency from a societal perspective, but the analytics of this and the preceding chapters suggest that firms should seek monopoly power because it offers hope of making above-normal profits. With a monopoly, product and market development costs can be recouped – and maybe more. The derivative lesson for business students is that, in their roles as entrepreneurs (or "intrapreneurs" – entrepreneurs within large firms), they should seek creative ways to develop their products and their markets. However, they also should seek creative and ethical ways to develop natural or artificial barriers. The development of products, markets, and entry barriers should go hand-in-hand – with perhaps as much or more attention given to the development of the latter. Entry barriers are crucial to profitability. They are what enable firms to control market supply – and therefore market price and profits. Without entry barriers, all firm expenditures of product and market development can be for naught as new entrants reduce any newly created product to a "commodity" – something everyone can produce such that nobody can recover development costs and make above-normal profits.

Conventional microeconomic analytics has branded (pun intended) branding, trade secrets, exclusive ownership of key resources, network effects, lock-ins, switching costs, patents, and copyrights as efficiency-impairing entry barriers that give rise to monopoly power. Business students should see them differently – as sources of above-normal profits. Their development also can be a means by which business students can put themselves on a career track to the executive suite. Managers who devote firm resources to the development of products that can be easily and quickly replicated may see themselves in stalled careers, at best.

Monopoly (or monopoly pricing power) is often presented in microeconomics courses as an unmitigated scourge on the market system. Production under (pure) monopolies is necessarily less "efficient" than production under (perfectly) competitive market conditions, which means monopolies necessarily (everywhere and always) lower the general welfare. While the deduction is true for the specified market conditions – the most notable being that the product is a *given*, or already exists when the analyses of perfect competition and monopoly begin – the conclusion is far too facile, and inappropriate when products and their markets have to be discovered and nurtured. Perfect competition may result in price being driven to marginal cost and to the minimum average cost, as explained in Chapter 9. However, under (perfect) competition, entrepreneurs have little (no) incentive to create and improve products in the first place.

Under monopoly market conditions, price may end up above marginal costs, with monopoly profits extracted, along with the creation of the identified inefficiency (deadweight loss) triangle. However, what can be overlooked is that the product exists and offers benefits to consumers. The existence of monopoly profits in some markets can also provide entrepreneurs with the incentive they need to make the needed up-front investments in product and market development, which can expand the welfare potential of markets.

This is not to say that all monopolies are "good," but it is to say that the existence of monopolies in market systems is not as "bad" as conventional microeconomic theory suggests. (For an extended, book-length discussion of these points, see McKenzie (2010). A shorter development of these points is available through Online Reading 10.3 – "In defense of monopoly.")

Further Reading Online

Reading 10.1: The Microsoft monopoly
Reading 10.2: The "endowment effect" and pricing
Reading 10.3: In defense of monopoly (*Regulation*, link available on the online resources website www.cambridge.org/mckenzie4)

Recommended Videos Online

1 Production and pricing under pure monopoly (Richard McKenzie, 32 minutes)

2 Problems with monopoly theory (Richard McKenzie, 30 minutes)

3 Perfect and imperfect price discrimination (Richard McKenzie, 29 minutes)

4 Market segmentation (Richard McKenzie, 25 minutes)

The Bottom Line

The key takeaways from Chapter 10 are the following:

1 As any other firm, a monopolist maximizes its profits where its marginal cost equals its marginal revenue.

2 The monopolist faces a downward-sloping demand curve, which means that its *MR* curve is also downward-sloping, but underneath its demand curve.

3 The source of a monopolist's ability to charge an above-competitive price comes from its ability to materially change market supply through its own production decisions.

4 The consequences of monopoly are higher prices and lower production levels than are possible under perfect competition.

5 A monopolist's ability to hike its price and profits is restricted by the elasticity of its demand, which is influenced by the closeness of substitutes for consumers and the costs of entry facing other producers.

6 A monopolist should set its price for the (short run and) long run with the same rule in mind: $MC = MR$.

7 A monopolist can make economic profits, but, in the short run, it also can incur economic losses. If these are expected to extend into the long run, the firm will exit.

8 For a monopolist to garner monopoly profits in the long run, it must be protected to some extent with costly entry barriers.

9 Monopoly power often results in inefficient production, when the monopolistic firm does not produce to the point at which its marginal cost equals the consumer's marginal benefit – the product's price. Consumers would prefer that more resources be used in the production of a monopolized good and would be willing to pay a price that exceeds the cost of production for additional units of the good. However, the profit-maximizing monopolist stops short of this point to maximize profit.

10 The new "network economy" often turns economic analysis on its head. This is especially true when it comes to discussions of "monopoly power." A market for a network good might tend toward a single seller. At the same time, the single seller may have little ability to profit from charging a high price because of the network effect.

11 A firm selling a network good will have to charge a very low (possibly a zero or negative price) initially to attract enough market share to achieve a critical level of network value. And, once a firm producing a network good achieves a significant market share, it runs the risk of providing an opening for new firms, if it attempts to profit by following the textbook monopoly practice of reducing output (which would reduce its network value) and charging a high price.

12 A monopolist can increase its profit (and market efficiency) through various forms of price discrimination; however, its ability to price-discriminate is constrained by the potential ability of consumers to resell the good.

13 Monopoly pricing power has at least one redeeming grace (unheralded by economists since Joseph Schumpeter): monopolies are a force for "creative destruction." As such, monopoly power is an under-appreciated market force for "creative production" (McKenzie 2010).

14 Monopolies can move to a competitive rate of return in the long run as the monopoly profits are eroded by technology changes that make monopoly products irrelevant or entrepreneurs find ways of circumventing barriers to entry.

Review Questions ▶▶

1 Many magazines offer multi-year subscriptions at a lower rate than one-year subscriptions. Explain various reasons for the logic of such a pricing decision.

2 Explain why $P > MR$ for a "price searcher." With the typical short-run cost curves, show equilibrium P and Q.

3 Explain the dilemma for a "price searcher" in choosing the optimal price. Explain intuitively (and graphically illustrate) the trade-off – and the reason that price-searching firms would like to price-discriminate.

4 If a monopolist incurs economic losses, what will it do in the short run? In the long run?

5 Explain why a monopolized industry will tend to produce less than a competitive industry.

6 Suppose a monopolist's demand curve increases. What will happen to the monopolist's price and output level?

7 "To retain its market power and above-normal profits over the long run, a firm must be protected by barriers to entry." Explain. List some restrictions on the mobility of resources that might help a firm retain monopoly power.

8 What do "switching costs" and "network effects" have to do with monopoly power?

9 Why should antitrust action not be taken against all monopolies?

10 Given the information in Table 10.2, copy and complete the table with the monopolist's marginal cost and marginal revenue schedules. Graph the demand, *MC*, and *MR* curves – and find the profit-maximizing point of production. Assuming this monopolistic firm faces fixed costs of $10 and must charge the same price for all units sold, how much profit does it make?

Table 10.2 Data for question 10

Quantity produced and sold	Price ($)	Total variable cost ($)	Marginal cost ($)	Marginal revenue ($)
1	12	5		
2	11	9		
3	10	14		
4	9	20		
5	8	28		
6	7	38		

11 On the graph you developed for question 10, identify the output and profits of a monopolist capable of perfect price discrimination.

12 Suppose another monopoly (make up your own numbers) is capable of imperfect price discrimination and divides its market into two segments. Graph the demands for these two market segments – and, in a third graph, the monopolist's combined *MR* curve. Using an *MC* curve in the third graph, determine the monopolist's profit-maximizing output level. Then, indicate the quantity and price of the product sold in each market segment.

13 If consumers of a network firm fear that it will become a true monopolist in the future, how does this fear impact the firm's current pricing policies?

14 How can antitrust enforcement in a market for a network good cause harm to consumers?

15 Why does popcorn cost so much at the movies?

16 Why do many bars have "happy hours" – hours generally in the late afternoon when drinks and appetizers are sold at discounts?

17 Why are the prices of printer ink cartridges so high relative to the prices of printers?

18 When a ski resort with some monopoly power is maximizing profit, price is greater than marginal cost. Thus, consumers are willing to pay more for additional lift tickets than the lifts cost to run. So why does the ski resort not charge a lower price per lift ticket and increase output?

19 Authors usually get a small fraction (say, 15 percent) of the gross revenue stream from any book they write, while the publisher gets what's left after royalty payments and all other costs. Why might authors and publishers of books (with some monopoly power) be at odds over the pricing of books? Would the publisher or the author(s) want the higher price? If the marginal cost of book production were zero, would the author(s) and the publisher then be in agreement over price?

20 Consider a good that is digital in nature – made totally of computer code ('1's and '0's; electrons) – software, for example. Suppose there are costs in developing the good and a market for the good which must be incurred before the first unit is sold. Assume also that there are strong network effects associated with the demand side of the good, and that the short-run and long-run marginal cost of production of the good is zero throughout the relevant range of production. Finally, assume there is no (low-cost) way to prevent piracy. If asked by the CEO of the company producing this good how the good should be priced in the short run and long run, what strategy would you recommend? How would the potential for switching costs or lock-in affect your recommendations?

11

Firm Strategy under Imperfectly
Competitive Market Conditions

Differences in tastes, desires, incomes and locations of buyers, and differences in the
use which they wish to make of commodities all indicate the need for variety and the
necessity of substituting for the concept of a "competitive ideal," an ideal involving both
monopoly and competition.

Edward Chamberlin[1]

We have so far focused on two distinctly different market structures: *perfect
competition* (characterized by producers who cannot influence price at all
because of extreme competition) and *pure monopoly* (in which there is only one
producer of a product with no close substitutes and whose market is protected by
prohibitively high barriers to entry). But neither of these theoretical structures
well describes most markets.

Even in the short run, firms typically compete with several others with similar
products. General Motors competes with Ford, Chevrolet, and a number of foreign producers. McDonald's competes with Burger King, Wendy's, Carl's Jr., The
Habit, and any number of other burger franchises, as well as with a host of other
chains in the fast-food restaurant category – for example, Dominos, Popeyes,
Arby's, Dairy Queen, and Taco Bell. And, in the long run, they may compete with
new companies that surmount the imperfect barriers to entry into their markets.

In a few words, most companies compete in imperfect markets that cause producers to be more efficient in their use of resources than under pure monopoly,
but less efficient than in perfect competition. Part A of this chapter develops a
broader theory of competition in markets for goods and services. Markets that
are less than perfectly competitive afford producers an opportunity to restrict
output, raise their prices, and increase profits, which can give rise to milder versions of the market inefficiencies discussed with pure monopoly in Chapter 10.

---

[1] Chamberlin, Edward, Monopolistic or Imperfect Competition?, *The Quarterly Journal of
Economics*, August 1937, Vol. 51, No. 4, pp. 557–580, https://doi.org/10.2307/1881679.
Reprinted by permission of Oxford University Press on behalf of the President and Fellows of
Harvard College.

As monopoly power increases, the specter of government regulation rises. Accordingly, toward the end of Part A, we revisit and apply the dominant theories on government regulation developed in Chapter 6.

Entrepreneurs constantly look for new and better products to bolster profits – and they scout for under-performing firms to buy at a low price, improve, and then sell for a higher price. So, managers need to be mindful of competition in the markets for their goods and services. But they must also be aware of another competitive arena: the market for corporate control – the topic in Part B. Whenever firms can make monopoly profits, even in the face of some competition, there is the ever-present principal–agent problem – in particular, that managers will use their discretion over firm resources to pocket some of the profits through pay or perks. The market for corporate control can discipline managers tempted to take advantage of their discretion. If managers misuse firm resources, then profits and stock price will be depressed, opening the firm to takeover by entrepreneurs who can buy the firm at low price with the intent of correcting the misuse of firm resources and elevating its stock price. We will cover the ways firms can be taken over and how managers can prevent such moves.

In Perspective 11, we take up a consequential but underrated problem: "the innovator's dilemma." It helps to explain why many established producers are inclined to stay with their tried-and-true products, signing (often deliberately) their market "death warrants" and being replaced by innovative new entrants.

Part A Theory and Public Policy Applications

One word of caution as we start into "real-world" market structures: such a study can be *frustrating*. Although models may incorporate more or less realistic assumptions about the behavior of real-world firms, the theories developed from them are somewhat conjectural. Real-world markets are complex phenomena that often do not lend themselves to hard-and-fast conclusions. This is because outcomes and decisions are so often *mutually interdependent*: outcomes depend on what other market participants do, and decisions depend on what they are expected to do. Behavior is something of a series of strategic games they play with one another, with each person's moves dependent upon how competitors are expected to react.

Accordingly, the market structures of monopolistic competition and oligopoly developed in this chapter require that we consider market movements as a series of interdependent actions and reactions – as is so often the case in games (and game theory) – in which outcomes are sometimes difficult to predict. Nevertheless, key insights can be developed – for example, when we consider how corporate takeovers can make imperfect markets more efficient in Part B.

It will be helpful to remember points from our discussion of perfect competition and pure monopoly: perfect competition, while "efficient" when the product already exists and price is the only margin for competition, can undercut consumer and social welfare in the long run (when benefits could be gained from the creation of new products and the upgrade of old products). There is little incentive for entrepreneurs to make up-front investments for product development; their costs cannot be recovered when markets are as "perfect" as assumed in perfect competition. On the other hand, monopoly pricing power can provide strong incentives for product innovation, because monopoly profits can inspire the creation of new products. Some friction on the movement of resources and prices can, in many unappreciated ways, be welfare-enhancing. However, there is surely some high level of monopoly power that is, on balance, destructive of consumer and social welfare through higher prices, lower output, and greater deadweight losses. One of the Holy Grails in economic theory is to find the optimal prevalence and level of monopoly power in market systems, which can promote innovation and guide the enforcement of antitrust laws. This might be found in the market structures considered in this chapter: monopolistic competition and oligopoly (or some variation of these market structures yet to be envisioned).

Monopolistic Competition

As we noted in our study of demand, the greater the number and variety of substitutes for a good or service, the greater its elasticity of demand – that is, consumers will be more responsive to a change in price. By definition, a monopolistically competitive market such as the fast-food industry produces many different products, most of which can substitute for each other. If Burger Bippy raises its prices, consumers can move to another restaurant with similar food and service. But a price hike is unlikely to cost Burger Bippy all of its customers, because of a preference for Burger Bippy products, consumer ignorance of alternatives, and the power of habit. It has some *monopoly power*; therefore, it can charge slightly more than the ideal competitive price, determined by the intersection of the marginal cost and demand curves. Burger Bippy cannot raise its prices much, however, without substantially reducing its sales.

Given a significant level of competition, the firm will face a relatively elastic demand curve – certainly more elastic than the pure monopolist's. The degree to which monopolistically competitive prices can stray from the competitive ideal depends on:

- the number of competitors;
- the ease with which existing competitors can expand their businesses to accommodate new customers (the cost of expansion);

- the ease with which new firms can enter the market (the cost of entry);
- the ability of firms to differentiate their products by location or by real or imagined characteristics (the cost of differentiation); and
- public awareness of price differences (the cost of gaining information on price differences).

Monopolistic Competition in the Short Run

In the short run, a monopolistically competitive firm may deviate little from the price–quantity combination produced under perfect competition. The demand curve for fast-food hamburgers in Figure 11.1 is highly, although not perfectly, elastic. Following the same rule as the perfect competitor and the pure monopolist, the monopolistically competitive burger maker produces where $MC = MR$. Because the firm's demand curve slopes downward, its MR curve slopes downward – as the pure monopolist's. The firm maximizes profits at Q_{mc} and P_{mc}, with a price only slightly higher and a quantity sold only slightly lower than under perfect competition (P_c and Q_c).[2] Market inefficiency, indicated by the shaded area, is modest.

The firm's short-run profits may be slight or substantial, depending on demand for its product and the number of producers in the market. In our example, profit is the area bounded by $ATC_1 P_{mc} ab$, found by subtracting total cost ($OATC_1 bQ_{mc}$) from total revenues ($OP_{mc} aQ_{mc}$), as with monopolies.

As before, these economic profits serve an important purpose: They give entrepreneurs an incentive to incur up-front product and market development costs.

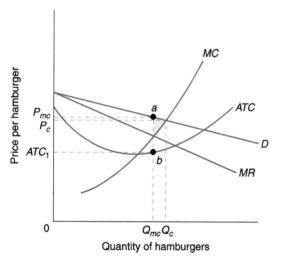

Figure 11.1 Monopolistic competition in the short run
As do all profit-maximizing firms, the monopolistic competitor will equate marginal revenue with marginal cost. It will produce Q_{mc} units and charge price P_{mc} (only slightly higher than the price under perfect competition). The monopolistic competitor makes a short-run economic profit equal to the area $ATC_1 P_{mc} ab$. The inefficiency of its slightly restricted production level is represented by the shaded area.

---

[2] Remember, the perfect competitor faces a horizontal (perfectly elastic) demand curve, which is also its price and marginal revenue. It also produces at the intersection of the MC and MR curves, which is where marginal cost equals price.

Unlike perfect competition, the prospects of profits offer some confidence that they can recover their up-front costs. Of course, much depends on how long the short-run profits can be expected to persist and the extent of the product and market development costs. When sufficiently large and persistent, these short-run profits will attract other producers into the market, because surmounting the barriers to entry into monopolistic competition is not prohibitively costly. When the market is divided up among more competitors, the individual firm's demand curve will shift downward, reflecting each competitor's smaller market share. As a result, the MR curve will shift downward as well. The demand curve will also become more elastic, reflecting the greater number of potential substitutes in the market. These changes are shown in Figure 11.2, where the increased competition results in quantity produced falling from Q_{mc2} to Q_{mc1}; and price falling from P_{mc2} to P_{mc1}.

Profits are eliminated when the price no longer exceeds the firm's average total cost. (As long as economic profit exists, new firms will continue to enter the market. Eventually the price will fall enough to eliminate economic profit.)[3] Notice that the firm is not producing and pricing at the minimum of its $LRAC$ curve (quantity Q_m) as the perfect competitor would (nor did it in the short run).[4] In this sense, the firm is producing below capacity by $Q_m - Q_{mc1}$ units.

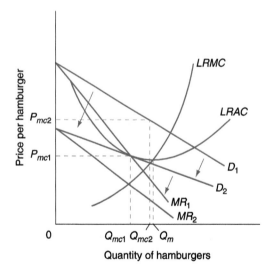

0   Q_{mc1} Q_{mc2} Q_m
Quantity of hamburgers

Price per hamburger

P_{mc2}

P_{mc1}

LRMC

LRAC

D_1

D_2

MR_1

MR_2

Figure 11.2 Monopolistic competition in the long run With short-run profits, firms will enter the monopolistically competitive market in the long run, shifting the monopolistic competitor's demand curve down from D_1 to D_2 and making it more elastic. Equilibrium will be achieved when the firm's demand curve becomes tangent to the downward-sloping portion of the firm's $LRAC$ curve at Q_{mc1}. At this point, price (shown by the demand curve) no longer exceeds average total cost; the firm is making zero economic profit. Unlike the perfect competitor, this firm is not producing at the minimum of the $LRAC$ curve, Q_m. In this sense, it is underproducing by $Q_m - Q_{mc1}$ units. This underproduction is also reflected in the fact that the price is greater than the marginal revenue.

[3] The monopolistic competitor will still have an incentive to stay in business, however. Economic profit, not book profit, falls to zero. Book profit will still be large enough to cover the opportunity cost of capital plus the risk cost of doing business.

[4] The perfect competitor produces at the minimum of the $LRAC$ curve because its demand curve is horizontal; therefore, the demand curve's point of tangency with the $LRAC$ curve is the low point of the curve.

In terms of price and quantity produced, monopolistic competition can never be as efficient as perfect competition. Perfectly competitive firms obtain their results partly because all of them are producing the same product. Consumers can choose from a great many suppliers, but they have no product options. In a monopolistically competitive market, on the other hand, consumers buy from a limited number of producers, but they can choose from a variety of slightly different products. For example, the pen market offers consumers a choice between felt-tipped, fountain, and ballpoint pens of many different styles. This variety in goods comes at a cost – the long-run price is above the minimum of the *LRAC* curve, as illustrated in Figure 11.2.

Because of the competition, firms must treat their customers with care. In fact, "customer service" is probably a key part of a firm's product. Firms can compete by the extent of the care they offer, but customer care can be expensive and is subject to diminishing returns. Moreover, customer treatment – or mistreatment – can exact a toll on a firm's employees, causing them to demand higher pay and hiking the firm's cost structure. Considering these costs, might there be an optimum amount of customer care which could vary among firms? In Online Reading 11.1, we develop the economic way of thinking about customer care and the lack thereof (with an emphasis on optimizing the "mistreatment" of customers).

Profits as Needed and Welfare-Enhancing Development Incentives

Many economists look upon the above market outcome (average cost above the minimum on the *LRAC* curve in Figure 11.2) as a form of *market inefficiency*. And, in a sense, in the theoretical world, it is. The graph presents a partial view of the role of economic profits in markets – as all graphs must show partial views of their subject matter. (After all, they represent a complex subject with only a few lines!) But this identified inefficiency is something of a theoretical mirage. It can't exist in real-world markets because the market conditions of perfect competition can't exist. (This is because numerous producers are unlikely to ever exist in a world beset with scarcity, and entry/exit costs can't be zero. And, as we have noted, the products in the market would never likely be developed under perfectly competitive market conditions because of the risk costs.)

Moreover, consumer welfare can be enhanced by product variations (at least up to some point), so that different consumers with different tastes can buy different products that come closer to matching their preferences. Put differently, consumer welfare can still be enhanced *because of the greater variety and upgrades inspired by short-run (and even long-run) economic profits*. Don't forget that a substantial percentage of products introduced in markets are failures, meaning they lose money for the developers/producers. This means that firms must be able to cover, in long-run equilibrium, the risk costs associated with failed products (or the *prospects* of failed products). Firms with multiple products – from Microsoft and Wendy's to Sony and Boeing – must have products on which they make economic profits to cover their losses on failed products. Thus, multiproduct firms need to find ways to protect some of their products from incursion by competitors through barriers such as patents, copyrights, network effects, scale economies, trade secrets, government regulations, and brands. Moreover, these market protections have social welfare benefits since they encourage product development and improvements.

Once again, a lesson to be drawn from this line of analysis is that entrepreneurs are well advised to work hard to make sure they have viable product designs that beat the existing and prospective competition. But they should also work on finding products that already have natural market-entry protections. If they don't, then the development of market-entry protections should go hand-in-hand with the development of the products. The market landscape is strewn with the carcasses of firms who thought a great deal about product development and paid little heed to market-entry protections.

Oligopoly

In an oligopoly – a market dominated by a few producers, into which entry is difficult – the demand curve facing an individual competitor will be less elastic than the monopolistic competitor's (as in Figure 11.3). If General Electric raises its price for LED light bulbs, consumers will have few alternatives. A price increase is less likely to drive away customers than under monopolistic competition, and the price–quantity combination achieved by the company will probably be further removed from the competitive ideal. In Figure 11.3, the oligopolist produces only Q_o units for a relatively high price of P_o, compared with the perfect competitor's price–quantity combination of Q_c and P_c. The shaded area representing inefficiency is relatively large.

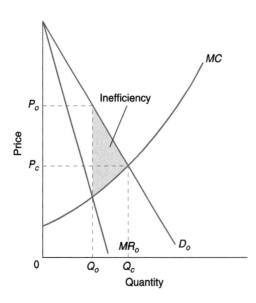

Figure 11.3 The oligopolist as monopolist With fewer competitors than the monopolistic competitor, the oligopolist faces a less elastic demand curve, D_o. Each oligopolist can afford to produce significantly less (Q_o) and to charge significantly more (P_o) than the perfect competitor (who produces Q_c at a price of P_c). The shaded area representing inefficiency is larger than that of a monopolistic competitor.

Exactly how an oligopolist chooses a price is not completely clear. We will examine a few of the major theories proposed. Because each oligopolist is a major factor in the market, their pricing decisions are *mutually interdependent*. The price asked by one will significantly affect the sales of the others. Hence, when one oligopolistic firm lowers its price, the others are likely to lower theirs, to prevent erosion of their market shares. The oligopolist may have to anticipate the pricing policies of others – how they will react to a change in price, and what this may mean for its own policy. In fact, oligopolistic pricing decisions resemble moves in a chess game. The thinking may be so complicated that no one can predict what will happen. Thus, theories of oligopolistic price determination tend to be context-specific, speculative, and confined almost exclusively to the short run. (In the long run, virtually anything can happen.)

The Oligopolist as Price Leader

Given the complexity of the pricing problem, the oligopolistic firm – particularly if it is the dominant firm in the market – may simply decide to behave like a monopolist, since it does have some monopoly power. (If the oligopolist were a pure monopoly, it would have little fear of losing business because of a change in price.) Alternatively, one producer may assume price leadership because it has the lowest costs of production; the others will have to follow its lead or be underpriced and run out of the market. Or the producer that dominates industry sales may assume leadership. Figure 11.4 depicts a situation in which all the firms are relatively small and of equal size, except for one large producer. The collective marginal cost curve of the small firms is shown in Figure 11.4(a), along with the market demand curve, D_m. The dominant producer's marginal cost curve (MC_d) is shown in Figure 11.4(b).

The dominant producer can see from Figure 11.4(a) that, at a price of P_1, the smaller producers will supply the entire market for the product. At P_1, the quantity demanded (Q_2) is exactly what the smaller producers are willing to offer. At P_1 or above, therefore, the dominant producer will sell nothing. At prices below P_1, however, the total quantity demanded exceeds the total quantity supplied by the smaller producers. For example, at a price of P_d, the total quantity demanded in Figure 11.4(a) is Q_3, whereas the total quantity supplied is Q_1. The dominant producer will be able to sell the difference, $Q_3 - Q_1$. For that matter, at every price below P_1, it can sell the difference between the quantity supplied by the smaller producers and the quantity demanded by the market.

As the price falls below P_1, the gap between supply and demand expands, so the dominant producer can sell more and more. If these gaps between quantity demanded and supplied are plotted on another graph, they will form the dominant producer's demand curve – as D_d in Figure 11.4(b). With its demand curve, the dominant producer can develop its accompanying marginal revenue curve – MR_d in Figure 11.4(b). Using its MC and MR curves, it establishes its profit-maximizing output level and price: Q_d and P_d.

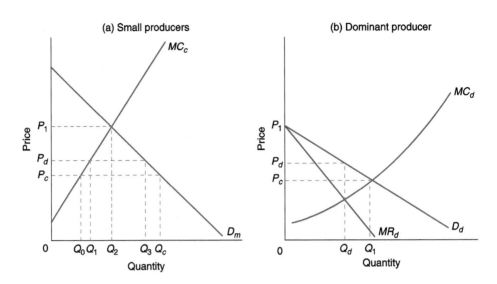

Figure 11.4 The oligopolist as price leader
The dominant producer who acts as a price leader will attempt to undercut the market price established by small producers (panel (a)). At price P_1, the small producers will supply the demand of the entire market, Q_2. At a lower price (e.g., P_d or P_c), the market will demand more than the small producers can supply. In panel (b), the dominant firm determines its demand curve by plotting the quantity it can sell at each price in panel (a). Then it determines its profit-maximizing output level (Q_d) by equating marginal cost with marginal revenue. It charges the highest price the market will bear for this quantity, forcing the market price down to P_d in panel (a). The dominant producer sells $Q_3 - Q_1$ units and the smaller producers supply the rest.

The dominant producer knows it can charge price P_d for quantity Q_d, because this price–quantity combination (and all others on curve D_d) represents a shortage not supplied by small producers at a particular price in Figure 11.4(a). As noted earlier, Q_d is the difference between the quantity demanded and the quantity supplied at price P_d. So, the dominant producer picks its price (P_d) and the smaller producers must follow.[5] If they try to charge a higher price, they will not sell as much as they want.

The Oligopolist in the Long Run

In an oligopolistic market, new potential competitors face significant barriers to entry; therefore, firms in oligopolistic industries can retain their short-run positions much longer than monopolistically competitive firms.

---

[5] Consider market equilibrium with and without the dominant producer. In the absence of the dominant producer, the market price will be P_1, the equilibrium price for a market composed of only the smaller producers. The dominant producer adds quantity Q_d, which causes the price to fall, forcing the smaller producers to cut back production to Q_1 in Figure 11.4(a).

Oligopoly is normally associated with such industries as the automobile, cigarette, and steel markets, which include some extremely large corporations.[6] In those industries, the financial resources required to establish production on a competitive scale may comprise a formidable barrier to entry. One cannot conclude that all new competition is blocked in an oligopoly, however. Many of the best examples of oligopolies are found in local markets with modest demand – for instance, drugstores, stereo shops, and lumber stores – in which only a few competitors exist, even though the financial barriers to entry can easily be overcome. Even in the national market, where the financial requirements for entry may be substantial, some large firms have the financial capacity to overcome barriers to entry. If firms in the electric light-bulb market exploit their short-run profit opportunities by restricting production and raising prices, outside firms can move into the light-bulb market and make a profit – as General Motors has moved into the market for electronics and robotics in recent years.

While oligopoly power is a cause for concern, the basis for competition is the relative ability of firms to enter a market where profits can be made, rather than the absolute size of the firms in the industry. The small regional markets of a century ago, isolated by lack of transportation and communication, were generally (far) less competitive than today's markets – even if today's firms are larger in an absolute sense. In the nineteenth century, the cost of moving into a faraway market effectively protected many local businesses from the threat of new competition.

Cartels: Incentives to Collude, to Cheat, and to Enter

In either a monopolistically competitive market or an oligopolistic market, firms may collude in an attempt to improve their profits by restricting output and raising the market price. In other words, they may agree to behave as though they were a *monopoly* – an arrangement called a **cartel**. The principal purpose of these anticompetitive efforts is to raise their prices and profits above competitive levels. But a cartel is not

> A **cartel** is an organization of independent producers intent on thwarting competition among themselves through the joint regulation of market shares, production levels, and prices.

a single, unified monopoly. The potential for monopoly profits provides a real incentive for competitors to collude – to conspire secretly to fix prices, production

---

[6] The automobile used to be a classic example of oligopoly in America – in the 1950s, with the dominance of General Motors, Ford, and Chevrolet. In recent decades, with dramatically reduced transaction costs and increased international trade, the industry is closer to monopolistic competition with many suppliers and a focus on product differentiation. That said, this market is still a great example of the evolution of industries over time and the "messiness" of the middle of the market structure spectrum.

levels, and market shares. However, after they have reduced market supply and raised the price, each has an incentive to chisel on the agreement. Each competitor will be tempted to cut prices in order to expand sales and profits. After all, if competitors are willing to collude for the purpose of improving their own welfare, they will probably be willing to chisel on cartel rules to enhance their welfare further. The incentive to cheat can easily cause a cartel to collapse – or even fail to form in the first place. If a cartel works for long, it is usually because some form of external cost (e.g., the threat of violence) is imposed on chiselers and barriers to entry (often from the government) make entry prohibitively costly.[7]

Although a cartel of a few firms is usually a more workable proposition than a cartel of many firms, even small groups may not be able to maintain a collusive agreement. Consider an oligopoly of only two producers called a **duopoly**. To keep the analysis simple, we assume here that entry of other competitors is impossible and each duopolist

A **duopoly** is an oligopolistic market shared by only two firms.

has the same constant marginal cost, which means that marginal cost and average cost are equal and can be represented by one horizontal curve. Figure 11.5 shows their combined MC curve, along with the market demand curve for the good. The two producers can maximize monopoly profits if they restrict total quantity to Q_m and sell it for price P_m. Dividing the total quantity sold between them, each will sell Q_1 at the monopoly price. Each will receive an economic profit equal to the area bounded by $ATC_1 P_m ab$, which is equal to total revenues $(P_m \times Q_1)$ minus total cost $(ATC_1 \times Q_1)$.

Once each firm has curbed production, each firm may reason that, by reducing the price slightly – to, say, P_1 – and perhaps disguising the price cut

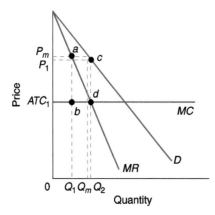

Figure 11.5 A duopoly in a two-member cartel
In an industry composed of two firms of equal size, firms may collude to restrict total output to Q_m and sell at a price of P_m. But having established this price–quantity combination, each has an incentive to chisel on the collusive agreement by lowering price slightly. For example, if one firm charges P_1, it can take the entire market, increasing its sales from Q_1 to Q_2. If the other firm follows suit to protect its market share, each will get a lower price and the cartel will likely collapse.

---

[7] A cartel may provide members with some private benefit that can be denied nonmembers. For example, local medical associations can deny nonmembers the right to practice in local hospitals. In this case, the cost of chiseling is exclusion from membership in the group.

through customer rebates or more attractive credit terms, it can capture the entire market and even raise production to Q_2. Each firm may imagine that its own profits can grow from the area bounded by ATC_1P_mab to the much larger area bounded by ATC_1P_1cd. This tempting scenario presumes, of course, that the other firm does not follow suit and lower its price. Each firm must also worry that, if it doesn't cheat, the other will cut price and capture most of the market share.

Thus, each duopolist has two incentives to chisel on the cartel. The first is offensive – to garner a larger share of the market and more profits. The second is defensive – to avoid a loss of market share and profits if the other cheats. Generally, firms that seek higher profits by forming a cartel will also have difficulty holding the cartel together because of these dual incentives. As each firm responds to the incentives to chisel, the two firms undercut each other and the price falls back toward (but not necessarily to) the competitive equilibrium price – at the intersection of the marginal cost and demand curves. Just how far the price will decline depends on their ability to impose penalties on each other for chiseling.

The strength and viability of a cartel depend on the number of firms in an industry, the freedom with which other firms can enter, and the costs of operating the cartel, detecting chiselers, and enforcing the rules. If firms differ in their production capabilities, the task of establishing each firm's share of the market is more difficult. If a cartel member believes it is receiving a smaller market share than it could achieve on its own, it has a greater incentive to chisel. Because of the built-in incentives for insiders to cheat and for outsiders to enter, the effectiveness of cartels is usually overrated. Even when "successful," their histories tend to be cyclical: periods in which output and prices are successfully controlled followed by periods of chiseling.[8]

Game Theory: Cartels and the Nash Equilibrium

Game theory is the study of how people make decisions when the payoff they receive depends on their own choices and the decisions of others. Throughout the book, we've seen how the Prisoner's Dilemma can be a helpful tool from game theory. Here, we use it to see the temptation to cheat on a cartel agreement with a simple payoff matrix.

Assume a duopoly, with firm A and firm B each providing jungle cruises in a remote tourist resort. The profits that each firm can earn depend on the price each charges. We restrict each firm's pricing to two possibilities: a high (monopoly) price and a low (competitive) price – with the four possible pricing combinations

---

[8] Cartels may have similar incentives to stifle innovation, but will likely run into the same (or greater) troubles in trying to keep the cartel together.

shown in the four cells of the payoff matrix in Table 11.1. In each cell, the profits of firm *A* are shown on the left and the profits of firm *B* are shown on the right. The two firms maximize their joint profits when each charges the high price for jungle cruises, yielding $1000 for each. But notice that, if firm *A* charges the high price, firm *B* will be able to earn $1200 by charging the low price. And if firm *A* charges the low price, firm *B* will make $400 charging the high price, but $500 charging the low price. Either way, it pays firm *B* to charge the low price. Exactly the same situation holds for firm *A*. The temptation then is for both of them to cheat on the agreement to charge the high price. The dilemma is, of course, that, while cheating is the best pricing strategy for both individually, it leads to the worse possible collective outcome for the two firms – total profits of $1000 instead of $2000.

The outcome in which both firms charge the low price is referred to as a *Nash equilibrium* – named after John Nash, whose work economists have followed since the 1950s and who won the Nobel Prize in Economics in 1994 for his contributions to game theory. (He was a distinguished Princeton University mathematician who suffered from mental illness for much of his career. His life and work in game theory was popularized in *A Beautiful Mind*, a bestselling book about the life of mathematician John Nash by Sylvia Nasar (1998) that became an excellent movie starring Russell Crowe in 2001.)

A Nash equilibrium occurs when each decision-maker has made the best decision for herself given the decisions that others have made – any unilateral change by a decision-maker would make her worse off. In the above Prisoner's Dilemma, when each firm is charging the low price, if either one of the firms shifted to a high price, its profits would fall by $100. So, the low-price/low-price outcome is a Nash equilibrium. The low-price decision is also what game theorists call a "dominant strategy": it yields the largest payoff to a decision-maker regardless of what others do. (Not every Nash equilibrium is the result of a dominant strategy. The "battle of the sexes" game from Chapter 2 is a counterexample: if someone changed their decision, it would pay others to change theirs as well.

Table 11.1 Game theory: cartel incentives and the Nash equilibrium

		Firm B	
		High price ($)	Low price ($)
Firm A	High price	1000/1000	400/1200
	Low price	1200/400	500/500

As good as the movie is, it misrepresents the Nash equilibrium and the implications of game theory for economics in a key scene, where Nash supposedly gets the idea for his equilibrium. He is in a bar with some friends. Three attractive women come in, but Nash and his friends agree that the blonde is the best looking of the three. In discussing the best strategy for possibly getting dates with the women, the friends decide that, if they all make a play for the blonde, none of them will likely be successful, so their best choice is to concentrate their attention on the other two. While this may have been the best strategy, it wasn't a Nash equilibrium. With Nash and his friends ignoring the blonde, the chance of getting a date with her goes up – and so the best payoff for each of them is to switch strategies and make a play for the blonde.[9]

Government-Supported Cartels

Government can either encourage or discourage the formation of a cartel. Through regulatory agencies that fix prices, determine market shares, and enforce cartel rules, government can keep cartel members or potential competitors from doing what comes naturally – chiseling. In doing so, government may be providing an important service to the industry, making cartels more likely and more durable. Perhaps this is why insurance companies often oppose deregulation of their rate structures. In seeking or welcoming regulation, an industry may calculate that it is easier to control one regulatory agency than a whole group of firms plus potential competitors.

In 1975, the airline industry opposed President Ford's proposal that Congress curtail the power of the Civil Aeronautics Board to set rates and determine airline routes. As the *Wall Street Journal* reported when Congress was debating airline deregulation (*Wall Street Journal* 1975):

The administration bill quickly drew a sharp blast from the Air Transport Association, which was speaking for the airline industry. The proposed legislation "would tear apart a national transportation system recognized as the finest in the world," the trade group said, urging Congress to reject it because it would cause "a major reduction or elimination of scheduled air service to many communities and would lead inevitably to increased costs to consumers."

---

[9] In another scene from the movie, Nash's professor tells him that his work discredits almost 200 years of economic theory. This comment is also in Nasar's book, in which she claims that the Nash equilibrium in a Prisoner's Dilemma "contradicts Adam Smith's metaphor of the Invisible Hand in economics" (Nasar 1998, 119). The suggestion here is that Smith was wrong in arguing that, when each person pursues his own interest, he is also serving the collective interest of others in the game. Exactly the opposite is true in a Prisoner's Dilemma – where the result of each person trying to do as well as possible is the minimization of the collective welfare. But Smith was careful to point out that the Invisible Hand worked only under certain conditions – those in which private property rights were enforced, markets were contestable, people were free to buy from and sell to those who made them the best offer, and public goods such as national defense and certain types of infrastructure were provided collectively.

The real reason the airlines opposed deregulation became clear in the early 1980s, when several airlines filed for bankruptcy. Partial deregulation, begun in 1979, increased competition, depressing fares and profits. Real fares have fallen significantly since deregulation and the big airlines have been forced to operate more efficiently in response to competitive pressures from small innovative airlines, trying to capture a larger share of the airline market with lower costs and prices.

Government can also suppress competition in many other ways that have nothing to do with price. For example, prohibiting the sale of hard liquor on Sunday can benefit liquor dealers, who might otherwise be forced by the market to stay open on Sundays. In Florida, a state representative who managed to get a law through the legislature permitting Sunday liquor sales was denounced by liquor dealers. As you would expect, domestic and global competitive pressures have weakened restrictions on liquor sales where those restrictions have been most severe (*The Economist* 2004).

Cartels with Lagged Demand

Our analysis of cartels has been based on the presumption of a "standard good." With the network effects and lagged demand introduced in Chapter 4, the pricing strategies of a cartel are potentially different. Remember that the value of a network good to individual consumers goes up as more consumers buy the good. The demand for a lagged-demand good can also rise as use of the product is extended and more people learn about the good and its value. When the market is split among two or more producers, each firm understands that, by lowering price, more goods will be sold currently, but even more goods will be sold in the future – when the benefits of the network effects and lagged demand kick in. However, each firm can reason that the additional future sales generated by its current price reduction could be picked up by one of the other producers. Thus, the benefits are external to the firm making the current sacrifice of a lower price. So, each producer can reason that it should not incur the current costs of a lower price for the benefit of others. Each producer individually has an impaired incentive to lower the price.

On the other hand, each producer can also see that all the producers have a collective incentive to lower the price currently. Why? To stimulate future demand and to raise their future price and profits. A cartel under such circumstances would organize to do what all the producers have an interest in doing: *lower* the price (rather than raise the price, as in conventional markets). The problem is that the incentive to go its own way or to chisel on the cartel remains strong for each firm – as is true in the conventional type of cartel – which suggests that consumers may not get the lower current price because of cartel cheating (Lee and Kreutzer 1982).

The Case of the Natural Monopoly

So far, our discussion of firms has assumed rising marginal costs. One argument for regulation, however, is based on the opposite characteristic. Industries such as electric utilities are considered a **natural monopoly**, meaning that the average and marginal costs of production decrease over the long run. That is, within the relevant range of the market demand, the

> A **natural monopoly** is a market structure characterized by a decline in the long-run average cost of production within the range of the market demand, which means that the market will be served most cost-effectively with only one producer.

LRMC and *LRAC* curves in Figure 11.6 slope downward. As a result, these firms tend naturally toward only one producer remaining viable in the market. Natural monopolies are seen as prime candidates for regulation because their ability to take advantage of massive economies of scale is efficient and desirable, but their (unregulated) dominance in the market would allow them to exert considerable monopoly power.

Figure 11.7 adds the demand and marginal revenue curves for electric power. A firm with decreasing costs will tend to expand production and lower its costs until it becomes large enough for its production decisions to influence price – that is, until it achieves monopoly power. Then it will choose to produce at the point at which all firms produce: where marginal cost equals marginal revenue. Thus, the monopolistic firm in Figure 11.7 will sell Q_m megawatts at an average price of P_m, generating monopoly profits in the process.

Although a firm with decreasing costs can expand until it is the major (or only) producer, it will not necessarily be able to price like a monopoly. Suppose a "natural monopoly" flexes its market muscle and charges P_m for Q_m units. Another firm, seeing the first firm's economic profits, may enter the industry, expand production, and charge a lower price, luring away customers. To protect its interests, the original firm will cut its price and expand production to lower its costs. It is difficult to say how far the price will fall and output will rise, but

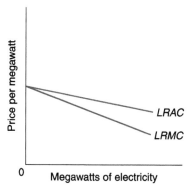

Figure 11.6 Long-run marginal and average costs in a natural monopoly

In a natural monopoly, long-run marginal cost and average costs decline continuously over the relevant range of production because of economies of scale. Although the *LRMC* and *LRAC* curves may eventually turn upward because of diseconomies of scale, the firm's market is not large enough to support production in this output range.

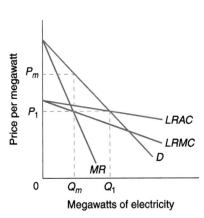

Figure 11.7 Creation of a natural monopoly
Even with declining marginal costs, the monopolist will produce at the point where marginal cost equals marginal revenue, making Q_m units and charging a price of P_m. Without barriers to entry, other firms could enter the market, causing the price to fall toward P_1 and the quantity produced to rise toward Q_1. But with sizable barriers to entry (at least from significant overhead costs), only one firm will dominate the industry indefinitely.

only one firm is likely to survive such a battle, selling to the entire market at a price that competitors cannot undercut. This price will be approximately P_1 in Figure 11.7.

If the price does fall to P_1 and only one firm survives, its total revenue will be $P_1 \times Q_1$. At this level, the firm's average cost is equal to P_1; therefore, the total cost of production (the average cost times the quantity sold) is equal to the firm's revenue. The firm is just covering its cost of production, including the owners' risk cost. Now alone in the market, the firm may think it can restrict output, raise its price, and reap an economic profit. Still, it faces the ever-present threat of some other company entering the market and underpricing its product. But, in practice, the existence of sizable barriers to entry often allows one firm to dominate indefinitely.

The Economics and Politics of Regulating Monopoly Power

Most industries are regulated to some extent – indirectly if not directly. And in many contexts, regulation is a primary consideration. In Chapter 6, we developed the basic theories for regulatory endeavors, which we revisit here: the public-interest theory and the economic theory. (We take up the special case for regulating banking and for extending bank regulations to "nonbank" financial institutions in Online Reading 11.2.)

The Public-Interest Theory of Monopoly Regulation

Regulation of monopoly has often been justified on the grounds that it is in the "public interest," meaning that it helps to achieve commonly acknowledged social goals. For economists, the focus of regulation is mostly to promote the public interest by increasing market efficiency.

Figure 11.8 shows a cartelized industry producing at an output level of Q_m and selling at a price of P_m. This output level is inefficient because the marginal benefit of the last unit produced (equal to its price) is greater than its marginal cost. Although consumers are willing to pay more than the cost of producing additional units, they are not given the opportunity to buy those units. The cartel's price–quantity combination creates economic profit for the owners (which may be considered inequitable), but also results in the loss of net benefits (deadweight loss) equal to the shaded triangular area *abc*.

Regulation can force firms to sell at lower prices and to produce and sell larger quantities. Ideally, firms can be made to produce Q_c units and to sell them at price P_c, which is the same price–quantity combination that could be achieved under highly competitive conditions. At this output level, the marginal benefit of the last unit produced is equal to its marginal cost.

Government regulators need not demand that a company produce Q_c units. All they have to do is require a company to charge no more than P_c. After this order has been given, the portion of the demand curve above P_c, along with the accompanying segment of the *MR* curve, becomes irrelevant. The firm simply is not allowed to choose a price–quantity combination above point *b* on the demand curve. The regulated firm becomes a "price taker" – this time, from the government – and so its demand and marginal revenue curves are equal and horizontal at P_c. The profit-maximizing producer will choose to sell at P_c – the maximum legal price. With marginal revenue guaranteed at P_c, the firm will equate marginal revenue with marginal cost and produce at Q_c, the efficient output level.

All this said, ideal results cannot be expected from the regulatory process. The cost of determining the ideal price–quantity combination can be extraordinarily high, if not prohibitive. Because regulators do not work for regulated industries, they will not know the details of a company's marginal cost or demand elasticity. The problem is particularly acute for regulators of monopolies because there are no competitors from which alternative cost estimates can be obtained. Furthermore, if prices are adjusted upward to allow for a company's higher costs, a regulated firm has a reduced incentive to control costs. The regulated price could conceivably end up being the monopoly price, with what-would-have-been

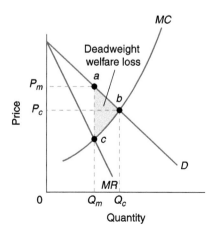

Figure 11.8 The effect of regulation on a cartelized industry

The profit-maximizing cartel will equilibrate at point *a*, producing only Q_m units and selling at a price of P_m. Since consumers want Q_c units and are willing to pay more than the marginal cost of production for them, Q_m is an inefficient production level. Under pure competition, the industry will produce at point *b*. Regulation can raise output and lower the price, ideally to P_c, thereby eliminating the deadweight welfare loss which results from monopolistic behavior and is equal to the shaded triangle *abc*.

monopoly profits converted into added costs (for example, higher pay and perks for managers of the regulated firm).

As we developed in Chapter 6, effective public policy always requires sufficient knowledge and adequately pure motives. Beyond the general concerns about any government intervention, the problem here is the need for highly specialized knowledge of production – about business and economics in general, and the regulated industry in particular. Moreover, where is one likely to gain this knowledge? From the industry to be regulated. And what is the probability that those with the knowledge will be objective in how they see the industry to be regulated? This is the sophisticated version of a concern called "capture of the regulatory body." A more cynical type of capture is also possible – if the regulated industry makes concerted efforts to influence regulators through favors or even bribes.

The cost of the regulatory process and the extent to which it can be harnessed by interest groups must both be emphasized. If regulation is truly to serve the public interest, it must increase the efficiency of the entire social system. That is, its benefits must exceed its costs. In practice, regulation often protects large and politically influential firms and industries against competition from smaller firms by imposing regulations that raise the costs of small firms more than those of large firms. Though most people assume that businesses oppose regulation, the truth is that many businesses pursue regulations that favor them. As discussed earlier in this chapter, the major airlines fought against the elimination of regulation in the 1970s. According to one study, businesses spend hundreds of billions of dollars a year resisting changes in regulation (both reductions and increases in regulation) because they benefited from the *status quo* (Crain and Hopkins 2001).

The Special Case for Regulating Natural Monopolies

Natural monopolies are often singled out as deserving special regulatory attention because, as we saw earlier, only a single producer will emerge in such a market. But from a purely theoretical perspective, the existence of a natural monopoly is insufficient justification for regulation. Unless there are significant barriers to entry into an industry and an inelastic market demand, natural monopolies should not be able to charge monopoly prices. In reply to this argument, proponents of regulation hold that some industries, such as electric utilities, require such huge amounts of capital that no competitor could be expected to enter the market to challenge the natural monopoly. This argument presumes, however, that electric power generation must take place on an extremely large scale. Such is not necessarily the case – as solar panels show. Further, if economic profits exist, many large corporations can raise the capital needed to produce electricity on a profitable scale.

Proponents of regulating natural monopolies also point to inefficient levels of output. Even if an unregulated industry produces Q_1 units and prices this output at P_1 (see Figure 11.9), it has not reached the efficient output level. This would be the level at which marginal cost equals marginal benefit – the point at which the MC curve intersects the demand curve: at Q_2 in Figure 11.9. Why does output fall short?

Given the market demand curve, the firm could sell an output of Q_2 for only P_2, earning total revenues of $P_2 \times Q_2$. Because the average cost of producing this output level – AC_1 on the vertical axis – would be greater than the price, total costs $(AC_1 \times Q_2)$ would be greater than total revenues. The loss to a firm that tried to produce at the efficient output level is shown by the shaded area on the graph. To produce at the efficient output level, a company would require a subsidy to offset this loss (which creates inefficiencies of its own because of the economic distortions created by the tax necessary to raise the revenue for the subsidy), or it would have to be able to price-discriminate, charging progressively lower prices for additional units sold.

After a firm is given a subsidy, its pricing and production decision must be closely monitored, since its incentive to control costs will be weakened. If the firm allows its cost curves to drift upward, the price it can charge will also rise. In Figure 11.10, the firm's cost curves shift up from $LRMC_1$ and $LRAC_1$ to $LRMC_2$ and $LRAC_2$. Following the rule that price should be set at the intersection of the $LRMC$ and demand curves, regulators permit the price to rise from P_1 to P_2. The firm's subsidized losses shrink from the shaded area $P_1 ATC_1 ba$ to $P_2 ATC_2 dc$, but the quantity produced also decreases from Q_1 to Q_2. Consumers are now getting fewer units at a higher price.

Thus, production may be equally efficient with or without regulation. Critics point to the U.S. Postal Service as an example of an industry that is closely regulated and subsidized, yet highly inefficient. If the postal industry were truly a natural monopoly, it would be a low-cost producer and would not need protection from competition. Proponents of regulation see the inefficiencies we have just demonstrated as an argument for even more careful scrutiny of a regulated firm's

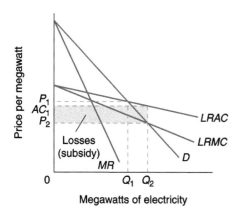

Figure 11.9 Underproduction by a natural monopoly

A natural monopolist that cannot price-discriminate will produce only Q_1 megawatts – less than Q_2, the efficient output level – and will charge a price of P_1. If the firm tries to produce Q_2, it will make losses equal to the shaded area, since its price (P_2) will not cover its average cost (AC_1).

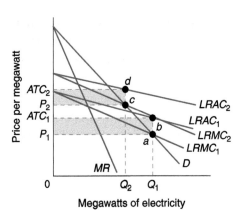

Figure 11.10 Regulation and increasing costs
If a natural monopoly is compensated for the losses incurred by operating at the efficient output level (the shaded area P_1ATC_1ba), it may monitor its costs less carefully. Its cost curves may shift up – from $LRMC_1$ to $LRMC_2$ and from $LRAC_1$ to $LRAC_2$. Regulators will then have to raise the price from P_1 to P_2 as production falls from Q_1 to Q_2. The firm will still have to be subsidized (by an amount equal to the shaded area P_2ATC_2dc) and consumers will be paying more for less.

cost – or for government control of production costs through nationalization. But how will this work in practice and what will this process cost?

Not all natural monopolies need subsidies to operate at an efficient output level. For all megawatts up to Q_1 in Figure 11.9, the unregulated firm can charge up to P_1 – a price that just covers its costs on those units. If its product cannot be easily resold, the firm can engage in price discrimination, charging slightly lower prices for the additional units beyond Q_1. As long as its marginal prices are on or below the demand curve and above the MC curve, the firm will cover its costs while moving toward the efficient output level – without giving other firms an incentive to move into its market.

Antitrust: Breaking up Monopoly Power

Should government attempt to break up monopolies? The theory is simple enough and the prospective benefits of antitrust activity are easy to understand. If the government prevents mergers that would result in too much market concentration – and breaks up existing monopolies that have too much monopoly power – then outcomes may well be more equitable and efficient.

But, in practice, key questions emerge: How do we measure monopoly power within markets? How long is it likely to persist if left alone? (Without protection from the government, monopoly power may eventually or quickly dissipate.) How costly will it be while it lasts – in terms of inequities and lost efficiency? What are the costs of the machinery of government needed to dissolve monopoly power? Thus, the decision whether to prosecute antitrust violations depends in part on the costs and benefits of such an action and whether the benefits justify the costs. As covered in Online Reading 3.4, the first seller of handheld calculators enjoyed a temporary monopoly of the U.S. market in 1969. Subsequently, the industry developed rapidly – and, in retrospect, it is clear that antitrust action would have been inappropriate.

To give another example from 1969, the Justice Department decided that an antitrust suit was warranted against IBM, which enjoyed a monopoly in the domestic computer market, dominated by large mainframe computers. After more than a decade, the Justice Department dropped the case in January 1982. The accumulated documentation from the proceedings filled a warehouse. The Justice Department and IBM devoted an untold number of lawyer-hours to the case. In the meantime, new firms producing minicomputers and microcomputers seriously eroded IBM's alleged monopoly – a trend that has continued since. Thus, the net benefits to society from the antitrust action against IBM were probably negative.

Similarly, the cost to prosecute Microsoft for antitrust violations (starting in 1998) seems also, in the long run, to outweigh the achieved benefits. The courts ruled that Microsoft is a "monopoly" in the operating system market. But the consumer benefits, in terms of lower prices and greater availability of products, which might result are still not obvious (McKenzie 2000). Microsoft's dominance in the operating system market continues to erode, with the resurgence in sales of Apple computers in the 2000s and the development of alternative computing platforms where Microsoft has yet to establish a significant foothold in smartphones and tablets. At the turn of the century, the company was likely on the horns of the "innovator's dilemma" we will describe in Part B – perhaps reluctant to devote corporate attention to creating its own market for mobile devices, maybe *because* of the dominance of its Windows operating system in the desktop and laptop computing markets. (If you're interested, we have much more to say about antitrust in Online Reading 11.5.)

IBM and Microsoft are among the strongest examples for proponents of antitrust. But antitrust efforts reach into more competitive market structures as well. Should Sprint be allowed to merge with JetBlue? Krogers with Albertsons? Staples with Office Depot? Why could Humana merge with United Healthcare but not with Aetna? The relevant questions are still the same: How much competition is enough to keep prices low? When do greater economies of scale give businesses a better opportunity to reduce costs and lower prices? How large are the barriers to entry for potential competitors?

Usually, the concern of antitrust is that consumers will be exploited by monopoly power in terms of higher prices and reduced quality. But, in recent years, the most attention in antitrust has been in the context of Big Tech (Google, Apple, Amazon, Facebook/Meta, Netflix, YouTube, and so on). Interestingly, the price of Google and Facebook to consumers is free in terms of money. Instead, the concerns are with respect to the price of (digital) advertising, the ability to profit through advertising revenues on content produced by other companies, the ability to gather and sell information on consumers, and the ability to "spread disinformation" and "harm democracy."

Finally, it's worth mentioning that government does not use antitrust against its own endeavors. As we've detailed in this chapter and earlier, government is quite fond of restricting competition to help interest groups (e.g., international trade restrictions), selling monopoly power (e.g., public schools with only one provider of class rings and graduation gowns), allowing noncompetitive structures (e.g., professional sports and NCAA revenue sports), and running its own entities with significant monopoly power (e.g., K-12 education). The irony is that government is famous for its antitrust efforts but is far busier creating and enhancing (rather than reducing) monopoly power.

The Economic Theory of Regulation

Beginning in the 1950s, "Public Choice" economists began to see regulation as a product of the supply of and demand for politically provided benefits (Stigler 1971; Breyer 1982). Firms have a demand for regulation that serves their private interests. For example, as we've seen, maintaining a cartel in a free market is difficult because colluders tend to cheat on the agreements – and, if somehow effective, new firms will enter the market unless barriers are prohibitively large (and they weren't so large to prevent multiple firms in the first place). In comparison, enforcing a collusive agreement through government regulation can be (much) more attractive. Government is seen as a supplier of regulatory services to industry – price fixing, restrictions on market entry, and so on. These services are offered to industries willing to pay for them – most notably, through campaign contributions. Regulators and politicians allocate the benefits among all the various private-interest groups, trying to equate political support and opposition at the margin.

To the extent that regulation benefits all regulated firms, whether or not they have contributed to the cost of procuring it, industries may consider regulation a "public good" which creates a free-rider problem – where others can enjoy the benefits without paying for it. Some firms will try to free-ride on others' efforts to secure regulation. If all firms free-ride, however, the collective benefits of regulation will be lost.

The free-rider phenomenon is particularly noticeable in large groups where the cost of organizing for collective action can be substantial. Someone must bear the initial cost of organization. Yet because the benefits of organization are spread more or less evenly over the group, the party that initiates the organization may incur costs greater than the benefits it receives. Thus, collective action may not be taken. Free-riding may explain why some large groups, such as administrative assistants, have not yet secured government protection. Everyone may be waiting for everyone else to act. Small groups may have much greater success because of their proportionally smaller organizational costs and larger individual benefits.

There are some exceptions to this rule. Several large groups, including truckers and farmers, have obtained a high degree of government regulation, whereas many highly concentrated groups, such as the electrical appliance industry, have not. In highly concentrated industries, it may be less costly to develop private cartels than to organize and secure government regulation. In industries composed of many firms, on the other hand, any one firm's share of the cost of securing regulation may be smaller than its share of the costs of establishing and enforcing a private cartel. Large groups control more sizable voting blocs than do small groups. Large groups may also have the advantage of established trade associations, whose help can be enlisted in pushing for protective legislation (Olson 1971, chapters 1 and 2).

In broad terms, the economic theory of regulation explains much about government policy – but this is one of its weaknesses. The theory is so broad that its usefulness as a predictor is limited. It does not enable economists to forecast which industries are likely to seek or achieve government regulation. Nor does it explain the political movement to deregulate the trucking and banking industries – or to regulate the environment. Neither of these trends appears to directly meet the demand of any particular business interest group. In general, any self-interested group will be better represented the larger its interest in the outcome, the smaller its size, the more homogeneous its position and objectives, and the more certain the outcome.

PERSPECTIVE 11
The "Innovator's Dilemma"

In our discussion of perfect competition, the product was a given (or assumed into existence), along with the firm's cost structure. Much of what firms actually do was assumed away to highlight how price and profits influence a firm's production decisions and scale of operation.

When markets are far removed from being perfectly competitive – when products are not given and the potential for innovation in product development abounds (as is true in most real-world markets) – a firm's strategies in reacting to competitors and product development are central management problems. Managers must think through the act-and-react play in "games" that have been central to our discussions in several chapters. In such "games," expectations of what others might do and what will pay off are important. In effect, this Perspective introduces another reality check, stressing that entrepreneurs often face perplexing dilemmas when considering their options on how to innovate – and, for that matter, whether to innovate. Contrary to many business commentaries, being an innovative company is not always synonymous with profit maximization.

As noted in Chapter 9, many business scholars and practitioners believe that "first movers" (the first persons or companies to develop product lines) have strong, strategic market advantages over later rivals. But Gerald Tellis and Peter Golder (2002) found that first movers were usually eclipsed by second, third, and later movers. Why do first movers so often lose their market leadership? The list of possible answers is quite long. For example, markets are constantly being revolutionized and dominant market positions cannot be held for long, given the rapidity of ongoing technological advances in products and production processes. If first movers behave like monopolies, hiking their prices and profits, they encourage new entrants. With large profit margins, they may fail to be sufficiently concerned about their costs. And although first movers have certain advantages, later entrants can have greater ones, including not having to identify and prove the economic viability of a nascent market. And so on.

We have no quibble with these explanations, but we hasten to add another, often-overlooked, line of argument: the retrenchment or demise of firms, especially those making monopoly profits, is often built into their success – what business professor Clayton Christensen (1997) calls the "innovator's dilemma" (McKenzie and Galar 2004).

To see the predicament of innovators, suppose that decades ago you were the first firm to sell a revolutionary new product – say, a mainframe computer – that was instantly very profitable because the product had considerable cost-saving value to buyers and you could charge monopoly prices. To maximize profits from the new technology, you would develop a corporate culture and incentive system to direct the energies of line workers and managers toward gradually refining, upgrading, and exploiting the known technology.[10] In defining your firm's internal control and development system, you determine what will be done in the firm, but also what will *not* be done. With R&D, you will likely limit the range of investigation, which could easily preclude research on revolutionary new product categories that do not rely directly on your firm's known technologies.

Of course, you could leave your business and R&D systems unconstrained, which means that employee energies can and will be directed in many ways. The problem is that you have a known product and production technology generating profits. If you leave your firm's R&D unfocused, your employees might discover or invent the next big product breakthrough – what will be seen in retrospect as a "disruptive technology." But you may have no more idea where the disruptive technology is coming from than anyone else – and you could waste considerable resources trying to find it. Furthermore, you would be diverting resources from the exploitation of your known technology. For many firms, the best option is to keep their focus on the known technology and direct its workers to refine and

---

[10] Organizational economist John Roberts carefully defines a firm's culture: "[I]t involves the fundamental shared values of the people in the firm, as well as their shared beliefs about why the firm exists, about what they are collectively and individually doing, and to what end. ... More significantly, it involves the norms of behavior that prevail in dealing with other members of the firm and with outsiders" (Roberts 2004, 18).

upgrade the known product with the intent of "mining" a relatively predictable R&D strategy. But by making a strategic decision to focus resources on "core competencies," the firm can intentionally leave the discovery and development of new, disruptive technologies to others.

We might imagine that the firm in an initially dominant market position can sit back and wait for the new technology to come onto the market – and then buy the firm that develops it or replicate it. But when new technologies first appear, it is not always clear that they are disruptive – that they will cause retreat or even the demise of the established firm and its products. New products and technologies are untested in terms of initial profitability and long-run survivability. No one can initially be sure that new products and technologies will ever be able to achieve long-run monopoly profits.

An established firm's internal culture and incentive systems may also constrain its movement into new markets and its adoption of new production technologies. They might efficiently exploit the known product and technology, but the established systems may not work so effectively in the development and exploitation of new products and technology. Of course, the established firm might frequently test its corporate flexibility, but such tests are costly and can be disruptive in themselves – as profits from known products and technologies can be lost in the process.[11]

To appreciate the innovator's dilemma, consider how you would appraise "conductive fabrics" – cloth with flexible and embedded (out-of-sight) wiring that can transmit electricity from human touch (just as computer touch screens have been able to do since the 1960s). For example, one can imagine emails being written on the legs of pants. In 2015, Google and Levi Strauss announced that they would explore the uses of the fabric through "Project Jacquard" (Dougherty 2015). Years later, the technology has many applications, but significant (and financially sound) uses of the technology are still speculative. Should other firms have diverted resources to advance these fabrics and expand their uses – away from other things where they have proven competency, such as speeding up search engines and making blue jeans? Should Microsoft, Amazon, or Apple follow Google's lead, knowing they will likely need to commit tens (if not hundreds) of millions of dollars to up-front development costs? Conductive fabrics could be "the next big thing," but maybe not – and, even if so, who knows when? In 2013,

---

[11] John Roberts (2004, 72) explains the cultural dilemma firms face – and draws out the nontrivial paradox that a firm operating at less than known maximum efficiency at every point in time might do better than "more efficient" firms over time: a company that mandates operating strictly according to *currently* defined best practices and has operations manuals that are always followed will struggle to generate potential improvements in best practices. One that allows more variation will rarely be using best practices at any given point in time in all its operations, but may do better on average and last longer.

Google thought that Google Glass (a computer screen smaller than an acorn that could fit on eyeglasses to display emails and web pages) might be immensely profitable, but the market has not been impressive so far. These are tough questions to answer, because there are so many unknowns about technology, and firm resources have many alternative uses.

The innovator's dilemma has been faced by many firms with mixed success. A good example is the predicament of IBM in the 1970s with its known mainframe computer technology. IBM was by far the most established mainframe computer producer in the world. When the PC emerged in the 1970s, neither Steve Jobs nor the people at Big Blue knew whether the PC would significantly challenge the market hegemony of the mainframe computer and IBM's dominance in the market. IBM also had a tightly directed corporate culture and incentive system – all directed toward enhancing and selling mainframe computers and related services. IBM could have chosen early in the 1970s to explore the PC market, but it was also reasonably worried that the diversion of corporate talent would be a waste, given that the PC might remain a sophisticated toy and never be a significant challenge to mainframes. IBM also could have reasoned (given the best but limited available information at the time) that it could sit back and wait for others to prove (or disprove) the viability of the PC market. Then, using its established market position and brand name, it could quickly take over the budding market. Needless to say, with its wait-and-see strategy and several crucial, mistaken market assessments, IBM was a late mover in PCs and never achieved the prominence and profitability it had in the mainframe market. In 2005, IBM finally gave up its pursuit and sold its PC division to Lenovo, a Chinese computer manufacturer.

This is not to say that IBM made the wrong decision in the 1970s to maintain its corporate focus on mainframe computers. In hindsight, one can say that *if* IBM had become an early player in the PC market and *if* it had not taken up other lines of new product development that turned out to be financial "dry holes" (which a less focused corporate culture could have allowed), *then* it could have been a much stronger company with PCs in the 1980s and 1990s. But those are two big "ifs." Who can say that IBM didn't, from the perspective of the 1970s, make decisions that maximized the value of the company's wealth – even if, by not initially responding to the PC technology, its decisions caused its exit from the market in 2005? Established companies that try new technologies are often unsuccessful.

Walmart entered the online video rental business in mid-2003, challenging Netflix, which had pioneered online video rentals in 1999. Market analysts were understandably concerned about Netflix's future, given Walmart's market savvy in "big-box" stores. However, in mid-2005, after investing tens of millions of dollars to promote its online video rental business and after waging a rental price war with Netflix (and Blockbuster), Walmart pulled out of the market with only 10 percent of the Netflix customer base – and set a new (presumably more profitable) course, referring its online customers to Netflix (Hansell 2005).

Sometimes, the efforts to innovate and expand are short-lived, amusing to outsiders, and only somewhat costly. Consider how somebody once thought these would be a good idea: Colgate Lasagna, Coors Sparkling Water, perfumes by Bic and Harley-Davidson, McPizza, Cosmo yogurt, Frito-Lay lemonade, and Cheetos lip balm. Beyond these relatively famous examples, one can imagine that the market landscape has been littered with failed and forgotten attempts by established firms to enter new markets. That said, even modest innovations can pay off immensely. Subway displayed its ingredients to consumers, who then picked what they wanted, leading to tremendous success.

Jeff Bezos's investment in "platforms" through Amazon has been revolution-ary. He has found a profitable way to reduce transaction costs, connecting buyers and sellers of all types to each other at lower cost. As such, Amazon has been a formidable competitor for brick-and-mortar stores. But it relies on other com-panies (e.g., UPS) to ship its products. And its warehouse model is under threat from more-mobile providers such as Uber. Should Amazon focus on its current strengths or look to operate airplanes, extend into drone delivery services, and/ or explore options in Uber's delivery space?

Likewise, Microsoft has invested heavily in OpenAI to develop ChatGPT with favorable early results. But can it continue to lead the field? Should it integrate ChatGPT with its search engine Bing to compete with Google? Should Google invest in similar ventures to fend off the challenge from Microsoft? Failure to innovate could lead to a (precipitous) drop in market share. But failing to invest well could be even more damaging.

The innovator's dilemma can also manifest itself in brand maintenance. The Ford Motor Company's Taurus was the top-selling automobile model in the United States for several years in the late 1980s and early 1990s. But Ford allowed the Taurus brand name to grow stale by not materially changing the car's appear-ance and features, perhaps worried about the risk associated with redesigning a top-selling design. By 2005, Ford had a line-up of largely uninspired designs that, according to one industry observer, was responsible for the company's loss of market share and its corporate debt being downgraded to "junk" status by Standard & Poor's (Ingrassia 2005).

Kodak, once dominant in the camera and film markets, is now a shadow of its former self – perhaps because it did not imagine the impact of digital cameras and picture files, especially with the rapid increase in hard-disk capacity, which dramatically reduced the price of storage space for digital pictures. (See Online Reading 11.3, which covers a brief history of Kodak's downfall.) Or maybe this was the best Kodak could do. Note that Intel, with a corporate culture focused on exploiting and enhancing microprocessor technology, decided to develop cameras that could spur the development of teleconferencing that would (profitably) be driven by computers with Intel microprocessors inside. The camera digression proved to be a "dry hole," much to the chagrin of former Intel CEO Andy Grove (Burgelman 2002).

Of course, companies have been known to reinvent themselves: IBM (from a mainframe and PC manufacturer into a business services firm), Nokia (from a conglomerate into a telecommunication firm), Nissan (from a failing car company in the late-1990s into a profitable company with inspired car designs by 2005), and Netflix (nimbly moving within the entertainment industry). But our point remains: many attempted conversions are failures – as are many of the product development diversions that are the pet projects of top executives (Roberts 2004, 274–280; Ghosn 2005; Ingrassia 2005). Former Apple CEO John Sculley was certain that its Newton personal electronic assistant would be worth the millions Apple devoted to its development. While the concept was good (as the Palm Pilot proved), the initial project was a disaster for Sculley and Apple (Roberts 2004, 273). Interestingly, Apple successfully returned to the Newton market with the iPod and iPhone that forced the retreat of the Palm Pilot.

In other words, contrary to advice often given that the "reinvention" of a failing company is the best strategy, a company's ultimate market retreat, if not demise, may be a company's best strategy for maximizing the wealth of its shareholders.[12] That is, instead of always seeking to maximize the life of a company with innovations in technology or market positioning, executives should at times use their failing companies as "cash cows" and drain the company of its technology and brand capital through limited investments in reinvention strategies.

---

[12] Roberts (2004, 67–73) argues that *nations* can also face the innovator's dilemma. Consider Japan. Before the 1990s, Japan had a business and government policy culture that was well set up to exploit known technologies that Japanese businesses could import and exploit to pursue a national goal of maximizing growth (with profits taking a secondary role). Business practices of providing permanent employment, which resulted in employee loyalty to their companies, as well as a financial system that limited stockholder control over firm growth goals, enabled the country to recover from World War II with remarkable rapidity. However, the country's business and government policy culture were ill-suited to cope with intensifying global competition. The country had to endure a prolonged lull in economic progress from the early 1990s because of the reluctance of business managers, workers, and policy-makers to accept the required changes in business practices and policies: "Indeed, it has taken a long time for the leaders there to begin to realize that the problems are not simple macroeconomic ones, but fundamental structural ones. Japan is still struggling to find a new way" (Roberts 2004, 70).

Part B Organizational Economics and Management

We have been concerned with competition among firms in final product markets. Managers are pressed to operate efficiently in competitive markets or face a loss of market share (and, perhaps, their jobs). But competition extends well in this realm. In the next chapter, we'll focus on competition and outcomes in input markets, especially labor. Here, we'll discuss how whole firms can be bought and sold – also a competitive market. In particular, entrepreneurs search for under-performing firms, because their resources can be redeployed for greater profits. This section of the chapter is about managing with an eye on the market for corporate control.

"Hostile" Takeover as a Check on Managerial Monopolies and Other Inefficiencies

It may appear that our discussion of monopolies applies only to "markets" and has little or nothing to do with the management of firms. But the theory of monopolies is directly applicable to management problems because firms often rely exclusively on internal departments (and their employees) to provide a variety of services, such as legal, advertising, accounting, IT, and the production of parts that are assembled into the firm's final goods. In such cases, the internal departments can act like little monopolies, cutting back on what they produce, reducing quality, and demanding a higher "price" (through the firm's budget processes).

Outsourcing is one way to avoid the inefficiencies of internal monopolies. It can improve a firm's profitability in two ways. First, it offers firms the opportunity to get some of their services cheaper from competitive outside bids. Second, it can encourage internal departments to work more efficiently if they are aware of the threat of being replaced by outside suppliers. For example, in 2004, Western Michigan University took bids to provide its custodial care from its existing union of sixty custodial workers and five outside firms. It chose to replace its current workers with those employed by Commercial Sanitation Management Services, reducing its costs by $1.5 million per year (Davis 2005).[13]

More broadly, managers can become complacent and allow their departments to act monopolistically (and inefficiently). They may become lax for other reasons as well, spending more on office perks than necessary, expanding the size of the firm beyond its core competencies, and generally being too lavish with shareholder profits. Top management may be tempted to take advantage of the

---

[13] For a clever, comedic, cynical, exaggerated version of this threat, check out: https://youtu.be/ZBdU9v5nLKQ.

Prisoner's Dilemma for shareholders. Each shareholder will likely shirk on monitoring the behavior of firm managers. Corporate takeovers, which threaten the jobs of management teams who disregard shareholder interests, represent an important check on management discretion.

Corporate takeovers occur for many reasons and in different ways. There may be complementarities in the production and distribution of the products of two firms that can be best realized by one firm. Two firms may find that they can realize economies of scale by combining their operations. Or one firm may be supplying another firm with the use of highly specific capital – and a merger reduces the threat of opportunistic behavior that would be costly to both (as covered in Chapter 7). Most takeovers are "friendly" – that is, the managements of the two firms work out a mutually agreeable arrangement. Indeed, takeovers occur for the same reason as any other market transaction: efficiencies are expected, meaning that both parties can be made better off. So, it should not be surprising that most takeovers are friendly.

But some takeovers are opposed by the management of the firms being taken over – as was the case, at least initially, in Oracle's takeover of PeopleSoft in 2004. These takeovers are described as "hostile" and are commonly seen as undesirable and inefficient. They are depicted as the work of corporate "raiders" who are only interested in turning a quick profit, disrupting productivity by forcing the targeted firms to take expensive and distracting defensive action. (Managers have found an array of legal means to defeat a takeover. These defensive maneuvers are covered in Online Reading 11.4.)

The Market for Corporate Control

If managers of target corporations always acted in the interest of their shareholders (the owners of the corporation), then a strong case could be made for regarding takeovers as inefficient. Managers of the target corporation would then oppose a takeover only if it failed to benefit their shareholders. Then again, if managers could always be depended upon to act in the interest of their shareholders, there would be no need for many of the concepts discussed in this book!

The strongest argument in favor of "hostile" takeovers is that they bring the interests of managers more in line with those of shareholders than would otherwise be the case. There is a "market for corporate control" that allows people who believe they can do a better job of managing a company (and maximizing shareholder return) to oust the existing management by outbidding them for the corporate stock. Although such takeover attempts are infrequent and not always successful, the mere threat of a takeover provides a strong disincentive for managers to pursue personal advantages at the expense of their shareholders. This disincentive suggests that the possibility of takeovers provides an efficiency advantage related to the primary concern of this section – why "hostile" takeovers are less hostile than commonly depicted.

A takeover can be opposed because it promotes efficiency. A management team that is doing a good job of managing a firm efficiently has little to fear from a rival management team taking over. The stock price of a well-managed firm will generally reflect this – and, thus, a corporate raider will not be able to profit from buying the firm's stock in the hope of increasing its price through improved management. A takeover is likely only when the existing managers are not running the firm efficiently because of incompetence, an inability (or unwillingness) to abandon old ways in response to changing conditions, or intentionally benefiting personally at the expense of shareholders. Under these circumstances, a takeover that promises to increase efficiency will not be popular with existing managers, because it threatens to put them out of work! Not surprisingly, managers whose jobs are threatened by a takeover will oppose it, seeing (and selling) it as "hostile."

The fact that pejorative terms such as "hostile takeover" and "corporate raiders" are so widely used testifies to the advantage of current managers over shareholders in promoting their interests through public debate. The costs are concentrated on a relatively small number of people – primarily the management team that loses its pay, perks, and privileges. Each member of this team will lose a great deal if the team is replaced and has a strong motivation to oppose a takeover. Even a grossly inefficient management team can be organized well enough to respond in unison to a takeover threat. This unified voice will usually characterize a takeover as damaging to the interests of the corporation, the shareholders, the community, and even the nation – and we would expect managers to be more vociferous the more inefficient their management.

But why is the media discussion of takeovers dominated by the managers who lose rather than by the shareholders who win? If a takeover is actually efficient, what about the voice of those who benefit? And there is plenty of evidence that the shareholders of the target company in a hostile takeover do win. For example, during the takeover wave in the 1980s, it was estimated that stock prices of targeted firms increased about 50 percent because of hostile takeovers, which suggests that the managers of the targeted firms may have destroyed a considerable amount of their corporations' value before being targeted for takeover (Jensen 1988).

As will be discussed later in this section, this increase in stock values does not necessarily *prove* that a takeover is efficient. The takeover could depress the stock prices of the firm that is taking over the target firm, for example.[14] But even if the takeover is not efficient, the shareholders of the target firm should favor it and

---

[14] Michael Jensen minces few words on what the data imply: "[T]he fact that takeover and LBO premiums [or added prices] average 50 percent above market price illustrates how much value public-company managers can destroy before they face a serious threat of disturbance. Takeovers and buyouts both create value and unlock value destroyed by management through misguided policies. I estimate that transactions associated with the market for corporate control unlocked shareholder gains (in target companies alone) of more than $500 billion between 1977 and 1988 – more than 50 percent of the cash dividends paid by the entire corporate sector over this same period" (Jensen 1989, 64–65).

counter the negative portrayal that company managers put forth. This seldom happens because there are typically many shareholders, few of whom have more than a handful of shares. Most shareholders have a diversified portfolio and are only marginally affected by changes in the price of any particular corporation's stock. The probability that the actions of a typical individual stockholder will have an impact is very low, approaching zero. Even if the overall gain to shareholders far exceeds the loss to management, the large number of shareholders and their diverse interests make it extraordinarily difficult for them to speak in unison. As indicated earlier, shareholders are disadvantaged because they are in a Prisoner's Dilemma with respect to influencing the terms of the debate on behalf of their collective benefit.

If shareholders and management were on equal footing at influencing the public perception of takeovers, almost no takeovers would be reported as hostile. Consider a hypothetical and analogous situation. Assume that you own a beautiful house on a high bluff overlooking the Pacific Ocean. You are extremely busy as a global entrepreneur and unable to spend much time at the house. Since the house and grounds require full-time professional attention, you hire a caretaker to manage the property. Assume that you pay the caretaker extremely well (because you want him to bear a cost from being fired for shirking and engaging in opportunism) and give him access to many of the property's amenities. He's happy with the job and you are pleased enough with his performance.

One day, a wealthy CEO makes you an offer on the house of $15 million, about 50 percent more than you thought you could sell it for. Although you were not interested in selling at $10 million, you find the $15 million offer quite attractive. For whatever reason, the house is worth more to the CEO than to you. It could be that the CEO values the property more than you because she will have more time to spend living in and enjoying the house. Or it could be because the CEO believes that a profit can be made on the house by bringing in a caretaker who will do a far better job managing the property, thus increasing its value to above $15 million. It makes little difference why the CEO values the house more – and you are ecstatic to sell at the price offered.

Imagine how surprised you would be if, as the sale of your house was being negotiated, the news media reported that your property was the target of a hostile takeover by a "house raider" interested only in personal advantage. What's so hostile about being offered a higher price for your property than you thought it was worth? And are you somehow worse off because the buyer also sees private benefit in the exchange?

But the media isn't interested in your opinion. Instead, reporters talk to your caretaker, who knows he will lose his job if the sale goes through. So, the caretaker reports that the sale is the result of a hostile move by an unsavory character. Obviously this is silly, and the media is not likely to report this (or any similar sale of a house) as a hostile takeover. But is this any sillier than reporting a corporate takeover as hostile when the owners of the corporation (the shareholders) are being offered a percent premium to sell their shares?

The two situations are not exactly the same, but they are similar enough to call into question the "hostility" of most takeovers. One important difference between the two situations is that, if such a report did start to circulate about the sale of your house, you would have the motivation and ability to clearly communicate that it was your house; you found the offer attractive; and there was nothing at all hostile about the sale. This difference explains why our example should not be taken as a criticism of the press. When there is one owner, as in the case of a house, the press can easily understand and report the owner's perspective. When there are thousands of owners, as in the case of corporations, it is much easier for reporters to obtain information about a corporation from its top managers.

The fact that there are many owners in the case of corporations is the basis for other differences between the sale of a house and a corporation. Just as reporters find it easier to rely on top management for information on a corporation, so do the owners of a corporation find it easier to rely on management to make most corporate decisions – even major decisions such as those which affect its sale. Obviously, the reason for granting a management team the power to act somewhat independently of shareholders is that shareholders are so large in number, so dispersed in location, and so diverse in interests that they cannot make the type of decisions needed to manage a corporation – or much else, for that matter. But as we have discussed in detail throughout the text, there are risks associated with letting agents (managers) act on behalf of principals (owners/shareholders). As the owner of the house, would you want your caretaker to negotiate the sale for you? Only if the caretaker were subject to a set of incentives that went a long way in aligning his interests in the sale with yours.

The Efficiency of Takeovers

Are hostile takeovers efficient? Not everyone believes so. Hostile takeovers are often imagined as ways to increase the wealth of people who are already rich at the expense of the corporation's workers (not just its managers), the corporation's long-run prospects, and the competitiveness of the general economy. For example, responding to a hostile takeover bid for Chrysler Corporation in the mid-1990s by Kirk Kerkorian, a major newspaper ran an editorial: "[W]hen Kerkorian was complaining about insufficient return to stockholders, the value of [his] investment in Chrysler had more than tripled, to $1.1 billion. That's not good enough? To satisfy his greed, Kerkorian seems prepared to endanger the jobs of thousands of Americans and the health of a major corporation so important to the economy" (*Atlanta Journal–Constitution* 1995).

This editorial comment ignores the efficiency effects of a corporate takeover. But, at the same time, the effect of a hostile takeover on economic efficiency is more complicated than has been suggested in this chapter so far. The stockholders clearly gain.[15] But what about common stockholders (whose earnings can vary with the success of their companies since they are residual claimants) and bond-holders (whose earnings are set by fixed interest rates) of the takeover corporation? Do they lose as the firm runs up debt to pay high prices for the stock of the acquired firm? Does the threat of a hostile takeover motivate managers to make decisions that boost profits in the short run but harm long-run profitability? What about when important parts of an acquired firm are spun off after a hostile takeover, leaving a much smaller firm and many of its workers laid off? These losses should be set against any gains that the shareholders of acquired firms receive. And isn't it possible that the losses are larger than the gains?

Winner's Curse

Those who own something that others are bidding for should expect their wealth to increase. So it is not surprising that takeover bids increase the wealth of the corporation's stockholders. But this is not necessarily true for the stockholders of a corporation mounting a takeover bid. In a competitive bidding process, it is possible to bid too much, and this may be true of the corporation making the winning bid. The winning bid is typically made by the bidder who is most optimistic about the value of the object of the bidding (Thaler 1992). This is no problem when bidding for something with highly subjective value (say, an antique piece of furniture), because the object is worth more to the winning bidder than to others. But when bidding for a productive asset (such as an offshore oil field) that is valued for its ability to generate a financial return, the value of the object is less dependent on who owns it.[16] Therefore, if the average bid is the best estimate of the value of the object, there is a good chance that the winning bid is too high.

---

[15] See Grinblatt and Titman (2002) for a review of the extensive literature on this topic. The evidence from the 1980s, when hostile takeovers were at their peak, suggests that the magnitude of the gains to the shareholders of a corporation that is targeted for a takeover is quite large. A study by the Office of the Chief Economist of the Securities and Exchange Commission (SEC) looked at 225 successful takeovers from 1981 to 1984 and found that the average premium to shareholders was 53.2 percent. In a follow-up study for 1985 and 1986, the premium was found to have dropped to an average of 37 percent and 33.6 percent, respectively. These averages probably understate the gains because they compare the stock price one month before the announcement of a takeover bid with the takeover price – and often the price begins increasing in response to rumors long before a formal offer is tendered (Jarrell, Brickley, and Netter 1988). These percentages represent huge gains in total dollars: $346 billion over the period 1977–86 in 1986 dollars (Jensen 1988, 21). This estimate applied to all mergers and acquisitions – not just "hostile" takeovers. But "hostile" or not, takeovers consistently increase the value of the acquired firm's stock – and probably increase it more when the takeover is opposed by management, because offering a higher price is a way around reluctant management.

[16] In general, of course, the value of the asset will depend to some degree on who owns it. The highest bidder will likely have good reason to believe that she is better able to utilize the asset to create value. In the case of an oil field, the possibilities for one owner to obtain more wealth than another are probably quite limited. In the case of a corporation, the importance of management no doubt provides more opportunity for some owners to run the business more profitably than others.

Economists have referred to this possible tendency to overbid as the "winner's curse." But for two good reasons, the winner's curse may not be all that prevalent here. First, people who are prone to fall victim to this curse are not likely to acquire (or retain) the control over wealth necessary to keep bidding on valuable property – and, certainly, not property as valuable as a corporation. Second, in many bidding situations, each bidder often receives information on how much others are willing to pay as the bidding process takes place and then adjusts his evaluation of the property accordingly. This is the case in corporate takeovers when offers to pay a certain price for a corporation's stock are made publicly.

So, we should expect that the winning bid for the stock of a corporation targeted for a takeover will (relatively) accurately reflect the value of the corporation to the winner and not greatly affect the wealth of the acquiring corporation's stockholders. We should also expect that a more competitive bidding process will yield a bid price closer to the actual stock value. And this is exactly what the evidence suggests.[17]

Bondholders

What about the possibility that the additional value realized by shareholders of a target corporation is at the expense of losses to bondholders? For example, a takeover could increase the risk that either the acquiring or the acquired firm will suffer financial failure, while also increasing the possibility that one or both will experience great profit. Shareholders stand to benefit from the profits if they occur, and so they can find the expected value of their stock increasing because of the increased risk. The additional risk cannot generate a similar advantage for bondholders because the return to bondholders is fixed. They lose if the corporation goes bankrupt, but they don't share in increased profits if the corporation does extremely well. According to several studies of takeovers in the 1960s to 1980s, however, takeovers do not impose losses on bondholders (Dennis and McConnell 1986; Lehn and Paulsen 1987). No doubt, some bondholders suffer small losses while others realize small gains. But the best conclusion is that, even in the worst case, any losses to bondholders are nowhere close to offsetting the gains to stockholders.

Takeover Mistakes

So far, we have been discussing the *average* wealth effect on shareholders and bondholders from takeovers. Just because the average wealth effect of a hostile takeover is positive does not mean that all such takeovers create wealth.

---

[17] According to a 1987 study by Gregg Jarrell and Annette Paulsen, stockholders of acquiring corporations realized an average gain of 1–2 percent on 663 successful bids from 1962 to 1985. Not surprisingly, as takeover activity increased, the return to acquiring firms decreased, with an average percentage return of 4.95 in the 1960s, 2.21 in the 1970s, and –0.04 (but statistically insignificant) in the 1980s (Jarrell and Paulsen 1989).

People make mistakes in the market for corporate takeovers, just as they do in other markets and all aspects of life. (And, of course, if buyers can make mistakes, then we have to admit that prospective sellers can too.) The relevant question is not whether people make mistakes, but whether they are subjected to *self-correcting forces* when they do.

To note, the bidders under the winner's curse should themselves be the target of a takeover. The evidence suggests that, in the case of hostile takeovers, they are. Economists Mark Mitchell and Kenneth Lehn asked, "Do bad bidders become good targets?" (Mitchell and Lehn 1990). Looking at takeovers between January 1980 and July 1988, they found that firms resulting from wealth-reducing take-overs (according to the response of stock prices) were more likely to be challenged with a subsequent takeover than firms where takeovers had proven to be wealth-increasing. The market for corporate control does not prevent mistakes, but it creates the information and motivation vital for correcting them when they occur.

Short-Run versus Long-Run Profits

If you are a corporate manager, you may be thinking that the threat of a takeover could motivate you to act in ways that increase the value of the corporate stock in the short run, but are harmful to profitability in the long run. Is it true that managers are less likely to be ousted in a hostile takeover if they concentrate on short-run profits at the expense of long-run profits?

The answer might be "Yes" if the prices of corporate stock reacted only to short-run profits. But should we expect only short-run performance reports to control stock prices? If they did, then there would be money to be made by investors who took the long view. If a stock's price were inflated by short-run gains that were not likely to continue into the future, then investors could sell the stock in anticipation that future performance wouldn't likely match current performance, which means that investors could buy the stock back when its price declined with dampening future gains, pocketing capital gains between the difference in the current sell price and the future buy-back price. If the stock were depressed because of the impact of current poor earnings that were not expected to continue into the future, then investors could buy the stock currently at the depressed price and sell the stock when its price reflected higher earnings in the future. The buying and selling of the stock imply that the company's long-term prospects are taken into account in the market price of the stock. (This will not be done perfectly, because of the costs of information on what will happen in the future and the ever-present uncertainties about what the future will bring.)

How should managers of the company be expected to make their decisions relating to short-term and long-term market forces? Consider a decision facing you as a manager about whether to commit to an expensive R&D project that will reduce profits over the near term but is expected to more than offset this loss with higher profits in the future. Should you be fearful that investing in this project will, because of the reduction in current profits, drive the price of your stock down, making your corporation more vulnerable to a hostile takeover? The answer is probably "No" – if your estimate of the long-run profitability of the project is correct. A takeover is unlikely for three reasons. First, the fact that price–earnings ratios vary widely between different stocks provides compelling evidence that stock prices reflect more than current profits. Second, studies indicate that a corporation's stock price generally increases when the corporation announces increased spending on investment and generally decreases with a reduction in investment spending (McConnell and Muscarella 1985). A study by Bronwyn Hall found that firms taken over by other firms did not have a higher ratio of R&D to sales than firms in the same industry that were not taken over.[18] Third, failing to make a profitable investment will make a firm *more* prone to takeover by those willing to make the investment.

The bottom line: There is no reason for managers to become short-sighted because of the threat of a hostile takeover. Indeed, the best protection against a takeover – hostile or otherwise – is to make decisions that increase the long-run profitability of the corporation, even if those decisions temporarily reduce profits.

Break-Ups

What about the fact that, after a corporation is taken over, it is sometimes broken up as the acquiring firm sells off divisions – often those that have been profitable? Isn't this disruptive and inefficient? There is no doubt that takeovers are disruptive, particularly when they result in parts of the acquired firm being spun off. But disruption is not necessarily inefficient. Indeed, any economy, any market, and any firm must respond rapidly to changing circumstances if they are to be efficient – and such responses are necessarily disruptive. Making the best use of resources in a world of advancing technologies, improved opportunities, and global competition requires continuous disruption. The alternative is stagnation and relative decline.

Many of the mergers that took place in the 1960s and 1970s created large conglomerate structures that, even if efficient at the time, soon ceased to be efficient. Increased global competition began rewarding smaller firms with quicker response times to changing market conditions. Technology reduced the synergies that might have existed at one point by having different products produced within the same firms. Transaction costs decreased for firms to buy inputs and components from other firms, thus increasing their ability to specialize in their core competencies.

---

[18] Hall's study is discussed in Jensen (1988).

In many cases, these changes made the divisions of the corporation worth more as separate firms than as parts of the whole. Many managers, however, prefer to be in charge of a large firm rather than a small one – and are reluctant to divest divisions worth more by themselves or as part of another organizational structure. This managerial reluctance of the 1960s, 1970s, and early 1980s was partly responsible for depressed stock prices. Corporate raiders were able to take advantage of the depressed prices by buying a controlling interest in conglomerates and increasing their total value by spinning off some of their divisions.[19]

Laid-Off Workers

Another complaint is when takeovers lead to downsizing and workers are laid off. The claim is that stockholders benefit at the expense of workers who lose their jobs. The fact that workers are laid off after hostile takeovers is consistent with the view that these takeovers promote *efficiency*. But the most natural thing in the world for managers to do when sheltered against the full rigors of competition is to let the workforce grow larger than efficiency requires. (This is most evident in government bureaucracies, which is partially attributable to the absence of a takeover option.) Which workers are most likely to be released – and how big is the cost to the workers when compared to the gain to shareholders?

Economic progress occurs most rapidly when there are strong pressures to produce the same output with less effort – that is, to lay off workers when they are no longer needed. This causes dislocations in the short run. But, in the long run, it increases the availability of the most valuable resource (human effort and brainpower) to expand output elsewhere in the economy. So, a strong argument can be made that one of the *advantages* of the market for corporate control is the increased pressure on managers to control the size of their workforce.

Some of the efficiencies derived from hostile takeovers (and therefore some of the benefits to corporate shareholders) are the result of workers losing their jobs. The evidence suggests that the workers most likely to lose their jobs are executives and managers, not line workers.[20] Moreover, even if many line workers are harmed in the case of losing their jobs from a takeover, it does not mean

---

[19] Others have explained the advantages of moving toward smaller and more focused firms with the existence of improved, more efficient, capital markets. These have made it more attractive for firms to substitute reliance on external capital markets with reliance on internal capital markets, which favors multidivision firms (Bhide 1990).

[20] In a study of sixty-two hostile takeover attempts from 1984 to 1996 (fifty of which were successful), layoffs were common, but seldom exceeded 10 percent of the workforce and were typically far less (Bhagat, Shleifer, and Vishny 1990). The probability of being laid off was 70 percent higher for white-collar workers than for blue-collar workers; the jobs of managers, not workers on the line, were more at risk. Moreover, layoffs at targeted firms that were not taken over were even greater (as a percentage of the workforce). This suggests that the threat of a takeover provides a strong incentive for efficiencies even when no takeover occurs.

that most of the workers harmed are necessarily made worse off by an economic *system* that encourages (or doesn't discourage) takeovers. Workers harmed in the case of their firm's takeover receive offsetting benefits from these efficiency improvements – for example, greater competition and a lower price for goods and services. More broadly, a system that promotes efficiency creates a range of outcomes that are helpful to society – even if any given worker would prefer to keep his inefficient job.

Will Monopoly Profits Last into the Very Long Run?

Finally, there is an important issue that we have sidestepped: whether monopolies once established (whatever their degrees of market power) can continue to make monopoly profits (whatever the level) and a higher-than-competitive rate of return on capital? Put another way, in our graphs, how long will the "box" representing monopoly profits persist?

The counterintuitive (and counterconventional) answer is "very likely not in the long run." Rather, the profit box will tend to shrink as the monopoly's rate of return moves toward (but maybe not all the way to) a competitive rate of return. We have made an obvious point that many people (including antitrust authorities) miss: in the long run, lots of things can happen. For example, technology can change, making monopolized products irrelevant. (Consider the post office's monopoly on first-class mail, which has been undermined by email and automatic bill payments.) And new firms can often move into (or alongside) monopolized markets, pushing prices down.

There is another rarely recognized force that will push the monopoly's rate of return toward a competitive rate of return – even when the monopolized product remains viable. This comes from *financial markets*: if a monopoly has an above-competitive rate of return, investors will flock to the firm's key assets and its stock, driving up their prices and driving down the rate of return for anyone that seeks to take over the firm. In short, the monopoly's profit stream going into its (viable) future will be capitalized into the monopoly's key assets and stock prices. This means that the initial owners of the monopoly can "make out like bandits" – all the more reason savvy entrepreneurs search for and invest in potential monopolies. The greater their potential monopoly profits – and the faster those profits can be capitalized – the more investment they will tend to make to develop their monopoly positions.

If you doubt this line of argument, consider Apple, which has developed some monopoly positions with (seemingly) lasting strength in an array of tech products (e.g., iPod, iPhone, and iPad). Then consider buying Apple stock. You will quickly realize that Apple's profits of the past and its potential profits into the future have already been (largely, but maybe not completely) capitalized into the value of the company's high-flying stock – making it, at this writing, the most highly valued company on the planet. To have hope of earning a higher-than-competitive rate of return, new Apple investors will have to make investments on their assessments of additional profits emerging from a string of new and innovative products coming out of the company. (And even those potential profits may have already been at least partially capitalized into the value of Apple stock.) Of course, new investors might "lose their shirts" on Apple stock if a new product stream falters, current competitors strengthen, or new competitors emerge.

Practical Lessons

Three key lessons emerge from the economic way of thinking developed in this chapter. The first is that the prospect of overcoming competitive pricing pressures through collusion among producers should be viewed for what it often is – a snare and a delusion. *If all firms agree to restrict production and follow through, then all producers can charge a higher price and make greater profits.* This is the snare. But the prospect of successful collusion is a delusion in most settings because the motivation behind the snare is greater profits. Producers attracted by the prospects of greater profits from collusive restrictions on industry output will likely pursue the opportunity to expand their productions when all producers have agreed to cut back on market supply. Whether from insiders cheating or outsiders entering, cartels emerge and collapse under the same force: greed!

Managers who devote their own time and firm resources to the development of industry cartels can wreck their careers because price fixing and other forms of collusion are illegal under U.S. and world antitrust laws. (See the review of antitrust laws in Online Reading 11.5.) The resources used in forming cartels will usually be a waste for two reasons: rampant cheating on cartel rules can be expected among cartel members; and, to the extent cartel members hold to their agreement, the higher price and profits will attract new entrants who can be expected to take up much of the production slack.

The second key lesson is that knowing models of market structure and the characteristics of one's markets can be helpful for thinking more clearly and profitably about business decisions. How many firms are in your product and input markets? Is there anything notable about the size and concentration of the players? Are costs in your industry tilted toward fixed or variable inputs – with a greater focus on merely covering variable costs at times? Do you have few (potential) customers, putting more pressure on any given bidding opportunity? Is there anything you can do to increase the barriers to entry or exit? And so on. (See Online Reading 11.6 about business strategy and market structure considerations.)

The third key lesson from this chapter comes from a myopic view of market competition. Business students naturally think of their firms' most serious competitive threat as other producers of the same or similar products – and other buyers of the same or similar resources. The threat of losing market share to competitors is understandably a pressing concern; however, business students should be ever-mindful of the threat from takeover entrepreneurs scanning the business landscape for opportunities. Firms operating with something close to maximum efficiency have little to fear, as the high buyout prices for efficiently operated firms should protect them from takeover entrepreneurs.

Rather, takeover entrepreneurs are most interested in mismanaged firms – and the greater the extent of mismanagement, the better (assuming the corrective policies for the mismanagement are transparent). Mismanaged firms harbor the potential for capital gains by replacing management teams, changing incentives, and adjusting organizational and financial structures. The operating rule of takeover entrepreneurs is simple: buy low and sell high! The size of mismanaged firms is of little consequence to many takeover entrepreneurs. Large mismanaged firms may require massive takeover funding, but such funding levels should be easily raised if there are profits to be made from correcting mismanagement on a large scale.

The rules are clear: well-managed firms don't allow for much of a spread between the buying and selling prices. Poorly managed firms do. As they ply their trade, takeover entrepreneurs (much abused by management teams displaced in takeovers) tend to do the world an economic favor: they redeploy the world's scarce resources more efficiently. Business students who work for grossly mismanaged firms should consider a career switch – to become a takeover entrepreneur (after first learning how to amass takeover capital and to correct mismanagement).

Of course, there are stock traders who never seek to buy out mismanaged firms. They simply short the stocks. They effectively borrow shares of mismanaged firms with the intent of repaying the shares they have shorted at a later date with shares that are bought at prices depressed by mismanagement revelations.

Further Reading Online

Reading 11.1: The value of "mistreating" customers

Reading 11.2: The special case for regulating banking

Reading 11.3: At Kodak, clinging to a future beyond film (*The New York Times*, link available on the online resources website www.cambridge.org/mckenzie4)

Reading 11.4: Hostile takeover defenses

Reading 11.5: Antitrust laws in the United States

Reading 11.6: Why economics has been fruitful for strategy (Scribd, link available on the online resources website www.cambridge.org/mckenzie4)

Recommended Videos Online

1 Monopolistic competition (Richard McKenzie, 27 minutes)

2 Oligopoly and cartels (Richard McKenzie, 34 minutes)

3 Natural monopoly (Richard McKenzie, 20 minutes)

4 Taxation and regulation of monopoly (Richard McKenzie, 23 minutes)

5 The innovator's dilemma (Richard McKenzie, 36 minutes)

6 Comedic/cynical on outsourcing (Despair.com, link available on the online resources website www.cambridge.org/mckenzie4)

The Bottom Line

The key takeaways from Chapter 11 are the following:

1 Firms in monopolistically competitive and oligopoly markets will follow the same production rule for profit maximization as perfect competitors and pure monopolies: produce where marginal cost and marginal revenue are equal.

2 Monopolistic competitors may earn zero economic profits in the long run, but they will not produce at the minimum of their *LRAC* curve.

3 The downward-sloping demand faced by a dominant producer in a market can be derived from the gaps between the quantity demanded and supplied at various prices by all other smaller producers.

4 The incentive to form cartels is also a chief cause for cartel failures: members are inclined to cheat on cartel production and pricing agreements.

5 At times, producers pursue government regulation because it can enable them to restrict their production and charge above-competitive prices.

6 Although our analysis of imperfect competition informs us about the working of real-world markets, it does not answer all of our questions. Thus, our conclusions regarding the pricing and production behavior of firms in monopolistically competitive and oligopolistic markets are tentative.

7 The "innovator's dilemma" puts successful firms in a difficult position, trying to decide whether to focus on core competencies or explore other opportunities that may (or may not) be successful.

8 The competitiveness of the capital market – including the market for entire firms – acts as a discipline on managers who might believe that they can take advantage of their discretionary authority. Capital markets also induce managers to find the most cost-effective methods of production.

Review Questions ▹▹

1 Under what circumstances could a monopolistic competitor earn an economic profit in the long run?

2 To achieve the efficiency of perfect competition, must a market consist of numerous producers? What other conditions are required?

3 "In an economy in which resources can move among industries with relative ease, a cartel attempting to maximize short-term profits will sow the seeds of its own destruction." Explain.

4 How do the costs of entering a market affect the chances of forming a workable cartel? How does the number of producers in a market affect the chances of maintaining a workable cartel?

5 How would a cartel in a market for a network good collude on price? Explain.

6 Describe the evolution of the markets for local newspapers and automobiles since World War II.

7 Should antitrust laws attempt to eliminate all forms of imperfect competition? Why or why not?

8 Explain the benefits and costs of an implied cartel – as manifested through "blue laws" (e.g., prohibiting auto sales on Sunday) or institutional prohibitions against steroids in athletics.

9 Using implied cartels (and perhaps other concepts from the course), discuss the historical evolution of the timing of "Black Friday" shopping.

10 What are some of the practical concerns in implementing antitrust laws and regulating the prices of a monopoly?

11 Suppose that the managers of a firm allow their internal departments to act as mini-monopolies or that managers pay their workers more than required by the labor market. What would tend to happen in capital markets?

12 Why would you expect the market for corporate control not to work well when there is a stock-market bubble of the type experienced in the late 1990s into the early 2000s? Can you explain some of the unethical management behavior and deceptive accounting practices that came to light in the early 2000s as the result, at least partially, of a breakdown in the market for corporate control?

13 Would you expect government-run organizations to be more or less efficient than privately owned firms? Explain your answer with reference to capital markets.

14 Richard Posner has argued that one of the "failures of capitalism" has come in the form of executive pay schemes that encouraged excessive risk-taking in financial markets. He argues for higher marginal tax rates on high-income-earning executives on the grounds that such rates will depress their take-home pay and discourage risk-taking. How do you evaluate his argument?

15 Consider two compensation schemes for financial executives: (1) executives are granted bonuses based on annual profits; and (2) executives are granted shares of company stock based on annual profits, but the shares cannot be sold for a specified number of years. Which pay scheme will result in greater risk-taking by executives? What is your reasoning?

12

Competitive and Monopsonistic Labor Markets

Labour, like all other things which are purchased and sold, and which may be increased or diminished in quantity, has its … market price.

David Ricardo

Professional football players earn more than ministers and nurses. Social workers with college degrees generally earn less than truck drivers, who may not have completed high school. The best full professor of history usually earns much less than a mediocre assistant professor of accounting.

Why do different occupations offer different salaries? Obviously not because of their relative worth as human beings. But just as there is a market for final goods and services – pencils, automobiles, and landscaping – there is a market for labor as a resource in the production process. In competitive labor markets, supply and demand are major forces in determining the wage rate in various labor markets. Accounting and history professors are in decidedly distinct markets, because neither can do the other's job well. If they could, history professors would likely seek an accounting professorship to double or even triple their salaries.

In Part A, we focus on how economic forces affect the wages paid and the number of employees hired. In particular, we develop the theory of wage determination under competitive and less-competitive labor market conditions. As such, we start by refining and extending our analysis in Chapter 3. Then, we discuss labor markets in which the employment and wage levels are influenced by monopolistic product markets, the clout of labor unions as cartels, and the market power of a single employer (or a few employers) with some control over wage rates.

Such models can also show how attempts to legislate wages (e.g., minimum-wage laws and other mandates related to labor) can affect a labor market. In Chapter 5, we explained how a government-imposed minimum wage generally undermines employment opportunities for covered workers in competitive labor markets.

At the end of Part A, we explore how a minimum wage can actually increase employment in noncompetitive labor markets (if set appropriately).

The general principles that govern product markets also govern labor markets, as well as markets for other resources such as land and capital. The use of land and capital has a price, called *rent* or *interest*, which is determined by supply and demand. And the relevant prices are determined within markets that are competitive to varying degrees. Furthermore, land, capital, and labor are all subject to the law of diminishing marginal returns. Beyond a certain point and given a fixed quantity of at least one resource, more land, labor, or capital will produce less and less additional output.

Because workers have minds of their own, with interests which are not the same as those of the people who hire them, there are important differences in the market for labor and the market for other inputs (e.g., turbines or asphalt) that warrant a separate consideration of labor markets. In this chapter, we discuss some of those considerations as we examine how much workers are paid, how they are paid, and how this can motivate performance. In Part B, we extend our earlier discussion of the benefits and pitfalls of tying worker pay to performance.

By concentrating on the economic determinants of employment – those that relate most directly to the production and promotion of a product – we do not mean to suggest that other factors are completely unimportant. Many noneconomic forces (e.g., race, sex, appearance, nepotism) may influence who is employed at what wage. Along these lines, in Perspective 12 we will describe two types of discrimination: "personal discrimination" (outcomes affected by preferences that are unrelated to productivity) and "statistical discrimination" (the probabilistic decisions of those making decisions with limited information).

Part A Theory and Public Policy Applications

The Demand for and Supply of Labor

As noted in Chapter 3, labor is a special kind of commodity, one in which people have a direct, personal stake. The employer buys this service (or rents this commodity) from workers at a price: the *wage rate* or *compensation rate* the laborer receives in exchange for his efforts. ("Wage" is a common term for the money exchanged in labor markets – particularly in per-hour contexts. "Compensation" is broader, including fringe benefits, deferred competition, and job characteristics.) In a competitive market, the interaction of supply and demand determines this price – as it does other prices. To understand why people earn what they do, we must first consider the determinants of the demand and supply of labor.

The Demand for Labor

As with the demand curve for a product, the demand curve for labor generally slopes downward. At higher wage rates, employers will hire fewer workers than at lower wage rates, all things equal.

> The **demand for labor** is the inverse relationship between the real wage rate and the quantity of labor employed during a given period, all else constant. It is derived from the underlying demand for the relevant product and dependent on the skill and productivity of workers and other factors.

The **demand for labor** stems partly from the demand for the good or service produced. If there were no demand for mousetraps, there would be no need – no demand – for mousetrap *makers*. This general principle applies to all kinds of labor in an open market. Plumbers, textile workers, and writers can earn a living because there is a demand for the services they offer. The greater the demand for the products and for the labor needed to produce it, the higher the wage rate, all else equal.

Thus, the demand for labor is said to be a "derived demand," since it is *derived* (in part) from the demand for the underlying product. This leads to some interesting implications and applications. First, at least from the employers' perspective, jobs are a means to an end, not an end to themselves. Firms don't hire workers for fun; they hire workers to produce goods and services, so that the owner can earn a rate of return on her investments. It follows that workers don't have an inherent right to any given job. Moreover, macroeconomic policy should aim to encourage productivity that results in jobs, rather than "creating jobs" *per se.*

Second, this implies that consumers have tremendous influence on the creation of jobs. Firms will not hire workers to satisfy an insufficient demand. For example, if you find a music star troubling, your real complaint is with the consumers who find her work entertaining. (If the current star didn't exist, another would rise to take her place and satisfy the demand.) Or consider a field where employees are paid millions of dollars to throw an orange sphere through an orange metal ring that is ten feet off the ground. The catalyst for this labor market is the millions of people who enjoy watching the orange sphere–ring game. Or consider the common complaint that Walmart drives "Ma-and-Pa" businesses out of the market. But really, it's the consumers who make this decision, by overwhelmingly choosing Walmart over "Ma-and-Pa."

> **Labor productivity** is how many units a worker can produce per unit of time (hour, week, month) with a given technology, amount of capital, etc.

Conditional on adequate demand for the goods or services, **labor productivity** – the quantity of output a laborer can produce in a given unit of time – becomes a critically important determinant of the demand for labor. In part, this is due to the skills of the worker, which connects to the supply of labor to be developed shortly. Other factors matter as well: the technology in use, the managerial efficiency of the firm, the institutional efficiency of relevant government policies, etc. The price of the final product helps us put a dollar value on a laborer's output, and his productivity determines how much he can produce. Together, labor productivity and the market price of what is produced determine the market value of labor to employers – and, ultimately, the employers' demand for labor. We can also predict that the demand for labor will rise and fall with changes in labor productivity and product price.

Suppose that mousetraps are sold in a competitive market where their price is set by the interaction of supply and demand. In the short run, mousetrap production is subject to diminishing marginal returns. When we developed a firm's cost structure in Chapters 7 and 8, we noted that output expands by smaller and smaller increments when more and more units of labor are added to a fixed quantity of plant and equipment. Initially, it is likely that there are increasing marginal returns when a variable resource is added to a fixed quantity of another resource. But the additional output from additional units of the variable resource must eventually reverse course. This is a technological fact of life.

In Chapter 9, we showed that firms in competitive markets will produce in the range where their marginal cost curves are upward-sloping – where they encounter diminishing returns. This is a matter of economic logic. Within the relevant range of production in competitive markets, firms will find their marginal product of labor diminishing as more workers are hired – a good reason firms must see their wage rate fall before hiring additional workers.[1] Additional workers simply can't add as much to output as prior workers – not because they are inherently less skilled or diligent, but rather because they are working with fixed plant and equipment in the short run.

Column (2) of Table 12.1 illustrates diminishing marginal returns for all workers. The first laborer contributes a marginal product (additional output) of six mousetraps per hour. From there, the marginal product of each additional laborer diminishes – from five to four to three, and so on.

The employer's problem, after production has reached the range of marginal diminishing returns, is to determine how many laborers to employ. She does so by considering the value of the marginal product of labor. Column (3) of Table 12.1 shows the market price of each mousetrap, which we assume here remains constant at $3. By multiplying this dollar price by the marginal product of each laborer in column (2), the employer arrives at the value of each laborer's

---

[1] Akin to income and substitution effects in consumer theory, firms have scale and substitution effects. For example, if the price of labor increases, firms will tend to produce less output, resulting in a lower scale of production and less demand for labor (and other inputs). And to the extent that they still continue to produce, they will look to substitute from the more expensive input (labor) to other inputs that have now become *relatively* less expensive (e.g., capital). Note that this provides two reasons for why the demand curve is downward-sloping.

Table 12.1 Computing the marginal value of labor

(1) Units of labor	(2) Marginal product of each laborer (per hour)	(3) Price of mousetraps in product market ($)	(4) Value of each laborer to employer (marginal *revenue* product) ((2) × (3)) ($)
First laborer	6	3	18
Second laborer	5	3	15
Third laborer	4	3	12
Fourth laborer	3	3	9
Fifth laborer	2	3	6
Sixth laborer	1	3	3

The **marginal revenue product** of labor is how much a worker generates in terms of revenue per unit of time. In simple terms, it is calculated by multiplying the marginal product of labor (how many units the worker generates) and the price of the product.

marginal product – their **marginal revenue product** in column (4). This is the highest amount that she will pay each laborer. She is willing to pay less (and thereby gain profit), but not more.

If the wage rate is $17.50 per hour, the employer will hire only one worker. She cannot justify hiring the second worker if she must pay $17.50 for an hour's work and receives only $15 worth of product in return. If the wage rate is $14.50, the employer can justify hiring two laborers. If the wage rate is lower still – say, $5.75 – the employer can hire as many as five workers.

Following this line of reasoning, we can conclude that the demand curve for the firm will slope downward (as the demand curves for other goods and services). That is, the lower the wage rate, all else constant, the greater the quantity of labor demanded. Theoretically, what is true of one employer must be true of all. So, the market demand curve for a given type of labor must also slope downward (as in Figure 12.1).[2] Profit-maximizing employers will not employ workers if they have to pay them more in wages than they are worth in the

---

[2] The reader may get the impression that the market demand curve for labor is derived by horizontally summing the value of marginal product curves of individual firms (represented by tables such as Table 12.1). Strictly speaking, this is not necessarily the case, primarily because the total number of workers hired by all firms can affect the supply of the final product (mousetraps), which can cause the market price of the final product to fall. The fall in the price of the final product can undercut the value of additional workers (since their value equals their marginal products multiplied by market price). This means that the true market demand curve can be more inelastic than the sum of all individual employer demand curves. However, these refinements are probably not worth the opportunity costs of developing them in a course like this.

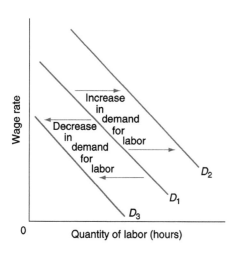

Figure 12.1 Shift in demand for labor
The demand for labor, as with all other demand curves, slopes downward. An increase in the demand for labor will cause a rightward shift in the demand curve from D_1 to D_2. A decrease will cause a leftward shift to D_3.

marketplace, which depends on their *productivity* and the *market value* of what they produce.

If the price of the product increases, the employer's demand for mouse-trap makers will shift – say, from D_1 to D_2 in Figure 12.1. Because the market value of the laborers' marginal product has risen, producers now want to sell more mousetraps and will hire more workers to produce them. If the price of mousetraps rises from $3 to $6, the value of each worker's marginal product doubles. At a wage rate of $15 per hour, an employer can now hire as many as four workers. (Similarly, if the price of the final product falls below $3, the demand for workers will also fall – with the demand curve shifting from D_1 to D_3 in Figure 12.1.)

When technological change improves worker productivity, the demand for workers may increase. If workers produce more, the value of their marginal product may rise, and employers may then be able to hire more of them. But an increase in worker productivity can also decrease the demand for labor. For instance, if worker productivity increases throughout the industry, more mouse-traps will be offered on the market, depressing the equilibrium price. The drop in price reduces the value of the workers' marginal product and may outweigh the favorable effect of the increase in productivity. In such cases, the demand for labor will fall. Consumers will pay less, but employees in the mousetrap industry will have fewer employment opportunities and earn less.[3]

---

[3] Scale and substitution effects provide another perspective here. With the price of capital reduced (through the technological advance), firms will be able to expand scale and increase output, using more labor and capital. On the other hand, firms will also be interested in substituting from relatively more expensive labor to the now-less-expensive capital.

The Supply of Labor

The supply curve for labor generally slopes upward. As depicted in Figure 12.2, at higher wage rates, more workers will be willing to work (at all or for more hours) than at lower wage rates. For example, if you survey your classmates, you will find that more of them would be willing to work for $50 per hour than for $20 per hour. (At $500 per hour, most people would be willing to work without hesitation, aside from lawyers, surgeons, and others whose opportunity cost can exceed $500 per hour!)

The **supply of labor** is the (usually positive) relationship between the real wage rate and the number of workers (or work hours) offered for employment during a given period, all else constant.

The **supply of labor** depends on the opportunity cost of a worker's time. She can use her time to construct mousetraps, do other jobs, go fishing, etc. Weighing the opportunity cost of each activity, the worker will allocate her time so that the marginal benefit of an hour spent doing one thing will equal the marginal benefit of time that could be used elsewhere. Workers will require a wage to compensate for the time lost from leisure activities such as fishing. To earn a given wage, a rational worker will give up the activities she values least. To allocate even more time to a job (and give up more valuable leisure activities), a worker will require a higher wage.

Given this cost–benefit trade-off, employers who want to increase production have two options: hire additional workers or ask current workers to work longer hours. Those who are currently working for $20 per hour must value time spent elsewhere at less than $20 per hour. To attract other workers (people who value their time spent elsewhere at more than $20 per hour), employers will have to increase the wage rate – perhaps to $22 per hour. To convince current workers to

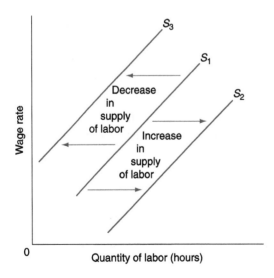

Figure 12.2 Shift in supply of labor
The supply curve for labor slopes upward. An increase in the supply of labor will cause a rightward shift in the supply curve from S_1 to S_2. A decrease in the supply of labor will cause a leftward shift from S_1 to S_3.

put in longer hours – to give up more attractive alternative activities – employers will also have to increase wage rates. In either case, the labor supply curve slopes upward. More labor is supplied at higher wages.[4]

The supply curve for labor will shift if the value of employee alternatives changes. For example, if the wage that mousetrap makers can earn in toy production goes up, the value of their time will increase. The supply of labor to the mousetrap industry would then decrease, shifting upward and to the left, from S_1 to S_3 in Figure 12.2. This shift in the labor supply curve means that less labor will be offered at any given wage rate. To hire the same quantity of labor – to keep mousetrap makers from transferring to the toy industry – the employer must increase the wage rate.

The same general effect will occur if worker valuation of leisure time changes. Because most people attach a high value to time spent with their families on holidays, employers who want to maintain operations on holidays generally have to pay a premium for workers' time. The supply curve for labor on holidays lies above and to the left of the regular supply curve. Conversely, if for any reason the value of worker alternatives decreases, the supply curve for labor will shift down to the right. If wages in the toy industry fall, for instance, more workers will want to move into the mousetrap business, increasing the labor supply in the mousetrap market.

Equilibrium in the Labor Market

A *competitive labor market* is one in which neither the individual employer nor the individual employee has the power to influence the wage rate. Such a market is shown in Figure 12.3. Given the supply curve S and the demand curve D, the wage rate will settle at W_1 and the quantity of labor employed will be Q_2. At this combination, defined by the intersection of the supply and demand curves, all of those who are willing to work for wage W_1 can find jobs.

The equilibrium wage rate is determined in much the same way as the prices of goods and services are established. At a wage rate of W_2, the quantity of labor that employers will hire is Q_1 whereas the quantity of workers willing to work is Q_3. In other words, at this wage rate a *surplus* of labor exists (unemployment). Note that all the workers in this surplus group (except the last one) are willing to work for less than W_2. That is, up to Q_3, the supply curve lies below W_2. The opportunity cost of their time is less than W_2. They can be expected to accept a

---

[4] The labor supply curve bends backward beyond some (high) wage rate. That is, beyond some wage rate, workers will choose to use some of their higher incomes to "buy" additional leisure, which means they will provide a lower quantity of labor to the market. (Imagine how many hours you would work per year if you were offered the same easy job paying $1 million per hour on January 1 every year.)

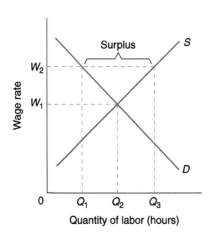

Figure 12.3 Equilibrium in the labor market
Given the supply and demand curves for labor, the equilibrium wage will be W_1 and the equilibrium quantity of labor hired will be Q_2. If the wage rate is W_2, a surplus of labor will develop (equal to the distance/difference between Q_3 and Q_1), exerting downward pressure on wages.

lower wage – and, over time, they will begin to offer to work for less than W_2. Other unemployed and employed workers must then compete by accepting still lower wages. In this manner, the wage rate will fall toward W_1. In the process, the quantity of labor that employers want to hire will expand from Q_1 toward Q_2. Meanwhile, the falling wage rate will convince some workers to take another opportunity, such as reading a book or getting another job. As they withdraw from this market, the quantity of labor supplied will decline from Q_3 toward Q_2. The quantity supplied will meet the quantity demanded (no labor surplus) at a wage rate of W_1.

In practice, the money wage rate may not fall. Instead, the general price level may increase while the money wage rate remains constant, reducing the *real* wage rate – that is, what the money wage rate will buy, accounting for inflation. This produces the same general effects: fewer laborers willing to work and more workers demanded by employers. When economists talk about wage increases or decreases, they mean changes in the *real* wage rate – the purchasing power of a worker's paycheck.[5]

Conversely, if the wage rate falls below W_1, the quantity of labor demanded by employers will exceed the quantity supplied, creating a *shortage*. Employers, eager to hire more workers at the lower wage, will compete for the scarce labor by offering higher wages. The quantity of labor offered on the market will increase, but these slightly higher wages will also cause some employers to reduce their hiring. In short, in a competitive market, the wage rate will rise toward the equilibrium wage rate (W_1).

---

[5] In practice, real wages may not adjust quickly enough, especially downwards. This ends up being a substantial catalyst for the macroeconomic troubles we'll describe in Online Chapter 4.

Why Wage Rates Differ

In a world of identical workers doing equivalent jobs under conditions of perfect competition, everyone would earn the same wage. In the real world, workers vary, jobs differ, and a range of factors reduce the competitiveness of labor markets. Therefore, some workers earn higher wages than others. Indeed, the differences in wages can be inordinately large. (Compare the hourly earnings of actor Tom Hanks and elementary school teachers.) Wages differ for many reasons, including working conditions, job characteristics, geography, and the inherent abilities and acquired skills of workers. After all of those have been held constant, we can discuss the impact of discrimination against individuals and various groups in Perspective 12.

Differences in Nonmonetary Benefits

So far, we have been speaking as though the wage rate were the key determinant of employment. What about job satisfaction and the way employers treat their employees? Some people accept lower wages to live in California or the Rockies. College professors forgo more lucrative work to be able to teach, write, gain tenure, and set their own work schedules. The congeniality of colleagues is another significant nonmonetary benefit that influences where and how much people work. Power, status, and public attention also figure into career decisions.

Some people would require greater wages to accept certain job characteristics. But when enough workers are neutral to (or even enjoy) those job characteristics, the market will not require greater compensation. Workers will simply self-select into characteristics they prefer and away from characteristics they dislike. In contrast, when a job characteristic is universally troubling – dangerous, disgusting, or distasteful – the market will require higher wages to compensate. These are called "compensating wage differentials."[6] For example, to install and maintain cell phone towers, most people are not at all interested in climbing to such heights. Those who are willing to take those risks will be compensated for what is universally seen as an unpleasant job characteristic. Likewise, part of the (higher) salaries of plumbers is due to the nature of some of their work.

More broadly, the trade-offs between the monetary and nonmonetary rewards of work will affect the wage rates for specific jobs. The more value people place on the nonmonetary benefits of a given job, the greater the labor supply. Added to wages, nonmonetary benefits could shift the labor supply curve from S_1 to S_2 in Figure 12.4, lowering the market wage rate from W_2 to W_1. Even though the

---

[6] To be more precise, they should be considered "compensating compensation differentials," since market adjustment can occur through fringe benefits, deferred compensation, other job characteristics, or wages.

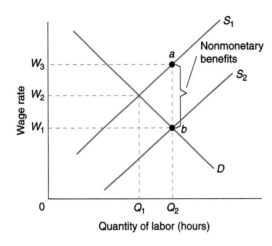

Figure 12.4 The effect of nonmonetary rewards on wage rates
The supply of labor is greater for jobs offering nonmonetary benefits – S_2 rather than S_1. Given a constant demand for labor, the wage rate will be W_2 for workers who do not receive nonmonetary benefits and W_1 for workers who do. Even though wages are lower when nonmonetary benefits are offered, workers are still better off, since they earn a total wage equal to W_3.

money wage rate is lower, workers are better off according to their own values. At a wage rate of W_1, their nonmonetary benefits equal the vertical distance between points a and b, making their full wage equivalent to W_3. The *full wage rate* is the sum of the money wage rate and the monetary equivalent of the nonmonetary benefits of a job.

Workers who complain that they are paid less than workers in other occupations often fail to consider their full wages (money wage plus nonmonetary benefits). The worker with a lower monetary wage may be receiving more nonmonetary rewards, including comfortable surroundings, freedom from intense pressure, flexibility with work hours, etc. The worker with the higher money wage may actually be earning a lower full wage than the worker with nonmonetary income. Certainly, many executives must wonder whether their high salaries compensate them for their loss of home life and leisure time – and professors who envy the higher salaries of coaches should recognize that a somewhat higher wage rate is necessary to offset the increased risk of being fired, less job flexibility, more travel, longer hours, etc.

Employers can benefit from providing employees with nonwage benefits. For example, a favorable working climate attracts more workers at lower wages. Although providing benefits is costly, doing so is worthwhile as long as providing the benefit serves to lower wages more than it raises other labor costs. Some nonwage benefits, such as air conditioning and low noise levels, also raise worker productivity. Needless to say, an employer cannot justify unlimited nonwage benefits. And employers will not pay more in wages – monetary or nonmonetary – than a worker is worth in terms of productivity. In a competitive labor market, they will tend to pay all employees a wage rate equal to the value added by the marginal employee – the last one hired.

Lax Work Demands as a Fringe Benefit

Lax work demands are a widely used but often unrecognized fringe benefit that varies across workplaces. It is easy to assume that the only way employers can remain competitive in pricing their final products is for employers to impose heavy work demands on their workers, which can lead to higher productivity (and a higher demand for workers). Lax work demands can do the opposite, which is why they should be avoided – or so it might be thought without considering the positive effect of lax work demands on the *supply* of labor.

Lax work demands can certainly reduce the demand for labor, but they can increase the supply of labor even more. Why? Workers may prefer to work under such conditions. The resulting lower wage rate could more than compensate employers for lost productivity. That is, employers might lose $1 an hour by lowering their work demands, but their wage rate might fall by even more – say, by $1.50 per hour – because of the increased labor supply. Workers can also be better off, on balance. Workers may lose $1.50 per hour in pay but gain $2 per hour in value from not having to work as hard. By relaxing work demands under such labor market conditions, employers can actually be *more* competitive in their final product markets because their overall labor costs are not as high as those of employers with more pressing work demands. Just as firms compete on wages and fringe benefits, employers also compete on the production demands placed on workers.

We have talked about "shirking" throughout the text in admittedly derogatory terms. This is only because we have implicitly assumed that "shirking" amounts to workers (and all agents) not working up to the demands placed on them and not meeting their contractual obligations to justify their wages. But employers must be ever-mindful that the division between lax work demands and shirking can be as thin as a knife's edge. That is, some shirking (relaxed work demands) is not shirking at all, but rather a fringe benefit that can enhance firm profitability. Keep this qualification in mind as you read our discussions of shirking in the rest of the chapter.

Differences among Markets

Differences in nonmonetary benefits explain only part of the observed differences in wage rates. Supply and demand conditions may differ between labor markets. As Figure 12.5(a) shows, given a constant supply of labor, a greater demand for labor will mean a higher wage rate. Conversely in Figure 12.5(b), given a constant demand for labor, a greater supply of labor will mean a lower wage rate. Depending on the relative conditions in different markets, wages may – or may not – differ significantly. In the labor market for "analytics," one finds both: high demand and relatively low supply – and thus high levels of compensation. All

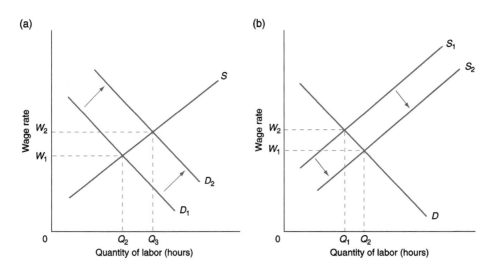

Figure 12.5 The effect of differences in supply and demand on wage rates
In competitive labor markets, higher demand for labor (D_2 in panel (a)) will bring a higher wage rate. A higher supply of labor (S_2 in panel (b)) will bring a lower wage rate.

things equal, you should want to work in a labor market with high demand, low supply, and few substitutes for your labor.

People in different lines of work may also earn different wages because consumers value the products they produce differently. Automobile workers may earn more than textile workers because people are willing to pay more for automobiles than for clothing. Consumer preferences contribute to differences in the value of the marginal product of labor and ultimately in the demand for labor.

But by themselves, relative product values cannot explain long-run differences in wages. Unless textile work offers compensating nonmonetary benefits, laborers in this industry will be attracted to higher wages elsewhere, perhaps in the automobile industry. The supply of labor in the automobile industry will rise and the wage rate will fall. In the long run, the wage differential will decrease or disappear. Certain factors may perpetuate the money wage differential in spite of competitive market pressures. Textile workers who enjoy living in South Carolina may resist moving to Detroit to manufacture automobiles. In this case, the nonmonetary benefits associated with the location of the textile work offset the difference in money wages. In addition, the cost of acquiring the skills needed for automobile work may act as a barrier to movement between industries – a problem we shall address shortly.

Differences among Workers

Differences in labor markets do not explain wage differences among people in the same line of work. *Differences among workers* must be responsible for this disparity. Some people are more attractive to employers. Employers must pay such workers more because their services are eagerly sought after, but they can afford to pay them more because their marginal product is greater.

Professional basketball star Stephen Curry earns an extremely high salary. The Golden State Warriors are willing to pay him well, both because of his popularity among fans – Curry's presence in the lineup attracts bigger crowds – and because he is immensely successful. Because a winning team generally garners (much) more support, Curry's presence indirectly boosts the team's earnings. In other words, Curry is in a labor submarket depicted by curve D_2 in Figure 12.5(a). Other players are in submarket D_1.

Differences in skill may also account for differences in wages. Most wages are paid not just for a worker's effort, but also for the use of what economists call **human capital**. We usually think of capital as plant and equipment – for instance, a factory building and the machines it contains. However, a capital good is most fundamentally defined as something produced or developed for use in the production of something else. In this sense, capital goods include the education or skill a person acquires for use in the production process. The educated worker, whether a top-notch mechanic or a registered nurse, holds within herself capital assets that earn a specific rate of return. In pursuing professional skills, the worker, in much the same way as the business entrepreneur, takes the risk that the acquired assets will become outmoded before they are fully used. Students who have majored in history expecting to teach have often found that their investment in human capital did not pay off. Many were unable to get teaching jobs in their chosen field; some have ended up as bartenders and cab drivers.

> **Human capital** is the acquired skills and productive capacity of workers.

Overtime Pay: an Unmitigated Benefit for Covered Workers?

In 2015, President Obama announced that his administration would increase the compensation of nearly 4.7 million Americans, writing in an op-ed for the *Huffington Post*, "We've got to keep making sure hard work is rewarded. Right now, too many Americans are working long days for less pay than they deserve" (Obama 2015). By government fiat, he required employers to pay an overtime premium (one-and-a-half times the hourly rate) to more workers – those on salary earning up to $50,400 per year. (Prior, salaried workers earning more than $23,660 per year had been exempt.)

Obama added that the new pay rule is "good for workers who want fair pay, and it's good for business owners who are already paying their employees what they deserve – since those who are doing right by their employees are undercut by competitors who aren't" (Obama 2015). The president and many other supporters of the new regulation presented the new pay rule as an unmitigated welfare gain for the affected workers – that workers will see their compensation go up by the amount of the added overtime pay. But is this likely? How might employers react to the new regulation? How might they be forced to react by competitive market pressures? (Employers and affected workers will face almost the same competitive pressures as before.)

As we explained in our analysis of mandated minimum wages in Chapter 5, employers have a number of margins on which they can adjust compensation packages in response to the new rule. How might employers in competitive labor markets be expected to react, for offensive and defensive reasons?

- First, because of their higher labor cost, employers will look to curb their count of covered workers. (This employment effect is likely to be muted by other adjustments employers can make.)
- Second, employers can reduce the fringe benefits (from vacation days to retirement contributions) of covered workers.
- Third, firms can eliminate or reduce the quality of valuable job characteristics (e.g., schedule flexibility).
- Fourth, they can increase the work demands imposed on covered workers.
- Fifth, many managers are paid in two parts: a salary and a bonus if sales targets are met. A forced increase in salary, through the imposed overtime pay, can lower the manager's bonus and (risk-adjusted) total compensation.

Such adjustments suggest that proponents of imposed overtime pay rules should be careful about what they advocate. Many salaried workers might receive an increase in one form of compensation (money pay) but decreases in other forms of compensation. Some salaried workers might gain in total compensation *on balance*, but other workers could easily lose. There will be net losses in total compensation if workers value the lost benefits more than they value the added money income (especially since money pay is usually subject to income taxation while nonmonetary benefits are not).

Monopsonistic Labor Markets

Competition is tough on those who must compete – not only as producers and consumers, but also as employers or workers. For example, firms would rather control competitive forces than be controlled by them. In labor markets, they would like to pay employees less than the market wage. But competition does not give them this choice. Similarly, competition for jobs prevents workers from earning more than the market wage. Thus doctors, truck drivers, and barbers have an interest in restricting competition in their labor markets. Acting as a group, they can acquire some control over their employment opportunities and wages.

As we saw in Chapter 11, it is feasible but unlikely that voluntary action alone is sufficient to allow for successful cartels. Such power is difficult to maintain without the support of the law or the threat of violence. Monopoly power is more promising, since it achieves the same outcomes without the hassles of holding a cartel together. As always, one group's exercise of power often leads to benefiting at the expense of others, market inefficiencies, lower social well-being, and other groups attempting to counteract it. In product markets, exercise of this power would come at the expense of consumers, who will have fewer goods and services to choose from at higher prices. Now, we examine the potential for employer and employee power in the labor market; the conditions that allow it to persist; its influence on the allocation of resources; and its effects on the real incomes of workers, consumers, and entrepreneurs.

The Monopsonistic Employer

Power is never complete; the forces of law, custom, and the market always circumscribe it. Within limits, employers can hire and fire, choose what to produce, and decide on what type of labor to employ. But certain laws restrict the conditions of employment as well as an employer's ability to discriminate among employees – for example, on the basis of race, sex, age, or religious affiliation. Competition imposes additional constraints. In a highly competitive labor market, an employer who offers below-market wages will be outbid by others who want to hire workers. Competition for labor pushes wages up to a certain level, forcing some employers to withdraw from the market but permitting others to hire at the going wage rate.[7] This is akin to the "price taker" in competitive product markets.

For the individual employer, then, the freedom of the competitive market is a highly constrained freedom. Not so, however, for the fortunate employers who enjoy the power of a **monopsony** – the sole or dominant employer/buyer of labor in a given market. (Monopsony is a cousin of *monopoly* – the single *seller* of a good and service.) A firm that is not a sole employer but dominates the market for a certain type of labor is said to have (degrees of) monopsony power. By reducing its demand for workers, monopsony power allows employers to suppress the wage rate.

> A pure **monopsony** is the sole buyer of a good, service, or resource protected by barriers to entry for other employers or barriers to exit for employees. Thus, monopsony power is the ability of a producer to alter the price of a resource by changing the quantity employed.

A classic example of *natural* monopsony is a nineteenth-century coal-mining company in a small town with no other industry. Once there, workers had few opportunities to go elsewhere, given limits in transportation and communication

---

[7] Competitors who do not hire also influence the wage rate; their presence on the sidelines keeps the price from falling far. If a firm lowers its wages, other employers may move into the market and hire away part of the workforce.

technology. Even so, to the extent that "word traveled" at all, the monopsonist had to be careful that it didn't get a reputation for exploiting workers or it would be unable to attract new workers from the outside. Sometimes, monopsony power is *artificial* and comes from the government. Examples include slavery, socialist or communist governments, and a military draft. Other times, it's allowed by the government, as in the case of professional sports leagues. Examples include player drafts, restrictions on free agency, salary caps, and so on.[8]

The Cost of Labor

Monopsony power reduces the costs of competitive hiring. Assume that the downward-sloping demand curve D in Figure 12.6 shows the market demand for workers, and the upward-sloping supply curve S shows the number of workers willing to work at various wage rates. If all firms act independently – that is, if they compete with one another – the market wage rate will settle at W_2 and the number of workers hired will be Q_2. At lower wage rates such as W_1, shortages will develop. As the market demand curve indicates, employers will be willing to pay more than W_1. If a shortage exists, the market wage will be bid up to W_2.

An increase in the wage rate will encourage more workers to seek jobs. As long as there is a shortage, the competitive bidding imposes costs on employers. The firm that offers a wage higher than W_1 forces other firms to offer a comparable wage to retain their current employees. If those firms want to acquire additional workers, they may have to offer an even higher wage. As they bid the wage up, firms impose reciprocal costs on one another – as at an auction.

Because any increase in wages paid to one worker must be extended to all, the total cost to all employers of hiring even one worker at a higher wage can be substantial when the employment level is already large. If the wage rises from W_1 to W_2 in Figure 12.6, the total wage bill for the first Q_1 workers also rises by the wage increase $(W_2 - W_1)$.[9]

Table 12.2 shows how the effect of a wage increase is multiplied when it must be extended to other workers. Columns (1) and (2) reflect the assumption that, as the wage rate rises, more workers will accept jobs. If only one worker is demanded, he can be hired for $20,000. The firm's total wage bill will also be $20,000 (column (3)). If two workers are demanded and the second worker will not work

---

[8] A monopolist with a competitive labor market is an interesting and somewhat counterintuitive example. The *monopoly* power in goods and services does not usually extend to *monopsony* power in the labor market. The firm will be able to charge consumers higher prices, but will be forced to compete as usual for labor services. In fact, we might expect workers at a monopoly to be paid *above* competitive wages. If they are not regulated, workers may be able to dip into the above-normal profits, often with the help of a union. If they are regulated, the firm's incentives to watch costs will be greatly reduced, as we described in Chapter 11.

[9] This assumes away the possibility of price discrimination that we described in Chapter 10.

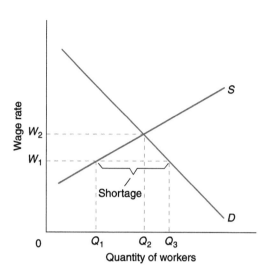

Figure 12.6 The competitive labor market
In a competitive market, the equilibrium wage rate will be W_2. Lower wage rates (such as W_1) would create a labor shortage and employers would offer a higher wage to compete for the available workers. In pushing up the wage rate to the equilibrium level, employers impose costs on one another. They must pay higher wages to new employees – and to all current employees – in order to keep them.

Table 12.2 Market demand for workers

(1) No. of workers willing to work	(2) Annual wage of each worker ($)	(3) Total wage bill ((1) × (2)) ($)	(4) Marginal cost of additional worker (change in (3)) ($)
1	20,000	20,000	20,000
2	22,000	44,000	24,000
3	24,000	72,000	28,000
4	26,000	104,000	32,000
5	28,000	140,000	36,000
6	30,000	180,000	40,000

for less than $22,000, the salary of the first worker must also be increased to $22,000. The additional cost of the second worker is therefore $24,000 (column (4)): $22,000 for his services plus the $2,000 raise that must be given to the first worker. The cost of additional workers can be similarly derived. When the sixth worker is added, she must be offered $30,000 and the other five workers must each be given a $2000 raise. The cost of adding this new worker – the **marginal cost of labor** – has risen to $40,000.

> The **marginal cost of labor** is the additional cost to the firm of expanding employment by one additional worker (or one additional hour).

Figure 12.7, based on columns (1), (2), and (4) of Table 12.2, shows the supply of labor and the marginal cost of labor graphically. The marginal cost curve for the monopsonist lies above the supply curve because the cost of each new worker hired (beyond the first worker) is greater than the worker's salary. (This

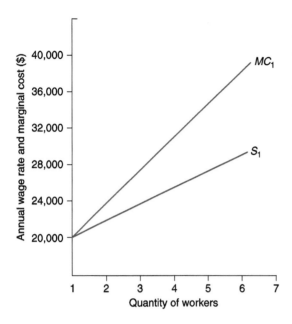

Figure 12.7 The marginal cost of labor
The marginal cost of hiring additional workers is greater than the wages that must be paid to the new workers; therefore, the marginal cost of labor curve lies above the labor supply curve.

is analogous to the marginal revenue curve *below* the demand curve for the *monopolist*.)

The Monopsonistic Hiring Decision

The monopsonistic employer does not get caught in this competitive bind. By definition, it is the only or dominant employer – and it can avoid competing with itself. Why bid up wages against yourself? Like a monopolist facing a market's product demand curve, the monopsonist can search through the various wage–quantity combinations on the labor supply curve for the one that maximizes profits. The monopsonist will keep hiring more workers as long as their contribution to revenues is greater than their additional cost – as the marginal cost of labor curve MC in Figure 12.8. To maximize profits, the monopsonist will hire until the marginal cost of the last worker hired equals his marginal value, as shown by the demand curve for labor. Given this, the monopsonist's optimal employment level will be Q_2, where the marginal cost and demand for labor curves intersect. Note that this level is lower than the competitive employment level, Q_3.

Why hire where marginal cost equals marginal value? Suppose the monopsonist employed fewer workers – say, Q_1. The marginal value of worker Q_1 would be high (point a), while her marginal cost would be low (point b). The monopsonist would be forgoing profits by hiring only Q_1 workers. Beyond Q_2 workers, the reverse would be true. The marginal cost of each new worker would be greater than her marginal value. Hiring more than Q_2 workers would reduce profits.

Figure 12.8 The monopsonist
The monopsonist will hire up to the point at which the marginal value of the last worker, shown by the demand curve for labor, equals his marginal cost. For this monopsonistic employer, the optimum number of workers is Q_2. The monopsonist must pay only W_1 for this number of workers – less than the competitive wage level of W_2.

After the monopsonist has chosen the employment level Q_2, it pays workers no more than is required by the labor supply curve, S. In Figure 12.8, the monopsonist pays only W_1 – much less than the wage that would be paid in a competitive labor market, W_2. In other words, the monopsonist hires fewer workers and pays them less than does an employer in a competitive labor market.

It is the monopsonistic firm's power to reduce the number of workers hired that enables it to hold wages below the competitive level. In a competitive labor market, if one firm attempts to cut employment and reduce wages, it will not be able to keep its business going: workers will depart to other employers willing to pay the going market wage. The individual firm is not large enough in relation to the entire labor market to exercise monopsony power; therefore, as a "wage taker," it must reluctantly accept the market wage (W_2) as a given.

Employer Cartels: Monopsony Power through Collusion

Envying the power of the monopsonist, competitive employers may attempt to organize a cartel. An *employer cartel* is an organization of employers that seeks to restrict the number of workers hired in order to lower wages and increase profits.

The usual way of lowering employment is to establish restrictive employment rules that limit the movement of workers from one job to another. Such rules tend to reduce the demand for labor. In Figure 12.9, demand falls from D_1 to D_2. As a result, the wage rate drops from W_2 to W_1, and employment falls from Q_3 to Q_2. Although the method of limiting employment is different from that used in monopsony, the effect is the same. Whether the monopsonistic firm equates marginal cost with marginal value (shown by curve D_1) or the employer cartel

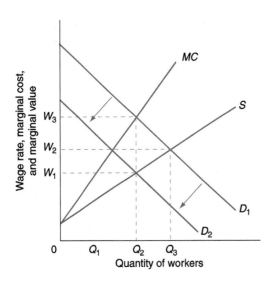

Figure 12.9 The employer cartel
To achieve the same results as a monopsonist, the employer cartel will devise restrictive employment rules that artificially reduce market demand to D_2. The reduced demand allows cartel members to hire only Q_2 workers at wage W_1 – significantly less than the competitive wage, W_2.

reduces the demand for labor (to D_2), employment still drops to Q_2. In both cases, workers earn a wage rate of W_1 – less than the competitive wage.

One industry in which employers have tried to cartelize the labor market is professional sports. Owners of teams have developed complex rules governing the hiring of athletes. In the National Football League (NFL), for example, teams acquire rights to negotiate with promising college players through an annual draft. After one team has drafted a player, no other team in the league can negotiate with him (unless he remains unsigned until the next year's draft). Teams can buy and sell draft rights as well as rights to players already drafted. But, within leagues, they are prohibited from competing directly with one another for player services. Violations of these rules carry stiff penalties, including revocation of a team's franchise.

The National Collegiate Athletic Association (NCAA) has done the same, to much greater effect, in their two primary "revenue sports": football and men's basketball. The cartel is prohibited from paying wages, with compensation limited to education, room, board, training, tutoring, and so on. While the compensation is not trivial, it pales in comparison to the marginal revenue product of these athletes at major colleges, especially the more prominent players (McKenzie and Sullivan 1987).[10]

In 2005, Apple's CEO Steve Jobs sealed a deal with Google's CEO Eric Schmidt not to recruit engineers from the other's firm. Intel and Adobe later joined the cartel. Supposedly, the deal suppressed the income of the two firms' engineers

---

[10] "Name, image, and likeness" (NIL) is now getting competitive levels of money to athletes, but colleges are still prohibited from paying players directly.

by up to $3 billion through 2014. The deal was investigated by the Justice Department and the companies were taken to court for violation of the country's antitrust laws. It was rendered an illegal collusion in 2014, requiring the companies involved to pay out damages to the estimated 64,000 affected workers of $325 million (Stempel 2014).

Monopsony and the Minimum Wage

In Chapter 5, we discussed the impact of the imposition of a federal minimum wage on competitive labor markets. We noted how a minimum wage would curb employment and cause employers to try to offset the added labor costs with reductions in fringe benefits and hikes in work demands. The analysis of a minimum wage under monopsony market conditions is straightforward; however, the employment consequence may be surprising.

Consider again Figure 12.9, used in our analysis of an employer cartel. Suppose that the monopsony (or the employer cartel) restricts labor market demand and pays a wage of W_1 and hires Q_2 workers because its marginal cost of labor is the MC curve. Now, suppose that the government imposes a minimum wage equal to W_2 – the competitive wage rate. Then W_2 becomes the monopsonist's marginal cost of labor curve up to the point where W_2 intersects D_1. (Like the "price taker," it now takes wage as given – from the government.)

Based on its new, regulated, marginal cost of labor (W_2), the monopsonist can increase its profits by hiring labor up to Q_3, the competitive equilibrium employment level. Note that, perhaps surprisingly, the imposition of the higher wage under monopsony causes employment to *rise* from Q_2 to Q_3. The monopsonist expands employment beyond Q_2 because it can make additional profits by doing so. (This is beyond what profits would otherwise have been, but not more than profits if the monopsonist remained unconstrained in its wage rate.) Moreover, there are no adjustments in fringe benefits or work demands that the monopsonist can make to mute the impact of the minimum wage. When competitive employers adjust their fringe benefits and work demands in response to the minimum wage, this is because the minimum wage set up an initial disequilibrium in the labor market. But the monopsonist does not end up in a disequilibrium: the quantity of labor demanded at W_2 is exactly equal to the quantity of labor supplied at W_2.

Does this mean that the minimum wage does not undercut the employment opportunities for the covered workers? Not necessarily. First, the minimum wage could be set so high – say, above W_3 in Figure 12.9 – that even monopsonies would curb their employment when faced with a minimum wage. Second, monopsonies could control a minor portion of all labor markets, meaning that the negative employment effects in competitive labor markets more than offset any possible positive employment effects in the more limited monopsony-controlled labor markets. The presence of some monopsonized markets could help explain why.[11]

Employee Cartels: Monopoly Power for Workers through Unions

In contrast to the potential monopsony power of employers over employees (when there are few who rent certain labor services), workers can gain monopoly power by collectively bargaining as one unit. A group of product sellers can collude to reduce quantity supplied and charge higher prices; a group of labor suppliers can reduce quantity to elevate wages.

We see this in Figure 12.10, which is equivalent to our development of monopoly power for sellers in Chapters 10 and 11 (see Figures 10.5 and 11.3). A competitive labor market will move toward equilibrium at P_c and Q_c. But a single provider of certain labor services – a monopolist of labor supply – will be able to reduce quantity, equating MR and MC at Q_o and charging P_u (on the firm's demand curve). An effective union – acting as a single, collective bargaining unit – will be able to accomplish the same outcome. (The cartel can also be depicted in a graph similar to Figure 12.9 – again, with D, MR, and MC_L, and, then, a reduction in supply to simulate the same outcome.)

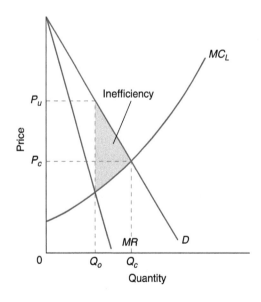

Figure 12.10 The employee cartel
A competitive labor market will move toward equilibrium at P_c and Q_c. A single seller of labor will be able to reduce quantity, equating MR and MC at Q_o and charging P_u (on the firm's demand curve). A union, acting as a monopolist of (labor) suppliers, will be able to accomplish the same outcome.

---

[11] As mentioned in Chapter 5, the measured negative employment effects of minimum-wage increases have generally been small. See Online Reading 5.5 for references to the econometric studies on the employment effects of the minimum wage.

As in Chapter 11, there is always an incentive to collude. But, unfortunately for those in the cartel, it is again difficult to establish and maintain a cartel. There is an incentive for insiders to cheat on the collusive agreement if formed. And there is an incentive for outsiders to enter the highly profitable settings where cartels have been successful. How to prevent cheating and entry? Violence or the threat of violence can be effective, especially in settings where extra-legal enforcement is feasible at relatively low cost (e.g., inner-city gangs with illegal drugs). Another option is to pursue government regulations that limit cheating and entry, allowing group members to enforce the cartel at low cost.

We see these same principles with labor unions – in essence, cartels in labor markets. Assume that union workers are earning compensation above marginal revenue product. (If not, why would they join the union and pay dues?) If they want even greater compensation, they might go on strike. But if they do, non-union workers would love to have the jobs just vacated, since they're only being paid a market wage. And union workers will be tempted to cross the picket lines, wanting to put food on their tables in the short run and worried about losing a job with above-market wages in the long run.

How to maintain the cartel in the face of the incentives for insiders to cheat and for outsiders to enter? Unions (especially those in blue-collar professions) have a notable history of using violence and threats. And unions are quite active in using government to restrict their competition in both labor and product markets. Unions want laws that increase the price of their competition, such as minimum wages,[12] "prevailing wage" laws,[13] and other employer mandates (of benefits they already have). They pursue laws that limit firms' ability to use nonunion labor: "project labor agreements," mandatory occupational licensing, and restrictions on immigration. They advocate laws that protect their jobs during strikes, make unionization relatively easy, mandate joining a union, and oppose secret ballots in union elections. They also pursue restrictions in product markets, looking to reduce foreign competition for the goods they make. Trade restrictions, as we covered in Chapter 6, increase the demand for domestic product. Since labor is a "derived demand," greater demand for product translates into greater demand for the labor which makes the product.

As we've described, firms cannot survive with significant inefficiencies in competitive markets. Paying workers above-market wages is a good example.

---

[12] Actually, it's not completely clear whether unions are helped or harmed by a higher minimum wage. On the one hand, the minimum wage bids up the price of potential substitutes – for example, two relatively unskilled workers replacing a union worker for some jobs. But a higher minimum also makes union membership relatively less attractive and less useful for dealing with any prospective monopsony power by employers.

[13] "Prevailing wage" laws are statewide versions of the federal "Davis–Bacon" law that places a minimum wage on skilled trades for jobs in public-sector infrastructure projects (Schansberg 2013).

Moreover, unions bring other inefficiencies: pay raises based on seniority rather than productivity, restrictive work rules, greatly reduced ability to fire shirkers and incompetent workers, etc. As such, we don't expect to see unions in competitive markets. Instead, we expect them to be in the two contexts where they are prevalent. First, unions are prominent in industries where firms have significant monopoly power – oligopolies and monopolies – and unions can bid into those profits. Historically, this is where unions have been most powerful – for example, in heavy manufacturing, transportation, and Hollywood.[14] But increasing competition in those industries has greatly reduced the power of unions in the past few decades.[15] Second, we expect to see unions in government. Since the rigors of competition are much less in the public sector and government endeavors are funded by the rationally ignorant voters we described in Chapter 6, it's not surprising that unions continue to be strong there – with about one-third of its workers in labor market cartels.[16]

PERSPECTIVE 12
Personal and Statistical Discrimination[17]

Before we discuss discrimination, we should revisit some of the many *other* reasons why wages and income differ:

1 *Human capital.* The job skills that people bring to the labor market can be endowed through natural ability or earned through investments in education, training, or job experience.
2 *Geographical location.* For example, because the cost of living is so much higher in New England than in the Southern U.S., incomes are higher there as well. Although it would be measured as an income differential, such differences in nominal income are irrelevant in comparing real income or purchasing power.

---

[14] Doctors (AMA), dentists (ADA), and lawyers (ABA) are in labor organizations that are equivalent to labor unions.

[15] A key piece of this puzzle in the U.S. was the deregulation of the transportation and communication industries in the late 1970s and early 1980s under Presidents Carter and Reagan. Economist Alfred Kahn led the charge to deregulate phones, trucks, trains, shipping, and airlines. This promoted competition, reduced prices, lowered transaction costs, and encouraged technological advance. This is arguably the most important economic story of the last fifty years in America – and, inarguably, the most underrated story.

[16] A combination of monopsony and union results in "bilateral monopoly power" – where each side has significant bargaining power. Another example is workers with highly specialized skills that are mostly useful in one industry. In such cases, there are only so many places for workers to work, but only so many of them who can be hired. Each side may find it challenging to find alternatives if this worker or this job disappears. In both cases, the net outcome, compared to competition, is not predictable without more information.

[17] For a more detailed discussion of these topics, see chapter 3 of *Poor Policy* (Schansberg 1996).

3 *Forms of compensation.* Since wages are only part of compensation (including fringe benefits, deferred compensation, and job characteristics), there may be differences in wages without differences in compensation and vice versa.

4 *Union membership.* Belonging to a labor market cartel should increase your income.

5 *Different preferences for "nonmarket activity" (schooling, household work, and leisure).* These help to determine whether people choose to work overtime, full time, part-time, or not at all. Individuals may have equal opportunities, but make different decisions concerning work hours and career investment, resulting in substantial income differentials (short-term and especially long-term).

Failing to account for such differences leads to unfortunate inferences. For example, newspapers often report that women earn far less than men, implying (or even saying) that the gap is caused by discrimination. (Today, the average woman earns about 82 percent of the average man in the United States; until the 1980s, this statistic had remained around 60 percent for decades.) However, this number does not account for differences in average job experience, training/education, representation in various job fields, etc. Because it fails to hold such important variables constant, the raw number tells us nothing about income differentials between equally qualified men and women. In a more useful comparison, at least by the early 1990s, June O'Neill (1994) found that twenty-seven- to thirty-three-year-old women who had not had a child earned 98 percent of that of their male counterparts.

Let's look at higher-education outcomes using the popular, simplistic metric. The average salaries for full-time faculty at U.S. four-year public colleges and universities in 2021–22 was $100,187 for men and $83,557 for women – about 20 percent more for men. If we look at different types of universities, the results are even more interesting. At the research-focused main campus of Indiana University in Bloomington, 1229 male faculty earn an average of $107,494, while 860 females earn an average of $85,618 – thus, 40 percent more males earning 25 percent higher incomes. At the teaching-focused regional campus of Indiana University in New Albany, 76 male faculty earn an average of $68,769, while 107 females earn $62,507 – thus, 40 percent more women earning 10 percent less income (O'Leary 2023). Are these schools engaging in personal discrimination against women? Is the campus in New Albany less discriminatory than Bloomington? Maybe, but this simplistic measure doesn't help us draw useful inferences.

Despite the obvious point that income varies for many reasons, the most popular topic concerning income differentials between groups is discrimination. When labor economists measure discrimination, they control for the variables discussed above. Whatever remains is considered "unexplained" differences in wages and is designated as the upper bound of possible discrimination. Here, we will focus on how discrimination occurs in product and labor markets – and we will discuss two key types of discrimination: personal and statistical.

Personal Discrimination

With a delicate and controversial subject, it is especially important to clearly define the terms to be used. We define prejudice as "prejudging" something or someone based on a belief or opinion. Discrimination would then be "prejudice in action." To discriminate, one must (1) have the underlying prejudice, (2) be in a position to turn the belief into action, and (3) be willing to bear the costs (if any) of those actions.[18]

"Personal discrimination" is a matter of indulging one's preferences concerning the buying or selling of goods and services or the choice of whom to employ. For instance, I might enjoy not hiring or promoting women. Or I might decide against buying something from a certain store simply because it is operated by a Korean or someone who went to a rival school. Or I might choose not to rent an apartment to someone because he is Jewish or supports a rival sports team. Both parties are cheated out of a mutually beneficial trade because of one party's personal prejudices.

This type of behavior is costly to those discriminated against. However, the degree of competition in a given market and the number of discriminatory firms determines the extent of the cost. For example, in Houston a few years ago, one gas-station owner decided to charge those with foreign automobiles a nickel more per gallon than the market rate. Since there were many gas stations in the city and only one station was participating, the cost was minimal to those discriminated against.

In addition, personal discrimination is somewhat costly to the one who discriminates. To indulge their tastes and preferences, they avoid good workers in favor of more-expensive or less-productive workers, forsake good tenants, turn away good customers, etc. The cost of such behavior tempers the desire to engage in it. Remember that discrimination is the willingness to put prejudicial opinions into action. The question then becomes: "Do I really want to lower my income in order to discriminate against someone?"

As long as the discrimination is limited to a few firms in a competitive market, the only significant result will be some segregation. Even if many firms discriminate, this gives nondiscriminating (profit-maximizing) entrepreneurs an incentive to enter the market and sell to (or hire) those who have been

---

[18] The second condition may seem trivial, but we want to narrow the field to discrimination in "markets." Although it's interesting to consider a bigot who has little contact with the subject of their bigotry, it's far more interesting to consider a bigot who is a landlord, a store owner, or an HR director.

discriminated against. As such, competition can weaken (but not necessarily eliminate) discriminatory practices.

Suppose that employers harbor a deep-seated prejudice against women, which depresses the market demand and wage rates for female workers. If women are just as productive as men, enterprising producers can hire women, pay them less than men, undersell the other suppliers, and take away part of their markets. Under competitive pressure, employers will start to hire women to keep their market shares. As a result, the demand for women workers will rise whereas the demand for men will fall. Such competition may not eliminate the wage differential between men and women, but it will at least reduce it.

When markets are less competitive, the costs of discrimination are lower, so we expect to find more of it, all else equal. In monopsonies, employers face little competition, so employment discrimination is more likely.[19] In monopolies, firms face little competition, allowing them to mess with all consumers, but perhaps certain consumers especially.

Sometimes government policy encourages discrimination by reducing its cost to zero. As we discussed in Chapter 11, when governments regulate a monopoly's prices and profits, they inadvertently provide an incentive for the firm to inflate its costs. If government is going to reduce my profits to "an acceptable level," why not lower profits myself by artificially raising costs? One way to do this is to indulge one's preferences concerning others – to engage in personal discrimination. The cost is zero since government would confiscate the "extra" profits anyway.

Another example is when government prevents a market from functioning normally – a "market distortion." For instance, as we saw in Chapter 5, an effective price floor on wages (a minimum wage) can create a surplus of workers (unemployment). With a surplus, employers can easily turn down any particular applicant because there are countless others looking for a job at the elevated wage. The employer can costlessly discriminate because of the surplus created by government. Another example is rent control which creates a housing shortage. With people waiting in line to get apartments at an artificially low price, landlords can costlessly choose those who fit their subjective preferences.

Government agencies are generally more interested in maximizing budgets than profits; they have an incentive to pursue (budget) size over efficiency. This inefficiency may include discriminatory hiring practices. If the goal is to expand budgets, bureaucrats may be unconcerned with hiring the best people for the job and may tend to hire less-efficient workers who fit their tastes and preferences.

---

[19] For reviews of the economic literature on labor market discrimination, see Alexis (1974), Marshall (1974), Cain (1986), Gunderson (1989), and Lang and Lehmann (2012).

This tendency can lead to discrimination against – or favoritism toward (e.g., nepotism) – individuals and groups. Further, their monopoly power can allow discriminatory selling practices. If everyone must purchase a product or service through a government monopoly, there is little incentive to please customers of any type – and an added incentive to scratch a discriminatory itch.

The point is not that government agencies or landlords in cities with rent control always discriminate – or that personal discrimination never occurs in competitive markets. Rather, it's that discrimination is less costly and therefore more likely in markets which are either less competitive or distorted by the government. Wage differences can result from personal discrimination – whether sexual, racial, religious, ethnic, or political. If such discrimination is widespread, enforcement of civil rights laws may be effective.[20] But competitive markets limit the inherent inefficiencies of discrimination and provide a strong financial incentive to override the prejudices of other market providers. In competitive markets, unless there are widespread discriminatory attitudes and an aversion to profit maximization, personal discrimination is unlikely to substantially affect individuals – and even less likely to be a significant factor for groups.

From economic analysis, we can see that promoting competition and eliminating government's market distortions is a useful way to curb discriminatory behavior. And if personal discrimination is at most a secondary cause of unfortunate economic outcomes, wisdom dictates a focus on primary causes such as human capital development.

Potential employees can be easily grouped according to identifiable group characteristics. But this can also lead to an *impersonal* form of discrimination based on groups to which an individual belongs rather than on individual merit. This leads us to a type of discrimination in which *everyone* participates.

Statistical Discrimination

Statistical discrimination (often described as "stereotyping") is talked about less frequently, although it is far more common – in fact, universal. For example, when you choose a can of beans at a store, do you select one with a dent in it (if it is the same price as an undented can)? Why not? Do you *know* there is something wrong with the dented can? Do you *know* there is nothing wrong with the undented can? If you are walking alone at night with three boisterous young men coming your way, do you get nervous? If possible, do you choose another

---

[20] Matters become more complex when discrimination is pervasive and/or backed by government. As an example of both: Imagine that you own a restaurant in the Deep South in the 1950s. You're not a bigot toward African-Americans, but many of your customers and workers are. If you serve or hire African-Americans, you may lose business or endure far worse consequences. Because the owner's labor demand is "derived" in part from the demand of other constituencies, he may be tempted to respond to their preferences.

path? Why? Do you know that the men intend to harm you? When you vote for offices at the bottom of a ballot, how do you decide? Name recognition, party affiliation, number of yard signs, incumbency or not? Do you *know* that your choices will be more effective than their opponents?

These decisions and many others have the following in common: there is incomplete (and asymmetric) information about the decision; information is costly to obtain; and the choice is of some importance. In other words, people often try to make the best decisions they can with highly imperfect information. (This is another application of imperfect information from our coverage in Chapter 5.)

Part of this decision-making process involves using group information to form "best guesses" about what individuals in a group will do. When Eric joined the Economics Department's intramural softball team in grad school at Texas A&M, he asked the captain what position to play. He looked at Eric for a moment and said: "You look like a right fielder." (Right field is where you put the worst player, since balls aren't often hit there.) Why did this happen? The captain had no idea how well or how poorly Eric played. But he knew that most individuals in the group Eric represents – tall, skinny guys with glasses – were not known for their athletic prowess. Until he observed Eric's "productivity," he had to play right field.

The same thing occurs in labor markets. Firms use signals of all types (group information) to do their best in selecting productive employees. Information is far from perfect; gathering information on prospective employees is costly; and hiring ineffective employees is a costly proposition. Grad schools look at grade point average (GPA), college attended, major, standardized test scores, course work, and letters of reference. Firms start with résumés – and after a screening process, they schedule an interview – again, trying to reduce the information asymmetries that make the decision so challenging.

Not all students who graduate with a 3.0 GPA are better workers than those with a 2.5 GPA. But, on average, a firm may have found this to be the case. Not all graduates of Princeton are more productive than those who went to "Northwest Idaho State University." But firms may have found Ivy League graduates to be more competent than obscure regional schools. A business may use a typing test for prospective clerical workers. If Michael can type 100 words per minute but suffers from "test anxiety" and can only type forty words per minute during a test, he is unlikely to get the job despite his ability.

Note that neither the employer nor the employee is happy about the failure of these signals to correctly predict productivity. For example, the firm wants to hire the best people available and the typing test will, in this instance, fail to find the most qualified person. But the key is that the firm must pay the cost of gathering credible, predictive information. Given these trade-offs – although mistakes will be made – this may still be the optimal way to find employees on average. Likewise, even if particular students from a less-highly-regarded university would be a great asset to a firm, they may be unable to signal their ability. Such workers "deserve better" in some sense, but will probably need to start at a lower position to demonstrate their true productivity. While "unjust" in an idealistic sense, statistical discrimination is comforting in that it is "nothing personal." Everyday people may simply be doing their best to make the best decisions and maximize profits in environments with limited information.

One final application: The growth of online courses provides opportunities and challenges for higher education. If the quality of such courses is (perceived to be) significantly lower by firms – either by the nature of online education or the ability of students to game the system – then the signal value of a college degree will decline and it will become less valuable as a statistical discrimination tool for students, companies, and society. How will the market adjust in the face of the relevant information problems? One would expect a feverish search for technological advances that limit student ability to game the system and/or firms pressuring colleges to note online classes on transcripts to increase information. Without one of these, the signal value of a college education will fall, leading students and firms to shy away from (online) higher education.

Part B Organizational Economics and Management

Paying for Performance

In Part A, our discussion was focused on how labor markets work – in particular, how the wage rate and other benefits are determined by the broad forces of supply and demand. In facilitating voluntary, mutually beneficial trades, markets must ultimately work with the interests of workers and firms in mind. The problem most firms must solve is how to get workers to do what they are supposed to do – to work effectively and efficiently together for the creation of firm profits. This is an extraordinarily difficult task. There is a lot of trial and error in business, especially as it relates to how workers are paid. At the same time, thinking conceptually about the payment/incentive problem can help firms moderate the extent of the errors.

One of the most fundamental rules of economics – and the *raison d'être* for the disciplines of organizational economics and management – is that, if you offer people a greater reward (monetary or not), they will tend to do more of whatever is being rewarded, all else equal. Some people find this proposition objectionable because it implies that people can, to one degree or another, be "bought." Admittedly, incentives may not matter in all forms of behavior or for all individuals. However, the proposition that incentives matter applies to a sufficiently wide range of behaviors to be considered a "rule" that managers are well advised to keep in mind. For example, pay someone a higher wage – such as time-and-a-half – and they will be likely to work longer days. Pay them double time, and they will even work holidays. There is some rate of pay at which a lot of people may work almost any time of the day or night on any day of the year.

This rule for incentives is not only applicable to the workplace. Parents know that one of the best ways to get their children to take out the garbage is to tie their allowance to the chore. When mentally ill, institutionalized patients are paid for the simple tasks they are assigned (e.g., sweeping a room or picking up trash), they perform them with greater regularity.[21]

Even pigeons, well known for having the lowest form of bird brain, respond to incentives. Granted, pigeons may never be able to grasp the concept of monetary rewards (offering them a dollar won't elicit much of a response), but they respond to food rewards. (Offer a nut in the palm of your outstretched hand and a whole flock will descend and maybe leave their mark on your shoulder!) From research, we know that pigeons are willing to work to get food pellets (measured by how many times they peck colored levers in their cages) – and they work harder if the reward for pecking is raised. Researchers have also been able to get pigeons to loaf on the job. How? Simply lower their rate of "pay."[22]

The importance of incentives may appear to encourage managers everywhere to link pay to some measure of performance. But, as noted earlier, the lone worker in a single proprietorship already has the "right" incentive. His reward is the same as the reward for the whole firm; the full cost of any shirking is borne by the worker/owner. However, such a congruence between the rewards of the owners and workers is duplicated nowhere else.

There are always "gaps" between the goals of owners and workers – and the greater the number of workers, the greater the potential gap in incentives. In (very) large firms, layers of bureaucracy separate workers from the owners; communications about the firm's goals are often imperfect; and each worker at the bottom of the firm's pyramid can reason that her (extremely limited) contributions to the firm's revenues and goals can easily go undetected. A recurring theme of this book is that, when monitoring is difficult, one can expect many workers to exploit opportunities to improve their own well-being at the expense

---

[21] For a review of the experimental literature on the connection between pay and performance of institutionalized patients, see Freed and Uren (2006).

[22] For a review of the relevant literature, see McKenzie and Tullock (1994, chapter 4).

of the firm and its owners. And the opportunities taken can result in substantial losses in worker output.

How can managers improve incentives, reduce shirking, and increase worker productivity? The well-known management guru Frederick Taylor (1895) strongly recommended piece-rate pay as a means of partially solving what he termed "the labor problem." But both management and labor largely ignored him at the time – for the good reasons we'll discuss below. In a word, pay for performance is easier said than done. And there are many ways of getting workers to perform that don't involve money pay. These are studied in various disciplines, including organizational behavior which draws on the principles of psychology. As such, managers should encourage workers at least occasionally, clearly define corporate goals, communicate goals in a clear and forceful manner, exert leadership, etc.

Southwest Airlines, one of the more aggressive, cost-conscious, and profitable airlines, motivates its workers by creating what one analyst (Lee 1994) called a "community ... resembling a 17th-century New England town more than a 20th-century corporation." The airline has shared values such as integrity, trust, and altruism (Lee 1994). But a company with a productive corporate culture is almost surely a company with strong incentives already in place to reward productivity. Without denigrating the corporate culture at Southwest, it should be noted that one reason it has the lowest average costs in the business is that its pilots and flight attendants are paid by the trip. This, along with a strong corporate culture, explains why Southwest's pilots and flight attendants hustle when the planes are on the tarmac. Indeed, Southwest has the shortest turn-around time in the industry. It pays for the crews to do what they can to get their planes back in the air quickly (Banks 1994, 107).

Motorola organizes its workers into teams and allows them to hire and fire their cohorts, determine training procedures, and set schedules. FedEx's corporate culture includes giving workers the right to evaluate their bosses and to appeal their own evaluations all the way to the CEO. It's understandable why FedEx delivery workers move at least twice as fast as U.S. postal workers: FedEx workers have incentives to do so, whereas postal workers do not.[23]

In a word, incentives matter! Incentive-paid workers simply gain more from extra work than do their salaried counterparts. Salaried workers are required to apply some minimal level of effort on the job. They can choose to work harder and produce more for the company. Their extra work might have some reward – a

---

[23] FedEx, UPS, and DHL track their delivery people on their routes, and their workers understand that their pay is tied to how cost-effective they are in their deliveries. Postal workers understand that they are not being so carefully monitored, mainly because there are no stockholders who can claim the profits from getting more work done. This more leisurely job environment is part of their compensation.

future raise or promotion – but such prospects are never certain. Many workers believe, with justification, that raises and promotions are more directly tied to seniority than how much they work. In contrast, the rewards of incentive-paid workers are much more immediate, direct, and contractual. Incentive-paid workers know that if they produce or sell more, their incomes will rise immediately and by a known amount. Accordingly, they have a greater incentive to apply themselves.[24]

Note also that incentive pay does more than just motivate greater effort. Different methods of pay are likely to attract different workers (Lazear 2000). Workers who are relatively unproductive, or who just don't want to compete aggressively, are likely to opt out of incentive-paid work, preferring salaried jobs. In short, workers who tend to be more productive can be expected to self-select into jobs with incentive pay. We should expect some firms to use incentive pay elements in many jobs simply to cull the unproductive workers. Job applicants who are willing to work hard will be able to convincingly communicate this to prospective employers by accepting the challenge of incentive pay.

We don't want to criticize the traditional, nonincentive methods for getting things done in business. Indeed, we discussed "teams" and the roles of honesty and trust earlier in the book. At the same time, we wish to stress a general and straightforward rule for organizing much production: *Give workers a direct, detectable stake in firm revenues or profits in order to raise revenues and profits. In a word, pay for performance.* One means of doing this is to make worker pay conditional on output: the greater the output from each worker, the greater the individual worker's pay.

"Piece-Rate" Pay (or Not)

Ideally, we might dispense with salaries (paid by the week, month, or year) and always pay by the "piece" (a "piece rate"). It would seem that firms would be eager to have the greater productivity and workers would enjoy the higher pay.

Many firms do pay piece rates. For example, hosiery mills pay by the number of socks completed. Most automobile salespeople are paid by the number of cars sold. Many lawyers are paid by the number of hours billed (and, presumably, services provided). Musicians are often paid by the number of concerts played. And so on.

But piece-rate pay is not so common; piece-rate workers make up a relatively small portion of the total workforce. There are relatively few workers in

---

[24] One early study found that incentive pay improved worker productivity by as much as 40 percent (Mangum 1962).

manufacturing and service industries whose pay is directly tied to each item or service produced. Professors are not paid by the number of students they teach. Office workers are not paid by the number of forms processed. Fast-food workers are not paid by the number of burgers flipped. Most people's pay is directly and explicitly tied to time on the job; they are generally paid by the hour, month, or year.

Admittedly, the pay of most workers has some indirect and implicit connection to production. Many workers know that, if they don't eventually add more to company revenues than they take home in pay, their jobs will be in considerable jeopardy. The question we find interesting is why piece rate – direct "pay for performance" – is not more widely used, given the positive incentives it can provide.

Many explanations for the absence of a piece-rate pay system are obvious and widely recognized.[25] The output of many workers cannot be reduced to "pieces." In such cases, no one should expect pay to be tied to that which cannot be measured with tolerable objectivity. Our work as university professors is hard to define and measure. In fact, observers might find it hard to determine when we are working, given that we may be doing nothing more than staring at a computer screen or talking with colleagues in the hallway. Measuring the "pieces" of what secretaries and executives complete is equally, if not more, difficult. Lincoln Electric, which has had considerable success with its pay-for-performance (as explained below), once tried to pay its typists by the keystroke. But the company quickly dropped this approach when one typist was caught constantly hitting a single key while she ate a sandwich on her lunch break (Roberts 2004, 42).

If a measure of "output" is defined when the assigned tasks are complex, the measure will not likely be all-inclusive. Some dimensions of the assigned tasks will not be measured, which means that incentives may be grossly distorted. Employees may work only to do those things that are defined and measured – and related to pay – at the expense of other parts of their assignments. If workers are paid by the number of parts produced, with the quality of individual parts not considered, some workers would be expected to sacrifice quality in order to increase their production count. If professors were paid by the number of students in their classes, you can bet they would spend less time at research and in committee meetings – and would be more lenient in the classroom. If middle

---

[25] For a review of arguments offered by psychologists against incentive pay plans, see Kohn (1993a, 1993b). Kohn sums up his argument as follows: "Do rewards motivate people? Absolutely. They motivate people to get rewards" (Kohn 1993b, 62). This suggests that the goals of the firm might not be achieved in the process, given the complexity of the production process and the resulting margins that workers can exploit.

managers were paid solely by units produced, they would produce a lot of units with little attention to costs or quality.[26]

Much output is the product of "teams" or groups of workers, extending at times to the entire plant or office. Pay is often not related to output because it may be difficult to determine which individuals are responsible for the "pieces" produced. Because we took up the problems of forming and paying teams in Chapter 9, here we remind readers only that team production creates special incentive problems. Having "small" teams, which makes each team member's contributions (or lack thereof) visible to others on the team, is one way to enhance incentives.

Piece-Rate Pay and Worker Risk

Not surprisingly, incentive schemes which enhance firm profits are not free of charge. According to one early study, 200 punch-press operators in Chicago who were paid piece rate earned 7 percent more than those paid a straight salary (Pencavel 1977). According to another study involving more than 100,000 workers in 500 manufacturing firms within two industries, the incomes of footwear workers on piece-rate or salary-plus-commission schemes were paid 14 percent more than those on salaries, with a differential ranging up to 31 percent for certain jobs. And the workers in the men's coats and suits industry on piece rate averaged 15 percent more than the salaried workers (Seiler 1984).[27]

Piece rates can be expected to raise the wages of covered workers for three basic reasons. First, it attracts more productive workers. Second, it provides stronger incentives to work harder for more minutes of each hour and for more hours during the workday. (Interestingly, these two effects look to reverse the adverse selection and moral hazard problems we described in Chapter 5.)

Third, the piece-rate workers are assuming some of the risk of production, which is influenced by factors beyond the workers' control. The greater average pay includes a *risk premium* intended to account for the prospects that income may not always match expectations. How much each worker produces will be determined by what the employer does to provide workers with a productive

---

[26] There is an old story from the days before the fall of communism in the former Soviet Union. Central planners gave production quotas to the managers of a glass factory. At first, they were incentivized by the pound, so they produced heavy glass. Then, they were paid by the square foot, so they produced thin (highly breakable) glass. This is also a useful story about why markets are often superior to central planning, since the market will incentivize such considerations more efficiently through prices and profit.

[27] The income differential between incentive-paid and salaried workers could be caused by different demands on their jobs. However, the cited studies looked at workers in comparable jobs or adjusted (by statistical means) for differences in jobs. Pencavel (1977) adjusts for differences in education, experience, race, and union status. Seiler (1984) adjusts for union, gender, location, occupation, type of product, and production methods.

work environment and what other workers are willing to do. One study has showed that a significant majority of workers covered under "output-related contracts" in the nonferrous foundries industry earn between 5 and 12 percent more than their counterparts who are paid strictly by their time at work. Of this pay differential, about one-fifth has been attributable to worker risk-bearing. So, a substantial share of the pay advantage for incentive workers is from the greater effort that covered workers expend (Petersen 1991).

When workers are paid by salary, incomes do not vary with firm output, which can go up and down for many reasons that are not under their control. For example, how many collars a worker can stitch to the bodies of shirts is dependent upon the flow of shirts through the plant, over which the workers doing the stitching have no control. Another example: a firm's ad campaigns can complement a worker's efforts to sell a good or service.

If paid by the work done, workers would also have to worry about how changes in the general economy would affect their workloads, production levels, and pay. When DuPont introduced an incentive compensation scheme for its fibers division in the late 1980s – under which a portion of worker incomes could be lost if profit goals were not achieved, but multiplied if profit goals were exceeded – the managers and employees were told to expect substantial income gains (Hayes 1988). However, when the economy turned sour in 1990, employee morale suffered as profits fell and workers were threatened with reduced incomes. The incentive program was canceled before the announced three-year trial period was up (Koening 1990). DuPont obviously concluded that it could buy back worker morale and production by not subjecting pay to factors that were beyond worker control. Each individual employee could reason that there was absolutely nothing she could do about the national economy. For that matter, she might rightfully worry that the free-riding of 20,000 other DuPont workers would put her income at risk.

When workers are paid by the piece, they are, in effect, asked to assume a greater risk, which shows up in the variability of their take-home pay. This means that piece-rate workers must be paid a higher *average* income than if they were offered a predictable wage. Without the higher average income for those working at a piece rate, workers would choose to work for employers paying a predictable wage. Those paying a piece rate would either be unable to hire anyone or would only be able to hire less-skilled workers.

The business lesson is simple: to get workers to accept incentive pay, employers must raise the pay. But for the piece-rate system to work and be profitable for the firm, the increase in expected worker productivity must exceed the risk premium that workers would demand. This means that a piece rate (or any other form of incentive compensation) will not be used when the risk premium required by workers is greater than the expected increase in productivity.

Even if workers are not particularly risk-averse, piece-rate pay systems may also be avoided because employers are likely to be in a better position to assume the risk of production variability than employees. This is because much of the variability in the output of *individual* workers will be "smoothed out" within a whole *group* of employees. When one worker's output is down, another worker's output will likely offset. Workers will, in effect, as a group, be able to buy themselves out of the risk. If each of the workers sees the risk cost of the piece-rate system at $500 and the employer sees the risk cost at $100, then each worker can agree to give up, say, $110 in pay for the rights to a constant income. The worker gains, on balance, $390 in nonmonetary income ($500 in risk cost reduction minus the $110 reduction in money wages). The employer gives up the piece-rate system simply because it can make a larger profit – $10 in this example – from each worker ($110 reduction in worker money wages minus the $100 increase in risk cost). Thus, one would expect piece-rate pay schemes to be more prevalent in larger firms that are more likely to be able to smooth out the variability.

Piece-rate (and other forms of incentive) pay also is more likely to be used in situations where the risk to workers is low relative to the benefits of the improved incentives. This means that they will tend to be used where production is not highly variable and where, in the absence of piece-rate pay, workers can easily exploit opportunities to shirk – when they cannot be easily monitored. For example, salespeople who are always on the road (nobody at the home office can monitor what they do on a daily basis) will tend to be paid, at least in part, by the "piece," in some form or another – say, on "commission," by the sale.

If business becomes more uncertain and less predictable with the growing complexity and globalization of business, we would expect the income gap between incentive-paid and salaried workers to widen. Employers will want to increase their competitive positions by giving their workers a greater incentive to work harder and smarter. Employers will want to shift a share of the growing business risk to their workers – at a price, of course – through greater reliance on commissions. At the same time, more workers might seek to move to salaried jobs to avoid greater risk. However, this will hold those salaries down, widening the gap between incentive-paid and salaried jobs.

Changing the Piece Rate?

Piece-rate pay systems can be used only when employers can make credible commitments to their workers to abide by the pay system that they establish and not to cut the *rate* in the *piece rate* when the desired results are achieved. Unfortunately, managers are all too often unable to make the credible commitment for the same reason that they might find the piece-rate system to be an attractive way to pay workers in theory. The basic problem is that workers *and* managers have incentives to engage in opportunistic behavior to the detriment of the other group.

Managers understand that many workers have a natural inclination to shirk their responsibilities, loaf on the job, and misuse company resources for personal gain. Managers also know that, if they tie worker pay to output, then output may be expected to expand: fewer workers will shirk. At the same time, the workers can reason that incentives also matter to managers. As is true of workers, managers are not always angels and can be expected, to one degree or another, to exploit *their* positions, achieving greater personal and business gain at the expense of their workers. Hence, workers can reason that, if they respond to the incentives built into the piece-rate system and produce more for more pay, then managers may change the deal. The managers can simply raise the number of pieces that workers must produce to get the previously established pay – or managers can simply dump what will then be excess workers.

Management specialist Edward Lawler reported that, during a strike at a manufacturing firm, a secretary was asked to take over a factory job and was paid on a piece-rate basis. Despite no previous experience, within days she was turning out 375 percent more output than the normal worker with ten years of experience who constantly complained that the work standards were too demanding (Lawler 1990, 58). The line workers were shirking despite the piece-rate pay, because they worried that the employer would reduce the per-piece rate if they produced as much as they could.

To clarify this point, suppose a worker is initially paid $500 per week, and during the course of the typical week she produces 100 pieces – for an average pay of $5 per piece. Management figures that the worker is spending some time shirking and that her output would be higher if she is paid $5 for each piece produced. If the worker responds by increasing her output to 150 pieces, management might lower the rate to $3.50 per piece. The worker would be paid $525 per week and the firm would take the overwhelming share of the gains from the greater effort of the worker. The worker would be working more diligently with little to show for what she had done. By heeding the piece-rate incentive, the worker could be inadvertently establishing a higher production standard.

These threats are real. In the 1970s, managers at a General Motors panel stamping plant in Flint, Michigan, announced that the company would allow workers to leave after they had satisfied daily production targets. Workers were soon leaving by noon. In response, management increased production targets. The result was a bitter workforce (Klein, Crawford, and Alchian 1978).

So, one reason that piece-rate systems aren't more widely used is that workers know that managers can abuse the systems, which means that workers will not buy into them at reasonable rates of pay. Indeed, a piece-rate system can have the exact opposite of the intended effect. Workers can reason that, if managers will raise the production requirements when they produce more in response to any established rate, then managers should be willing to lower the production requirements when the workers lower their production after the piece-rate system is established. Hence, the establishment of the piece-rate system can lead to a *reduction* in output as workers cut back on production.

Does this mean that managers can never raise the production standard for any given pay rate? Of course not. Workers should be concerned only if the standard is changed because of something *they* – the workers – did. If management in some way increases the productivity of workers independent of their effort (e.g., introduces computerized equipment or rearranges the flow of the materials through the plant), then the piece-rate pay standard can be raised and workers should not object. They are still getting value for their effort and are not worse off. What managers must avoid doing is changing the foundations of the work and then taking more in terms of a lower *pay rate* than they are due, which effectively means violating the spirit of the contract with their workers.

More broadly, the lesson of this discussion is *not* that piece-rate pay incentives can't work. Rather, the lesson is that getting the piece-rate pay system right can be quite tricky. Managers must convincingly *commit* themselves to the established piece rate and not exploiting the workers. The best way for managers to be believable is to create a history of living up to their commitments. Back to the topic of honesty from Chapter 5, they should create a valuable reputation with their workers, which is all the more important when performance targets are imprecise (Baker, Gibbon, and Murphy 1994).

Lincoln Electric's Pay System

Lincoln Electric, a major producer of arc-welding equipment in Cleveland, makes heavy use of piece-rate pay. As Roberts (2004) and Miller (1992) have stressed, their pay system continues to contribute to worker productivity for several reasons:

- First, the company has a target rate of return for shareholders, with deviations adding to or subtracting from year-end bonuses, which often amount to 100 percent of base pay.
- Second, employees largely own the firm, a fact that reduces the likelihood that piece rates will be changed.
- Third, management understands the need for credible commitments. According to one manager, "When we set a piecework price, that price cannot be changed just because, in management's opinion, the worker is making too much money. ... Piecework prices can only be changed when management has made a change in the method of doing that particular job and under no other conditions. If this is not carried out 100 percent, piecework cannot work" (Miller 1992, 117).

- Fourth, Lincoln pursues a permanent employment policy. Permanent employees are guaranteed only 75 percent of normal hours, and management can move workers into different jobs in response to demand changes. Also, workers have agreed to mandatory overtime when demand is high (the firm doesn't have to hire workers in peak demand periods). In other words, workers and management have agreed to share some of the risk.

- Fifth, to combat quality problems, each unit produced is stenciled with the initials of the workers who produced it. If a unit fails after delivery because of flaws in production, the responsible workers can lose as much as 10 percent of their annual bonus.

- Sixth, large inventories are maintained to smooth out differences in the production rates of different workers.

- Finally, with its reward system heavily weighted to performance pay, Lincoln has attracted workers motivated by monetary rewards and willing to work hard. Workers who aren't so motivated don't apply – or if they try it and aren't willing to keep up with the pace of co-workers, they resign to work elsewhere. The importance of this self-selection became clear when the company bought plants in other countries and instituted its piece-rate pay system, only to learn that the workers at the foreign plants had not self-selected to respond to Lincoln's pay system. The result was that the company's acquisitions were failures simply because its piece-rate system did not inspire the effort experienced in the Cleveland plant (Bartlett and O'Connell 1998).

Two-Part Pay Systems

There are innumerable ways of paying people to encourage performance. A two-part pay contract – *salary plus commission* – is a compromise between straight salary and straight commission. For example, a worker for a job placement service can be paid a salary of $4000 per month, plus 10 percent of the fees received for any placement. If the recruiter can be expected to place two workers per month and the placement fee is $15,000, the worker's expected monthly income is $7000 ($4000 plus 10 percent of $30,000).

This form of payment can be mutually attractive to the placement firm and its recruiters because it accomplishes a few important objectives. First, the system can be a way by which workers and their employers share the risks to reflect the way that placements depend on the actions of both workers and the employer. Whereas each worker understands that her placements are greatly affected by how hard and smart she works, each also knows that productivity is related to what all other workers and the employer do (often to a nontrivial degree). Worker income is dependent on, for example, how much the employer advertises, seeks to maintain a good image for the firm, and develops the right incentives for *all* workers to apply themselves.[28]

Employees have an interest in everyone working as a team and working productively, just as the employer does. Productive work by all can increase firm output, worker pay, and job security. As a consequence, although each worker may, in one sense, "prefer" all income in the form of a guaranteed fixed monthly check, the worker also has an interest in commission pay – *if everyone else is paid commission and if perverse incentives are avoided.* Hence, a pay system that is based, to a degree, on commission can raise the incomes of all workers. Put another way, to the extent that one worker's income is dependent upon other workers' efforts, we should expect workers to favor a pay system that incorporates strong production incentives for all workers.

With the two-part pay system, workers are given some security in that they can count on a minimum income level – $4000 per month in our example. The workers shift some of their risk to their employer. But the employer risk need not equal the sum of the risks that the workers avoid. This is because, as noted earlier, the employer usually hires many people, and the variability of the income of the employer is not likely to be as great as the variability of individual workers' income.

Getting Workers to Reveal Asymmetric Information

Crucial to manager performance is the problem of getting workers to deal honestly when their pay is at stake. For example, consider the manager whose sales force works "in the field" – far removed from headquarters. Salespeople are difficult to monitor and they know a great deal more about the sales potential of their territories than the managers at headquarters. How do managers get salespeople to reveal the potential of their districts when they know that the information will affect their performance criteria and the combination of salary and commission in their compensation package? If the manager at headquarters simply asks the salespeople how much they can sell in their areas, the salespeople will likely understate the sales potential. After all, some understatement harbors the potential of raising their salary and commission rate.

One solution is to offer the sales personnel a menu of salary and commission rates. Consider the set of three salary–commission rate combinations illustrated in Figure 12.11 – with salary on the vertical axis and sales on the horizontal axis. One pay package has a high salary (S_1) and a low commission rate, which

---

[28] Another application is referral bonuses that are paid if the new employee gets through a ninety-day probationary period. Workers have a stronger incentive to refer better candidates – and then to help the new employees be successful.

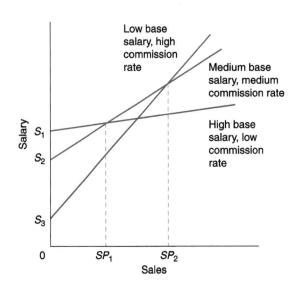

Figure 12.11 Menu of two-part pay packages By varying the base salary and the commission rate, employers can get salespeople to reveal more accurately the sales potential of their districts. A salesperson who believes that the sales potential of his district is great will take the income path that starts at a base salary of S_3. The salesperson who is unimpressed by the sales potential of his district will choose the income path that starts at S_1.

is described by the low slope of the straight, upward-sloping compensation line that emerges from S_1 on the vertical axis. Another pay package has a lower salary component (S_2) and a higher commission rate; a third has an even lower salary (S_3) and an even higher commission rate.

What's a salesperson to do? Lying about the sales potential of her territory won't help. Indeed, the salesperson isn't even asked to tell the truth. All she must do is choose from among the compensation packages in a way that she, not the manager, believes will maximize total pay. The salesperson who sees little prospect for sales will choose the package with the salary of S_1 and be compensated for the limited sales potential by a high salary. The salesperson who believes that the sales potential will be greater than SP_1 (on the horizontal axis) but less than SP_2 will choose the package with a salary of S_2. The salesperson who believes that "the sky is the limit" (a sales potential greater than SP_2) will choose the package with the low salary of S_3. This is the approach for establishing salary–commission contracts at IBM (Milgrom and Roberts 1992, 400–402). It's not a sure-fire way of making salespeople totally honest, but it can improve the managerial decision – all that real-world managers can hope to achieve.

Our focus in this chapter has been exclusively on labor, but labor is hardly the only resource. Firms need plant and equipment, which they can buy or lease. In Online Reading 12.1, we explain how the Irvine Company, a major real estate company in Southern California, structures its contracts for rental property in shopping malls to maximize profitability for itself and its tenants.

One-Time Bonuses versus Annual Raises

In 2015, the *New York Times* reported on findings from Aon Hewitt, a global consulting firm that focuses on employee compensation issues. In a survey of more than 1000 firms, Hewitt researchers found a "drastic" decline in employee raises as a part of their compensation packages and a concomitant rise in the use of annual bonuses. In 1980, raises as a share of "payroll budgets" were 10 percent. By 2001, that share had shrunk to 4.3 percent. In 2014, the share had decreased to 2.9 percent, a decline in share of more than two-thirds.

For much of this period, "one-off annual bonuses" rose from a 3.9 percent share of payroll budget in 1988 to 8 percent in 1998 and 12.7 percent in 2014. In her article's lead, the *NY Times* reporter readily deduced: "continued efforts to keep costs down have pushed employers to increasingly turn to one-off bonuses and non-monetary rewards at the expense of annual pay raises" (Cohen 2015). Later, she gave emphasis to her lead: "Employers like one-shots precisely because they are temporary. They save money over the long run because they don't lock in raises, giving managers greater control over budgets, particularly during downturns" (Cohen 2015). The reporter concluded that the trade-off between raises and bonuses was a decided win–lose deal: managers and stockholders gained at the expense of their workers, brought on by the poor bargaining position of workers.

Given the usual presumption of voluntary, mutually beneficial trades in markets, we hope you will consider such articles with a critical and skeptical eye, keeping several issues in mind:

- First, the data on the growth of bonuses help to explain why measured real money-wage gains of workers have not risen any more than they have (and could have fallen for many workers). The bonuses, which are not counted as "wages" in some data series, could have compensated – or more than compensated – for any loss in real wage growth.
- Second, the reporter doesn't seem to understand that a shift from money-wage raises to bonuses could easily have been a win–win for firms *and* their workers. If firms gain flexibility in shifting to bonuses, the gains to workers in their total compensation could have been greater *than they otherwise would have been*. In fact, labor markets likely pressured firms to share the gains (in increased flexibility and productivity) with their workers in this way.
- Third, and most importantly, the reporter is assuming the presence of significant monopsony power and the ability of firms to foist their preferences on workers – rather than a competitive labor market where firms are necessarily responsive to workers. Why would one imagine monopsony power here – or in any given context?

We make no pretense that these issues can be settled here. What we can say is that the reporter jumped far too quickly to the conclusion that firm compensation trends necessarily imply that firms gain at the expense of workers. Especially when labor markets are competitive, such assertions are difficult to defend.

Practical Lessons

An unstated admonition from this chapter is that an employer should consider becoming a monopsony in its local labor (or any other resource) market. Expanding production in a given labor market to where the firm becomes a dominant monopsony employer in a local market can mean that the employer is increasing its wage bill by more than it might if it spread out production over several local labor markets.

But monopsony analysis can be misleading. Taken uncritically, it can suggest to business students that being a monopsony employer of labor (or any other resource) can yield a competitive advantage. After all, as our graphical analysis suggests, a monopsony can pay workers a wage rate lower than would be paid if the market were fully competitive. Such can indeed be the case, but only when the monopsony is somehow assumed into existence or magically imposed on a local labor market with all other employers removed.

But firms that become large employers are *not* magically imposed on local labor markets. They generally grow within their labor markets as they expand the reach of their sales through attractive product development and pricing. As they grow in sales, firms usually increase their demands for labor within their local markets and increase the overall demand for labor. Their growth causes them to *increase* the wage rate that they and other firms pay – above the competitive levels that would have prevailed. The upward press of wage rates paid can make for a competitive cost disadvantage for the growing firms. Hence, to keep their labor costs under control and their product prices competitive, would-be monopsonists should avoid dominating their local labor markets by expanding production in other markets within the country or across the globe where wage rates are relatively low and where expanding firms can have minimal upward influence on local wage rates.

As such, there are two good reasons for large firms to have plants in various locations. First, the spread of production facilities enables them to spread their production risks. For example, this reduces the chance that a natural disaster in a given locale will wipe out their ability to continue in business even for a brief time. Second, the spread of production across various locales can reduce labor costs by not becoming demand-elevating monopsonies in given labor markets.

Further Reading Online

Reading 12.1:   Incentives in the Irvine Company rental contracts

Recommended Videos Online

1   Intro to labor markets (Richard McKenzie, 35 minutes)
2   Competitive labor markets (Richard McKenzie, 37 minutes)

3 Monopsony labor markets (Richard McKenzie, 32 minutes)

4 Labor market discrimination (Richard McKenzie, 25 minutes)

5 Menu of two-part pay options (Richard McKenzie, 12 minutes)

6 Relocating workers and two-part pay (Richard McKenzie, 16 minutes)

7 A cheap employee is … a cheap employee (Freakonomics, link available on the online resources website www.cambridge.org/mckenzie4)

8 Why does the most monotonous job in the world pay $1 million? (Freakonomics, link available on the online resources website www.cambridge.org/mckenzie4)

9 The true story of the gender pay gap (Freakonomics, link available on the online resources website www.cambridge.org/mckenzie4)

10 What can Uber teach us about the gender pay gap? (Freakonomics, link available on the online resources website www.cambridge.org/mckenzie4)

11 Mike Rowe: Learning from dirty jobs (TED, link available on the online resources website www.cambridge.org/mckenzie4)

12 Working stiffed (*The Daily Show*, link available on the online resources website www.cambridge.org/mckenzie4)

The Bottom Line

The key takeaways from Chapter 12 are the following:

1 The demand for labor is influenced by the worker's productivity and the price of the worker's product.

2 Suppliers of labor (workers) are influenced significantly by the nonmonetary benefits of employment, as well as by their opportunity costs – the value they place on their next-best alternative to employment.

3 In a competitive labor market, wage rates are determined by the interaction of willing suppliers of labor (employees) and demanders of labor (employers).

4 In competitive labor markets, wage rates above the intersection of supply and demand give rise to market surpluses, which cause the wage rate to fall toward equilibrium. Wage rates below the intersection of supply and demand give rise to market shortages, which cause the wage rate to rise.

5 Monopsony power can lead to wages less than marginal revenue product. But wages can be low for several reasons, especially from low marginal revenue product. When thinking about the extent of monopsony power, the question is the number of options available to workers.

6 Monopsonists will maximize profits by hiring workers up to the point that the marginal cost of the last worker equals her marginal value. Monopsonists can pay less than the competitive wage rate because it can restrict the market demand for labor.

7 Unions are a collusion of workers into a single bargaining unit – a cartel of labor suppliers who look to benefit by increasing wages. As such, they are

prone to the problems that other cartels face: cheating by insiders and entry by outsiders.

8 Unions can limit entry through the use of threats, violence, and a legislative agenda that limits competition in their product and labor markets.

9 Workers who are paid for performance incur a risk cost, which can explain why they often earn more than workers who are paid a straight salary. In addition, workers who are paid for performance are also induced to produce more, which enables them to earn more.

10 For piece-rate pay systems to result in an increase in worker production, employers must be credible in committing to the same rate of pay when workers increase their output.

11 Although paying for performance sounds nice, providing the "right" pay for the "right" performance is not easily resolved by managers. Accordingly, there are profits to be made from getting incentives right as surely as there are profits to be made from getting product designs right.

12 One reason for employers paying workers in two parts – salary plus some form of commission (or tie-in to performance) – is that both employer and employee can gain.

Review Questions ▸▸

1 Explain why compensation isn't often significantly greater than, or less than, marginal revenue product of labor (MRP_L). Provide an exception to each.

2 What are some of the causes of an increase (or decrease) in the marginal revenue product of a given worker?

3 The demand for labor is a "derived demand." Explain this and provide an application to illustrate this principle's importance.

4 Are most firms "wage takers" or "wage searchers" in the market for labor? Explain each and then defend your choice.

5 The government requires employers to pay time-and-a-half for some labor in excess of 40 hours per week. How should managers be expected to react to this law? What effect should such a law have on the quantity of labor demanded? Why?

6 How does union support for child labor restrictions align with the private interests of union members? Explain using supply and demand graphs.

7 Suppose the government requires employers to pay a minimum wage of $15 per hour to workers over twenty-one years of age. What effect should such a law have on the employment opportunities and wage rates of persons under twenty-one and over twenty-one?

8 How can government mandates that employers provide their workers with particular fringe benefits make workers worse off? (Imagine an absurd mandated benefit to see the point more easily.) How do such mandates affect the supply and demand curves for labor? What happens to the market wage and employment level?

9 What is the difference between "lax work demands" and "shirking"? Where do you see this tension in your workplace?

10 When would employers relax work demands on their employees? Develop a supply and demand for labor graph that shows how relaxed work demands can be profitable to employers. When would employers stop relaxing their work demands?

11 Can a monopolist (in a good or service) take advantage of their pricing power to reduce compensation to workers in a competitive labor market? If so, how so? If not, why not?

12 Is it possible (or even likely) that a monopolist (in a good or service) would compensate its workers at above-market wage rates? Why or why not?

13 Can you think of a market (other than labor) where input providers face monopsony power? How can one distinguish the lower prices from monopsony power from the lower costs associated with economies of scale?

14 Do less-skilled or more-skilled workers face more monopsony power? What are some of the job options for less-skilled workers in a city? What are some of the job options for someone with more skills (that match their skills reasonably well)?

15 Do firms have monopsony power over immigrants? Does it matter whether the immigrants are legal or illegal? What other details would matter in determining the level of monopsony power?

16 In Figure 12.8 we graphed a monopsonist and in Figure 12.9 we graphed a cartel of firms acting as a monopsonist. In Figure 12.10 we graphed a single seller of labor. Draw the graph for a cartel of labor suppliers who reduce supply that is similar to Figure 12.9.

17 In what contexts are unions more likely to be successful? Why were private-sector unions more successful fifty years ago?

18 Aside from discrimination, list a number of reasons why wages/income differ by individual. Why is it important to recognize these differences?

19 What is "personal discrimination"? What limits its practice? To the extent that one believes discrimination is a problem, what are some market characteristics and government policies to avoid?

20 Assume that I operate a high-rise building in a large city and have decided to include a thirteenth floor. Given discrimination against this number by people

with certain religious beliefs, how will the market respond as firms consider leasing office space from me on this floor? Does it matter whether consumers have the same prejudice against the number? Who will lease the space, and will they pay at or below market prices? What should I as the owner do?

21 What must one assume to assert that certain minority groups endure (systemic) personal discrimination by banks because they have higher loan rejection rates? What is a more likely explanation? What is a better statistic to use here?

22 What is "statistical discrimination"? Why does it occur? Apply it to a labor market context with an example.

23 In June 2018, many people were upset that the U.S. Transportation Security Administration (TSA) searched a ninety-six-year-old woman who was about to board a plane. Discuss the pros and cons of this event in light of "statistical discrimination."

24 Workers paid on a piece-rate basis often use the term "rate buster" for someone who responds to the piece rate by turning out lots of output. How does a reputation by management for honesty and credibility help eliminate the problem reflected by the term?

25 Is it possible that piece-rate pay can make firms less profitable even when it decreases worker shirking and increases worker productivity? Explore with a graph using the supply and demand for labor.

Select Bibliography

Alchian, Armen A. and Harold Demsetz, 1973. The property rights paradigm, *Journal of Economic History* 33: 17

Anderson, Terry L. and Peter J. Hill, 2004. *The Not So Wild, Wild West: Property Rights on the Frontier*, Stanford, CA: Stanford University Press

Ariely, Dan, 2010. *Predictably Irrational: The Hidden Forces that Shape Our Decisions*, Revised and Expanded Edition, New York: HarperCollins

Aristotle, *Ethics*, vol. 8, no. 9

Barringer, Felicity, 2015. World's aquifers losing replenishment race, researchers say, *New York Times*, June 25, www.nytimes.com/2015/06/26/science/worlds-aquifers-losing-replenishment-race-researchers-say.html?smprod=nytcore-ipad&smid=nytcore-ipad-share&_r=0

Becker, Gary S. and Kevin M. Murphy, 1988. A theory of rational addiction, *Journal of Political Economy* 96: 675–700

Bentley, Arthur, 1967. *The Process of Government*, Cambridge, MA: Belknap Press, Harvard University Press (first published 1908, University of Chicago Press)

Brandenburger, Adam M. and Barry J. Nalebuff, 1996. *Co-Opetition*, New York: Currency/Doubleday

Brennan, Jason, 2016. *Against Democracy*, Princeton, NJ: Princeton University Press

Brickley, James A. and Frederick H. Dark, 1987. The choice of organizational forms: the case of franchising, *Journal of Financial Economics* 18: 401–420

Caplan, Bryan, 2007. *The Myth of the Rational Voter: Why Democracies Choose Bad Policies*, Princeton, NJ: Princeton University Press

Coase, Ronald H., 1988. *The Firm, the Market, and the Law*, Chicago, IL: University of Chicago Press: 33–55 (reprinted from Coase 1937, 386–405)

David, Paul A., 1985. Clio and the economics of QWERTY, *American Economic Review* 75: 332–337

Fast, N. and N. Berg, 1971. *The Lincoln Electric Company*, Harvard Business School Case, Cambridge, MA: Harvard Business School Press

Hardin, Garrett, 1968. The tragedy of the commons, *Science* 62: 1243–1254

Hayek, F. A., 1945. The use of knowledge in society, *American Economic Review* 35: 519–530

Jensen, Michael, 1988. Takeovers: their causes and consequences, *Journal of Economic Perspectives* 2: 21–48

  1989. Eclipse of the public corporation, *Harvard Business Review* 67: 61–74

Jensen, Michael and William H. Meckling, 1976. Theory of the firm: managerial behavior, agency costs and ownership structure, *Journal of Financial Economics* 3: 325–328

Kanter, Rosabeth M., 1973. *Commitment and Community: Communes and Utopias in Sociological Perspective*, Cambridge, MA: Harvard University Press

Klein, Benjamin, Robert Crawford, and Armen Alchian, 1978. Vertical integration, appropriable rents, and the competitive contracting process, *Journal of Law and Economics* 21: 297–326

Knight, Frank H., 1921. *Risk, Uncertainty, and Profit*, Boston, MA: Houghton Mifflin (republished 1971, University of Chicago Press)

Kohn, Alfie, 1993b. Why incentive plans cannot work, *Harvard Business Review*, September-October: 54–63

Kolko, Gabriel, 1963. *The Triumph of Conservatism: A Reinterpretation of American History, 1900–1916*, New York: Free Press

Lazear, Edward, 1979. Why is there mandatory retirement?, *Journal of Political Economy* 87: 1261–1284

2000. Performance pay and productivity, *American Economic Review* 90: 1346–1361

Lee, Dwight R. and David Kreutzer, 1982. Lagged demand and a perverse response to threatened property rights, *Economic Inquiry* 20: 579–588

Lessig, Lawrence, 2001. *The Future of Ideas: The Fate of the Commons in a Connected World*, New York: Random House

Levitt, Stephen D. and Stephen J. Dubner, 2005. *Freakonomics: A Rogue Economist Explores the Hidden Side of Everything*, New York: William Morrow (revised edition, 2006)

Liebowitz, Stan J. and Stephen E. Margolis, 1999. *Winners, Losers, and Microsoft: How Technology Markets Choose Products*, Oakland, CA: Independent Institute (reprinted from: Liebowitz, Stan J. and Stephen E. Margolis, 1990. The fable of the keys, *Journal of Law and Economics* 33: 1–25)

Maslow, A. H., 1954. *Motivation and Personality*, New York: Harper & Row

McKenzie, Richard B., 1996. In defense of academic tenure, *Journal of Institutional and Theoretical Economics* 152: 325–341

2000. *Trust on Trial: How the Microsoft Case is Transforming the Rules of Competition*, Boston, MA: Perseus

2008. *Why Popcorn Costs So Much at the Movies, and Other Pricing Puzzles*, Heidelberg: Springer/Copernicus

McKenzie, Richard B. and Dwight R. Lee, 2008. *In Defense of Monopoly: How Market Power Fosters Creative Production*, Ann Arbor, MI: University of Michigan Press

McKenzie, Richard B. and Thomas Sullivan, 1987. The NCAA as a cartel: an economic and legal reinterpretation, *Antitrust Bulletin* 3: 373–399

Micklethwait, John and Adrian Wooldridge, 2003. *The Company: A Short History of a Revolutionary Idea*, New York: The Modern Library

Milgrom, Paul and John Roberts, 1992. *Economics, Organization and Management*, Englewood Cliffs, NJ: Prentice Hall

Miller, Gary J., 1992. *Managerial Dilemmas: The Political Economy of Hierarchy*, New York: Cambridge University Press

von Mises, Ludwig, 1962. *The Ultimate Foundations of Economic Science: An Essay on Method*, Princeton, NJ: D. Van Nostrand

Moore, Gordon E., 1994. The accidental entrepreneur, *Engineering & Science* 62: 23–30

Murray, Charles, 1988. *In Pursuit of Happiness and Good Government*, New York: Simon and Schuster

Nalbantian, Haig R. and Andrew Schotter, 1997. Productivity under group incentives: an experimental study, *American Economic Review* 87: 314–341

Olson, Mancur, 1971. *The Logic of Collective Action: Public Goods and the Theory of Groups*, Cambridge, MA: Harvard University Press

Ostrom, Elinor, 2000. Collective action and the evolution of social norms, *Journal of Economic Perspectives* 14: 137–158

Radford, R. A., 1945. The economic organization of a POW camp, *Economica* 12: 189–201

Read, Leonard E., 1983. I, Pencil, *The Freeman*, November (originally published 1958 in *The Freeman*), https://fee.org/resources/i-pencil

Roberts, John, 2004. *The Modern Firm: Organizational Design for Performance and Growth*, New York: Oxford University Press

Rubin, Paul H., 1978. The theory of the firm and the structure of the franchise contract, *Journal of Law and Economics* 21: 223–233

  2002. *Darwinian Politics: The Evolutionary Origin of Freedom*, New Brunswick, NJ: Rutgers University Press

Schansberg, D. Eric, 1996. *Poor Policy: How Government Harms the Poor*, Boulder, CO: Westview Press.

  2011. Envisioning a free market in health care, *Cato Journal* 31(1): 27–58

  2013. Who prevails with the prevailing wage?, *Indiana Policy Review* (Summer): 2–5

  2014. The economics of health care and health insurance, *The Independent Review* 18(3): 401–420

  2021. The limits of democracy, *Cato Journal* 41(3): 637–656

Smith, Adam, 1937. *An Inquiry into the Nature and Causes of the Wealth of Nations*, New York: Modern Library (originally published 1776)

Stigler, George J., 1971. The theory of economic regulation, *Bell Journal of Economics* 2: 3–21

Taylor, Frederick W., 1895. A piece rate system, *American Society of Mechanical Engineers Transactions* 16: 856–893

Tellis, Gerald and Peter Golder, 2002. *Will and Vision: How Late Comers Grow to Dominate Markets*, New York: McGraw-Hill

Thaler, Richard H., 2015b. *Misbehaving: The Making of Behavioral Economics*, New York: W. W. Norton

Thaler, Richard H. and Cass R. Sunstein, 2008. *Nudge: Improving Decisions about Health, Wealth, and Happiness*, New Haven, CT: Yale University Press

Tichy, Noel M. and Stratford Sherman, 1993. Jack Welch's lessons for success, *Fortune*, January 25: 86–93

Tullock, Gordon, 1967. The welfare costs of tariffs, monopolies, and theft, *Western Economic Journal* 5: 224–232

Williamson, Oliver E., 1967. Hierarchical control and optimum size firms, *Journal of Political Economy* 75: 123–138

Index